LOGICS

JOHN NOLT
University of Tennessee, Knoxville

Wadsworth Publishing Company
I(T)P® An International Thomson Publishing Company

Belmont, CA • Albany, NY • Bonn • Boston • Cincinnati • Detroit • Johannesburg
London • Madrid • Melbourne • Mexico City • New York • Paris • San Francisco
Singapore • Tokyo • Toronto • Washington

Philosophy Editor: Peter Adams
Assistant Editor: Clayton Glad
Editorial Assistant: Greg Bruek
Project Editor: Gary Mcdonald
Production: Greg Hubit Bookworks
Print Buyer: Barbara Britton

Advertising Project Manager: Joseph Jodar
Designer: John Edeen
Copy Editor: Margaret Moore
Cover Designer: Randall Goodall
Compositor: Thompson Type
Printer: Quebecor Printing / Fairfield

For more information, contact Wadsworth Publishing Company,
10 Davis Drive, Belmont, CA 94002, or electronically at
http://www.thomson.com/wadsworth.html

International Thomson Publishing Europe
Berkshire House 168–173
High Holborn
London WC1V7AA, England

International Thomson Editores
Campos Eliseos 385, Piso 7
Col. Polanco
11560 México D.F., México

Thomas Nelson Australia
102 Dodds Street
South Melbourne 3205
Victoria, Australia

International Thomson Publishing Asia
221 Henderson Road
#05–10 Henderson Building
Singapore 0315

Nelson Canada
1120 Birchmount Road
Scarborough, Ontario
Canada M1K 5G4

International Thomson Publishing Japan
Hirakawacho Kyowa Building, 3F
2-2-1 Hirakawacho
Chiyoda-ku, Tokyo 102, Japan

International Thomson Publishing GmbH
Königswinterer Strasse 418
53227 Bonn, Germany

International Thomson Publishing
    Southern Africa
Building 18, Constantia Park
240 Old Pretoria Road
Halfway House, 1685 South Africa

Library of Congress Cataloging-in-Publication Data
Nolt, John Eric.
    Logics / John Nolt.
        p. cm.
    Includes index.
    ISBN 0-534-50640-2
    1. Logics. I. Title.
BC71.N55   1997
160—dc20   96-32646

To Karen, Jenna, and Ben

CONTENTS

PREFACE

This book has many uses. Chapters 1, 2, 3, 4, 6, 7, and 8 provide the basics for a one-term introduction to formal logic. But later chapters contain an ample stock of advanced material as well, allowing for a variety of two-course sequences. It may also do duty for a second course alone, in which the early chapters provide review and the later chapters a selection of topics.

Regardless of how it is used, this book is designed to meet several specific needs. There is, first of all, the need to convey to students some of the diversity of recent developments in logic. Logic, as the title is intended to suggest, is no longer just logic but *logics*—a study of a multitude of systems developed for an impressive variety of applications. Though classical predicate logic is still the centerpiece, it is by no means all, or even most, of the subject. From the beginning, this book makes the presuppositions of classical logic explicit and points to alternatives.

Second, this is a text that seeks to balance the formal and philosophical with the practical. A wide range of formal topics is covered, and there is frequent reference to their philosophical roots. But in no case do I treat any system as *merely* a formal object. Logic is, first and foremost, the study of reasoning, and its life-blood is the elucidation of particular arguments. Thus, even where this book examines exotic formal systems, practical understanding of inference is always the primary concern.

Third, to facilitate understanding, each system is introduced, first, by way of concrete problems that motivate it and then by an account of its semantics. Proof theory, though usually historically prior, is relegated to third place, since much that is puzzling about proofs can be elucidated semantically, whereas relatively little that is puzzling about semantics can be illuminated by proofs. The ultimate step for each system is an ascent to the vantage point of metatheory, where the deepest understanding may be achieved.

In doing semantics, some metatheory is, of course, unavoidable. The main issue is how explicit to be about it. I have been very explicit. Metatheory baffles many students chiefly because the rules of the game are rarely explained. In the first five sections of Chapter 5 I have endeavored to explain them.

With respect to metatheory itself, my aim has been to err on the side of too much help, rather than not enough. I hope, however, that that aim is not incompatible with elegance. Detailed explanations generally precede the more difficult metaproofs, but the metaproofs themselves are as simple and nontechnical as I can make them.

I would like to thank those students and colleagues at the University of Tennessee, Knoxville, who helped to shape this book—especially Hilde Nelson, Eddy Falls, and Scott Nixon, who read nearly the entire manuscript, tested numerous exercises, and provided many valuable suggestions, corrections, and clarifications. David Reisman, Molly Finneseth, Annette Mendola, George Davis, John Fitzpatrick, Betsy Postow, Jack Thompson, and John Zavodny also contributed important corrections. Wadsworth's careful reviewers caught many a mistake, omission, or unclear phrase. For this I thank John Bickle, East Carolina University; Robert L. Causey, University of Texas at Austin; John Clifford, University of Missouri; Glenn J. Ross, Franklin and Marshall College; Catherine Shamey, Santa Monica College; and James Van Evra, University of Waterloo. Their thoughtful suggestions have made this a better book than I could have written alone.

PART I

INFORMAL LOGIC

CHAPTER 1

INFORMAL LOGIC

This chapter introduces logic from an intuitive, or **informal,** point of view. In later chapters, as we examine not specific arguments but argument forms, we will look back at the concepts introduced here from various formal viewpoints. The informal stance, however, is fundamental. It is the milieu out of which the study of logic emerges and to which, ultimately, it must return—on pain of losing its roots and becoming irrelevant to the concerns that produced it.

1.1 WHAT IS LOGIC?

Logic is the study of reasoning. Reasoning is a process of thought, but there exists no uncontroversial method for studying thought. As a result, contemporary logic, which likes to think of itself as founded on hard (though perhaps not empirical) facts, has nothing to say about thought. Instead, logicians study certain excrescences of thought: verbalized bits of reasoning—arguments.

An **argument** is a sequence of declarative sentences, one of which is intended as a **conclusion;** the remaining sentences, the **premises,** are intended to prove or at least provide some evidence for the conclusion. The premises and conclusion express **propositions**—which may be true or false—as opposed to questions, commands, or exclamations. Nondeclarative sentences may sometimes suggest premises or conclusions, but they never *are* premises or conclusions.

Declarative sentences are not themselves propositions. Some theorists have held that propositions are assertions made by sentences in particular contexts; others, that they are the meanings of sentences or the thoughts sentences express. But it is generally agreed that between sentences and propositions there is an important difference. The sentence "I am a woman" uttered by me expresses a different proposition than the same sentence uttered by you. When I utter the sentence, the proposition I assert is false; if you are a woman, when you utter the

3

sentence you assert a true proposition. Even if you are not a woman, the proposition you assert by uttering this sentence is different than the one I assert by uttering it; your proposition is about you, mine about me.

Logicians, however, tend in practice to ignore the differences between sentences and propositions, studying the former as if they were the latter. This practice presupposes that each argument we study is uttered in a fixed context (a given speaker in a given circumstance), since only relative to such a fixed context does each sentence in the argument express a unique proposition. To illustrate, consider the following argument:

> All women are mortal.
> I am a woman.
> ∴ I am mortal.

The symbol '∴' means "therefore" and is used to mark the conclusion. The speaker might be you now, or me at age 13, or Queen Victoria reflecting on her imminent death. It doesn't matter who the speaker is, but we do presuppose that there is a *single* speaker, not several, so that, for example, 'I' in the second premise refers to the same person as 'I' in the conclusion. We also keep fixed some other presuppositions about the context: that, for example, the speaker is consistently using the English language—not some Alice-in-Wonderland tongue in which familiar words have unfamiliar meanings—and that demonstrative words like 'this' or 'that' have clear and unambiguous reference.

Having by fiat frozen these aspects of context, we have obliterated the difference between sentences and propositions and can proceed to treat sentences as if they were the propositions they express. (In this book we shall sometimes use the word 'statement' to designate sentences whose context has thus been frozen.) In this way we shift our focus from such elusive entities as assertions, meanings, or thoughts, to sentences, which can be pinned down on paper and dissected neatly into discrete components.

Contemporary logic thus replaces thoughts, meanings, or acts with symbols—letters, words, phrases, and sentences. Whether that is an illuminating or useful strategy, you will be able to judge for yourself by the time you finish this book. But this much is undeniable: Logicians have learned a great deal about systems of symbols—and much that is astonishing, unexpected, or useful, as we shall see.

Our definition of 'argument' stipulated that an argument's premises must be *intended* to give evidence for the conclusion. But an argument need not actually give evidence. There are bad arguments as well as good ones. Consider this:

> Humans are the only rational beings.
> Rationality alone enables a being to make moral judgments.
> ∴ Only humans are ends-in-themselves.

Now this is an argument, but it's bad. (Of course, no famous Western philosopher would ever *really* have reasoned this way!) Intuitively, the reason it's bad is that we can't see what the capacity for moral judgment has to do with being an end-in-itself. Still, bad as it is, it's an argument; the author intended the first two propositions (sentences) to be taken as evidence for or proof of the third, and that's all that being an argument requires.

Let's now consider a good one. I'll begin with a claim. The claim is that in certain matters your will is not free. In fact there is one act you cannot initiate no matter how strong your will. The act is this: to criticize all and only those people who are un-self-critical. For example, consider yourself. Are you going to criticize yourself or not? If you do, then you will criticize someone who is self-critical (namely, you)—and so you're not criticizing only the un-self-critical. On the other hand, if you don't criticize yourself, then you fail to criticize someone who is un-self-critical (namely, you again)—and so you don't criticize all the un-self-critical. So either way you fail.[1]

Now consider your thoughts as you read the previous paragraph. (I assume you read it with comprehension; if not, now might be a good time to try again.) When I first made the claim, unless you had read this sort of thing before, you were probably puzzled. You wondered, among other things, what I was up to. At a certain point (or maybe not a certain point—maybe slowly), a light went on and you saw it. The dawning of that light is insight.

A good argument, when it works, gives you insight. It enables you to see why the conclusion is true—not "see" in a literal sense, of course, but "in your mind's eye." What was wrong with the bad argument given above was that it didn't yield any insight at all. It puzzled us and offered no resolution to our puzzlement.

Here I am talking about thought (insight, puzzlement, dawning lights, and so on), when I said just a few paragraphs back that we were going to talk about symbol systems. That's because I want to make vivid a certain contrast. There is much to be noticed about the experience—the phenomenology—of argumentation. But contemporary logicians try to explain as much as possible of what makes an argument good or bad without using mentalistic jargon, which they view with suspicion. They prefer to talk about symbols.

The previous argument showed us something about insight, but it's rather flashy for an introductory illustration; let's consider a more mundane and time-worn example:

All men are mortal.
Socrates is a man.
∴ Socrates is mortal.[2]

---

[1] The reasoning here is identical to the reasoning of Russell's barber paradox and to the core of the argument by which we will prove the halting problem unsolvable (see Section 10.5).

[2] The origin of this argument is a mystery to me. It appears in many logic textbooks, going way back in history, so presumably it has a classical source. The obvious source would be Aristotle, since Aristotle invented formal logic, but an Aristotle scholar assures me that this argument is nowhere to be found among the Philosopher's works.

This is good too, if not so good as our last example. It could, I suppose, convey some insight to a sheltered three-year-old. Its virtues, according to hoary tradition, are these:

1. Its premises are true.
2. Its reasoning is valid.

Now obviously, these virtues don't by themselves add up to a prize-winning argument. There are other things we'd like—such as significance, substance, relevance to some larger context—but the two listed above *are* virtues. Arguments that lack them are not likely to convey insight into true conclusions. So they are as good a place as any to start if we want to understand what makes an argument good.

Virtue 1, however, is the business of just about everybody but the logician. To tell whether or not a given premise is true (except for logically true or logically false propositions, cases to which we will later return), we must turn to science, conscience, or common sense—not to logic.

1.2 VALIDITY AND COUNTEREXAMPLES

That leaves us with virtue 2, the one that generally interests logicians. Most logicians have belonged to a school of thought known as the **classical tradition.** In the first four parts of this book we will consider logic from the classical perspective, though in the fifth we shall step outside of it. To say that an argument is **valid** is, according to the classical tradition, to say that there is no way for the conclusion not to be true while the premises are true. We'll sometimes put this in terms of "possible situations": There is no possible situation in which the premises are true but the conclusion isn't.

The Socrates argument is valid, for there is no possible situation in which all men are mortal, Socrates is a man, and Socrates is not mortal; we can't even coherently think such a thing.

The end-in-itself argument is **invalid** (i.e., not valid), for there is a possible situation in which the premises are true and the conclusion isn't. That is, it is possible that humans are the only rational beings and that rationality alone enables a being to make moral judgments but that humans are not the only ends-in-themselves. One way this is possible is if being an end-in-itself has nothing to do with the ability to make moral judgments, but rather is linked to some more general capacity, such as sentience or the ability to live and flourish. Thus perhaps other critters are also ends-in-themselves even if the argument's premises are true.

A possible situation in which an argument's premises are true and its conclusion is not true is called a **counterexample** to the argument. We may define validity more briefly simply by saying that a valid argument is one without a counterexample.

When we speak of possible situations, the term 'possible' is to be understood in a very broad sense. To be possible, a situation need not be something we can bring about; it doesn't even have to obey the laws of physics. It just has to be something we can **coherently conceive**—that is, it has to be thinkable and describable without self-contradiction.

Thus, intuitively,[3] to tell whether or not an argument is valid, we try to conceive or imagine a possible situation in which its premises are true and conclusion is untrue. If we succeed (i.e., if we can describe a counterexample), the argument is invalid. If we fail, then either we have not been imaginative enough or the argument is valid. This makes logicians nervous; they'd like to have a test that doesn't rely on human ingenuity; much of this book will be devoted to explaining what they do about this anxiety and how their efforts fare.

But most people are not so skittish. We appeal to counterexamples almost unconsciously in everyday life. Consider this mundane argument:

> They said on the radio that it's going to be a beautiful day today.
> ∴   It *is* going to be beautiful today.

One natural (albeit cynical) reply is, "They could be wrong." This reply demonstrates the invalidity of the argument by describing a counterexample—that is, a possible situation in which the conclusion ('It's going to be a beautiful day today') is untrue even though the premise ('They said so on the radio') is true: namely, the situation in which the forecasters are wrong.

A counterexample need not be an actual situation, though it might; it is enough that the situation be conceptually possible. Thus it need not be *true* that the forecasters are wrong; to see the invalidity of the argument, we need only realize that it is *possible* they are wrong.

To give a counterexample, then, is merely to tell a kind of story. The story needn't be true, but it must be conceptually coherent. The cynical respondent to our argument above hints at such a story with the remark "They could be wrong."

That's enough for casual conversation. But for logical analysis it's useful to be more explicit. A well-stated description of a counterexample should contain three elements:

1. Affirmations of all the argument's premises.
2. A denial of the argument's conclusion.
3. An explanation of how this can be—that is, how the conclusion can still be untrue while the premises are all true.

If we flesh out the cynic's counterexample to make all of these elements explicit, the result might be something like this:

> They said on the radio that it's going to be a beautiful day today. But they are wrong. A cold front is moving in unexpectedly and will bring rain instead of a beautiful day.

---

[3] When I say 'intuitively', I mean from an informal point of view. We are still talking about thoughts here, not symbols. This is typical of informal logic. The formal, symbolic approach begins with the next chapter.

All three elements are now present. The first sentence of this "story" affirms the premise. The second denies the conclusion. The third explains how the conclusion could be untrue even though the premise is true.

This is not, of course, the only possible situation that would make the premises but not the conclusion true. I made up the idea of an unexpected cold front more or less arbitrarily. There are other counterexamples as well. Maybe an unexpected *warm* front will bring rain. Or maybe there will be an unexpected dust storm. Or maybe the radio announcer knew it was going to be an awful day and flat out lied. Each of these scenarios is a counterexample. This is typical; invalid arguments usually have indefinitely many counterexamples, each of which is by itself sufficient to show that the argument is invalid.

Let's consider another example. Is the following argument valid or invalid?

> All philosophers are freethinkers.
> Al is not a philosopher.
> ∴   Al is not a freethinker.

To answer, we try to imagine a counterexample. Is there a way for the conclusion not to be true while the premises are true? (To say that the conclusion is not true, of course, is to say that Al *is* a freethinker.) A moment's thought should reveal that this is quite possible. Here's one counterexample:

> All philosophers are freethinkers and Al is not a philosopher, but Al is nevertheless a freethinker, because there are some freethinking bricklayers who are not philosophers, and Al is one of these.

Again all three elements of a well-described counterexample are present. The statement 'All philosophers are freethinkers and Al is not a philosopher' affirms both of the premises. The statement 'Al is nevertheless a freethinker' denies the conclusion, and the remainder of the story explains how this can be so. The story is perfectly coherent, and thus it shows us how the conclusion could be untrue even if the premises were true.

Notice again that the counterexample need not be an actual situation. It's just a story, a scenario, a fiction. In fact, it isn't true that all philosophers are freethinkers, and maybe it isn't true that Al (whoever Al is) is a freethinker, either. That doesn't matter; our story still provides a counterexample, and it shows that the argument is invalid, by showing how it *could be* that the conclusion is untrue while the premises are true.

Notice, further, that we needn't have said that Al is a bricklayer; for purposes of the example, he could have been an anarcho-communist or some other species of freethinker—or an unspecified kind of freethinker. The details are flexible; what counts, however we formulate the details, is that our "story" is coherent and that it makes the premises true and the conclusion untrue.

Let's consider another argument:

> All philosophers are freethinkers.
> Al is a philosopher.
> ∴   Al is a freethinker.

This has no counterexample. If we affirm the premises, then we cannot without lapsing into incoherence deny the conclusion. If all philosophers are freethinkers and Al is one of the philosophers, then he must be a freethinker. This argument is valid.

That, of course, doesn't mean it's a good argument in all respects. On the contrary, some philosophers are dogmatically religious, so the first premise is false, which makes the argument unconvincing. But still the reasoning is valid.

Sometimes what appears to be a counterexample turns out on closer examination not to be. Unless the mistake is trivial (e.g., the story fails to make all the premises true or fails to make the conclusion untrue), the problem is often that the alleged counterexample is subtly incoherent and hence impossible. To return to the argument about Socrates, suppose someone said

> The argument is invalid because we can envision a situation in which all men are mortal and Socrates is a man, but Socrates is nevertheless immortal because he has an immortal soul.

This story does seem to make the premises of the argument true and the conclusion false. But is it really intelligible? If having an immortal soul makes one immortal and the man Socrates has an immortal soul, then not all men are mortal. The story is incoherent; it contradicts itself. It is therefore not a genuine counterexample, since a counterexample is a *possible* situation; that is, its description must be conceptually coherent.

Some additional invalid arguments with accompanying counterexamples are listed below. Keep in mind that invalid arguments generally have many counterexamples so that the counterexamples presented here are not the only ones. Note also that each counterexample contains all three elements (though sometimes more than one element may be expressed by the same sentence). The three elements, once again, are

1. Affirmations of all the argument's premises.
2. A denial of the argument's conclusion.
3. An explanation of how this can be—that is, how the conclusion can be untrue while the premises are all true.

In each case, the counterexample is a logically coherent story (not an argument) that shows how the conclusion could be untrue while the premises are true, thus proving that the argument is invalid. Notice how each of the counterexamples below performs this function:

Invalid Argument

> Sandy is not a man.
> ∴ Sandy is a woman.

Counterexample

> Sandy is neither a man nor a woman but a hamster.

Invalid Argument

> If the TV is unplugged, it doesn't work.
> The TV is not working.
> ∴ It's unplugged.

Counterexample

> If the TV is unplugged it doesn't work, and it's not working. However, it is plugged in. The reason it's not working is that there's a short in the circuitry.

Invalid Argument

> All charged particles have mass.
> Neutrons are particles that have mass.
> ∴ Neutrons are charged particles.

Counterexample

> All charged particles have mass, but so do some uncharged particles, including neutrons.

Invalid Argument

> The winning ticket is number 540.
> Beth holds ticket number 539.
> ∴ Beth does not hold the winning ticket.

Counterexample

> The winning ticket is number 540; Beth is holding both ticket 539 and ticket 540.

Invalid Argument

> There is nobody in this room taller than Amy.
> Bill is in this room.
> ∴ Bill is shorter than Amy.

Counterexample

> Bill and Amy are the only ones in this room, and they are the same height.

Invalid Argument

> Sally does not believe that Eve ate the apple.
> ∴ Sally believes that Eve did not eat the apple.

Counterexample

> Sally has no opinion about the story of Eve. She doesn't believe that Eve ate the apple, but she doesn't disbelieve it either.

Invalid Argument

> Some people smoke cigars.
> Some people smoke pipes.
> ∴ Some people smoke both cigars and pipes.

Counterexample

> There are pipe-smokers and cigar-smokers, but nobody smokes both pipes and cigars, so the two groups don't have any members in common.

Invalid Argument

> Some people smoke cigars.
> ∴ Some people do not smoke cigars.

Counterexample

> There are people, and all of them smoke cigars. (If everybody does, then some people do and so the premise is true!)

Invalid Argument

> We need to raise some money for our club.
> Having a bake sale would raise money.
> ∴ We should have a bake sale.

Counterexample

> We need to raise money for the club, and having a bake sale would raise money, but so would other kinds of events, like holding a car wash or a telethon. Some of these alternative fund-raising ideas better suit the needs of the club and the abilities of its members, and so they are what should be done instead of a bake sale.

Invalid Argument

> Kate hit me first.
> ∴   I had to hit her back.

Counterexample

> Kate hit the (obviously immature) arguer first. But the arguer could have turned the other cheek or simply walked away; there was no need to hit back.

Let's take stock. What launched our discussion of counterexamples was talk of validity, and what led us to validity was a look at the two virtues of a good argument, namely:

1. The premises are true.
2. The reasoning is valid.

Logicians sometimes suggest that these two virtues are sufficient for a good argument. I have already expressed doubts about this. But we can see why someone might believe it if we consider the two virtues together. To say that the reasoning is valid is to say that there is no counterexample—that is, there is no way for the conclusion not to be true while the premises are true. Now, if we add virtue 1—namely, that the premises *are* true—we see that the two virtues together add up to a guarantee of the truth of the conclusion. An argument that has both virtues—true premises and valid reasoning—is said to be **sound.** Sound reasoning certifies that its conclusion is true.

If that's all we want from reasoning, then virtues 1 and 2 are all we need. In the classical logical tradition, it has been customary to ask for no more. But I think we generally want more. We want insight, significance, cogency . . . well, at least we want **relevance.** Virtues 1 and 2 don't even give us that—as we shall see in the next section.

Exercise 1.2

Classify the following arguments as valid or invalid. For those that are invalid, describe a counterexample, making sure that your description includes all three elements of a well-described counterexample. Take each argument as it stands; that is, don't alter the problem by, for example, adding premises.

1. No plants are sentient.
   All morally considerable things are sentient.
   ∴ No plants are morally considerable.
2. All mathematical truths are knowable.
   All mathematical truths are eternal.
   ∴ All that is knowable is eternal.
3. Most geniuses have been close to madness.
   Blake was a genius.
   ∴ Blake was close to madness.

4.   Most of the sentences in this book are true.
      Most of the sentences in this book are about logic.
  ∴   There are true sentences about logic in this book.

5.   A high gasoline tax is the most effective way to reduce the trade deficit.
      We need to reduce the trade deficit.
  ∴   We need a high gasoline tax.

6.   Some angels are fallen.
  ∴   Some angels are not fallen.

7.   To know something is to be certain of it.
      We cannot be certain of anything.
  ∴   We cannot know anything.

8.   The surface area of China is smaller than the surface area of Russia.
  ∴   The surface area of Russia is larger than the surface area of China.

9.   Some men are mortal.
  ∴   Some mortals are men.

10.   The witnesses said that either one or two shots were fired at the victim.
      Two bullets were found in the victim's body.
  ∴   Two shots were fired at the victim.

11.   People do climb Mount Everest without oxygen tanks.
  ∴   It is possible to climb Mount Everest without oxygen tanks.

12.   Some fools are greedy.
      Some fools are lecherous.
  ∴   There are some fools who are both lecherous and greedy.

13.   No one has ever lived for 200 years.
  ∴   No one ever will.

14.   DNA contains the code of life.
      Life is sacred.
  ∴   It is wrong to manipulate DNA.

15.   There are fewer than a billion people in the whole United States.
      New York is only a part of the United States.
  ∴   There aren't a billion people in New York.

1.3 RELEVANCE

Consider the following rather lyrical argument:

      I've heard of Wartburg, Tennessee.
  ∴   There's no tree that's not a tree.

Pretty bad—but it has both of the virtues discussed in the previous section: The premise is true, and the reasoning is valid. Of course the conclusion doesn't *follow* from the premise. But that wasn't how we defined validity—following from the premises. We defined it as the absence of a counterexample. And there is no counterexample here.

The queerness resides in the conclusion: 'There's no tree that's not a tree'. This conclusion can't be untrue; it's true in any possible situation, no matter what the world is like. Hence there is no possible situation in which the premise is true and the conclusion is not (simply because, regardless of the premises, there is no possible situation in which the conclusion is not true). So the argument has no counterexample; it is valid. Further, since the premise is true, it is sound. Still, it is a dumb argument.

Not that it leads to an incorrect conclusion. The conclusion *can't* be untrue; it's true in all possible situations. So here as elsewhere, soundness guarantees truth. What's wrong with this argument is that the conclusion derives no support from the premise. The premise is irrelevant; the conclusion could stand on its own.

The conclusion is a **logical truth,** a statement true in all possible situations. And the argument is an illustration of the general rule that *any argument whose conclusion is logically true is automatically valid, no matter what the premises.* A logical truth must be true no matter what we assume; so it is a valid conclusion from anything.

But since this argument is bad nevertheless, we may infer that at least one additional virtue is required for good reasoning: relevance. But what is relevance? In recent years a whole field of logic, relevance logic, has emerged to attempt to answer this question. We shall consider it in some detail in Section 16.3. Unfortunately, there seem to be as many relevance logics as relevance logicians, so the discipline is in disarray. But the need for relevance is clear.

There is another kind of inference in which the need for relevance stands out starkly: an argument with inconsistent premises. A set of propositions (or a single proposition) is **inconsistent** if there is no possible situation in which they are all true (or in which it is true). The proposition

There is a tree that's not a tree.

is inconsistent. So is this set of propositions:

Albert is a pirate.
Albert is not a pirate,

and the more complex set:

He's either here or in Chicago.
He's not here.
He's not in Chicago.

Including any such inconsistent proposition or set of propositions among the premises of an argument makes the argument automatically valid. For example, the argument

Albert is a pirate.
Albert is not a pirate.
∴   Albert plays golf.

is valid. Since there is no possible situation in which both premises are true, there is no possible situation in which both premises are true and the conclusion is not true; hence there is no counterexample. Any attempt to describe a situation in which both premises are true will result in incoherence. More generally, *any argument with inconsistent premises is valid.*

This sounds disastrous, but it isn't. It doesn't mean you can prove whatever you want just by assuming an inconsistency. To prove in the fullest sense means (at least) to have a sound argument—to reason validly from *true* premises. But inconsistent premises cannot all be true. So arguments with inconsistent premises never prove anything and are therefore harmless. Yet they are odd because, though valid, they may lack relevance.

Relevance logicians reject the classical tradition's definition of validity, arguing that validity should by definition imply relevance so that we can reject such perverse examples as those recently contemplated. This is an appealing idea. The problem comes, as I noted before, in the attempt to work out the details. No one has hit upon a relevance-preserving definition of validity that has gained widespread acceptance.

It might be useful, however, to take a stab at saying what relevance is. One criterion that might be taken as an indicator of relevance is this: *Any idea that occurs in the conclusion also occurs in at least one of the premises.* In other words, every idea in a conclusion must "come from" somewhere, that is, from one or more of the premises. Conclusions should be "summations" of the premises. They should consist of elements of the premises recombined in a way that, ideally, produces insight. Consider, for example, this typical deductive argument:

> All courses numbered less than 400 are undergraduate courses.
> No undergraduate course can be taken for graduate credit.
> ∴   No course numbered less than 400 can be taken for graduate credit.

The fundamental ideas in the conclusion are 'course numbered less than 400' and 'being taken for graduate credit'. The first of these ideas comes from the first premise and the second from the second. Each has its origin in a premise, and this accounts, at least in part, for the conclusion's relevance.

Notice that I did not list the terms 'no' and 'can' as expressing ideas. These terms represent logical relationships, and they belong to a class of words that we shall call **logical operators.** (Some authors call them **syncategorematic** terms.) Roughly, a word is a logical operator if it expresses, not a specific idea itself, but a way of modifying or combining ideas. Some common logical operators are 'all', 'some', 'most', 'no', 'not', 'if . . . then', 'or', 'unless', and 'and'. Thus, though a relevant conclusion may not introduce ideas not contained in the premises, it may use logical operators to recombine the premises' ideas in new ways. (Precisely which such combinations preserve relevance is one of the controversial issues in relevance logic.)

Contrast the previous relevant and valid argument with this argument, which is both fallacious and irrelevant:

> Smoking is harmful.
> ∴   Smoking should be illegal.

There are two fundamental ideas in the conclusion—and perhaps a third. The two obvious ones are 'smoking' and the notion of being 'illegal'. Depending on how we count, we might also treat 'should' as an idea, though some logicians would consider it a logical operator. No matter. The inference is clearly irrelevant, because although the term 'smoking' in the conclusion has its origin in the premise, the term 'illegal' comes from nowhere—and that's a hallmark of irrelevance.

Notice that we could make the inference relevant by adding a premise connecting the idea of harm to the idea of illegality:

> Anything that is harmful should be illegal.
> Smoking is harmful.
> ∴   Smoking should be illegal.

The conclusion is now relevantly drawn. The terms 'illegal' and 'should' (if we want to count the latter as expressing an idea) come from the first premise, and the term 'smoking' comes from the second. We have also strengthened the reasoning; the argument is now valid. The added premise, however, is false. And so, though valid, the argument is unsound.

Arguments with logically true conclusions or inconsistent sets of premises provide the most glaring examples of validity (in the classical sense) without relevance. But logically true statements and inconsistent premise sets are relatively rare in actual reasoning. Most of the statements with which we reason are **contingent**—that is, true in some possible situations and false in others. When we reason with contingent statements, there is less dissonance between classical logic and relevance logic. Still, differences remain, as we shall see in Section 16.3.

Exercise 1.3

Classify the following arguments as valid or invalid, using the informal concept of validity. For those that are invalid, describe a counterexample. Then discuss whether or not the argument's premises are relevant to its conclusion.

1.   Joe is a mathematician.
      ∴   Joe is a mathematician.
2.   Joe is a mathematician.
       Joe is not a mathematician.
      ∴   Joe is weird.
3.   Joe is a mathematician.
      ∴   Joe is not both a mathematician and not a mathematician.
4.   Olaf has been vaporized into incandescent plasma.
      ∴   Olaf is dead.
5.   All men are mortal.
       Socrates is Greek.
       Socrates is a man.
      ∴   Socrates is mortal.

1.4 ARGUMENT INDICATORS

We have defined an argument as a sequence of declarative sentences, one of which is *intended* as a conclusion that the others, the premises, are *intended* to support. In this section we consider the grammatical cues by which speakers of English communicate such intentions. The most important of these are **argument indicators**, words or phrases that signal the presence and communicate the structure of arguments. These fall into two classes: premise indicators and conclusion indicators. A **premise indicator** is an expression such as 'for', 'since', and 'because' that connects two statements, signifying that the one to which it is immediately attached is a premise from which the other is inferred as a conclusion. So, for example, in the sentence

The soul is indestructible because it is indivisible.

the premise indicator 'because' signals that the statement 'it is indivisible' (where 'it' refers to the soul) is a premise supporting the conclusion 'the soul is indestructible'. Premise indicators can also occur at the beginnings of sentences, but the rule still holds: The statement to which the premise indicator is attached is the premise; the other is the conclusion. Hence, for example, in the sentence

Since numbers are nonphysical, nonphysical objects exist.

the word 'since' shows that the statement 'numbers are nonphysical' is a premise leading to the conclusion 'nonphysical objects exist'.

Conclusion indicators are words or phrases that signify that the statement to which they are attached is a conclusion that follows from previously stated premises. English is rich in conclusion indicators. Some of the most common are 'therefore', 'thus', 'so', 'hence', 'then', 'it follows that', 'in conclusion', 'accordingly', and 'consequently'. In the following argument, for example, 'hence' indicates that the third statement, 'God exists', is a conclusion from the first two:

Without God, there can be no morality. Yet morality exists. *Hence* God exists.

But the same thing can be signaled by a premise indicator:

God exists, *for* without God there can be no morality, and morality exists.

or by a mix of premise and conclusion indicators:

Without God there can be no morality. *Then* God exists, *since* morality exists.

These are three different expressions of the same argument. There are many others. Notice that the conclusion (in this case, 'God exists') may occur at the end, or at the beginning, or in the middle of the argument, depending on the arrangement of argument indicators. All three positions are common in ordinary speech and writing. But for logical analysis it is customary to list the premises first and the conclusion, prefixed by '∴', last, as we have been doing. This is called **standard form.**

Arguments may also be stated without indicators, in which case we must rely on subtler clues of context, intonation, or order to discern their structure. Most often when argument indicators are lacking the conclusion is given first, followed by the premises. Here is an example:

> There is no truth without thought. Truth is a correspondence between thought and reality. And a correspondence between two things cannot exist unless the things themselves exist.

Here the first statement is a conclusion from the remaining two.

Like most English words, many of the terms we use for argument indicators have more than one meaning. So not every occurrence of 'since', 'because', 'thus', and so on is an argument indicator. If someone says, "I got down on my hands and knees and *thus* I escaped beneath the smoke," it is unlikely that she is offering an argument. 'Thus' here means "in this way," not "it follows that." The speaker is not attempting to prove that she escaped. Similarly, in the sentence '*Since* the summer began, there hasn't been a drop of rain', the word 'since' indicates temporal duration, not a logical relationship between premise and conclusion. Neither sentence is an argument.

Sometimes arguments are not completely stated. A premise may be omitted because it is so obvious that it need not be stated (or, more sinisterly, because the arguer is trying to get listeners to take it for granted without thinking). Likewise, a conclusion may be omitted because it is very obvious, or because the arguer wants listeners to draw it for themselves and thus perhaps be more inclined to accept it. This argument, for example, has an implicit premise:

> The moon has no atmosphere and therefore cannot support life.

The unstated premise is, of course, that an atmosphere is needed to support life. (Notice also that the conclusion is only partly stated; its subject, having been mentioned already in the premise, is not repeated.) The argument, stated in full, is

> An atmosphere is needed to support life.
> The moon has no atmosphere.
> ∴ The moon cannot support life.

Here is an argument with an implicit conclusion:

> Ailanthus trees have smooth bark, but the bark of this tree is rough.

The full argument is

> Ailanthus trees have smooth bark.
> The bark of this tree is rough.
> ∴ This tree is not an ailanthus tree.

Arguments are sometimes confused with conditional statements. A **conditional statement** is an assertion that one thing is the case if another thing is, for example:

If three is an even number, then it is divisible by two.

A conditional asserts neither of its components. This statement, for example, asserts neither that three is even nor that it is divisible by two, but the latter is the case *if* the former is. In this way the statement differs significantly from the following argument, which is formed from the same components:

Since three is an even number, it is divisible by two.

In an argument, both the premises and the conclusion are categorically asserted. A person who utters these words is saying (absurdly) that three is even and that three is divisible by two.

The point here is that 'if' and certain related terms, such as 'unless' and 'only if', are *not* premise indicators. Instead, they form compounds that function as single statements. We shall have more to say about them in the next chapter.

Exercise 1.4

Some of the following passages are arguments, some are not. Some of the arguments are incomplete, lacking a premise, or a conclusion, or both. Rewrite each argument in standard form, supplying implicit premises or conclusions. For those passages that are not arguments, write 'not an argument'.

1. Uranium is heavier than iron, because gold is heavier than iron and uranium is heavier than gold.
2. Since anyone under 18 is a juvenile and juveniles are not allowed on the premises, Sally is not allowed on the premises.
3. If there is a storm warning, the siren sounds. So there is no storm warning, since the siren is not sounding.
4. Savage could not have been the thief. The thief was over six feet tall. But Savage is only 5'8".
5. We went to Indianapolis; then we went to Chicago.
6. The water froze, and when water freezes the temperature must be at or below zero degrees Celsius.
7. Different cultures have different conceptions of rationality. Hence rationality itself takes many forms, for what a culture *conceives* as rational *is* rational for that culture.
8. Alice has a National Rifle Association sticker on her windshield. It is likely, therefore, that she opposes gun control.
9. Because all things other than pleasure are valued only for the pleasure they produce, but pleasure is valued for its own sake, only pleasure is intrinsically valuable. For a thing is intrinsically valuable if and only if it is valued for its own sake.
10. I lied because I was afraid you would hate me if I told the truth.

1.5 USE AND MENTION

Before we move on to formal logic, it will be useful to explain a convention used throughout this text. Since contemporary logic studies systems of symbols, logicians must often talk about specific symbols or strings of symbols. To do this, we need names for these symbols or strings. We shall form names for symbols or strings by enclosing them in single quotation marks.

If we take an ordinary name, for example, and flank it with single quotation marks, the result is a new name—one that names the old name. Thus, for example, the following sentence is true:

'Smog' is a four-letter word.

But this is false:

Smog is a four-letter word.

Smog is not a word at all; it is a form of air pollution. In the first sentence the word 'smog' is mentioned but not used; in the second it is used but not mentioned. In logic we usually mention specific symbols by using their quotation names in the manner of the first sentence. This is why single quotation marks have appeared and will continue to appear so frequently in this book.

Failure to observe the use/mention distinction can lead to confusion or nonsense. Consider

The King refers to Elvis.

Which king? And why would he want to do that? But, of course, what is intended is

'The King' refers to Elvis.

That is, the phrase 'The King' or, more completely, 'The King of Rock and Roll' is used to refer to the man Elvis Presley. The confusion arises from a failure to indicate that the phrase 'The King' is merely being mentioned, not used.

Here's an example that is purely nonsensical:

Contains four words does not contain four words

—at least until appropriate quotation marks are added, when it becomes this simple and obvious truth:

'Contains four words' does not contain four words.

Indeed not; it contains only three.

Quotation marks are likewise needed for mentioning letters, numerals, and other symbols. Thus we may (correctly) write

'10' is a numeral that names the number 10.

Numerals are symbols. They can be written or printed. The numeral '10', for example, consists of a vertical stroke followed by a circle. But numbers are something else again. They are not shapes or marks and cannot themselves be written—though they may be named. The names of the number ten are legion. They include not only the Arabic numeral '10' but also the Roman numeral 'X', the formula '8 + 2', the English word 'ten', and so on. Ten is not any of these things, but the unique thing that they all name.

To summarize, when you see single quotation marks, look between them: The word or phrase, symbol or formula that you see written there is, precisely as written, the thing being mentioned. Where there are no quotation marks, the words in the sentence are being *used,* and you generally have to look elsewhere to find what is being *mentioned.*

When we are using one language to study another, the one we use is called the **metalanguage** and the one being studied—i.e., mentioned—is called the **object language.** For example, when native speakers of English study Hebrew, they usually converse about Hebrew grammar, style, wording, and so on in English. Here English is the metalanguage and Hebrew is the object language. In the succeeding chapters, we shall study various logical languages. Each, as we study it in turn, will become our object language; but the metalanguage will always be English. We will, however, from time to time import exotica, such as Greek letters for variables, or some notation from mathematics into our metalanguage, so it will be a specialized or technical form of English.

Exercise 1.5

One or more of the following sentences is true as it stands; others are not true unless quotation marks are added. Supply quotation marks where necessary to make them true.

1. Logic begins with an L.
2. The numbers 2 and -2 are both solutions to the equation $x^2 = 4$.
3. The argument some dogs are collies therefore some collies are dogs is valid.
4. The number four has many names.
5. Instead of the word therefore we may write the symbol $\therefore$.

CLASSICAL PROPOSITIONAL LOGIC

CLASSICAL PROPOSITIONAL LOGIC: SYNTAX

An argument form is a pattern of reasoning common to many arguments. Studying forms enables us to understand whole classes of arguments at once. In this chapter we introduce a symbolic language capable
of exhibiting simple argument forms: the language of propositional
logic. We investigate its **syntax** (grammar) in this chapter and its **semantics** (meaning-structures) in the next in order to develop mathematically rigorous methods to check for validity and related properties.

2.1 ARGUMENT FORMS

In Chapter 1 we approached logic from an **informal** point of view, considering
arguments as they occur in natural language. Here we begin the study of **formal
logic,** whose subject matter is **argument forms**—patterns of reasoning shared by
many different arguments. Here is a simple argument form:

> If P, then Q
> P
> ∴ Q

This form is known by its medieval Latin name, ***modus ponens.***[1] The letters 'P'
and 'Q' function as place-holders for declarative sentences. We shall call such
letters **sentence letters.** We say that an argument is an **instance** of a form comprised
of sentence letters (or, simply, that it *has* that form) if it is obtainable from the
form by replacing the sentence letters with sentences, each occurrence of the same

---

[1] This is an abbreviation of the longer term '*modus ponendo ponens*', which,
loosely translated, means the mode of proving an assertion by assuming an assertion (the nonconditional premise).

letter being replaced by the same sentence.[2] The following argument, for example, is an instance of the form modus ponens in which 'P' is replaced by 'the fetus is a person' and 'Q' by 'abortion is murder':

> If the fetus is a person, then abortion is murder.
> The fetus is a person.
> ∴   Abortion is murder.

Since the number of declarative sentences is potentially infinite, the form represents infinitely many different arguments, all with the same structure. Another example of the form modus ponens is

> If Clara won't get the raise, then she'll quit.
> She won't get the raise.
> ∴   She'll quit.

What is significant about this form is that any argument that has it is valid. Since there are infinitely many such arguments, to know that they all are valid is to possess knowledge that is in a sense infinite. But can we really *know* that each instance of modus ponens is valid?

One possible approach to such knowledge is to insert random sentences in place of 'P' and 'Q' and check the resulting arguments for validity by trying to formulate counterexamples. But this case-by-case approach, though it might ultimately convince us, is logically inconclusive. Even in an entire human lifetime we could check only a finite number of instances; there will always be infinitely many that we have never examined. Maybe some of these, so strange and complex that we would never think to check them, are *in*valid. Maybe even some of the ones we have checked are invalid, and failures of imagination have prevented us from noticing!

A more sophisticated approach is to move to a more abstract level of thought. We might, for example, reason this way: No matter which sentences 'P' and 'Q' stand for, whenever 'if P, then Q' is true and 'P' is true, then 'Q' has to be true as well. Here we focus on the general pattern of the reasoning, on the form, rather than the form's instances. In this way we might be able to "see" that the form itself guarantees the validity of its instances. But this sort of "seeing," or intuition, is still fallible and hence still subject to doubt.

---

[2] Notice, however, that this definition does not rule out replacing different letters with the same sentences. Just as in the mathematical equation '$x + y = y + x$' we may legitimately replace both 'x' and 'y' by '2' to obtain the instance '$2 + 2 = 2 + 2$', so in the form modus ponens, for example, we might replace both 'P' and 'Q' by the same sentence, say 'People have souls'. The result

> If people have souls, then people have souls.
> People have souls.
> ∴   People have souls.

is, like '$2 + 2 = 2 + 2$', trivial and uninteresting. But, like all instances of modus ponens, it is valid.

These doubts can be *wholly* dispelled, but not without a deeper understanding of the grammatical structure (**syntax**) and meaning (**semantics**) of argument forms. This understanding will enable us to see why some arguments are valid and others not, and it will yield rigorous techniques for settling questions of validity and related issues.

We begin with some syntactic fundamentals. First, the order of the premises and minor variations in wording that do not alter meaning are irrelevant to an argument's form. Thus with regard to the previous argument, for example, we may omit the 'then', reverse the premises, and adjust the wording a bit without altering the meaning. The result

> Clara won't get the raise.
> If she won't get the raise, she'll quit.
> ∴   She'll quit.

still counts as an instance of modus ponens.

However, the order of components within a sentence *does* matter. To illustrate this, it will be useful to introduce some terminology. An "if . . . then" statement, such as 'if she won't get the raise, she'll quit', is called a **conditional statement,** or often just a **conditional.** The sentence following the 'if' is the **antecedent,** and the sentence following the 'then' (or simply the remainder if the 'then' is missing) is the **consequent** ('consequen*t*' with a 't', not consequen*ce*). If we exchange the antecedent and the consequent within the conditional, as in this argument:

> If she quits, Clara won't get the raise.
> She won't get the raise.
> ∴   She'll quit.

the result is no longer modus ponens. Instead, this argument has the form

> If Q, then P
> P
> ∴   Q

Because the second premise 'P' affirms the consequent of the conditional premise 'If Q, then P', this form is called **affirming the consequent.** (For parallel reasons, modus ponens is sometimes called **affirming the antecedent.**)

Moreover, the argument itself, unlike the two previous arguments, is *in*valid. Here is a counterexample: The boss is a scrooge; Clara won't get the raise, period, whether she quits or not. But she won't quit, because she needs the job to feed her kids.

At least one instance of affirming the consequent, then, is invalid. A form like modus ponens all of whose instances are valid is called a **valid form.** Any form that, like affirming the consequent, has at least one invalid instance is called an **invalid form.**

But not every instance of an invalid form need be invalid. Here is a valid instance of affirming the consequent:

If some men are saints, then some saints are men.
Some saints are men.
∴   Some men are saints.

This is valid, however, not *because* it is an instance of affirming the consequent, but rather because the second premise and the conclusion say essentially the same thing. The conclusion therefore follows from the second premise alone. The first premise is superfluous.

Because invalid forms may have valid instances, knowing that a form is invalid tells us little about the validity of a particular instance of that form. We may safely assume that having that form does not make the instance valid, but it may be valid nevertheless in virtue of structure not represented in the form (such as the equivalence of the second premise and conclusion in the previous example).

In algebra, the equation '$x + y = y + x$' has precisely the same meaning as the equation '$z + w = w + z$'. Likewise in logic, the use of different sentence letters makes no difference to the form. We could also write modus ponens, for example, as

If R, then S
R
∴   S

Similarly, we might express affirming the consequent as

If P, then Q
Q
∴   P

Hence, although exchanging letters within the conditional alone changed modus ponens into affirming the consequent, consistent replacement of letters throughout a form does not alter the form. The preceding form, for example, results from our original version of affirming the consequent by replacing 'P' by 'Q' and 'Q' by 'P' everywhere they occur. Thus it still counts as affirming the consequent.

We need to be cautious, however, if we obliterate distinctions between letters. If in the preceding form, we replace 'P' by 'Q', and make no other changes, we get

If Q, then Q
Q
∴   Q

This form is still affirming the consequent, but it is also affirming the antecedent. We might call it "affirming both the consequent and the antecedent"!

For brevity, logicians have invented symbols to represent logically significant terms, that is, **logical operators.**[3] We shall represent 'if . . . then', for example, by the symbol '→'. So instead of 'if P then Q', from now on we may write 'P → Q'. To save space, we often write an entire form on one line. In this format we shall

---

[3] This is not, of course, an exact definition, but as we shall see later (especially in Section 9.4), the exact definition of 'logical operator' is a matter of dispute.

use the symbol '⊢', often called the **turnstile,** instead of '∴', and separate the premises with commas. Thus modus ponens, for example, is written as 'P → Q, P ⊢ Q'. An argument form written in this format is called a **sequent.**

'If . . . then' is not the only logical operator. In this chapter we consider four others. These correspond roughly to the English expressions 'it is not the case that', 'and', 'or', and 'if and only if', which we represent respectively by the symbols '~', '&', '∨', and '↔'.[4] (Often 'and' is accompanied by the word 'both' and 'or' by the word 'either'; these additions are usually for clarity or emphasis and do not affect the logical meaning.) What is common to all five operators is that they apply to propositions to produce more complex propositions. That is why the form of logic considered in this chapter is known as **propositional logic.** In later chapters we will consider operators that apply to entities of other types.

The operators 'if . . . then', 'and', 'or', and 'if and only if' are called **binary** or **dyadic operators,** because they combine two statements into a new statement. We may, for example, use the operator 'and' to combine the separate statements 'it is Wednesday' and 'it is hot' into a new statement 'it is Wednesday and it is hot'. The operator 'it is not the case that', by contrast, applies to only one proposition at a time and hence is **monadic** or **unary.** We may, for example, affix it to the sentence 'it is Wednesday' to form the new sentence 'it is not the case that it is Wednesday'.

The operator expressed by the symbol '~' is called the **negation operator,** and a proposition resulting from its application is called a **negative proposition** or **negation.** The symbol '&' is the **conjunction operator;** it combines two propositions, called **conjuncts,** into a **conjunction.** Similarly, '∨' is the **disjunction operator;** it combines two propositions, called **disjuncts,** into a **disjunction.** The **biconditional operator** '↔' is the least familiar of the five. It combines two propositions, which we shall call **constituents,** into a **biconditional.** A biconditional asserts the equivalence of its components in the sense that if either one is true, so is the other.

These five operators can be combined with sentence letters to produce an infinity of argument forms. The central aim of formal propositional logic is to establish methods for deciding which of these forms are valid and which are not.

As a first step toward this goal, we might attempt to evaluate forms informally, by the method of counterexamples explained in Section 1.2. That is, given a sequent, we might by trial and error attempt to produce invalid instances— instances for which there is a possible situation that makes the premises true but

---

[4] Just as mathematicians use both '·' and '×' to represent multiplication, so logicians sometimes use other symbols to represent these operators:

Logical Operator	Alternative Symbol(s)	
It is not the case that	−	¬
And	•	∧
Or	(none)	
If . . . then	⊃	
If and only if	≡	

the conclusion untrue. The hope would be that either we find an invalid instance, thus showing the sequent to be invalid, or we fail to find an invalid instance, but as a result of our search become familiar enough with the sequent to see that it is valid.

Consider, for example, the sequent 'P ∨ Q ⊢ P ↔ Q'. To test its validity informally, we consider instances, more or less at random. Suppose we take this instance:

> Either it is a skunk or it is a badger.
> ∴   It is a skunk if and only if it is a badger.

Now it is not difficult to formulate a counterexample. Consider a possible situation in which the animal referred to by the word 'it' is a skunk but not a badger. Then the premise is certainly true, but the conclusion is false. For the conclusion asserts that if it's a skunk it's also a badger, and vice versa, but in the situation we are envisioning (which is perfectly possible) it is a skunk but not a badger.

If we try to find an invalid instance of the sequent 'P → Q, ~Q ⊢ ~P', by contrast, we meet with repeated failure. (This sequent, incidentally, is called *modus tollens*—i.e., mode of denying, or **denying the consequent.**) Consider this instance:

> If you press the accelerator, the engine speeds up.
> It is not the case that the engine speeds up.
> ∴   Therefore, you are not pressing the accelerator.

We might at first attempt a counterexample along these lines: Maybe the engine is malfunctioning or simply turned off so that even though you are pressing the accelerator it is not speeding up. This, of course, is a possible situation. But it is not a counterexample, because it is a situation in which the first premise is false. Or maybe the engine is not speeding up, though whenever you press the accelerator it does speed up. But then you are certainly not pressing the accelerator. This, once again, is a possible situation, but it is not a counterexample because it is a situation in which the conclusion is true.

By repeated failures to find a counterexample, both with this instance and with other instances of modus tollens, we might eventually gain confidence in the validity of the form itself and maybe even see why it is valid. This method, how-ever, is intuitive and imprecise. It relies heavily on inventiveness and the powers of imagination. And since for all of us these powers are limited, it does not guarantee a correct answer—or any answer at all. There are better methods, as we shall soon see.

Exercise 2.1.1

Check the following forms for validity informally by attempting to construct an instance that has an obvious counterexample. If you can do so, write out the instance and describe the counterexample that shows it to be invalid. If not, or if you see that the argument is valid, simply write 'valid' for that form.

1. P → Q, ~P ⊢ ~Q

2. $P \vdash P \& Q$
3. $P \& Q \vdash P$
4. $P \vee Q \vdash P$
5. $P \vdash P \vee Q$
6. $P \to Q \vdash Q \to P$
7. $P \to Q \vdash P \to \sim\sim Q$
8. $P \leftrightarrow Q \vdash Q \leftrightarrow P$
9. $P \leftrightarrow Q \vdash P \& Q$
10. $P, \sim P \vdash Q$

Exercise 2.1.2

Given that modus ponens is also called affirming the antecedent and modus tollens is also called denying the consequent, what is the name of the sequent in problem 1 of Exercise 2.1.1?

2.2 FORMALIZATION

In this section we present the syntax (grammar) of the language of propositional logic. Fundamental to an understanding of syntax is the notion of the *scope* of a logical operator. The **scope** of a particular occurrence of an operator consists of that occurrence of the operator itself, together with whatever it is operating on. Consider, for example, the following pair of English sentences:

It is not the case that boron is both a compound and an element.

Boron is a compound, and it is not the case that it is an element.

In the first sentence—which, incidentally, is true—the negation operator applies to the entire conjunction 'boron is both a compound and an element', or, more explicitly, 'boron is a compound and boron is an element'. Thus the scope of the negation operator is the entire sentence. In the second sentence, which is false, the negation operator applies only to the subsentence 'it [boron] is an element'. Its scope is thus only the second conjunct of the second sentence—that is, the sub-sentence 'it is not the case that it [boron] is an element'.

In representing the forms of these two sentences in the language of propositional logic, we need some conventions for indicating scope. For this purpose, we borrow from algebra the idea of using brackets as punctuation. Using brackets, we can represent the form of the first of the two sentences above as '~(C & E)'. The second is then symbolized as 'C & ~E'.

In algebra, the negative sign '−' is presumed to apply just to the term it immediately prefixes, unless brackets are used to extend its scope. Thus the expression '−3 + 5' represents the number 2, because '−' applies just to the numeral '3'. But in the expression '−(3 + 5)', the '−' applies to '(3 + 5)' so that this expression represents the number −8. We use brackets similarly in logic. The negation sign is presumed to apply to whatever formula it immediately prefixes, unless we extend its scope with brackets.

Brackets are also needed to determine scope when two or more binary operators occur in the same formula. Suppose you receive the following announcement in the mail:

> You have won ten thousand dollars and a Caribbean cruise or a dinner for two.

You might well be puzzled, for this announcement is ambiguous. Using 'T' for 'you have won ten thousand dollars', 'C' for 'you have won a Caribbean cruise', and 'D' for 'you have won a dinner for two', we may symbolize the sentence either as 'T & (C ∨ D)' or as '(T & C) ∨ D'. There is a big difference. If the first formula represents what is meant, you have won ten thousand dollars, plus a cruise or a dinner. If (as is most likely) the second formula represents what is meant, then, even if the announcement is true, you probably have won only a dinner.

This sort of multiplicity of meaning is called **scope ambiguity.** In the first formula, the scope of the conjunction operator is the whole formula and the scope of the disjunction operator is just the second conjunct. In the second formula, the scope of the disjunction operator is the whole formula and the scope of the conjunction operator is just the first disjunct. Without brackets, the scopes of the two operators are indeterminate and, as with the English sentence, it is not clear what is meant.

Because one of the purposes of propositional logic is to clarify thought, its grammatical rules prohibit expressions such as 'T & C ∨ D', which are ambiguous in just the way the contest announcement is, because of the absence of brackets. To prevent such ambiguities, each binary operator in a grammatical formula must be accompanied by a pair of brackets that indicate its scope. There is only one exception: We may omit a pair of brackets that surround everything else in a formula, since brackets in this position are not needed to prevent ambiguity. Thus, instead of '(T & (C ∨ D))', which is strictly correct, having a pair of brackets for each of the formula's two binary operators, we may, if we like, write 'T & (C ∨ D)', as we did in the preceding example, dropping the outermost brackets, the ones that indicate the scope of the '&'.

Negation requires no brackets of its own. We can negate any part of the formula '(C ∨ D)', for example, simply by appropriate placement of the negation operator. The possible locations for a single negation operator are as follows: '~(C ∨ D)', '(~C ∨ D)', '(C ∨ ~D)'. The brackets that come with the '∨' (which we have kept here in the second and third formulas, even though we could have omitted them), together with the placement of '~' suffice to define the scopes of both '~' and '∨'. Even when we iterate negations, as in '~~P' ("it is not the case that it is not the case that P"), no brackets are needed. Because '~' applies to the smallest whole formula to its right, the scope of the leftmost occurrence of '~' is the whole formula and the scope of the rightmost occurrence of '~' is '~P'.

All formulas of propositional logic contain sentence letters as their ultimate constituents. Thus sentence letters are called **atomic** formulas, and, by analogy, formulas consisting of more than just a single sentence letter are called **complex,** or **molecular,** formulas.

Recall that the scope of an occurrence of a logical operator is that occurrence of the operator together with all the parts of the formula to which it applies. More precisely, it is the smallest formula containing that occurrence of the operator (which often is only a part of a larger formula). Each molecular formula has one and only one operator whose scope is that entire formula. This operator is called the formula's **main operator,** and it defines the formula's fundamental form. The main operator of the formula '(P & (Q ∨ R))', for example, is '&'. The formula as a whole is thus a conjunction, though its second conjunct is a disjunction. In the formula '~(P → (Q ∨ R))' the main operator is '~'. This formula is therefore negative; more specifically, it is the negation of a conditional whose consequent is a disjunction. Recognition of the main operator in a formula is crucial in constructing semantic trees or planning proof strategies, procedures that are discussed in the next two chapters.

The task of representing the forms of arguments in propositional logic is complicated by the fact that there are many ways of expressing the logical operators in natural language. English has, for example, many ways of expressing negation. Usually, of course, instead of saying 'it is not the case that', we simply append 'not' to the sentence's verb. 'It is not the case that I am going' sounds better as 'I am not going'. But we use the more awkward wording to emphasize that from a logical point of view negation is an operation that applies to a whole sentence, not just to a verb.

Prefixes such as 'non-', 'im-', 'in-', 'un-', 'a-', 'ir-', and so on may also express negation. But not always. 'He is incompetent' is arguably synonymous with 'it is not the case that he is competent', but 'gasoline is inflammable' does not mean the same thing as 'it is not the case that gasoline is flammable'! Likewise, 'she uncovered the dough' does not mean the same thing as 'it is not the case that she covered the dough'. Negation is not the only kind of opposition.

To determine whether we are dealing with true negation or some other form of opposition, we must ask whether what we are dealing with can be adequately expressed by the phrase 'it is not the case that'. If so, it is negation. If not, it is something else.

Conjunction may be expressed not only by the terms 'and' or 'both . . . and', but also by 'but', 'nevertheless', 'furthermore', 'moreover', 'yet', 'still', and so on. These terms connote differing nuances of contrast or connection, yet like 'and' they all perform the logical operation of linking two sentences into a compound sentence that affirms them both. Even a semicolon between two sentences may express conjunction in English.

English sentences with compound subjects or predicates are usually treated in propositional logic as conjunctions of two complete sentences. Hence we think of the sentence 'Sal and Jeff were here' as abbreviating 'Sal was here and Jeff was here' and the sentence 'Sal danced and sang' as abbreviating 'Sal danced and Sal sang'.

Often where two sentences are linked by a word that expresses conjunction, we may question whether to treat them as a conjunction or as separate sentences. From a logical point of view it makes little difference. The argument 'He's big and he's mean, so he's dangerous' is equally well rendered into propositional logic as 'B & M ⊢ D' or as 'B, M ⊢ D'. Neither sequent is valid.

Conditionals also have important variants. They can, for example, be presented in reverse order, provided that the antecedent remains attached to the 'if'. The statement 'if it rains, it pours', for example, can also be expressed as 'it pours if it rains'. The form is in each case the same: 'R → P'. In either order, the antecedent is always the clause prefixed by 'if'.

There is one exception. Where 'if' is preceded by the term 'only', what it prefixes is the consequent, not the antecedent. The following four sentences, for example, all assert the same (true) conditional proposition:

If you are pregnant, then you are female.

You are female if you are pregnant.

Only if you are female are you pregnant.

You are pregnant only if you are female.

In each case, 'you are pregnant' is the antecedent and 'you are female' the consequent. The form of all four is the same: 'P → F'. If we reverse antecedents and consequents, we get four sentences of the form 'F → P'. These, too, all affirm the same proposition, but it is a different proposition from that affirmed by the first group of four, a proposition that is (fortunately) not in all cases true.

If you are female, then you are pregnant.

You are pregnant if you are female.

Only if you are pregnant are you female.

You are female only if you are pregnant.

Many people find it difficult to keep the meanings of 'if' and 'only if' distinct. Keep in mind that 'if' always prefixes antecedents and 'only if' always prefixes consequents, and you should have no trouble.

Given these remarks about 'if' and 'only if', it ought to be clear that the biconditional operator 'if and only if' may be understood as a conjunction of two conditionals, one expressed by 'if', the other by 'only if'. Hence 'P ↔ Q' just means '(P → Q) & (Q → P)'. We could therefore dispense with the symbol '↔' and treat all biconditionals as conjunctions of two conditionals in this way. But we retain '↔', partly in deference to tradition, partly because it saves writing.

Apart from the optional addition of 'either', the term 'or' has few variants in English. We may regard it, however, as a component of the important term 'neither . . . nor'. Etymologically, this is a contraction of 'not either . . . or'; it thus expresses negated disjunction. The sentence 'it will neither snow nor rain', for example, may be symbolized as '~(S ∨ R)'. It is also acceptable to symbolize this statement as '~S & ~R', which is logically equivalent to '~(S ∨ R)', though this symbolization has the disadvantage of failing to reflect the English etymology.

The term 'unless' may be thought of as expressing another two-operator combination, a conditional with a negated antecedent. 'We will starve unless we eat' says the same thing as 'if we do not eat, we will starve'. We may thus symbolize the sentence as '~E → S'. Alternatively, 'unless' may be understood simply as expressing disjunction, in which case it prefixes the first disjunct. So we may also symbolize 'we will starve unless we eat' as 'E ∨ S'. These two symbolizations are equally correct.

Exercise 2.2.1

Formalize each of the sentences below, using the following interpretation scheme:

P — the peasants revolt   Q — the queen hesitates
R — the revolution will succeed   S — the slaves revolt

1. Either the peasants will revolt or the slaves will revolt.
2. Both the peasants and the slaves will revolt.
3. The peasants and the slaves will not both revolt.
4. If the peasants revolt, then the revolution will not succeed.
5. The peasants revolt if and only if they don't fail to revolt.
6. Only if the peasants revolt will the slaves revolt.
7. The revolution will succeed only if the queen hesitates.
8. If the peasants revolt and the queen hesitates, the revolution will succeed.
9. If the peasants revolt, then the revolution will succeed if the queen hesitates.
10. The revolution will not succeed unless the queen hesitates.
11. The peasants will revolt whether or not the queen hesitates.
12. The revolution will succeed if the slaves and the peasants both revolt.
13. If either the peasants or the slaves revolt and the queen hesitates, then the revolution will succeed.
14. If the peasants revolt but the slaves don't, the revolution will not succeed, and if both the peasants and the slaves revolt, the revolution will succeed.
15. If the peasants revolt if and only if the slaves revolt, then neither will revolt.

Exercise 2.2.2

Use premise and conclusion indicators to determine the premises and conclusions of the following arguments, then symbolize them in the formal notation of propositional logic using the sentence letters whose interpretation is specified below. (The forms of all of these arguments, incidentally, are valid in classical logic.)

Sentence Letter	Interpretation
B	Descartes believes that he thinks
E	Descartes exists
K_1	Descartes knows that he thinks
K_2	Descartes knows that he exists
J	Descartes is justified in believing he thinks
T	Descartes thinks

1. If Descartes thinks, then he exists; for he doesn't both think and not exist.

2. If Descartes thinks, then he exists. Hence he does not think, because he does not exist.
3. Descartes is justified in believing that he thinks if he knows that he thinks. But he is not justified in believing that he thinks, so he does not know that he thinks.
4. If Descartes knows that he thinks, then he exists. For if he knows that he thinks, then he thinks; and if he thinks, then he exists.
5. Descartes does not exist. For either he knows that he exists or he doesn't exist; and he doesn't know that he exists.
6. Descartes believes that he thinks. If he does not think, he does not believe that he thinks. Therefore Descartes thinks.
7. If Descartes thinks, then he knows that he exists, and if he knows that he exists, then he exists. Therefore, if Descartes thinks, then he both knows that he exists and really does exist.
8. If Descartes does not exist, then he doesn't think; so if he thinks, it is not the case that he does not exist.
9. Descartes neither exists nor does not exist. Therefore Descartes thinks.
10. Descartes knows that he thinks if and only if (1) he believes that he thinks, (2) he is justified in believing that he thinks, and (3) he does in fact think. Therefore, if Descartes does not think, then he does not know that he thinks.

2.3 FORMATION RULES

The formulas of propositional logic have a grammar, and that grammar (or syntax) may be precisely articulated as **formation rules.** Formation rules define what counts as a formula by giving general directions for assembling formulas out of simple symbols, or characters. They are the rules of grammar for a formal language. In order to state the formation rules for propositional logic, we need first to define the **character set** for propositional logic—that is, the alphabet and punctuation marks from which the formulas of its language are constructed. We stipulate that a **character** for the language of propositional logic is anything belonging to one of the following four sets:

Sentence letters:	Capital letters from the English alphabet
Numerals:	0 1 2 3 4 5 6 7 8 9
Logical operators:	~ & ∨ → ↔
Brackets:	( )

The only novelty here is the numerals. These are used to form subscripts for sentence letters when we want to use the same letter for two different sentences and need a means to keep the letters distinct. Moreover, without subscripts we could symbolize no more noncompound sentences than we have capital letters—that is, twenty-six. And though we are unlikely in practice to need more than twenty-six letters at once, a system of logic should not be subject to such arbitrary restrictions.

With these ideas in mind, we are ready to state the **formation rules**—the rules of grammar for the language of propositional logic; they define the notion of a grammatical formula by telling how to construct such formulas, starting with sentence letters, and combining them with the operators and brackets.

Formation Rules for Propositional Logic

1. Any sentence letter, with or without a sequence of numerals as a subscript, is a formula.
2. If Φ is a formula, then so is ~Φ.
3. If Φ and Ψ are formulas, then so are $(\Phi \,\&\, \Psi)$, $(\Phi \lor \Psi)$, $(\Phi \to \Psi)$ and $(\Phi \leftrightarrow \Psi)$.

Anything that is not a formula by finitely many applications of these rules is not a formula. Notice that in stating the formation rules, we use Greek letters (which belong to the metalanguage (see Section 1.5), *not* to the language of propositional logic). They are variables that stand for formulas of propositional logic. The Greek indicates generality. For example, 'Φ' and 'Ψ' in rule 3 stand for *any* formulas, no matter how simple or complex. When they are combined with operators and brackets into a complex expression, this expression stands for any formula obtainable by replacing the Greek letters with formulas. Thus, for example, the expression '$(\Phi \,\&\, \Psi)$' stands for '(P & Q)', '(~R & S)', '((P ∨ R) & (Q → ~~S))', and so on. Use of English letters here would be inappropriate, since they would too easily be confused with individual expressions of the object language.[5] In contrast to such expressions as '(P & Q)', expressions containing Greek letters, such as '$(\Phi \,\&\, \Psi)$', are not formulas. Rather, they are metalinguistic devices used for referring to whole classes of formulas.

Repeated (recursive) application of the formation rules enables us to construct a great variety of formulas. So, for example, 'P' and 'Q' are formulas by rule 1. Hence by rule 3, '(P ∨ Q)' is a formula. Now by rule 1 again 'R' is a formula, from which it follows by rule 2 that '~R' is a formula and again by rule 2 that '~~R' is a formula. Hence, since both '(P ∨ Q)' and '~~R' are formulas, by rule 3 '((P ∨ Q) → ~~R)' is a formula. And since this is a formula, by rule 2 again, '~((P ∨ Q) → ~~R)' is also a formula. And so on! In this way we can build up formulas as complex as we like.

---

[5] To see this more clearly, suppose that instead of rule 2 we wrote:

    2'   If 'P' is a formula, then so is '~P'.

Then the rule would tell us only how to generate this one formula '~P'. It would not tell us how to generate '~~P' or '~Q'. If, by contrast, we put the rule this way:

    2"   If P is a formula, then so is ~P

we would be mixing the object language and the metalanguage confusingly. It's not clear what this means. The Greek says exactly what we want while avoiding these problems.

Notice that the only formation rule that introduces brackets is rule 3. This means that the only legitimate function of a pair of brackets is to delineate the scope of some binary operator. In particular, brackets are not used to indicate the scopes of either sentence letters or the negation operator. Thus, for example, none of the following expressions count as formulas:

(P)   ~(P)   (~P)   ~(~P)   **(All wrong!)**

Exercise 2.3

Some of the following expressions are formulas of propositional logic. Others are not. For those that are, explain how they are built up by the formation rules. For those that aren't, explain why they can't be built up by the formation rules.

1. (P) ∨ (Q)
2. (P & Q)
3. P & Q
4. ~~~P
5. ~(P ∨ (Q & S))
6. (Φ → Ψ)
7. ((P & Q) ∨ (R & S))
8. P
9. (P → P)
10. (P & Q & R)

3

CLASSICAL PROPOSITIONAL LOGIC: SEMANTICS

3.1 TRUTH CONDITIONS

In this chapter we examine *semantics* of classical propositional logic. **Semantics** is the study of meaning. The logical meaning of an expression is usually understood as its contribution to the truth or falsity of sentences in which it occurs. By rigorously characterizing the meanings (in this sense) of the logical operators, we deepen our understanding of validity and related concepts.

Logicians have traditionally defined meaning in terms of possible truth. To know the meaning of a sentence, they have assumed, is to know which possible situations or circumstances make it true and which make it false. For example, if we wished to check a student's understanding of the sentence 'The government is an oligarchy', we might describe various possible political arrangements, asking each time whether the government described was an oligarchy. The pattern of the student's responses to these scenarios would quickly reveal whether she knows what 'The government is an oligarchy' means.

Or, to take a more sophisticated example, philosophers sometimes debate what is meant by such sentences as 'James knows that God exists'. To clarify their understanding, they ask whether or not the sentence would be true in various possible situations. Suppose, for example, that James has been brought up from earliest childhood to believe in God. Would that make it true that he knows God exists? Suppose he has had a mystical vision in which it seemed to him that God gave him a message. Would that make it true? Suppose that he has had such a vision and that God really did give him the message. The point of these queries is to clarify the meaning of the sentence 'James knows that God exists'—or, more broadly, to clarify the meaning of the predicate 'knows' in application to religious assertions. And the general assumption of the inquiry is that to know the meaning of a sentence or term is to know which possible situations make that sentence true or that term truly applicable.

This assumption is often expressed by saying that the meaning of a term is its **truth conditions.** The truth conditions for a term are rules that specify the possible situations in which sentences containing that term are true and the possible situations in which sentences containing that term are false.

In this section we give a truth-conditional semantics for the five logical operators introduced in Chapter 2. That is, we explain their meanings in terms of the possible situations in which sentences containing them are true and the possible situations in which sentences containing them are false.

In doing so, we shall employ the concept of *truth value.* A **truth value** is a kind of semantic quantity that characterizes propositions. For now, we assume that there are only two truth values: **true,** or **T,** and **false,** or **F.** A true proposition has the value T and a false proposition the value F. Moreover, we assume that in each possible situation each proposition has one, and only one, of these truth values. This assumption is called the **principle of bivalence.** Logics based on the principle of bivalence and the assumption that meaning is truth conditions are called **classical.** The dominant logics in Western thought have been classical.

Some philosophers have held that classical logic is universally the best form of logic, or even the only true logic. This book dissents from that view. In Part V we shall explore reasons for thinking that the principle of bivalence, though appropriate for some applications of logic, is less appropriate for others. We shall consider truth values other than T and F and the possibility that sentences may have more than one truth value, or none at all. And in Section 16.2, we question even the idea that meaning has anything to do with truth. There we explore a semantics that defines the meanings of terms, not as their truth conditions, but as their **assertibility conditions**—the conditions under which statements containing these terms are confirmable by adequate evidence. And beyond that we shall glimpse still more radical ways of departing from the classical tradition. Each of these novel semantic assumptions alters our conception of what valid reasoning is. For now, however, we present the semantics of the logical operators in the classical way, as bivalent truth conditions.

We begin with classical logic for two reasons. First, it is highly established in the Western logical tradition—our tradition. Second, it is, from a semantic viewpoint at least, the simplest logic, and it is best to start with what is simple.

Our immediate task, then, is to define the meanings of the five logical operators in terms of their truth conditions. We begin with the conjunction operator. If we conjoin two sentences—say, 'it is Wednesday' and 'it is hot'—we obtain a single sentence ('it is Wednesday and it is hot') that is true if and only if both original sentences were true, and false otherwise. Hence the truth conditions for conjunction may be stated as follows:

> The truth value of a conjunction is T in a given situation iff the truth value of each of its conjuncts is T in that situation.

and

> The truth value of a conjunction is F in a given situation iff one or both of its conjuncts does not have the value T in that situation.

(The term 'iff' is a commonly used abbreviation for 'if and only if'.) To understand these truth conditions is, by the lights of classical logic, to understand what conjunction means.

All of this is well and good if we aim to state the truth conditions for conjunction when applied to statements of natural language. But we have taken a step of abstraction into formal logic. We are no longer concerned primarily with sentences, like 'it's Wednesday and it's hot', but with formulas, like 'W & H'. Simple sentences have been replaced with sentence letters. But a sentence letter, such as 'W', has in itself no meaning and is neither true nor false. Of course we can *give* it a meaning by associating it with a particular statement of natural language. But this we do differently in different contexts. For one problem 'W' may mean "it's Wednesday," for another "Water is H_2O." So what can it mean to talk about a situation that makes a mere formula like 'W & H' true?

Two things are needed to make talk about possible situations intelligible in formal propositional logic. The first is an interpretation of the sentence letters. **Interpretations** are given by associating sentence letters with statements of natural language. The interpretation of a sentence letter may vary from problem to problem, but within a given problem we keep the interpretation fixed. Thus we may stipulate, for example, that (for the duration of this example) 'W' means "it's Wednesday" and 'H' means "it's hot." Let us now, in fact, stipulate this. The second thing we need to make sense of the notion of a possible situation is the concept of a valuation:

DEFINITION A **valuation** of a formula or set of formulas of propositional logic is an assignment of one and only one of the truth values T and F to each of the sentence letters occurring in that formula or in any formula of that set.

For a formula, such as 'W & H', that contains two sentence letters, there are four valuations, as shown in the following table:

W	H
T	T
T	F
F	T
F	F

That is, both 'W' and 'H' might be true, 'W' might be true and 'H' false, 'W' might be false and 'H' true, and both 'W' and 'H' might be false. Given an interpretation of the sentence letters, each valuation defines a situation. For example, given the interpretation stipulated above, the valuation that assigns T to both 'W' and 'H' defines a possible situation in which it is both Wednesday and hot. Similarly, the valuation that assigns T to 'W' and F to 'H' defines a possible situation in which it is Wednesday but not hot, and so on.

Stipulation of the interpretation, however, though obviously essential for applying logic to natural language, is inessential from a purely formal point of view. To state truth conditions for the logical operators, we need only to say how the truth values of sentences containing them depend on the truth values of their components, not what the components themselves have been interpreted to mean. Hence truth conditions for formal logic need concern themselves only with valuations, not with interpretations. A valuation alone is not a possible situation, but merely a pattern of truth values—the empty form, as it were, of a possible situation. It has the advantage, however, of being an entity definable with mathematical precision. If we disregard particular interpretations of sentence letters and think of abstract valuations rather than possible situations, we enter a realm of formal thought where everything is sharply defined and clear. The truth conditions for conjunction now look like this:

> The truth value of a conjunction is T on a given valuation iff the truth value of each of its conjuncts is T on that valuation.

and

> The truth value of a conjunction is F on a given valuation iff one or both of its conjuncts does not have the value T on that valuation.

Because these more abstract truth conditions are stated in terms of valuations, they are often referred to as **valuation rules.**

Valuation rules will appear so often from now on that it will be useful to abbreviate them. We shall use the script letter "$\mathcal{V}$" to stand for valuations, and, as in the previous section, Greek capital letters will stand for formulas. Instead of the cumbersome phrase 'the value assigned to Φ by $\mathcal{V}$', we shall write "$\mathcal{V}(\Phi)$'. Thus, to say that $\mathcal{V}$ assigns the value T to Φ, we write simply "$\mathcal{V}(\Phi) = T$'. Using this notation, we may state the valuation rules for conjunction more compactly as follows:

$\mathcal{V}(\Phi \ \& \ \Psi) = T$ iff both $\mathcal{V}(\Phi) = T$ and $\mathcal{V}(\Psi) = T$.
$\mathcal{V}(\Phi \ \& \ \Psi) = F$ iff either $\mathcal{V}(\Phi) \neq T$ or $\mathcal{V}(\Psi) \neq T$, or both.[1]

---

[1] We could also state the second rule this way:

$\mathcal{V}(\Phi \ \& \ \Psi) = F$ iff either $\mathcal{V}(\Phi) = F$ or $\mathcal{V}(\Psi) = F$, or both.

But then a question might arise regarding the truth value of '$\Phi \ \& \ \Psi$' if somehow Φ or Ψ lacked truth value or had some value other than T or F. Defining the falsity of the conjunction in terms of the untruth, rather than the falsity, of its components makes conjunctions bivalent even if their components are not. Bi-

The same idea may be expressed in tabular form, listing the four possible combinations of truth value for Φ and Ψ on the left and the resulting truth value for Φ & Ψ on the right:

Φ	Ψ	Φ & Ψ
T	T	T
T	F	F
F	T	F
F	F	F

This is called a **truth table.** Truth tables are, perhaps, easier to read than valuation rules. But, unlike the rules, they have the disadvantage of not being generalizable to more advanced forms of logic. Rules will prove more useful in the long run, which is why we emphasize them here.

Let's now examine the truth conditions for the negation operator. If we attach it to a sentence—say, 'It's snowing'—we get a negated sentence: for example, 'It is not the case that it's snowing'. If the sentence is true, its negation is false. If the sentence is false, its negation is true. This is vividly apparent when negation is iterated. The sentence 'It is not the case that it is not the case that it's snowing', for example, is just an elaborate way of saying 'It's snowing'; any situation in which one sentence is true is a situation in which the other is true, and in any situation in which one sentence is false, the other is false as well. Two negations "cancel out," producing a statement with the same meaning as the original. By the same principle, three negations have the same effect as one, four likewise cancel out, and so on. Negation, then, is simply an operation that inverts truth value. Hence the truth conditions for negation may be stated precisely as follows:

$$\mathcal{V}(\sim\!\Phi) = \text{T iff } \mathcal{V}(\Phi) \neq \text{T.}$$
$$\mathcal{V}(\sim\!\Phi) = \text{F iff } \mathcal{V}(\Phi) = \text{T.}$$

This, according to classical logic, is the meaning of negation. We can also represent these rules in a truth table. Since the negation operator is monadic, applying to a single formula rather than to two, there are only two cases to consider instead of four: the case in which that formula is true and the case in which it is false. The table shows that $\sim\!\Phi$ has the value listed in the right column when Φ has the value listed to the left:

---

valence is thus built into the valuation rules themselves. In fact, throughout this book I consistently define all semantic ideas in terms of truth and untruth, rather than truth and falsehood. This saves a good bit of trouble in the metatheoretic work of Chapter 5 and facilitates a smooth transition to nonclassical logics in Part V.

Often both valuation rules are stated together in a very compact fashion, as follows:

$$\mathcal{V}(\Phi \ \& \ \Psi) = \text{T iff both } \mathcal{V}(\Phi) = \text{T and } \mathcal{V}(\Psi) = \text{T; otherwise, } \mathcal{V}(\Phi \ \& \ \Psi) = \text{F.}$$

Our formulation says exactly this, but it is more explicit about what "otherwise" means.

Φ	~Φ
T	F
F	T

Let's now consider the truth conditions for 'or'. 'Or' has two meanings. It can mean "either . . . or . . . and possibly both" or "either . . . or . . . and not both." The first meaning is called **inclusive disjunction** and the second **exclusive disjunction**. This ambiguity is unfortunate. Suppose, for example, that on a true–false quiz you find the statement

Four is either an even number or a square number.

What should you answer? Four is both even and square. So, you might argue, it is not *either* even or square—that is, not just one of these two things—it's *both*. In that case you would mark the statement false. On the other hand, you might think that since four is even (and also since it's square), it's true that it is even or square. In that case you would mark the statement true.

In neither case would you be wrong, and in neither case would you have misunderstood anything. But if you marked the statement false, that would mean you understood the 'or' exclusively, and if you marked it true, that would mean you understood it inclusively.

This problem might be less acute if we were speakers of Latin. In Latin there are two words for 'or': '*vel*' and '*aut*'. In most contexts, '*vel*' more naturally expresses the idea "either . . . or . . . and possibly both" (the inclusive sense), and '*aut*' tends to mean "either . . . or . . . and not both" (the exclusive sense of 'or'). In English we sometimes resolve the ambiguity by using the compound term 'and/ or' for the inclusive sense. But both 'or' by itself and 'either . . . or' generally admit of both readings. When we use them, we or our listeners may not know exactly what we mean.

This situation would be intolerable in a formal logical language. Formal logic aims at precision. Its operators must have clear and unambiguous meanings. Therefore, when we introduce an operator like '∨' we must stipulate precisely what it means. Logicians usually have found the inclusive sense of 'or' more useful, and so, by convention, that is the sense they have given to the operator '∨'. In fact, '∨' is just an abbreviation for '*vel*'.

Apart from cases in which both disjuncts are true (the cases on which the inclusive and exclusive senses of 'or' disagree), the truth conditions for 'or' are clear. If one disjunct is true and the other false (e.g., 'either the sun is a star or the moon is'), then the whole disjunction is true. And if both disjuncts are false (e.g., 'either the moon is a star or the earth is'), then the disjunction is false. Hence the valuation rules for the operator '∨' are as follows:

$\mathcal{V}(\Phi \vee \Psi) = T$ iff either $\mathcal{V}(\Phi) = T$ or $\mathcal{V}(\Psi) = T$, or both.
$\mathcal{V}(\Phi \vee \Psi) = F$ iff both $\mathcal{V}(\Phi) \neq T$ and $\mathcal{V}(\Psi) \neq T$.

The corresponding truth table is:

Φ	Ψ	Φ ∨ Ψ
T	T	T
T	F	T
F	T	T
F	F	F

The logical operator '∨', then, accurately symbolizes the English 'or' only when 'or' is used in the inclusive sense. In spite of this, we need not introduce a special symbol for exclusive disjunction, since 'P or Q', where 'or' is intended in the exclusive sense, may be symbolized in our notation as '(P ∨ Q) & ~(P & Q)'—that is, "either P or Q, but not both P and Q."

In formalizing arguments involving disjunction, we will for the sake of simplicity and consistency treat the disjunctions as inclusive, except when there is strong reason not to. But on those fairly frequent occasions when the meaning of 'or' is unclear, we should keep in mind that this policy is essentially arbitrary.

We now turn to the truth conditions for conditional statements. Under what conditions is Φ → Ψ true? Let's consider the case in which the antecedent Φ is false (we assume nothing about the consequent Ψ). Now, though Φ is false, the conditional invites us to consider what is the case *if* Φ, hence to suppose Φ true. This, however, yields a contradiction, from which (as we saw in Section 1.3) any proposition validly follows. Take a specific instance: The statement 'Napoleon conquered Russia' is false. Given this, it is (in a certain sense) true, for example, that if Napoleon conquered Russia, then Caesar conquered the universe. Indeed, if Napoleon conquered Russia, then anything you like is true—because the fact is that Napoleon didn't conquer Russia. Thus it appears that when Φ is false, Φ → Ψ is true, regardless of the truth value of Ψ.

Let us next consider the case in which the consequent Ψ is true. Then, whether or not Φ is true, Ψ is true (trivially). Take a specific instance: The statement 'Iron is a metal' is true. Then any conditional containing 'Iron is a metal' as its consequent is true. For example, 'If today is Tuesday, then iron is a metal' would be true—because whether or not it is Tuesday (i.e., regardless of the truth value of the antecedent), iron *is* a metal. Thus in general we may infer that Φ → Ψ is true when Ψ is true, regardless of the truth value of Φ.

We have now concluded that Φ → Ψ is true whenever Φ is false or whenever Ψ is true. Together these conclusions account for three of the four truth combinations for Φ and Ψ; that is, Φ → Ψ is true whenever Φ and Ψ are both true, or Φ is false and Ψ is true, or Φ and Ψ are both false. The only remaining case is the one in which Φ is true and Ψ false. But in this case the conditional is clearly false. If, for example, it is Tuesday and the weather is not hot, then the conditional 'if it is Tuesday, then it is hot' is obviously false.

To summarize, we have concluded that Φ → Ψ is true if Ψ is true (regardless of the truth value of Φ), Φ → Ψ is also true if Φ is not true (regardless of the truth value of Ψ), and Φ → Ψ is false if Φ is true and Ψ is not true. This covers all possible cases. Hence the truth conditions for '→' are as follows:

$\mathcal{V}(\Phi \rightarrow \Psi) = T$ iff either $\mathcal{V}(\Phi) \neq T$ or $\mathcal{V}(\Psi) = T$, or both.
$\mathcal{V}(\Phi \rightarrow \Psi) = F$ iff both $\mathcal{V}(\Phi) = T$ and $\mathcal{V}(\Psi) \neq T$.

The corresponding truth table is

Φ	Ψ	$\Phi \rightarrow \Psi$
T	T	T
T	F	F
F	T	T
F	F	T

The conditional defined by these truth conditions is called the **material conditional.**

If you were unconvinced by the reasoning that led us to the truth conditions for the material conditional, you are not alone. Many logicians (your author among them) are troubled by this reasoning.

Consider, once again, the last line on the truth table, the case in which Φ and Ψ are both false. I argued that the conditional was true in that case, since its antecedent contradicts the facts, and from a contradiction anything follows. Now surely conditionals are *sometimes* true when their antecedents and consequents are both false. The statement

(A) If you are less than an inch tall, then you are less than a foot tall.

for example, is uncontroversially true, though (taking 'you' as referring to you) its antecedent and consequent are both false. But the antecedent and consequent of the following statement are also both false, and yet, unlike statement (A), this statement seems false:

(B) If you have no lungs, then you can breathe with your eyeballs.

If, as these examples suggest, English conditionals are sometimes true and sometimes false when their antecedents and consequents are both false, then the truth value of an English conditional must not be determined solely by the truth values of its components. Something else must figure into the truth conditions.

An operator which forms compounds whose truth value is strictly a function of the truth values of the components is said to be **truth-functional.** The symbols '&', '~', '∨', and the material conditional as defined by the truth conditions above are truth-functional. But we have seen evidence that suggests that 'if ... then' is not a truth-functional operator and hence is not the material conditional.

Intuitively, what makes statement (A) true is not that its antecedent contradicts the facts, but that it is necessary, given that you are less than an inch tall, that you are also less than a foot tall. Correspondingly, what makes statement (B) false seems to be the lack of just such a necessary connection: It is not necessary, given that you have no lungs, that you can breathe with your eyeballs. This suggests that an English statement of the form 'if P then Q' is true if and only if such a necessary connection exists, regardless of the truth values of the components.

The truth conditions for the material conditional take into account only the truth values of the antecedent and consequent, not the presence or lack of such a necessary connection. This leads to anomalies not only in the case in which the antecedent and consequent are both false, but also in the case in which the antecedent is false and the consequent true. In that case a material conditional is true. But consider this statement:

If there are no people, then people exist.

Once again, contrary to the truth conditions for the material conditional, this seems false, and once again, the necessary connection is lacking. This case, in fact, is especially anomalous, since here the antecedent does not merely fail to necessitate the consequent—it actually necessitates the negation of the consequent.

Further anomalies occur in the case in which the antecedent and consequent are both true. Consider this example:

If the Mississippi contains more than a thimbleful of water, then it is the greatest river in North America.

The Mississippi contains considerably more than a thimbleful of water and it is the greatest river in North America, so both the antecedent and consequent are true. If it is a material conditional, it is therefore true. Yet many English speakers would say that this conditional is false. It seems false, once again, because it is not *necessary* given merely that the Mississippi contains more than a thimbleful of water that it is the greatest river in North America.

Thus English conditionals seem to be true only when there is a necessary connection between antecedent and consequent, whereas the truth conditions for material conditionals ignore all such connections, taking into account only the truth values of the antecedent and consequent.

What, then, of the reasoning by which I arrived at the truth conditions for the material conditional in the first place? It is sound—as applies to the material conditional, but not to English conditionals. I claimed, for example, that when the consequent Ψ of $\Phi \rightarrow \Psi$ is true, then whether or not Φ is true, Ψ is true. But this claim tacitly ignores the possibility that the truth or falsity of Φ might necessitate the falsity of Ψ so that (taking this necessary connection into account) it would be wrong to conclude that Ψ is true whether or not Φ is true. Thus I arrived at the truth conditions for the material conditional by implicitly assuming that such necessary connections do not affect the conditional's truth value.

A similar assumption underlies my reasoning in the case in which the antecedent is false. I claimed that when Φ is false, the supposition that Φ is true yields a contradiction, from which any proposition validly follows. Thus, given that Φ is false, if Φ then Ψ, that is, $\Phi \rightarrow \Psi$ is true—for any proposition Ψ. Thus I assumed that what determines the truth value of the conditional is simply the contradiction of its antecedent with the facts, rather than a necessary connection, or lack thereof, between the antecedent and consequent.

It was, therefore, by assuming that such necessary connections do not affect the truth value of the conditional that I arrived at the truth conditions for the material conditional. But this assumption seems false for at least some English conditionals. The material conditional is therefore not just another way of writing the English 'if . . . then'.[2]

But then if our aim is to evaluate arguments, which we normally formulate in English, why bother with the material conditional?

Part of the answer is historical. Beginning with the work of the Scottish philosopher David Hume (1711–1776), many thinkers, among them some of the founders of contemporary logic, have doubted the intelligibility of this idea of necessary connection. As a result, many have found the material conditional (whose truth conditions, though odd, are at least exact) preferable to English conditionals, whose truth conditions seem bound up with the suspect notion of necessity. Indeed, logicians have long dreamed of an ideal language, free of all ambiguity, unclarity, and dubious metaphysics; and the replacement of the English conditional by the material conditional offered hope of progress toward that goal. Early in this century, Bertrand Russell, Ludwig Wittgenstein, and other prominent philosophers held that with the creation of such a language the perennial philosophical problems, which they regarded as linguistic confusions, would simply dissolve. There is indeed much to be said for the replacement of murkier notions by clearer ones, but in the end we may be left wondering whether we have really solved the problems or merely changed the subject.

In any case, these early thinkers had little choice but to embrace the material conditional. They needed some sort of conditional operator, and it was not until midcentury that logicians began to formulate rigorous and illuminating truth conditions involving ideas of necessary connection. Moreover, the material conditional does mimic English conditionals fairly well in many cases. Like English conditionals, it is always false when its antecedent is true and its consequent false; and in the other cases its truth value sometimes agrees and sometimes disagrees with that of English conditionals. Certainly, it offers the best approximation to English conditionals among truth-functional operators. Moreover, its truth conditions are simple and precise. For these reasons, the material conditional has become the standard conditional of logic and mathematics.

Lately, however, logicians have formulated a variety of alternative truth conditions that seem to reflect more adequately the meanings of English conditionals. We shall consider some of these in later chapters. Unfortunately, none of these alternatives has won universal acclaim as the true meaning of 'if . . . then'. That is why we still bother with the material conditional.

This having been said, however, it must be admitted that the common textbook practice of symbolizing 'if . . . then' in English as the material conditional (a practice in which this textbook too has indulged) is not wholly defensible. The material conditional is at best a rough approximation to 'if . . . then', and some patterns of reasoning valid for the one are not valid for the other. We shall be more

---

[2] That, at least, is my view. Some logicians still insist that English conditionals *are* material conditionals. They say unabashedly that statements like 'if you have no lungs, then you can breathe with your eyeballs' are true. We can see why they say this by understanding what they mean by 'if . . . then', but I do not think that that is what the rest of us usually mean by 'if . . . then'.

careful about the difference between the material conditional and English conditionals for the remainder of this chapter. When considering instances of argument forms containing the material conditional, we shall not translate the material conditional back into English as 'if . . . then', but instead retain the symbol '→' as a reminder that its meaning lies solely in its truth conditions, not in what we normally mean by 'if . . . then'.

It remains to discuss the truth conditions for the biconditional operator '↔', which we have associated with the English expression 'if and only if'. Since, as we saw in Section 2.2, 'if' prefixes antecedents and 'only if' prefixes consequents, the statement form

Φ if Ψ

may be symbolized as Ψ → Φ, and the form

Φ only if Ψ

as Φ → Ψ. Thus the biconditional, as its name implies, can be understood as a pair of conditionals—more precisely, as a conjunction of two conditionals. As a conjunction, it is true if both conditionals are true, and it is false if either or both are untrue. Now if Φ and Ψ are either both true or both untrue, both conditionals are true (by the valuation rules for '→'). But if Φ is true and Ψ untrue, then Φ → Ψ is untrue; and if Φ is untrue and Ψ true, then Ψ → Φ is untrue. In either of these cases, the biconditional is false. Thus the truth conditions for the biconditional are as follows:

$\mathcal{V}(\Phi \leftrightarrow \Psi) = \text{T}$ iff either $\mathcal{V}(\Phi) = \text{T}$ and $\mathcal{V}(\Psi) = \text{T}$, or $\mathcal{V}(\Phi) \neq \text{T}$ and $\mathcal{V}(\Psi) \neq \text{T}$.
$\mathcal{V}(\Phi \leftrightarrow \Psi) = \text{F}$ iff either $\mathcal{V}(\Phi) = \text{T}$ and $\mathcal{V}(\Psi) \neq \text{T}$, or $\mathcal{V}(\Phi) \neq \text{T}$ and $\mathcal{V}(\Psi) = \text{T}$.

These rules yield the following truth table:

Φ	Ψ	Φ ↔ Ψ
T	T	T
T	F	F
F	T	F
F	F	T

The biconditional, in other words, is true if the two constituents have the same truth value and false if they differ in truth value.

Because the truth conditions for '↔' are just those for a conjunction of two material conditionals, '↔' is often called the **material biconditional** operator, and where Φ ↔ Ψ is true, Φ and Ψ are called **material equivalents.** Two formulas, then, are **materially equivalent** on a valuation if and only if they have the same truth value on that valuation.

The material biconditional shares with the material conditional the oddity of ignoring necessary connections between its components. If its components are either both true or both untrue a material biconditional is true, regardless of the existence or lack of existence of necessary or relevant connections between the

TABLE 3.1
Valuation Rules for Propositional Logic

For any formulas Φ and Ψ and any valuation $\mathcal{V}$:

1. $\mathcal{V}(\sim\Phi) = T$ iff $\mathcal{V}(\Phi) \neq T$;
     $\mathcal{V}(\sim\Phi) = F$ iff $\mathcal{V}(\Phi) = T$.

2. $\mathcal{V}(\Phi \mathbin{\&} \Psi) = T$ iff both $\mathcal{V}(\Phi) = T$ and $\mathcal{V}(\Psi) = T$;
     $\mathcal{V}(\Phi \mathbin{\&} \Psi) = F$ iff either $\mathcal{V}(\Phi) \neq T$ or $\mathcal{V}(\Psi) \neq T$, or both.

3. $\mathcal{V}(\Phi \vee \Psi) = T$ iff either $\mathcal{V}(\Phi) = T$ or $\mathcal{V}(\Psi) = T$, or both;
     $\mathcal{V}(\Phi \vee \Psi) = F$ iff both $\mathcal{V}(\Phi) \neq T$ and $\mathcal{V}(\Psi) \neq T$.

4. $\mathcal{V}(\Phi \rightarrow \Psi) = T$ iff either $\mathcal{V}(\Phi) \neq T$ or $\mathcal{V}(\Psi) = T$, or both;
     $\mathcal{V}(\Phi \rightarrow \Psi) = F$ iff both $\mathcal{V}(\Phi) = T$ and $\mathcal{V}(\Psi) \neq T$.

5. $\mathcal{V}(\Phi \leftrightarrow \Psi) = T$ iff either $\mathcal{V}(\Phi) = T$ and $\mathcal{V}(\Psi) = T$, or $\mathcal{V}(\Phi) \neq T$ and $\mathcal{V}(\Psi) \neq T$;
     $\mathcal{V}(\Phi \leftrightarrow \Psi) = F$ iff either $\mathcal{V}(\Phi) = T$ and $\mathcal{V}(\Psi) \neq T$, or $\mathcal{V}(\Phi) \neq T$ and $\mathcal{V}(\Psi) = T$.

---

components. Thus (importing '$\leftrightarrow$' into English) the following statements, however odd, are both true:

Life evolved on earth $\leftrightarrow$ Ronald Reagan was president of the United States.

Grass is purple $\leftrightarrow$ grass is colorless.

The first statement is true because both of its components are true, the second because both of its components are false. Obviously, then, '$\leftrightarrow$' differs from 'if and only if', just as '$\rightarrow$' differs from 'if . . . then'. The material biconditional and English biconditionals do agree, however, when one component is true and the other false; here the biconditional itself is surely false.

To summarize: The meanings of the five truth-functional operators of propositional logic are given by the rules in Table 3.1. These rules constitute the complete semantics for classical propositional logic. For each operator there is a rule telling when formulas of which it is the main operator are true and a rule telling when those formulas are false. Together this pair of rules implies each such formula is false if and only if it is not true. Hence collectively the valuation rules embody the principle of bivalence—the principle that each formula is either true or false, but not both, on all valuations.

The rules are numbered 1–5. We will use this numbering for future reference.

Exercise 3.1

The five operators discussed in this section are a somewhat arbitrary selection from among many possible truth-functional operators, some of them expressible by common words or phrases of English. Invent symbols and formulate truth tables and a valuation rule for binary operators expressible by these English terms (you may find it easier to do the truth tables first):

1. exclusive 'or'
2. '... unless ...'
3. 'neither ... nor ...'
4. 'not both ... and ...'; this is sometimes called the nand operator.

3.2 TRUTH TABLES

The valuation rules tell us what the operators of propositional logic mean. But they do more than that. They also enable us to understand why in some cases one formula must be true if others are true; that is, they enable us to understand why some argument forms are valid—and not merely to understand, but to confirm our understanding by calculation. Because propositional logic makes such calculations possible, it is sometimes called the **propositional calculus.**

In Chapter 1 we said that an argument is valid iff it has no counterexample—that is, iff there is no possible situation in which its premises are true but its conclusion is untrue. In this chapter we have shifted our attention from specific arguments to argument forms. For forms, too, we may define a notion of counterexample:

> DEFINITION A **counterexample** to a sequent or argument form is a valuation on which its premises are true and its conclusion is not true.

This notion of a counterexample is closely related to the earlier one. Given a counterexample to a sequent, we can always convert it to a counterexample to an argument that is an instance of that sequent by giving an appropriate interpretation to the form's sentence letters.

Consider, for example, the invalid sequent 'P ∨ Q ⊢ Q'. The valuation $\mathcal{V}$ such that $\mathcal{V}('P') = T$ and $\mathcal{V}('Q') = F$ is a counterexample to this sequent. For since $\mathcal{V}('P') = T$, by the valuation rule for disjunction $\mathcal{V}('P \vee Q') = T$. But $\mathcal{V}('Q') = F$. That is, $\mathcal{V}$ is a valuation that makes the premise 'P ∨ Q' of this sequent true and its conclusion 'Q' untrue. Now any interpretation that correlates 'P' with a true statement and 'Q' with a false one produces an instance of this sequent that has a counterexample. And, indeed, this counterexample will describe an *actual* situation. (An actual situation is, of course, a kind of possible situation; anything actual can be coherently described.) For example, suppose we interpret 'P' by the true statement 'People are mammals' and 'Q' by the false statement 'Quail are mammals'. Then (retaining the '∨' symbol) this interpretation yields the following instance of the sequent:

People are mammals ∨ Quail are mammals.
∴ Quail are mammals.

And in the actual situation the premise is true but the conclusion isn't.

Conversely, given a counterexample to an instance of a sequent, we can always construct a counterexample to the sequent by assigning to its sentence letters the truth values of the corresponding sentences in the counterexample to the instance. Consider, for example, this argument, which is an instance of the sequent 'P ⊢ P & Q':

> Bill is a prince.
> ∴   Bill is a prince & Jill is a queen.

Here is a counterexample to this argument:

> Bill is a prince, but Jill, the miller's daughter, is a poor but honest maiden, not a queen.

This counterexample makes 'Bill is a prince' true and 'Jill is a queen' false. We can turn it into a counterexample to the sequent by ignoring our interpretation of the sentence letters and assigning these truth values directly to the corresponding sentence letters themselves. The result is the valuation $\mathcal{V}$ such that $\mathcal{V}(\text{'P'}) = T$ and $\mathcal{V}(\text{'Q'}) = F$, which is a counterexample to the sequent.

In this way we can always convert a counterexample to an instance of a sequent into a counterexample to the sequent itself, and vice versa. This realization leads us to a new understanding of the concept of a valid argument form. In Section 2.1, we defined a valid argument form as a form all of whose instances are valid arguments. Thus an argument form is valid iff none of its instances have counterexamples. But we have just seen that for each possible situation that is a counterexample to an instance there is a valuation that is a counterexample to the form, and vice versa. Therefore, to say that no instances of the form have counterexamples is equivalent to saying that the form itself has no counterexamples. Thus we may equally well define validity for an argument form as follows:

DEFINITION A sequent or argument form is **valid** iff there is no valuation on which its premises are true and its conclusion is not true.

Likewise, since an invalid form is just one that has an instance with a counterexample, and since there is a counterexample to some instance iff the form has a counterexample, we may likewise redefine the concept of invalidity for an argument form:

DEFINITION A sequent or argument form is **invalid** iff there is at least one valuation on which its premises are true and its conclusion is not true.

We shall rely on these new definitions from now on. Central to both is the concept used by the valuation rules to define truth conditions: the concept of a valuation. Thus these definitions illuminate the relationship between the concepts of validity and invalidity and the valuation rules. The remainder of this chapter shows how to utilize this relationship to develop computational tests for validity and other semantic properties.

As a first step in this direction we note that, given a valuation, the valuation rules enable us to calculate the truth value of a formula or set of formulas from the truth values assigned to their component sentence letters. For example, given the valuation $\mathcal{V}$ such that $\mathcal{V}(\text{'P'}) = T$, $\mathcal{V}(\text{'Q'}) = T$, and $\mathcal{V}(\text{'R'}) = F$, we can calculate the truth value of the formula 'P $\rightarrow$ (Q & ~R)' as follows. Since $\mathcal{V}(\text{'R'}) \neq T$, by the valuation rule for negation, $\mathcal{V}(\text{'~R'}) = T$. And since both $\mathcal{V}(\text{'Q'}) = T$ and $\mathcal{V}(\text{'~R'}) = T$, by the valuation rule for conjunction $\mathcal{V}(\text{'Q & ~R'}) = T$. And, finally, since both $\mathcal{V}(\text{'P'}) = T$ and $\mathcal{V}(\text{'Q & ~R'}) = T$, by the valuation rule for the material conditional, $\mathcal{V}(\text{'P} \rightarrow \text{(Q & ~R)'}) = T$.

We may list the results of such calculations for all the valuations of a formula or set of formulas on a truth table. If we do this for the set of formulas that comprises a sequent, the table will display all the possible valuations of the premises and conclusion, each as a single horizontal line. We can then, simply by scanning down the table, check to see if there is a line (i.e., a valuation) on which the premises are true and the conclusion is false. If so, that line represents a counterexample to the sequent and the sequent is invalid. If not, then (since all the valuations of the sequent are displayed on the table) there is no counterexample and the sequent is valid. Here at last is a simple, mathematically rigorous test for validity, one that relies on neither intuition nor imagination!

Let's try it out. Our example will be a sequent expressing modus ponens, where '$\rightarrow$' is now explicitly understood as the material conditional. This sequent contains only two sentence letters, so it has four possible valuations (both 'P' and 'Q' true, 'P' true and 'Q' false, 'P' false and 'Q' true, both 'P' and 'Q' false), which we list in the two leftmost columns of the table. Then, beneath each formula of the sequent, we write its truth value on each of those valuations, like this:

P	Q	P $\rightarrow$ Q,	P	$\vdash$ Q
T	T	T	T	T
T	F	F	T	F
F	T	T	F	T
F	F	T	F	F

Each horizontal line represents a single valuation. For example, the second line from the bottom represents the valuation $\mathcal{V}$ such that $\mathcal{V}(\text{'P'}) = F$ and $\mathcal{V}(\text{'Q'}) = T$. To the right, below each formula of the sequent, is listed the truth value of that formula on $\mathcal{V}$. On this valuation, for example, 'P $\rightarrow$ Q' is true. Since the truth table is a complete list of valuations, if there is a valuation on which the premises are true and the conclusion is not, it will show up as a line on the table. In this case, there is no such line, that is, no counterexample. (The only valuation on which both premises are true is the first one listed, the valuation $\mathcal{V}$ such that $\mathcal{V}(\text{'P'}) = T$ and $\mathcal{V}(\text{'Q'}) = T$. But on this valuation the form's conclusion 'Q' is true.) Thus modus ponens is valid for the material conditional.

Affirming the consequent, which is sometimes confused with modus ponens, is, as we saw in Section 2.1, intuitively *in*valid. Its truth table confirms our intuitions:

P	Q	P → Q,	Q	⊢ P
T	T	T	T	T
T	F	F	F	T
F	T	T	T	F
F	F	T	F	F

On the third valuation listed in the table the premises 'P → Q' and 'Q' are both true, but the conclusion 'P' is false. This valuation is therefore a counterexample to the sequent, proving it invalid.

We can use the counterexample displayed in the truth table to construct instances of the sequent that are invalid arguments. Since the valuation which makes 'P' false and 'Q' true provides a counterexample, we need merely substitute any sentence that is actually false for 'P' and any sentence that is actually true for 'Q' to obtain an invalid instance. Since these are the truth values these sentences have in the actual situation, a description of the actual situation constitutes a counterexample to that instance. Let 'P', for example, be the false sentence 'Logic is a kind of biology' and 'Q' the true sentence 'Logic is an intellectual discipline'. Then we obtain this instance:

> Logic is a kind of biology → Logic is an intellectual discipline.
> Logic is an intellectual discipline.
> ∴ Logic is a kind of biology.

The premises of this argument are true and its conclusion false in the actual situation.

This technique sometimes yields puzzling instances whose conditional premise, though actually true, seems false if we confuse '→' with 'if . . . then'. But keeping the truth conditions for '→' distinctly in mind resolves the puzzlement.

To obtain the values listed under the formulas in the preceding tables, we just copied them from one of the leftmost columns (if the formula was a sentence letter) or derived them directly from the valuation rules (in the case of the conditional formulas). With more complex formulas, however, we may need to apply the valuation rules successively, a step at a time, to calculate truth values for whole formulas.

Consider the sequent '(P & Q) ∨ (~P & ~Q) ⊢ ~P ↔ ~Q'. (To give this some intuitive content, we might interpret 'P' as the statement 'The princess dines' and 'Q' as the statement 'The queen dines'. This makes the argument: Either the princess and queen both dine or neither dines; therefore the princess does not dine if and only if the queen does not dine.) We begin the table for this sequent as before by listing the four possible valuations of the two sentence letters 'P' and 'Q' in the two leftmost columns. Now we use the valuation rules to calculate truth values, starting with the sentence letters and working our way up to more and more complex formulas. The first step is to copy the 'P' column at the left of the table under each occurrence of the sentence letter 'P' in the formulas and the 'Q' column under each occurrence of 'Q'. Where 'P' or 'Q' are directly preceded by '~', however, we know that their truth values will be reversed, so in these cases we reverse each truth value in the column we copy. The table now lists the truth values for all sentence letters or negated sentence letters in the formulas:

P	Q	(P	&	Q)	∨	(~P	&	~Q)	⊢	~P	↔	~Q
T	T	T		T		F		F		F		F
T	F	T		F		F		T		F		T
F	T	F		T		T		F		T		F
F	F	F		F		T		T		T		T

Notice that we have written the columns for negated sentence letters under the negation signs. In general, whenever we are listing the truth values for a complex formula, we write them under the operator whose scope is that formula.

The next step is to use the valuation rules to calculate the truth values for the formulas directly joining those whose truth values we have already identified. In the case of the premise, these are the two conjunctions 'P & Q' and '~P & ~Q'. Remembering that a conjunction is true iff both conjuncts are true, we place a 'T' beneath '&' on lines where the sentence letters it joins are both true and an 'F' in all other cases. In the case of the conclusion, the operator joining the '~P' and '~Q' is the biconditional, and its scope is the entire conclusion. This biconditional is true on those lines in which '~P' and '~Q' have the same truth value and false where they differ in truth value. We write these values beneath the symbol '↔'. The truth table now looks like this:

P	Q	(P	&	Q)	∨	(~P	&	~Q)	⊢	~P	↔	~Q
T	T	T	T	T		F	F	F		F	T	F
T	F	T	F	F		F	F	T		F	F	T
F	T	F	F	T		T	F	F		T	F	F
F	F	F	F	F		T	T	T		T	T	T

One step in our calculation remains. The premise is a disjunction of the two conjunctions whose truth values we have just determined. A disjunction is true if and only if one or both of its disjuncts are true; otherwise, it is false. Using this rule, we write the appropriate truth values beneath the symbol '∨':

P	Q	(P	&	Q)	∨	(~P	&	~Q)	⊢	~P	↔	~Q
T	T	T	T	T	T	F	F	F		F	T	F
T	F	T	F	F	F	F	F	T		F	F	T
F	T	F	F	T	F	T	F	F		T	F	F
F	F	F	F	F	T	T	T	T		T	T	T

We also circle the column under the main operator of each formula. Only the circled values, the ones listing the truth values for whole formulas, matter. The other columns of truth values on the table are merely part of the calculation by which the circled values were obtained.

As before we read the table by scanning down the columns of truth values for whole formulas (the circled columns), looking for a valuation on which the premise but not the conclusion is true. There isn't any; that is, there is no counterexample. So the sequent is valid.

When a sequent contains two sentence letters, there are four valuations of that sequent and hence four lines on the truth table. But not all argument forms contain two sentence letters. Some contain only one, some three or more. Where the number of sentence letters in a sequent is n, the number of valuations of the sequent, and the number of lines on its truth table, is 2^n. Thus a sequent containing only one sentence letter has $2^1 = 2$ valuations, a sequent containing three has $2^3 = 8$ valuations, a sequent containing four has $2^4 = 16$ valuations, and so on.

It is useful to list the valuations in a standard order. Our convention is as follows: List all the sentence letters of the sequent horizontally in the top left corner of the table *in alphabetical order*. (Where the letters have superscripts the order remains alphabetical, but letters with lower superscripts are written before those with higher superscripts, and letters with no superscripts come first of all.)

Then list the valuations under these letters as follows. Beneath the *rightmost* letter, write a column of alternating 'T's and 'F's, beginning with 'T', continuing downward until you have written 2^n 'T's and 'F's, where n is the total number of sentence letters. Then under the next rightmost letter, write another column of 'T's and 'F's, beginning with 'T', but doubling the number alternated. In other words, write two 'T's, two 'F's, and so on, downward until again you have written 2^n 'T's and 'F's. Now moving to the next rightmost letter (if one remains) and beginning, as always, with 'T' (because, after all, truth deserves priority over falsehood), write another column of 2^n T's and F's, doubling the alternation again (four 'T's, four 'F's, and so on). Keep moving to the left, doubling the number of the alternation between T's and F's until each letter has a column of 'T's and 'F's beneath it. For the three letters 'P', 'Q', and 'R', for example, the listing of valuations looks like this:

P	Q	R	
T	T	T	
T	T	F	
T	F	T	
T	F	F	
F	T	T	
F	T	F	
F	F	T	
F	F	F	

Argument forms containing many sentence letters are tested for validity in just the same way as argument forms containing only one or two. Consider, for example, the sequent '(P & Q) → R ⊢ (P → R) & (Q → R)'. Once again, we simply recopy the columns for the sentence letters from the columns to the left, then calculate the values for formulas of successively larger scope by using the valuation rules, and finally circle the columns under the main operators. Here is the result:

P	Q	R	(P	&	Q)	→	R	⊢	(P	→	R)	&	(Q	→	R)
T	T	T	T	T	T	T	T		T	T	T	T	T	T	T
T	T	F	T	T	T	F	F		T	F	F	F	T	F	F
T	F	T	T	F	F	T	T		T	T	T	T	F	T	T
T	F	F	T	F	F	T	F		T	F	F	F	F	T	F
F	T	T	F	F	T	T	T		F	T	T	T	T	T	T
F	T	F	F	F	T	T	F		F	T	F	F	T	F	F
F	F	T	F	F	F	T	T		F	T	T	T	F	T	T
F	F	F	F	F	F	T	F		F	T	F	T	F	T	F

The table shows that two valuations are counterexamples to this sequent: the valuation on which 'P' is true and 'Q' and 'R' are false, and the valuation on which 'P' is false, 'Q' true, and 'R' false. Thus the sequent is invalid.

The significance of these counterexamples can be made clearer by considering a specific interpretation. Let 'P' stand for 'The match is lighted', 'Q' for 'You drop the match into a can of gasoline', and 'R' for 'An explosion occurs'. Then the first counterexample represents a situation in which the match is lighted but you don't drop it into a can of gasoline so that no explosion occurs, and the second counterexample represents a situation in which the match is not lighted and you do drop it into a can of gasoline but once again no explosion occurs.

Let's now consider the truth table for the sequent 'Q ⊢ P → P'. Like some of the examples discussed in Section 1.3, this sequent lacks relevance; yet it is clearly valid, as its truth table shows:

P	Q	Q	⊢	P	→	P
T	T	T		T	T	T
T	F	F		T	T	T
F	T	T		F	T	F
F	F	F		F	T	F

The sequent is valid because there is no valuation on which the premise is true but the conclusion is not. This, however, is due to a peculiarity of the conclusion: It is true on all valuations; it cannot in any way be false. In Section 1.3 we noted that a logical truth, that is, a *statement* true in all possible situations, validly follows from any set of premises. 'P → P' is, of course, a symbolic formula, not a statement. But if we supply it with an interpretation by assigning to 'P' some specific statement (*any* statement will do), then 'P → P' expresses a logical truth. In a sense, then, 'P → P' itself, though a formula and not a statement, is logically true. A formula that is logically true in this sense is said to be **valid**:

> DEFINITION A **valid formula** is a formula true on all of its valuations.

Up until now we have applied the term 'valid' exclusively to arguments or argument forms, not to formulas. Since it is important not to confuse the formulas with argument forms, perhaps we ought to use some other term here to avoid confusion. Yet there is a substantial justification for applying the term 'valid' to both. For a valid formula is in effect a valid sequent with no premises. That is, we may think of a valid formula as a formula which may legitimately function as a conclusion without any premises at all. Since there is no valuation on which this "conclusion" is not true, there is no valuation on which the (nonexistent) premises are true and the "conclusion" is not true, and hence no counterexample. A valid formula may thus be regarded as a limiting case of a valid sequent.

Actually, in propositional logic we do have a term that substitutes nicely for 'valid formula'. The term is 'tautology':

> DEFINITION A **tautology** is a formula whose truth table displays a column consisting entirely of 'T's under its main operator.

In elementary propositional logic, a tautology (or **tautologous formula**) and a valid formula are the same thing. But valuations in more advanced forms of logic are not always expressible by truth tables. Thus in later chapters we shall encounter valid formulas that are not tautologies. 'Valid formula' is the more general and widely applicable of the two terms.

Truth tables make it graphically clear why a tautology validly follows from any set of premises. Such an inference is valid because it has no counterexample. It can't have a counterexample (that is, a valuation on which the premises are true but the conclusion is not) because a tautologous (valid) conclusion is true on all valuations.

In Section 1.3 we also noted that any argument with an inconsistent set of premises is valid. The corresponding notions of inconsistency for a formula or set of formulas are as follows:

> DEFINITION A *formula* is **inconsistent** iff there is no valuation on which it is true.
>
> DEFINITION A *set of formulas* is **inconsistent** iff there is no valuation on which all the formulas in the set are true.

Inconsistent formulas may also be called **self-contradictory formulas** or **contradictions.** With regard to truth tables, a formula is inconsistent if and only if the column under its main operator contains only 'F's, and a set of formulas is inconsistent if and only if there is no horizontal line on which all formulas show a 'T' beneath their main operators.

In Section 1.3 we observed that any conclusion follows from an inconsistent set of premises. The medievals called this principle *ex falso quodlibet*—"from a falsehood, anything you please." (Actually, this is misleading; the phrase better fits the relation between the antecedent and consequent of the material conditional; a false antecedent materially implies whatever you please. But a merely *false* premise or premise set does not validly imply all conclusions. From the premise 'The Earth is flat', for example, we cannot validly deduce whatever we please. We can, however, do so from an *inconsistent* premise or premise set.) Ex falso quodlibet may be plainly depicted on a truth table. The premises of the sequent 'P, ~P ⊢ Q', for example, constitute an inconsistent set:

P	Q		P,	~P	⊢	Q
T	T		T	F		T
T	F		T	F		F
F	T		F	T		T
F	F		F	T		F

By scanning down the table, we see that there is no horizontal line (valuation) on which both premises are true so that the set consisting of the two premises is inconsistent. Obviously, then, there is no valuation on which both premises are true while the conclusion is not true. So the sequent is valid.

Corresponding to the two notions of inconsistency defined above are the following two notions of consistency:

DEFINITION A *formula* is **consistent** iff it is true on at least one valuation.

DEFINITION A *set of formulas* is **consistent** iff there is at least one valuation on which all the formulas in the set are true.

The truth table of a consistent formula has at least one 'T' in the column beneath its main operator. The truth table of a consistent set of formulas contains at least one horizontal line on which there is a 'T' beneath the main operator of every formula of the set. Some authors use the term '**satisfiable**' instead of 'consistent'.

Formulas which are consistent but not valid are said to be **contingent**:

DEFINITION A formula is **contingent** iff it is true on some of its valuations and not true on others.

TABLE 3.2
Semantic Classification of Formulas

Type of Formula	Definition	Truth-Table Indication
Valid (Tautologous)	True on all valuations	Column under main operator contains only 'T's
Contingent	True on at least one but not all valuations	Column under main operator contains both 'T's and 'F's
Inconsistent	True on no valuations	Column under main operator contains only 'F's

TABLE 3.3
Semantic Classification of Sets of Formulas

Type of Set	Definition	Truth-Table Indication
Consistent	There is at least one valuation on which all formulas in the set are true	Horizontal line on which all formulas in the set have 'T's under their main operators
Inconsistent	There is no valuation on which all formulas in the set are true	There is no horizontal line on which all formulas in the set have 'T's under their main operators

All formulas fall into one of the three categories: valid, contingent, or inconsistent. These are summarized in Table 3.2. A consistent formula, of course, is just one that is not inconsistent. It is therefore either valid or contingent. We could also, therefore, have divided all formulas into the two classifications, "consistent" and "inconsistent," instead of into the three categories described in Table 3.2. For *sets* of formulas this twofold classification is generally the most useful. See Table 3.3.

Truth tables are useful for detecting one other semantic relationship that is of great importance—logical equivalence:

DEFINITION Two formulas are **logically equivalent** iff they have the same truth value on every valuation of both.

With respect to truth tables, two formulas are logically equivalent if and only if the columns under their main operators are identical. Consider, for example, the formulas '~(P ∨ Q)' and '~P & ~Q', which as we saw in Section 2.2 are both ways of symbolizing 'neither P nor Q'. They are logically equivalent, as we can see by placing them both on the same truth table:

P	Q	~	(P	∨	Q)		~P	&	~Q
T	T	F	T	T	T		F	F	F
T	F	F	T	T	F		F	F	T
F	T	F	F	T	T		T	F	F
F	F	T	F	F	F		T	T	T

The truth table reveals their equivalence in that the columns under their main operators (the circled columns) are identical.

Logical equivalence is significant for several reasons. For one thing, logically equivalent formulas validly imply one another. That is, an inference from either as premise to the other as conclusion is valid. There can be no counterexample because since the two formulas have the same truth values on all valuations, there is no valuation on which the premise but not the conclusion of such an inference is true.

Further, since in classical logic meaning is truth conditions and since logically equivalent formulas have identical truth conditions, it follows that logically equivalent formulas have, for the purposes of classical logic, the same meaning. Thus '~(P ∨ Q)' and '~P & ~Q' are equally adequate symbolizations for 'neither P nor Q' because from the viewpoint of classical logic they are synonymous. 'Neither . . . nor', in other words, is not ambiguous. Rather, these formulas are two ways of expressing the single meaning that 'neither . . . nor' has in English. The logical meaning of 'neither . . . nor' is, in other words, simply the pattern of truth values the table for each of these formulas displays.

The material conditional formula 'P → Q' is equivalent to both '~P ∨ Q' and '~(P & ~Q)', as the following table shows:

P	Q	P	→	Q		~P	∨	Q		~	(P	&	~Q)
T	T		T			F	T	T		T	T	F	F
T	F		F			F	F	F		F	T	T	T
F	T		T			T	T	T		T	F	F	F
F	F		T			T	T	F		T	F	F	T

This means that so far as logic is concerned 'P → Q', '~P ∨ Q', and '~(P & ~Q)' all have the same meaning. Thus, whenever we symbolize a statement as 'P → Q', we could as well symbolize it as '~P ∨ Q' or as '~(P & ~Q)'. It follows that the material conditional is a needless redundancy. We could exclude it from the language of propositional logic and still be able (using '&' or '∨', and '~') to say everything we could say before. This is true even for very complex formulas. If, for example, we consistently replace formulas of the form Φ → Ψ with formulas of the form ~Φ ∨ Ψ, then instead of writing

P → (Q → R)

we would write

$$\sim P \lor (\sim Q \lor R)$$

Likewise, we could eliminate '↔' by taking formulas of the form $\Phi \leftrightarrow \Psi$ as abbreviations for more complex but equivalent formulas, say, those of the form $(\Phi \ \& \ \Psi) \lor (\sim\Phi \ \& \ \sim\Psi)$ (see problem 1 of Exercise 3.2.4). This would leave us with only three operators: '$\sim$', '$\&$', and '$\lor$'.

We could reduce our vocabulary still further, either by rewriting $\Phi \ \& \ \Psi$ as $\sim(\sim\Phi \lor \sim\Psi)$ or by rewriting $\Phi \lor \Psi$ as $\sim(\sim\Phi \ \& \ \sim\Psi)$ (see problems 2 and 3 of Exercise 3.2.4), thus eliminating either '$\&$' or '$\lor$'. Only two of the five operators, then, are really needed—either '$\sim$' and '$\&$' or '$\sim$' and '$\lor$'. And either of these pairs can be further reduced to a single operator, though not to one of the familiar five. This final reduction requires either the operator 'neither . . . nor', which is written as a downward pointing arrow, '↓', or as the operator 'not both . . . and', sometimes called 'nand', and written simply as '|'. (Neither symbol belongs to the language of propositional logic as we defined it in Section 2.3; thus to do this reduction we would have to adopt a new set of formation rules.) The truth tables for these operators are as follows:

Φ	Ψ	$\Phi \downarrow \Psi$		Φ	Ψ	$\Phi \mid \Psi$
T	T	F		T	T	F
T	F	F		T	F	T
F	T	F		F	T	T
F	F	T		F	F	T

Here we consider the reduction of '$\&$' and '$\sim$' to '|', leaving the reduction to '↓' as an exercise. This reduction depends on the equivalence of $\sim\Phi$ to $\Phi \mid \Phi$ and the equivalence of $\Phi \ \& \ \Psi$ to $\sim(\Phi \mid \Psi)$, that is, $(\Phi \mid \Psi) \mid (\Phi \mid \Psi)$, which the following truth tables illustrate:

Φ	$\sim\Phi$	$\Phi \mid \Phi$
T	F	F
F	T	T

Φ	Ψ	$\Phi \ \& \ \Psi$	$(\Phi \mid \Psi)$	$\mid$	$(\Phi \mid \Psi)$
T	T	T	F	T	F
T	F	F	T	F	T
F	T	F	T	F	T
F	F	F	T	F	T

(In each case we represent two separate formulas on the same table to show their equivalence.) Thus we can see that any formula has an equivalent whose sole operator is '|'. We can express the conditional 'P → Q', for example, first in terms of '~' and '&':

~(P & ~Q)

Then the negation sign prefixing 'Q' may be eliminated in terms of '|':

~(P & (Q|Q))

(The order in which we eliminate particular occurrences of '~' and '&' is arbitrary.) Next we eliminate the '&' in terms of '|':

~((P | (Q|Q)) | (P | (Q|Q)))

And finally, we eliminate the initial negation:

((P | (Q|Q)) | (P | (Q|Q))) | ((P | (Q|Q)) | (P | (Q|Q)))

The material conditional! In principle, we could by such means express every formula of propositional logic solely in terms of the operator '|'. The unreadability of the result explains why in practice we don't. Thus we will stick with the traditional five operators, chiefly because, though redundant, they give us a reasonably comprehensible language.

Yet here we have learned something remarkable: We can say much with paltry means if we are willing to tolerate long formulas. Humans generally are not; but, as we shall see in Chapter 10, computers have a different opinion.

Exercise 3.2.1

Use truth tables to test the following argument forms for validity. Write either 'valid' or 'invalid' beside the table to indicate the answer.

1. $P \vee Q, P \vdash Q$
2. $P \vee Q, \sim P \vdash Q$
3. $P \rightarrow Q \vdash \sim Q \rightarrow \sim P$
4. $P \rightarrow Q \vdash Q \rightarrow P$
5. $P \rightarrow Q, \sim P \vdash \sim Q$
6. $P \rightarrow Q, \sim Q \vdash \sim P$
7. $P \vdash Q \rightarrow P$
8. $\sim Q \vdash Q \rightarrow P$
9. $P \vdash P \rightarrow Q$
10. $\sim(P \rightarrow Q) \vdash P \& \sim Q$
11. $P \vee Q \vdash P \leftrightarrow Q$
12. $P \& Q \vdash P \leftrightarrow Q$
13. $P \& Q \vdash Q \& P$
14. $P \vee Q, P \rightarrow R, Q \rightarrow R \vdash R$
15. $P \vee Q, Q \vee R \vdash P \vee R$
16. $P \rightarrow Q, Q \rightarrow P \vdash P \leftrightarrow Q$

17. P ⊢ ~(P & ~P)
18. ~(P & Q) ⊢ ~P & ~Q
19. ~(P ∨ ~P) ⊢ Q
20. P ⊢ (P → Q) → (P & Q)

Exercise 3.2.2

Use truth tables to determine whether the following formulas are valid, contingent, or inconsistent. Write your answer beside the table.

1. P → ~P
2. P → ~~P
3. P ↔ ~~P
4. P ↔ ~P
5. (P ∨ Q) ∨ (~P & ~Q)
6. P & ~~P
7. P ∨ P
8. (P & (P → Q)) → Q
9. (P ∨ Q) ↔ (Q ∨ P)
10. (P → Q) ↔ (~P ∨ Q)

Exercise 3.2.3

Use truth tables to determine whether the following sets of formulas are consistent or inconsistent. Write your answer beside the table.

1. P → Q, Q → ~P
2. P ↔ Q, Q ↔ ~P
3. P ∨ Q, ~P, ~Q
4. P & Q, ~P
5. ~(P & Q), P ∨ Q

Exercise 3.2.4

1. Use a truth table to verify that 'P ↔ Q' is logically equivalent both to '(P → Q) & (Q → P)' and to '(P & Q) ∨ (~P & ~Q)'.
2. Use a truth table to verify that 'P & Q' is logically equivalent to '~(~P ∨ ~Q)'.
3. Use a truth table to verify that 'P ∨ Q' is logically equivalent to '~(~P & ~Q)'.
4. Use a truth table to verify that 'Q ∨ P' and '~Q → P', which are both ways of symbolizing 'P unless Q', are equivalent.
5. Find equivalents for the forms ~Φ and Φ & Ψ in terms of '↓', and show that they are logical equivalents by constructing the appropriate truth tables.
6. Find a logical equivalent for Φ ∨ Ψ in terms of '↓', and demonstrate the equivalence with a truth table. Do the same thing in terms of '|'.

3.3 SEMANTIC TREES

A semantic tree is a device for displaying all the valuations on which the formula or set of formulas is true. Since classical logic is bivalent, the valuations on which the formula or set of formulas is false are then simply those not displayed. Thus trees do the same job as truth tables. But they do it more efficiently; especially for long problems, a tree generally requires less computation and writing than the corresponding truth table. A truth table for a formula or sequent containing n sentence letters has 2^n lines. For $n = 10$, for example, $2^n = 1024$—a good many more lines than we are likely to want to write. But a tree for a formula or sequent with ten sentence letters (or even more) may fit easily within a page. Moreover, as we shall see in Section 7.4, trees have the advantage of being straightforwardly generalizable to predicate logic, which truth tables are not.

Suppose, for instance, that we want a list of the valuations on which the formula '~P & (Q ∨ R)' is true. To obtain this by the tree method, we write the formula and then begin to break it down into those smaller formulas which, according to the valuation rules, must be true in order to make '~P & (Q ∨ R)' true. Now '~P & (Q ∨ R)' is a conjunction, and a conjunction is true iff both of its conjuncts are true. So we write '~P & (Q ∨ R)', then check it off (to indicate that it has been analyzed), and write its two conjuncts beneath it, like this:

> √ ~P & (Q ∨ R)
>   ~P
>   Q ∨ R

A formula which has been checked off is in effect eliminated. We need pay no further attention to it. What remains, then, are the two formulas '~P' and 'Q ∨ R'. '~P' is true on just those valuations on which 'P' is false. But we still need to analyze 'Q ∨ R'.

Now, whereas a conjunction can be true in only one way (both conjuncts are true), there are two ways in which a disjunction can be true: Either the first disjunct is true or the second disjunct is true (or both—but this possibility is in effect already included in the other two, as will be explained shortly). Hence to analyze 'Q ∨ R', we check it and split our list into two branches, the first representing valuations in which 'Q' is true, the second representing valuations on which 'R' is true, as follows:

> √ ~P & (Q ∨ R)
>   ~P
> √ Q ∨ R)
>
>   ╱   ╲
>   Q   R

It is because lists may "branch" in this way that the structures we create by this procedure are called semantic *trees*. (But these trees grow downward!) When all formulas other than sentence letters or negated sentence letters have been checked off, as they have here, the tree is finished. This tree contains two "branches," or *paths,* one running from '~P & (Q ∨ R)' to 'Q', the other from '~P & (Q ∨ R)' to 'R'.

DEFINITION A **path** through a tree (in any stage of construction) is a complete column of formulas from the top to the bottom of the tree.

Now we scan along each path, looking for sentence letters or negated sentence letters. Along the first path we find '~P' and 'Q'. This shows that '~P & (Q ∨ R)' is true on those valuations which make both '~P' and 'Q' true, that is, those valuations which make 'P' false and 'Q' true. But 'R' does not appear either by itself or negated along the first path. This indicates that if 'P' is false and 'Q' true, '~P & (Q ∨ R)' is true, regardless of whether 'R' is true or false. The first path, then, represents these two valuations:

P	Q	R
F	T	T
F	T	F

Checking the second path for sentence letters or negated sentence letters, we find '~P' and 'R'. This means that '~P & (Q ∨ R)' is also true on valuations in which 'P' is false and 'R' is true, regardless of the truth value of 'Q', which does not appear, either alone or negated, along that path. Hence the second path represents these valuations:

P	Q	R
F	T	T
F	F	T

Notice that there is some redundancy here. Both paths represent the valuation on which 'P' is false and both 'Q' and 'R' are true. This is what I meant when I said a few paragraphs back that the possibility of both disjuncts being true is in effect already included in the possibilities of either disjunct being true. Thus together the two paths represent three valuations, not four:

P	Q	R
F	T	T
F	T	F
F	F	T

These are precisely the lines of the truth table on which '~P & (Q ∨ R)' is true; they represent all the valuations which make this formula true. In this way the tree procedure accomplishes exactly what truth tables do.

Sometimes as we are constructing a tree, we find that a formula and its negation both appear on the same path. Since no valuation can make both a formula and its negation true, this means that the path does not represent any valuation. It is merely a failed attempt to find valuations that make the formulas of the initial list true. Such a path is considered "blocked" or "closed," and this is indicated by writing an 'X' beneath it.

Consider, for example, the tree for the formula '~(P & Q) & P'. Since this formula is a conjunction, after writing it we check it and analyze it into its two conjuncts, like this:

$\checkmark$ ~(P & Q) & P
   ~(P & Q)
   P

Now '~(P & Q)' is true iff 'P & Q' is false. By valuation rule 2, 'P & Q' is false iff either 'P' or 'Q' or both are untrue—that is, by valuation rule 1, iff either '~P' or '~Q' or both are true. Thus we may check '~(P & Q)' and split our list into two branches, the first representing valuations on which '~P' is true, the second representing valuations on which '~Q' is true:

$\checkmark$ ~(P & Q) & P
   ~(P & Q)
   P

  ~P   ~Q
  X

We have placed an 'X' at the bottom of the left branch because the path it represents—the path extending from '~(P & Q) & P' to '~P'—contains both 'P' and '~P' and must be closed. This path represents no valuations. The path that follows the right branch, however, does not close. On it we find 'P' and '~Q'. Since these are the only letters in our initial formula, '~(P & Q) & P', that formula is true on only one valuation, namely, the valuation on which 'P' is true and 'Q' is false.

Sometimes all paths close. This indicates that the initial formula or set of formulas is not true on any valuations, that is, is inconsistent. Consider, for example, the formulas 'P ∨ Q', '~P', and '~Q', which together form an inconsistent set. We may set them down in a vertical list and apply the same procedure as above:

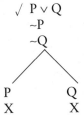

  $\checkmark$ P ∨ Q
    ~P
    ~Q

 P   Q
 X   X

When we check 'P ∨ Q' and analyze it into its two truth possibilities, 'P' and 'Q', we see that each of the resulting paths contains both a formula and its negation: 'P' and '~P' on the path that branches to the left, 'Q' and '~Q' on the path that branches to the right. So we place an 'X' at the bottom of each path to indicate that it is closed. With both paths closed, there is nothing more to be done. The tree is complete, and it shows that there are no valuations on which the formulas of our initial list ('P ∨ Q', '~P', and '~Q') are all true.

In summary, then, to construct a semantic tree, list the formula or set of formulas to be tested in a single column. Then check off a complex formula on the list, writing at the bottom of the list simpler formulas that would have to be true if this complex formula were true. If the complex formula can be true in more than one way, split the list and display formulas representing each of these ways on a separate "branch." Then repeat this procedure for other complex formulas in the list. Eventually along each path of the tree one of two things will occur. Either (1) all the formulas along that path of the tree will be simplified into sentence letters or negations of sentence letters or (2) some formula and its negation both will appear. In the first case, the path displays one or more valuations on which the initial formula or set of formulas is true—namely, those valuations on which isolated sentence letters along that path are assigned the letter T, negated sentence letters along that path are assigned the value F, and sentence letters not appearing either negated or unnegated along the path are assigned either T or F. In the second case, the path is a dead end and represents only a failed attempt to construct a valuation. We close it with an 'X'.

The following terminology will be helpful:

DEFINITION A *path* is **finished** if it is closed or if the only unchecked formulas it contains are sentence letters or negations of sentence letters so that no more rules apply to its formulas. A *tree* is **finished** if all of its paths are finished.

DEFINITION An **open path** is a path that has not been ended with an 'X'.

DEFINITION A **closed path** is a path that has been ended with an 'X'.

DEFINITION A formula **occurs on** a path if (1) it is on that path and is not merely a subformula of some other formula on that path and (2) it is unchecked.

In order to apply the tree procedure formally, we need to specify exact rules by which complex formulas are to be analyzed into simpler components. There is nothing surprising here. The tree rules simply mimic the valuation rules. This is why trees are called *semantic* trees. They are simply a perspicuous way of displaying the semantics for any formula or (finite) set of formulas.

There are ten tree rules, two for each of the valuation rules (that is, one for the truth clause and one for the falsity clause of each rule). Each tree rule is listed, along with the clause of the valuation rule to which it corresponds, in Table 3.4. The trees we have done so far have exemplified the negation, conjunction, negated conjunction, and disjunction rules.

The conjunction rule, for example, was the one we used to analyze '~(P & Q) & P' into its components:

1.   √ ~(P & Q) & P   Given
2.   ~(P & Q)   1 &
3.   P   1 &

Here we have repeated the first step of the tree for '~(P & Q) & P', annotating it by numbering and labeling the lines—a procedure which, having named the rules, we will follow from now on. Line 1 is marked 'given' to indicate that it is the given formula. Lines 2 and 3 are marked '1 &' to show that they are obtained from line 1 by the conjunction rule.

In the second step of this tree, we used the negated conjunction rule to show that there are two ways in which 'P & Q' can be false—namely, if 'P' is false or if 'Q' is false.

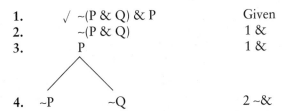

Finally, we complete the tree by closing the left branch with the negation rule. From now on we will annotate the 'X' by writing the line numbers on which we found the formula and its negation, which closed the path—in this case, lines 3 and 4:

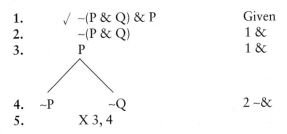

As noted previously, this tree shows that '~(P & Q) & P' is true on only one valuation—namely, the valuation on which 'P' is true and 'Q' is false.

Because a tree for a formula, a set of formulas, or a sequent displays all the information contained in a truth table for that formula, set of formulas, or sequent, any test that can be performed by a truth table can also be performed by a tree. To test a sequent for validity, for example, we must determine whether there is a valuation that makes its premises but not its conclusion true. This would, of course, be a valuation on which both the sequent's premises and the negation of

TABLE 3.4
The Ten Tree Rules

Valuation Rule	Corresponding Tree Rule
1 $\mathcal{V}(\sim\!\Phi) = T$ iff $\mathcal{V}(\Phi) \neq T$.	**Negation** (~) If an open path contains both a formula and its negation, place an 'X' at the bottom of the path.
$\mathcal{V}(\sim\!\Phi) = F$ iff $\mathcal{V}(\Phi) = T$.	**Negated Negation** (~~) If an open path contains an unchecked formula of the form ~~Φ, check it and write Φ at the bottom of every open path that contains this newly checked formula.
2 $\mathcal{V}(\Phi\ \&\ \Psi) = T$ iff both $\mathcal{V}(\Phi) = T$ and $\mathcal{V}(\Psi) = T$.	**Conjunction** (&) If an open path contains an unchecked formula of the form ($\Phi\ \&\ \Psi$), check it and list Φ above Ψ at the bottom of every open path that contains this newly checked formula.
$\mathcal{V}(\Phi\ \&\ \Psi) = F$ iff either $\mathcal{V}(\Phi) \neq T$ or $\mathcal{V}(\Psi) \neq T$, or both.	**Negated Conjunction** (~&) If an open path contains an unchecked formula of the form ~($\Phi\ \&\ \Psi$), check it and split the bottom of each open path containing this newly checked formula into two branches; at the end of the first write ~Φ, and at the end of the second write ~Ψ.
3 $\mathcal{V}(\Phi \lor \Psi) = T$ iff either $\mathcal{V}(\Phi) = T$ or $\mathcal{V}(\Psi) = T$, or both.	**Disjunction** ($\lor$) If an open path contains an unchecked formula of the form ($\Phi \lor \Psi$), check it and split the bottom of each open path containing this newly checked formula into two branches; at the end of the first write Φ, and at the end of the second write Ψ.
$\mathcal{V}(\Phi \lor \Psi) = F$ iff both $\mathcal{V}(\Phi) \neq T$ and $\mathcal{V}(\Psi) \neq T$.	**Negated Disjunction** (~$\lor$) If an open path contains an unchecked formula of the form ~($\Phi \lor \Psi$), check it and list ~Φ above ~Ψ at the bottom of every open path that contains this newly checked formula.

its conclusion are true. We may construct a tree to search for just such valuations by starting with the argument's premises and the negation of its conclusion.

Let's test the sequent 'P → (Q & (R ∨ S)) ⊢ P → Q'. Since it contains four sentence letters, the truth table would take $2^4 = 16$ lines—a laborious task. The tree method is much more efficient. We list the premise and the negation of the conclusion, labeling them as such to the right, and then analyze them by mechanically applying the tree rules. Here is the result:

TABLE 3.4
The Ten Tree Rules (*continued*)

Valuation Rule	Corresponding Tree Rule
4 $\mathcal{V}(\Phi \to \Psi) = T$ iff either $\mathcal{V}(\Phi) \neq T$ or $\mathcal{V}(\Psi) = T$, or both.	**Conditional ($\to$)** If an open path contains an unchecked formula of the form ($\Phi \to \Psi$), check it and split the bottom of each open path containing this newly checked formula into two branches; at the end of the first write ~Φ, and at the end of the second write Ψ.
$\mathcal{V}(\Phi \to \Psi) = F$ iff both $\mathcal{V}(\Phi) = T$ and $\mathcal{V}(\Psi) \neq T$.	**Negated Conditional (~$\to$)** If an open path contains an unchecked formula of the form ~($\Phi \to \Psi$), check it and list Φ above ~Ψ at the bottom of every open path that contains this newly checked formula.
5 $\mathcal{V}(\Phi \leftrightarrow \Psi) = T$ iff either $\mathcal{V}(\Phi) = T$ and $\mathcal{V}(\Psi) = T$, or $\mathcal{V}(\Phi) \neq T$ and $\mathcal{V}(\Psi) \neq T$.	**Biconditional ($\leftrightarrow$)** If an open path contains an unchecked formula of the form ($\Phi \leftrightarrow \Psi$), check it and split the bottom of each open path containing this newly checked formula into two branches; at the end of the first list Φ above Ψ, and at the end of the second list ~Φ above ~Ψ.
$\mathcal{V}(\Phi \leftrightarrow \Psi) = F$ iff either $\mathcal{V}(\Phi) = T$ and $\mathcal{V}(\Psi) \neq T$, or $\mathcal{V}(\Phi) \neq T$ and $\mathcal{V}(\Psi) = T$.	**Negated Biconditional (~$\leftrightarrow$)** If an open path contains an unchecked formula of the form ~($\Phi \leftrightarrow \Psi$), check it and split the bottom of each open path containing this newly checked formula into two branches; at the end of the first list Φ above ~Ψ, and at the end of the second list ~Φ above Ψ.

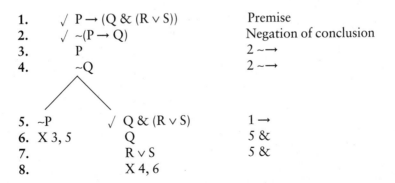

Both paths close, so there is no valuation which makes the premises but not the conclusion true. Hence the sequent is valid.

Notice that we closed the right branch without analyzing 'R ∨ S'. This is permissible. Any path may be closed as soon as a formula and its negation both appear on it. Analyzing 'R ∨ S' would have split this path into two new paths, but each of these still would have contained both 'Q' and '~Q' and hence each still would have closed. Closing a path as soon as possible saves work.

It also saves work to apply nonbranching rules first. When I began the tree, I had the choice of analyzing either 'P → (Q & (R ∨ S))' or '~(P → Q)' first. I chose the latter, because it is a negated conditional, and the negated conditional rule does not branch. If I had analyzed 'P → (Q & (R ∨ S))', which is a conditional, first, then I would have had to use the conditional rule, which does branch. Then when I analyzed '~(P → Q)', I would have had to write the results twice, once at the bottom of each open path. Analyzing 'P → (Q & (R ∨ S))' first is not wrong, but it requires more writing, as can be seen by comparing the resulting tree with the previous tree:

| 1. | ✓ P → (Q & (R ∨ S)) | | Premise |
| 2. | ✓ ~(P → Q) | | Negation of conclusion |

3.	~P	✓ Q & (R ∨ S)	1 →
4.	P	P	2 ~→
5.	~Q	~Q	2 ~→
6.	X 3, 4	Q	3 &
7.		R ∨ S	3 &
8.		X 5, 6	

Yet this tree, though more complicated, gives the same answer as the first. There is, then, some flexibility in the order of application of the rules. But in general it is best where possible to apply nonbranching rules before the branching ones.

Let's next test the sequent '(P ↔ Q) ⊢ ~(P ↔ R)' for validity. Once again we list the premises and the negation of the conclusion so that the tree searches for counterexamples. In this case the conclusion is a negation, so its negation is a double negative. Here is the tree:

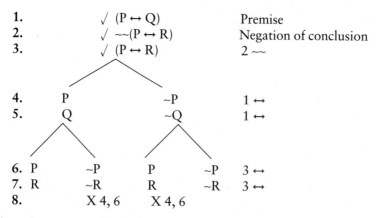

1.	✓ (P ↔ Q)		Premise
2.	✓ ~~(P ↔ R)		Negation of conclusion
3.	✓ (P ↔ R)		2 ~~

| 4. | P | ~P | 1 ↔ |
| 5. | Q | ~Q | 1 ↔ |

6.	P	~P	P	~P	3 ↔
7.	R	~R	R	~R	3 ↔
8.		X 4, 6	X 4, 6		

The leftmost and rightmost branches remain open. The leftmost branch reveals that the premise '(P ↔ Q)' is true and the conclusion '~(P ↔ R)' false (because its negation is true) on the valuation on which 'P', 'Q', and 'R' are all true. This valuation, in other words, is a counterexample to the sequent. The rightmost branch reveals that the valuation on which 'P', 'Q', and 'R' are all false is also a counterexample. Thus the sequent is invalid.

If we begin a tree, not with premises and a negated conclusion, but with a single formula or set of formulas, as we did in the first examples of this section, the tree tests this formula or set of formulas for consistency. If all paths close, there is no valuation on which the formula or set of formulas is true, and so that formula or set is inconsistent. If one or more paths remain open after the tree is finished, these represent valuations on which the formula or all members of the set are true, and so the formula or set is consistent.

Trees may also be used to test *formulas* for validity. The easiest way to do this is to search for valuations on which the formula is not true. If no such valuations exist, then the formula is valid. Thus we begin the tree with the formula's negation. If all paths close, there are no valuations on which its negation is untrue so that the original formula is true on all valuations. Consider, for example, the formula '(P → Q) ↔ ~(P & ~Q)'. When we negate it and do a tree, all paths close:

1.	√ ~((P → Q) ↔ ~(P & ~Q))		Negation of formula
2.	√ (P → Q) √ ~(P → Q)		1 ~↔
3.	√ ~~(P & ~Q) √ ~(P & ~Q)		1 ~↔
4.	P & ~Q 3 ~~		
5.	P 4 & P		2 ~→
6.	~Q 4 & ~Q		2 ~→
7.	~P Q 2 → ~P ~~Q		3 ~&
8.	X 5, 7 X 6, 7 X 5, 7 X		6, 7

Therefore, since there is no valuation on which '~((P → Q) ↔ ~(P & ~Q))' is true, '(P → Q) ↔ ~(P & ~Q)' is true on all valuations, that is, valid.

Notice that I closed the rightmost path before '~~Q' was fully analyzed. This is a legitimate use of the negation rule. If the path had not closed, however, the tree would not be finished until the negated negation rule was applied to '~~Q'.

Here is a list of some of the ways in which trees may be used to test for various semantic properties:

> **To determine whether a sequent is valid,** construct a tree starting with its premises and the negation of its conclusion. If all paths close, the sequent is valid. If not, it is invalid and the open paths display the counterexamples.

To determine whether a formula or set of formulas is consistent, construct a tree starting with that formula (or set of formulas). If all paths close, that formula (or set of formulas) is inconsistent. If not, it is consistent, and the open paths display the valuations that make the formula (or all members of the set) true.

To determine whether a formula is valid, construct a tree starting with its negation. If all paths close, the formula is valid. If not, then the formula is not valid, and the open paths display the valuations on which it is false.

To determine whether a formula is contingent, construct two trees, one to test it for consistency and one to test it for validity. If the formula is consistent but not valid, then it is contingent.

Constructing trees is just a matter of following the rules, but there are a few common errors to avoid. Keep these in mind:

The rules for constructing trees apply only to whole formulas, not to their parts. Thus, for example, the use of ~~shown below is not permissible:

1. √ P → ~~Q   Given
2. √ P → Q   1 ~~   **(Wrong!)**

Although using ~~ on subformulas does not produce wrong answers, it is never necessary and technically is a violation of the double negation rule. Trying to apply other rules to parts of formulas, however, often does produce wrong answers.

A rule applied to a formula cannot affect paths not containing that formula. Consider, for example, the following incomplete tree:

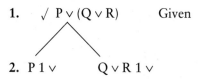

Here the formula 'Q ∨ R' at the end of the right-branching path remains to be analyzed. The next step is to apply the disjunction rule to this formula. In doing so, we split this right-branching path but add nothing to the path at the left, for it does not contain 'Q ∨ R' and is in fact already finished.

The negation rule applies only to formulas on the same path. In the following tree, for example, both 'P' and '~P' appear, but neither path closes because the formulas don't appear on the same path:

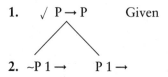

To summarize: A finished tree for a formula or a set of formulas displays all the valuations on which that formula or all members of that set are true. Thus trees do the same work as truth tables, but in most cases they do it more efficiently. Moreover, as we shall see in later chapters, they may be used for some logics to which truth tables are inapplicable.

Exercise 3.3.1

Redo Exercises 3.2.1, 3.2.2, and 3.2.3 using trees instead of truth tables.

Exercise 3.3.2

1. How might trees be used to prove that two formulas are logically equivalent? Explain.
2. To prove a formula valid using trees, we construct a tree from its negation. Is there a way to prove a formula valid by doing a tree on that formula without negating it? Explain.

3.4 VALUATIONS AND POSSIBLE SITUATIONS

We saw in Section 2.1 that while any instance of a valid form is a valid argument, not every instance of an invalid form is an invalid argument. We noted, for example, that this instance of the invalid sequent affirming the consequent is in fact a valid argument:

> If some men are saints, then some saints are men.
> Some saints are men.
> ∴   Some men are saints.

How can this be? The answer lies in the distinction between valuations and possible situations.

Suppose we let 'S_1' stand for 'Some men are saints' and 'S_2' for 'Some saints are men'. Then we can represent the form of the argument as '$S_1 \to S_2, S_2 \vdash S_1$'. Here is its truth table:

S_1	S_2	$S_1 \to S_2,$	S_2	$\vdash S_1$
T	T	T	T	T
T	F	F	F	T
F	T	T	T	F
F	F	T	F	F

The valuation in which 'S_1' is false and 'S_2' true is a counterexample to the *sequent* or *argument form*. But the corresponding situation—the one in which 'Some men are saints' is false and 'Some saints are men' is true—isn't a counterexample to the *argument* because it isn't a *possible* situation. The very idea of a situation in which some men are saints but it is not the case that some saints are men (i.e., no saints are men) is nonsense. Of course we can easily find other interpretations of 'S₁' and 'S₂'—and consequently other instances of this form—to which the valuation that makes 'S₁' false and 'S₂' true provides a genuine counterexample, even an *actual* counterexample. But on this particular interpretation, that valuation corresponds to an *im*possible situation. (Incidentally, so does the valuation that makes 'S₁' true and 'S₂' false.) An *im*possible situation, if it even makes sense to talk about such a thing, cannot be a counterexample.

Depending on how we interpret the sentence letters, then, a particular valuation may or may not correspond to a possible situation. For many interpretations, all valuations correspond to possible situations. For example, if we let 'S₁' stand for 'It is sunny' and 'S₂' for 'It is Sunday', every line on the truth table above (every valuation) represents a possible situation, and the valuation on which 'S₁' is false and 'S₂' true represents a counterexample to the argument as well as to the form. In such cases, the statements corresponding to the sentence letters are said to be **logically independent.** But where the statements corresponding to the sentence letters logically imply one another or exclude one another, in various combinations, some valuations represent impossible situations.

Such nonindependent statements as 'Some men are saints' and 'Some saints are men' have interrelated semantic structures that are not represented in propositional argument forms in which they are symbolized simply as sentence letters. (In this case, the semantic structures in question are relationships among the logical meanings of the words 'some', 'men', and 'saints'.) In Chapter 6 we shall begin to formalize the semantic structures of such statements, and we shall redefine the notion of a valuation so that it reflects more of these semantic structures and yields a more powerful and precise logic. Later we shall explore ways of creating logics that are more powerful and precise still. But at no point shall our concept of a valuation become so sophisticated that a valuation may never represent an impossible situation—which is to say that at no point do we ever achieve a formal semantics or formal logic that reflects all the logical dependencies inherent in natural language.

Certain consequences of this disparity between valuations and possible situations, between formal and informal logic, will haunt us throughout this book:

An invalid sequent may have valid instances. The reason for this we have already seen. The counterexamples to the sequent may on some interpretations represent impossible situations so that there are no possible situations which make the corresponding argument's premises true while its conclusion is untrue. No argument is valid *because of* having an invalid form, but an argument may be valid *in spite of* having an invalid form, because of elements of its semantic structure not represented in the form.

A contingent formula may have valid or inconsistent instances. A contingent formula is true on some valuations and false on others. But on some interpretations either the valuations on which the contingent formula is true or those on which it is false may all correspond to impossible situations. In the former case, the interpretation yields an inconsistent instance. In the latter, provided that at least one of the valuations on which the formula is true corresponds to a possible situation, the interpretation yields a valid instance. Example: 'P & Q' is a contingent formula, but the instance 'Some women are mortal & Nothing is mortal' is an inconsistent statement, and the instance 'Every woman is a woman & Every mortal is a mortal' is a valid statement (logical truth). (Check the truth table of 'P & Q' to see which valuations correspond to impossible situations in each case.)

A consistent formula or set of formulas may have inconsistent instances. That is, though there is a valuation that makes the formula or set of formulas true, there may not be a possible situation that makes a particular instance of that formula or set of formulas true, again because the situation corresponding to that valuation may be impossible. Example: The set consisting of the formulas 'P' and 'Q' is consistent, but if we interpret 'P' as 'Smoking is permitted' and 'Q' as 'Smoking is forbidden', the set of statements for which these letters stand is inconsistent.

All of this sounds discouraging. Nevertheless:

All instances of a valid sequent are valid arguments. A valid sequent has no valuation on which its premises are true but its conclusion is not true. Some valuations may on a particular interpretation correspond to impossible situations. Yet since a valid sequent has no valuations representing situations (possible or impossible) in which the premises are true and the conclusion is false, none of its valuations represents a possible situation that is a counterexample to the instance. Hence, if a sequent is valid, all of its instances must be valid as well. Valid sequents are, in other words, perfectly reliable patterns of inference.

All instances of a valid formula are logical truths. A valid formula is a formula true on all valuations. Even if on a given interpretation some valuations of such a formula do not represent possible situations, the formula is still true on all the others and hence true in all the situations that are possible. Therefore any statement obtained by interpreting a valid formula must be true in all possible situations. That is, it must be a logical truth.

All instances of an inconsistent formula are inconsistent statements. An inconsistent formula is true on no valuations. Hence, even if on a given interpretation some of its valuations represent impossible situations, still the formula is true on none of the remaining valuations which represent possible situations. Therefore any statement obtained by interpreting an inconsistent formula is not true in any possible situation.

Under the same interpretation, logically equivalent formulas have as their instances logically equivalent statements. Logically equivalent formulas are formulas whose truth value is the same on all valuations. Once again, even if a given interpretation rules out some of these valuations as impossible, still the formulas will have the same truth value in the remaining valuations—the ones representing possible situations. Hence any two statements obtained by interpreting them will have the same truth values in all possible situations. That is, they will be equivalent statements.

To summarize: Formal validity (for both formulas and sequents), inconsistency, and equivalence are reliable indicators of their informal counterparts. Formal invalidity, contingency, and consistency are not.

4

CLASSICAL PROPOSITIONAL LOGIC: INFERENCE

4.1 CHAINS OF INFERENCE

Most people can at best understand arguments that use about three or four premises at once. For more complicated arguments, we generally break the argument down into more digestible chunks. Beginning with one or two or three premises, we draw a subconclusion, which functions as a stopping point on the way to the main conclusion the argument aims to establish. This subconclusion summarizes the contribution of these premises to the argument so that they may henceforth be forgotten. This subconclusion is then combined with a few more premises to draw a further conclusion, and the process is repeated, step by small step, until the final conclusion emerges. The following example illustrates the utility of breaking complex inferences down into smaller ones:

> The meeting must be held on Monday, Wednesday, or Friday.
> At least four of these five people must be there: Al, Beth, Carla, Dave, and Em.
> Em can't come on Monday or Wednesday.
> Carla and Dave can't both come on Monday or Friday, though either of them could come alone on those days.
> Al can come only on Monday and Friday.
> ∴ The meeting must be held on Friday.

The argument is difficult to understand all at once, but it becomes easy if analyzed into small steps. For example, from the premises

Em can't come on Monday or Wednesday.

and

Al can come only on Monday and Friday.

we can deduce the subconclusion

Neither Al nor Em can come on Wednesday.

And from this subconclusion together with the premise

At least four of these five people must be there: Al, Beth, Carla, Dave, and Em.

we can further conclude

The meeting can't be held on Wednesday.

In addition, from the premises

Em can't come on Monday or Wednesday.

and

Carla and Dave can't both come on Monday or Friday, though either of them could come alone on those days.

we can conclude

Em and either Carla or Dave can't come on Monday.

Putting this together with the premise

At least four of these five people must be there: Al, Beth, Carla, Dave, and Em.

yields the conclusion

The meeting can't be held on Monday.

Combining this with the previously derived conclusion that the meeting can't be held on Wednesday and with the premise

The meeting must be held on Monday, Wednesday, or Friday.

we get the conclusion

The meeting must be held on Friday.

Thus we analyze a complicated and forbidding inference into a sequence of simple inferences. The result of this process is summarized below in a more compact form, which we shall call a **proof**. A proof begins with the premises, or **assumptions,** of the unanalyzed argument, listed on separately numbered lines. We indicate which statements are assumptions by writing an 'A' to the right of each. Each successive conclusion is written on a new numbered line, with the line numbers of the premises (either assumptions or previous conclusions) from which it was deduced listed to the right. Here is our reasoning recorded as a proof:

1.	The meeting must be held on Monday, Wednesday, or Friday.	A
	At least four of these five people must be there: Al, Beth,	
2.	Carla,Dave, and Em.	A
3.	Em can't come on Monday or Wednesday.	A
	Carla and Dave can't both come on Monday or Friday, though	
4.	either of them could come alone on those days.	A
5.	Al can come only on Monday and Friday.	A
6.	Neither Al nor Em can come on Wednesday.	3, 5
7.	The meeting can't be held on Wednesday.	2, 6
8.	Em and either Carla or Dave can't come on Monday.	3, 4
9.	The meeting can't be held on Monday.	2, 8
10.	The meeting must be held on Friday.	1, 7, 9

The series of conclusions is listed on lines 6–10. None of these conclusions is drawn from more than three premises. Each inference is plainly valid. The proof ends when the desired conclusion is reached. In the remainder of this chapter, we explore a more formal version of this proof technique.

Exercise 4.1

Analyze each of the following arguments into simple inferences involving at most three premises each, and write the analyzed argument as a proof. Each inference in this proof should be obviously valid in the informal sense of validity discussed in Chapter 1, but it need not exemplify any prescribed formal rule. (Some simple formal inference rules are introduced in the next section.) There is not just one right answer; each argument may be analyzed in many ways.

1. If the person exists after death, then the person is not a living body.
    The person is not a dead body.
    Any body is either alive or dead.
    The person exists after death.
    ∴ The person is not a body.
2. x is an odd number.
    $x + y = 25$.
    $x > 3$.
    $30/x$ is a whole number.
    $x < 10$.
    ∴ $y = 20$.
3. You will graduate this semester.
    In order to graduate this semester, you must fulfill the humanities requirement this semester.
    You fulfill the humanities requirement when and only when you have taken and passed either (1) two courses in literature and a single course in either

philosophy or art or (2) two courses in philosophy and a single course in either literature or art.

You have taken and passed one art course but have taken no courses in philosophy or literature.

You have time to take at most two courses this semester.

Among the philosophy courses, only one is offered at a time when you can take it.

∴   You will take two literature courses this semester.

4.2 SIMPLE FORMAL INFERENCE RULES

In this section we introduce the idea of a proof, not for an argument but for a sequent or argument *form*. The idea, once again, is to break a complicated or dubious inference down into smaller inferences, each of which has a simple form. In formal proofs we require that these smaller inferences have one of a well-defined set of forms that we already recognize as valid. In the system of formal logic that we shall adopt there are ten such forms. The most familiar of them is modus ponens (introduced in Section 2.1).

To illustrate, let's construct a formal proof to demonstrate the validity of the sequent:

$$P \rightarrow (Q \rightarrow (S \rightarrow T)), P, P \rightarrow Q, S \vdash T$$

The first step is to write the assumptions in a numbered list, indicating that they are assumptions by writing an 'A' to the right of each:

1. $P \rightarrow (Q \rightarrow (S \rightarrow T))$ A
2. P A
3. $P \rightarrow Q$ A
4. S A

Then we look for familiar inference patterns among the premises. For example, from premises 2 and 3, we may infer by modus ponens the conclusion Q. So we write this as a conclusion, listing to the right the line numbers of the premises from which it was inferred and the form or rule of inference by which it was inferred:

5. Q 2, 3 modus ponens

The formula 'P', which is assumed on line 2, is also the antecedent of the conditional assumption on line 1. Though the consequent of this conditional is a complex formula, rather than a single sentence letter, we still recognize here another instance of modus ponens. So we draw the conclusion:

6. $Q \rightarrow (S \rightarrow T)$ 1, 2 modus ponens

(We have dropped the unnecessary outer brackets, as usual, and will continue to do so without comment from now on.) Now lines 5 and 6 can be combined to obtain yet another conclusion:

    7. $S \rightarrow T$ 5, 6 modus ponens

And lines 4 and 7 yield the conclusion:

    8. T 4, 7 modus ponens

This is the conclusion we wanted to establish. And now we have succeeded. For by showing that it is possible to get from the assumptions of the sequent to its conclusion by simple steps of valid reasoning, we have shown that the sequent itself is valid.

To see why it is valid, consider a preliminary conclusion C_1 validly drawn from some initial set of premises. Now let new premises be used together with C_1 to validly draw a second conclusion C_2. Since C_1 was validly drawn, by the definition of validity C_1 is true on any valuation on which the original premises are true. And similarly, since C_2 validly follows from C_1 together with the new premises, C_2 is true on any valuation on which both C_1 and the new premises are true. But since C_1 is true on *any* valuation on which the original premises are true, C_1 is true on any valuation on which the original premises *and also* the new premises are true. Hence, since C_2 is true on any valuation on which both C_1 and the new premises are true, C_2 is true on any valuation on which both the initial premises and the new premises are true. That is, the inference from the initial premises together with the new premises to C_2 is valid. Further, if we were to add still more premises and validly draw yet a third conclusion C_3, the same reasoning would show that the inference combining all three sets of premises to the conclusion C_3 is also valid. And so it goes. Thus, by stringing together valid inferences, we prove the validity of the inference whose premises are all the assumptions made along the way and whose conclusion is the final conclusion of the string.

In the rest of this section, we shall show how to break down any valid sequent in propositional logic into a sequence of simple and (more or less) obviously valid patterns of reasoning. Such sequences, as exemplified by lines 1–8 above, are called **proofs**. Modus ponens is not the only pattern used in proofs. We shall construct proofs in propositional logic by the so-called natural deduction method, which utilizes ten distinct patterns of reasoning, or **rules of inference** (or **inference rules**), of which modus ponens is one. (There are many other methods of proof, which use different types and numbers of rules, though for classical logic, at least, they all yield the same results. Some of the alternative methods are discussed in Section 4.5.)

Proofs, of course, are only as credible as their inference rules. As we introduce each rule, we shall verify its validity using the semantics developed in Chapter 3. This will enable us to see that our proof technique is **sound**—that is, that if we start with assumptions true on some valuation, we shall always, no matter how many times we apply these rules, arrive at conclusions that are likewise true on that valuation. Thus a proof establishes that there are no counterexamples to the sequent of which it is a proof; it is a third formal method (in addition to truth tables and trees) for showing that a sequent is valid. In Section 5.10 we shall show that the entire system of rules introduced here is not only sound but also **complete**—that is, capable of providing a proof for every valid sequent of propositional logic.

Our first inference rule, modus ponens, may be stated as follows:

Given any conditional and its antecedent, infer its consequent.

Or, using the Greek letters of Section 2.3:

Given $\Phi \to \Psi$ and Φ, infer Ψ.

Φ and Ψ may be any formulas, simple or complex. For example, in the inference from assumptions 1 and 2 to conclusion 6 in the proof above, Φ is 'P' and Ψ is 'Q $\to$ (S $\to$ T)'.

Modus ponens is clearly valid, as we can see by examining its truth table. That is, no matter what the truth values of Φ and Ψ may be, it can never happen that $\Phi \to \Psi$ and Φ are true but Ψ is untrue:

Φ	Ψ	Φ	$\to$	Ψ,	Φ	$\vdash$	Ψ
T	T	T	T	T	T		T
T	F	T	F	F	T		F
F	T	F	T	T	F		T
F	F	F	T	F	F		F

In addition to modus ponens, we shall introduce nine other rules, for a total of ten—two for each of the five logical operators. For each operator one of the two rules, called an **introduction rule,** allows us to reason to (introduces) conclusions in which that operator is the main operator. The second rule allows us to reason from premises in which that operator is the main operator; it is known as the operator's **elimination rule,** because it enables us to break a premise into its components, thus "eliminating" the operator.

Modus ponens is the elimination rule for the conditional. Given a formula Φ, it allows us to "eliminate" the conditional operator from $\Phi \to \Psi$ and wind up just with Ψ. In doing proofs, then, we shall call modus ponens **conditional elimination,** which we abbreviate as '$\to$E'. Officially, we state the rule of modus ponens as follows:

Conditional Elimination ($\to$E)   Given ($\Phi \to \Psi$) and Φ, infer Ψ.

The introduction rule for the conditional has some special features which are best appreciated only after some practice with the other rules. We shall therefore consider it later.

Perhaps the simplest rules are those for conjunction. Indeed, these may seem utterly trivial. Here is the conjunction elimination rule:

Conjunction Elimination (&E)   From (Φ & Ψ), infer either Φ or Ψ.

That is, we may "eliminate" a conjunction by inferring one or the other of its conjuncts. (We can, if we like, infer both, but that takes two applications of the rule.) Conjunction elimination is sometimes known as **simplification.** This rule is obviously valid. The only way Φ & Ψ can be true on a valuation is if both of its conjuncts are true on that valuation. Hence there is no valuation on which Φ & Ψ is true and either of its conjuncts is untrue.

The following proof for the sequent 'R $\rightarrow$ (P & Q), R $\vdash$ Q' exemplifies both &E and $\rightarrow$E:

1.	R $\rightarrow$ (P & Q)	A
2.	R	A
3.	P & Q	1, 2 $\rightarrow$E
4.	Q	3 &E

As before, we begin by writing the assumptions on numbered lines (lines 1 and 2) and marking them with an 'A' to indicate that they are assumptions. '$\rightarrow$E' (modus ponens) applied to lines 1 and 2 gets us the conclusion 'P & Q' at line 3, and from this by conjunction elimination we obtain the desired conclusion 'Q'.

Let's now consider the conjunction introduction rule. This rule enables us to infer conclusions whose main operator is a conjunction:

Conjunction Introduction (&I)   From Φ and Ψ, infer (Φ & Ψ).

Conjunction introduction is also called **conjunction** or (more rarely) **adjunction**. It allows us to join any two previously established formulas together with '&'. If these formulas are true, then by the valuation rule for '&' the resulting conjunction must be true as well, and so clearly the rule is valid. We may illustrate both &E and &I by constructing a proof for the sequent 'P & Q $\vdash$ Q & P'. (This sequent is hardly less obviously valid than the rules themselves, but it nicely illustrates their use.)

1.	P & Q	A
2.	P	1 &E
3.	Q	1 &E
4.	Q & P	2, 3 &I

Starting with the assumption 'P & Q', we break it into its components at lines 2 and 3 by &E, then introduce the desired conclusion by &I (whose purpose, remember, is to create conjunctive conclusions) at line 4. Intuitively, the reasoning is this: Given that the conjunction 'P & Q' is true, 'P' is true and 'Q' is true as well. But then the conjunction 'Q & P' is also true.

The order in which the premises are listed is irrelevant to the application of a rule of inference. Thus, even though 'P' is listed on line 2 of this proof and 'Q' on line 3, we may legitimately infer 'Q & P', in which 'Q' comes first.

Moreover, the use of two different Greek letters in stating a rule does not imply that the formulas designated by those letters must be different. In the &I rule, for example, Φ and Ψ can stand for *any* formulas without restriction—even for the same formula. The following proof of the trivial but valid sequent 'P $\vdash$ P & P' illustrates this point:

1.	P	A
2.	P & P	1, 1 &I

Here we apply the rule of &I (from Φ and Ψ, infer (Φ & Ψ)) to a case in which both Φ and Ψ are 'P'. That is, we infer from 'P' and 'P' again the conclusion 'P & P'. Since we have used 'P' twice, we list line 1 twice in the annotation. Though odd, this sort of move is quite legitimate, not only for &I but (where applicable) for other rules as well. Given, for example, that the sun is hot, it validly follows that the sun is hot and the sun is hot—though we are not likely to have much use for that conclusion.

The elimination and introduction rules for the biconditional are closely related to those for conjunction. This is not surprising since 'P ↔ Q' has the same truth conditions as the conjunction '(P → Q) & (Q → P)'. Thus, like the conjunction rules, the biconditional rules simply break the complex formula into its conditional components or assemble it from these components:

Biconditional Elimination (↔E)   From (Φ ↔ Ψ), infer either (Φ → Ψ) or (Ψ → Φ).

Biconditional Introduction (↔I)   From (Φ → Ψ) and (Ψ → Φ), infer (Φ ↔ Ψ).

As with conjunction elimination, the biconditional elimination rule gives us a choice of which of the two components to infer. This rule is used here in a proof of 'P ↔ Q, P ⊢ P & Q':

1.	P ↔ Q	A
2.	P	A
3.	P → Q	1 ↔E
4.	Q	2, 3 →E
5.	P & Q	2, 4 &I

We "eliminate" the biconditional at line 3, obtaining one of its component conditionals, 'P → Q'. Next we use modus ponens (→E) at line 4 to obtain 'Q', one of the conjuncts of our desired conclusion. The other conjunct, 'P', was already given as an assumption. Conjunction introduction enables us to combine these conjuncts into our conclusion at line 5.

The following proof of '(P → Q) → (Q → P), P → Q ⊢ P ↔ Q' illustrates the use of the other biconditional rule, biconditional introduction:

1.	(P → Q) → (Q → P)	A
2.	P → Q	A
3.	Q → P	1, 2 →E
4.	P ↔ Q	2, 3 ↔I

We next consider the disjunction introduction rule (sometimes called the **addition** rule):

Disjunction Introduction (∨I)   From Φ, infer either (Φ ∨ Ψ) or (Ψ ∨ Φ).

That is, given any formula, we may infer its disjunction (as either first or second disjunct) with any other formula. If, for example, my best friend is Jim, then it is certainly true that either my best friend is Jim or my best friend is Sally. And it is obvious from the valuation rule for 'v' that this pattern is valid in general, for whenever either disjunct of any disjunction is true, the disjunction itself is also true.

The following proof of '(P v Q) → R, P ⊢ R v S' illustrates the use of vI:

1.	(P v Q) → R	A
2.	P	A
3.	P v Q	2 vI
4.	R	1, 3 →E
5.	R v S	4 vI

To use the conditional assumption '(P v Q) → R' we must "eliminate" the conditional by →E. But to do this we must first obtain its antecedent, 'P v Q'. Since we are given 'P' as an assumption, we can infer 'P v Q' simply by applying vI at line 3. This enables us to derive 'R' at line 4. The conclusion we want to reach, however, is 'R v S'. But this can be deduced from 'R' by applying vI once again, this time to line 4.

The disjunction elimination rule, vE, allows us to draw conclusions from disjunctive premises, provided that we have established certain conditionals:

Disjunction Elimination (vE)   From (Φ v Ψ), (Φ → Θ), and (Ψ → Θ), infer Θ.

Disjunction elimination is also known as **constructive dilemma**. It is valid, as can be seen by inspection of this truth table:

Φ	Ψ	Θ	(Φ v Ψ),	(Φ → Θ),	(Ψ → Θ)	⊢	Θ
T	T	T	T	T	T		T
T	T	F	T	F	F		F
T	F	T	T	T	T		T
T	F	F	T	F	T		F
F	T	T	T	T	T		T
F	T	F	T	T	F		F
F	F	T	F	T	T		T
F	F	F	F	T	T		F

Consider, for example, the argument

> *ABCD* is either a rectangle or a parallelogram.
> If *ABCD* is a rectangle, then it is a quadrilateral.
> If *ABCD* is a parallelogram, then it is a quadrilateral.
> ∴   *ABCD* is a quadrilateral.

We may symbolize this argument as 'R v P, R → Q, P → Q ⊢ Q'. Its proof is a single step of vE:

1.	R v P	A

2. $R \to Q$ A
3. $P \to Q$ A
4. Q   1, 2, 3 ∨E

Here Φ is 'R', Ψ is 'P', and Θ is 'Q'. Notice that since ∨E uses three premises, we must cite three lines to the right when using it. Sometimes the same line is cited twice, as in the proof of 'P ∨ P, P → Q ⊢ Q':

1. $P \vee P$ A
2. $P \to Q$ A
3. Q   1, 2, 2 ∨E

In this proof, Φ and Ψ are both 'P' and Θ is 'Q'. The first premise is, of course, redundant, but redundancy does not affect validity.

The most interesting uses of ∨E are those in which the conditional premises necessary for proving the conclusion are not given as assumptions but must themselves be proved. This, however, requires the use of the rule →I, which is introduced in the next section.

The negation elimination rule, which is sometimes called the **double negation rule,** allows us to "cancel out" double negations when these have the rest of the formula in their scope:

Negation Elimination (~E)   From ~~Φ, infer Φ.

This rule, too, is obviously valid. For by the valuation rule for '~', if ~~Φ is true, then ~Φ is false and hence Φ is true. To say, for example, that I am not not tired is the same thing as to say that I am tired. Here is an example of the use of negation elimination, in the proof of 'P → ~~Q, P ⊢ Q':

1. $P \to$ ~~Q   A
2. P   A
3. ~~Q   1, 2 →E
4. Q   3 ~E

Neither the negation elimination rule nor any of the other rules allow us to operate inside formulas. It is a mistake, for example, to do the proof just illustrated this way:

1. $P \to$ ~~Q   A
2. P   A
3. $P \to Q$ 1 ~E (**wrong!**)
4. Q   2, 3 →E

Negation elimination operates only on doubly negated formulas. 'P → ~~Q' is a conditional, not a doubly negated formula. We must use conditional elimination to separate '~~Q' (which *is* a doubly negated formula) from the conditional before negation elimination can be applied.

It is not really invalid to eliminate double negations inside formulas; it's just not a legitimate use of our negation elimination rule. We never need to use it this way, because our elimination rules always enable us to break formulas down (where this may validly be done) so that the double negation sooner or later appears on a line by itself and hence becomes accessible to the negation elimination rule. We could be more liberal, permitting elimination of double negations inside formulas, but only at the expense of complicating some of our metatheoretic work later on. Conservatism now will pay off later.

Finally, we should note that there is no one correct way to prove a sequent. If the sequent is valid, then it will have many different proofs, all of them correct, but varying in the kinds of rules used or in their order of application. Often, however, there is one simplest proof, more obvious than all the rest. In constructing proofs, good logicians strive for simplicity and elegance and thus make their discipline an art.

Exercise 4.2

Construct proofs for the following sequents:

1. $P \rightarrow Q, Q \rightarrow R, P \vdash R$
2. $P \rightarrow (Q \rightarrow R), P, Q \vdash R$
3. $P \& Q, P \rightarrow R \vdash R$
4. $P \rightarrow Q, P \rightarrow R, P \vdash Q \& R$
5. $(P \& Q) \rightarrow R, P \rightarrow Q, P \vdash R$
6. $P \& Q \vdash Q \vee R$
7. $P \vdash (P \vee Q) \& (P \vee R)$
8. $P, ((Q \& R) \vee P) \rightarrow S \vdash S$
9. $P \vdash P \vee P$
10. $P \vdash (P \vee P) \& (P \& P)$
11. $P \rightarrow (Q \rightarrow R), P \rightarrow (R \rightarrow Q), P \vdash Q \leftrightarrow R$
12. $P \leftrightarrow Q, (P \rightarrow Q) \rightarrow R \vdash R$
13. $\sim\sim(P \leftrightarrow (Q \& R)), P \vdash R$
14. $(P \rightarrow Q) \rightarrow \sim\sim(Q \rightarrow P), P \rightarrow Q \vdash Q \leftrightarrow P$
15. $P \leftrightarrow \sim\sim Q, P \& R \vdash Q \vee S$
16. $P \vee Q, Q \rightarrow P, P \rightarrow P \vdash P$
17. $P \vee Q, Q \rightarrow \sim\sim R, P \rightarrow \sim\sim R \vdash R \vee S$
18. $(P \& (Q \vee R)) \leftrightarrow S, P, \sim\sim R \vdash S$
19. $P \rightarrow P \vdash P \leftrightarrow P$
20. $Q \vdash Q \vee (\sim\sim Q \leftrightarrow P)$

4.3 HYPOTHETICAL DERIVATIONS

We have now encountered eight of the ten rules. I saved the remaining two until last because they make use of a special mechanism: the hypothetical derivation. A hypothetical derivation is a proof made on the basis of a temporary assumption, or **hypothesis,** which we do not assert to be true, but only suppose for the sake of argument. Hypothetical reasoning is common and familiar. In planning a vacation, for example, one might reason as follows:

> Suppose we stay an extra day at the lake. Then we would get home on Sunday. But then it would be hard to get ready for school on Monday.

Here the arguer is not asserting that she and her audience will stay an extra day at the lake, but is only supposing this to see what follows. The conclusion, that it will be hard to get ready for school on Monday, is likewise not asserted or believed. The point is simply that this conclusion would be true *if* the hypothetical supposition were true.

Her reasoning presupposes two unstated assumptions, used respectively to derive the second and third sentences. These are

1. If we stay an extra day at the lake, then we get home on Sunday.

and

2. If we get home on Sunday, then it will be hard to get ready for school on Monday.

Using 'S' for 'we stay an extra day at the lake,' 'H' for 'we get home on Sunday', and 'M' for 'it will be hard to get ready for school on Monday', we may formalize this reasoning as follows:

1.	$S \rightarrow H$	A
2.	$H \rightarrow M$	A
3.	$\mid$ S	H (for $\rightarrow$I)
4.	$\mid$ H	1, 3 $\rightarrow$E
5.	$\mid$ M	2, 4 $\rightarrow$E

(Assumptions 1 and 2 correspond to the implicit statements 1 and 2 above. Statements 3, 4, and 5 represent the first, second, and third sentences of the stated argument, respectively.)

I have done something novel beginning with S on line 3, the line that represents the supposition or hypothesis that we stay an extra day at the lake. Instead of labeling S as an assumption ('A'), I have marked it with the notation 'H (for →I)'. This indicates that 'S' is a hypothesis ('H'), made only for the sake of a conditional introduction ('→I') argument and not (like 1 and 2) really assumed and asserted to be true. Moreover, I have drawn a vertical line to the left of 'S' extending to all subsequent conclusions derived from 'S'. This line specifies that the reasoning to its right is hypothetical—that statements 3, 4, and 5 are not genuinely asserted, but only considered for the sake of argument.

This hypothetical reasoning has a purpose. In granting assumptions 1 and 2, we see that we can derive 'M' from 'S'; this means the conditional 'S → M' must be true. This conditional, which symbolizes the English sentence 'if we stay an extra day at the lake, then it will be hard to get ready for school on Monday', is both the point of the argument and its implicit final conclusion. But this conditional is not deduced directly from our assumptions, nor from any of the statements listed in the argument, either singly or in combination. Rather, we know that 'S → M' is true because (given our assumptions) we showed in the hypothetical reasoning (or **hypothetical derivation**) carried out in lines 3–5 that 'M' follows logically from 'S'. It is this *reasoning*, not any single statement or set of statements, that shows 'S → M' is true. To indicate this, and to draw the argument's final conclusion, we add a new line to the previous reasoning, as follows:

1.	S → H	A
2.	H → M	A
3.	$\quad$ S	H (for →I)
4.	$\quad$ H	1, 3 →E
5.	$\quad$ M	2, 4 →E
6.	S → M	3–5 →I

The annotation of line 6 indicates that we have drawn the conclusion 'S → M' from the hypothetical derivation displayed on lines 3–5. The rule used is the rule of **conditional introduction** (→I), commonly known as **conditional proof.** It may be stated as follows:

> **Conditional Introduction or Conditional Proof (→I)**   Given a hypothetical derivation of Ψ from Φ, end the derivation and infer (Φ → Ψ).

In our example, Φ is 'S' and Ψ is 'M'.

A hypothetical derivation itself begins with a hypothesis, or temporary assumption, and ends when a desired conclusion has been reached. In this case the conclusion of the hypothetical derivation was 'M'. Its duration is marked by indentation and a vertical line to the left. Since in this problem the point of the hypothetical derivation was to show that 'M' followed from 'S', the hypothetical derivation (and hence the vertical line) ends with 'M'. A conclusion inferred from a hypothetical derivation is not part of the hypothetical derivation, and hence the vertical line does not extend to it. The conclusion, 'S → M' ('if we stay an extra day at the lake, then it will be hard to get ready for school on Monday'), is not merely hypothetical; it is something the arguer actually asserts and presumably believes.

Conditional introduction is, of course, the rule that enables us to prove conditional conclusions. We do this by hypothesizing the antecedent of the conditional and reasoning hypothetically until we derive the conditional's consequent. At that point the hypothetical derivation ends. We then apply conditional introduction to our hypothetical derivation to obtain the conditional conclusion. This proof of 'P ⊢ Q → (P & Q)' provides another example:

1.	P	A
2.	$\quad$ Q	H (for →I)
3.	$\quad$ P & Q	1, 2 &I
4.	Q → (P & Q)	2–3 →I

The sequent's conclusion, 'Q → (P & Q)', is a conditional, so after listing the assumption 'P' as usual, we hypothesize the antecedent 'Q' of this conditional at line 2. A single step of &I at line 3 enables us to derive its consequent, 'P & Q', thus completing the hypothetical derivation. We then get the desired conclusion by applying conditional introduction to the hypothetical derivation at line 4.

Conditional introduction is used in proving biconditional conclusions as well as conditional conclusions. But in proving biconditionals we often need to employ it twice in order to prove each of the two conditionals that comprise the biconditional before we assemble these components into the biconditional conclusion. The following proof of the sequent 'P & Q ⊢ P ↔ Q' illustrates this technique:

1.	P & Q	A
2.	⎸ P	H (for →I)
3.	⎸ Q	1 &E
4.	P → Q	2–3 →I
5.	⎸ Q	H (for →I)
6.	⎸ P	1 &E
7.	Q → P	5–6 →I
8.	P ↔ Q	4, 7 ↔I

Here the conclusion we wish to obtain is 'P ↔ Q'. The rule for proving biconditional conclusions is ↔I, but to use ↔I to get 'P ↔ Q' we must first obtain its "component" conditionals, 'P → Q' and 'Q → P'. We do this in lines 2–4 and 5–7, respectively, by first hypothesizing each conditional's antecedent, next hypothetically deriving its consequent (which in each case involves a simple step of &E from our assumption), and finally applying →I to the resulting hypothetical derivation (at lines 4 and 7, respectively). Having obtained the two component conditionals, we complete the proof with a step of ↔I at line 8.

A step or two of conditional introduction is often used to provide the conditionals needed for drawing conclusions from a disjunctive premise by ∨E. This proof of 'P ∨ P ⊢ P' provides an example that is both elegant and instructive:

1.	P ∨ P	A
2.	⎸ P	H (for →I)
3.	P → P	2–2 →I
4.	P	1, 3, 3 ∨E

Our assumption is the disjunctive premise 'P ∨ P'. The standard rule for drawing conclusions from disjunctive premises is ∨E: From (Φ ∨ Ψ), (Φ → Θ), and (Ψ → Θ), infer Θ. If we take Φ, Ψ, and Θ all to be 'P', this becomes: From 'P ∨ P', 'P → P', and 'P → P', infer 'P'. Thus we see that if we can prove 'P → P', we can use it twice with our assumption 'P ∨ P' to deduce the desired conclusion 'P'. But how do we prove 'P → P'? That's where →I comes in. We hypothesize this conditional's antecedent at line 2 and aim to derive its consequent. The hypothetical derivation is the simplest possible, for its hypothesis and conclusion are the very same statement 'P'. There is no need to apply any rules. In hypothesizing 'P', we have already in effect concluded 'P'; the hypothetical derivation ends as soon as it begins at line 2. We then use →I to derive 'P → P' at line 3 and ∨E to obtain 'P' at line 4.

Let's consider one more example of the use of →I in preparation for a step of ∨E. In this case the sequent to be proved is 'P ∨ Q, R ⊢ (P & R) ∨ (Q & R)':

1.	P ∨ Q	A
2.	R	A
3.	⎸ P	H (for →I)
4.	⎸ P & R	2, 3 &I
5.	⎸ (P & R) ∨ (Q & R)	4 ∨I
6.	P → ((P & R) ∨ (Q & R))	3–5 →I
7.	⎸ Q	H (for →I)
8.	⎸ Q & R	2, 7 &I
9.	⎸ (P & R) ∨ (Q & R)	8 ∨I
10.	Q → ((P & R) ∨ (Q & R))	7–9 →I
11.	(P & R) ∨ (Q & R)	1, 6, 10 ∨E

To use the disjunctive premise 'P ∨ Q' to obtain the conclusion '(P & R) ∨ (Q & R)' by ∨E, we need two conditional premises: 'P → ((P & R) ∨ (Q & R))' and 'Q → ((P & R) ∨ (Q & R))'. These are conditionals, so we use →I to prove each, the first in lines 3–6, the second in lines 7–10. Once the two conditionals have been established, a single step of ∨E at line 11 completes the proof.

In proving conditionals whose antecedents contain further conditionals, we sometimes need to make two or more hypothetical suppositions in succession. For example, to prove 'P ⊢ (Q → R) → (Q → (P & R))', we hypothesize the conclusion's antecedent 'Q → R' and then aim to deduce its consequent 'Q → (P & R)'. But this consequent is itself a conditional so that we must introduce a second hypothesis, the second conditional's antecedent, 'Q'. This enables us to deduce 'Q → (P & R)' by →I. And since this is proved under the initial hypothesis '(Q → R)', a final step of →I yields the conclusion '(Q → R) → (Q → (P & R))'. Here is the proof in full:

1.	P	A
2.	⎸ Q → R	H (for →I)
3.	⎸ ⎸ Q	H (for →I)
4.	⎸ ⎸ R	2, 3 →E
5.	⎸ ⎸ P & R	1, 4 &I
6.	⎸ Q → (P & R)	3–5 →I
7.	(Q → R) → (Q → (P & R))	2–6 →I

Notice that though the antecedent of '(Q → R) → (Q → (P & R))' is also a conditional, 'Q → R', we do not attempt to prove this conditional by hypothesizing 'Q' and deriving 'R'. The antecedent of a conditional conclusion, no matter how complex, typically figures in a proof as a single hypothesis (line 2 in the proof above) and is not itself proved.

Finally, *after a hypothetical derivation ends, all the formulas contained within it are "off limits" for the rest of the proof.* They may not be used or cited later, because they were never genuinely asserted, but only hypothetically entertained. The following attempted proof of the invalid sequent 'P, Q → ~P ⊢ P & ~P' illustrates how violations of this restriction breed trouble. (If you don't see that this sequent is invalid, check it with a truth table.)

1. P   A
2. Q → ~P   A
3. | Q   H (for →I)
4. | ~P   2, 3 →E
5. Q → ~P   3-4 →I
6. P & ~P   1, 4 &I (**Wrong!**)

All rules are used correctly through step 5, though steps 3–5 are redundant, since all they do is prove 'Q → ~P', which was already given as an assumption at line 2. Step 6, however, is mistaken, since it uses the formula '~P', which appears in the hypothetical derivation at line 4, after that hypothetical derivation has ended. '~P', however, was never proved; it was merely derived from the supposition of 'Q'. It cannot be cited after the hypothetical derivation based on 'Q' ends at step 4. Violation of this restriction may result in "proofs" of invalid sequents, as it does here. These, of course, are not really proofs, since in a proof the rules must be applied correctly.

However, *any nonhypothetical assumption or nonhypothetical conclusion and any hypothesis or conclusion within a hypothetical derivation that has not yet ended may be used to draw further conclusions.* So, for example, in the proof of 'P ⊢ (Q → R) → (Q → (P & R))', which was given just before the preceding example, it is permissible to use the hypothesis 'Q → R' (line 2) at line 4 of the hypothetical derivation that begins with 'Q' (line 3), because the hypothetical derivation beginning with 'Q → R' has not yet ended.

A proof is not complete until all hypothetical derivations have ended. If we were to leave a hypothetical derivation incomplete, then its hypothesis would be an additional assumption in the reasoning; but, being marked with an 'H' instead of an 'A', it might not be recognized as such.

To summarize: →I is the rule most often used for proving conditional conclusions. To prove a conditional conclusion Φ → Ψ, hypothesize its antecedent Φ and reason hypothetically to its consequent Ψ. Then, citing this entire hypothetical derivation, deduce Φ → Ψ by →I. The conclusion Φ → Ψ does not belong to the hypothetical derivation, so the vertical line that began with Φ does not continue to Φ → Ψ, but ends with Ψ.

It is perhaps not so obvious as with the nonhypothetical rules that →I is valid. To recognize its validity, we must keep in mind that the hypothetical derivation from Φ to Ψ must itself have been constructed using valid rules. This means that if a valuation makes true both the proof's assumptions and Φ, as well as any other hypotheses whose derivations had not ended when Φ was supposed, then it also makes Ψ true. That is, there is no valuation that makes these assumptions and hypotheses true and also makes Φ true but Ψ untrue. In other words, there is no valuation that makes these assumptions and hypotheses true and Φ → Ψ untrue.[1] But this means that the inference from these assumptions or hypotheses to Φ → Ψ is valid. Hence the rule →I, which allows us to conclude Φ → Ψ from these as-

---

[1] This reasoning appeals implicitly to the valuation rule for the conditional.

sumptions and hypotheses, is itself valid; it never leads from true premises to an untrue conclusion.

We next consider the rule for proving negative propositions: negation introduction, ~I, often known as **indirect proof** or *reductio ad absurdum* (reduction to absurdity). Negation introduction is the rule for proving negated conclusions. To prove ~Φ, hypothesize Φ and validly derive from Φ an "absurdity"—that is, a conclusion known to be false. Since the derivation is valid, if Φ and any additional assumptions or hypotheses used in the derivation were true, the derived conclusion would have to be true as well. Therefore, since the derived conclusion is false, either Φ or some other assumption or hypothesis used to derive it must be false. So, if these other assumptions or hypotheses are true, it must be Φ that is false. Hence ~Φ follows from these other assumptions or hypotheses.

But how can we formally ensure that the conclusion we derive from Φ is false? One way is to require that the conclusion be inconsistent. Inconsistencies of the form 'Φ & ~Φ', for example, fill the bill. Actually, any inconsistency would do, but so as not to unduly complicate our rule, we shall require that the conclusion of the hypothetical derivation always have this one form. This restriction, as we shall see in Section 5.10, does not prevent us from proving any valid sequent. Therefore we will state the negation introduction rule as follows:

> **Negation Introduction (~I)** Given a hypothetical derivation of any formula of the form (Ψ & ~Ψ) from Φ, end the derivation and infer ~Φ.

The following proof of 'P → Q, ~Q ⊢ ~P', a sequent expressing modus tollens, uses this rule. Here Φ is 'P' and Ψ is 'Q':

1. P → Q		A
2. ~Q		A
3.	P	H (for ~I)
4.	Q	1, 3 →E
5.	Q & ~Q	2, 4 &I
6. ~P		3–5 ~I

Having listed the assumptions on lines 1 and 2, we note that the desired conclusion is a negation, '~P'. To prove this conclusion by ~I, then, we hypothesize 'P' at line 3—not, as before, for →I, but rather for ~I—and try to derive an "absurdity." This is accomplished at line 5, where it is established that, given the assumptions 'P → Q' and '~Q', 'P' leads to absurdity. Therefore, given these assumptions, 'P' must be false, which is what we conclude at line 6 by asserting '~P'.

Formal indirect proofs are, of course, not *merely* formal. They may be used to represent specific natural language arguments. So, for example, if we let 'P' stand for 'A person is defined by her genome' and 'Q' for 'Identical twins are the same person', the reasoning represented by this proof is as follows. It is assumed at line 1 that if a person is defined by her genome, then identical twins are the same person and at line 2 that identical twins are not the same person. The argument aims to show that a person is not defined by her genome (line 6). To prove this, we suppose for the sake of argument at line 3 that a person *is* defined by her genome. We do not, of course, really assert this; we suppose it only to reduce it to absurdity and so prove its negation. Together with assumption 1, this supposition leads at line 4 to the conclusion that identical twins are the same person. And this conclusion, together with assumption 2, yields the absurd conclusion that identical twins both are and are not the same person. Having shown, given assumptions 1 and 2, that the supposition that a person is defined by her genome leads to absurdity, we conclude on the strength of these assumptions alone that a person is not defined by her genome. This final conclusion is recorded on line 6.

The following proof of the sequent '~(P ∨ Q) ⊢ ~P' provides another example of the application of ~I. Recall that '~(P ∨ Q)' means "neither P nor Q."

1.	~(P ∨ Q)	A
2.	P	H (for ~I)
3.	P ∨ Q	2 ∨I
4.	(P ∨ Q) & ~(P ∨ Q)	1, 3 &I
5.	~P	2–4 ~I

With respect to our statement of the negation introduction rule, Φ here is 'P' and Ψ is 'P ∨ Q'. Once again the conclusion to be proved is '~P'. So, after listing the assumption, we hypothesize 'P' and aim for some contradiction. The trick is to see that we can obtain 'P ∨ Q', which contradicts our assumption, by applying ∨I to 'P'. The contradiction (absurdity) is reached at line 4 by &I. 'P' having led to an absurdity, we deduce '~P' at line 5.

Negation introduction may also be used, in combination with negation elimination, to prove unnegated conclusions. To prove an unnegated conclusion Θ, we may hypothesize ~Θ, derive an absurdity, and apply ~I. But since ~I adds a negation sign to the hypothesis that is reduced to absurdity, it enables us to conclude only ~~Θ, not the desired conclusion Θ. However, from ~~Θ we can deduce Θ by negation elimination and so complete the proof. The following proof of '~(P & ~Q), P ⊢ Q' uses this strategy.[2] In this case Θ is 'Q'; with respect to the formal statement of the ~I rule, Φ is '~Q' and Ψ is 'P & ~Q':

1.	~(P & ~Q)	A
2.	P	A
3.	~Q	H (for ~I)
4.	P & ~Q	2, 3 &I
5.	(P & ~Q) & ~(P & ~Q)	1, 4 &I
6.	~~Q	3–5 ~I
7.	Q	6 ~E

Negation introduction is often combined with conditional introduction, as in this proof of the sequent, 'P → Q ⊢ ~Q → ~P', which expresses the pattern of inference called **contraposition**:

1.	P → Q	A
2.	~Q	H (for →I)

---

[2] To see why this form ought to be valid, recall that '~(P & ~Q)' is equivalent to 'P → Q'.

3.		P	H (for ~I)
4.		Q	1, 3 →E
5.		Q & ~Q	2, 4 &I
6.	~P		3–5 ~I
7.	~Q → ~P		2–6 →I

Having written our assumption, we note that the conclusion for which we are aiming, '~Q → ~P', is a conditional. So we hypothesize its antecedent at line 2 for →I, aiming to derive its consequent, '~P'. But '~P' is a negation, and ~I is the rule for proving negations. So, to set up a derivation of '~P', we hypothesize 'P' at line 3 for ~I and try to deduce a contradiction. The contradiction is obtained at line 5, which enables us to use ~I at line 6 to get '~P'. Having now derived '~P' from '~Q', we can deduce '~P → ~Q' by →I at line 7 to complete the proof.

Negation introduction is used in a peculiar way in the proof of the principle *ex falso quodlibet,* the principle expressed by the sequent 'P, ~P ⊢ Q'. (We demonstrated the validity of this sequent using a truth table in Section 3.2.)

1.	P		A
2.	~P		A
3.		~Q	H (for ~I)
4.		P & ~P	1, 2 &I
5.	~~Q		3–4 ~I
6.	Q		5 ~E

'Q' is an unnegated conclusion, but ~I enables us to prove it nevertheless. To do so, we must reduce '~Q' to absurdity to obtain '~~Q', from which 'Q' follows by ~E.

What is genuinely peculiar about this proof is that '~Q' is not used in the derivation of the contradiction 'P & ~P'. The contradiction comes directly from assumptions 1 and 2. This undermines the notion that it is '~Q' that is being reduced to absurdity, for the absurdity lies in the assumptions, not in '~Q'. This pattern of reasoning is, however, legitimate in classical logic. Having assumed an absurdity, we can reduce *any* formula to absurdity: All formulas validly follow.

Validly—but not relevantly. There is no counterexample to the sequent 'P, ~P ⊢ Q', but many instances of this sequent are irrelevant. Relevance logicians, who advocate a notion of validity stricter than the classical notion, would reject step 5 of this proof as invalid. Since the hypothesis '~Q' was not used in the derivation of the contradiction, they argue, no conclusion concerning '~Q' can legitimately be drawn. We note their protest here but set it aside. They will get their say in Section 16.3. In the meantime, we will accept such peculiar uses of ~I as valid.

We next consider a proof of the sequent 'P ∨ Q, ~P ⊢ Q', which expresses the pattern of inference called **disjunctive syllogism**. This proof also employs the irrelevant use of ~I illustrated in the previous problem. Because this sort of irrelevant move is unavoidable in proofs of disjunctive syllogism, many relevance logicians like disjunctive syllogism no better than they like ex falso quodlibet.

```
 1. P ∨ Q                       A
 2. ~P                          A
 3. |       P                   H (for →I)
 4. |   |       ~Q              H (for ~I)
 5. |   |       P & ~P          2, 3 &I
 6. |      ~~Q                  4–5 ~I
 7. |       Q                   6 ~E
 8. P → Q                       3–7 →I
 9. |       Q                   H (for →I)
10. Q → Q                       9, 9 →I
11. Q                           1, 8, 10 ∨E
```

Our first assumption is a disjunction; to use it we need ∨E. But to use ∨E with 'P ∨ Q' to obtain the conclusion 'Q', we need these two conditionals: 'P → Q' and 'Q → Q'. These we obtain by →I, the first in lines 3–8, the second in lines 9–10. To prove 'P → Q', we hypothesize its antecedent 'P' at line 3. We now have hypothesized 'P' and assumed '~P' so that we can obtain any conclusion we please. We want 'Q', the consequent of 'P → Q', in order to complete our conditional proof. To get it, we hypothesize '~Q' for reduction to absurdity. As in the previous example, however, we derive the absurdity (at line 5), not from this hypothesis but from previous (and irrelevant) assumptions. Nevertheless, this allows us to conclude '~~Q' at line 6 by ~I, from which we obtain 'Q' at line 7. The hypothetical derivation at lines 3–7 has thus established 'P → Q', a fact we record at line 8. The proof of 'Q → Q' at lines 9–10 is trivial. Having obtained the necessary premises at lines 1, 8, and 10, we finish with a step of ∨E.

Although there are many (indeed, infinitely many!) different proofs for each valid sequent, there is often one way that is the simplest and most direct. Finding that way is a matter of strategy. Often the best strategy for a proof can be "read" directly from the form of the conclusion—that is, from the identity of its main operator, as Table 4.1 indicates.

It is common, as we have seen in some of the examples worked earlier, for different strategies to be used successively in different stages of a proof. To illustrate how Table 4.1 provides guidance in doing this, let's prove the sequent 'P ∨ Q ⊢ Q ∨ P'. We begin by noting that the conclusion of this sequent is of the form Φ ∨ Ψ. The first suggestion in the table for conclusions of this form is to use ∨I if either Φ or Ψ (i.e., in this instance 'P' or 'Q') is present as a premise. But we have neither premise, so this suggestion is inapplicable. We then try the second suggestion, which is applicable if there is a premise of the form Θ ∨ Δ. 'P ∨ Q' is such a premise. The table then recommends proving as subconclusions the conditionals Θ → (Φ ∨ Ψ) and Δ → (Φ ∨ Ψ) (i.e., in this case 'P → (Q ∨ P)' and 'Q → (Q ∨ P)'). A **subconclusion** is simply a conclusion useful for obtaining the main conclusion. It may be, but is not always, the conclusion of a hypothetical derivation.

Now the task is to prove the two subconclusions 'P → (Q ∨ P)' and 'Q → (Q ∨ P)'. These are both of the form Φ → Ψ. So we consult Table 4.1 regarding strategies for proving conclusions of this form. The table recommends in each case

TABLE 4.1
Proof Strategies

If the conclusion or sub-conclusion you are trying to prove is of the form:	Then try this strategy:
~Φ	Hypothesize Φ and work toward a subconclusion of the form Ψ & ~Ψ in order to obtain ~Φ by ~I.
Φ & Ψ	Prove the subconclusions Φ and Ψ separately and then join them by &I.
Φ ∨ Ψ	If either Φ or Ψ is a premise, simply apply ∨I to obtain Φ ∨ Ψ. Otherwise, if there is a disjunctive premise Θ ∨ Δ, try proving the two conditionals Θ → (Φ ∨ Ψ) and Δ → (Φ ∨ Ψ) as subconclusions and then using ∨E to obtain Φ ∨ Ψ. If neither of these strategies works, then hypothesize ~(Φ ∨ Ψ) and work toward a subconclusion of the form Θ & ~Θ in order to obtain Φ ∨ Ψ by ~I and ~E.
Φ → Ψ	Hypothesize Φ and work toward the subconclusion Ψ in order to obtain the conditional by →I.
Φ ↔ Ψ	Prove the subconclusions Φ → Ψ and Ψ → Φ; then use ↔I to obtain Φ ↔ Ψ.

to hypothesize the antecedent, derive the consequent, and then use →I. We are now working on two levels. Though our ultimate strategy is to use ∨E, our immediate strategy is to use →I to obtain both 'P → (Q ∨ P)' and 'Q → (Q ∨ P)'. We begin the proof of the first of these conditionals by hypothesizing 'P' (line 2 in the proof below).

Now our goal is to prove yet another subconclusion: 'Q ∨ P'. This, again, is of the form Φ ∨ Ψ. So once again we consult Table 4.1 for strategies for proving conclusions of this form. But now, since we have hypothesized 'P', we can follow the first suggestion for disjunctive conclusions, obtaining 'Q ∨ P' directly by ∨I.

This enables us to prove 'P → (Q ∨ P)' by →I, completing our →I strategy. The second conditional, 'Q → (Q ∨ P)', can now be proved in the same way (lines 5–7 below). Now with both conditionals available, we simply apply ∨E (at line 8 below), completing both our initial strategy and the proof. Here is the result:

1.	P ∨ Q	A
2.	P	H (for →I)
3.	Q ∨ P	2 ∨I
4.	P → (Q ∨ P)	2–3 →I
5.	Q	H (for →I)
6.	Q ∨ P	5 ∨I

7. $Q \rightarrow (Q \vee P)$ 5–6 →I
8. $Q \vee P$ 1, 4, 7 ∨E

Though the form of the conclusion usually determines the best overall strategy for the proof, the details depend on the forms of the premises. It is almost always necessary to break the premises into their components using the appropriate elimination rules. Sometimes when no promising strategy is apparent, breaking down the premises in this way makes the path to the conclusion clear. As the preceding example illustrates, disjunctive premises typically demand a disjunction elimination strategy. Where $\Phi \vee \Psi$ is the disjunctive premise and Θ is the desired conclusion, this strategy requires the conditionals $\Phi \rightarrow \Theta$ and $\Psi \rightarrow \Theta$, which must usually be proved by →I before ∨E can be applied.

Sometimes none of the strategies listed in Table 4.1 seems to work. In that case, consider what additional premises would enable you to prove the conclusion, and see if these can be proved in some way. In many cases, such premises can be proved by ~I.

The following proof of '$\sim P \rightarrow Q \vdash P \vee Q$' illustrates this point:

1. $\sim P \rightarrow Q$ A
2. $\sim (P \vee Q)$ H (for ~I)
3. P H (for ~I)
4. $P \vee Q$ 2 ∨I
5. $(P \vee Q) \& \sim (P \vee Q)$ 2, 4 &I
6. $\sim P$ 3–5 ~I
7. Q 1, 6 →E
8. $P \vee Q$ 7 ∨I
9. $(P \vee Q) \& \sim (P \vee Q)$ 2, 8 &I
10. $\sim\sim (P \vee Q)$ 2–9 ~I
11. $P \vee Q$ 10 ~E

Having written the assumption at line 1, we note that the conclusion is of the form $\Phi \vee \Psi$ and consult Table 4.1 regarding conclusions of this form. But we are not given either disjunct as a premise, nor are we given a disjunctive premise, so the first two strategies for disjunctive conclusions are inapplicable. We therefore follow the third, hypothesizing the negation of this conclusion at line 2 and hoping to derive an absurdity. But which absurdity? Thinking ahead, we see that if we had the premise '$\sim P$', then by →E with 1 we could get 'Q', from which we could obtain '$P \vee Q$' by ∨I. This would contradict our hypothesis, providing the desired absurdity. Hence we can solve the problem if we can prove '$\sim P$'. Since '$\sim P$' is of the form $\sim\Phi$, Table 4.1 recommends using ~I as the strategy for proving it. So we hypothesize 'P' at line 3, attempting to derive an absurdity. This is achieved at line 5, which enables us to conclude '$\sim P$' at line 6. The rest of the proof then proceeds according to the strategy just outlined. Solving difficult problems in propositional logic often requires just this sort of thinking ahead.

This proof of '$P \leftrightarrow \sim Q \vdash \sim (P \leftrightarrow Q)$' uses a similar double ~I strategy, which requires the same sort of advance planning:

1.	P ↔ ~Q	A
2.	P ↔ Q	H (for ~I)
3.	P → ~Q	1 ↔E
4.	~Q → P	1 ↔E
5.	P → Q	2 ↔E
6.	Q → P	2 ↔E
7.	Q	H (for ~I)
8.	P	6, 7 →E
9.	~Q	3, 8 →E
10.	Q & ~Q	7, 9 &I
11.	~Q	7–10 ~I
12.	P	4, 11 →E
13.	Q	5, 12 →E
14.	Q & ~Q	11, 13 &I
15.	~(P ↔ Q)	2–14 ~I

Since the sequent's conclusion is '~(P ↔ Q)', which has the form ~Φ, we hypothesize 'P ↔ Q' at line 2 in order to reduce it to absurdity. No strategy is apparent at this point, so we use ↔E to break the two biconditionals into their components at lines 3–6, hoping that this will help us see how the absurdity might be derived. And it does, for we now note that if we could prove '~Q', then using line 4 we could get 'P', and with 'P' together with line 5 we could get 'Q'. Then we would have both 'Q' and '~Q'—which would provide the absurdity that we need to derive from the hypothesis 'P ↔ Q'. But before we can do any of this, we must prove '~Q'. Since this is a negated formula, the appropriate strategy is ~I. So we hypothesize 'Q' at line 7 in order to reduce it to absurdity. We obtain the absurdity at line 10, and that yields '~Q' at line 11. We then proceed to the final absurdity as planned.

The ten rules of inference are summarized in Table 4.2.

Exercise 4.3

Construct a proof for each of the following sequents:

1. P → Q, P ⊢ Q ∨ R
2. (P ∨ Q) → R ⊢ P → R
3. P → Q, P → R ⊢ P → (Q & R)
4. P → Q ⊢ (P & R) → Q
5. P ↔ Q, Q ↔ R ⊢ P ↔ R
6. P → (Q → R) ⊢ (P & Q) → R
7. (P & Q) → R ⊢ P → (Q → R)
8. P → Q ⊢ (Q → R) → (P → R)
9. P ⊢ Q → (R → (S → ((P & Q) & (R & S))))
10. ~~P ∨ ~~Q ⊢ P ∨ Q
11. (P & Q) ∨ (P & R) ⊢ P
12. (P & Q) ∨ (P & R) ⊢ Q ∨ R
13. P → Q, P → ~Q ⊢ ~P

TABLE 4.2
Summary: The Ten Rules of Inference

Negation Elimination (Double Negation) (~E)   From ~~Φ, infer Φ.

Negation Introduction (Reductio ad Absurdum, Indirect Proof) (~I)   Given a hypothetical derivation of any formula of the form (Ψ & ~Ψ) from Φ, end the derivation and infer ~Φ.

Conjunction Elimination (Simplification) (&E)   From (Φ & Ψ), infer either Φ or Ψ.

Conjunction Introduction (Conjunction) (&I)   From Φ and Ψ, infer (Φ & Ψ).

Disjunction Elimination (Constructive Dilemma) (∨E)   From (Φ ∨ Ψ), (Φ → Θ), and (Ψ → Θ), infer Θ.

Disjunction Introduction (Addition) (∨I)   From Φ, infer either (Φ ∨ Ψ) or (Ψ ∨ Φ).

Conditional Elimination (Modus Ponens) (→E)   Given (Φ → Ψ) and Φ, infer Ψ.

Conditional Introduction (Conditional Proof) (→I)   Given a hypothetical derivation of Ψ from Φ, end the derivation and infer (Φ → Ψ).

Biconditional Elimination (↔E)   From (Φ ↔ Ψ), infer either (Φ → Ψ) or (Ψ → Φ).

Biconditional Introduction (↔I)   From (Φ → Ψ) and (Ψ → Φ), infer (Φ ↔ Ψ).

---

14. P → ~P ⊢ ~P
15. P, ~Q ⊢ ~(P → Q)
16. ~(P & Q) ⊢ P → ~Q
17. P ↔ Q ⊢ ~P ↔ ~Q
18. (P & ~Q) ∨ (~P & Q) ⊢ ~(P ↔ Q)
19. P ∨ Q ⊢ ~(~P ∨ ~Q)
20. ~P ⊢ P → Q

4.4 THEOREMS AND SHORTCUTS

A remarkable feature of the hypothetical rules is that they enable us to prove conclusions without assumptions. Consider, for example, this simple proof of the assumptionless sequent '⊢ P → P':

1. | P   H (for →I)
2. P → P   1–1 →I

But this is reasonable, for 'P → P' is a tautology—that is, a valid formula. It is true on all valuations—that is, no matter what the facts are—and hence is true regardless of what we assume, or whether we assume anything at all. Each of the formula's instances—the statement 'If the pie is done, then the pie is done', for example—is true come what may. (Even in a world where there are no pies, it is true that if the pie is done, then the pie is done!) Conclusions provable without assumptions are called **theorems**. And, as we shall see in Section 5.10, all the theorems of propositional logic are tautologies, and vice versa.[3]

The formula '~(P & ~P)', which expresses the **principle of noncontradiction**, is also a theorem, which is equally easy to prove:

```
1. |      P & ~P          H (for ~I)
2. ~(P & ~P)              1–1 ~I
```

Here we needn't draw any conclusions in order to reduce the hypothesis to absurdity; the hypothesis *is* an absurdity!

Slightly more difficult to prove than these theorems is the **law of excluded middle** as expressed by the sequent '⊢ P ∨ ~P':

```
1. |        ~(P ∨ ~P)               H (for ~I)
2. |    |        P                  H (for ~I)
3. |    |      P ∨ ~P               2 ∨I
4. |    |   (P ∨ ~P) & ~(P ∨ ~P)    1, 3 &I
5. |      ~P                        3–4 ~I
6. |     P ∨ ~P                     5 ∨I
7. |   (P ∨ ~P) & ~(P ∨ ~P)         1, 6 &I
8. ~~(P ∨ ~P)                       1–7 ~I
9. P ∨ ~P                           8 ~E
```

Here we prove 'P ∨ ~P' by reducing its negation, '~(P ∨ ~P)', to absurdity. The trick is to see, after hypothesizing '~(P ∨ ~P)', that we could contradict this hypothesis by a simple step of ∨I (line 6) if we could prove '~P'. But '~P' is a negated formula, so we hypothesize 'P' at line 3 in an effort to reduce it to absurdity. This absurdity emerges at line 4, enabling us to deduce '~P' at line 5 and so complete the strategy as planned.

As a final example, we shall prove the theorem '⊢ (P → Q) → (~Q → ~P)'. The strategy here, an indirect proof nested within two conditional proofs, calls for three hypotheses:

```
1. |   P → Q                        H (for →I)
2. |    |      ~Q                    H (for →I)
3. |    |    |    P                  H (for ~I)
4. |    |    |    Q                  1, 3 →E
5. |    |    |    Q & ~Q             2, 4 &I
6. |    |      ~P                    3–5 ~I
7. |     ~Q → ~P                     2–6 →I
8. (P → Q) → (~Q → ~P)              1–7 →I
```

---

[3] See Exercise 5.10.2, problem 2.

When we prove a sequent, whether or not it is a theorem, we show it to be a reliably valid inference pattern—a fact which can be used to shorten proofs. Consider, for example, the sequent 'P ⊢ ~~P', which expresses an inference pattern that like ~E is often called **double negation.** Its proof is as follows:

1.	P	A
2.	~P	H (for ~I)
3.	P & ~P	1, 2 &I
4.	~~P	1–2 ~I

Having proved this sequent, we have in effect proved the validity of all sequents of the form **Φ ⊢ ~~Φ**, where **Φ** is any formula whatsoever—sequents such as 'P ∨ Q ⊢ ~~(P ∨ Q)', 'P → ~R ⊢ ~~(P → ~R)', '~Q ⊢ ~~~Q', and so on. We shall call these *variants* of the original sequent. More precisely, a **variant** of a sequent is a sequent formed by replacing one or more of its sentence letters by formulas, each occurrence of the same sentence letter being replaced by the same formula. *(Note, however, that only sentence letters may be replaced, not larger parts of the formula.)* Take, for example, 'P ∨ Q ⊢ ~~(P ∨ Q)'. This is a variant of the sequent 'P ⊢ ~~P' because it is the result of replacing each occurrence of the sentence letter 'P' in 'P ⊢ ~~P' by 'P ∨ Q'. To prove 'P ⊢ ~~P' is in effect to prove 'P ∨ Q ⊢ ~~(P ∨ Q)' as well, since the proof of the latter mimics the proof of the former precisely; we simply replace each occurrence of 'P' in the proof of 'P ⊢ ~~P' with 'P ∨ Q', leaving everything else the same:

1.	P ∨ Q	A
2.	~(P ∨ Q)	H (for ~I)
3.	(P ∨ Q) & ~(P ∨ Q)	1, 2 &I
4.	~~(P ∨ Q)	1–2 ~I

Any other variant of 'P ⊢ ~~P' can be proved by the same sort of replacement. Thus, having proved 'P ⊢ ~~P', we have in effect shown how to prove each instance of the general rule of double negation:

From **Φ**, infer ~~**Φ**.

This rule is thus just as legitimate as our ten basic introduction and elimination rules. There is no reason not to give it some abbreviation, say 'DN', and allow it to be used in proofs. This will save work. Consider, for example, this proof of the sequent '~~Q → R, Q ⊢ R':

1.	~~Q → R	A
2.	Q	A
3.	~Q	H (for ~I)
4.	Q & ~Q	2, 3 &I
5.	~~Q	3–4 ~I
6.	R	2, 5 →E

Steps 2–5 just repeat the form of the proof of double negation given above. Instead of going to all of this trouble, from now on we may simply write:

1.	~~Q → R	A
2.	Q	A
3.	~~Q	2 DN
4.	R	1, 3 →E

Any previously proved sequent may be used as a rule of inference in this way. Such rules are called **derived rules** because their justification is derived from the ten rules we have taken as basic. Derived rules do not enable us to prove any sequent that cannot already be proved by the original ten. They merely shorten proofs and save work.

Though any previously proved sequent can be used as a derived rule, we shall be selective in the ones we name and abbreviate for use. Too many rules can be cumbersome. The derived rules listed in Table 4.3 suffice for an elegant proof for just about any sequent we might encounter. We have not actually proved them all—yet. Those that remain unproved are left as exercises.

From now on we may freely use the derived rules listed in Table 4.3. The following proof of '~(~P ∨ Q) ⊢ ~(P → Q)' provides a further illustration of the use of derived rules:

1.	~(~P ∨ Q)	A
2.	P → Q	H (for ~I)
3.	~~P & ~Q	1 DM
4.	~Q	3 &E
5.	~P	2, 4 MT
6.	~~P	3 &E
7.	~P & ~~P	5, 6 &I
8.	~(P → Q)	2–7 ~I

The overall strategy is reductio (indirect proof). Notice that there is no need to use ~E on line 6 before proceeding to the contradiction. '~P & ~~P' is just as good a contradiction as 'P & ~P'.

TABLE 4.3
Some Important Derived Rules

Derived Rule(s)	Name	Abbreviation
From Φ → Ψ and ~Ψ, infer ~Φ.	Modus Tollens	MT
From Φ → Ψ, infer ~Ψ → ~Φ.	Contraposition	CP
From Φ ↔ Ψ and Φ, infer Ψ. From Φ ↔ Ψ and Ψ, infer Φ.	Biconditional Modus Ponens	↔MP
From Φ ↔ Ψ and ~Ψ, infer ~Φ. From Φ ↔ Ψ and ~Φ, infer ~Ψ.	Biconditional Modus Tollens	↔MT

(continued)

TABLE 4.3
Some Important Derived Rules (*continued*)

Derived Rule(s)	Name	Abbreviation
From $\Phi \vee \Psi$ and $\sim\Phi$, infer Ψ. From $\Phi \vee \Psi$ and $\sim\Psi$, infer Φ.	Disjunctive Syllogism	DS
From $\Phi \rightarrow \Psi$ and $\Psi \rightarrow \Theta$, infer $\Phi \rightarrow \Theta$.	Hypothetical Syllogism	HS
From Φ, infer $\sim\sim\Phi$.	Double Negation	DN
From $\sim(\Phi \vee \Psi)$, infer $\sim\Phi \mathbin{\&} \sim\Psi$. From $\sim\Phi \mathbin{\&} \sim\Psi$, infer $\sim(\Phi \vee \Psi)$. From $\sim(\Phi \mathbin{\&} \Psi)$, infer $\sim\Phi \vee \sim\Psi$. From $\sim\Phi \vee \sim\Psi$, infer $\sim(\Phi \mathbin{\&} \Psi)$. From $\Phi \vee \Psi$, infer $\sim(\sim\Phi \mathbin{\&} \sim\Psi)$. From $\sim(\sim\Phi \mathbin{\&} \sim\Psi)$, infer $\Phi \vee \Psi$. From $\Phi \mathbin{\&} \Psi$, infer $\sim(\sim\Phi \vee \sim\Psi)$. From $\sim(\sim\Phi \vee \sim\Psi)$, infer $\Phi \mathbin{\&} \Psi$.	De Morgan's Laws	DM
From $\Phi \mathbin{\&} \Psi$, infer $\Psi \mathbin{\&} \Phi$. From $\Phi \vee \Psi$, infer $\Psi \vee \Phi$.	Commutation	COM
From $(\Phi \mathbin{\&} \Psi) \mathbin{\&} \Theta$, infer $\Phi \mathbin{\&} (\Psi \mathbin{\&} \Theta)$. From $\Phi \mathbin{\&} (\Psi \mathbin{\&} \Theta)$, infer $(\Phi \mathbin{\&} \Psi) \mathbin{\&} \Theta$. From $(\Phi \vee \Psi) \vee \Theta$, infer $\Phi \vee (\Psi \vee \Theta)$. From $\Phi \vee (\Psi \vee \Theta)$, infer $(\Phi \vee \Psi) \vee \Theta$.	Association	ASSOC
From $(\Phi \mathbin{\&} \Psi) \vee \Theta$, infer $(\Phi \vee \Theta) \mathbin{\&}$ $\quad (\Psi \vee \Theta)$. From $(\Phi \vee \Theta) \mathbin{\&} (\Psi \vee \Theta)$, infer $\quad (\Phi \mathbin{\&} \Psi) \vee \Theta$. From $(\Phi \vee \Psi) \mathbin{\&} \Theta$, infer $(\Phi \mathbin{\&} \Theta) \vee$ $\quad (\Psi \mathbin{\&} \Theta)$. From $(\Phi \mathbin{\&} \Theta) \vee (\Psi \mathbin{\&} \Theta)$, infer $(\Phi \vee \Psi)$ $\quad \mathbin{\&} \Theta$.	Distribution	DIST
From $\Phi \rightarrow \Psi$, infer $\sim\Phi \vee \Psi$. From $\sim\Phi \vee \Psi$, infer $\Phi \rightarrow \Psi$. From $\Phi \rightarrow \Psi$, infer $\sim(\Phi \mathbin{\&} \sim\Psi)$. From $\sim(\Phi \mathbin{\&} \sim\Psi)$, infer $\Phi \rightarrow \Psi$.	Material Implication	MI
From Φ and $\sim\Phi$, infer any formula Ψ.	Ex Falso Quodlibet	EFQ

Exercise 4.4.1

Sequents representing some of the derived rules discussed in this section have been proved in the text (Sections 4.2–4.4), but a number of the derived rules have not been so verified. Complete the verification of these derived rules by proving the following sequents, using only the ten basic rules:

Sequent	Corresponding Derived Rule
1. $P \leftrightarrow Q, P \vdash Q$	Biconditional Modus Ponens
2. $P \leftrightarrow Q, Q \vdash P$	Biconditional Modus Ponens
3. $P \leftrightarrow Q, \sim Q \vdash \sim P$	Biconditional Modus Tollens
4. $P \leftrightarrow Q, \sim P \vdash \sim Q$	Biconditional Modus Tollens
5. $P \vee Q, \sim Q \vdash P$	Disjunctive Syllogism
6. $\sim(P \vee Q) \vdash \sim P \mathbin{\&} \sim Q$	De Morgan's Law
7. $\sim P \mathbin{\&} \sim Q \vdash \sim(P \vee Q)$	De Morgan's Law
8. $\sim(P \mathbin{\&} Q) \vdash \sim P \vee \sim Q$	De Morgan's Law
9. $\sim P \vee \sim Q \vdash \sim(P \mathbin{\&} Q)$	De Morgan's Law
10. $P \vee Q \vdash \sim(\sim P \mathbin{\&} \sim Q)$	De Morgan's Law
11. $\sim(\sim P \mathbin{\&} \sim Q) \vdash P \vee Q$	De Morgan's Law
12. $P \mathbin{\&} Q \vdash \sim(\sim P \vee \sim Q)$	De Morgan's Law
13. $\sim(\sim P \vee \sim Q) \vdash P \mathbin{\&} Q$	De Morgan's Law
14. $(P \mathbin{\&} Q) \mathbin{\&} R \vdash P \mathbin{\&} (Q \mathbin{\&} R)$	Association
15. $P \mathbin{\&} (Q \mathbin{\&} R) \vdash (P \mathbin{\&} Q) \mathbin{\&} R$	Association
16. $(P \vee Q) \vee R \vdash (P \vee Q) \vee R$	Association
17. $P \vee (Q \vee R) \vdash (P \vee Q) \vee R$	Association
18. $(P \mathbin{\&} Q) \vee R \vdash (P \vee R) \mathbin{\&} (Q \vee R)$	Distribution
19. $(P \vee R) \mathbin{\&} (Q \vee R) \vdash (P \mathbin{\&} Q) \vee R$	Distribution
20. $(P \vee Q) \mathbin{\&} R \vdash (P \mathbin{\&} R) \vee (Q \mathbin{\&} R)$	Distribution
21. $(P \mathbin{\&} R) \vee (Q \mathbin{\&} R) \vdash (P \vee Q) \mathbin{\&} R$	Distribution
22. $P \rightarrow Q \vdash \sim P \vee Q$	Material Implication
23. $\sim P \vee Q \vdash P \rightarrow Q$	Material Implication
24. $P \rightarrow Q \vdash \sim(P \mathbin{\&} \sim Q)$	Material Implication
25. $\sim(P \mathbin{\&} \sim Q) \vdash P \rightarrow Q$	Material Implication

Exercise 4.4.2

Prove the following theorems using either basic or derived rules:

1. $\vdash P \rightarrow (P \vee Q)$
2. $\vdash (P \mathbin{\&} Q) \rightarrow P$
3. $\vdash P \rightarrow \sim\sim P$
4. $\vdash P \rightarrow (Q \rightarrow (P \mathbin{\&} Q))$
5. $\vdash P \rightarrow ((P \rightarrow Q) \rightarrow Q)$
6. $\vdash \sim(P \vee Q) \rightarrow \sim P$
7. $\vdash \sim(P \leftrightarrow \sim P)$
8. $\vdash P \rightarrow (Q \vee \sim Q)$
9. $\vdash (P \leftrightarrow Q) \vee (P \leftrightarrow \sim Q)$
10. $\vdash (P \rightarrow Q) \leftrightarrow \sim(P \mathbin{\&} \sim Q)$

Exercise 4.4.3

Reprove the sequents of Exercise 4.3, using derived rules to shorten the proofs wherever possible.

4.5 ALTERNATIVE PROOF TECHNIQUES
AND THE LIMITATIONS OF PROOFS

Our system of ten inference rules is only one of many proof systems for classical predicate logic. All do the same work—that is, prove the same sequents—so choice among them is largely a matter of taste and style. For the austere, there is the system which uses only two rules—modus ponens (our →E) and tautology introduction:

> **Tautology Introduction (TI)**   Any tautology may be asserted at any line of a proof.

Tautology introduction is in effect a derived rule of our system (though we have not used it as such), since every tautology is a theorem.

A proof of the sequent 'P ∨ Q, ~P ⊢ Q' in this system might look like this:

1. $P \lor Q$ A
2. $\sim P$ A
3. $(P \lor Q) \rightarrow (\sim P \rightarrow Q)$ TI
4. $\sim P \rightarrow Q$ 1, 3 →E
5. Q 2, 4 →E

This system works because each valid sequent corresponds to a conditional tautology created by taking its premises successively as antecedents for its conclusion. For example, if $\Phi_1, \Phi_2, \Phi_3 \vdash \Psi$ is a valid sequent, then $(\Phi_1 \rightarrow (\Phi_2 \rightarrow (\Phi_3 \rightarrow \Psi)))$ is the corresponding tautology. To prove the sequent using just modus ponens and TI, we assume $\Phi_1, \Phi_2,$ and Φ_3, assert $(\Phi_1 \rightarrow (\Phi_2 \rightarrow (\Phi_3 \rightarrow \Psi)))$ by TI, and derive successively $\Phi_2 \rightarrow (\Phi_3 \rightarrow \Psi), \Phi_3 \rightarrow \Psi$, and finally Ψ by modus ponens. It is not difficult to see that this proof procedure works for any valid sequent, regardless of the number of premises.

The main drawback of this method is that tautologies are not immediately recognizable by their form. If, for example, we are presented with an invalid sequent, say, 'P → Q, Q ⊢ P', we may attempt a proof along these lines:

1. $P \rightarrow Q$ A
2. Q A
3. $(P \rightarrow Q) \rightarrow (Q \rightarrow P)$ TI **(Wrong!)**
4. $Q \rightarrow P$ 1, 3 →E
5. P 2, 4 →E

But this proof is erroneous, for '$(P \rightarrow Q) \rightarrow (Q \rightarrow P)$' is not tautologous. We may, however, be unable to confirm that it is not tautologous without doing a truth table, a tree, or a proof using another system of rules! Thus in application this proof system must often be supplemented by some independent test for tautologousness. Though technically there is nothing wrong with such a system, it is not very practical.

But the austere need not despair. If instead of the TI rule, which permits the introduction of any tautology, we allow introduction of tautologies only of a limited number of *recognizable* forms, we can still create a system that will prove all valid sequents. Such, for example, is the system that has as its inference rules only →E and the introduction of tautologies of one of the following three forms:

Ax1 $\Phi \to (\Psi \to \Phi)$

Ax2 $(\Phi \to (\Psi \to \Theta)) \to ((\Phi \to \Psi) \to (\Phi \to \Theta))$

Ax3 $(\sim\!\Psi \to \sim\!\Phi) \to ((\sim\!\Psi \to \Phi) \to \Psi)$[4]

These forms are called **axiom schemas.** (An axiom is a fundamental principle from which other less fundamental principles are derived.) There are other sets of axiom schemas which also suffice to prove all valid sequents. This particular set is formulated only in terms of negation and the conditional; it must be augmented by definitions introducing the other operators to be capable of proving sequents containing them. A disjunction $\Phi \vee \Psi$, for example, is defined as $\sim\!\Phi \to \Psi$, a logically equivalent conditional whose antecedent is negated. This means that any instance of either of these two forms may be replaced by the corresponding instance of the other—regardless of whether the initial instance is a whole formula or just a subformula. So, for example, this definition allows us to move from the premise

$$(\sim\!P \to \sim\!Q) \to ((\sim\!P \to Q) \to P)$$

(which, incidentally, is an instance of Ax3) to the conclusion

$$(\sim\!P \to \sim\!Q) \to ((P \vee Q) \to P)$$

by replacing '$\sim\!P \to Q$' with '$P \vee Q$'. Definitions such as these are called **contextual definitions** or **definitions in use,** because they give directions for replacing not merely the defined term, but an entire formula or subformula containing that term, by an abbreviating formula, and vice versa. The operators '$\sim$' and '$\to$' are regarded in this axiom system as **primitive** operators; only they are mentioned in the formation rules. Those introduced by definition are known as **defined** operators. Formulas containing defined operators are regarded as mere abbreviations for formulas containing only primitive operators.

The full set of definitions for the defined operators is as follows:

$\Phi \vee \Psi$	$=_{df}$	$\sim\!\Phi \to \Psi$
$\Phi \mathbin{\&} \Psi$	$=_{df}$	$\sim\!(\Phi \to \sim\!\Psi)$
$\Phi \leftrightarrow \Psi$	$=_{df}$	$(\Phi \to \Psi) \mathbin{\&} (\Psi \to \Phi)$

The symbol '$=_{df}$' is a metalinguistic abbreviation meaning "is by definition."

Notice that the definition of '$\leftrightarrow$' mentions the operator '$\&$'. It must therefore be supplemented by the definition of '$\&$' if expressions containing '$\leftrightarrow$' are to be reduced to primitive terms. Formulas of the form $\Phi \leftrightarrow \Psi$ abbreviate formulas of the form $(\Phi \to \Psi) \mathbin{\&} (\Psi \to \Phi)$, which in turn (by the definition of '$\&$') abbreviate formulas of the form $\sim\!((\Phi \to \Psi) \to \sim\!(\Psi \to \Phi))$.

---

[4] These axiom schemas are from Elliott Mendelson, *Introduction to Mathematical Logic,* 3rd ed. (Monterey, CA: Wadsworth & Brooks/Cole, 1987), p. 29.

In a proof, the definitions may be used as rules of inference, though they differ from the deduction rules presented earlier in this chapter in that they may be applied to subformulas as well as to whole formulas. When the definition of an operator is used, either to introduce or to eliminate that operator, we indicate this by writing to the right of the new formula the line number of the formula to which the definition was applied, followed by 'Df' to indicate that the step is being made by definition and by an occurrence of the operator itself to indicate which definition is being used.

This simple proof 'Q ⊢ P ∨ Q' illustrates the use of both an axiom and a definition:

1. Q   A
2. Q → (~P → Q)   A1
3. ~P → Q   1, 2 →E
4. P ∨ Q   3 Df∨

In step 2 we introduce an instance of axiom schema 1 in which Φ is 'Q' and Ψ is '~P'. The conclusion follows directly by modus ponens (→E) and the definition of '∨'.

Here is a proof of hypothetical syllogism, 'P → Q, Q → R ⊢ P → R':

1. P → Q   A
2. Q → R   A
3. (P → (Q → R)) → ((P → Q) → (P → R))   Ax2
4. (Q → R) → (P → (Q → R))   Ax1
5. P → (Q → R)   2, 4 →E
6. (P → Q) → (P → R)   3, 5 →E
7. P → R   1, 6 →E

In step 3 we use a simple instance of axiom schema 2 in which Φ is 'P', Ψ is 'Q', and Θ is 'R'. In step 4 we introduce an instance of axiom schema 1 in which Φ is 'Q → R' and Ψ is 'P'. The conclusion then follows by three steps of modus ponens. In virtue of this proof, hypothetical syllogism may henceforth be used as a derived rule.

As a final illustration, we shall prove '~~P ⊢ P', which establishes ~E as a derived rule in this axiom system:

1. ~~P   A
2. ~~P → (~P → ~~P)   Ax1
3. ~P → ~~P   1, 2 →E
4. (~P → ~~P) → ((~P → ~P) → P)   Ax3
5. (~P → ~P) → P   3, 4 →E
6. (~P → ((~P → ~P) → ~P) → ~P) → ((~P → (~P → ~P)) →
    (~P → ~P))   Ax2
7. ~P → ((~P → ~P) → ~P)   Ax1
8. (~P → (~P → ~P)) → (~P → ~P)   6, 7 →E
9. ~P → (~P → ~P)   Ax1
10. ~P → ~P   8, 9 →E
11. P   5, 10 →E

Because this axiom system has just three axiom schemas and only one inference rule, there is little to work with. Proofs tend to be longer and more complicated than those in natural deduction systems. This can be alleviated, however, by the introduction of derived rules. Axiom systems, though perhaps cumbersome to reason with, are generally easy to reason about. Thus axiom systems are often preferred for metatheoretic work. But that is the subject of the next chapter.

It can be shown (though we shall not show it) that each of the ten basic rules of our natural deduction system is a derived rule of this axiom system. Thus any sequent provable in the former is provable in the latter. Likewise, it is easy to show that each instance of each axiom of this system is a theorem of our natural deduction system. Since the natural deduction system also contains →E, this means that any sequent provable in the axiom system is also provable in the natural deduction system—provided there is always some way within the natural deduction system to mimic definitional inferences. This, too, can be shown. Therefore the two systems prove exactly the same sequents.

Deduction can also be pursued in an algebraic fashion. The idea here is to treat logical equivalences as identities. Thus, for example, the commutation law,

$$(\Phi \mathbin{\&} \Psi) \leftrightarrow (\Psi \mathbin{\&} \Phi)$$

which expresses a logical equivalence, may be thought of as asserting that propositions of the forms $\Phi \mathbin{\&} \Psi$ and $\Psi \mathbin{\&} \Phi$ are *identical*. In algebra, terms denoting identical objects may be substituted one for another wherever they occur. Thus, for example, since $3x = x+x+x$, the expressions '$3x$' and '$x+x+x$' may be used interchangeably. In algebraic deduction, logically equivalent formulas are similarly interchangeable. Hence, for instance, using the commutation law above, we may from the premise

$$\sim(P \mathbin{\&} Q) \rightarrow R$$

directly infer the conclusion

$$\sim(Q \mathbin{\&} P) \rightarrow R$$

Algebraic equivalence rules may be combined with natural deduction rules to form hybrid logical systems. There are also systems which combine natural deduction rules with axioms. Indeed, the number of deductive systems adequate to classical propositional logic (or any other interesting logic, for that matter) is infinite. We have chosen the natural deduction approach and will stick with that throughout this book, because among all the systems of classical logic it seems most nearly to approximate the ways people ordinarily reason.

In comparison to truth tables and trees, however, all of these proof techniques have two serious disadvantages: (1) They test only for validity, not for invalidity, and (2) even for valid arguments they do not guarantee an answer.[5] We

---

[5] Proof techniques can be modified or elaborated to ameliorate or, in some cases, eliminate these disadvantages, but only at the cost of making them more complicated or less natural.

may prove a sequent to be valid, but proofs are not designed to reveal invalidity. If we try to prove a sequent and fail, that does not show the sequent is invalid. Maybe we did not try hard enough. Thus, given a sequent whose validity is in question, trying to prove it settles the question only if the sequent is valid and we do in fact find a proof.

Moreover, because proof rules can be applied or axioms introduced in any order, they may be applied repeatedly without ever reaching the desired conclusion, even if that conclusion validly follows from the premises. Proof, in other words, may elude us, even though proofs exist.

Because of these disadvantages, this book does not emphasize proofs, though they are the most familiar and widely recognized way of doing logic. We shall concentrate instead on the more powerful semantic techniques—valuation rules, truth tables, and trees—and their generalizations for more advanced logical systems.

Exercise 4.5.1

Prove instances of Ax1, Ax2, and Ax3 as theorems within our natural deduction system.

Exercise 4.5.2

Prove the following sequents within the axiom system presented in this section:

1. $\vdash P \to P$
2. $\vdash (\sim P \to P) \to P$
3. $P, \sim P \vdash Q$
4. $P \to (Q \to R), Q \vdash P \to R$

CHAPTER 5

CLASSICAL PROPOSITIONAL LOGIC: METATHEORY

5.1 INTRODUCTION TO METALOGIC

Metalogic is the logical study of formal logical systems. In metalogic we study one or more formal languages (e.g., the language of propositional logic) which, being the objects of our study, are called **object languages.** We must, of course, use language to talk about an object language, but the language we use is usually not the object language itself. We call it the **metalanguage.** Virtually everything said in a logic textbook, except for the problems and exercises, is formulated in the metalanguage. Our metalanguage is English augmented with an assortment of variables (e.g., Greek letters) and other technical devices.

Chapter 4 covered proofs formulated and carried out in an object language, the language of propositional logic. The proofs we shall construct in this chapter will be proofs about the object language, formulated and carried out in the metalanguage. The conclusions of these proofs are called **metatheorems,** and the proofs themselves are called **metaproofs.** Reasoning in metaproofs often mirrors reasoning in the object language. Similar inference rules (e.g., modus ponens) may be used, though usually they are used without comment, rather than being explicitly cited and annotated. Over the years, logicians have developed a peculiar style and rhetoric for expressing metatheorems. Part of what you will be learning here is that style and rhetoric.

To prove a metatheorem, we begin with a set of premises and construct a proof linking them to some desired conclusion, just as in a formal language. In a typical exercise in propositional logic, however, both the premises and the conclusion are explicitly given. For metatheorems, only the conclusion is given; you are not told exactly which premises to use. Part of your work is to decide which premises are needed. Premises for metatheorems are typically definitions or previously proved metatheorems. Occasionally some principles of arithmetic or algebra are also used. It's usually easy to tell which definitions to use; they will nearly always be the definitions of the concepts employed in the metatheorem. The definitions we will need to prove metatheorems in this chapter are the ones introduced in Chapters 2–4.

Consider, for example, how to prove the elementary metatheorem that '~~P' is a formula (of the language of propositional logic). The main concept used in this metatheorem is the concept of a formula. So we need to locate the definition of a formula, which will function as a premise in the proof. The appropriate definition is embodied in the formation rules (see Section 2.3). From rule 1 it follows that 'P' is a formula. And since 'P' is a formula, by rule 2 '~P' is also a formula. Once we have shown that '~P' is a formula, it follows, again by rule 2, that '~~P' is a formula—so we have our conclusion. Notice that the only premises used were rules 1 and 2, and that rule 2 was used twice. Here's the proof in good metatheoretic style:

METATHEOREM: '~~P' is a formula.

PROOF: By formation rule 1, 'P' is a formula, whence it follows by rule 2 that '~P' is a formula, and again by rule 2 that '~~P' is a formula.   QED

The letters 'QED' at the end stand for *quod erat demonstrandum*, a Latin phrase meaning "which was to be proved." This is the logician's equivalent of a high five. When you finish proving a metatheorem, writing these letters gives you a little rush.

Metatheorems differ greatly in form and content. Here is another simple metatheorem that uses the valuation rules, rather than the formation rules:

METATHEOREM: 'P → ~P' is consistent.

PROOF: Since (by the definition of a valuation), a valuation is simply an assignment of one of the values T or F to the sentence letters of a formula, there is a valuation $\mathcal{V}$ of the formula 'P' such that $\mathcal{V}('P') = F$ and hence $\mathcal{V}('P') \neq T$. By valuation rule 4 (the rule for the conditional), if $\mathcal{V}('P') \neq T$, then $\mathcal{V}('P \rightarrow \sim P') = T$. Hence there is a valuation (namely

> $\mathcal{V}$) on which 'P → ~P' is true. It follows (by the definition of consistency) that 'P → ~P' is consistent.   QED

This metatheorem simply puts into words what a truth table or tree would reveal. But for that very reason it may be useful as an illustration of metatheoretic style. Simple metatheorems may just be summaries or reminders of what we already know; that is the case, too, with the next one.

But this next metatheorem is more general in scope. It combines the definition of a valuation, the formation rules, and the valuation rules to get the conclusion that all formulas have exactly one of the values T or F on each of their valuations:

> **METATHEOREM (Bivalence):** Each formula of propositional logic is either true or false, but not both, on each of its valuations.
>
> **PROOF:** Consider any formula Φ of propositional logic and any valuation $\mathcal{V}$ of Φ. Since Φ is a formula, Φ is either atomic or complex. If Φ is atomic, then the definition of a valuation stipulates that $\mathcal{V}$ assigns it one, but not both, of the values T or F. If Φ is complex, then by formation rules 2 and 3 it must have one of five forms: ~Φ, (Φ & Ψ), (Φ ∨ Ψ), (Φ → Ψ), or (Φ ↔ Ψ). Now the valuation rule for each of these forms stipulates that $\mathcal{V}$ assigns Φ the value F iff $\mathcal{V}$ does not assign Φ the value T.[1] No matter whether Φ is atomic or complex, then, $\mathcal{V}$ assigns to Φ one, but not both, of the values T or F.   QED

Though simple, this metatheorem is important for it confirms that our semantics is bivalent—that is, classical.

Exercise 5.1

Prove the following metatheorems:

1. '(P → (Q ∨ (R ∨ ~S)))' is a formula.
2. '(P → ~P)' is true on the valuation in which 'P' is false.

---

[1] The valuation rule for conjunction, for example, is:

$\mathcal{V}(\Phi$ & $\Psi) = T$ iff both $\mathcal{V}(\Phi) = T$ and $\mathcal{V}(\Psi) = T$;
$\mathcal{V}(\Phi$ & $\Psi) = F$ iff either $\mathcal{V}(\Phi) \neq T$ or $\mathcal{V}(\Psi) \neq T$, or both.

The conditions under which $\mathcal{V}(\Phi$ & $\Psi) = F$ are precisely those under which it is not the case that $\mathcal{V}(\Phi$ & $\Psi) = T$. (Check that the other rules imply that complex formulas of other forms too are false iff they are not true.)

5.2 CONDITIONAL PROOF

In formal logic, different kinds of proofs require different strategies. The same is true in metalogic. Indeed, the same principles of strategy apply to both kinds of reasoning. In both cases, strategy is governed mainly by the structure of the conclusion. For example, if the conclusion is a conditional statement (i.e., a statement of the form $\Phi \rightarrow \Psi$), then the best strategy is usually **conditional proof.** The object language version of conditional proof was covered in Section 4.3, where it is called conditional introduction ($\rightarrow$I). Here we discuss conditional proof in the metalanguage.

In a conditional proof we suppose the antecedent Φ for the sake of argument and use it, perhaps together with other assumptions, to derive the consequent Ψ. The argument in which we derive Ψ is **hypothetical,** in the sense that it depends on the supposition of the antecedent Φ, which we need not assert to be true. Because of its hypothetical character, I like to think of this argument as a kind of fiction. However, if we succeed in validly deriving the consequent Ψ from the antecedent Φ, then we certainly know this:

If Φ is true, then Ψ is true.

That is, we know that $\Phi \rightarrow \Psi$. Since we know this whether or not Φ is true, the conclusion $\Phi \rightarrow \Psi$, unlike the hypothetical conclusion Ψ, does not depend on the truth of the supposition Φ. Hence we are entitled to **discharge** this supposition— that is, not to regard it as one of the assumptions on which the proof of $\Phi \rightarrow \Psi$ rests. (It was, after all, made only "for the sake of argument.")

Formal systems usually have some notational device to indicate the discharging of suppositions, and some even have ways of setting off the hypothetical argument. In the system of Chapter 4, the discharging of suppositions is indicated by the ending of the line to the left of the hypothetical derivation. Metatheory dispenses with these devices. I find it helpful, however, to adopt the convention of indenting the proof when a supposition is introduced and ending the indentation when it is discharged. The hypothetical argument is thus set off clearly from the rest of the argument. This convention is consistently employed below.

Let's consider a simple example of a metatheorem employing a conditional proof strategy. The metatheorem is this:

If the set of premises of a valid sequent is consistent, then so is the conclusion.

This metatheorem is a conditional statement, so to prove it we will use conditional proof. We begin by supposing the antecedent:

(A) The set of premises of a valid sequent is consistent.

Our immediate goal is to prove the consequent:

(C) The conclusion of the sequent is consistent.

If we can do so, then we can discharge the supposition (A) and assert the desired conditional statement (A) → (C).

The problem now becomes how to derive (C) from (A). The argument is not immediate, so we need some additional assumptions.[2] As noted above, these are likely to be definitions of major terms used in the metatheorem. Two major terms used here are 'valid' and 'consistent'. The latter is used in two senses; statement (A) concerns the consistency of a set of object language formulas, and statement (C) concerns the consistency of a single object language formula, the conclusion. So the next step is to look up the definitions of these terms. These definitions are as follows:

(1) A sequent is valid iff there is no valuation on which its premises are true and its conclusion is not true.
(2) A set of formulas is consistent iff there is at least one valuation in which all members of the set are true.
(3) A single formula is consistent iff there is at least one valuation in which it is true.

(These definitions are statements in the metalanguage concerning sequents or formulas of the object language.)

Now the path of reasoning from (A) to (C) is easy to see. Since the sequent in question is valid, by (1) there is no valuation on which its premises are true and its conclusion is not true. But since the set of its premises is consistent, by (2) there is at least one valuation on which these premises are all true. Hence on that valuation (if no other) the sequent's conclusion is not untrue—that is, it is true. But, then by definition (3), the sequent's conclusion is consistent—which is the conclusion (C) that we were trying to prove.

That, of course, was just the hypothetical argument. Having completed the hypothetical argument, we still need to discharge supposition (A) and assert our conclusion (A) → (C). Here's what it looks like when we assemble the pieces:

METATHEOREM: If the set of premises of a valid sequent is consistent, then so is the conclusion.

PROOF: Suppose (for conditional proof) that the set $\Phi_1, \ldots, \Phi_n$ of premises of some valid sequent with conclusion Ψ is consistent. Then (by the definition of consistency for a set) there is at least one valuation $\mathcal{V}$ on which $\Phi_1, \ldots, \Phi_n$ are all true. But (by the definition of validity) there is no valuation on which $\Phi_1, \ldots, \Phi_n$ are all true and Ψ is not true. Thus Ψ is not untrue

---

[2] By the way, be sure to keep straight which argument we are talking about at which time. We are talking about two arguments: a metatheoretical one that we are constructing and a formal one, technically a sequent, in the object language that the metatheoretical argument is about. Metatheory is always working on two levels like this, and that's one of the things that makes metatheory difficult.

> on $\mathscr{V}$ and so must be true on $\mathscr{V}$. Hence (by the definition of consistency) Ψ is consistent.
>
> Therefore, if the set of premises of a valid sequent is consistent, then so is the conclusion.   QED

The indented part is the hypothetical argument, the "logical fiction." We need not know or care whether there is any such object language sequent as we are supposing here (though in this case, of course, there are many). The hypothetical argument takes us from the antecedent (A) to the consequent (C) of our conclusion. Then the antecedent is discharged (indicated by ending the indentation) and the conditional conclusion is asserted to complete the proof.

I have used parenthetical remarks to indicate where definitions are invoked in the proof. In most metatheoretical writing, these remarks would be omitted; it is assumed that the reader is sophisticated enough to realize that the argument is by definition. But it helps when you are learning metatheory to remind yourself of what you are doing by incorporating such remarks.

Notice how I used Greek letters as variables in the metalanguage. Such variables provide clear reference and help to condense the prose. I used Greek because I didn't want the variables that belong to the metalanguage to be confused with the P's, Q's, and so on that are part of the formal object language we are talking about. If, for example, I had used the letter

P

instead of

Ψ

in the metatheorem, someone might have thought the conclusion was meant specifically to be the atomic formula 'P'. The metatheorem, however, does not specify the form of the conclusion. To designate object language formulas without specifying their identity, we need special variables in our metalanguage. And since we don't want to confuse these **metavariables**—that is, variables of the metalanguage—with object language formulas, it's best to use a wholly distinct alphabet. That's the reason for the Greek. When no such confusion could arise, however, we will sometimes use the more familiar English letters as metavariables.

The purpose of the notation '$\Phi_1, \ldots, \Phi_n$' should be clear. This is just a way of designating a list of some unspecified number (n) of formulas. We stipulate that this notation allows the possibility that the list has no members so that n might be 0, unless otherwise specified. If $n = 0$, then by convention every valuation makes $\Phi_1, \ldots, \Phi_n$ true, since there is nothing to make true. (The convention in question is a convention that governs universally quantified statements—that is, statements about *all* members or *every* member of a class—in classical logic generally. In this case the particular statement at issue—'Every valuation makes $\Phi_1, \ldots, \Phi_n$ true'—is a statement of the metalanguage. Further explanation of this convention must await a full treatment of the semantics of quantifiers, which is given in Section 7.2.)

One final point about this metatheorem: Its hypothetical argument follows a pattern that is very common in metalogical reasoning:

Unpacking — Logical manipulation — Repacking

Unpacking means replacing the terms given in the metatheorem (in this case in its antecedent) with their definitions. The following statements in the proof constituted the unpacking:

> Then (by the definition of consistency for a set) there is at least one valuation $\mathcal{V}$ on which $\Phi_1, \ldots, \Phi_n$ are all true. But (by the definition of validity) there is no valuation on which $\Phi_1, \ldots, \Phi_n$ are all true and Ψ is not true.

When you begin to prove metatheorems, it is best to look up relevant definitions as you unpack and to word your unpacking as nearly like the definition as is possible. This prevents errors.

One common error in unpacking is to introduce the symbol $\mathcal{V}$ without specifying whether it stands for some particular valuation (as in the preceding example) or for all valuations. Always be sure to specify what it stands for.

Moreover, remember that there is no such thing as truth per se in formal logic. That is, a formula is never merely true or false; it is true or false on *some* valuation or, perhaps, on *all* valuations. Make sure as you unpack that with each mention of truth or falsity you specify the valuation(s) to which it applies.

Once the given terms are unpacked, a conclusion is drawn from them by logical inference. This is the stage of logical manipulation:

> Thus Ψ is not untrue on $\mathcal{V}$ and so must be true on $\mathcal{V}$.

The logical step here is simply the elimination of a double negation. The final stage, repacking, puts the newly derived conclusion back into defined terms:

> Hence (by the definition of consistency) Ψ is consistent.

Watch for this pattern, and imitate it where appropriate. It is common not only in conditional proof but in many other forms of metalogical reasoning as well.

Some metatheorems are biconditional in form. Since a biconditional is, in effect, simply two conditionals, proofs of biconditional metatheorems often take the form of two conditional proofs. That is the case in the next metatheorem:

METATHEOREM: A sequent is valid if and only if the set containing its premises and the negation of its conclusion is inconsistent.

PROOF: Suppose (for conditional proof) that $\Phi_1, \ldots, \Phi_n \vdash \Psi$ is a valid sequent. Then (by the definition of validity) there is no valuation in which its premises $\Phi_1, \ldots, \Phi_n$ are all true and its conclusion Ψ is not true. From this it follows by valuation rule 1 that there is no valuation on which $\Phi_1, \ldots, \Phi_n$ and $\sim\!\Psi$ are all true—that is, (by the definition of consistency) that the set $\{\Phi_1, \ldots, \Phi_n, \sim\Psi\}$ is inconsistent.

Hence we have shown that if a sequent is valid, then the set consisting of its premises and the negation of its conclusion is inconsistent.

Now suppose (again for conditional proof) that the set $\{\Phi_1, \ldots, \Phi_n, \sim\Psi\}$ is inconsistent. This means that there is no valuation on which $\Phi_1, \ldots, \Phi_n$ and $\sim\Psi$ are all true. Hence (by valuation rule 1) there is no valuation on which $\Phi_1, \ldots, \Phi_n$ are true and Ψ is not true, which is to say that the sequent $\Phi_1, \ldots, \Phi_n \vdash \Psi$ is valid.

Thus, if the set containing a sequent's premises and the negation of its conclusion is inconsistent, then that sequent is valid. In summary, we have shown that a sequent is valid *if and only if* the set containing its premises and the negation of its conclusion is inconsistent.   QED

The proof consists of two conditional proofs, whose conclusions are assembled into the biconditional at the end. Again, I am saying more here than the usual sparse metalogical style permits. At most what is actually written when this kind of proof appears in a journal article is the two hypothetical arguments (indicated here by the indentations). The rest would be understood as implicit. With this example it is also possible to combine the two proofs into a series of biconditional inferences—something like this:

PROOF: $\Phi_1, \ldots, \Phi_n \vdash \Psi$ is a valid sequent iff there is no valuation in which its premises $\Phi_1, \ldots, \Phi_n$ are all true and its conclusion Ψ is false. But this is the case iff there is no valuation on which $\Phi_1, \ldots, \Phi_n$ and $\sim\Psi$ are all true, that is, iff $\{\Phi_1, \ldots, \Phi_n, \sim\Psi\}$ is inconsistent.   QED

This style of proof is fairly common. The curly brackets '{' and '}' are the conventional marks used to indicate the members of a set. We will employ this convention from now on. For more on sets, see Section 7.1.

Exercise 5.2

Prove the following metatheorems by conditional proof:

1. If formula Φ is valid, then $\sim\Phi$ is inconsistent.
2. If Φ and Ψ are formulas and Φ is inconsistent, then $(\Phi \& \Psi)$ is inconsistent.
3. If $\Phi_1, \ldots, \Phi_n \vdash \Psi$ is a valid sequent whose premises $\Phi_1, \ldots, \Phi_n$ are all valid, then its conclusion Ψ is also a valid formula.
4. If the set of premises of a sequent is inconsistent, then that sequent is valid.
5. A formula Φ is inconsistent if and only if $\sim\Phi$ is a valid formula.

5.3 REDUCTIO AD ABSURDUM

Conditional proof is a very common proof strategy in metatheorems. It may be used whenever a metatheorem is conditional in form. However, not all metatheorems are conditionals, and so some require other strategies. Another common strategy is **reductio ad absurdum**—also called **indirect proof**. The object language version of this strategy, which is embodied in the negation introduction rule (~I), was covered in Section 4.3. This is a powerful technique, which is used primarily in proving negative conclusions but may be used with conclusions of any form.

The trick of a reductio is to suppose the denial of the conclusion you want to prove and then show that that supposition validly implies a contradiction. Typically the contradiction will be a metalinguistic statement of the form (Φ and not-Φ), but occasionally other sorts of contradictions are used—for example, the arithmetic statement '0 = 1' or a statement to the effect that a thing is not identical to itself. Now any supposition which—perhaps together with other statements that are given as true—validly implies a contradiction must be false. For by the definition of validity it is impossible for all the premises of a valid inference to be true while its conclusion is false. But a contradictory conclusion is certainly false. Hence at least one of the premises that validly implies it must be false. Therefore, given that the other premises used to derive the contradiction are true, we may discharge the supposition (which, recall, was the denial of our intended conclusion) and assert this intended conclusion itself.

As in a conditional proof, the argument from the supposition to the contradiction is hypothetical; it is a fiction based on a supposition which we needn't believe. (In a reductio we certainly don't believe our supposition, since what we are trying to prove is precisely its opposite!) And, as in conditional proof, we will set off this fiction by indenting it. Here is a simple metatheorem whose proof uses a reductio strategy:

METATHEOREM: There is no invalid sequent with an inconsistent set of premises.

PROOF: Suppose for reductio that there is an invalid sequent with an inconsistent premise set $\{\Phi_1, \ldots, \Phi_n\}$. Since the sequent is invalid, there is (by the definition of invalidity) some valuation $\mathscr{V}$ on which $\Phi_1, \ldots, \Phi_n$ are all true and the argument's conclusion is not true. But since $\Phi_1, \ldots, \Phi_n$ are true on $\mathscr{V}$, $\{\Phi_1, \ldots, \Phi_n\}$ is consistent (by the definition of consistency for a set), which contradicts our supposition.

Consequently, there is no invalid argument with an inconsistent set of premises.   QED

The hypothetical argument begins with the supposition of the denial of the intended conclusion. This is shown by the hypothetical argument to lead to the contradiction that $\{\Phi_1, \ldots, \Phi_n\}$ is both consistent and inconsistent. So the supposition is discharged (ending the indentation), and the desired conclusion is asserted as proved.

Exercise 5.3

Prove the following metatheorems by reductio ad absurdum:

1. There is no valid sequent with a consistent set of premises and an inconsistent conclusion.
2. There is no formula Φ such that Φ and $\sim\!\Phi$ are each inconsistent.
3. There is no invalid sequent with a valid conclusion.
4. The formula '(P & ~P)' is inconsistent.
5. The form 'P ⊢ P ∨ Q' is valid.
6. '(P)' is not a formula. (Hint: Suppose for reductio that 'P' is a formula; then it must have been constructed only by successive application of the three formation rules so that one of these rules must be the last to have been applied. You can then contradict this supposition by showing for each of the formation rules that it could not have been the last rule used to construct something of the form '(P)'.)
7. Any sequent of the form $\Phi \vdash \Phi$ is valid.

5.4 MIXED STRATEGIES

The metatheorems we have considered so far are extremely simple. More interesting metatheorems use several different strategies, one nested inside another. For example, in deriving the consequent from the antecedent in the hypothetical argument of a conditional proof, we might need to use a reductio strategy so that we nest a reductio argument inside a conditional proof. Here is an example:

> **METATHEOREM:** If the conclusion of one valid sequent is Φ and the conclusion of a second valid sequent is $\sim\!\Phi$, then the set consisting of all the premises of both sequents is inconsistent.
>
> PROOF: Suppose for conditional proof that the conclusion of one valid sequent is Φ and the conclusion of a second valid sequent is $\sim\!\Phi$.
>
> > Now suppose for reductio that the set consisting of all the premises of both sequents is consistent. That is (by the definition of consistency for sets), there is some valuation $\mathscr{V}$ which makes each member of this set true.

Then all the premises of both sequents are true on $\mathcal{V}$; and, since both sequents are valid, it follows by the definition of validity that neither the conclusion Φ nor the conclusion $\sim\Phi$ is untrue on $\mathcal{V}$. Therefore both $\mathcal{V}(\Phi) = T$ and $\mathcal{V}(\sim\Phi) = T$. But since $\mathcal{V}(\Phi) = T$, by valuation rule 1, $\mathcal{V}(\sim\Phi) \neq T$, and so we have a contradiction.

Thus, contrary to our reductio supposition, the set consisting of all the premises of both sequents is inconsistent.

So, if the conclusion of one valid sequent is Φ and the conclusion of a second valid sequent is $\sim\Phi$, then the set consisting of all the premises of both sequents is inconsistent.   QED

The trick in proving this metatheorem is to pay careful attention to the form of the conclusion, that is, the metatheorem itself. The metatheorem is a conditional whose antecedent is

(A) The conclusion of one valid sequent is Φ and the conclusion of a second valid sequent is $\sim\Phi$.

and whose consequent is

(C) The set consisting of all the premises of both sequents is inconsistent.

So to prove this conditional, we suppose (A) for conditional proof (thus beginning the proof with an indentation to indicate that we are engaged in a logical fiction) and from (A) derive (C). Then we discharge (A) and assert the conditional conclusion (the last statement of the proof).

But how can we derive (C) from (A)? The clue to follow here is that (C) is a negative statement; it says that a certain set is inconsistent, that is, not consistent. Negative conclusions are usually best proved by reductio. So within the hypothetical argument of the conditional proof, we use a reductio strategy. We thus suppose the denial of (C) for reductio. This is our second supposition, so we indent a second time; we are now engaged in a "fiction within a fiction"—something like the play performed inside Shakespeare's comedy *A Midsummer Night's Dream*. We then proceed from (A) by simple definition, as in the previous examples, and a contradiction follows quickly. This contradiction brings the "inner" fiction to an end. We discharge the reductio supposition and conclude that its negation is true. But this negative conclusion is precisely the conclusion (C) that we were aiming for.

Exercise 5.4

Prove the following metatheorems by using reductio arguments inside conditional proofs:

1. If the conclusion of a valid sequent is inconsistent, then the set of premises is inconsistent as well.

2. If the conclusion Ψ of a sequent $\Phi_1, \ldots, \Phi_n \vdash \Psi$ is valid, then the sequent itself is valid.
3. If new premises $\Phi_{n+1}, \ldots, \Phi_m$ are added to a valid sequent $\Phi_1, \ldots, \Phi_n \vdash \Psi$, then the resulting sequent $\Phi_1, \ldots, \Phi_n, \Phi_{n+1}, \ldots, \Phi_m \vdash \Psi$ is valid.
4. If $\Phi_1, \ldots, \Phi_m \vdash \Psi$ and $\Psi, \Psi_1, \ldots, \Psi_n \vdash \Theta$ are valid sequents, then $\Phi_1, \ldots, \Psi_m, \Psi_1, \ldots, \Psi_n \vdash \Theta$ is a valid sequent.

5.5 MATHEMATICAL INDUCTION

The final metatheoretic strategy that we will consider is mathematical induction. The name is really a misnomer; mathematical induction is a form of deductive reasoning, not inductive reasoning. In fact, it's just an iterated form of modus ponens. Mathematical induction is used when we want to prove that each member of a series of items has a certain property. A series is a linear list, in which there is a first item, a second item, and so on. Mathematical induction works on both finite series (which have a last item) and infinite series (which do not). An infinite series is a series ordered like the natural numbers (the whole numbers beginning with 1); that is, it has a first item and each item of the series has a successor (e.g., after the second item there is a third), but the series itself never ends. Many items that concern us in logic can be arranged into series. For example, rule 2 of the formation rules generates an infinite series of negated formulas for each sentence letter so that from rule 2 alone we can see that there are infinitely many formulas. Using the sentence letter 'P', for example, we have the series

$$P, \quad \sim P, \quad \sim\sim P, \quad \sim\sim\sim P, \ldots$$

(the dots indicate that the series continues infinitely). Let us call this series S.

Now suppose that we want to prove that each item of S has the property of being a formula. Of course, that's obvious from the formation rules, but we are concerned with how to give a proper proof of it. The proof requires mathematical induction. To prove by mathematical induction that each item of a series has a given property F, we prove two things:

(1) That the first item of the series has F and
(2) That for any n, if the nth item of the series has F, then so does the $(n + 1)$st.

The proof of (1) is called the **basis case** of the induction; the proof of (2) is called the **inductive step**. If we can prove these two things, then our work is done, for together they logically imply the conclusion that every object in the series has the property, even if the series is infinite. To see this, note that (2) is a universal statement which implies each of the following instances:

If item 1 has F, then so does item 2.

If item 2 has F, then so does item 3.

If item 3 has F, then so does item 4.

. . . and so on.

But (1) tells us that item 1 has F. So by modus ponens, together with the first statement, item 2 has F. But then by modus ponens, together with the second statement, item 3 has F, and so on. Thus by infinitely many steps of modus ponens it follows that each item in the series has F. Of course we can't actually carry out infinitely many steps of modus ponens. That's why we have the special principle of mathematical induction. (We wouldn't need it if all we ever had to worry about were finite series.) This principle stipulates that if we have proved (1) and (2), we can conclude straightaway that each item of the series has F; we needn't bother with modus ponens. The validity of the principle is obvious.

In proofs by mathematical induction, the basis case is usually trivial. The inductive step justifies the universally quantified conditional (2). The strategy is always conditional proof. We suppose for conditional proof that some arbitrary nth item of the series has F (this supposition is called the **inductive hypothesis**) and prove from this supposition that the $(n + 1)$st item has F as well. That proves the conditional, and since the item considered was arbitrary, we can universally generalize the conditional.

Now in the problem we are considering, F is the property of being a formula. We want to prove that every item of series S has this property. The basis case must establish that 'P' is a formula (which follows immediately from formation rule 1), and the inductive step must show that if one item in the series is a formula, the result of prefixing it with a negation sign is also a formula (which follows immediately from formation rule 2). Hence the proof is easy. Here it is in proper metatheoretic form:

METATHEOREM: Each item of series S is a formula.

PROOF:

Basis Case: The first item of S is 'P', which (by formation rule 1) is a formula.

Inductive Step: Suppose that the nth item of S is a formula. (This is the inductive hypothesis; it initiates the conditional proof.) Now the $(n + 1)$st item is the result of prefixing the nth with a negation sign. Therefore (by formation rule 2 and the inductive hypothesis) the $(n + 1)$st item of S is a formula.

Thus (by conditional proof) it follows that if the nth item of S is a formula, then so is the $(n + 1)$st. Hence (by mathematical induction) each item of S is a formula.   QED

Again, this is more explicit than the usual metatheoretic style. In professional writing, the labels 'Basis Case' and 'Inductive Step' and the parenthetical remarks would be omitted, as would the last two sentences, which explicitly use conditional proof and mathematical induction to draw the conclusions.

Mathematical induction enables us to prove that each item in a sequence has a given property F. In the previous example, F was the property of being a formula.

In the next example, F is the property of being logically equivalent to 'P', and the sequence is:

P,   (P & P),   ((P & P) & P),   (((P & P) & P) & P), . . .

We shall call this series *T*. What we want to show, in other words, is that each member of *T* has the property of being logically equivalent to 'P'. In this sequence, for each number n ($n > 0$), the $(n + 1)$st item is a conjunction whose first conjunct is the nth item and whose second conjunct is 'P'.

We begin by recalling that two formulas are logically equivalent iff they have the same truth value on every valuation of both. Since no formula of *T* contains any sentence letter other than 'P', there are only two valuations to consider: the valuation on which 'P' is true and the valuation on which 'P' is false. The proof proceeds as follows:

METATHEOREM: Each item of series *T* is logically equivalent to 'P'.

PROOF:

Basis Case: The first item of *T* is 'P', which (trivially) has the same truth value as 'P' on any valuation. Hence the first item of *T* is logically equivalent to 'P'.

Inductive Step: Suppose that the nth item Φ of *T* is logically equivalent to 'P'. That is, Φ is true on any valuation on which 'P' is true and false on any valuation on which 'P' is false. Now the $(n + 1)$st item is of the form $(\Phi \And P)$. On any valuation on which 'P' is true, therefore, both conjuncts of $(\Phi \And P)$ are true; similarly, on any valuation on which 'P' is false, both conjuncts of $(\Phi \And P)$ are false. Thus, by the valuation rule for conjunction, $(\Phi \And P)$ is true on any valuation on which 'P' is true and false on any valuation on which $(\Phi \And P)$ is false. Thus 'P' has the same truth value as $(\Phi \And P)$ on every valuation of both, and so $(\Phi \And P)$, which is the $(n + 1)$st item in the series, is logically equivalent to 'P'.

Thus (by conditional proof) it follows that if the nth item of *T* is logically equivalent to 'P', then so is the $(n + 1)$st. Hence (by mathematical induction) each item of *T* is logically equivalent to 'P'.   QED

Let's consider one more metatheorem that uses mathematical induction. In this case, we will be concerned with the following sequence of formulas, which we shall call *T*:

P_1, $(P_1 \vee P_2)$, $((P_1 \vee P_2) \vee P_3)$, $(((P_1 \vee P_2) \vee P_3) \vee P_4)$, . . .

For each number n greater than 0, the $(n + 1)$st item of this sequence is obtained from the nth by disjoining it with the letter 'P' subscripted with the numeral for $n + 1$. Our problem is to prove that for each such n, the tree constructed using the

nth item as its initial list contains exactly n paths. That is, F is the rather complex property of *being a disjunction whose tree contains the number of paths designated by the numeral that subscripts its second disjunct*. Despite the complexity of this property, mathematical induction operates in precisely the same way as in the previous metatheorem. Here is the proof:

METATHEOREM: For all n, the tree constructed by using the nth item of T as its initial list has exactly n paths.

PROOF:

Basis Case: The first item of T is 'P_1'. Since 'P_1' is atomic, the tree constructed by using it as the initial list is finished as soon as 'P_1' is written, and it contains one path.

Inductive Step: Suppose (inductive hypothesis) that the tree constructed by using the nth item of T as its initial list has exactly n paths. Now the $(n + 1)$st item is obtained from the nth by disjoining it with 'P' subscripted by the numeral for $n + 1$. Thus, when the $(n + 1)$st item is used as the initial list of a tree, the only possible first move is to check it and branch to the nth item on the left and to 'P' subscripted by the numeral for $n + 1$ on the right. The right path is then finished, since the initial formula is checked and 'P' with its subscript is atomic. And the left path below the initial formula will consist simply of the tree for the nth item of T, which by hypothesis has exactly n paths. Hence the whole tree must contain exactly $n + 1$ paths.

Thus we have shown (by conditional proof) that if the tree constructed by using the nth item of T as its initial list has exactly n paths, then the tree constructed by using the $(n + 1)$st item of T as its initial list has exactly $n + 1$ paths. So (by mathematical induction) for all n, the tree constructed by using the nth item of T as its initial list has exactly n paths.   QED

To summarize: We have considered three important strategies for metalinguistic proofs: conditional proof, reductio ad absurdum, and mathematical induction. These strategies may be nested within one another in various combinations, but each always produces an argument of the same form. Which form to use is determined by the structure of the conclusion: For a conditional conclusion, use conditional proof; for a negative conclusion and some conclusions of other forms, use reductio; for a conclusion about a series of things, use mathematical induction. The essentials of these forms are expressed in the following templates. These templates may be used quite literally and mechanically in setting up proofs, but filling in the arguments (represented in each case by a box containing a sketchy outline of the argument) may require creativity.

Template for Conditional Proof

> **METATHEOREM:** If [ANTECEDENT], then [CONSEQUENT]
>
> PROOF: Suppose for conditional proof that [ANTECEDENT]
>> Unpacking
>> Logical Manipulation
>> Repacking
>
>> Therefore [CONSEQUENT]
>
> Hence (by conditional proof) if [ANTECEDENT], then [CONSEQUENT].

Template for Reductio

> **METATHEOREM:** [CONCLUSION]
>
> PROOF: Suppose for reductio that [DENIAL OF CONCLUSION]
>> Unpacking
>> Logical Manipulation
>
>> Therefore [CONTRADICTION]
>
> Hence (by reductio) [CONCLUSION].

Template for Mathematical Induction

> **METATHEOREM:** All members of [SERIES] have property F
>
> PROOF:
>
> **Basis Case:**
>> (Style of argument here varies but is often trivial.)
>
> Therefore the first member of [SERIES] has property F.
>
> **Inductive Step:**
>> Suppose that the nth member of [SERIES] has property F
>>> Unpacking
>>> Logical Manipulation
>>> Repacking
>
>> Therefore the $(n + 1)$st member of [SERIES] has property F.
>
> Hence (by conditional proof) we have shown that for any n, if the nth member of [SERIES] has property F, so does the $(n + 1)$st. Consequently (using mathematical induction to combine this conclusion with the conclusion of the basis case) all members of [SERIES] have property F.

Exercise 5.5

Prove the following metatheorems:

1. Every member of the following sequence is a formula:

$$(P \rightarrow P), \quad (P \rightarrow (P \rightarrow P)), \quad (P \rightarrow (P \rightarrow (P \rightarrow P))), \ldots$$

2. Every member of the sequence of problem 1 is valid.
3. Every member of the following sequence is contingent:

$$P, \quad {\sim}P, \quad {\sim}{\sim}P, \quad {\sim}{\sim}{\sim}P, \ldots$$

4. Each member of the following sequence of formulas

$$P_1, \quad (P_2 \rightarrow P_1), \quad (P_3 \rightarrow (P_2 \rightarrow P_1)), \quad (P_4 \rightarrow (P_3 \rightarrow (P_2 \rightarrow P_1))), \ldots$$

   is true in any valuation on which 'P$_1$' is true. (Hint: For each n, the $(n + 1)$st member of the series is a conditional whose antecedent is 'P' subscripted by the numeral for $n + 1$, and whose consequent is the nth member.)
5. If Ψ is a valid formula, then every member of the following sequence is a valid formula:

$$\Psi, \quad (\Psi \vee P_1), \quad ((\Psi \vee P_1) \vee P_2), \quad (((\Psi \vee P_1) \vee P_2) \vee P_3), \ldots$$

(Hint: Use mathematical induction inside a conditional proof.)

5.6 ALGORITHMS

An **algorithm**[3] is a fully determinate computational procedure. A **fully determinate** procedure is one that leaves nothing to chance or human discretion; any two people (or computers) carrying out the procedure (on the same symbols) would carry out the same steps in the same order. Algorithms are **computational** in the sense that they are operations on symbols; that is, an algorithm takes a sequence of symbols and converts it into a sequence of symbols. One simple algorithm is the familiar procedure for adding a column of numbers. The process begins, for instance, with a sequence of symbols that looks like this:

$$
\begin{array}{r}
27 \\
82 \\
+\ \underline{13}
\end{array}
$$

---

[3] The word "algorithm" (occasionally spelled "algorism") is a corruption of the name of the ninth-century Arabic mathematician Al-Khawarazmi. Al-Khawarazmi is most noted for bringing what we now call "Arabic" numerals from India to the Arab world, whence they were later transmitted to the West. He also wrote a famous textbook illustrating many algorithms (or "Al-Khawarazmisms"!).

This initial symbol sequence is called the **input** to the algorithm. Then you perform a series of precise, well-defined operations that yield a new sequence of symbols, namely,

122

This is the **output,** or answer. The steps comprising the algorithm consist of adding the individual digits (starting in the rightmost column), carrying the appropriate numbers, and so on. This procedure, of course, works with any finite column of numbers as input so that once you learn the algorithm, you can, at least in principle, add any column of numbers.

The symbols or characters that an algorithm operates on need not be numerals. The automatic "search and replace" operations available on most word processors, for example, are simple algorithms that operate on the character set of a computer (which includes the English alphabet), rather than just on numerals. Say you want to replace all occurrences of the word 'Milton' in a document with the word 'Shakespeare'. You put the cursor at the beginning of the document and invoke the algorithm. The computer then runs through the entire document from beginning to end, making the replacements you indicated. In this case, the input to the algorithm consists of three symbol sequences: 'Milton', 'Shakespeare', and the initial document. The output is the revised document, in which the word 'Shakespeare' has replaced the word 'Milton'. Here again the algorithm is a *general* procedure; it operates not only on these three symbol sequences, but (in principle at least— ignoring the memory limitations of computers) on any three sequences of letters.[4] This is why mathematicians sometimes refer to algorithms as **general procedures.**

The concept of an algorithm carries with it some important presuppositions, which are not always explicitly recognized. First, *each algorithm is defined only over a prescribed character set, that is, a specified alphabet of symbols.* Though both sequences of numerals and strings of ordinary text are symbol sequences, you can do addition only on sequences of numerals, not on strings of text. That is, the generality of an algorithm is not absolute; it is limited by the kinds of symbols the algorithm is designed to deal with. More specifically, each algorithm presupposes a fixed character set upon which it works.

A **character set** is simply a finite set of discrete symbols. It may be as simple as the binary alphabet of a computer (which has only two fundamental symbols, often represented as 0 and 1)[5] or as complex as the typographical system of English

---

[4] When the input to an algorithm consists of more than one sequence of symbols, as it does here, these may be regarded as a single sequence in which the three elements are listed in some conventional order (for example: term to be replaced, term to replace it, document). We might in practice need additional symbols (such as spaces, commas, or other special symbols) between successive members of the sequence so that we can tell where one ends and the next begins. But by this means, any finite set of sequences can be treated as a single sequence. Therefore we lose no generality by thinking of an algorithm as operating always on a *single* sequence of symbols.

[5] Simpler still are character sets containing only one character; the abaci discussed in Section 10.1 use in effect only a single character type: the counters that are manipulated in their registers.

(which includes letters, both upper and lower case, numerals, punctuation marks, etc.). Logicians, of course, are most interested in the character sets of logical languages. The character set for propositional logic, for example, consists of the twenty-six capital letters of the English alphabet, the ten numerals 0–9 (for subscripts), right and left parentheses, and the five characters for the logical operators. Among the most prominent algorithms applied to sequences of these symbols (formulas or lists of formulas) are truth tables and trees.[6]

The character set presupposed by any particular algorithm must be finite; that is, it must not contain an infinite number of fundamental symbols. We shall sometimes talk about infinite *sequences* of characters, but the character set itself must be finite. (Thus these infinite sequences always contain repeated characters.) This is a genuine limitation, though it might not seem so at first, for there are symbol systems that can be interpreted as having infinitely many characters. Consider, for example, the dial of a nondigital watch. If the hands move continuously—instead of in discrete jumps or ticks—then each configuration of the hands might be thought of as a character representing a time. But between any two distinct positions of a given hand, there is always an intermediate position so that there are infinitely many of these "characters." Such characters (or sequences of them) would not, therefore, be appropriate input for an algorithm. We'd have to digitize them—that is, represent them in a symbol system with a finite character set, before we could apply anything that could legitimately be called an algorithm.

The character set must not only be finite; *its symbols must be distinct* as well. This does not preclude some variation. For example, all the following constitute tokens of the letter 'U' in the character set of English:

U *U* 𝒰 u ᵤ U u U u

But what about this?

Is it a 'U', or an 'O' that didn't quite get closed at the top? In reality, there are borderline cases—symbol tokens that could be classified either of two or more ways. But the conception of an algorithm presupposes that such things don't happen, that each individual symbol is distinct and uniquely classifiable.

*In addition, inputs to and outputs from algorithms must be **sequences** of symbols.* That is, they must be arrayed in a distinct linear order, like the text you are now reading. By convention the sequential order of this text is from left to

---

[6] Actually, truth tables and trees are not quite algorithms as we use them, since we allow some choice as to which rule to apply next in a tree or which subformula to analyze next in a truth table. Only if we adopted rules that rigidly determined the order of these operations would trees and truth tables be algorithms, strictly speaking. We could adopt such rules, just to make truth tables and trees conform to the definition of an algorithm, but that would be more trouble than it would be worth.

right and from the top to the bottom of the page, but other conventions could be used, as they are in some languages. Below are some symbols from the English character set that are not arranged in any clear sequential order:

$$B$$
$$R$$
$$X \qquad N$$
$$T$$
$$Q \qquad V$$
$$Z^C$$

This sort of thing could not be input or output for an algorithm, unless we established some convention that would impose a sequential order on it.

Moreover, *all input sequences are presumed to be finite.* Infinite sequences, like the sequence of numerals used for counting,

1, 2, 3, 4, 5, 6, 7, 8, 9, 10, 11, 12, . . .

cannot be input to an algorithm (though each individual member of the sequence, being itself a *finite* string of symbols, could be).

Finally, *an algorithm need not be defined over all the finite sequences of symbols from its prescribed character set.* Many algorithms work with only certain very specific sorts of sequences. In the case of truth tables and trees, for example, the sequences must be formulas or lists of formulas, that is, sequences generated by the formation rules. There are infinitely many ill-formed or nonsensical sequences of characters of propositional logic, such as

)) → P (

for which the truth-table algorithm is not defined. In general, we designate those symbol sequences for which an algorithm *is* defined as its **permissible** symbol sequences.

Noting the limitations of algorithms gives us a clearer conception of their nature. An algorithm can apply only to finite, linear sequences of absolutely distinct symbols—and only to those that count as permissible sequences of the prescribed character set.[7]

A final and crucial feature of algorithms is that they may be either terminating or nonterminating. A **terminating** algorithm is one that, given any permissible input, will always yield its output after a finite number of steps. A **nonterminating** algorithm is one that for at least one permissible input does not yield its entire output after any finite number of steps. The procedure for adding columns of numbers, for example, is a terminating algorithm. But the algorithm for counting

---

[7] Philosophers—especially those who want to identify thought with algorithmic process—have not always kept these presuppositions in mind. The human mind operates with sensory input and behavioral output that, at least on the face of it, seems not to satisfy all of these presuppositions.

(using a given numeral, usually '1', as the starting point or input) is nonterminating. It's a fully definite computational procedure, but it never achieves completion.

Logicians are interested in algorithms because they want to know how much of logic can be reduced to mechanical computational procedures. Early in this century, some philosophers and mathematicians hoped that all the theses of logic and mathematics could eventually be brought within the reach of terminating algorithms—that the truth or falsity of any statement of logic or mathematics could be decided by finite calculations. They thought this could be accomplished by completely *formalizing* logic and mathematics—that is, expressing them in symbol systems—and then devising the appropriate algorithms to operate on these symbol systems. Accordingly, this line of research was called **formalism.** Formalists hoped to encode various fields of logic and mathematics in **axioms** (fundamental assumptions) expressed in a logical language, and then to apply finite computational procedures (usually envisioned at the time as rules of inference) to these axioms to determine the truth or falsity of any question expressible in the system.

But formalism failed. We now know that it is impossible to answer all logical questions by finite computations, and we shall prove this when we consider the undecidability of predicate logic. Nevertheless, for some restricted systems of logic, the formalist dream can be realized. Propositional logic is one such system. For all questions of validity (for both formulas and sequents), invalidity, consistency, and so on, we have terminating algorithms (truth tables and trees) which give the answers.

Here we are concerned with trees. It is obvious that the tree test is—or can easily be transformed into—an algorithm (see footnote 6). What is not so obvious is that it terminates for all inputs consisting of any finite list of sentences whatsoever. That requires proof. Our task in the next section is to construct a metatheorem that proves this.

5.7 DECIDABILITY

What we want to prove ultimately is that propositional logic is decidable. What it means to say that a logic is **decidable** is that there exists a terminating algorithm which determines for each sequent of the logic whether or not it is valid. Such an algorithm is called a **decision procedure** or a **solution to the decision problem** for the logic. What we shall show is that the tree test is a decision procedure for propositional logic.[8] To do so, we need to establish that

(1) the tree test for propositional logic is in fact a *terminating* algorithm,

(2) if the tree test classifies the sequent as valid (i.e., all paths of its finished tree close), then that sequent *is* valid, and

---

[8] We could have shown this for the truth-table test as well. In fact, for the truth-table test it's obvious. We focus on trees, however, because the tree test can be straightforwardly generalized to predicate logic; the truth-table test can't be.

(3) if a sequent *is* valid, the tree test classifies that sequent as valid (i.e., all paths of its finished tree close).

We will prove proposition (1) in this section, proposition (2) in Section 5.8, and proposition (3) in Section 5.9. Proposition (2) expresses the **soundness** of the tree test; the test is sound in the sense that if it classifies a sequent as valid, the sequent is in fact valid. Proposition (3) expresses the test's **completeness**; the test is complete in that it does not fail to classify any valid sequents as valid. Uniting the conditionals (2) and (3) into a single biconditional, we get a statement that expresses the full accuracy of the tree test:

(4) The tree test classifies a sequent as valid (i.e., all paths close) if and only if that sequent *is* valid.

Our first task is to prove that the tree test always terminates. The reason it terminates is that whenever we apply a rule to a formula, each of the new formulas produced by the rule is shorter (i.e., contains fewer characters) than the original formula. Now formulas are not infinitely divisible; like material substances they have smallest units, or atoms—namely, atomic formulas. Hence this shortening process cannot go on forever. Eventually it has to stop.

This is the right idea, but it misses something: Although formulas grow shorter and shorter within each path, the *number of paths* increases each time we apply a branching rule. In applying branching rules, might we not spawn so many new paths that we create more work than we complete and hence never finish? In other words, even though no single path may ever grow infinitely long, might we not generate so many new paths that the tree continues to grow—perhaps by becoming "bushier and bushier"—without end?

In fact this cannot happen. But that is not so obvious; it requires proof.

Our reasoning will fall into several parts, which we will express as **lemmas** (short proofs preliminary to a major result). In lemma 1 we will show that because of the shortening of formulas, each individual path in a tree must come to an end. Then, to alleviate the concern that the tree might continue to grow forever anyway (e.g., by multiplication of paths), we will prove in lemma 3 that in order to grow endlessly it would have to have an unending path, which lemma 1 will have shown to be impossible. Before proving lemma 3, we shall prove another lemma, lemma 2, which provides a fact needed in proving lemma 3. Finally, we'll combine lemmas 1 and 3 into a metatheorem that proves the tree test always terminates. Before embarking on our proofs, we need some definitions.

> DEFINITION 1 The **character count** of an open path is the total number of characters (logical operators, sentence letters, and parentheses—numerical subscripts don't count) contained in unchecked formulas on that path. The character count of a closed path is zero.

NOTE: *For purposes of calculating the character count, the formation rules must be followed strictly. This means that outer brackets may not be dropped; they are included in the count.*

DEFINITION 2 A path P_2 is a **one-step extension** of a path P_1 iff P_2 is obtained from P_1 by applying a single tree rule to some unchecked formula or (in the case of the negation rule) pair of unchecked formulas of P_1.

Each application of a branching rule produces two one-step extensions of a path, but application of a nonbranching rule produces only one one-step extension. One-step extensions created by some rules (for example, the disjunction or double negation rules) contain only one more formula than the path they extend. But one-step extensions created by others (for example, the conjunction or biconditional rules) contain two more formulas than the path they extend.

We can now launch our proofs. We first prove lemma 1, which shows in effect that if an initial list has a finite character count (which is always the case), then any path it generates must be finitely long as well.

Lemma 1: If the character count of the tree's initial list is n, then each path of the tree must be finished after at most n applications of the tree rules to formulas on that path.

PROOF: Suppose the character count of the tree's initial list is n. Now when any of the rules is applied to a formula on a path P, each of the resulting one-step extensions of P has a character count at least one less than the character count of P (check this for each of the rules).[9] Further, the minimum character count for any path is zero.[10] Thus, since the character count of the initial list is n, and each application of a rule decreases the character count of the resulting one-step extensions by at least one, at most n applications of the rules can be made to formulas on a path before that path is finished.

---

[9] The biconditional rule, for example, allows us to check a formula of the form $(\Phi \leftrightarrow \Psi)$ and create one one-step extension to which we add Φ and Ψ and another to which we add $\sim\Phi$ and $\sim\Psi$. The formula $(\Phi \leftrightarrow \Psi)$ has three characters in addition to those in Φ and Ψ, namely, '(', '$\leftrightarrow$', and ')'. (Outer brackets are included in the character count!) But the first one-step extension omits all three of these characters, keeping only Φ and Ψ, whereas the second adds only two characters in addition to those in Φ and Ψ, namely, two occurrences of '$\sim$'. Thus, since a checked formula no longer counts, application of the biconditional rule reduces the character count along the first one-step extension by three and along the second one-step extension by one. Similar reductions of the character count occur with all the other rules.

[10] The character count of a path drops to zero if the path closes; if it doesn't close, the path must nevertheless be finished by the time its character count reaches zero, since by that time all formulas are checked and so no further rules can be applied. Actually, the character count of an open path cannot drop as far as zero, since some unchecked atomic formulas or negations of atomic formulas remain on the path.

> Hence, if the character count of the tree's initial list is n, then each path of the tree must be finished after at most n applications of the tree rules to formulas on that path.   QED

Having shown that all paths must be finite, we must still prove that the tree can't grow forever by endless proliferation of these finite paths. To make these ideas precise, we add two more definitions.

> **DEFINITION 3** A path P is **infinitely prolongable** iff there exists an infinite series $P_0, P_1, \ldots$ of paths such that $P_0 = P$ and, for each n, P_{n+1} is a one-step extension of P_n.

That is, a path is infinitely prolongable iff the tree rules can be applied to make it grow endlessly longer. This is just what lemma 1 rules out; that is, so long as the initial list has a finite character count, lemma 1 tells us that it cannot produce an infinitely prolongable path. But we are still concerned about a tree growing endlessly in some other way—for example, by becoming infinitely "bushy." The next definition gives precision to this worry. It captures the idea of infinite growth in general.

> **DEFINITION 4** A path P is **nonterminating** iff there exists an infinite series $T_0, T_1, \ldots$ such that $T_0 = P$ and, for each n, T_{n+1} is the result of applying a single rule to an unchecked formula or (in the case of the negation rule) pair of unchecked formulas somewhere in T_n.

The infinite series $T_0, T_1, \ldots$ is a series of trees (or partial trees) generated by applying rules starting with P, but not confining application of the rules to only one path. Thus a path is nonterminating iff starting with that path we can apply tree rules to formulas (perhaps among various branches into which that path splits) forever. Nontermination is an apparently broader concept than infinite prolongability; a path might, it seems, be nonterminating by being able to grow endlessly more "bushy," as well as by growing endlessly longer. Actually, however, this apparent difference is illusory, as we'll prove in lemma 3. But to prove lemma 3, we first need to prove lemma 2:

> **Lemma 2:** If P is a nonterminating path, then P has a nonterminating one-step extension.
>
> **PROOF:** Suppose (for conditional proof) that P is a nonterminating path. That is, there is an infinite series $T_0, T_1, \ldots$ such that $T_0 = P$ and, for each n, T_{n+1} is the result of applying a single

rule somewhere in T_n. Thus in particular T_1 is the result of applying a single rule to a formula or pair of formulas of P. Since no single application of a rule can split a path into more than two paths, T_1 contains at most two paths—maybe only one.

> Now suppose for reductio that P does not have a nonterminating one-step extension. This means that no path of T_1 is nonterminating. Hence there can't be an infinite succession of rule-applications starting with any path of T_1. But since T_1 has at most two paths, it follows that there can't be an infinite succession of rule-applications to T_1 itself, since the total number of rule-applications for T_1 is just the total number for its paths, and this number, being the sum of at most two finite quantities, is finite. Hence there is no infinite series $T_0, T_1, \ldots$ such that $T_0 = P$ and, for each n, T_{n+1} is the result of applying a single rule somewhere in T_n, in contradiction to what we concluded earlier.

Hence, contrary to our supposition, P does have a nonterminating one-step extension.

Thus we have shown that if P is a nonterminating path, then P has a nonterminating one-step extension.

The next lemma, which shows that a path can't grow infinitely in any sense without being infinitely prolonged, is historically known as König's lemma:

Lemma 3 (König's Lemma): If L is a nonterminating path, then L is infinitely prolongable.

PROOF: Suppose (for conditional proof) that L is a nonterminating path. This means that there exists an infinite series $T_0, T_1, \ldots$ of trees such that $T_0 = L$ and, for each n, T_{n+1} is the result of applying a single rule somewhere in T_n. We now define an infinite series $P_0, P_1, \ldots$ of paths such that $P_0 = L$ and, for each n, P_{n+1} is a one-step extension of P_n. First let $P_0 = L$. Now by lemma 2, P_0 has at least one nonterminating one-step extension. Call it P_1. (If there is more than one, let P_1 be the leftmost.) Now again by lemma 2, since P_1 is nonterminating, it must have a nonterminating one-step extension P_2, and so on ad infinitum. Clearly, then, $P_0, P_1, \ldots$ is an infinite series of paths such that $P_0 = L$ and, for each n, P_{n+1} is a one-step extension of P_n. But this means that L is infinitely prolongable.

Thus we have shown that if L is a nonterminating path, then L is infinitely prolongable.

We are ready at last to combine lemmas 1 and 3 into the major result of this section:

METATHEOREM (Decidability): Any tree for any finite list of formulas of propositional logic is finished after some finite number of applications of the tree rules.

PROOF: Suppose for reductio that this is not the case—that there is a finite list L of formulas of propositional logic which yields a tree that is not finished after any finite number of applications of the rules. This means that, starting with L, rules can be applied infinitely so that there is an infinite series $T_0, T_1, \ldots$ such that $T_0 = L$ and, for each n, T_{n+1} is the result of applying a single rule somewhere in T_n. L, that is to say, is nonterminating. Hence by lemma 3, L is infinitely prolongable. But since L is a finite list of formulas, it must have a finite character count, n. Hence by lemma 1 each path of L's tree must be finished after at most n applications of tree rules to formulas on that path, where n is finite. So L is not infinitely prolongable, and we have a contradiction.

Therefore the tree for any finite list of formulas of propositional logic is finished after some finite number of applications of the tree rules.   QED

Since sequents are always finite lists, and they remain finite when we negate their conclusions, it follows that the tree test peformed on a sequent will always finish in a finite number of steps. The tree test is, in other words, a terminating algorithm.

5.8 SOUNDNESS OF THE TREE TEST

A test for validity is said to be **sound** if whenever that test classifies a sequent as valid, it is in fact valid. In this section, we will show that the tree test is sound.[11] We shall do this proof in two stages. First we will prove as a metatheorem that any tree constructed from a consistent initial list has an open path. Then we will derive

---

[11] This is a different use of the term than when we speak of a *sound* argument—that is, a valid argument with true premises. The soundness of the tree rules (or of the rules of inference; see Section 5.10) implies nothing at all about the truth or falsity of the premises. It is unfortunate that the same word 'sound' is used in both of these ways, but the usage is so firmly established in the logical literature that there is no point in bucking it.

the soundness result explicitly as a **corollary**—that is, a result that follows easily from something previously established.

To prove the conditional that if an initial list is consistent, then it always yields an open path, we suppose for conditional proof that we have a consistent initial list. We then unpack the notion of consistency as truth on some valuation, which we shall call $\mathcal{V}$. The heart of the argument is to show that each time we apply a tree rule, the resulting tree contains a path P whose formulas are all true on $\mathcal{V}$. But since all of P's formulas are true on $\mathcal{V}$, P cannot be closed because it cannot contain both a formula and its negation (since these could not both be true on $\mathcal{V}$). Hence P must be an open path.

That's the proof in a nutshell. Here it is in greater detail:

METATHEOREM: If an initial list of formulas is consistent, then there is an open path through any (finished or unfinished) tree obtainable from that list by the tree rules.

PROOF: Suppose (for conditional proof) that some initial list of formulas, call it L, is consistent.

This means that there is some valuation $\mathcal{V}$ on which all the members of L are true. Now let T be any tree obtainable from L by the tree rules. To create T, a series $T_1, \ldots, T_z$ of trees was successively constructed, whose first member T_1 was L, whose final member T_z is T, and whose $(n + 1)$st member $T_{n + 1}$, for each n $(1 < n \leq z)$, was obtained from the nth, T_n, by the application of a single tree rule. We shall prove that each member of this series contains an open path, whence it follows that T itself (i.e., T_z) contains an open path. To prove this, it suffices to show that every tree in the sequence contains a path whose formulas are all true on $\mathcal{V}$. For if all formulas of a path are true on $\mathcal{V}$, then (by valuation rule 1) that path cannot contain both a formula and its negation, and hence must be open. To prove that each tree in the series contains a path all formulas of which are true on $\mathcal{V}$, we use mathematical induction:

Basis Case: The first member of the series is T_1, which is L itself, and by hypothesis each member of L is true on $\mathcal{V}$.[12]

Inductive Step: Suppose (inductive hypothesis) that the nth item T_n of the series (where $n < z$) contains a path P all of whose formulas are true on $\mathcal{V}$. Now the $(n + 1)$st item, $T_{n + 1}$, is formed by a single application of a rule

---

[12] When I say that this is true "by hypothesis," I refer to the fact that we are operating under the supposition (for conditional proof) that L is consistent, which means there must be a valuation on which all of its members are true. We have labeled that valuation "$\mathcal{V}$". Thus each member of L is true on $\mathcal{V}$.

to T_n. There are two possibilities concerning the point of application of this rule: Either the formula or formulas to which the rule is applied are on P or they are not. If the rule is applied to formulas on P, then by the inductive hypothesis these formulas are true on $\mathcal{V}$. Hence the rule used can't have been the negation rule, which closes paths, since a formula and its negation cannot both be true on $\mathcal{V}$. So it must have been one of the other nine rules. Now, when applied to a formula on a path whose formulas are all true on some valuation, each of these rules produces at least one one-step extension of that path whose formulas are all true on that valuation. (It is easy to check this for each rule, and you should do so.[13]) So at least one of the one-step extensions of P is a path of T_{n+1} whose formulas are all true on $\mathcal{V}$. If, on the other hand, the formula or formulas to which the rule is applied are not on P, then nothing will be added to P in moving from T_n to T_{n+1}. Hence in this case P itself is a path of T_{n+1} whose formulas are all true on $\mathcal{V}$. So either way T_{n+1} contains a path whose formulas are all true on $\mathcal{V}$.

Thus (by conditional proof) we have shown that for any n ($n <$ z), if T_n contains a path whose formulas are all true on $\mathcal{V}$, so does T_{n+1}. So (by mathematical induction) each tree in the sequence $T_1, \ldots, T_z$ contains a path whose formulas are all true on $\mathcal{V}$. Hence T (T_z) must itself contain a path whose formulas are all true on $\mathcal{V}$. Hence (as explained above) T contains an open path.

Hence we have shown (by conditional proof) that if L is consistent, then there is an open path through any (finished or unfinished) tree T obtainable from L by the tree rules.   QED.

We now use this metatheorem to prove that the tree test is sound. A test for validity is sound, once again, if whenever that test classifies a sequent as valid, that sequent is in fact valid. What it means for the tree test to **classify a sequent as valid** is that, given the premises and the negation of the conclusion as an initial list, we

---

[13] Take, for example, the disjunction rule ∨. Suppose this is applied to a formula $\Phi \lor \Psi$ which occurs on a path all of whose formulas are true on some valuation $\mathcal{V}$. Then, since $\Phi \lor \Psi$ itself is true on $\mathcal{V}$, by the valuation rule for disjunction either Φ or Ψ must be true on $\mathcal{V}$. Therefore, since the rule ∨ produces two one-step extensions of the path, one of which appends Φ to it and the other of which appends Ψ, all the formulas of at least one of these one-step extensions of the path must be true on $\mathcal{V}$.

get a tree all of whose paths close. The argument from our metatheorem to sound-ness is relatively simple:

COROLLARY (Soundness): If the tree test classifies a sequent as valid, it is in fact valid.

PROOF: Suppose (for conditional proof) that the tree test classifies a sequent $\Phi_1, \ldots, \Phi_n \vdash \Psi$ as valid. This means that the tree's initial list is $\Phi_1, \ldots, \Phi_n, \sim\Psi$ and that all paths of the tree close. But by the previous metatheorem, if that initial list is consis-tent, then there is an open path through any tree constructed from it. Since all paths close, there is no open path through the finished tree. So (by modus tollens), the initial list is inconsis-tent. But then by the metatheorem proved at the end of Section 5.2, the sequent is valid.

Therefore, if the tree test classifies a sequent as valid, it is in fact valid. QED

A radical skeptic might wonder what this soundness proof really proves. If, for example, someone had doubts about the validity of sequents proved by →I, those doubts would hardly be allayed by a metatheorem established by con-ditional proof—that is, the same pattern of reasoning at a different linguistic level. As a response to such a person, the metaproof would be in some sense circular—assuming the validity of one of the very patterns whose validity it purported to prove.

Metatheoretic proofs are not, however, intended as responses to radical skep-tics. To a person who doggedly doubts the elementary rules of logic, there is no effective *logical* response. Rather, the point of this soundness proof is to show, given a prior understanding of logic, that any sequent judged valid by the tree test is valid on classical semantics—the semantics described in Chapter 3. The sound-ness proof provides not a wholesale assurance that classical reasoning is irrefut-able, but the more modest assurance that the tree rules validate only sequents they ought to validate, given classical semantics. It presupposes, moreover, a willingness to use what are in effect the rules of classical logic in the metalanguage. But what alternative is there? If we did not grant the validity of some sort of reasoning somewhere, we would never accept any conclusion and never come to systematic insight about anything. That is the radical skeptic's game, but it is a game that precludes much intellectual adventure.

Exercise 5.8.1

In the proof of the main metatheorem of this section, it is necessary to verify for each tree rule other than ~ that when applied to a path whose formulas are all true on some valuation $\mathcal{V}$, it yields at least one one-step extension of that path whose formulas are all true on $\mathcal{V}$ or on some expansion of $\mathcal{V}$. I did this for the ∨ rule in footnote 13. Write out the necessary verifications for the rules ~~, &, ~&, ~∨, →, ~→, ↔, and ~↔.

Exercise 5.8.2

Using the metatheorem of this section as an assumption, prove the following corollaries:

1. If the tree test classifies a formula as inconsistent, it is in fact inconsistent.
2. If the tree test classifies a formula as valid, it is in fact valid.
3. If a formula is contingent, the tree test classifies it as contingent.

5.9 COMPLETENESS OF THE TREE TEST

In this section we prove the completeness of the tree test. A test for validity of sequents is **complete** iff it classifies all the valid sequents as valid; in other words, if a sequent *is* valid, the test classifies that sequent as valid. To prove that the tree test is complete, we proceed as we did in proving that it is sound. That is, we first prove a general metatheorem and then append a simple corollary that proves the completeness result.

The general metatheorem is expressed as the following conditional:

> If there is an open path through a finished tree, then its initial list is consistent.

To prove this conditional, the first step is to suppose for conditional proof that there is an open path P through a finished tree. We then show how to construct a valuation $\mathcal{V}$ on which all the members of P are true. But given that all members of P—including the initial list itself—are true on $\mathcal{V}$, by the definition of consistency the initial list is consistent.

In showing how to construct $\mathcal{V}$, we first define the notion of formula length. The **length** of a formula is the number of characters it contains, excluding subscripts. Thus, for example, the length of '~(P & Q)' is 6 and the length of '~~P_{12}' is 3. Here is the proof in full regalia:

> **METATHEOREM:** If there is an open path through a finished tree, then its initial list is consistent.
>
> **PROOF:** Suppose (for conditional proof) that there is an open path P through a finished tree. Since this tree is finished, any formula

of P having length 3 or more has been checked.[14] Now consider the valuation $\mathcal{V}$ which makes formulas of length 1 (sentence letters) occurring on P true and all other sentence letters false.[15] Since P is open and the tree is finished, P cannot contain both an atomic formula and its negation. So all formulas of P having length 1 or 2 are true on $\mathcal{V}$.[16] We use this fact to show that all formulas of P are true on $\mathcal{V}$ and hence that all members of the initial list are true on $\mathcal{V}$ (since these are formulas of any path, including P). To do so, we proceed by reductio:

> Suppose for reductio that some formula of P is not true on $\mathcal{V}$. Then there must be some formula Φ of P which is not true on $\mathcal{V}$, such that all formulas of P shorter than Φ are true on $\mathcal{V}$. Now the length of Φ is at least 3, for otherwise Φ would be true on $\mathcal{V}$, as noted above. And since the tree is finished and P is open, some rule has been applied to Φ.[17] Except for the negation rule (which closes paths and hence could not have been applied on P), applying any rule to any formula yields only shorter formulas. Hence P contains at least one formula shorter than Φ that is obtained from Φ by one of the rules. But since Φ is the shortest formula on P that is not true on $\mathcal{V}$, all formulas shorter than Φ on P are true on $\mathcal{V}$. Hence all formulas on P obtained from Φ by the rules are true on $\mathcal{V}$. But it is a property of each of the rules that if they yield only true formulas on some path, then the formula to which they were applied is true. (Check this for each

---

[14] That is, only atomic formulas or negations of atomic formulas remain unchecked. This must be the case, since otherwise more rules could be applied on P, which is open, and so the tree would not be finished.

[15] Recall that formulas count as occurring on a path only if they are listed there as whole formulas, not if they are merely parts of other formulas.

   The point of making all sentence letters that do not occur on P false is that some sentence letters in the initial list may not occur either negated or unnegated along the path. This signifies that, given the other truth values determined by the path, their truth value does not affect the truth of formulas of the initial list. For the sake of definiteness, we define $\mathcal{V}$ in a way that makes those sentence letters false, but this choice is arbitrary. Our definition also, of course, makes sentence letters whose negations occur on P false, and this is not arbitrary.

[16] Formulas of length 1 (sentence letters) are true because they are assigned the value T by $\mathcal{V}$ directly. And formulas of length 2 (negated sentence letters) are true because, since their sentence letters do occur on path P, these sentence letters have been assigned the value F by $\mathcal{V}$.

[17] We know this because a finished path by definition contains no unchecked sentences of length 3 or more. Any checked sentence is a sentence to which a rule has been applied.

rule.[18]) Hence Φ itself must be true on 𝒱. But by hypothesis Φ is not true on 𝒱, and so we have a contradiction. This contradiction shows that our reductio hypothesis (namely, that some formula of P is not true on 𝒱) is false; hence all formulas of P are true on 𝒱, whence it follows (as noted above) that the initial list was consistent.

But all of this was proved under the assumption (for conditional proof) that the finished tree contains an open path. Hence in sum what we have proved is that if a finished tree contains an open path, then the tree's initial list was consistent.   QED

COROLLARY (Completeness): If a sequent is valid, the tree test classifies that sequent as valid.

PROOF: Suppose that $\Phi_1, \ldots, \Phi_n \vdash \Psi$ is a valid sequent. It follows by the metatheorem proved at the end of Section 5.2 that the set $\{\Phi_1, \ldots, \Phi_n, \sim\Psi\}$ is inconsistent. But by the previous metatheorem, if there is an open path through the finished tree whose initial list is this set, then that initial list is consistent. Hence (by modus tollens) there is no open path through the tree constructed by using $\Phi_1, \ldots, \Phi_n, \sim\Psi$ as the initial list. But this is to say that the tree test classifies the sequent $\Phi_1, \ldots, \Phi_n \vdash \Psi$ as valid.

Therefore, if a sequent is valid, then the tree test classifies that sequent as valid.   QED

Exercise 5.9

Using the metatheorem of this section as an assumption, prove the following corollaries:

1. If a formula is inconsistent, then the tree test classifies it as inconsistent.
2. If a formula is valid, then the tree test classifies it as valid.
3. If the tree test classifies a formula as contingent, then it is contingent.

---

[18] If, for example, the rule & is applied to a conjunction Φ & Ψ, it will produce the formulas Φ and Ψ on each path below it. But by the valuation rule for conjunction, if these two formulas are true, then Φ & Ψ itself must be true. Similarly, if ∨ is applied to a disjunction Φ ∨ Ψ, each new path it produces will contain either Φ or Ψ. But by the valuation rule for disjunction, if either of these two formulas is true, then Φ ∨ Ψ is true. Thus, if either of these rules yields only true formulas along a given path, then the formula to which it is applied must be true. The same result holds for the other rules.

5.10 SOUNDNESS AND COMPLETENESS
OF THE NATURAL DEDUCTION RULES

Having shown that the tree test is sound and complete—that it classifies a sequent as valid iff it is in fact valid—our next task is to show that the ten natural deduction rules presented in Sections 4.2 and 4.3 are also sound and complete. A system of *inference rules* is **sound** iff each sequent provable by these rules is valid, and it is **complete** iff each valid sequent is provable by the rules. The soundness of these ten basic inference rules provides a guarantee that no sequent provable by these rules has a counterexample. The completeness of these rules guarantees that they alone suffice to prove every valid sequent expressible in the language of propositional logic.

The ten rules by themselves, however, do not constitute a decision procedure, since applications of the rules need not terminate. Consider, for example, the following infinite "proof" that uses only the rules &I and &E:[19]

1.	P & Q	A
2.	P	1 &E
3.	Q	1 &E
4.	P & Q	2, 3 &I
5.	P	4 &E
6.	Q	4 &E
7.	P & Q	5, 6 &I
8.	P	7 &E
9.	Q	7 &E

.
.
.

This pattern can clearly be iterated ad infinitum. Nobody would do this in practice, of course, but it is a common experience in working with inference rules to reason in circles, repeatedly deriving what you have already proved or assumed. This simple example shows that in principle you could do so forever.

So inference rules by themselves are not a decision procedure in the way truth tables or trees are. It is, however, possible to design a terminating algorithm for generating proofs by rigorously specifying the order of application of the inference rules. One way to do this is to make proofs mimic trees. If a sequent is valid, we know from the completeness of the tree test that all the paths of the tree for that sequent close. The tree procedure is closely akin to a reductio (~I) proof in which the negation of the conclusion is shown to lead to contradiction. If we had a terminating algorithm for reliably converting trees for valid sequents into such proofs, then by using it we could avoid the kind of infinite regress illustrated

---

[19] I put the word 'proof' in quotation marks because an infinite structure like this is not a genuine proof. A proof always has a final line on which its conclusion is displayed.

above. The whole procedure would, however, be parasitic upon the tree test. That is, we would need to construct a tree first to determine whether or not the sequent was valid; then, if all paths closed, we would convert that tree into a proof. For invalid sequents, whose paths do not all close, prior performance of the tree test would prevent us from attempting a proof. Thus an algorithm for converting trees of valid sequents to proofs would have little value in itself, since once we have determined the validity of a sequent by the tree test, it is redundant to construct a proof.

Yet such an algorithm would have at least one valuable implication: It would demonstrate the completeness of the ten basic rules. For if we could convert any tree for a valid sequent into a proof of that sequent, then the following would be true:

(1) If the tree test classifies a sequent as valid, then that sequent can be proved using only the ten basic inference rules.

Putting this together with the completeness of the tree test (which we proved in the previous section):

(2) If a sequent is valid, the tree test classifies that sequent as valid,

we obtain the conclusion:

(3) If a sequent is valid, then that sequent can be proved using only the ten basic inference rules.

But (3) asserts that the rules are complete. Since we have already proved (2), to prove the completeness of the inference rules, then, we need only prove (1)—that is, to show how to convert a tree for a valid sequent (a tree all of whose paths close) into a proof that uses only the ten rules. Before defining a general method for doing this, let's do the conversion for some specific examples.

Our first example is the valid sequent 'P & Q ⊢ P ∨ R'. Our aim is to show how to convert the tree for this sequent into a proof. We shall do this by constructing the tree and the corresponding proof side by side. The first step of the tree test is to write the initial list, consisting of the premises and the negation of the conclusion. The tree test reveals the inconsistency of this initial list (assuming the sequent it represents is valid) by showing that each possible way in which all of its formulas might be true leads to contradiction. We may think of this as a reductio strategy in which the negation of the conclusion is hypothesized in order to show that, given the premises, it leads to absurdity. Thus we can begin to construct a proof that mimics the tree test by assuming the sequent's premises and hypothesizing the negation of its conclusion for indirect proof. Thus, for the sequent 'P & Q ⊢ P ∨ R', the tree and the corresponding proof begin as follows:

Tree			Corresponding Proof		
1. P & Q	Premise		1. P & Q		A
2. ~(P ∨ R)	Neg. Concl.		2. | ~(P ∨ R)		H (for ~I)

In the tree, both formulas require nonbranching rules so that the order of application is unimportant. Let's begin by analyzing 'P & Q'. The corresponding move in the proof is to apply &E twice:[20]

3.	P	1 &	3.		P	1 &E
4.	Q	1 &	4.		Q	1 &E

The occurrence of 'P & Q' in the tree should now be checked off. The next step in constructing the tree is to check '~(P ∨ R)' and analyze it into '~P' and '~R' using the ~∨ rule. In the proof these same formulas may be deduced by converting '~(P ∨ R)' into '~P & ~R' by De Morgan's law (DM) and then using two steps of &E:

5.	~P	1 ~∨	5.		~P & ~R	2 DM
6.	~R	1 ~∨	6.		~P	5 &E
			7.		~R	5 &E

DM, of course, is a derived rule, not one of the ten basic rules. We saw in Section 4.4, however, that derived rules are merely abbreviatory devices; anything proved with derived rules can also be proved with the ten basic rules so that the use of derived rules here is legitimate.

Both 'P' and '~P' now appear on the tree's one path. The next step in the tree, therefore, is to close this path using the negation rule. We shall think of the 'X' that closes the path as representing a contradictory formula—specifically, 'P & ~P'. The proof also contains both 'P' and '~P'; thus the corresponding move in the proof is to derive 'P & ~P' by &I:

7. X	3, 5	8.		P & ~P	3, 6 &I

The tree, which represents only the derivation of a contradiction from the premises and the hypothesis of the negated conclusion, is now complete. But to finish the proof we need to end the hypothetical derivation and deduce the conclusion. This takes two more steps, one of ~I and one of ~E:

9.	~~(P ∨ R)	1–8 ~I
10.	P ∨ R	9 ~E

We have now converted the tree for the sequent 'P & Q ⊢ P ∨ R' into a proof of that sequent.

This example was unusually simple, since the tree did not branch. When trees branch, the corresponding proofs involve uses of ∨E within the overall ~I strategy, and things become more complicated. Take, for example, the valid sequent 'P ∨ Q, ~P ⊢ Q', which expresses one version of disjunctive syllogism. As before, we begin the tree by listing the premises and negation of the conclusion, and we begin the corresponding proof by assuming the premises and hypothesizing the negation of the conclusion:

---

[20] Only the first application of &E, the one at line 3, is essential to the proof, but we are concerned here with proofs that mimic trees, not with proofs that are maximally compact. The extra steps are harmless.

Tree		Corresponding Proof		
1. P ∨ Q	Premise	1.	P ∨ Q	A
2. ~P	Premise	2.	~P	A
3. ~Q	Neg. Concl.	3. |	~Q	H (for ~I)

The next step of the tree is to check the disjunction and break it into its components, drawing out the consequences of each component separately along distinct paths. However, if the initial list is inconsistent (as this one is), then each path closes because each contains a contradiction. Thus, if a disjunction Φ ∨ Ψ occurs in a tree with an inconsistent initial list, the tree will show that Φ and Ψ each lead to contradiction, which shows that the disjunction itself, together with the other statements on its path, implies a contradiction.

To mimic this in a proof, we need to prove Φ → Θ and Ψ → Θ, for some contradiction Θ, then use ∨E to derive Θ directly from Φ ∨ Ψ. Thus a single application of the ∨ rule in the tree becomes a disjunction elimination (∨E) with two subsidiary conditional proofs in the corresponding proof (here Φ is 'P', Ψ is 'Q', and Θ is 'P & ~P'):

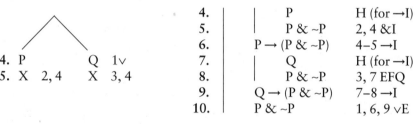

4.	| | P	H (for →I)
5.	| | P & ~P	2, 4 &I
6.	| P → (P & ~P)	4–5 →I
7.	| | Q	H (for →I)
8.	| | P & ~P	3, 7 EFQ
9.	| Q → (P & ~P)	7–8 →I
10.	| P & ~P	1, 6, 9 ∨E

The two conditional proofs constructed in preparation for ∨E represent the two branches of the tree. The hypothetical derivation at lines 4–5 of the proof represents the left branch of the tree. The 'X' on the left branch of the tree corresponds to the contradiction 'P & ~P' at line 5 of the proof. The hypothetical derivation at lines 7–8 represents the right branch of the tree, and the contradiction 'P & ~P' in the proof (line 8) represents 'X' that ends the right branch of the tree. But here 'P & ~P' is obtained, not by &I from 'P' and '~P', but by the derived rule EFQ (ex falso quodlibet; see Section 4.4) from 'Q' and '~Q'.

This use of EFQ is important. Though different formulas (such as 'P' and '~P' or 'Q' and '~Q') may lead us to close paths in the tree, each occurrence of 'X' must be represented by the same contradictory formula in the proof. This is because each of the two conditionals used in ∨E (here the conditionals appearing at lines 6 and 9) must have the same consequent. So to apply ∨E (which we do here at line 10) we need to derive the same contradiction from each hypothesis. EFQ will always enable us to do this. (EFQ is, of course, not one of the ten basic rules, but we saw above that use of derived rules here is legitimate.) *In fact, to standard-ize our procedure, we shall arbitrarily stipulate that 'X' in any tree always repre-sents the formula 'P & ~P' in the proof.*

The conditionals on lines 6 and 9 of the proof and the conclusion derived by ∨E at line 10 do not correspond to any particular formulas in the tree. They are, rather, part of the apparatus of disjunction elimination, which ensures that contra-dictions derived along different branches of the tree also follow from the formula from which those branches stem.

As in the previous example, the tree represents only the derivation of a contradiction from the hypothesized negation of the sequent's conclusion. To complete the proof, we must end this hypothetical derivation and apply final steps of ~I and ~E:

11.	~~Q	3–10 ~I
12.	Q	11 ~E

Indeed, any proof derived from a tree by the method illustrated here must end in this way.

The full algorithm for converting trees for valid sequents into proofs may be stated as follows:

1. List the premises of the sequent as assumptions, then hypothesize the negation of the conclusion.
2. Derive 'P & ~P' from this hypothesis by converting each step in the tree into a series of proof steps as described in Table 5.1.
3. Deduce the double negation of the sequent's conclusion by ~I, and then deduce the conclusion itself by ~E.

Table 5.1, as noted in step 2, provides instructions for converting each application of a tree rule into a series of steps in the proof. It remains only to verify that this algorithm performs as advertised.

TABLE 5.1
Instructions for Converting Trees for Valid Sequents into Proofs

Tree Rule	Corresponding Step(s) in Proof
Negation (~) If an open path contains both a formula Φ and its negation, place an 'X' at the bottom of the path.	Deduce from Φ and ~Φ the contradiction 'P & ~P', either directly by &I (if Φ is 'P') or by EFQ.
Negated Negation (~~) If an open path contains an unchecked formula of the form ~~Φ, check it and write Φ at the bottom of every open path that contains this newly checked formula.	Deduce Φ from ~~Φ by ~E.
Conjunction (&) If an open path contains an unchecked formula of the form (Φ & Ψ), check it and list Φ above Ψ at the bottom of every open path that contains this newly checked formula.	Apply &E twice to (Φ & Ψ) to obtain Φ and Ψ on separate lines.

(continued)

TABLE 5.1
Instructions for Converting Trees for Valid Sequents into Proofs (*continued*)

Tree Rule	Corresponding Step(s) in Proof
Negated Conjunction (~&) If an open path contains an unchecked formula of the form ~(Φ & Ψ), check it and split the bottom of each open path containing this newly checked formula into two branches; at the end of the first write ~Φ, and at the end of the second write ~Ψ.	Apply DM to ~(Φ & Ψ) to obtain ~Φ ∨ ~Ψ, then apply the directions for disjunction to ~Φ ∨ ~Ψ.
Disjunction (∨) If an open path contains an unchecked formula of the form (Φ ∨ Ψ), check it and split the bottom of each open path containing this newly checked formula into two branches; at the end of the first write Φ, and at the end of the second write Ψ.	Hypothesize Φ, aiming to derive 'P & ~P' and then deduce Φ → (P & ~P) by →I. Next, hypothesize Ψ, again derive 'P & ~P', and then obtain Ψ → (P & ~P) by →I. Finally, use ∨E to deduce 'P & ~P' from (Φ ∨ Ψ), Φ → (P & ~P), and Ψ → (P & ~P). This procedure always works if the sequent being tested on the tree is valid, since in that case all the paths below (Φ ∨ Ψ) must close, and each closed path is converted into a derivation of 'P & ~P' in the proof (see negation rule). If there are further applications of branching rules below (Φ ∨ Ψ), these will also be converted into derivations of 'P & ~P' by further applications of the procedure for disjunction.
Negated Disjunction (~∨) If an open path contains an unchecked formula of the form ~(Φ ∨ Ψ), check it and list ~Φ above ~Ψ at the bottom of every open path that contains this newly checked formula.	Apply DM to ~(Φ ∨ Ψ) to obtain ~Φ & ~Ψ, then use &E twice to obtain ~Φ and ~Ψ on separate lines.
Conditional (→) If an open path contains an unchecked formula of the form (Φ → Ψ), check it and split the bottom of each open path containing this newly checked formula into two branches; at the end of the first write ~Φ, and at the end of the second write Ψ.	Apply MI to (Φ → Ψ) to obtain ~Φ ∨ Ψ, then apply the directions for disjunction to ~Φ ∨ Ψ.

(continued)

TABLE 5.1
Instructions for Converting Trees for Valid Sequents into Proofs (*continued*)

Tree Rule	Corresponding Step(s) in Proof
Negated Conditional (~→) If an open path contains an unchecked formula of the form ~(Φ → Ψ), check it and list Φ above ~Ψ at the bottom of every open path that contains this newly checked formula.	From ~(Φ → Ψ), reason as follows (line numbers are represented by letters, starting with 'a'): a ~(Φ → Ψ) b ┃ ~Φ ∨ Ψ H (for ~I) c ┃ Φ → Ψ b MI d ┃ (Φ→Ψ)&~(Φ→Ψ) a, c &I e ~(~Φ ∨ Ψ) b–d ~I f ~~Φ & ~Ψ e DM g ~~Φ f &E h Φ g ~E i ~Ψ f &E (Here Φ is proved at line h and ~Ψ at line i.)

Biconditional (↔) If an open path contains an unchecked formula of the form (Φ ↔ Ψ), check it and split the bottom of each open path containing this newly checked formula into two branches; at the end of the first list Φ above Ψ, and at the end of the second list ~Φ above ~Ψ.	From (Φ ↔ Ψ), reason as follows:
	a Φ ↔ Ψ
	b ┃ ~((Φ & Ψ) ∨ (~Φ & ~Ψ)) H (for ~I)
	c ┃┃ Φ H (for ~I)
	d ┃┃ Ψ a, c ↔MP
	e ┃┃ (Φ & Ψ) c, d &I
	f ┃┃ (Φ & Ψ) ∨ (~Φ & ~Ψ) e ∨I
	g ┃┃ (Φ & Ψ) ∨ (~Φ & ~Ψ) &
	   ┃┃ ~((Φ & Ψ) ∨ (~Φ & ~Ψ)) b, f &I
	h ┃ ~Φ c–g ~I
	i ┃ ~Ψ a, h ↔MT
	j ┃ ~Φ & ~Ψ h, i &I
	k ┃ (Φ & Ψ) ∨ (~Φ & ~Ψ) j ∨I
	l ┃ (Φ & Ψ) ∨ (~Φ & ~Ψ) &
	   ┃ ~((Φ & Ψ) ∨ (~Φ & ~Ψ)) b, k &I
	m ~~((Φ & Ψ) ∨ (~Φ & ~Ψ)) b–l ~I
	n (Φ & Ψ) ∨ (~Φ & ~Ψ) m ~E
	Then apply the directions for disjunction to (Φ & Ψ) ∨ (~Φ & ~Ψ).

Negated Biconditional (~↔) If an open path contains an unchecked formula of the form ~(Φ ↔ Ψ), check it and split the bottom of each open path containing this newly checked formula into two branches; at the end of the first list Φ above ~Ψ, and at the end of the second list ~Φ above Ψ.	From ~(Φ ↔ Ψ), reason as follows: a ~(Φ ↔ Ψ) b ┃ ~((Φ & ~Ψ) ∨ (~Φ & Ψ)) H (for ~I) c ┃ ~(Φ & ~Ψ) & ~(~Φ & Ψ) b DM d ┃ ~(Φ & ~Ψ) c &E e ┃ Φ → Ψ d MI f ┃ ~(~Φ & Ψ) c &E g ┃ ~~Φ ∨ ~Ψ f DM h ┃ ~Ψ ∨ ~~Φ g COM i ┃ ~(Ψ & ~Φ) h DM j ┃ Ψ → Φ i MI

(continued)

TABLE 5.1
Instructions for Converting Trees for Valid Sequents into Proofs (*continued*)

Tree Rule	Corresponding Step(s) in Proof

$$
\begin{array}{lll}
\text{k} & \Phi \leftrightarrow \Psi & \text{e, j} \leftrightarrow\text{I} \\
\text{l} & (\Phi \leftrightarrow \Psi) \mathbin{\&} \sim(\Phi \leftrightarrow \Psi) & \text{a, k \&I} \\
\text{m} \;\; \sim\sim((\Phi \mathbin{\&} \sim\Psi) \vee (\sim\Phi \mathbin{\&} \Psi)) & & \text{b--l } \sim\text{I} \\
\text{n} \;\; (\Phi \mathbin{\&} \sim\Psi) \vee (\sim\Phi \mathbin{\&} \Psi) & & \text{m } \sim\text{E}
\end{array}
$$

Then apply the directions for disjunction to
$(\Phi \mathbin{\&} \sim\Psi) \vee (\sim\Phi \mathbin{\&} \Psi)$.

METATHEOREM: If the tree test classifies a sequent as valid, then that sequent can be proved using only the ten basic inference rules.

PROOF: Suppose that the tree test classifies a sequent $\Phi_1, \ldots, \Phi_n \vdash \Psi$ as valid. Then all paths of the tree whose initial list is $\Phi_1, \ldots, \Phi_n, \sim\Psi$ close. To construct a proof of $\Phi_1, \ldots, \Phi_n \vdash \Psi$ using only the ten basic inference rules, apply the algorithm described earlier. Now either the tree contains applications of branching rules or it does not. If it does not, then it is evident by inspection of the algorithm that each formula in the tree obtained by the tree rules is deduced from the initial assumptions and the hypothesis in the proof, and that where the final 'X' appears in the tree, the corresponding formula derived in the proof is 'P & ~P'. Hence the portion of the proof corresponding to the tree is just a straightforward derivation of 'P & ~P' from the assumptions $\Phi_1, \ldots, \Phi_n$ and the hypothesis $\sim\Psi$. If, on the other hand, the tree employs branching rules, the formulas that begin new branches of the tree constitute additional hypotheses in the proof.[21] Yet, since each path of the tree closes, each of these hypothetical derivations still ends with 'P & ~P'. So, in accordance with the procedures for disjunction and for the other branching rules, each time a branching rule is applied to some formula Θ in the tree, the portion of the proof generated by the algorithm is a derivation by $\vee$E of 'P & ~P' from Θ. Even if the branches themselves branch, the result is the same, since 'P & ~P' will be derived in the portion of the proof corresponding to each branch and hence

---

[21] In the case of the two rules for the biconditional, $\leftrightarrow$ and $\sim\leftrightarrow$, which produce branches beginning with two formulas each, the hypothesis corresponding to each branch in the proof is a single formula—the conjunction of these two formulas.

(by ∨E) from the formula from which the subbranches originate. Thus, whether or not the tree branches, the portion of the proof corresponding to the tree as a whole is a derivation of 'P & ~P' from the assumptions $\Phi_1, \ldots, \Phi_n$ and the hypothesis ~Ψ. Therefore we may apply step 3 of the algorithm (obtain ~~Ψ by ~I and then Ψ by ~E), completing the proof of Φ_1,

$\Phi_n \vdash Ψ$. Though portions of the proof may use derived rules, these can be replaced as explained in Section 4.4 by derivations using only the ten basic rules. In this way we obtain a proof of $\Phi_1, \ldots, \Phi_n \vdash Ψ$ using only the ten basic rules.
Therefore, if the tree test classifies a sequent as valid, then that sequent can be proved using only the ten basic inference rules.   QED

COROLLARY (Completeness of the Inference Rules): If a sequent is valid, then that sequent can be proved using only the ten basic inference rules.

PROOF: From the completeness of the tree test, we know that if a sequent is valid, then the tree test classifies it as valid. Together with the previous metatheorem, this implies that if a sequent is valid, then that sequent can be proved using only the ten basic rules.   QED

Finally, we shall show that the system consisting of the ten basic inference rules is sound—that is, that any sequent provable by these rules is valid. We have already seen in Sections 4.2 and 4.3 that each rule individually is valid—that is, that there is no counterexample to any instance of any of these rules. To prove a sequent, however, we apply these rules successively. We must, then, show that invalidity does not somehow creep into a proof as a result of this succession. In order to show this, it will be useful to define the notion of a **corresponding sequent** to a line of a proof.

DEFINITION The **corresponding sequent** for a given line of a proof is the sequent whose conclusion is the formula on that line, and whose premises are all the assumptions and all the hypotheses whose derivations have not yet ended that are listed on that line or at any previous lines.

The corresponding sequent for a given line is in effect what is proved at that line. To illustrate, consider this proof of 'P → Q, ~Q ⊢ ~P'. Corresponding sequents are listed to the right.

Line of Proof			Corresponding Sequent
1. P → Q		A	P → Q ⊢ P → Q
2. ~Q		A	P → Q, ~Q ⊢ ~Q
3.		P	H (for ~I)	P → Q, ~Q, P ⊢ P
4.		Q	1, 3 →E	P → Q, ~Q, P ⊢ Q
5.		Q & ~Q	2, 3 &I	P → Q, ~Q, P ⊢ Q & ~Q
6. ~P		3–5 ~I	P → Q, ~Q ⊢ ~P

Since all hypothetical derivations must end before a proof is finished, the corresponding sequent for the last line of any proof is just the sequent whose premises are the proof's assumptions and whose conclusion is the proof's conclusion—that is, the sequent to be proved. Thus, if we can show that the corresponding sequent for *any* line of any proof is valid, it will follow that the corresponding sequent for *the last line* of any proof is valid, and hence that any sequent provable by the ten basic inference rules is valid. Actually, since inference rules may apply to any earlier lines, it is easier to prove something apparently a little stronger than this—namely, that each line and all lines preceding it correspond to valid sequents. This can be done by mathematical induction on the number of lines in the proof. The induction appeals frequently to the following lemma, which was problem 4 of Exercise 5.4:

> **LEMMA:** If $\Phi_1, \ldots, \Phi_m \vdash \Psi$ and $\Psi, \Psi_1, \ldots, \Psi_n \vdash \Theta$ are valid sequents (where $m \geq 0$ and $n \geq 0$), then $\Phi_1, \ldots, \Phi_m, \Psi_1, \ldots, \Psi_n \vdash \Theta$ is a valid sequent.

Here is the induction itself:

> **METATHEOREM:** Let P be any proof using only the ten basic inference rules; then for each line of P, the corresponding sequents for all lines up to and including that line are valid.
>
> PROOF: The lines of P form a series, so we may proceed by mathematical induction. The property which we show belongs to each line is rather convoluted. It is the property of being a line of P such that the corresponding sequents for it and all previous lines are valid.
>
> **Basis Case:** The first line of any proof is always the assumption or hypothesis of some formula Ψ. Since there are no lines previous to this first line, the corresponding sequent is $\Psi \vdash \Psi$. This is clearly valid (see problem 7 of Exercise 5.3). Hence the first line of P has the property of being such that the corresponding sequents for it and all previous lines are valid.
>
> **Inductive Step:** Suppose that the corresponding sequents of all lines up to and including the nth line are valid. We must show that the

corresponding sequents of all lines up to and including the $(n + 1)$st line are valid. To do this, it suffices to show just that the corresponding sequent for the $(n + 1)$st line is valid. Now in a proof using only the ten basic inference rules there are only twelve ways in which the $(n + 1)$st line can be obtained: It may be an assumption, or a hypothesis, or a conclusion obtained by one of the ten basic rules. If it is an assumption or hypothesis Ψ, then the corresponding sequent must also have Ψ as both premise and conclusion (though it may have other premises as well), and so this sequent is clearly valid. (This follows from problem 7 of Exercise 5.3 together with problem 3 of Exercise 5.4.) Now we must show for each of the ten rules that when applied to lines whose corresponding sequents are valid this rule produces a line whose corresponding sequent is valid. We shall do this for ~E, →E, and ~I, leaving the remaining seven cases as exercises. *First, we show that if ~E is applied to a line whose corresponding sequent is valid, the resulting conclusion is a line whose corresponding sequent is valid.* To do this, we proceed by conditional proof.

Suppose ~E is applied to a line whose corresponding sequent is valid. Now since ~E is applied to this line, the formula it contains must be of the form ~~Θ. Since the conclusion of the corresponding sequent for this line must be the formula that appears on this line, the corresponding sequent must have the form $\Phi_1, \ldots, \Phi_m \vdash$ ~~Θ, where $m \geq 0$. Now ~E has been applied to ~~Θ to obtain Θ. Therefore the sequent corresponding to the line obtained by ~E is of the form $\Phi_1, \ldots, \Phi_m, \Psi_1, \ldots,$ $\Psi_n \vdash \Theta$, where $n \geq 0$. (Here $\Psi_1, \ldots, \Psi_n$ are any hypotheses or assumptions that may have been introduced after the line at which ~~Θ appears.[22]) Now since $\Phi_1, \ldots, \Phi_m \vdash$ ~~Θ is valid, and we saw in Section 4.2 that ~~$\Theta \vdash \Theta$ is valid, it follows by the lemma that $\Phi_1, \ldots, \Phi_m \vdash \Theta$ is valid. (In terms of the lemma, Ψ is ~~Θ and $n = 0$.) And since $\Phi_1, \ldots, \Phi_m \vdash \Theta$ is valid, by problem 7 of Exercise 5.3, $\Phi_1, \ldots, \Phi_m, \Psi_1, \ldots, \Psi_n \vdash \Theta$ is valid.

Hence we have shown that if ~E is applied to a line whose corresponding sequent is valid, the resulting conclusion is a line whose corresponding sequent is valid. *Next, we shall show, again by conditional proof, that if →E is applied to a pair of lines, each of whose corresponding sequents is valid, the result is a line whose corresponding sequent is valid.*

---

[22] Notice that none of the original hypotheses or assumptions $\Phi_1, \ldots, \Phi_m$ can be dropped, since that would indicate that ~~Θ appears in a hypothetical derivation that has ended, so that neither ~E nor any other rule may be applied to it.

Suppose that →E is applied to two lines each of whose corresponding sequents is valid. The formulas on these lines are therefore of the forms $\Phi \rightarrow \Psi$ and Φ, and their corresponding sequents have the forms $\Phi_1, \ldots, \Phi_m \vdash \Phi \rightarrow \Psi$ and $\Delta_1, \ldots, \Delta_n \vdash \Phi$, where $m \geq 0$ and $n \geq 0$. The line obtained by the application of →E is of the form Ψ, and its corresponding sequent has the form $\Psi_1, \ldots, \Psi_p \vdash \Psi$, where $p \geq 0$ and $\Phi_1, \ldots, \Phi_m$ and $\Delta_1, \ldots, \Delta_n$ are included among $\Psi_1, \ldots, \Psi_p$.[23] Now we saw in Section 4.2 that $\Phi \rightarrow \Psi, \Phi \vdash \Psi$ is a valid form. Hence, since $\Phi_1, \ldots, \Phi_m \vdash \Phi \rightarrow \Psi$ is valid, it follows by the lemma that $\Phi_1, \ldots, \Phi_m, \Phi \vdash \Psi$ is valid. Given this and the fact that $\Delta_1, \ldots, \Delta_n \vdash \Phi$ is valid, it follows again by the lemma that $\Phi_1, \ldots, \Phi_m, \Delta_1, \ldots, \Delta_n \vdash \Psi$ is valid. But since $\Phi_1, \ldots, \Phi_m$ and $\Delta_1, \ldots, \Delta_n$ are included among $\Psi_1, \ldots, \Psi_p$, from this by problem 3 of Exercise 5.4 we may infer that $\Psi_1, \ldots, \Psi_p \vdash \Psi$ is valid. But this is the corresponding sequent for the line obtained by →E.

Therefore, if →E is applied to a pair of lines, each of whose corresponding sequents is valid, the result is a line whose corresponding sequent is valid. Finally, we show that *if ~I is applied to a series of lines all of whose corresponding sequents are valid, the result is a line whose corresponding sequent is valid.*

Suppose that ~I is applied to a series of lines all of whose corresponding sequents are valid. For ~I to be applicable, the first such line must contain a hypothesized formula Φ and the last must contain a contradiction $\Psi \mathbin{\&} {\sim}\Psi$ that is derived from Φ. The corresponding sequent of this last line must therefore have the form $\Phi, \Phi_1, \ldots, \Phi_m \vdash \Psi \mathbin{\&} {\sim}\Psi$, where $m \geq 0$. Since we have supposed this sequent to be valid, there is no valuation on which $\Phi, \Phi_1, \ldots, \Phi_m$ are all true and $\Psi \mathbin{\&} {\sim}\Psi$ is untrue. But since $\Psi \mathbin{\&} {\sim}\Psi$ is untrue on all valuations, there is no valuation on which $\Phi, \Phi_1, \ldots, \Phi_m$ are all true. Hence by valuation rule 1, there is no valuation on which $\Phi_1, \ldots, \Phi_m$ are all true and ${\sim}\Phi$ is not true. Therefore the sequent $\Phi_1, \ldots, \Phi_m \vdash {\sim}\Phi$ is valid. But since application of ~I ends the hypothetical derivation from Φ, leaving only $\Phi_1, \ldots, \Phi_m$ as the assumptions or hypotheses whose derivations have not ended, this sequent is just the corresponding sequent for the line obtained by ~I.

---

[23] The reason for this inclusion is explained in the previous footnote.

Therefore, if ~I is applied to a series of lines all of whose corresponding sequents are valid, the result is a line whose corresponding sequent is valid. Similar results may be obtained for each of the remaining seven rules: &I, &E, vI, vE, →E, ↔I, and ↔E. Hence no matter by which of the twelve possible ways the ($n + 1$)st line is obtained, the corresponding sequent for the ($n + 1$)st line is valid.

Therefore, if the corresponding sequents of all lines of P up to and including the nth line are valid, then so are the corresponding sequents for all lines up to and including the ($n + 1$)st. Hence by mathematical induction, for each line of P, the corresponding sequents for all lines up to and including that line are valid.   QED

From this result, the soundness of the ten rules follows as a corollary:

COROLLARY (Soundness of the Ten Basic Inference Rules): If a sequent can be proved using only the ten basic inference rules, then that sequent is valid.

PROOF: Let $\Phi_1, \ldots, \Phi_n \vdash \Psi$ be a sequent provable using only the ten basic rules. Then there exists a proof of this sequent whose assumptions are $\Phi_1, \ldots, \Phi_n$ and whose last line contains the formula Ψ. Since all hypothetical derivations used in this proof must have ended before the last line, the corresponding sequent for this last line is just $\Phi_1, \ldots, \Phi_n \vdash \Psi$ (see definition of corresponding sequent). But by the previous metatheorem, the corresponding sequent for any line of any proof is valid. Hence $\Phi_1, \ldots, \Phi_n \vdash \Psi$ is valid.

Hence, if a sequent can be proved using only the ten basic inference rules, then that sequent is valid.   QED

Having shown that the ten basic inference rules are sound and complete (i.e., that they enable us to prove a sequent of propositional logic iff it is valid), we now know that they enable us to prove exactly the sequents we should be able to prove, given the classical notion of validity.

Exercise 5.10.1

Prove for each of the rules &I, &E, vI, vE, →E, ↔I, and ↔E that if applied to lines whose corresponding sequents are valid, they yield a conclusion whose corresponding sequent is valid.

Exercise 5.10.2

1. A set of rules is **consistent** iff there is no formula Φ such that both Φ and $\sim\Phi$ are provable as theorems from these rules. Use the soundness of the ten basic inference rules to prove that these rules are consistent.
2. Use the soundness and completeness of the ten basic inference rules to prove that a formula of propositional logic is valid (tautologous) iff it is a theorem.

CLASSICAL PREDICATE LOGIC

CLASSICAL PREDICATE LOGIC: SYNTAX

6.1 QUANTIFIERS, PREDICATES, AND NAMES

Propositional logic is the study of how validity and related properties arise from formal configurations of the operators '~', '&', '∨', '→', and '↔'. But these are not the only logical operators. Other expressions also contribute to validity. Consider, for example, the argument

All women are mortal.
Cleopatra is a woman.
∴   Cleopatra is mortal.

This is clearly valid in the informal sense described in Chapter 1. But what makes it valid? None of the five propositional operators are seen to occur here so that if we were to attempt a symbolization in propositional logic, the best we could do would be something like 'P, Q ⊢ R'. But this sequent represents any argument with two premises, and it is invalid. Plainly there is some syntactic and semantic structure within these sentences that accounts for the argument's validity, but just as plainly propositional logic does not enable us to represent it.

The atoms of propositional logic are sentence letters. But, as in the preceding argument, the sentences these letters represent have internal components—subjects, predicates, and modifiers of various sorts—whose arrangement may affect the argument's validity. To adequately conceptualize such arguments, we need ways of representing this "subatomic" structure. We must turn up the power of our conceptual microscope, as it were, to reveal details where previously we had seen only structureless units. Predicate logic, then, is the study of this "subatomic" realm.

We give the microscope its first twist by teasing out the structure of the argument's initial premise:

All women are mortal.

Ideally, formalization produces intelligible connections to previous work. So it is progress of a sort to recognize that the same thing could be said by the more awkward sentence:

For any thing, if it is a woman, then it is mortal.

Though more awkward, this makes a potentially illuminating connection, since it contains a conditional—something we already know how to formalize. Hence we could begin the process of formalization like this:

For any thing (it is a woman → it is mortal).

Now the term 'thing' and the two occurrences of the word 'it' are simply place-holders—variables standing for any individual whatsoever. We could therefore replace them with a symbol formally recognized as a **variable**—say, 'x':

For any x (x is a woman → x is mortal).

The variable 'x' may stand for any object. We shall use the lowercase letters 'u' through 'z' as variables in this way.

Next we adopt the symbol '$\forall$' to stand for the English words 'for any' or 'for all'. This symbol is called the **universal quantifier.** We may now write

$\forall x(x$ is a woman → x is mortal).

This is still a specific sentence, though written in a motley hybrid of logic and English. It says exactly what our original sentence said—namely, that all women are mortal.

Two fragments of English remain: 'is a woman' and 'is mortal'. In English grammar these are called "predicate phrases"; in logic we just call them **predicates.** We next adopt a new category of symbols: capital letters, to stand for predicates. Like the sentence letters of propositional logic, these are place-holders that have variable interpretations; they don't mean anything until we assign them an interpretation, and we may assign them different interpretations in different contexts. Here we will use 'W' to stand for 'is a woman' and 'M' for 'is mortal'. In predicate logic it is customary to write the predicate first followed by the subject so that 'x is a woman', for example, is symbolized as 'Wx'.[1] Thus we obtain

---

[1] This curious backwardness is the fault of Gottlob Frege, who invented predicate logic late in the nineteenth century. Frege thought of predicates as designating functions which produce truth values when applied to objects. Function symbols in mathematics are usually written before the names of objects to which they apply, and Frege adopted this mathematical convention.

$$\forall x(Wx \to Mx)$$

This is a formula of predicate logic. Unlike the other expressions we wrote to produce it, this formula is not a sentence, but (like the formulas of propositional logic) a representation of a sentence form. By itself, it has no specific meaning, though when we assign meanings to the predicate letters (as we have done) it does mean something—in this case, "All women are mortal."

The remaining two sentences of our argument both contain the name 'Cleopatra'. We shall use lowercase letters 'a' through 't' as names for people or things, so 'c' is the obvious choice for Cleopatra. Since, as we noted above, subjects customarily are written after predicates, 'Cleopatra is a woman' becomes 'Wc' and 'Cleopatra is mortal' is 'Mc'. Thus the entire argument may be formalized as the sequent '$\forall x(Wx \to Mx)$, Wc $\vdash$ Mc'.

Now it is obvious that from '$\forall x(Wx \to Mx)$' we may validly deduce 'Wc $\to$ Mc'—in English:

> All women are mortal.
> $\therefore$ If Cleopatra is a woman, then Cleopatra is mortal.

And from 'Wc $\to$ Mc' and the second premise 'Wc', the conclusion 'Mc' follows by modus ponens ($\to$E). So already we have begun to see more clearly why the argument is valid. But we will leave the detailed analysis of inference in predicate logic for later chapters. Our goal in this chapter is to become familiar with the language of predicate logic and develop the skill of formalization.

Let's consider some variations. Suppose we want to formalize 'Everything is mortal'. That means that for any x, x is mortal—in symbols:

$$\forall x Mx$$

We might also want to say that everything is immortal. (This is not true, of course, but we might want to say it anyway.) This is to say of each thing that it is *not* mortal.[2] So 'Everything is immortal' means

> For any x, x is not mortal.

Now 'Mx' says that x is mortal, so '$\sim Mx$' says that x is not mortal. Therefore the formula we want is

$$\forall x \sim Mx$$

Notice that 'Everything is immortal' is just another way of saying that nothing is mortal. We could also say that nothing is a woman in the same way: '$\forall x \sim Wx$'.

It would be wrong to symbolize 'Nothing is mortal' with the quantifier and negation sign reversed as

---

[2] We assume here that 'immortal' means simply "deathless" so that it makes sense to say of nonliving as well as living things that they are immortal—as, for example, when we speak of "the immortal words of Shakespeare" or "the immortal realm of ideas." If, instead, we use 'mortal' to mean "living and doomed to die" and 'immortal' to mean "living and deathless," then 'immortal' does not mean the same thing as 'not mortal'—unless we confine the domain of discourse (see Section 7.2) to living things.

$\sim\forall x Mx$

This is a perfectly intelligible formula, but what it says is "it is not the case that for all x, x is mortal"—or, more compactly, "not everything is mortal." This statement, unlike 'Nothing is mortal', is compatible with the existence of some mortal things.

Consider now the sentence

No women are mortal.

This means

For any x, if x is a woman, then x is not mortal.

That is,

$\forall x(Wx \longrightarrow \sim Mx)$

'No' in this context is thus analyzed into universal quantification over a conditional whose consequent is negated.

In addition to '$\forall$', which means "for any" or "for all," predicate logic contains a second quantifier, '$\exists$', which means "for at least one." The English word it is most commonly used to symbolize is 'some'. Consider, for example, the sentence

Some fathers are gorillas.

This means the same thing as

For at least one x, x is a father and x is a gorilla.

Using 'F' for the predicate 'is a father' and 'G' for 'is a gorilla', we may symbolize this sentence as

$\exists x(Fx \,\&\, Gx)$

which is an existentially quantified conjunction. Actually, in English, the word 'some' tends to mean "at least two," so there may be some slippage of meaning in the formalization. This slippage is usually not too troublesome, but it should not be forgotten. The English expressions 'there is' and 'there exists' are perhaps better translations of '$\exists$' than 'some' is. Hence the preceding formula can also be read as

There is an x such that x is a father and x is a gorilla.

or

There exists an x such that x is a father and x is a gorilla.

Accordingly, '$\exists$' is called the **existential quantifier.**

We might also want to say (because it is true) that some fathers aren't gorillas. This means

There exists an x such that x is a father and x is not a gorilla.

which in symbolic terms is

$\exists x(Fx \,\&\, \sim Gx)$

Notice that it is wrong to render the true statement 'some fathers aren't gorillas' as

$\sim\exists x(Fx \,\&\, Gx)$

This is the denial of 'some fathers are gorillas'. In English it says

It is not true that some fathers are gorillas.

which is to say that no fathers are gorillas—which, of course, is false.[3] But this itself tells us something interesting: Statements beginning with 'no' can be rendered into predicate logic in either of two equivalent ways. For example, we can symbolize the statement 'No women are mortal' either with the universal quantifier as

$\forall x(Wx \rightarrow \sim Mx)$

as we did earlier, or with the existential quantifier as

$\sim\exists x(Wx \,\&\, Mx)$

These are two equivalent ways of saying "no W are M," just as '$\sim(P \lor Q)$' and '$\sim P \,\&\, \sim Q$' are in propositional logic two equivalent ways of saying "neither P nor Q."

Notice that the universal quantifier tends to go with the conditional operator, whereas the existential quantifier tends to go with the conjunction. Existential quantifiers are, in fact, rarely if ever applied to conditional statements, because the result would be something we would almost never have occasion to say. Consider, for example, the statement 'There exists a unicorn with one horn'. Using 'U' for 'is a unicorn' and 'H' for 'has one horn', this is correctly symbolized as an existentially quantified conjunction:

$\exists x(Ux \,\&\, Hx)$

That is, "There exists an x such that x is a unicorn and x has one horn." This, of course, is false, since unicorns don't exist. Suppose, however, that we *incorrectly* formulated this same statement using the conditional operator instead of the conjunction, that is,

$\exists x(Ux \rightarrow Hx)$ **(Wrong!)**

Now what we have said is something true but *very* strange: There exists something such that *if* it is a unicorn, then it has one horn. We are not saying that anything is a unicorn, nor are we saying that anything has a horn. (The statement we were trying to formalize said both of these things.) The sort of object described by this erroneous formulation might be anything at all. It is true of my neighbor's cat, or the state of Alaska, or even the number 47 that *if* it is a unicorn, then it has one horn.

---

[3] At least as of this writing. Gorillas being endangered, it may soon to our sorrow become true.

The point is that when you apply an existential quantifier to a conditional, you say something so strange that it is virtually certain not to be what you mean. So, if you find yourself formalizing a statement that way, think again.

But universal quantifiers typically do govern conditionals, and they are seldom applied to conjunctions. *It is wrong, for example, to formalize 'All women are mortal'* as

$\forall x(Wx \mathbin{\&} Mx)$

This means "for all x, x is both a woman and mortal"—that is, the whole universe consists of nothing but mortal women (a much less pleasing prospect than the actual arrangement—and nothing like what we meant to say). However, universally quantified conjunctions are occasionally useful, as in the statement

Everything is located in space and time.

Using 'S' for 'is located in space' and 'T' for 'is located in time', this is

$\forall x(Sx \mathbin{\&} Tx)$

Both existential and universal quantifiers can be combined with the other propositional operators as well—in infinite variety. The sentence

Everything is either mortal or not mortal,

for example, combines disjunction, negation, and universal quantification as follows:

$\forall x(Mx \vee {\sim}Mx)$

That is a logical truth—not to be confused with the contingent statement

Either everything is mortal or everything is immortal,

which is a disjunction whose disjuncts are both universally quantified statements:

$\forall xMx \vee \forall x{\sim}Mx$

And, of course, much greater complexity is possible. One way to increase the complexity of an English sentence is to add adjectives. Adjectival modification in English is usually represented by a conjunction in predicate logic. Thus, for example, in the sentence

All mortal women are located in space and time,

the modification of the noun 'women' by the adjective 'mortal' is represented in predicate logic by a conjunction of two predicates. We may render this as

For any x, if x is mortal and x is a woman, then x is located in space and x is located in time,

which goes over into predicate logic as

$\forall x((Mx \mathbin{\&} Wx) \rightarrow (Sx \mathbin{\&} Tx))$

Some English predicates, such as 'loathes', are transitive, taking both a subject and an object. These need two names to make a complete sentence and hence are called **two-place predicates.** The usual convention is to write them in the order predicate-subject-object. So, for example, the statement 'Beth loathes Carl' may be formalized (using 'b' for 'Beth', 'c' for 'Carl', and 'L' for loathes) as 'Lbc'. Two-place predicates may be combined with quantifiers and the propositional operators for still greater variety of expression. Here are some examples:

English Sentence	Formalization
Carl loathes Beth.	Lcb
Carl loathes himself.	Lcc
Carl loathes everything.	$\forall x Lcx$
Something loathes Carl.	$\exists x Lxc$
Something loathes itself.	$\exists x Lxx$
Beth loathes nothing.	$\forall x \sim Lbx$ or $\sim \exists x Lbx$
Beth does not loathe everything.	$\sim \forall x Lbx$
Something loathes something.	$\exists x \exists y Lxy$

For 'Beth loathes nothing', there are two equivalent formulations, each equally correct. There are various equivalent ways of writing the others as well, but I have given the simplest or most obvious formalization in each case. One way to obtain an equivalent formalization of any quantified formula is to replace the quantified variable with a different one. '$\exists x Lxx$' and '$\exists y Lyy$', for example, say the same thing. The replacement, however, must be uniform. We may not replace some occurrences of a variable and not others. The expression '$\exists x Lyy$', for example, does not mean the same thing as '$\exists x Lxx$'. In fact, it is not even a formula, as we shall see in the next section.

The last formula in the list, '$\exists x \exists y Lxy$', boasts two existential quantifiers, an arrangement which requires two different variables. Read literally, it means "there exists an x such that there exists a y such that x loathes y" or (what comes to the same thing) "for at least one x and at least one y, x loathes y."

It is important to note that, as in mathematics, different variables may stand for the same object. '$\exists x \exists y Lxy$' may be true, for example, because 'Lcc' is true—that is, because Carl loathes himself. If so, 'x' and 'y' both stand for Carl.

Moreover, the same variable stands for the same thing only so long as it is governed by the same occurrence of a quantifier. The variable 'x' in '$\exists x Lxx$' stands for the same individual or individuals in each of its occurrences. That is why it means "something loathes *itself*." But consider the statement

Something loathes itself and something doesn't loathe itself,

or, perhaps more colloquially,

There are things that loathe themselves and things that don't.

This may be formalized as

$\exists x Lxx \ \& \ \exists x \sim Lxx$

Here the first three occurrences of 'x', being governed by the first existential quantifier, refer to the things that loathe themselves, and the second three occurrences, being governed by the second existential quantifier, refer to the things that don't. Thus two occurrences of the same variable must refer to the same thing only if they are governed by the same quantifier. Some people find this confusing and would prefer to formalize this conjunction as

$\exists x Lxx \ \& \ \exists y \sim Lyy$

That's fine. But so is the first way we did it.

It is not fine, however, to have two quantifiers governing the same variable, as in '$\forall x \forall x Lxx$'. Here we can't tell which variable is governed by which quantifier. We shall not even count such expressions as formulas.

When universal and existential quantifiers occur in the same sentence, the sentence is usually ambiguous. Consider the sentence 'Something loathes everything'. This has the following two meanings:

1. There is some one being (think of Dante's Lucifer, for example) that loathes everything, or
2. Everything is loathed, but not necessarily by the same being in each case. (Thus Beth may be loathed by Carl, Carl by himself, and so on, though perhaps no one being loathes everything.)

Because the founders of predicate logic were trying to create an ideal language, formulas of predicate logic are, by design, perfectly unambiguous. Consequently, when we formalize 'Something loathes everything', we must decide on one or the other of these meanings. The difference between them is reflected in the formalism by the ordering of the quantifiers. Converting each reading into semilogical English, we obtain

1. There exists an x such that for any y, x loathes y.
2. For any y, there exists an x such that x loathes y.

These, when formalized, become

1. $\exists x \forall y Lxy$
2. $\forall y \exists x Lxy$

By forcing us to choose one meaning or the other, predicate logic sensitizes us to ambiguities of natural language that might otherwise go unnoticed.

Ambiguity that arises from mixing universal and existential quantifiers in English is called a **quantifier scope ambiguity**. Because English grammar allows much greater flexibility in the placement of quantifiers within a sentence than do the formation rules of predicate logic (which we shall consider in the next section), it has no reliable way of indicating their scope (the part of the sentence they govern). But, as we shall see, the scope of a quantifier in a formula of predicate logic is always definite and clear.

The order of the quantifiers matters, however, only when universal and existential quantifiers are mixed. There is no difference in meaning, for example, between '$\forall x \forall y Lxy$' and '$\forall y \forall x Lxy$'. They both express the thesis of universal loathing: Everything loathes everything.

Two-place predicates do not always represent transitive verbs. Some represent predicate phrases of other sorts. The phrase 'is north of', for example, would typically be formalized as a two-place predicate. We might, for instance, write 'Knoxville is north of Atlanta' as 'Nka'.

Some predicates have three or even more places. The English phrase 'is between' links three names, as in the sentence 'Nashville is between Memphis and Knoxville', which may be written as 'Bnmk'. There is no overall convention governing the order of the names in such cases; what matters is that within a given context we keep the order consistent.

Predicates with two or more places are called **relational** or **polyadic** predicates. Those with only one place are, by contrast, said to be **nonrelational** or **monadic**. Sentence letters are, as we shall see in the next section, sometimes regarded as zero-place predicates.

One final word about formalization: *Keep quantifiers as close as possible to the variables they govern.* This prevents mistakes. Consider, for example, the sentence 'All lovers are happy', which is correctly formalized, using 'L' for 'lovers' and 'H' for 'is happy', as '$\forall x (\exists y Lxy \rightarrow Hx)$'—that is, "for all x, if there exists a y such that x loves y, then x is happy." Here the existential quantifier is inside the brackets, taking the narrowest possible scope—as it should be. (Since the universal quantifier governs the variable 'x', which occurs in both the antecedent and the consequent of the conditional, it must contain the whole conditional within its scope.) Sometimes beginners in predicate logic are tempted to draw the existential quantifier out of the conditional, like this: $\forall x \exists y (Lxy \rightarrow Hx)$. **This is wrong!** What it says is that for any x there exists a y such that if x loves y then x is happy. This, given the meaning of the material conditional, is true in any possible situation in which each x loves nothing. It does not even come close to saying that all lovers are happy.

This mistaken formula exhibits another warning signal that should have prevented us from writing it in the first place. It contains an existentially quantified conditional, and existentially quantified conditionals, as we noted earlier, have meanings so strange that they are virtually never what we intend to say.

Exercise 6.1

Using the following interpretation, formalize the arguments below in predicate logic. (All are valid.)

Names	Sentence Letters	One-Place Predicates	Two-Place Predicates
a — Al	H — happiness is maximized	A — is an act	L — loves
b — Beth		B — is blameworthy	R — respects
c — Carl		G — is good	

(continued)

Names	Sentence Letters	One-Place Predicates	Two-Place Predicates
h — healing s — sleeping t — theft		F — is fortunate J — is just P — is praiseworthy	

1. Beth is fortunate. So is Carl. Therefore both Carl and Beth are fortunate.
2. Theft is not praiseworthy, but blameworthy. Hence theft is blameworthy.
3. Healing is good. So something is good.
4. Healing is a good act. Therefore some acts are good.
5. Everything is good. Consequently theft is good.
6. Theft is not good. Therefore not everything is good.
7. Everything good is praiseworthy. Healing is good. Therefore healing is praiseworthy.
8. All just things are praiseworthy. All praiseworthy things are good. Therefore any just thing is good.
9. Healing is a praiseworthy act. Nothing praiseworthy is blameworthy. Therefore, healing is not blameworthy.
10. Healing is good, but theft is not. Therefore some things are good and some things aren't.
11. Everything is good and everything is just. Therefore everything is both good and just.
12. Either everything is praiseworthy or everything is blameworthy. So everything is either praiseworthy or blameworthy.
13. If everything is good, then happiness is maximized. So, since happiness is not maximized, not everything is good.
14. Not all acts are just. Therefore there are acts that are not just.
15. Not every act is just. Hence some acts are unjust.
16. Some acts are just. Nothing just is blameworthy. Therefore some acts are not blameworthy.
17. If all acts are just, then happiness is maximized. So, if happiness is not maximized, then some acts are not just.
18. Sleeping is an act, but it is not praiseworthy and it is not blameworthy. Therefore some acts are neither praiseworthy nor blameworthy.
19. No acts are both praiseworthy and blameworthy. Theft is a blameworthy act. Therefore theft is not praiseworthy.
20. All acts that are not good are blameworthy. No good acts are blameworthy. Therefore acts are blameworthy if and only if they are not good.
21. If Beth loves and respects Al, then Al is fortunate. But then Beth does not love Al, since Al is not fortunate, though Beth respects him.
22. Although Carl doesn't love Beth, Al does. Therefore Beth is loved.
23. Beth loves everything. Everything loves Beth. It follows that Al loves Beth and Beth loves Al.
24. Al loves both himself and Beth, since everything loves everything.

25. Since Al loves Beth, something loves something.
26. Everything loves itself. Hence Beth and Al both love themselves.
27. Nothing loves anything. So Al loves neither himself nor Beth.
28. Al loves anything that Beth loves. Beth loves Al. Therefore Al loves something.
29. If happiness is maximized, then there is some one thing that loves everything. Carl is unloved. So happiness is not maximized.
30. To love a thing is to respect it. So, since Beth loves Al, Beth respects Al.
31. There is nothing which both Al and Carl love. Al loves Beth. Hence Carl doesn't.
32. All those who love themselves respect themselves. All those who love anything love themselves. Beth loves Al. Therefore Beth respects herself.
33. Beth does not love Al. For Al loves everything if and only if Beth loves Al. And Al does not love Carl.
34. For any two things x and y, if x loves y, then y does not love x. Therefore nothing loves itself.
35. Al respects a thing if and only if it does not respect itself. Ergo, happiness is maximized.

6.2 SYNTAX FOR PREDICATE LOGIC

In this section we formalize the language of predicate logic, as we did for the language of propositional logic in Section 2.3. We begin by listing the character set for predicate logic, which consists of six distinct categories of characters:

Logical operators:[4]	~ & ∨ → ↔ ∀ ∃
Brackets:	( )
Names:	lowercase letters 'a' through 't'
Variables:	lowercase letters 'u' through 'z'
Predicates:	uppercase letters
Numerals:	0 1 2 3 4 5 6 7 8 9

As in propositional logic, the numerals are used for subscripts, which may be added to predicates, names, or variables. Though seldom used in practice, subscripts are needed to ensure that the language contains enough symbols for very complex problems.

An **atomic formula** is a predicate followed by zero or more names. (A predicate followed by zero names is just a sentence letter, as in propositional logic.) If

---

[4] As with the propositional operators, there is some variety in the notation for quantifiers. Sometimes brackets are used so that 'for any x' is written as '$(\forall x)$' and 'for at least one x' as '$(\exists x)$', but the brackets are superfluous. When brackets are used, the symbol '∀' may be omitted so that 'for any x' is written simply as '(x)'.

the number of names following a predicate in an atomic formula is n, then that predicate is an n-place predicate.

As in Section 2.3, we will define the notion of a formula recursively by a set of formation rules. Before stating the rules, however, it will be useful to introduce some new notation into the metalanguage. We will use uppercase Greek letters as usual, to stand for formulas. But from now on these will be used for predicates as well. And we will use lowercase Greek letters—'α', 'β', 'χ', 'δ', and so on—to represent unspecified variables or names.

We sometimes need to describe in a general way the substitution of names or variables for one another within a formula. We might wish, for example, to describe the sort of transformation that turns the formula 'Laa' into the quantified formula '∃xLxa'. The transformation is achieved in this instance by replacing the first 'a' with 'x' and prefixing the result with '∃x'. But to describe this transformation in general (i.e., for other formulas as well as this one) we might say this:

> Let Φ be a formula containing some name α and $\Phi^\beta/_\alpha$ (read "Φ with β replacing α") be the result of replacing one or more occurrences of α in Φ by some variable β not already in Φ. Then transform Φ into $\exists\beta\Phi^\beta/_\alpha$.

With regard to the specific instance given above, α stands for 'a', β for 'x', Φ for 'Laa', $\Phi^\beta/_\alpha$ for 'Lxa', and $\exists\beta\Phi^\beta/_\alpha$ for '∃xLxa'. The Greek, however, enables us to describe this transformation so generally that it could be applied to any formula containing a name. Formation rule 4 uses precisely this transformation to define the construction of grammatically correct quantified formulas. Here is the complete list:

Formation Rules for Predicate Logic

1. Any atomic formula is a formula.
2. If Φ is a formula, so is ~Φ.
3. If Φ and Ψ are formulas, so are (Φ & Ψ), (Φ ∨ Ψ), (Φ → Ψ), and (Φ ↔ Ψ).
4. If Φ is a formula containing a name α, then any expression of the form $\forall\beta\Phi^\beta/_\alpha$ or $\exists\beta\Phi^\beta/_\alpha$ is a formula, where $\Phi^\beta/_\alpha$ is the result of replacing one or more occurrences of α in Φ by some variable β not already in Φ.

Anything that is not a formula by finitely many applications of these rules is not a formula.

Rules 2 and 3 are the same as for propositional logic. Rule 1 expands the corresponding rule of propositional logic, for the class of atomic formulas now includes not only sentence letters but any n-place predicate followed by n names.

As in propositional logic, rule 3 is the only rule that introduces brackets. Brackets, therefore, occur only with binary operators. We retain the convention that outer brackets may be dropped so that instead of '(∃xFx & ∃xGx)', for example, we may write '∃xFx & ∃xGx'. However, the brackets in a formula such as '∃x(Fx & Gx)' are not outer brackets (since the quantifier occurs outside of them) and may not be dropped.

Variables are introduced only by rule 4, and each variable is attached to a particular occurrence of a quantifier. Expressions such as 'Lxx', '∃xLxy', and

'(∃xFx & Gx)' are therefore not formulas. (In the last of these, the variable attached to 'G' has no corresponding quantifier, since the scope of the existential quantifier is just '∃xFx'.)

Moreover, in a formula each variable occurs at least twice—once following its quantifier and at least once again where it has replaced a name. Thus, for example, '∃xLaa' is not a formula, since 'x' does not have a second occurrence.

The phrase 'by some variable β not already in Φ' in rule 4 ensures that quantifiers of the same variable never have overlapping scopes. So, for example, 'Laa' is a formula by formation rule 1, from which it follows by rule 4 that '∃xLxa' is a formula, but we may *not* conclude from this by another application of rule 4 that '∃x∃xLxx' is a formula, since 'x' already occurs in '∃xLxa'. Rule 4 does, however, license the conclusion that '∃y∃xLxy' is a formula, since 'y' does not already occur in '∃xLxa'. Quantifiers of *different* variables, then, may have overlapping scopes.

Two quantifiers of the same variable may occur in the same formula, provided their scopes do not overlap. For example, by formation rule 1, both 'Fa' and 'Gb' are formulas. Applying rule 4 to each of these, we deduce that '∀xFx' and '∃xGx' are both formulas. And then, applying rule 3 to these two, we obtain the conclusion that '(∀xFx & ∃xGx)' is a formula. In this formula there are two quantifiers of 'x', but their scopes do not overlap.

The formation rules are used, as in propositional logic, to verify that formalizations are grammatical—that is, that they make sense in the language of predicate logic. Take, for example, the expression '∃x∀y(Fxy ↔ ~Gx)'. We can see that this is a formula as follows:

'Fab' and 'Ga' are both formulas by formation rule 1. Since 'Ga' is a formula, '~Ga' is a formula by rule 2. But then since 'Fab' and '~Ga' are both formulas, by rule 3 '(Fab ↔ ~Ga)' is a formula. From this it follows by rule 4 that '∀y(Fay ↔ ~Ga)' is a formula, and again by rule 4 that '∃x∀y(Fxy ↔ ~Gx)' is a formula.

Exercise 6.2.1

Some of the expressions below are formulas; others are not. For those that are, tell how they are constructed from the formation rules, as in the example immediately above. For those that are not, explain why they are not.

1. ∀xLxx
2. ∃x∀xLxx
3. ∃aFa
4. ∃xFa
5. ∀x∀y(Lxy ↔ Lyx)
6. (Laa)
7. ~∀x~Fx
8. (∃xFx → ∃xFx)
9. (P → ∃xFx)
10. Lab → Lba

Exercise 6.2.2

Formalize the sentences below, using the indicated interpretation, and check your formalization with the formation rules to make sure that it results in a genuine formula.

Names	One-Place Predicates	Two-Place Predicates
a — Aristotle	F — is a feminist	R — ridicules
n — Nietzsche	G — is Greek	S — is smarter than
p — Plato	P — is a philosopher	W — wrote

1. Aristotle is Greek.
2. Plato is a Greek feminist.
3. If Plato is a feminist, then someone is a Greek feminist.
4. No Greeks are feminists.
5. All feminists are philosophers.
6. All Greek feminists are philosophers.
7. Aristotle wrote something.
8. Aristotle wrote everything.
9. Aristotle wrote nothing.
10. Nietzsche ridicules everything that Plato wrote.
11. Nietzsche ridicules all feminists.
12. Nietzsche ridicules everyone smarter than he is.
13. Some Greeks are philosophers and some are not.
14. Some Greeks both are and are not philosophers.
15. Nietzsche ridicules a thing if and only if it does not ridicule itself.
16. Some philosophers ridicule themselves.
17. Some philosophers ridicule everything.
18. All things that are ridiculed ridicule their ridiculers.
19. If one thing is smarter than a second, then the second is not smarter than the first.
20. Nietzsche ridicules all Greek philosophers.

6.3 IDENTITY

Another logical operator which is often employed in predicate logic is '=', a symbol familiar from mathematics. But unlike any logical operator we have so far considered, '=' is a predicate—a two-place predicate, to be precise. What makes it a logical operator, rather than an ordinary predicate, like 'F' or 'L', is that its meaning is fixed. It always means "is identical to" or "is the same thing as," whereas other predicates are interpreted to mean different things in different contexts. Also, in deference to custom, it is written between the two names to which it applies, rather than before them as with other two-place predicates. But this syntactic arrangement may create some confusion when identities are negated. For example, let 'a' stand for 'Alice' and 'b' for 'Bob'. Then the formula '~a = b' means "Alice is not Bob." Beginners sometimes mistakenly read this as saying "not-Alice is identical to Bob," but this misconstrues the scope of the negation operator. As with any atomic formula, the negation operator's scope extends over the entire formula. Besides, what on earth is not-Alice?

To avoid this misreading, some authors introduce brackets around the identity formula, like this: ~(a=b). But this requires more writing and further differentiates '=' from other two-place predicates. Another solution, often used in mathematics, is to abbreviate '~a = b' as 'a ≠ b', but this has the disadvantage of obscuring logical form. The double negation of 'a = b', for example, becomes '~a ≠ b', which no longer looks like a double negation and, moreover, invites the same sorts of misreadings that '~a = b' does. We shall therefore use neither the brackets nor the slash in our object language, though we shall sometimes use '≠' in the metalanguage.

In adding the identity predicate to our language, we need to modify our definition of atomic formulas. That definition should now read:

> Any predicate followed by zero or more names or any formula of the form α = β, where α and β are names, is an **atomic formula.**

The formation rules then remain the same. The identity predicate in combination with the other operators enables us to express a wealth of new concepts.

Else, Other Than, Except: The expressions 'else', 'other than', and 'except' often express the idea of difference, that is, nonidentity. The statement 'God is more perfect than anything else', for example, can be symbolized as '∀x(~x = g → Pgx)', reading 'g' as "God" and 'P' as "more perfect than". Notice that the statement 'God is more perfect than anything', '∀xPgx', is absurd, since it implies that God is more perfect than himself, that is, 'Pgg'. The notion that God is more perfect than anything else is inexpressible without the identity predicate.

The terms 'other than' and 'except' work similarly. The statement 'Al will go with anyone other than Beth', for example, may be symbolized as '∀x(~x = b → Gax)'. This formula may also symbolize the sentence 'Al will go with anyone except Beth'. 'Except', however, often carries an implication of exclusion so that 'Al will go with anyone *except* Beth' may mean not only that Al will go with anyone who is not Beth, but also that Al will not go with Beth. If so, then a better formalization is '∀x(~x = b → Gax) & ~Gab'—or, more compactly, '∀x(~x = b ↔ Gax)'. [This compact formulation is equivalent to the first, since '~Gab' is equivalent to '∀x(Gax → ~x = b)'.] This might even be what is meant in some contexts by the sentence 'Al will go with anyone *other than* Beth'. But neither 'other than' nor 'except' always carries this implication of exclusion. If, for example, we know that Al will go with anyone who is not Beth but are unsure of whether he would go with Beth, we might still say, "Al will go with anyone except Beth," without thereby committing ourselves on the question of whether he will go with Beth. English uses of 'except' and 'other than' are thus potentially ambiguous.

'Else', 'other than', and 'except' can also be applied to more than one individual. The sentence 'Everyone except Al and Beth is happy', for example, may be represented as '$\forall x((\sim x = a \ \& \sim x = b) \rightarrow Hx)$'—or, if it is meant to assert that Al and Beth are not happy, as '$\forall x((\sim x = a \ \& \sim x = b) \rightarrow Hx) \ \& \ (\sim Ha \ \& \sim Hb)$', which, in most compact terms, is '$\forall x((\sim x = a \ \& \sim x = b) \leftrightarrow Hx)$'.

Superlatives.   Expressions such as 'the greatest', 'the fastest', 'the most expensive', 'the most perfect', and so on are called **superlatives.** They are used to denote the highest degree of a comparative quality. The comparative expressions associated with the superlatives just mentioned are, respectively, 'greater', 'faster', 'more expensive', and 'more perfect'. Superlatives can be analyzed in terms of comparatives together with the identity predicate. To say that Al is the fastest runner, for example, is to say that Al is faster than all *other* runners—that Al is a runner who is faster than all runners who are not Al. Using 'a' for 'Al', 'R' for 'is a runner', and 'F' for 'is faster than', this goes over into predicate logic as '$Ra \ \& \ \forall x((Rx \ \& \sim x = a) \rightarrow Fax)$'. Other statements containing superlatives may be analyzed similarly. The statement 'There is no largest number', for example, may be written as '$\sim \exists x(Nx \ \& \ \forall y((Ny \ \& \sim y = x) \rightarrow Lxy))$', reading 'is a number' for 'N' and 'is larger than' for 'L'.

Only.   Etymologically, 'only' is a contraction of 'onely'. To say that a particular individual has a certain property *onely* is to say that it alone has that property—that anything that has that property is identical with it. Thus the statement 'Only Al is happy' may be formalized as '$Ha \ \& \ \forall x(Hx \rightarrow x = a)$'—or, more compactly, as '$\forall x(Hx \leftrightarrow x = a)$'. 'Only' is tricky with multiple individuals. It might seem that we could formalize 'Only Al and Beth are happy' as '$\forall x(Hx \leftrightarrow (x = a \ \& \ x = b))$', but this says that a thing is happy if and only if it is *both* Al and Beth. If Al and Beth are different individuals, this is absurd. What is really meant is '$\forall x(Hx \leftrightarrow (x = a \lor x = b))$', but we are misled because in English we say 'and' instead of 'or'.

At Least.   Since the existential quantifier means 'for at least one', the formalization of the expression 'at least one' is simple. The statement 'There is at least one mind', for example, is formalized as '$\exists x Mx$', where 'M' means "is a mind." But what about 'There are at least two minds'? An obvious suggestion is '$\exists x \exists y(Mx \ \& \ My)$'. This, however, will not do, because nothing guarantees that the variables 'x' and 'y' designate different objects. In fact, this is just a redundant way of saying $\exists x Mx$; the two formulas are equivalent. To guarantee that x and y are distinct, we need to say so. A proper formalization is '$\exists x \exists y((Mx \ \& \ My) \ \& \sim x = y)$'. Similarly, we can formalize 'There are at least three minds' as '$\exists x \exists y \exists z(((Mx \ \& \ My) \ \& \ Mz) \ \& \ ((\sim x = y \ \& \sim y = z) \ \& \sim x = z))$', and so on.

At Most.   Suppose we want to say that there is at most one mind. This means that no two distinct things are minds; that is, if we choose any object x and any object y and they turn out both to be minds, then they are identical. Thus one way to formalize this statement is '$\forall x \forall y((Mx \;\&\; My) \rightarrow x = y)$'. Another way to go at it is to notice that 'There is at most one mind' is the denial of 'There are at least two minds'. This produces the formalization '$\sim\exists x \exists y((Mx \;\&\; My) \;\&\; \sim x = y)$'. The two formalizations are equivalent and equally correct.

But both formalizations are ungainly for formalizing 'at most' with numbers larger than one. 'There are at most two minds', for example, is '$\forall x \forall y \forall z((Mx \;\&\; My) \;\&\; Mz) \rightarrow ((x = y \lor y = z) \lor x = z))$' by analogy with the first method, '$\sim\exists x \exists y \exists z(((Mx \;\&\; My) \;\&\; Mz) \;\&\; ((\sim x = y \;\&\; \sim y = z) \;\&\; \sim x = z))$' by analogy with the second. The first formula says that for any things x, y, and z that are minds, at least two of them are identical. The second says that there do not exist three distinct minds.

A simpler and more subtle formalization of 'There are at most two minds' is '$\exists x \exists y \forall z(Mz \rightarrow (z = x \lor z = y))$'. That is, there are objects x and y such that anything that is a mind is one of these. This does not assert that x and y are distinct (so they might be the same thing), nor does it assert that they are minds (only that *if* there are minds, then they are identical with either x or y). Thus it is compatible with there being one mind or no minds, as well as two. But it is not compatible with there being three, since it asserts that every mind is one or the other of x or y. It is thus equivalent to both of our earlier formulations of 'There are at most two minds'.

Using this more subtle formalization scheme, 'There is at most one mind' is simply '$\exists x \forall y(My \rightarrow y = x)$', and 'There are at most three minds' is '$\exists x \exists y \exists z \forall w(Mw \rightarrow ((w = x \lor w = y) \lor w = z))$'. This is the simplest way to express 'at most' in predicate logic.

We can also say there is at most one *thing*—where 'thing' is not a predicate but a place-holder for a variable. (Certain mystics hold something like this.) One simple formalization is '$\exists x \forall y \; y = x$'. Can you think of others?

Numerical Quantifiers. How can we say there is *exactly* one mind? This means that there is at least one mind and at most one mind so that one formalization is '$\exists x Mx \;\&\; \exists x \forall y(My \rightarrow y = x)$'. A more compact way of saying the same thing is '$\exists x \forall y(My \leftrightarrow y = x)$'. This combines into a single quantified biconditional the statement 'there is at least one mind'—which is normally just '$\exists x Mx$' but may be equivalently written as '$\exists x \forall y(y = x \rightarrow My)$'—and 'there is at most one mind'—'$\exists x \forall y(My \rightarrow y = x)$'.

Generalizing, we may formalize 'There are exactly two minds' as '$\exists x \exists y(\sim x = y \;\&\; \forall z(Mz \leftrightarrow (z = x \lor z = y)))$'. This formula says that there are two distinct objects x and y and that a thing is a mind if and only if it is identical to one of these. 'There are exactly three minds' is '$\exists x \exists y \exists z(((\sim x = y \;\&\; \sim y = z) \;\&\; \sim x = z) \;\&\; \forall w(Mw \leftrightarrow ((w = x \lor w = y) \lor w = z)))$'—and so on. In this way we can formalize **numerical quantifiers**, which are phrases of the form 'there are exactly n ...', where 'n' stands for a number.

Russell's Theory of Definite Descriptions. France is no longer a monarchy. What, then, are we to make of the sentence 'The present king of France is bald'? Is it true or false—and what makes it so? Bertrand Russell's consideration of this and similar examples led him early in this century to the theory of descriptions that bears his name and still stands out as a paradigm of logical analysis. A **definite description,** according to Russell, is a phrase of the form 'the so-and-so'. Examples are 'the present king of France', 'the positive square root of two', 'the supreme being', and 'the woman I met last week'.

Russell's quarry was the logical form of sentences containing definite descriptions. Superficially, a sentence like 'The present king of France is bald' seems to be of subject-predicate form, with the definite description 'the present king of France' functioning as a name. Thus we might symbolize it as 'Bk', where 'B' means "is bald" and 'k' means "the present king of France." But difficulties ensue, for if 'the present king of France' is a name, what does it name, and what determines whether or not what it names is bald? These questions lead into dim metaphysics. (What sort of entity *is* the present king of France, anyway?)

Logical paradox is not far behind. Presumably the statement 'The present king of France is bald' is false—from which it follows that 'The present king of France is not bald', that is, '~Bk' is true. But there is no present king of France of whom it can be said that he is not bald. Hence 'The present king of France is not bald' also seems false. Is '~Bk', then, both true and false?

The problem, according to Russell, lies in thinking that the logical form of 'The present king of France is bald' is 'Bk'. Definite descriptions, he argues, are not simple names; sentences containing them have a logical structure quite different from their surface grammar. A statement of the form 'The F is G' means

1. There is at least one F, and
2. it alone is F, and
3. it is G.

In symbols this is

$$\exists x((Fx \ \& \ \forall y(Fy \to y = x)) \ \& \ Gx)^5$$

Applied to the statement 'The present king of France is bald', Russell's analysis dissolves the purported name 'k' into a complex of logical relationships involving the one-place predicate 'is presently king of France'. Using 'K' to represent this predicate and 'B' for 'is bald', this statement becomes

(A) $\exists x((Kx \ \& \ \forall y(Ky \to y = x)) \ \& \ Bx)$

Translating back into English we get

1. There is at least one thing which is presently king of France,
2. it alone is presently king of France, and
3. it is bald.

---

[5] We could compress this to '$\exists x(\forall y(Fy \leftrightarrow y = x) \ \& \ Gx)$', but we shall stick with the formulation above—which is Russell's—because it is the most widely used.

This, as we expect, is false, since the first conjunct claims falsely that there is a present king of France. Since (A) is false, its negation,

(B) $\sim\exists x((Kx \ \& \ \forall y(Ky \rightarrow y = x)) \ \& \ Bx)$,

that is,

(i) It is not the case that there is at least one present king of France, who alone is presently king of France, and who is bald,

is true. This accounts for the intuition that 'The present king of France is not bald' is true. But what of the intuition that this same sentence is false? That is also right, according to Russell! For the sentence is ambiguous; it can also mean

(ii) There is at least one present king of France, who alone is presently king of France, and who is not bald,

that is, in symbols:

(C) $\exists x((Kx \ \& \ \forall y(Ky \rightarrow y = x)) \ \& \ \sim Bx)$

Statement (ii) and its formalization (C) are both false for the same reason that (A) is: There is no present king of France. The difference between (B) and (C) lies in the scope of the negation operator. The ambiguity is therefore a matter of scope, like the ambiguities that arise from the mixing of universal and existential quantifiers in English. Formalization reveals the ambiguity and untangles conflicting intuitions; the English sentence that appears to be both true and false is from a logical point of view really two sentences. What troubled us, then, was merely a grammatical illusion.

In summary, Russell shows how certain sentences containing expressions that seem to refer to nonexistent entities can be analyzed into formulas containing only well-understood quantifiers and predicates. This both dispels logical paradox and forestalls a metaphysical snipe hunt.

Exercise 6.3

Formalize each of the following arguments using the interpretation indicated below. The arguments, by the way, are all valid.

Names	One-Place Predicates	Two-Place Predicates
a — Al	C — is a carpenter	B — is a brother of
b — Bud	D — is a doctor	L — loves
c — Cindy	H — is happy	R — is richer than
d — Deb	S — is a smoker	
e — Ed	W — writes novels	

1. Bud is Al. Therefore, if Bud is a carpenter, so is Al.
2. Al and Bud are identical, but Al is not Cindy. So Cindy is not Bud.
3. Al is Bud. So Bud is Al.
4. Al is not Al. Hence Cindy is a carpenter who writes novels.
5. Al is a brother of Cindy's. Cindy is not one of Al's brothers. Therefore Al is not Cindy.
6. Since Al is a carpenter and Cindy is not, at least two things exist.
7. Cindy's only brother is Al. Ed writes novels. Al doesn't. So Ed isn't a brother of Cindy's.
8. Everything except Al loves Cindy. Therefore Ed loves Cindy, since Al is a carpenter, but Ed isn't.
9. Al loves Cindy, but really the only thing one loves is oneself. It follows that Cindy loves Al.
10. If one thing is richer than a second, then the two are not identical. Therefore nothing is richer than itself.
11. Cindy is the richest doctor. Deb is a doctor. Therefore, unless Cindy is Deb, Cindy is richer than Deb.
12. There is at most one thing. Hence Al and Bud are one and the same thing.
13. There are at most two things. Something other than Cindy is happy. Therefore there are exactly two things.
14. All who are loved are happy. Something that is unhappy loves Al. So Al is not the only thing that exists.
15. Only Al and Ed love Cindy. Cindy loves Al but not Ed. Cindy is loved only by her brothers. Therefore Cindy has exactly two brothers.
16. Except for Cindy and Bud, everything is happy. Al is unhappy. Hence Al is either Cindy or Bud.

(Hint: The remaining problems all use Russell's theory of descriptions.)

17. The brother of Cindy is happy. Therefore Cindy has a brother.
18. Al is the only one who writes novels. Al is happy. Therefore the writer of novels is happy.
19. Al is one of Cindy's brothers and he is happy. Ed is one of Cindy's brothers and he is not happy. Therefore it is not true that the brother of Cindy is happy.
20. The doctor is a nonsmoker. Therefore it is not the case that the doctor is a smoker.

6.4 FUNCTIONS

An *n*-place predicate is an expression which forms a sentence when applied to *n* names. But in both natural and mathematical languages there are expressions which form names when applied to names. These expressions are **function symbols**. Like predicates, function symbols may apply to one name or to many. There are even zero-place function symbols, but these are just names themselves.

Consider, for example, the English expression 'the father of'. When prefixed to the name of a person, this expression produces a new name that denotes a different person. If, for example, we prefix it to the name 'Martin Luther King, Jr.' to produce the expression 'the father of Martin Luther King, Jr.', this new expression is a complex name denoting the individual Martin Luther King, Sr. 'The father of' is a one-place function symbol.

Or, to take a different example, consider the expression 'the sum of . . . and . . .', which is represented in mathematics by the symbol '+'. Applied to the names of two numbers, this symbol produces a complex name which denotes a third number. Thus the expression 'the sum of two and three'—or in mathematical notation '2 + 3'—is a complex name for the number five. Thus either expression—'the sum of . . . and . . .' or '+'—is a two-place function symbol.

In both natural and formal languages functional notation is quite varied. Some function symbols are written before the names to which they apply. An example is the mathematical symbol '−', used as a one-place function to mean "negative." Such function symbols are said to be written in **prefix** position. Other function symbols, such as '¢' (which, when applied to a numeral, yields the name of a price in cents), are written after the names to which they apply; these are said to be written in **postfix** position. Two-place function symbols, like '+', are often written in **infix** position—that is, between the names to which they apply.

The objects denoted by the names to which a function symbol is applied on a specific occasion are called **arguments** of the function.[6] The object denoted by the complex symbol consisting of the function symbol and the names to which it applies is called the **value** of the function. Thus for the expression '2 + 3' the arguments are 2 and 3 (in that order) and the value is 5.

Corresponding to each function symbol is a **domain** of objects to which the symbol applies and a **range** of objects which the resulting complex names denote. The domain is the set of possible arguments and the range the set of possible values. The domain of the expression 'the father of' is the set of all sons and daughters; its range is the set of all fathers. The domain of '+' is the set of all pairs of numbers; its range is the set of all numbers.

The range and domain may contain very different sorts of objects. For example, the expression 'the birthday of' is a one-place function symbol which when applied to the name of a person produces a complex expression that names a date. Thus its range is the set of people and its domain is a set of dates. Here are some examples of function symbols, along with the kinds of objects that constitute their domains and ranges:

Function Symbol	Number of Places	Domain	Range
the mother of	1	children	mothers
the square of	1	numbers	numbers

(continued)

---

[6] This is a wholly new use of the term 'argument'. It has nothing to do with the by now familiar use, according to which an argument is a set of premises together with a conclusion.

Function Symbol	Number of Places	Domain	Range
¢	1	numbers	prices
the prime factors of	1	positive whole numbers	sets of prime numbers
the midpoint between . . . and . . .	2	pairs of points	points
× (the product of . . . and . . .)	2	pairs of numbers	numbers

Perhaps the most important thing to remember about function symbols is this: *An expression counts as a function symbol only if it has a unique denotation for every object in its domain.* The expression 'the child of' is not a function symbol over the domain of people because some people have no children and some have more than one; hence, when prefixed to the name of a person, this expression does not always produce a uniquely referring name. The expression 'the child of' is a function symbol, however, relative to the domain of parents who have one and only one child. If prefixed to the name of any person in that domain, it does produce a uniquely referring name. Or, to take another example, the familiar arithmetic operators '+', '−' (used to indicate subtraction), and '×' (multiplication) are all two-place function symbols (provided, in the case of subtraction, that negative numbers are included in the range). But '/' (the division sign) is not a function symbol, for the expression '1/0', for example, is denotationless, since division by zero is undefined.

The domains of the function symbols we shall consider here will always be the same as the domain of quantification—that is, the domain of the particular valuation we are considering (see Section 7.2). For this reason, we will accept as function symbols only expressions which when applied to the name of a member of this domain yield a complex name that refers to a member of that domain. We shall not consider function symbols like 'the birthday of', whose ranges are not included in their domains.

We shall take as function symbols the same letters we use for names—lowercase letters 'a' through 't'. These are always written before the names of their arguments, which are surrounded by small brackets. Multiple argument names are separated by commas. Thus, for example, if 'f' means "the father of" and 'a' means "Alice", then 'f(a)' is a complex name meaning "the father of Alice." Likewise, if 'm' means "the midpoint between" and 'a' and 'b' denote points, then 'm(a,b)' means "the midpoint between a and b."

The arguments of function symbols may be quantified. So, for example, where 'm' means "is the mother of", the sentence 'Everyone loves their mother' may be symbolized as

$\forall x L x m(x)$

which, literally transcribed, means "For all x, x loves the mother of x." (We here assume a domain of people.) Here are some further examples, using 'm' for 'the mother of', 'L' for 'loves', and 'o' for 'Olaf':

Sentence	Formalization
Olaf loves his mother.	Lom(o)
Olaf loves his maternal grandmother.	Lom(m(o))
Olaf loves someone's mother.	$\exists x$Lom(x)
Olaf's maternal grandmother loves his mother.	Lm(m(o))m(o)
Nobody is his/her own mother.	~$\exists x\ x$ = m(x)

When adding function symbols to predicate logic, we must again modify our definition of a name. Instead of defining a name simply as any lowercase letter 'a' through 't', we give the following recursive definition, which allows the complex names formed by function symbols to count officially as names:

1. Any lowercase letter 'a' through 't' is a name.
2. If ϕ is an n-place function symbol and $\alpha_1, \ldots, \alpha_n$ are names, then $\phi(\alpha_1, \ldots, \alpha_n)$ is a name.

Anything not obtainable by repeated application of clauses 1 and 2 is not a name. The recursiveness of this definition allows us to construct names in which other names are nested, as in some of the preceding examples. The formation rules and other definitions remain the same.

Exercise 6.4

Translate the following arguments into predicate logic with functions. Assume that the domain of discourse is the set of nonnegative integers $\{0, 1, 2, \ldots\}$. (All of these arguments are valid—and sound!)

Name	One-Place Function Symbols	Two-Place Function Symbols	One-Place Predicates	Two-Place Predicates
o — zero	f — the square of	p — the product of (i.e., "times")	E — is even	G — is greater than
i — one	s — the successor of (i.e., the next number after)		O — is odd	L — is less than

1. The square of zero is even. Therefore something is even.
2. The square of one is odd. Therefore the square of something is odd.
3. Zero times the successor of zero is zero. The successor of zero is one. One is odd. Therefore there is an odd number whose product with zero is zero.

4. The successor of any odd number is even. One is odd. Therefore the successor of one is even.

5. For any two numbers x and y, the product of x and y equals the product of y and x. The product of zero and any number is zero. Therefore the product of any number and zero is zero.

6. The square of any number is its product with itself. Zero times any number is zero. Therefore the square of zero is zero.

7. For any two numbers, the first is greater than the second if and only if the second is less than the first. The successor of a number is greater than that number. Therefore every number is less than its successor.

8. The successor of zero does not equal the successor of the successor of zero. Hence zero does not equal the successor of zero.

9. Every number is distinct from its successor. Thus there are at least two things.

10. One is the square of one. One is odd. No odd numbers are even. Therefore not all square numbers are even.

11. Zero is even. So every number has a successor.

12. Since any number's successor is greater than that number, there is no greatest number. For no number is its own successor, and if one number is greater than another, the second is not greater than the first.

CHAPTER 7

CLASSICAL PREDICATE LOGIC: SEMANTICS

This chapter introduces the classical semantics and the tree test for predicate logic. As a preliminary, however, we begin with a little elementary set theory, since set theory is the basis for the semantics.

7.1 SETS AND *n*-TUPLES

To understand the semantics of predicate logic, it is necessary to know a bit about sets. This section provides only that bit. It is not a general introduction to set theory.[1]

A **set** is a multiplicity of objects considered without regard to order or repetition. Small sets are usually represented by listing the names of the objects that comprise them (their **members**), separated by commas and surrounded by curly brackets. Thus, for example, the set consisting of the numbers one, two, and three is represented by the notation '{1, 2, 3}'.

To say that a set is a multiplicity considered *without regard to order* means, for example, that the set {2, 1, 3} is the same set as the set {1, 2, 3}—that is, {2, 1, 3} = {1, 2, 3}. In other words, the order in which the names are listed does not matter. To say that the objects are considered *without regard to repetition* means that repeated names are superfluous. Thus, for example, the set {1, 2, 2, 1, 3} is identical to the set {1, 2, 3}. In general, sets with the same members, regardless of how those members are listed, are identical.

---

[1] One of the best introductions to elementary set theory is Robert R. Stoll, *Set Theory and Logic* (San Francisco: W. H. Freeman, 1961).

Set identity is also insensitive to the ways in which the members of the sets are described or named. So, for example, the set {2, 5} is the same set as the set {1 + 1, 5}. The fact that the number two is described in two different ways makes no difference to the set.

It is, we should admit, a bit misleading to say that a set is a multiplicity of objects, since in some cases a set has only one member and in one case—the empty or null set—it has none. Sets with only one member are called **unit sets** or **singletons**. The set {Socrates}, for example, is the unit set of Socrates—that is, the set whose sole member is Socrates. However, {Socrates} and Socrates are not the same. The former is a set, the latter an Athenian philosopher. The former has one member, Socrates; but Socrates—who is an individual, not a set—has no members in the set-theoretic sense.

We shall use the obvious notation '{ }' to designate the empty set, though often '∅' or 'Λ' are used. Since sets having the same members are identical, there is only one empty set—for any two empty sets, having the same members (i.e., no members at all), must be identical.

The lowercase Greek letter epsilon, 'ε', is used in set theory to mean "is a member of." Thus '1 ε {1, 2, 3}' and 'Socrates ε {Socrates}' are true statements, but '0 ε {1, 2, 3}' and 'Socrates ε { }' are false. In general, to indicate that it is not the case that A ε B, we may write 'A ∉ B'.

Sets may contain other sets. The set {{1, 2}, {3}}, for example, has two members, the sets {1, 2} and {3}. Thus {1, 2} ε {{1, 2}, {3}} and {3} ε {{1, 2}, {3}}, but, for example, 1 ∉ {{1, 2}, {3}}, though 1ε {1, 2}.

Sets which are infinite or too big to specify as lists may usually be defined by one-place predicate phrases. For example, the set of all mathematicians is defined by the phrase 'is a mathematician'. For this, it is common to use the notation '{x|x is a mathematician}', which is read as "the set of all x such that x is a mathematician." Thus, for example, since Descartes is a mathematician, the statement 'Descartes ε {x|x is a mathematician}' is true.

Another way to specify infinite sets, if their members have a natural order, is to list the first few members within curly brackets and follow them with three dots, indicating that the list is to be continued infinitely. Thus, for example, we may denote the set of all natural numbers (whole numbers greater than 0) either as '{x|x is a natural number}' or as '{1, 2, 3, . . .}'. However, in the second case the ordering serves only as a convenient way to indicate which objects we are talking about. It does not mean that the integers are ordered within the set.

If we wish to consider *ordered* lists (provided these are finite), we shall use instead the concept of an *n*-tuple. The simplest example of an *n*-tuple is an ordered pair. An **ordered pair** is (unsurprisingly) a pair of objects taken in a certain order, but without regard to how the objects are described. For example, the ordered pair consisting of the numbers one and two, in that order, is different from the ordered pair consisting of the numbers two and one, in that order. We denote ordered pairs by listing their members in order and separated by commas in between angle brackets. Thus the first of these pairs is <1, 2> and the second is <2, 1>.

The manner of description of the objects makes no difference to the identity of the pair. So, for example, given that $x = \sqrt{2}$, <1, x^2> is the same pair as <1, 2>.

In addition to ordered pairs, there are ordered triples, ordered quadruples, and so on. In general, ordered lists of *n* items are called ordered ***n*-tuples.** There are also ordered one-tuples, but only in a trivial sense, since there is no order to consider when there is only one item. Ordered one-tuples, unlike unit sets, are the same thing as the object they contain. Thus, for example, <Socrates> = Socrates; and, more generally, for any object x, $<x> = x$.

Repetition matters with ordered *n*-tuples. The pair <1, 1>, for example, is not the same as the triple <1, 1, 1>; the former is a list of two items, the latter of three.

A set of ordered *n*-tuples, for some specific *n*, is an ***n*-place relation.** For example, this infinite set of ordered pairs of natural numbers

$$\{<1, 2>, <2, 3>, <3, 4>, <4, 5>, \ldots\}$$

is a two-place relation. It is called the **successor** relation on the natural numbers, since it contains all pairs of natural numbers such that the second item of each pair is the number that comes after, or succeeds, the first.

Here is another infinite two-place relation on natural numbers:

$$\{<1, 2>, <1, 3>, <2, 3>, <1, 4>, <2, 4>, <3, 4>, \ldots\}$$

This one is the **less-than** relation, since it is the set of all pairs of natural numbers such that the first item in the pair is less than the second.

Or, to take yet another example, this finite set of ordered triples of truth values is a three-place relation:

$$\{<T, T, T>, <T, F, F>, <F, T, F>, <F, F, F>\}$$

It is the set of all triples of truth values such that the third item of each pair is the truth value of any conjunction whose two conjuncts have, respectively, the first two items as values. We may therefore think of this three-place relation as the conjunction relation.

There are also nameless random or arbitrary relations, such as this three-place relation on the natural numbers:

$$\{<1, 147, 3>, <3, 3, 2>, <82, 9, 1>\}$$

Relations may be null, in which case they are just the empty set. For example, the two-place both-less-than-and-greater-than relation on the natural numbers is null, since there is no pair of natural numbers such that the first item in the pair is both less than and greater than the second item.

Exercise 7.1

Tell which of the following statements are true and which are false, and explain why.

1. $\{1, 2\} = \{2, 1\}$
2. $\{1, 2\} = \{2, 1, 2\}$
3. $\{1\} = 1$
4. $<1, 2> = <2, 1>$

5. $<1, 1> = 1$
6. If $x = 1$, then $\{1, x\} = \{1\}$.
7. If $x = 1$, then $<1, x> = <x, x>$.
8. $1 \, \varepsilon \, \{1\}$
9. $<1, 2> \, \varepsilon \, \{<1, 2>, <2, 4>\}$
10. $1 \, \varepsilon \, \{<1, 2>, <2, 4>\}$
11. $\{x|x=1\} = \{1\}$
12. $1 \, \varepsilon \, \{x|x \text{ is a number}\}$
13. $\{1, 2\} \, \varepsilon \, \{x|x \text{ is a number}\}$
14. $\{<2, 3>\}$ is a two-place relation.
15. $\{<1>, <2>\} = \{1, 2\}$

7.2 SEMANTICS FOR PREDICATE LOGIC

In laying out the semantics for propositional logic, we assumed that the logical meaning of a term is given by the truth conditions for sentences containing it. We retain that assumption here. Therefore our task in this section is to describe truth conditions for sentences containing names, predicates, and quantifiers.

We shall divide this task into three components: first, an informal description of the semantics of predicate logic; second, an informal account of two kinds of interpretations for this semantics; and finally a detailed formal presentation of the semantics.

We begin our informal description of the semantics with a look at simple subject-predicate sentences. Take the sentence 'Bertrand [Russell] is a philosopher', which we may symbolize as 'Pb'. The following points seem fairly obvious:

1. The name 'Bertrand' denotes an individual object: the man Bertrand Russell.
2. The predicate 'is a philosopher' in effect denotes a set: the set of all philosophers.
3. The sentence 'Bertrand is a philosopher' is true in a given situation if and only if the object denoted by the name in that situation is a member of the set denoted by the predicate in that situation.

Since Bertrand is in the actual situation a member of the set of all philosophers, principle 3 implies (correctly) that the sentence 'Bertrand is a philosopher' is actually true. But we are talking here of the English sentence. What of the corresponding formula 'Pb'?

In propositional logic, the sentence letters have no truth value of their own but are assigned various truth values on various valuations. Moreover, their interpretation is not fixed but varies from problem to problem. We specify an interpretation by associating sentence letters with ordinary statements. A valuation and an intepretation together define a possible situation.

The same thing is true in predicate logic, but valuations and interpretations are somewhat more complex, for, like sentence letters, the names and predicates of predicate logic have no values on their own and (except for the identity predicate) no fixed interpretation. Their values are assigned by a valuation. But these values cannot be truth values, for predicates and names are neither true nor false. Rather, as items 1 and 2 above suggest, the value of a name is an object and the value of a one-place predicate is a set. Hence a valuation for predicate logic assigns objects to names and sets of objects to one-place predicates.

The set assigned to a one-place predicate may be empty. For example, the predicate phrase 'is an even prime number other than 2' applies to nothing at all and hence denotes the empty set. Thus, if we wanted to represent this predicate phrase by a corresponding predicate in predicate logic, we would assign to that predicate the empty set.

As item 3 suggests, a valuation for predicate logic assigns truth conditions of the following sort to simple subject-predicate sentences:

> A formula consisting of a one-place predicate followed by a name is true on a given valuation if and only if the value assigned to that name (the object denoted by the name) on that valuation is a member of the value assigned to the predicate (the set denoted by the predicate) on that valuation.

The truth conditions for atomic formulas containing predicates of more than one place (relational predicates) are only slightly more complex. Consider the relational predicate 'was a teacher of'. This predicate is true of just those pairs of individuals such that the first was a teacher of the second. So, for example, it is true of <Socrates, Plato>, but not of <Plato, Socrates>, since Socrates was Plato's teacher, but not vice versa. If we suppose that Socrates was his own teacher, this predicate is also true of the pair <Socrates, Socrates>. In general, then, a two-place predicate denotes a set, not of individuals, but of ordered pairs of individuals— that is, a two-place relation.

Accordingly, a valuation for predicate logic assigns to each two-place predicate a two-place relation. And the truth conditions for such a sentence look something like this:

> A formula consisting of a two-place predicate followed by two names is true on a given valuation if and only if the pair consisting of the values assigned to those names (the objects they denote) in the order of the names' occurrence is a member of the value assigned to the predicate (the set of ordered pairs of individuals it denotes) on that valuation.

What has just been said of two-place predicates can be generalized to all relational predicates. To each three-place predicate a valuation assigns a set of ordered triples, to each four-place predicate a set of ordered quadruples, and so on—and the truth conditions for sentences formed from these more complex relational predicates function analogously.

Like one-place predicates, relational predicates may be empty. If we assign the empty set to a relational predicate, that indicates that nothing in the domain has the corresponding relation to anything. If the predicate means "loves," for example, assigning it the empty set means contemplating a loveless situation.

Unlike ordinary two-place predicates, the two-place identity predicate '=' has an unvarying interpretation. It always denotes an **identity relation:** the set of all pairs of the form $\langle d, d \rangle$, where d is a member of the valuation's domain (the notion of a domain is introduced below). But it comes to the same thing to think of the identity predicate as forming a true sentence whenever the names flanking it denote the same object, and a false sentence otherwise. That is how we shall express the truth conditions for the identity predicate in the valuation rules below.

Zero-place predicates (sentence letters) are treated exactly as in propositional logic; a valuation assigns to a zero-place predicate a truth value. Valuations in predicate logic thus include the valuations of propositional logic, while going beyond them.

That brings us to quantifiers. Consider the sentence 'Everything is messy'. Using the predicate 'M' for 'is messy', we can symbolize it as '$\forall x Mx$', but this is highly ambiguous. Just what is meant by 'everything'? Uttered by a parent upon entering a child's room, the sentence may refer to the room's contents. Uttered by a corporate accountant, it may refer to all aspects of the corporation's finances. Uttered by an environmentalist, it may denote contents of the biosphere. Uttered by a cosmologist, it may characterize reality at large. Thus 'everything' has different meanings in different contexts. Context, in other words, determines the **universe** or **domain** of the discourse for ordinary language.

Now our aim is to formulate the truth conditions for quantified statements—that is, to characterize the possible situations in which these statements are true and those in which they are false. And we have begun to see that to define situations sharply enough to state these truth conditions, we must say exactly which objects are involved in those situations; we must, in other words, specify their domains.

Suppose that we take the domain of the statement 'Everything is messy' to be the objects in a certain child's room. This statement's meaning is now clear: Each object in the room is messy. (This might be the case, for example, if the child has decorated each object in the room with peanut butter.) Now, to keep things simple, let's suppose further that the child's room contains only four objects: Dolly, Bear, Truck, and Ball. Then, assuming that these constitute the domain for a given situation, the statement 'Everything is messy' is true in that situation if and only if in it each of the following statements is true:

Dolly is messy.

Bear is messy.

Truck is messy.

Ball is messy.

Correlatively, 'Everything is messy' is untrue in a situation with the same domain if and only if at least one of these four statements is untrue.

Valuations in predicate logic, then, not only must assign values to names and predicates; but in addition, as this example illustrates, they must specify the domain of discourse over which the quantifiers are to be interpreted.

This domain figures into the truth conditions for the existential as well as for the universal quantifier. The existentially quantified statement 'Something is messy', for example, is true in a situation whose domain consists just of Dolly, Bear, Truck, and Ball iff at least one of the four statements listed above is true. The domain delimits the set of objects among which the 'something' of this statement is to be found.

Mixing predicate logic and English we might say that '∃x x is messy' is true in a situation iff some statement of the form 'a is messy' is true in that situation, where 'a' is a name of some object in the situation's domain. Likewise, '∀x x is messy' is true in a situation iff every statement of the form 'a is messy' is true for any name 'a' of an object in the relevant domain.

Indeed, given this domain, we can think of '∀x x is messy' as shorthand for the conjunction:

Dolly is messy & Bear is messy & Truck is messy & Ball is messy.

And similarly, we may regard '∃x x is messy' as abbreviating the disjunction:

Dolly is messy ∨ Bear is messy ∨ Truck is messy ∨ Ball is messy.

This analysis eliminates quantifiers altogether, reducing them to the familiar operators of propositional logic. The Austrian philosopher and logician Ludwig Wittgenstein advocated just such a reduction in his influential work *Tractatus Logico-Philosophicus* (1921). But this reduction depends on two assumptions that are not always true:

1. Each object in the domain has a name (for otherwise we cannot formulate the conjunction or disjunction into which a quantified statement is to be analyzed), and

2. The number of objects in the domain is finite (for otherwise the conjunction or disjunction into which the quantified statement is to be analyzed has infinitely many conjuncts or disjuncts, and we have not given meanings to such infinite statements).

These assumptions are unnecessary encumbrances, and so contemporary logicians generally reject Wittgenstein's analysis. They see quantifiers as playing a role not reducible to that of conjunction or disjunction: namely, expressing general statements about domains whose objects need be neither named nor finite in number. We shall see shortly how that is accomplished.

First, however, we should note that differences in the domain may result in significant differences in formalization. If, for example, the domain is limited to people, then the existential quantifier may be read as "somebody" and the universal quantifier as "everybody." The statement 'Everybody is happy', for example, is then just '∀xHx'. But if the domain contains things other than people, then the quantifiers range over these other things as well, and this reading is no longer permissible. To assert 'Everybody is happy' given a domain including nonpersons, we must distinguish the people from the nonpeople. This can be done by using the predicate 'P' to represent 'is a person'. 'Everybody is happy' then becomes '∀x(Px → Hx)'—that is, "every person is happy." Similarly, the statement 'Somebody is happy' is '∃x(Px & Hx)'.

We have so far seen that a valuation in predicate logic consists of two parts:

1. A **domain** or "universe" of discourse, the set of objects out of which situations are to be constructed, and
2. An assignment of appropriate values to predicates and names.

The values assigned to predicates and names are called their **extensions.** The concept of an extension is a generalization of the concept of denotation—a concept that is most at home when applied to names. Each name denotes a particular individual. But we can also think of one-place predicates as denoting sets of individuals, n-place predicates as denoting sets of n-tuples of individuals, and even sentence letters as denoting truth values.[2] This, however, stretches the ordinary concept of denotation uncomfortably. Generally, we shall use the technical term 'extension' to designate all of these kinds of values.

The two parts of a particular valuation together comprise a structure capable of modeling possible situations of a certain form. In fact, valuations in predicate logic are often called **models.** Just as a set of toy soldiers may model a battle, a map may model a stretch of terrain, or a configuration of electrical potentials in a computer may model almost anything, so a valuation (that is, a domain plus assignments of extensions from that domain to names and predicates) may model possible situations. It usually makes little difference which objects we choose to comprise the domain, since most often they are only stand-ins for the things they model. We shall usually work with domains of numbers, but that is merely for convenience. The important property of a domain is how many objects it contains, for that limits the complexity of situations we can model. *The domain of a valuation must contain at least one object, but there is no maximum. Even infinite domains are permitted.*

A valuation becomes a model of a particular possible situation when it is interpreted. To interpret a model, we associate formal names and predicates with English names or predicate phrases. But we may also consider uninterpreted models. To illustrate, let's construct a valuation for the formula '(Ma & Lab) & ~Fa'.

We shall take as the domain for this valuation the set of numbers {1, 2, 3}, and we shall assign to the names 'a' and 'b' the numbers 1 and 2, respectively. Thus we are modeling possible situations involving three entities, two of which have the names 'a' and 'b' and one of which is unnamed. *There is no requirement that everything be named.*

Further, let's assign to the one-place predicate 'M' the set {1, 2}. This means that 'M' is true of 1 and 2 but not of 3. One-place predicates may also be empty; that is, they may apply to nothing in the domain so that their extension is the empty set { }. Suppose we assign the empty set to the one-place predicate 'F'; that means that nothing in the domain (i.e., nothing in the situations we are modeling) has the property indicated by this predicate.

Finally, let's assign the set {<1, 1>, <1, 2>, <2, 2>} to the two-place predicate 'L'. This indicates that these three pairs stand in the relation indicated by 'L'— whatever that is.

---

[2] Gottlob Frege, who invented the modern concept of an extension while he was inventing predicate logic, thought of truth values in this way. A true sentence, he held, denotes The True and a false sentence denotes The False.

When, as in this example, we have not associated any particular meanings. with names or predicates, the model is **uninterpreted.** Like a valuation in propositional logic, an uninterpreted model in predicate logic is not a representation of a possible situation, but something more abstract: a representation of a form that many possible situations could share.

A name in an uninterpreted model arbitrarily designates whatever object is assigned to it, as in the following diagram:

Reference in an Uninterpreted Model

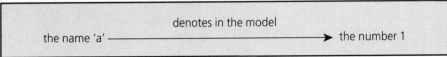

An uninterpreted model comes to represent a specific possible situation when we interpret it by associating English names or predicate phrases with the formal names and predicates. Thus we might let 'a' mean "Al" and 'b' mean "Beth". Then the number 1 stands for Al in our model and 2 stands for Beth. We have not said what 3 stands for; it merely represents some unspecified object. Further, let's interpret 'M' to mean "is mortal," 'F' to mean "is a fish," and 'L' to mean "loves." Since we have assigned the set {1, 2} to 'M', the situation we are considering is one in which Al and Beth are both mortal, but the unspecified object is not. Nothing in this situation is a fish, since the value assigned to 'F' is { }. And, finally, since the value assigned to 'L' is {<1, 1>, <1, 2>, <2, 2>}, our situation is one in which Al and Beth both love themselves and he loves her, though his love is unrequited. The unspecified object neither loves nor is loved by anything.

When we interpret a model in this way, so that the objects in the domain are stand-ins for other objects, we shall call it a **surrogate model.** Unlike an uninterpreted model, a surrogate model stands for a specific possible situation. In a surrogate model, reference relations become a bit more complicated:

Reference in a Surrogate Model

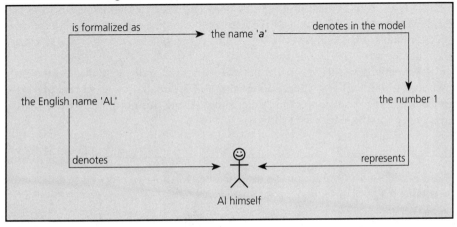

We can also create models that are not merely models but the reality itself. To do this we let the domain consist of the actual objects of our English discourse. Thus, instead of {1, 2, 3}, we might select the domain {Al, Beth, Carl}. Now 'a' denotes Al himself, rather than a stand-in. This kind of interpreted model is called a **natural model**.

Reference in a Natural Model

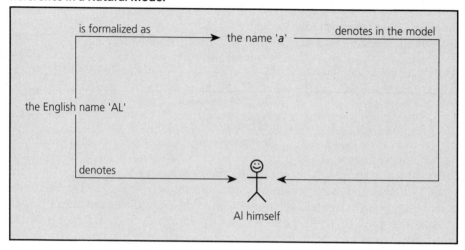

Natural models are defined by associating English expressions with relevant predicates and names and then assigning those predicates and names the objects and sets they actually denote.

To summarize, models may be either uninterpreted or interpreted. Uninterpreted models represent the forms of possible situations; interpreted models represent specific possible situations. There are two kinds of interpreted models: surrogate models, in which the objects of the domain stand for something other than themselves, and natural models, in which the objects in the domain are the very objects denoted by the corresponding English terms.

Just as propositional logic can be done entirely by assigning truth values to meaningless sentence letters, so predicate logic can be done entirely with uninterpreted models. Usually, however, we will interpret our models in order to clarify their significance.

We may now consider the formal semantics for predicate logic. Let σ be any predicate or name. Then where $\mathcal{V}$ is a valuation, we shall use the expression '$\mathcal{V}(\sigma)$' to designate the extension that $\mathcal{V}$ assigns to σ. Using this notation, we may define the concept of a valuation as follows:

DEFINITION A **valuation** or **model** for a formula or set of formulas of predicate logic consists of

> 1. A nonempty set $\mathcal{D}$ of objects, which is called the **domain,** and
> 2. An assignment to each predicate or name σ in that formula or set of formulas an extension $\mathcal{V}(\sigma)$ which meets the following conditions:
>   - i. If σ is a name, $\mathcal{V}(\sigma)$ is a member of $\mathcal{D}$.
>   - ii. If σ is a zero-place predicate, $\mathcal{V}(\sigma)$ is one (but not both) of the values T or F.
>   - iii. If σ is a one-place predicate, $\mathcal{V}(\sigma)$ is a set of members of $\mathcal{D}$.
>   - iv. If σ is an n-place predicate ($n > 1$), $\mathcal{V}(\sigma)$ is a set of ordered n-tuples of members of $\mathcal{D}$.

Note once again that although the domain must contain at least one member, the sets mentioned in items iii and iv may be empty.

Like propositional logic, predicate logic is truth-functional; that is, the truth values of complex formulas are determined from the truth values of simpler formulas by a set of valuation rules. The valuation rules for the quantifiers, however, introduce some novelties.

Consider, for example, the formula '$\forall x Fx$'. It seems initially reasonable to suppose, as Wittgenstein did, that this formula is true if and only if Fα is true for any name α—that is, if 'Fa', 'Fb', 'Fc', and so on are all true, where this list includes a statement of the form Fα for each name α. If we drop Wittgenstein's idea that a universally quantified statement is a conjunction and allow the list to be infinite, the resulting understanding of the quantifier is called the **substitutional interpretation.** But the substitutional interpretation is still problematic if the domain contains unnamed objects, because it treats these objects as if they don't exist. Consider, for example, the valuation on the domain $\{1, 2, 3\}$ on which the names 'a' and 'b' name 1 and 2 respectively, 3 is unnamed, and the extension of 'F' is $\{1, 2\}$. Then Fα is true for all names α, but '$\forall x Fx$' ought to be false, since 'F' is not true of the unnamed object 3. The substitutional interpretation, however, would make '$\forall x Fx$' true.

To remedy this problem, we adopt slightly different truth conditions: '$\forall x Fx$' is true if and only if

1. Fα is true for every name α that already has an extension, *and*
2. Fβ would still be true for any new name β that has not yet received an extension, no matter which object from the domain we assigned to β.

This modified quantifier semantics is called the **objectual interpretation,** because it takes direct account of the objects in the domain, not merely of their names. It is the standard quantifier semantics for classical predicate logic.

Like the substitutional interpretation, the objectual interpretation implies that '$\forall x Fx$' is true if and only if each member of a list of sentences of the form Fα is true. But on the objectual interpretation the names α are not limited to our current vocabulary; they may also be new names added by expanding our current vocabulary to name formerly unnamed objects. Thus an object in the domain need not actually be named in order to count for quantificational purposes. It is enough that it could in principle be named. Of course, we wouldn't want to name it with a name that already denotes something else, since that name would then become ambiguous. So the **potential names** of an object are limited to those it already has and those we might give it that do not already name something else. Let's put this in formal terms:

DEFINITION Let $\mathcal{V}$ be any valuation, d any object in the domain of $\mathcal{V}$, and α any name. Then α is a **potential name** of d with respect to $\mathcal{V}$ if and only if $\mathcal{V}$ does not assign some extension other than d to α. (In other words, α is a potential name of d if and only if either $\mathcal{V}(\alpha) = d$ or $\mathcal{V}$ assigns nothing to α.)

When we name an object that previously had been nameless, we expand our valuation. So we need to define the idea of an expansion as well:

DEFINITION Let $\mathcal{V}$ be any valuation, d any object in the domain of $\mathcal{V}$, and α any potential name of d with respect to $\mathcal{V}$. Then the **expansion** $\mathcal{V}_{(\alpha, d)}$ of $\mathcal{V}$ with respect to α and d is the valuation which has the same domain as $\mathcal{V}$ and assigns the same extensions to the same predicates and names, but which *also* assigns to α the extension d, if $\mathcal{V}$ does not already assign α an extension. If $\mathcal{V}$ already assigns the extension d to α, then $\mathcal{V}_{(\alpha, d)}$ is just $\mathcal{V}$.

Notice that the definition of an expansion permits expansions of a valuation with respect to names that already have extensions. We shall call these **trivial expansions,** since they leave the original valuation unaltered. Expansions which assign extensions to names that previously did not have them we shall call **nontrivial expansions.** A trivial expansion is *not,* of course, an expansion in the ordinary sense. But this terminological twist will help us to formulate the valuation rules for the quantifiers. To illustrate, consider again the formula '∃xFx'. This should be true if some formula of the form Fα is true, where α is a name that already has an extension, but it should also be true if 'F' is true only of some nameless object to which we could assign a potential name. We can say this using our new terminology, as follows:

'∃xFx' is true on a valuation $\mathcal{V}$ if and only if for some object d in the domain of $\mathcal{V}$, and some potential name α of d, Fα is true on $\mathcal{V}_{(\alpha, d)}$.

Here $\mathcal{V}_{(\alpha, d)}$ is either $\mathcal{V}$ itself [if $\mathcal{V}(\alpha) = d$] or a valuation just like $\mathcal{V}$ except that it also assigns the extension d to α (if $\mathcal{V}$ assigns no extension to α). This is the idea behind rule 10 below. Rule 9 works similarly.

We may now state the valuation rules:

Valuation Rules for Predicate Logic

For all valuations $\mathcal{V}$:

1. If Φ is a one-place predicate and α is a name, then $\mathcal{V}(\Phi\alpha) = \text{T}$ iff $\mathcal{V}(\alpha) \; \varepsilon$ $\mathcal{V}(\Phi)$;
   $\mathcal{V}(\Phi\alpha) = \text{F}$ iff $\mathcal{V}(\alpha) \; \not\varepsilon \; \mathcal{V}(\Phi)$.

2. If Φ is an n-place predicate ($n > 1$) and $\alpha_1, \ldots, \alpha_n$ are names, then
   $\mathcal{V}(\Phi\alpha_1, \ldots, \alpha_n) = \text{T}$ iff $<\mathcal{V}(\alpha_1), \ldots, \mathcal{V}(\alpha_n)> \varepsilon \; \mathcal{V}(\Phi)$;
   $\mathcal{V}(\Phi\alpha_1, \ldots, \alpha_n) = \text{F}$ iff $<\mathcal{V}(\alpha_1), \ldots, \mathcal{V}(\alpha_n)> \not\varepsilon \; \mathcal{V}(\Phi)$.

3. If α and β are names, then $\mathcal{V}(\alpha = \beta) = \text{T}$ iff $\mathcal{V}(\alpha) = \mathcal{V}(\beta)$;
   $\mathcal{V}(\alpha = \beta) = \text{F}$ iff $\mathcal{V}(\alpha) \neq \mathcal{V}(\beta)$.

For the next five rules, Φ and Ψ are any formulas:

4. $\mathcal{V}(\sim\Phi) = \text{T}$ iff $\mathcal{V}(\Phi) \neq \text{T}$;
   $\mathcal{V}(\sim\Phi) = \text{F}$ iff $\mathcal{V}(\Phi) = \text{T}$.

5. $\mathcal{V}(\Phi \;\&\; \Psi) = \text{T}$ iff both $\mathcal{V}(\Phi) = \text{T}$ and $\mathcal{V}(\Psi) = \text{T}$;
   $\mathcal{V}(\Phi \;\&\; \Psi) = \text{F}$ iff either $\mathcal{V}(\Phi) \neq \text{T}$ or $\mathcal{V}(\Psi) \neq \text{T}$, or both.

6. $\mathcal{V}(\Phi \vee \Psi) = \text{T}$ iff either $\mathcal{V}(\Phi) = \text{T}$ or $\mathcal{V}(\Psi) = \text{T}$, or both;
   $\mathcal{V}(\Phi \vee \Psi) = \text{F}$ iff both $\mathcal{V}(\Phi) \neq \text{T}$ and $\mathcal{V}(\Psi) \neq \text{T}$.

7. $\mathcal{V}(\Phi \rightarrow \Psi) = \text{T}$ iff either $\mathcal{V}(\Phi) \neq \text{T}$ or $\mathcal{V}(\Psi) = \text{T}$, or both;
   $\mathcal{V}(\Phi \rightarrow \Psi) = \text{F}$ iff both $\mathcal{V}(\Phi) = \text{T}$ and $\mathcal{V}(\Psi) \neq \text{T}$.

8. $\mathcal{V}(\Phi \leftrightarrow \Psi) = \text{T}$ iff either $\mathcal{V}(\Phi) = \text{T}$ and $\mathcal{V}(\Psi) = \text{T}$, or $\mathcal{V}(\Phi) \neq \text{T}$ and $\mathcal{V}(\Psi) \neq \text{T}$;
   $\mathcal{V}(\Phi \leftrightarrow \Psi) = \text{F}$ iff either $\mathcal{V}(\Phi) = \text{T}$ and $\mathcal{V}(\Psi) \neq \text{T}$, or $\mathcal{V}(\Phi) \neq \text{T}$ and $\mathcal{V}(\Psi) = \text{T}$.

For the next two rules, $\Phi^\alpha/_\beta$ stands for the result of replacing each occurrence of the variable β in Φ by α, and $\mathcal{D}$ is the domain of $\mathcal{V}$.

9. $\mathcal{V}(\forall\beta\Phi) = \text{T}$ iff for all potential names α of all objects d in $\mathcal{D}$,
   $\mathcal{V}_{(\alpha,d)}(\Phi^\alpha/_\beta) = \text{T}$;
   $\mathcal{V}(\forall\beta\Phi) = \text{F}$ iff for some potential name α of some object d in $\mathcal{D}$,
   $\mathcal{V}_{(\alpha,d)}(\Phi^\alpha/_\beta) \neq \text{T}$.

10. $\mathcal{V}(\exists\beta\Phi) = \text{T}$ iff for some potential name α of some object d in $\mathcal{D}$,
    $\mathcal{V}_{(\alpha,d)}(\Phi^\alpha/_\beta) = \text{T}$;
    $\mathcal{V}(\exists\beta\Phi) = \text{F}$ iff for all potential names α of all objects d in $\mathcal{D}$,
    $\mathcal{V}_{(\alpha,d)}(\Phi^\alpha/_\beta) \neq \text{T}$.

Rules 4–8 constitute the semantics for propositional logic, which is thus included in the semantics for predicate logic. But predicate logic contains more: Rules 1–3 give the semantics for atomic formulas containing names, and rules 9 and 10 present the semantics for quantifiers.

Rule 1 stipulates that a formula consisting of a one-place predicate followed by a name is true if the extension assigned to the name (i.e., an object) is a member of the extension assigned to the predicate (i.e., a set of objects). Consider the formula 'Pa', interpreted to mean "Al is a predator." This means that 'Pa' is true if Al is a member of the set of predators—or, rather, if the object modeling Al on our valuation is a member of the set of objects that models the predators. 'Pa' is false, by contrast, iff the extension of 'a' is not a member of the extension of 'P'.

According to rule 2, a formula consisting of an n-place predicate followed by n names is true if the n-tuple consisting of the extensions assigned to the names (arranged in the same order as the names) is a member of the extension assigned to the predicate (i.e., a set of ordered n-tuples). Consider the formula 'Lab', interpreted to mean "Al loves Beth." This means that 'Lab' is true if the pair <Al, Beth> is a member of the set of pairs such that the first loves the second—or, rather, if the pair of objects modeling Al and Beth on our valuation is a member of the set of pairs that models the relation "loves". 'Lab' is false iff this is not the case.

Rule 3 says that an identity statement is true iff the names flanking the identity sign have the same extension and false iff they don't. The '=' in the expression '$\mathcal{V}(\alpha) = \mathcal{V}(\beta)$' is an expression of the metalanguage, not the identity predicate of the object language.

In propositional logic, the valuation rules are just the rules for constructing truth tables. But the more complex semantics of predicate logic cannot be presented in a neat tabular form. Since domains may be of any size and may consist of any objects, each formula or set of formulas has infinitely many valuations; thus we cannot represent all of its valuations on a finite table, as we could in propositional logic. Still, we can use the semantics to calculate the truth values of formulas from the values (extensions) assigned to their parts, just as we did in propositional logic.

Listed below is a set of formulas:

1. Fa & Fb
2. a=d
3. $\forall x Fx$
4. $\exists x Fx$
5. $\exists x(Fx \& Gx)$
6. $P \rightarrow Q$
7. $Q \rightarrow \forall x Fx$
8. Lab
9. $\exists x \exists y Lxy$
10. $\forall x \exists y Lxy$

Now consider the following valuation $\mathcal{V}$ of these formulas:

Domain = {1, 2, 3, 4, 5}
$\mathcal{V}$('a') = 1
$\mathcal{V}$('b') = 2
$\mathcal{V}$('d') = 1
$\mathcal{V}$('P') = T
$\mathcal{V}$('Q') = F
$\mathcal{V}$('F') = {1, 2, 3}
$\mathcal{V}$('G') = {4, 5}
$\mathcal{V}$('L') = {<1, 2>, <2, 1>, <4, 4>, <5, 4>}

Which of formulas 1–10 is true and which is false on this valuation? The solutions are as follows:

1. Since 1 ε {1, 2, 3}, $\mathcal{V}$('a') ε $\mathcal{V}$('F'). So by rule 1, $\mathcal{V}$('Fa') = T. Likewise, since 2 ε {1, 2, 3}, $\mathcal{V}$('b') ε $\mathcal{V}$('F'). So again by rule 1, $\mathcal{V}$('Fb') = T. Hence by rule 5, $\mathcal{V}$('Fa & Fb') = T.

2. $\mathcal{V}$('a') = $\mathcal{V}$('d') = 1. Hence by rule 3, $\mathcal{V}$('a = d') = T.

3. The name 'c', since it is not assigned any denotation by $\mathcal{V}$, is a potential name of 4 with respect to $\mathcal{V}$. So consider the nontrivial expansion $\mathcal{V}_{('c',4)}$ of $\mathcal{V}$. Since 4 $\notin$ {1, 2, 3}, $\mathcal{V}_{('c',4)}$('c') $\notin$ $\mathcal{V}_{('c',4)}$('F'). Hence by rule 1, $\mathcal{V}_{('c',4)}$('Fc') ≠ T. So by rule 9, $\mathcal{V}$('∀xFx') = F.

4. Since $\mathcal{V}$('a') = 1, $\mathcal{V}_{('a',1)}$ is a trivial expansion of $\mathcal{V}$, and 'a' is a potential name of 1 with respect to $\mathcal{V}$. Since 1 ε {1, 2, 3}, $\mathcal{V}_{('a',1)}$('a') ε $\mathcal{V}_{('a',1)}$('F'). So by rule 1, $\mathcal{V}_{('a',1)}$('Fa') = T. Hence by rule 10, $\mathcal{V}$('∃xFx') = T.

5. No member of the domain {1, 2, 3, 4, 5} is an element of both $\mathcal{V}$('F'), i.e., {1, 2, 3} and $\mathcal{V}$('G'), i.e., {4, 5}. Hence there is no potential name α and object d in {1, 2, 3, 4, 5} such that $\mathcal{V}_{(α,d)}$('Fα & Gα') = T. (For if $\mathcal{V}_{(α,d)}$('Fα & Gα') = T, then by rule 5, both $\mathcal{V}_{(α,d)}$('Fα') = T and $\mathcal{V}_{(α,d)}$('Gα') = T, which by rule 1 would mean that d would be in both {1, 2, 3} and {4, 5}, which is impossible.) Therefore by rule 10, $\mathcal{V}$('∃x(Fx & Gx)') = F.

6. $\mathcal{V}$('P') = T and $\mathcal{V}$('Q') = F so that $\mathcal{V}$('Q') ≠ T; it follows by rule 7 that $\mathcal{V}$('P → Q') = F.

7. $\mathcal{V}$('Q') ≠ T; it follows by rule 7 that $\mathcal{V}$('Q → ∀xFx') = T.

8. Since <1, 2> ε {<1, 2>, <2, 1>, <4, 4>, <5, 4>}, <$\mathcal{V}$('a'), $\mathcal{V}$('b')> ε $\mathcal{V}$('L'). Thus by rule 2, $\mathcal{V}$('Lab') = T.

9. In problem 8 we saw that $\mathcal{V}$('Lab') = T. But then since $\mathcal{V}$('b') = 2, $\mathcal{V}_{('b',2)}$('Lab') = T and 'b' is a potential name of 2 with respect to $\mathcal{V}$. So by rule 10, $\mathcal{V}$('∃yLay') = T. Moreover, since $\mathcal{V}$('a') = 1, $\mathcal{V}_{('a',1)}$('∃yLay') = T and 'a' is a potential name of 1 with respect to $\mathcal{V}$. Hence again by rule 10, $\mathcal{V}$('∃x∃yLxy') = T.

10. The name 'c', not being assigned any denotation by $\mathcal{V}$, is a potential name of 3 with respect to $\mathcal{V}$. So consider the nontrivial expansion $\mathcal{V}_{('c',3)}$ of $\mathcal{V}$. Now there is no member d of the domain {1, 2, 3, 4, 5} such that <3, d> ε $\mathcal{V}$('L'). Hence by rule 2 there is no potential name α and object d in {1, 2, 3, 4, 5} such that $\mathcal{V}_{('c',3)(α,d)}$('Lcα') = T. Hence by rule 10, $\mathcal{V}_{('c',3)}$('∃yLcy') ≠ T. Therefore by rule 9, $\mathcal{V}$('∀x∃yLxy') = F.

In problem 10 we use the notation '$\mathcal{V}_{('c',3)(α,d)}$' to stand for the expansion of $\mathcal{V}_{('c',3)}$ with respect to an unspecified name α and object d. $\mathcal{V}_{('c',3)}$ itself, of course, is the expansion of $\mathcal{V}$ with respect to 'c' and 3. It is often necessary to consider expansions of expansions (and expansions of expansions of expansions . . . and so on!) when working with multiple quantifiers.

Exercise 7.2.1

Some additional formulas are listed below. Which of them are true and which are false on the valuation given on page 198? (Show your work as in the solutions to that example.)

1. Fa → Fb
2. ~a = b
3. ∀xGx

4. $\exists x Gx$
5. $\exists x {\sim} Gx$
6. ${\sim}\exists x Gx$
7. $\forall x(Fx \lor Gx)$
8. $\forall x {\sim}(Fx \,\&\, Gx)$
9. $\exists x Lxx$
10. $\exists y \forall x Lxy$

We have so far ignored function symbols. Though we shall not need to use the semantics of function symbols in this book, for completeness we consider them briefly here.

In addition to assigning the usual extensions to predicates and names, a valuation of a formula or set of formulas containing function symbols assigns to each function symbol an *n*-place function. An **n-place function** *f* is a set of ordered pairs that meets two conditions:

1. The first item in each pair is an ordered *n*-tuple.
2. For any pairs $<x, y>$ and $<x, z>$ in f, $y = z$.

For example, the two-place addition function on the natural numbers is the set

$$\{<<1, 1>, 2>, <<1, 2>, 3>, <<2, 1>, 3>, <<2, 2>, 4>, <<1, 3>, 4>, \ldots\}$$

Each pair in this set has as its first item a pair of numbers, whose sum is the second item. For a given pair $<<x, y>, z>$, x and y are **arguments** of the function, and z is the **value** for those arguments.

Since a one-tuple is just the object it contains, a one-place function is just a set of ordered pairs—that is, a simple relation. Thus, for example, the one-place successor function is the set

$$\{<1, 2>, <2, 3>, <3, 4>, <4, 5>, \ldots\}$$

(Notice that the one-place successor function and the two-place successor relation discussed in Section 7.1 are in fact the same set.) Here the first member of each pair is the argument and the second is the value for that argument.

Condition 2 of the definition of a function requires that each argument yield a unique value. Thus, for example, since $<2, 3>$ is a member of the successor function, there can be no member of the form $<2, x>$, where $x \neq 3$.

The semantics for function symbols in predicate logic is defined by the valuation rule for function symbols, which assigns an extension to a complex name by considering the extensions of its parts. The rule is

For any *n*-place function symbol ϕ and any names $\alpha_1, \ldots, \alpha_n$, $\mathcal{V}(\phi(\alpha_1, \ldots, \alpha_n)) = d$ iff $<<\mathcal{V}(\alpha_1), \ldots, \mathcal{V}(\alpha_n)>, d> \in \mathcal{V}(\phi)$.

Here $\mathcal{V}(\phi)$ is the *n*-place function assigned by $\mathcal{V}$ to ϕ, and d is the value of that function for the arguments $\mathcal{V}(\alpha_1), \ldots, \mathcal{V}(\alpha_n)$. Since an *n*-place function has only one value for each *n*-tuple of arguments, there is only one object d that the complex name $\phi(\alpha_1, \ldots, \alpha_n)$ denotes.

Let's take a specific example. Suppose some valuation $\mathscr{V}$ assigns to the two-place function symbol 'f' the addition function mentioned above. Further, for the names 'a' and 'b', let $\mathscr{V}('a') = 1$ and $\mathscr{V}('b') = 2$. We wish to use the valuation rule for function symbols to determine the extension of the complex name 'f(a, b)'. The rule stipulates that

$$\mathscr{V}('f(a, b)') = d \text{ iff } <<\mathscr{V}('a'), \mathscr{V}('b')>, d> \varepsilon \, \mathscr{V}('f')$$

But since $\mathscr{V}('a') = 1$, $\mathscr{V}('b') = 2$, and $\mathscr{V}('f') = \{<<1, 1>, 2>, <<1, 2>, 3>, <<2, 1>, 3>, <<2, 2>, 4>, <<1, 3>, 4>, \ldots\}$, this means that

$$\mathscr{V}('f(a, b)') = d \text{ iff } <<1, 2>, d> \varepsilon \{<<1, 1>, 2>, <<1, 2>, 3>, <<2, 1>, 3>, <<2, 2>, 4>, <<1, 3>, 4>, \ldots\}$$

Now the only number d such that $<<1, 2>, d> \varepsilon \{<<1, 1>, 2>, <<1, 2>, 3>, <<2, 1>, 3>, <<2, 2>, 4>, <<1, 3>, 4>, \ldots\}$ is 3. Hence

$$\mathscr{V}('f(a, b)') = 3$$

Or, again, suppose that 's' is a one-place function symbol to which $\mathscr{V}$ assigns the successor function and that 'a' is a name such that $\mathscr{V}('a') = 2$. To calculate $\mathscr{V}('s(a)')$, we apply the rule as follows:

$$\mathscr{V}('s(a)') = d \text{ iff } <<\mathscr{V}('a')>, d> \varepsilon \, \mathscr{V}('s')$$

However, since a one-tuple of a given object is just that object itself, it follows that

$$\mathscr{V}('s(a)') = d \text{ iff } <\mathscr{V}('a'), d> \varepsilon \, \mathscr{V}('s')$$

And since $\mathscr{V}('a') = 2$ and $\mathscr{V}('s') = \{<1, 2>, <2, 3>, <3, 4>, <4, 5>, \ldots\}$, we have

$$\mathscr{V}('s(a)') = d \text{ iff } <2, d> \varepsilon \{<1, 2>, <2, 3>, <3, 4>, <4, 5>, \ldots\}$$

But the only d such that $<2, d> \varepsilon \{<1, 2>, <2, 3>, <3, 4>, <4, 5>, \ldots\}$ is 3. Hence

$$\mathscr{V}('s(a)') = 3$$

Exercise 7.2.2

Let 'a', 'b', and 'c' be names, 's' a one-place function symbol, and 'f' a two-place function symbol, and let

$$\mathscr{V}('a') = 1$$
$$\mathscr{V}('b') = 2$$
$$\mathscr{V}('c') = 3$$
$$\mathscr{V}('s') = \{<1, 2>, <2, 3>, <3, 4>, <4, 5>, \ldots\}$$
$$\mathscr{V}('f') = \{<<1, 1>, 2>, <<1, 2>, 3>, <<2, 1>, 3>, <<2, 2>, 4>, <<1, 3>, 4>, \ldots\}$$

Use the valuation rule for functions (together in problem 5 with the valuation rule for identity) to calculate the following values. Show your work in the way exemplified above.

1. $\mathcal{V}(\text{'s(b)'})$
2. $\mathcal{V}(\text{'s(s(a))'})$
3. $\mathcal{V}(\text{'f(a, a)'})$
4. $\mathcal{V}(\text{'f(a, s(a))'})$
5. $\mathcal{V}(\text{'s(b) = c'})$

7.3 USING THE SEMANTICS

We now consider how to use the semantics of predicate logic to prove metatheorems about such important properties as consistency and validity. The material in this section presupposes familiarity with Sections 5.1–5.4.

The metalinguistic terms 'consistent', 'valid', and so on have the same definitions in predicate logic as in propositional logic. Thus, for example, a sequent in predicate logic is *valid* if and only if there is no valuation on which its premises are all true and its conclusion is untrue. But valuations are no longer merely lines on a truth table. Still, the general idea is the same: The truth values of complex formulas are determined by the values assigned to their components. The following metatheorems illustrate how the valuation rules can be used to determine validity, consistency, and so on.

METATHEOREM: The sequent 'Lab ⊢ Lba' is invalid.

PROOF: Let $\mathcal{V}$ be the valuation on domain $\{1, 2\}$ such that

$$\mathcal{V}(\text{'a'}) = 1$$
$$\mathcal{V}(\text{'b'}) = 2$$
$$\mathcal{V}(\text{'L'}) = \{<1, 2>\}$$

Since $<1, 2> \, \varepsilon \, \{<1, 2>\}$, clearly $<\mathcal{V}(\text{'a'}), \mathcal{V}(\text{'b'})> \, \varepsilon \, \mathcal{V}(\text{'L'})$, and so by valuation rule 2, $\mathcal{V}(\text{'Lab'}) = \text{T}$. However, $<2, 1> \, \not\varepsilon \, \{<1, 2>\}$ so that $<\mathcal{V}(\text{'b'}), \mathcal{V}(\text{'a'})> \, \not\varepsilon \, \mathcal{V}(\text{'L'})$. Thus by rule 2, $\mathcal{V}(\text{'Lba'}) \neq \text{T}$. Thus, since $\mathcal{V}(\text{'Lab'}) = \text{T}$ and $\mathcal{V}(\text{'Lba'}) \neq \text{T}$, it follows (by the definition of validity) that 'Lab ⊢ Lba' is not valid, that is, invalid.   QED

The strategy for proving a sequent invalid is simply to produce a counterexample. The challenge, then, is to understand the problem well enough to see how the premises could be true while the conclusion is untrue. Once you see this, it's a fairly routine job, requiring care but little insight, to construct the appropriate valuation and show using the valuation rules that it is a counterexample. In the preceding problem, if we think of 'L' as 'loves', 'a' as 'Al', and 'b' as 'Beth', then the counterexample is obvious: It's perfectly possible for Al to love Beth without her loving him. We then construct a valuation which expresses the form of this situation. An uninterpreted model suffices for a counterexample, though usually we will suggest an interpretation that makes it a surrogate model, as we just did here.

The best strategy for proving a sequent valid is usually reductio. We suppose that the sequent is not valid and then deduce a contradiction. The reasoning proceeds through the usual stages of unpacking and logical manipulation, as in the following example:

METATHEOREM: The sequent 'Fa ⊢ ∃xFx' is valid.

PROOF: Suppose for reductio that this sequent is not valid, that is, there is some valuation $\mathcal{V}$ such that $\mathcal{V}('Fa') = T$ and $\mathcal{V}('∃xFx') \neq T$. Since $\mathcal{V}('Fa') = T$, by valuation rule 1 $\mathcal{V}('a') \varepsilon \mathcal{V}('F')$. Now since $\mathcal{V}$ is a valuation of 'Fa', $\mathcal{V}$ must assign some extension d to 'a'. Therefore 'a' is a potential name of d with respect to $\mathcal{V}$ and $\mathcal{V}_{('a',d)}('Fa') = T$. It follows by rule 10 that $\mathcal{V}('∃xFx') = T$. But we supposed that $\mathcal{V}('∃xFx') \neq T$, and so we have a contradiction. Therefore the sequent 'Fa ⊢ ∃xFx' is valid.   QED

The reductio strategy also serves for proving the validity of formulas, as the following example illustrates:

METATHEOREM: '∀x(Fx → Fx)' is a valid formula.

PROOF: Suppose for reductio that '∀x(Fx → Fx)' is not valid. Then there is some valuation $\mathcal{V}$ such that $\mathcal{V}('∀x(Fx → Fx)') \neq T$. Hence by rule 9, there is some potential name α of some object d in the domain of $\mathcal{V}$ such that $\mathcal{V}_{(\alpha,d)}('F\alpha → F\alpha') \neq T$. Thus by rule 7, $\mathcal{V}_{(\alpha,d)}('F\alpha') = T$ and $\mathcal{V}_{(\alpha,d)}('F\alpha') \neq T$, which is absurd. Hence, contrary to our supposition, '∀x(Fx → Fx)' is valid.   QED

In this last problem, after stating the reductio hypothesis we used the valuation rules to analyze the formula into its components until we reached a contradiction. This is a standard strategy.

To prove the consistency of a set of formulas, by contrast, we construct a valuation on which they are all true. The strategy here is similar to the strategy for showing a sequent to be invalid:

METATHEOREM: The set {'∃xFx', '∃x~Fx'} is consistent.

PROOF: Let $\mathcal{V}$ be the valuation on domain {1, 2} such that

$$\mathcal{V}('F') = \{1\}$$

Now the name 'a', since it is not assigned any denotation by $\mathcal{V}$, is a potential name of 1 with respect to $\mathcal{V}$. So consider the nontrivial expansion $\mathcal{V}_{(\text{'a'},1)}$ of $\mathcal{V}$. Since 1 ε {1}, by rule 1, $\mathcal{V}_{(\text{'a'},1)}$('Fa') = T. Hence by rule 10, $\mathcal{V}$('∃xFx') = T. Further, because 'a' is not assigned any denotation by $\mathcal{V}$, it is also a potential name for 2. So we may also consider the expansion $\mathcal{V}_{(\text{'a'},2)}$ of $\mathcal{V}$. Since 2 ɛ̸ {1}, $\mathcal{V}_{(\text{'a'},2)}$('a') ɛ̸ $\mathcal{V}_{(\text{'a'},2)}$('F'). So by rule 1, $\mathcal{V}_{(\text{'a'},2)}$('Fa') ≠ T; and so by rule 4, $\mathcal{V}_{(\text{'a'},2)}$('~Fa') = T. Hence by rule 10, $\mathcal{V}$('∃x~Fx') = T. Thus we have shown both that $\mathcal{V}$('∃xFx') = T and that $\mathcal{V}$('∃x~Fx') = T, whence it follows (by the definition of consistency for a set) that {'∃xFx', '∃x~Fx'} is consistent.   QED

This proof is easy to understand intuitively. We create a valuation containing two objects, one of which is F and the other of which is not F. Clearly on this valuation, something is F and something is not F, and so the valuation shows the set to be consistent. We could have used $\mathcal{V}_{(\text{'b'},2)}$ instead of $\mathcal{V}_{(\text{'a'},2)}$ for our second expansion of $\mathcal{V}$, but there is no reason not to consider two different expansions with respect to the same name, so long as we are looking at separate formulas or subformulas whose quantifiers do not overlap.

To prove inconsistency, it's usually best to suppose consistency and proceed by reductio:

METATHEOREM: The formula '∀xFx & ∃x~Fx' is inconsistent.

PROOF: Suppose for reductio that '∀xFx & ∃x~Fx' is consistent, that is, there is some valuation $\mathcal{V}$ on which '∀xFx & ∃x~Fx' is true. Then by rule 5 both $\mathcal{V}$('∀xFx') = T and $\mathcal{V}$('∃x~Fx') = T. Since $\mathcal{V}$('∃x~Fx') = T, by rule 10 there is some potential name α of some object d in the domain of $\mathcal{V}$ such that $\mathcal{V}_{(\alpha,d)}$(~Fα) = T. Hence by rule 4, $\mathcal{V}_{(\alpha,d)}$(Fα) ≠ T. Therefore by rule 9, $\mathcal{V}$('∀xFx') ≠ T. But we said above that $\mathcal{V}$('∀xFx') = T, and so we have a contradiction.
Consequently, '∀xFx & ∃x~Fx' is inconsistent.   QED

To summarize, problems such as those we have been doing are usually most efficiently handled by one of two general strategies:

1. *To prove sequents invalid, formulas or sets consistent, or formulas contingent, construct appropriate valuations, and then show, using the valuation rules, that these valuations make the desired truth-value assignments.* To prove a sequent invalid, the appropriate valuation is one which makes its premises true and its conclusion untrue (a counterexample). To prove a formula consistent, use a valuation which makes it true. To prove a set of formulas consistent, use a valuation which makes

all members of the set true. And to prove a formula contingent, use two valuations, one which makes the formula true and one which makes it untrue.

2. *To prove sequents or formulas valid and formulas or sets inconsistent, proceed by reductio.* Begin, as usual, by supposing the denial of the desired metatheorem. Then unpack this supposition, using the definition of its central term (e.g., 'valid', 'inconsistent'). This unpacking will yield a statement about some valuation $\mathcal{V}$. (For example, if the supposition is that a certain sequent is not valid, then unpacking will yield the statement that there is some valuation $\mathcal{V}$ on which the sequent's premises are true and its conclusion is untrue.) Now further unpack this statement about $\mathcal{V}$, using the valuation rules to analyze the truth conditions for complex formulas into the truth conditions of their simpler components. The desired contradiction should eventually emerge from this analysis.

The next metatheorem follows strategy 2, but the result is a bit surprising. If we interpret 'a' as meaning "God," for example, the metatheorem seems to assert that it is a logical truth that God exists (more literally, that there is something identical to God).

METATHEOREM: '$\exists x \; x = a$' is a valid formula.

PROOF: Suppose for reductio that '$\exists x \; x = a$' is not valid, that is, there is some valuation $\mathcal{V}$ such that $\mathcal{V}(\text{'}\exists x \; x = a\text{'}) \neq T$. Then by rule 9 there is no potential name α of an object d such that $\mathcal{V}_{(\alpha, d)}(\alpha = a) = T$. Now by the definition of a valuation, $\mathcal{V}$ must assign to 'a' some denotation $\mathcal{V}(\text{'a'})$ of which it is a potential name. So in particular, putting 'a' for α and $\mathcal{V}(\text{'a'})$ for d so that $\mathcal{V}_{(\alpha, d)}$ is just $\mathcal{V}$, it follows that $\mathcal{V}(\text{'a = a'}) \neq T$. But since (obviously) $\mathcal{V}(\text{'a'}) = \mathcal{V}(\text{'a'})$, by rule 3, $\mathcal{V}(\text{'a = a'}) = T$—and so we have a contradiction.

Hence, contrary to our supposition, '$\exists x \; x = a$' is valid.   QED

Theology on the cheap! Unfortunately, however, if we interpret 'a' as meaning "the Easter Bunny," we get a similar result. This shocking anomaly reveals that classical predicate logic cannot adequately represent names that do not or might not denote, for it tacitly presupposes that every name denotes some existing thing. This presupposition is embodied in the definition of a valuation, which stipulates that each name be given some object in the domain as its extension. This prejudices the question of whether or not there is anything corresponding to the name. Once we understand how this prejudice is built into the semantics, it is easy to see why according to that semantics '$\exists x \; x = a$' is valid.

But, having accepted this result, we must admit that predicate logic is inapplicable to expressions containing names that do not or might not name. Thus from the validity of '$\exists x\ x = a$' we cannot legitimately infer that it is a logical truth that God exists, for God's existence is a matter of dispute, and so 'a' cannot legitimately be interpreted as naming God.

There are forms of logic, called **free logics,** which dispense with the presupposition that all names denote—at the cost of additional complexities. Logicians have generally found it easier to presuppose that all the names they are using denote than to grapple with these complexities. I concur, at least for pedagogical purposes, which is why I don't begin with free logics. But we'll look into them in Section 15.1.

In addition to the presupposition that each name names, predicate logic has yet another presupposition that creates somewhat dubious valid formulas. This is the assumption, stated in the definition of a valuation, that the domain is non-empty. Given this assumption, there are no valuations in which nothing exists. Yet it seems in some sense possible for nothing to exist—particularly in certain restricted domains of quantification. So here again some modification may be desirable. That modification, too, will be discussed in Section 15.1.

Predicate logic has some other rough edges, the most prominent of which involves statements of the form 'All F are G' where the extension of 'F' is the empty set. Consider, for example, the statement 'All frogs over a hundred feet tall are green', where 'F' means "is a frog over a hundred feet tall" and 'G' means "is green." (There are, I assume, no frogs over a hundred feet tall.) Is this statement true or false?

The question is baffling, for English has no clear conventions to deal with such cases. On the one hand, the fact that there are no frogs that tall seems to make the statement false. But, on the other, since the set of all such frogs is empty, it is true of each thing x that *if* x is a frog over a hundred feet tall, then x is green—at least when we read 'if . . . then' as the material conditional—because for each thing x it is false that it is a frog over a hundred feet tall. Thus understood, this sentence—and, indeed, every quantified conditional whose antecedent term is similarly empty—is true. Hence it is also true that all frogs over a hundred feet tall are red—and yellow, and pink, and colorless . . . ! This is the understanding that prevails, given the conventions of predicate logic. Thus, for example, the sequent '$\sim\exists x Fx \vdash \forall x(Fx \rightarrow Gx)$' is valid. We leave the proof as an exercise.

It is possible to prove results of greater generality than those so far considered. The next metatheorem establishes that for any variable β, the expressions $\sim\exists\beta$ and $\forall\beta\sim$ are equivalent in the sense that any formula beginning with one keeps its truth value if we replace it with the other. (Intuitively this is right, since both expressions mean "for no β.") This equivalence is important; in the next section we use it to justify the tree rule for negated existential statements.

METATHEOREM: For any two formulas of the forms $\sim\exists\beta\Phi$ and $\forall\beta\sim\Phi$ and any valuation $\mathcal{V}$, $\mathcal{V}(\sim\exists\beta\Phi) = \mathcal{V}(\forall\beta\sim\Phi)$.

PROOF: By valuation rule 10 there are two possibilities: either $\mathcal{V}(\sim\exists\beta\Phi)$ = T or $\mathcal{V}(\sim\exists\beta\Phi)$ = F. We consider each in turn.

> Suppose, first, that $\mathcal{V}(\sim\exists\beta\Phi) = T$. Then by valuation rule 4, $\mathcal{V}(\exists\beta\Phi) \neq T$. Hence by rule 10 there is no potential name α of an object d in the domain of $\mathcal{V}$ such that $\mathcal{V}_{(\alpha,d)}(\Phi^\alpha/_\beta) = T$. Thus by rule 4, $\mathcal{V}_{(\alpha,d)}(\sim\Phi^\alpha/_\beta) = T$ for all potential names α of objects d in the domain of $\mathcal{V}$. It follows by rule 9 that $\mathcal{V}(\forall\beta\sim\Phi) = T$ so that $\mathcal{V}(\sim\exists\beta\Phi) = \mathcal{V}(\forall\beta\sim\Phi)$.
>
> Hence we have shown that if $\mathcal{V}(\sim\exists\beta\Phi) = T$, then $\mathcal{V}(\sim\exists\beta\Phi) = \mathcal{V}(\forall\beta\sim\Phi)$. Suppose, then, to consider the second case, that $\mathcal{V}(\sim\exists\beta\Phi) = F$. It follows by rule 4 that $\mathcal{V}(\exists\beta\Phi) = T$. Then by rule 10 there is a potential name α of an object d such that $\mathcal{V}_{(\alpha,d)}(\Phi^\alpha/_\beta) = T$. Hence by rule 4, $\mathcal{V}_{(\alpha,d)}(\sim\Phi^\alpha/_\beta) \neq T$. But then by rule 9, $\mathcal{V}(\forall\beta\sim\Phi) = F$ so that once again $\mathcal{V}(\sim\exists\beta\Phi) = \mathcal{V}(\forall\beta\sim\Phi)$.
>
> Hence we have shown that if $\mathcal{V}(\sim\exists\beta\Phi) = F$, then $\mathcal{V}(\sim\exists\beta\Phi) = \mathcal{V}(\forall\beta\sim\Phi)$. Since the same conclusion follows in either case, it must be the case that $\mathcal{V}(\sim\exists\beta\Phi) = \mathcal{V}(\forall\beta\sim\Phi)$.   QED

The strategy here is often called **constructive dilemma,** or **argument by cases.** We begin with a disjunctive premise—in this case either $\mathcal{V}(\sim\exists\beta\Phi) = T$ or $\mathcal{V}(\sim\exists\beta\Phi) = F$—and prove that each of its disjuncts leads to the same conclusion. (These subsidiary proofs may be thought of as conditional proofs.) Then it follows that that conclusion must be true.

To those already familiar with object language systems of deduction, like the one presented in Chapter 8, these metatheoretic proofs may seem extravagant. The former rely on a small number of simple syntactic rules, whereas our metaproofs use more cumbersome semantic methods. But these semantic methods are more powerful. Object language proofs can establish the validity of sequents, but not their invalidity. If we construct a proof for a sequent, we know it is valid; but if we can't, we don't know anything. The sequent might be invalid, or we might just not have hit upon the way to prove it. Using the semantic techniques of this section, we can prove both validity and invalidity—and deal as well with the related concepts of consistency, contingency, and so on. Moreover, the semantics presented in this section provides the background needed to understand trees in predicate logic. And trees handle much of what we have been doing here with metatheorems while avoiding much of the cumbersomeness.

Exercise 7.3

Prove the following metatheorems, using the valuation rules and appropriate definitions:

1. '$\forall x Fx \vdash Fa$' is a valid sequent.
2. '$\exists x Fx \vdash \forall x Fx$' is an invalid sequent.
3. '$\exists x \sim x = a$' is a consistent formula.
4. The formula '$\exists x(Fx \ \& \sim Fx)$' is inconsistent.
5. The formula '$\forall x Fx \lor \exists x \sim Fx$' is valid.

6. The formula '$\exists x Fx$' is contingent.
7. The sequent 'Fa ⊢ $\forall x Fx$' is invalid.
8. '$\sim a = a$' is inconsistent.
9. '$\sim \exists x\ x = x$' is inconsistent.
10. For any two formulas of the forms $\exists \beta \sim \Phi$ and $\sim \forall \beta \Phi$ and any valuation $\mathcal{V}$, $\mathcal{V}(\exists \beta \sim \Phi) = \mathcal{V}(\sim \forall \beta \Phi)$.

7.4 TREES FOR PREDICATE LOGIC

The tree test for predicate logic retains all the tree rules for propositional logic (Section 3.3) and adds six more—two each to deal with the two quantifiers and the identity predicate. As in propositional logic, the purpose of a tree is to display valuations on which all the formulas of the initial list are true. However, while trees in propositional logic display all such valuations, trees in predicate logic do not. Formulas true on one valuation in predicate logic are true on infinitely many others (we can always, for example, replace the objects in the domain of that valuation by other surrogate objects), whereas in propositional logic the number of valuations of a given set of formulas is finite.

Still, a tree in predicate logic displays all the general classes of valuations on which its initial list of formulas might be true—and, as in propositional logic, each open path of a finished tree can be interpreted as displaying at least one valuation on which the initial list is true. Moreover, as in propositional logic, if all paths close, the initial list is inconsistent.

We shall begin our examination of trees in predicate logic by considering the tree rule governing unnegated existentially quantified formulas. An existentially quantified formula $\exists \beta \Phi$ is true on a valuation $\mathcal{V}$ iff there is an object d in the domain such that for some potential name α of d, $\Phi^\alpha/_\beta$—the result of replacing every occurrence of β in Φ by α—is true on $\mathcal{V}$. So to display in a tree the way in which an existentially quantified formula can be true, we give d a name α and assert $\Phi^\alpha/_\beta$. To ensure that α is a potential name for d, no matter which object d is, we require that α be new to the path so that no value has been assigned to it by valuations of the initial list. Thus the rule may be stated as follows:

Existential Rule (∃)   If an unchecked formula of the form $\exists \beta \Phi$ appears on an open path, check it. Then choose a name α that does not yet appear anywhere on that path and write $\Phi^\alpha/_\beta$, the result of replacing every occurrence of β in Φ by α, at the bottom of every open path that contains the newly checked formula.

We shall illustrate the use of this rule by constructing a tree for the sequent '$\exists x Fx$ ⊢ Fa':

1. $\sqrt{\exists x Fx}$ Premise
2. ~Fa   Negation of conclusion
3. Fb   1 ∃

Once we introduce the new name 'b' by ∃ at 3, there is nothing more to be done. The unchecked formulas are atomic, and no further rules apply. So the tree is finished, and its one path has not closed. This indicates that the sequent is invalid.

What counterexample is displayed here? Recall that a counterexample is a valuation that makes the premises true and the conclusion untrue, and a valuation in predicate logic has two components: a domain and an assignment of extensions to predicates and names. In general, we shall take the domain of the valuation defined by an open path to consist just of the objects mentioned by name in the formulas on that path. Here, for example, the only names appearing in the formulas of the open path are 'a' and 'b'. Since in uninterpreted models the identity of the objects in the domain is a matter of indifference, we'll let them be numbers. To keep things simple and uniform, let's stipulate that in all problems the name 'a' denotes the number 1, 'b' the number 2, 'c' the number 3, and so on.[3] Thus, if an open path on a tree contains the names 'a' and 'b', and no others, as in our example, the domain of the valuation defined by that path is {1, 2}.

The stipulation announced in the previous paragraph already determines the extensions assigned to 'a' and 'b'. They are 1 and 2, respectively. To complete the counterexample, we need only to specify the extension of the one-place predicate 'F'.

In general, extensions are assigned to predicates in the following ways: For any atomic formula that occurs unnegated on the path, if it is a zero-place predicate, then the valuation assigns that predicate the extension T; if it is a one-place predicate followed by a name, then the number denoted by that name is in the extension of that predicate; and if it is an n-place predicate followed by n names, then the n-tuple of numbers denoted by those names in the order of their occurrence is a member of the extension of the predicate. Zero-place predicates which either do not appear on the path or appear negated on the path are assigned the value F; and single numbers or n-tuples not explicitly included in a predicate's extension by the occurrence of the corresponding atomic sentence on the path are assumed not to be in that predicate's extension.

Therefore, since 'Fb' appears on the path, the number 2, which is the object denoted by 'b', is in the extension of 'F'. And since there is no atomic formula of the form Fα on the path for any other name α, 2 is the only member of the extension of 'F'. The extension of 'F', therefore, is {2}.

Accordingly, the valuation $\mathcal{V}$ defined by the open path of this tree is

Domain of $\mathcal{V}$ = {1, 2}
$\mathcal{V}$('a')   = 1
$\mathcal{V}$('b')   = 2
$\mathcal{V}$('F')   = {2}

---

[3] We could also give naming conventions for subscripted names, but we won't bother since in practice we won't use them.

It is easy to see, using the valuation rules of predicate logic, that this is a valuation on which '∃xFx' is true and 'Fa' is false and hence a counterexample.

This is, of course, an uninterpreted valuation. To give it some intuitive content, we might convert it into a surrogate valuation by taking 'a' to mean "Al", 'b' to mean "Beth," and 'F' to mean, say, "is female." Thus the number one is a surrogate for Al and two is a surrogate for Beth. Then the specific possible situation it represents is a situation involving only Al and Beth in which Beth is female, but Al isn't. And that situation is a clear counterexample to the argument

> Something is female.
> ∴ Al is female.

Thus we can see intuitively, as well as formally, why the sequent '∃xFx ⊢ Fa' is invalid.

Let's now turn to the rules for negated quantifiers:

Negated Existential Rule (~∃)   If an unchecked formula of the form ~∃βΦ appears on an open path, check it and write ∀β~Φ at the bottom of every open path that contains the newly checked formula.

Negated Universal Rule (~∀)   If an unchecked formula of the form ~∀βΦ appears on an open path, check it and write ∃β~Φ at the bottom of every open path that contains the newly checked formula.

These rules convert negated existential or universal statements into quantified negations, which can then be analyzed with the rules for unnegated existential or universal formulas. The negated existential rule depends on the fact that '~∃α' and '∀α~' are equivalent, which was proved as a metatheorem near the end of Section 7.3. Similarly, the negated universal rule depends on the equivalence of '~∀α' and '∃α~' (see problem 10 of Exercise 7.3).

The tree for the sequent '~∃xFx ⊢ ∀x~Fx' provides a simple illustration of the use of the ~∃ rule:

1. √~∃xFx   Premise
2. ~∀x~Fx   Negation of conclusion
3. ∀x~Fx   1 ~∃
4. ×   2, 3 ~

Here application of ~∃ to the formula at line 1 produces an immediate contradiction and closes the path. The sequent is valid. There is no counterexample.

Notice that the annotation at line 4 specifically mentions that the ~ rule was used to close the path. In predicate logic there are two path-closing rules: the familiar rule ~ and a new rule, ~=, which will be introduced shortly. It is useful, therefore, to begin to get into the habit of specifying which rule we are using when closing a path.

The tree for the sequent 'Fa & Ga ⊢ ∀x(Fx & Gx)' illustrates the use of the ~∀ rule:

1.	√Fa & Ga	Premise
2.	√~∀x(Fx & Gx)	Negation of conclusion
3.	Fa	1 &
4.	Ga	1 &
5.	√∃x~(Fx & Gx)	2 ~∀
6.	√~(Fb & Gb)	5 ∃

7. ~Fb 6 ~&   ~Gb 6 ~&

At this point all nonatomic formulas are checked, and there is nothing left to do, so the tree is complete. This tree has two open paths, but both represent the same valuation $\mathscr{V}$:

Domain of $\mathscr{V}$	=	{1, 2}
$\mathscr{V}$('a')	=	1
$\mathscr{V}$('b')	=	2
$\mathscr{V}$('F')	=	{1}
$\mathscr{V}$('G')	=	{1}

And this valuation is a counterexample to the sequent. If we interpret 'a' to mean "Al," 'b' to mean "Beth," 'F' to mean "is foolish," and 'G' to mean "is greedy," then the sequent says that since Al is foolish and greedy, everyone is foolish and greedy. The valuation defined by the tree represents a conterexample to this inference. The counterexample is a situation involving only Al and Beth in which Al is both foolish and greedy but Beth is neither.

The final quantifier rule is the rule for the unnegated universal quantifier. What makes a universally quantified statement ∀βΦ true on a valuation $\mathscr{V}$ is that each **instance** of the form $\Phi^\alpha/_\beta$ is true, where $\Phi^\alpha/_\beta$ is the result of replacing all occurrences of β in Φ by a potential name α of an object in the domain. This suggests that the tree rule for the universal quantifier should enable us to produce an instance of the quantified formula for each object in the domain.

However, in constructing trees, we construct the domain associated with each open path as we go. Since existential formulas may introduce new names onto the path, we cannot in all cases be sure what the ultimate domain will be until the path is complete. (Of course, if the path closes, there is no domain to worry about.) Therefore, even if we instantiate a universal formula for each name currently on the path (that is, apply the ∀ rule for each such name), so long as the path is not finished, that is no guarantee the path contains each instance of the universal formula required to make that formula true. New objects may be added to the domain later. Thus we cannot be sure that we are done using a universal formula until the path is finished. *This means that, unlike other formulas, universal formulas should not be checked when we apply their tree rule.*

Ultimately, unless the path closes, we should obtain an instance of each universal formula for each name on the path. But what if we need to apply the universal rule to a formula on a path that does not yet contain any names at all? For an answer, we must recall the stipulation contained within the definition of a valuation that the domain must be nonempty. There must, in other words, be at least one object in the domain. We therefore introduce a new name for that object and instantiate the quantified formula using that name.

The universal rule may thus be stated as follows:

Universal Rule (∀)   If a formula of the form ∀βΦ appears on an open path and α is a name that occurs in a formula on that path, write Φ^α/$_β$ (the result of replacing all occurrences of β in Φ by α) at the bottom of the path. If no formula containing a name appears on the path, then choose some name α and write Φ^α/$_β$ at the bottom of the path. In either case, *do not* check ∀βΦ.

Let's use the tree for the sequent '∀x(Fx → Gx), ∀xFx ⊢ Ga' to illustrate this rule:

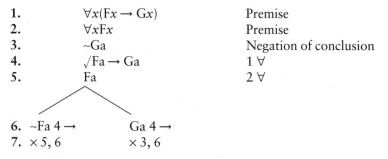

1.	∀x(Fx → Gx)	Premise
2.	∀xFx	Premise
3.	~Ga	Negation of conclusion
4.	√Fa → Ga	1 ∀
5.	Fa	2 ∀

6. ~Fa 4 →	Ga 4 →
7. × 5, 6	× 3, 6

Since the only name on the path is 'a', this is the name used to instantiate the quantified formulas on lines 1 and 2 by ∀. The results appear at lines 4 and 5. Note that neither universal formula is checked. Since both paths close, the sequent is valid.

The sequent '∀xFx ⊢ ∃xFx' provides an example of the use of ∀ on a path initially containing no names:

1. ∀xFx   Premise
2. √~∃xFx   Negation of conclusion
3. ∀x~Fx   2 ~∃
4. Fa   1 ∀
5. ~Fa   3 ∀
6. ×   4, 5

At line 4, since no name yet appears on the path, we choose the new name 'a' and instantiate '∀xFx' with 'a' to obtain 'Fa'. But at line 5, since 'a' now appears at line 4, we use 'a' again to instantiate '∀x~Fx'. This yields a contradiction and closes the path, showing the sequent to be valid.

Consider now the tree for the sequent '∃xFx & ∃xGx ⊢ ∃x(Fx & Gx)':

1.	$\sqrt{}\exists x Fx \,\&\, \exists x Gx$	Premise
2.	$\sqrt{}\mathord{\sim}\exists x(Fx \,\&\, Gx)$	Negation of conclusion
3.	$\sqrt{}\exists x Fx$	1 &
4.	$\sqrt{}\exists x Gx$	1 &
5.	Fa	3 ∃
6.	Gb	4 ∃
7.	$\forall x\mathord{\sim}(Fx \,\&\, Gx)$	2 ∼∃
8.	$\sqrt{}\mathord{\sim}(Fa \,\&\, Ga)$	7 ∀
9.	$\sqrt{}\mathord{\sim}(Fb \,\&\, Gb)$	7 ∀

| 10. | ∼Fa 8 ∼&   ∼Ga 8 ∼& |
| 11. | × 5, 10 ∼ |

| 12. | ∼Fb 9 ∼&   ∼Gb 9 ∼& |
| 13. | ×   6, 12 ∼ |

Note, first, that in each of its applications (lines 5 and 6) the rule ∃ introduces a *new* name. Notice, too, that the universal formula at line 7 is unchecked. But since it has been instantiated for each name on the path (at lines 8 and 9), nothing further can be done with it (∀ introduces a new name only if the path does not yet contain any names). All the other unchecked formulas are atomic. Therefore the tree is finished.

The open path represents the following valuation $\mathcal{V}$:

Domain of $\mathcal{V}$ = {1, 2}
$\mathcal{V}$('a') = 1
$\mathcal{V}$('b') = 2
$\mathcal{V}$('F') = {1}
$\mathcal{V}$('G') = {2}

When multiple quantifiers are present, there must be multiple applications of the quantifier rules, as the tree for the sequent '$\forall x\forall y(Fxy \rightarrow \mathord{\sim}Fyx) \vdash \mathord{\sim}\exists x Fxx$' illustrates:

1.	$\forall x\forall y(Fxy \rightarrow \mathord{\sim}Fyx)$	Premise
2.	$\sqrt{}\mathord{\sim}\mathord{\sim}\exists x Fxx$	Negation of conclusion
3.	$\sqrt{}\exists x Fxx$	2 ∼∼
4.	Faa	3 ∃
5.	$\forall y(Fay \rightarrow \mathord{\sim}Fya)$	1 ∀
6.	$\sqrt{}Faa \rightarrow \mathord{\sim}Faa$	5 ∀

| 7. | ∼Faa 6 →   ∼Faa 6 → |
| 8. | × 4, 7 ∼   × 4, 7 ∼ |

The sequent is valid.

Trees for predicate logic may also contain sentence letters, as in propositional logic. Here is the tree for '~∃xFx → P, ~Fa ⊢ P':

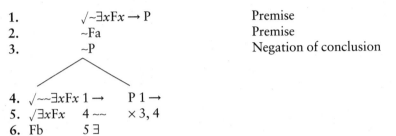

1.	√~∃xFx → P	Premise
2.	~Fa	Premise
3.	~P	Negation of conclusion

4.	√~~∃xFx 1 →		P 1 →	
5.	√∃xFx 4 ~~		× 3, 4	
6.	Fb 5 ∃			

Note the introduction of the new name 'b' at step 6. ∃ requires a new name and does not allow us to conclude 'Fa'. Thus the left path remains open. It represents the following valuation 𝒱:

Domain of 𝒱 = {1, 2}
𝒱('a')   = 1
𝒱('b')   = 2
𝒱('F')   = {2}
𝒱('P')   = F

The tree tests for consistency, contingency, the validity of formulas, and other semantic properties are the same as in propositional logic. The following tree, for example, tests the *formula* '~(∀x~Fx & ∃xFx)' for validity:

1.	√~~(∀x~Fx & ∃xFx)	Negation of given formula
2.	√∀x~Fx & ∃xFx	1 ~~
3.	∀x~Fx	2 &
4.	√∃xFx	2 &
5.	Fa	4 ∃
6.	~Fa	3 ∀
7.	×	5, 6 ~

The formula is valid. Note that I apply ∃ at line 5 before applying ∀ at line 6. As a general policy, this saves work. If I had applied ∀ first, I would have had to introduce a new name with it and then introduce a second new name with the application of ∃ to line 4. Then I would have had to apply ∀ to line 3 again for this second new name. The path still would have closed, but the way I did it is much simpler.

Next, we consider an example unlike any that we have so far examined—the tree for the sequent '∀x∃yCxy ⊢ Caa':

1.	∀x∃yCxy	Premise
2.	~Caa	Negation of conclusion
3.	√∃yCay	1 ∀
4.	Cab	3 ∃
5.	√∃yCby	1 ∀
6.	Cbc	5 ∃

7. $\sqrt{\exists y Ccy}$ 1 $\forall$
8. Ccd 7 $\exists$

       .
        .
         .

This tree goes on forever. Each time we instantiate the universal formula at line 1, we get a new existential formula. Then we must apply $\exists$ to this existential formula. But that produces a new name, and we must go back and instantiate 1 again with that new name. This produces yet another existential formula, and the cycle begins anew. Yet the infinite path specifies a counterexample. The counterexample is the valuation $\mathcal{V}$ such that

$$\text{Domain of } \mathcal{V} = \{1, 2, 3, 4, \ldots\}$$
$$\mathcal{V}(\text{'a'}) = 1$$
$$\mathcal{V}(\text{'b'}) = 2$$
.
.
.
$$\mathcal{V}(\text{'C'}) = \{<1, 2>, <2, 3>, <3, 4>, \ldots\}$$

Both the domain and the extension of 'C' are infinite sets, and infinitely many names (indicated by the three dots) receive extensions.

To understand this example intuitively, think of 'C' as meaning "is caused by." Then the premise '$\forall x \exists y Cxy$' means that everything is caused by something—that is, everything has a cause—and the conclusion means "a is caused by itself." The counterexample, then, represents a situation in which everything has a cause and the succession of causes is infinite. We might think of the numbers in the domain as representing events. Then for each number n, $n + 1$ represents the cause of n. In this situation it is true that each event has a cause, but false that event a is self-caused. Hence it is clear that the sequent is invalid.

Yet the tree itself can never be completed. We can see intuitively the answer it would give if we could complete it: The sequent is invalid. But in fact the tree test is in this case nonterminating. That fact is profoundly significant, but we shall not explore its significance until Chapter 10.

In the meantime, we have two other tree rules to consider—the identity rules. An identity statement—that is, a statement of the form $\alpha = \beta$—is true iff α and β name the same object. Hence anything that is true of the object named by α must also be true of the object named by β. Thus, if one of these names occurs in a formula, we should be able to substitute the other name for it without changing that formula's truth value. This leads us to the rule for unnegated identity statements:

Identity (=)   If a formula of the form $\alpha = \beta$ appears on an open path, then if another formula Φ containing either α or β appears unchecked on that path, write at the bottom of the path any formula not already occurring (checked or unchecked) on the path which results from replacing one or more occurrences of either of these names by the other in Φ. Do not check either α = β or Φ.

The stipulation that the formula obtained should not have occurred previously, either checked or unchecked, on the path, prevents repetition—and hence useless work.

Notice that, like a universally quantified statement, an identity statement is never checked. This is because, like a universally quantified statement, an identity statement may be reused repeatedly as new formulas to which it is applicable are added to the path. This tree for the sequent 'a = b, Lab ⊢ Lba' illustrates its use:

1.	a = b	Premise
2.	Lab	Premise
3.	~Lba	Negation of conclusion
4.	Lbb	1, 2 =
5.	~Lbb	1, 3 =
6.	×	4, 5

At step 3 we replace the 'a' in 'Lab' by 'b' to obtain 'Lbb'. Similarly, at step 4 we replace the 'a' in '~Lba' by 'b' to obtain '~Lbb'.

Getting the tree to close this quickly requires some foresight; many of the substitutions of 'a' for 'b' or 'b' for 'a' that we could have made would not help in closing the tree. However, by making all possible substitutions of this sort in all the unchecked formulas of the tree, we would eventually hit upon one that would close the tree. But such "blind" substitution is inefficient; intelligent planning is better.

The negated identity rule is encouragingly simple:

Negated Identity (~=)   Close any open path on which a formula of the form ~α = α occurs.

Clearly any formula of the form ~α = α is inconsistent, which is what justifies this rule. The tree for the sequent 'a = b ⊢ b = a' illustrates the rule:

1.	a = b	Premise
2.	~b = a	Negation of conclusion
3.	~b = b	1, 2 =
4.	×	3 ~=

The sequent is valid. At step 3 we replace the occurrence of 'a' in '~b = a' by 'b' to obtain '~b = b', which closes the tree by ~=.

Consider now the tree for the sequent 'Fa, Fb ⊢ a = b':

1. Fa   Premise
2. Fb   Premise
3. ~a = b   Negation of conclusion

Nothing more can be done here. Neither the identity rule nor the negated identity rule applies to formulas of the form $\sim\alpha = \beta$, where α and β are different names. So the tree is finished and the sequent is invalid. The open path represents the following valuation:

Domain = {1, 2}
$\mathcal{V}$('a')   = 1
$\mathcal{V}$('b')   = 2
$\mathcal{V}$('F')   = {1, 2}

Finally, let's consider the sequent '~a = b, ~b = c ⊢ ~a = c':

1. ~a = b   Premise
2. ~b = c   Premise
3. √~~a = c   Negation of conclusion
4. a = c   3~~
5. ~c = b   1, 4 =
6. ~b = a   2, 4 =

The only identity statement here is at line 4. We apply this statement to each formula to which it can be applied, but still the tree does not close. Hence the sequent is invalid.

When open paths contain unnegated identity statements, we must modify our conventions regarding how open paths define valuations. The formula 'a = c' can be true only if 'a' and 'c' name the same object. To ensure that, we adopt the following stipulation: *When formulas of the form $\alpha = \beta$ appear on an open path, the extension assigned to each name is the lowest number assigned to any name with which it is identified, either directly or via a series of intermediate identity statements.* Names not occurring in identity statements, however, have their usual denotations. For example, in the tree above, 'a' would normally denote 1 and 'c' would normally denote 3. But since 'a = c' appears on the open path, we change the denotation of 'c' to the lesser denotation 1. Thus the valuation specified by this tree is

Domain = {1, 2}
$\mathcal{V}$('a')   = 1
$\mathcal{V}$('b')   = 2
$\mathcal{V}$('c')   = 1

This is clearly a counterexample.

Though I have dropped a number of hints along the way, I have not yet said explicitly how to determine whether a tree is finished. I do so now: A tree in predicate logic is finished when either all of its paths close or no more rules can be applied to any of the formulas left on its open paths. No more rules apply to the formulas of a path when each formula on that path

1. is checked, or
2. is an atomic formula *not* of the form α = β, or
3. is the negation of an atomic formula (including formulas of the form ~α = β), or
4. is a universal formula to which the rule ∀ has been applied for each name on the path, or
5. is a formula of the form α = β which has been applied to each formula Φ (not including α = β itself) that contains either the name α or the name β to produce every possible consequence obtainable by the identity rule.

Whenever you produce a tree that contains open paths, check each path with this five-item list to make sure that the tree is really finished.

Table 7.1 summarizes the six new tree rules for predicate logic with identity, along with the valuation rules to which they correspond (for a similar summary of the tree rules for propositional logic, see Table 3.4 in Section 3.3):

Order of Application

In propositional logic the order in which rules were applied made no difference, except as a matter of keeping things simple. We get the correct answer if we apply the rules correctly, no matter what the order of application. In predicate logic this is no longer true: *Order of application matters.* If we apply rules in the wrong order, we may get an infinite tree even if the tree can be closed. Consider, for example, the inconsistent set {∀x∃yFyx, ∃x∀y~Fyx}. (To see informally that this set is inconsistent, think of 'F' as meaning "is the father of." Then the first of the two formulas says that everything has a father and the second that something is fatherless.) Now suppose we test the set for inconsistency by applying the rules in the following *incorrect* order:

1. ∀x∃yFyx	Given		
2. √∃x∀y~Fyx	Given		
3. √∃yFya	1 ∀	Wrong!	
4. Fba	3 ∃	Wrong!	
5. √∃yFyb	1 ∀	Wrong!	
6. Fcb	5 ∃	Wrong!	
7. √∃yFyc	1 ∀	Wrong!	
8. Fcd	7 ∃	Wrong!	

.
.
.

We can continue applying ∀ to 1 and then ∃ to the resulting formula forever. Yet since the set is inconsistent the tree ought to close. In fact, it does close if we apply the rules in a different order:

1. ∀x∃yFyx	Given
2. √∃x∀y~Fyx	Given
3. ∀y~Fya	2 ∃

TABLE 7.1
The Correspondence Between Valuation Rules and Tree Rules

Valuation Rule	Corresponding Tree Rule
$\mathcal{V}(\exists\beta\Phi) = $ T iff for some potential name α of some object d in $\mathfrak{D}$, $\mathcal{V}_{(\alpha,d)}(\Phi^{\alpha}/_{\beta}) = $ T.	**Existential Quantification ($\exists$)** If an unchecked formula of the form $\exists\beta\Phi$ appears on an open path, check it. Then choose a name α that does not yet appear anywhere on that path and write $\Phi^{\alpha}/_{\beta}$, the result of replacing every occurrence of β in Φ by α, at the bottom of every open path that contains the newly checked formula.
$\mathcal{V}(\exists\beta\Phi) = $ F iff for all potential names α of all objects d in $\mathfrak{D}$, $\mathcal{V}_{(\alpha,d)}(\Phi^{\alpha}/_{\beta}) \neq $ T.	**Negated Existential Quantification ($\sim\exists$)** If an unchecked formula of the form $\sim\exists\beta\Phi$ appears on an open path, check it and write $\forall\beta\sim\Phi$ at the bottom of every open path that contains the newly checked formula.
$\mathcal{V}(\forall\beta\Phi) = $ T iff for all potential names α of all objects d in $\mathfrak{D}$, $\mathcal{V}_{(\alpha,d)}(\Phi^{\alpha}/_{\beta}) = $ T.	**Universal Quantification ($\forall$)** If a formula of the form $\forall\beta\Phi$ appears on an open path and α is a name that occurs in a formula on that path, write $\Phi^{\alpha}/_{\beta}$ (the result of replacing all occurrences of β in Φ by α) at the bottom of the path. If no formula containing a name appears on the path, then choose some name α and write $\Phi^{\alpha}/_{\beta}$ at the bottom of the path. In either case, *do not* check $\forall\beta\Phi$.
$\mathcal{V}(\forall\beta\Phi) = $ F iff for some potential name α of some object d in $\mathfrak{D}$, $\mathcal{V}_{(\alpha,d)}(\Phi^{\alpha}/_{\beta}) \neq $ T.	**Negated Universal Quantification ($\sim\forall$)** If an unchecked formula of the form $\sim\forall\beta\Phi$ appears on an open path, check it and write $\exists\beta\sim\Phi$ at the bottom of every open path that contains the newly checked formula.
$\mathcal{V}(\alpha = \beta) = $ T iff $\mathcal{V}(\alpha) = \mathcal{V}(\beta)$.	**Identity (=)** If a formula of the form $\alpha = \beta$ appears on an open path, then if another formula Φ containing either α or β appears unchecked on that path, write at the bottom of the path any formula not already occurring (checked or unchecked) on the path which results from replacing one or more occurrences of either of these names by the other in Φ. Do not check either $\alpha = \beta$ or Φ.
$\mathcal{V}(\alpha = \beta) = $ F iff $\mathcal{V}(\alpha) \neq \mathcal{V}(\beta)$; more to the point than this general rule is this more specific consequence of it: $\mathcal{V}(\alpha = \alpha) = $ F iff $\mathcal{V}(\alpha) \neq \mathcal{V}(\alpha)$.	**Negated Identity ($\sim=$)** Close any open path on which a formula of the form $\sim\alpha = \alpha$ occurs.

4. $\sqrt{}\exists y Fya$	1 $\forall$
5. Fba	4 $\exists$
6. ~Fba	3 $\forall$
7. $\times$	5, 6

The problem with the first tree was that we never used line 2; we simply ignored it. If, instead, we switch back and forth among the usable lines, rather than getting stuck in some subset of them, we can guarantee that trees whose initial lists are inconsistent will always close. (This will not, however, always prevent infinite trees for *consistent* initial lists.) The simplest way to do this is to impose a prescribed order on the application of rules. One such order is specified below. Apply every rule you can under item A before going to item B; apply every rule you can under item B before going to item C; and so on. When you finish with item F, go back and start at the beginning of the list again, and repeat this procedure until the tree is finished.

A. Path-closing rules (~, ~=)
B. Nonbranching rules other than =, $\exists$, and $\forall$ (that is, the rules ~~, &, ~v, ~→)
C. Branching rules (i.e., the rules v, →, ~&, ↔, ~↔)
D. =
E. $\exists$
F. $\forall$

Using this order of application rigidly and mechanically will guarantee that the tree will close if its initial list is inconsistent. (We prove this in Section 9.2.) But sometimes you can get the tree to close more quickly by deviating from the prescribed order. I did this in the second tree above (the one that closes). At the beginning (line 3) I followed the prescribed order. Unable to apply any rules from items A through D, I applied $\exists$, as directed in item E. At that point the only unchecked formulas left were universal, so I moved to item F, applying $\forall$ to line 1 at line 4. So far so good; I was still conforming to the prescribed order. But if I had continued to do so, I would have applied $\forall$ again at line 5 to get '~Faa' from line 3, for the procedure is to apply every rule possible under item F before going back to the beginning of the list. But instead I skipped that step—knowing that the formula '~Faa' would not be useful in closing the tree—and went back up to item E, applying $\exists$ at line 5. If I had followed the order of application exactly, my tree would have had one extra line ('~Faa', inserted between the current lines 4 and 5), but still it would have closed. Instead, I thought ahead and saved a step.

In practice, you can usually ignore the prescribed order of application. If a tree is going to close, intelligence and forethought usually reveal a way to close it without resorting to this clumsy and inefficient procedure.

But in theory, this prescribed order officially governs tree construction. By assuming that the rules are always applied in this order, we will be able to show that the tree test detects inconsistency (or validity) without fail; that is, it never goes on infinitely if the initial list is inconsistent. This assumption is essential to the completeness proof of Section 9.2. If we don't constrain rule application, the tree test becomes incomplete.

Exercise 7.4.1

Construct a tree for each of the following sequents to decide whether it is valid. If it is invalid, specify one of the valuations defined by an open path of its tree that serves as a counterexample.

1. $\forall x Fx \vdash Fa$
2. $\exists x Fx \vdash \forall x Fx$
3. $Fa \vdash \exists x Fx$
4. $Fa \vdash \forall x Fx$
5. $\sim\exists x\sim Fx \vdash \forall x Fx$
6. $\forall x Fx \vdash \sim\exists x\sim Fx$
7. $\forall x\sim Fx \vdash \sim\forall x Fx$
8. $\sim\forall x Fx \vdash \forall x\sim Fx$
9. $\sim\exists x(Fx \mathbin{\&} Gx) \vdash \sim Fa$
10. $Fa \rightarrow Gb, \forall x\sim Fx \vdash \sim Gb$
11. $\forall x(Fx \rightarrow Gx), \sim\exists x Gx \vdash \sim Fa$
12. $\forall x(Fx \rightarrow Gx), \forall x Gx \vdash Fa$
13. $\forall x Fx \rightarrow \forall x Gx, \sim\exists x Gx \vdash \exists x\sim Fx$
14. $\exists x(Fx \mathbin{\&} Gx) \vdash \exists x Fx \mathbin{\&} \exists x Gx$
15. $\forall x Fx \lor \forall x Gx \vdash \forall x(Fx \lor Gx)$
16. $\forall x(Fx \lor Gx) \vdash \forall x Fx \lor \forall x Gx$
17. $\exists x(Fx \mathbin{\&} \sim Fx) \vdash P$
18. $\exists x Fx \mathbin{\&} \exists x\sim Fx \vdash P$
19. $\forall x\forall y(Lxy \rightarrow Lyx), \exists x Lax \vdash \exists x Lxa$
20. $\exists x\exists y Lxy \vdash \exists x Lxx$
21. $\exists x\forall y Lxy \vdash \forall x\exists y Lyx$
22. $\forall x(Fx \rightarrow \forall y Gy), Fa \vdash \forall x Gx$
23. $\forall x(\exists y Gy \rightarrow Fx), Ga \vdash \forall x Fx$
24. $Fa, Gb \vdash a = b$
25. $Fa, \sim Fb \vdash \sim a = b$
26. $\forall x(Fx \rightarrow Gx), \sim Fa \vdash \exists x\sim x = a$
27. $Lab \vdash \exists x\exists y\sim x = y$
28. $\vdash \forall x\ x = x$
29. $\vdash \forall x\forall y(x = y \rightarrow y = x)$
30. $\vdash \forall x\forall y\forall z((x = y \mathbin{\&} y = z) \rightarrow x = z)$

Exercise 7.4.2

What follows is one of many versions of the famous ontological argument for the existence of God:

> God is (by definition) the most perfect being. Anything that exists is more perfect than anything that does not exist. Therefore, God exists.

Formalize this argument using the name 'g' for 'God' and the two-place predicate 'P' for 'is more perfect' (hint: review the treatment of superlatives in Section 6.3). Then use a tree to test the argument for validity. Explain what the tree test shows.

Trees with Function Symbols

The addition of function symbols to predicate logic requires no additional tree rules, but because it expands our notion of a name (see Section 6.4), complex names formed with function symbols may now be used with the universal quantifier and identity rules. There are four points to keep in mind:

1. *For the purposes of the universal quantifier rule ($\forall$), each complex name formed by a function symbol is a name; a path is therefore not complete until the quantifier rule has been applied for each of these names that occurs on that path. In the formula 'Lom(m(o))', for example, there are three names:*

    $$m(m(o)) \qquad m(o) \qquad o$$

    The universal quantifier rule applies to all three.
2. *When instantiating universally quantified formulas, instantiate all names containing no function symbols first, then all names containing one function symbol, then all names containing two function symbols, and so on—unless you can see a quick way to close the path by not doing so. This ensures that you don't go on infinitely instantiating, having skipped a name that might close the path. If you break this rule, the tree test may fail to give an answer even for valid arguments.*
3. *The universal quantifier rule ($\forall$), when applied to paths containing no names, and the existential quantifier rule ($\exists$) produce only noncompound names; that is, the names used to replace the variables when these rules are applied never contain function symbols.*
4. *The identity rules (= and ~=) may be used with either simple or complex names.*

Consider, for example, the tree for the sequent '$\forall x\, Lf(x)x \vdash Lf(f(a))f(a)$':

1	$\forall x\, Lf(x)x$	Premise
2.	$\sim Lf(f(a))f(a)$	Negation of conclusion
3.	$Lf(f(a))f(a)$	1 $\forall$
4.	$\times$	2, 3 $\sim$

At step 3 we apply the universal rule, replacing both occurrences of the variable 'x' in '$Lf(x)x$' by the name '$f(a)$'. This closes the tree, showing that the sequent is valid. Note that here we instantiate with '$f(a)$' before instantiating with 'a', taking advantage of the 'unless' clause in rule 2 above.

The following tree tests the sequent '$\exists x\, Lxf(x) \vdash Lof(o)$' for validity:

1.	$\sqrt{}\,\exists x\, Lxf(x)$	Premise
2.	$\sim Lof(o)$	Negation of conclusion
3.	$Laf(a)$	1 $\exists$

We apply the existential rule as usual to line 1, introducing a new name 'a'. This leaves only atomic formulas. The tree shows that in a domain containing four objects (corresponding to the four names, 'o', '$f(o)$', 'a', and '$f(a)$') there is an obvious counterexample. Technically, we need to specify the value of the function f for each object in the domain. Since 'f(o)' and 'f(a)' designate objects in the domain, a complete valuation will specify the extensions of 'f(f(o))', 'f(f(f(o)))', 'f(f(a))', and so on. But since these expressions do not occur in any formula in the tree, the extension we assign to them doesn't matter, so we may as well just set their extensions all conventionally as 1.

An important law governing functions is that for any argument they yield a unique value. The formula '$\exists x \forall y(y = f(a) \leftrightarrow y = x)$' expresses this law for one-place functions. It is valid, as the following tree reveals:

1. $\checkmark \sim \exists x \forall y(y = f(a) \leftrightarrow y = x)$ Negation of given formula
2. $\forall x \sim \forall y(y = f(a) \leftrightarrow y = x)$ 1 $\sim \exists$
3. $\checkmark \sim \forall y(y = f(a) \leftrightarrow y = f(a))$ 2 $\forall$
4. $\checkmark \exists y \sim (y = f(a) \leftrightarrow y = f(a))$ 3 $\sim \forall$
5. $\checkmark \sim (b = f(a) \leftrightarrow b = f(a))$ 4 $\exists$

6. $b = f(a)$ 5 $\sim \leftrightarrow$ $\sim b = f(a)$ 5 $\sim \leftrightarrow$
7. $\sim b = f(a)$ 5 $\sim \leftrightarrow$ $b = f(a)$ 5 $\sim \leftrightarrow$
8. $\times$ 6, 7 $\sim$ $\times$ 6, 7 $\sim$

Exercise 7.4.3

Demonstrate the validity of the sequents formalized in Exercise 6.4 by constructing a tree for each.

CHAPTER 8

CLASSICAL PREDICATE LOGIC: INFERENCE

Predicate logic adds three new operators to those of propositional logic: the two quantifiers and the identity predicate. This chapter presents a natural deduction system for predicate logic by adding six new inference rules—an introduction rule and an elimination rule for each of the three new operators. We then consider the role of function symbols in proofs.

8.1 EXISTENTIAL INTRODUCTION

The ten inference rules and all the derived rules for propositional logic are retained in predicate logic. Some proofs of predicate logic use only these propositional rules. The sequent 'Fa, Fa $\rightarrow \forall x$Fx, $\forall x$Fx $\rightarrow \forall x$Gx $\vdash \forall x$Gx', for example, can be proved simply by two steps of $\rightarrow$E:

1.	Fa	A
2.	Fa $\rightarrow \forall x$Fx	A
3.	$\forall x$Fx $\rightarrow \forall x$Gx	A
4.	$\forall x$Fx	1, 2 $\rightarrow$E
5.	$\forall x$Gx	3, 4 $\rightarrow$E

More commonly, however, proofs in predicate logic employ one or more of the six new inference rules required by the introduction of the quantifiers and the identity predicate. We shall consider each of these new rules in turn, beginning in this section with the quantifier rules.

Perhaps the simplest quantifier rule is the introduction rule for the existential quantifier, $\exists$I, which introduces existentially quantified conclusions. The basic idea is obvious: Whatever is true of a named object is true of something. If, for example, it is true of Alice that she is a frisbee player, then something is a frisbee player. In symbols: 'Fa ⊢ ∃xFx'. Similarly, given that Alice likes herself, we may draw any of three conclusions: that Alice likes something (namely herself), that something (Alice again!) likes Alice, and that something (guess who) likes itself. Symbolically:

> Laa ⊢ ∃xLax
> Laa ⊢ ∃xLxa
> Laa ⊢ ∃xLxx

All of these inferences, and others of a similar nature, are licensed by the ∃I rule, which may be expressed formally as follows:

Existential Introduction (∃I)   Let Φ be any formula containing some name α and $Φ^β/_α$ be the result of replacing at least one occurrence of α in Φ by some variable β not already in Φ. Then from Φ infer $∃βΦ^β/_α$.

Each of the three sequents above may be proved by a single step of ∃I. With respect to the first of these sequents, Φ is 'Laa', α is 'a', β is 'x', and $Φ^β/_α$ is 'Lax'. For the other two, α, β, and Φ are the same, but $Φ^β/_α$ is 'Lxa' or 'Lxx', respectively. The proof of the first sequent looks like this:

> 1. Laa   A
> 2. ∃xLax   1 ∃I

The proofs of the other two sequents are the same, except for the identity of the formula on line 2. Thus ∃I may sometimes be applied to the same formula in several different ways.

   ∃I may also be applied to complex formulas, as in this proof of the sequent 'Fa, Ga ⊢ ∃x(Fx & Gx)':

> 1. Fa   A
> 2. Ga   A
> 3. Fa & Ga   1, 2 &I
> 4. ∃x(Fx & Gx)   3 ∃I

Notice that in performing ∃I we must add the outer brackets that had been dropped by convention from the conjunction. If we do not do so, the result, '∃xFx & Gx', is not a formula.

   ∃I never introduces more than one quantifier at a time. To prove a conclusion with two existential quantifiers, we need two steps of ∃I. Consider, for example, this argument:

> Alice despises Bill and Bill despises Alice.
> ∴   There are two things that despise each other.

In symbols: 'Dab & Dba ⊢ ∃x∃y(Dxy & Dyx)'. Because the conclusion contains two existential quantifiers, the proof uses two steps of ∃I:

1. Dab & Dba   A
2. ∃y(Day & Dya)   1 ∃I
3. ∃x∃y(Dxy & Dyx)   2 ∃I

Since the quantifier added by ∃I is always the leftmost one, quantifiers must be introduced in reverse order, from right to left. So in this problem we quantify the name 'b' at line 2, using the variable '*y*', before quantifying the name 'a' using the variable '*x*'. If we had applied ∃I to the name 'a' first, replacing it with the variable '*y*', the result would have been '∃x∃y(Dyx & Dxy)', which is not the conclusion we symbolized, though it is its equivalent and does follow validly by ∃I from the premise.

Notice that the variable introduced by the ∃I rule may not already occur in Φ. Thus we could not at line 3 have inferred '∃y∃y(Dyy & Dyy)', since that would violate the formal statement of the rule. The purpose of the qualification 'not already in Φ' in that statement is to prevent just such an introduction of two quantifiers on the same variable with overlapping scopes. Such an expression is not even a formula, as was explained in Section 6.2.

Proof of the sequent 'Fa & Ga ⊢ ∃xFx & ∃xGx' also requires two uses of ∃I, though here because the scopes of the two quantifiers do not overlap, we may use the same variable in each case without violating either the ∃I rule or the formation rules:

1. Fa & Ga   A
2. Fa   1 &E
3. Ga   1 &E
4. ∃xFx   2 ∃I
5. ∃xGx   3 ∃I
6. ∃xFx & ∃xGx   4, 5 &I

However, the premise 'Fa & Ga' must be dissected into its conjuncts 'Fa' and 'Ga' before ∃I can be applied in order to obtain the conjuncts of the conclusion.

Sometimes the use of ∃I is less obvious and direct, as in the reductio strategy used in this proof of '~∃xFx ⊢ ~Fa':

1. ~∃xFx   A
2. │ Fa   H (for ~I)
3. │ ∃xFx   2 ∃I
4. │ ∃xFx & ~∃xFx   1, 3 &I
5. ~Fa   2–4 ~I

Here, since the conclusion '~Fa' is negative, we hypothesize 'Fa' for indirect proof at line 2. Then at line 3 we obtain by ∃I a statement that contradicts assumption 1. The resulting contradiction enables us to deduce the desired conclusion by ~I at line 5.

Sometimes ∃I is combined in complex ways with other rules. In this proof of 'Fa ∨ Gb ⊢ ∃xFx ∨ ∃xGx', for example, it is used with ∨E:

1.	Fa ∨ Gb	A
2.	⎜ Fa	H (for →I)
3.	⎜ ∃xFx	2 ∃I
4.	⎜ ∃xFx ∨ ∃xGx	3 ∨I
5.	Fa → (∃xFx ∨ ∃xGx)	2–4 →I
6.	⎜ Gb	H (for →I)
7.	⎜ ∃xGx	6 ∃I
8.	⎜ ∃xFx ∨ ∃xGx	7 ∨I
9.	Gb → (∃xFx ∨ ∃xGx)	6–8 →I
10.	∃xFx ∨ ∃xGx	1, 5, 9 ∨E

The replacement here of both 'a' and 'b' by the same variable 'x' is legitimate because of the nonoverlapping scopes of the two existential quantifiers.

But a quantified variable may replace only one name at a time (though it may replace several occurrences of that name). The inference illustrated below violates the ∃I rule by attempting to replace two different names:

1.	Tab	A
2.	∃xTxx	1 ∃I **(Wrong!)**

From the premise that Alice is taller than Bob, it certainly does not follow that something is taller than itself!

Exercise 8.1

Prove the following sequents, using ∃I and the inference rules of propositional logic:

1. Lab ⊢ ∃xLxb
2. Lab ⊢ ∃xLax
3. Laa ⊢ ∃xLxx
4. Lab ⊢ ∃x∃yLxy
5. Fa ∨ Ga ⊢ ∃x(Fx ∨ Gx)
6. Fa ∨ Ga ⊢ ∃xFx ∨ ∃xGx
7. ~∃x∃yRxy ⊢ ~Rab
8. ~∃x∃yRxy ⊢ ~Raa
9. ⊢ Fa → ∃xFx
10. ~∃xFx ⊢ ∃x~Fx

8.2 EXISTENTIAL ELIMINATION

The elimination rule for the existential quantifier, ∃E, is the rule which enables us to reason from existential premises. It is the most complicated of the quantifier rules because, like →I and ~I, it employs a hypothetical derivation. As usual, the idea is best explained by example. Consider the argument

> Some fish are guppies.
> ∴   Some guppies are fish.

We may represent this as the sequent '$\exists x(Fx \ \& \ Gx) \vdash \exists x(Gx \ \& \ Fx)$'. This sequent is valid. But how might we break it down into simple inferences that also have application elsewhere? The premise asserts that some fish (i.e., at least one) are guppies, but it does not identify this fish or (if there is more than one) these fish. Yet their identities are not really germane to the inference; the conclusion ought to follow no matter who or what they are. So we might as well choose some individual arbitrarily and suppose that it is one of these fish that are guppies. We might then reason as follows:

> Take Al here and suppose that he is one of these fish that are guppies. Then Al is a fish. Moreover, Al is a guppy as well. Therefore Al is both a guppy and a fish. So some guppies are fish.

But now since we have shown that guppies are fish from the supposition (hypothesis) that Al is a fish that is a guppy, and since (apart from this supposition) we have assumed nothing specifically about Al, then no matter which object or objects are actually the fish that are guppies, it must be the case that some guppies are fish.

I have indented the hypothetical part of the argument—the part based on the supposition that Al is one of the fish that are guppies. Since we are not told which objects are both fish and guppies, we call on Al to serve as a **representative individual**—that is, a stand-in for each of a certain set of objects—in this case the objects that are both fish and guppies. We suppose, then, that Al is both a fish and a guppy. We shall call the statement 'Al is both a fish and a guppy' a **representative instance** of 'Some fish are guppies', since it takes the representative individual Al to be an instance of that premise. Now by a dull but valid argument we deduce from this supposition the conclusion that some guppies are fish. But this conclusion is at first derived only hypothetically—that is, only from the hypothesis that Al is one of the fish that are guppies. That hypothesis, however, may be wildly false (Al might, for example, be my pet rattlesnake). Yet—and this is the crux of the reasoning—so long as we have made no additional assumptions about Al, the steps of the hypothetical argument must apply as well to the actual individuals of unknown identity that are both fish and guppies—that is, to all the individuals Al represents. In other words, if we had names for these individuals, we could substitute their names for Al's in the argument and still draw the same conclusion. Hence the conclusion deduced hypothetically (provided that it does not mention Al, who is only a stand-in) may be asserted nonhypothetically—even if the hypothesis from which it was originally drawn is false. In our example, the conclusion is that some guppies are fish. So we reassert this conclusion nonhypothetically—not because *Al* is a fish and a guppy, but because the hypothetical derivation shows that this conclusion must be true no matter which object or objects are both fish and guppies.

Formally, the reasoning looks like this:

1.	$\exists x(Fx \ \& \ Gx)$	A
2.	Fa & Ga	H (for $\exists$E)
3.	Fa	2 &E
4.	Ga	2 &E
5.	Ga & Fa	3, 4 &I
6.	$\exists x(Gx \ \& \ Fx)$	5 $\exists$I
7.	$\exists x(Gx \ \& \ Fx)$	1, 2–6 $\exists$E

The conclusion '$\exists x(Gx \ \& \ Fx)$' is derived twice—once hypothetically, from the supposition 'Fa & Ga', and a second time nonhypothetically (this time by the rule $\exists$E). This is always the case in applications of $\exists$E. What justifies the step of $\exists$E (the conclusion's change of status from hypothetical to nonhypothetical) is that in the hypothetical derivation we could substitute *any* name for the name of the representative individual (in this case 'a') and still reach that conclusion. Thus, in this proof, no matter which individuals are both F and G (provided only that at least one is, which we assumed at line 1), the conclusion '$\exists x(Fx \ \& \ Gx)$' must be true.

It is crucial for the application of $\exists$E that the name of the representative individual not appear in any assumptions or hypotheses other than the supposition of the representative instance in which it is introduced and that it not appear in the conclusion of the hypothetical argument from that supposition, for otherwise there would be no guarantee that our hypothetical reasoning applies indifferently to any of the unknown objects the representative individual represents. There would be no guarantee, in other words, that the representative individual is truly representative.

In annotating an inference by $\exists$E (see line 7 above), we always cite the line of the existential premise to which it was applied (in this case line 1), together with the lines of the hypothetical derivation in which the desired conclusion is derived from the supposition of a representative instance of that existential premise (here, lines 2–6).

The $\exists$E rule is stated formally below. If you have followed the discussion so far, you should see the need for the various qualifications that make it rather ugly:

Existential Elimination ($\exists$E)   Let $\exists\beta\Phi$ be any existential formula, Ψ any formula, and α any name that occurs neither in Φ nor in Ψ. And let $\Phi^\alpha/_\beta$ be the result of replacing all occurrences of the variable β in Φ by α. Then, given a derivation of Ψ from the hypothesis $\Phi^\alpha/_\beta$, end the hypothetical derivation and from $\exists\beta\Phi$ infer Ψ, provided that α does not occur in any other hypothesis whose hypothetical derivation has not ended or in any assumption.

In the proof given above, $\exists\beta\Phi$ is '$\exists x(Fx \ \& \ Gx)$', β is 'x', Ψ is '$\exists x(Gx \ \& \ Fx)$', α is 'a', and $\Phi^\alpha/_\beta$ is 'Fa & Ga'.

In summary, to use an existential premise $\exists\beta\Phi$ to prove a conclusion Ψ, we hypothesize a representative instance $\Phi^\alpha/_\beta$ of that premise and derive Ψ

hypothetically. So long as α does not appear in any other hypothesis whose derivation has not ended, nor in any assumption, nor in Φ or the conclusion Ψ, we
may then end the hypothetical derivation and infer Ψ by ∃E. As justification for
this step, we cite the line on which the existential premise ∃βΦ occurs and the lines
of the hypothetical derivation in which Ψ is derived from $\Phi^{\alpha}/_{\beta}$.

This proof of the sequent '∃xLxx ⊢ ∃x∃yLxy' provides another example of
the use of ∃E:

1.	∃xLxx	A
2.	Laa	H (for ∃E)
3.	∃yLay	2 ∃I
4.	∃x∃yLxy	3 ∃I
5.	∃x∃yLxy	1, 2–4 ∃E

We hypothesize a representative instance of the premise '∃xLxx' at line 2. From
this we derive the conclusion '∃x∃yLxy' at line 4. ∃E then enables us to end the
hypothetical derivation and assert '∃x∃yLxy' on the strength of the assumption
'∃xLxx' alone.

In the examples we have examined so far, the conclusion Ψ obtained by ∃E
is an existential formula. But in general Ψ may have any form. In the case of the
sequent '∃x(Fx & ~Fx) ⊢ P', for example, it is the sentence letter 'P'. The premise
of this sequent, '∃x(Fx & ~Fx)', is self-contradictory, and so of course it implies
anything.

1.	∃x(Fx & ~Fx)	A
2.	Fa & ~Fa	H (for ∃E)
3.	Fa	2 &E
4.	~Fa	2 &E
5.	P	3, 4 EFQ
6.	P	1, 2–5 ∃E

We take 'Fa & ~Fa' as the representative instance of '∃x(Fx & ~Fx)' at line 2. The
hypothetical derivation uses the derived rule EFQ (see Section 4.4). Notice that all
the restrictions on ∃E are met: 'a' does not occur in any hypothesis other than 2,
nor in any assumption, nor in 'P'.

Violating these restrictions breeds trouble. Consider, for example, this erroneous reasoning:

1.	∃x(Fx & Gx)	A	
2.	Fa & Ga	H (for ∃E)	
3.	Fa	2 &E	
4.	Fa	1, 2–3 ∃E	**(Wrong!)**

Everything is fine down to the last step. But the conclusion Ψ—that is, 'Fa'—of
the hypothetical derivation contains 'a', the name of the representative individual.
So this conclusion is not, as it ought to be, provable regardless of which individual
is both F and G. Hence the step of ∃E at line 4 is illegitimate. It is no surprise, then,
that the resulting sequent, '∃x(Fx & Gx) ⊢ Fa', is invalid. From the assumption

that some fish are guppies it does not follow that Al is a guppy (Al might not be a fish at all)!

We also brew trouble if we use as the name of the representative individual a name that already occurs in an assumption or in a hypothesis whose hypothetical derivation has not ended, as in this reasoning:

1.	$\exists x Lxa$	A
2.	Laa	H (for $\exists E$)
3.	$\exists x Lxx$	2 $\exists I$
4.	$\exists x Lxx$	1, 2–3 $\exists E$ **(Wrong!)**

Here the name 'a' occurs in the assumption. Therefore, in taking 'a' as our representative individual at line 2, we have chosen an individual that is not truly representative. Suppose 'L' means "loves" and 'a' means "Al." Then the assumption at line 1 says that something loves Al. But we are not told what this "something" is. By supposing at line 2 that it is Al himself (instead of a truly representative individual about whom we previously had assumed nothing), we illegitimately introduce information about this individual's identity. This enables us to derive an excessively strong conclusion at line 4. For from the premise that something loves Al, it does not follow that Al loves himself.

If a premise begins with two existential quantifiers, then two uses of $\exists E$ are required. We shall illustrate this double usage with a proof of the sequent '$\exists x \exists y Lxy \vdash \exists y \exists x Lyx$'. The premise and the conclusion of this sequent are equivalent. They say exactly the same thing—which is why the sequent is valid.

1.	$\exists x \exists y Lxy$	A
2.	$\exists y Lay$	H (for $\exists E$)
3.	Lab	H (for $\exists E$)
4.	$\exists x Lax$	3 $\exists I$
5.	$\exists y \exists x Lyx$	4 $\exists I$
6.	$\exists y \exists x Lyx$	2, 3–5 $\exists E$
7.	$\exists y \exists x Lyx$	1, 2–6 $\exists E$

At line 2 we hypothesize '$\exists y Lay$' as a representative instance of '$\exists x \exists y Lxy$'. Then at line 3 we hypothesize 'Lab' as a representative instance of '$\exists y Lay$'. Now we have two representative individuals, denoted by the names 'a' and 'b'. Since neither our conclusion '$\exists y \exists x Lyx$' nor any assumption or hypothesis other than line 3 contains 'b', when $\exists E$ is used at line 6 all the restrictions on the $\exists E$ rule are satisfied. Similarly, since neither '$\exists y \exists x Lyx$' nor any assumption or hypothesis whose derivation has not ended other than line 2 contains 'a', the use of $\exists E$ at line 7 is legitimate.[1]

Our next example illustrates the use of $\exists E$ within an indirect proof. The sequent we shall prove in this case is '$\sim\exists x (Fx \vee Gx) \vdash \sim\exists x Fx$':

---

[1] The hypothetical derivation from line 3 has ended by line 7 (indeed, it ends at line 5) so that the fact that its hypothesis contains 'a' is of no concern when we apply the $\exists E$ rule at line 7.

1. ~∃x(Fx ∨ Gx)   A
2. | ∃xFx   H (for ~I)
3. | | Fa   H (for ∃E)
4. | | Fa ∨ Ga   3 ∨ I
5. | | ∃x(Fx ∨ Gx)   4 ∃I
6. | | ∃x(Fx ∨ Gx) & ~∃x(Fx ∨ Gx)   1, 5 &I
7. | ∃x(Fx ∨ Gx) & ~∃x(Fx ∨ Gx)   2, 3–6 ∃E
8. ~∃xFx   2–7 ~I

The conclusion is negative, so we employ indirect proof, hypothesizing '∃xFx' for ~I at line 2. Then at line 3 we hypothesize a representative instance of '∃xFx' for ∃E. The contradiction obtained at line 6 from this second hypothesis is shown by ∃E at line 7 to follow just from '∃xFx' together with the asssumption. This allows us to reject '∃xFx' and affirm '~∃xFx' by ~I at line 8.

We conclude our discussion of ∃E with another proof that uses ∃E within an indirect proof. Here, however, the contradiction most directly obtainable from the representative instance contains the name of the representative individual. We therefore use EFQ to derive a contradiction not containing this name before applying ∃E. The sequent in this case is the theorem '⊢ ~∃x(Fx ↔ ~Fx)':

1. | ∃x(Fx ↔ ~Fx)   H (for ~I)
2. | | Fa ↔ ~Fa   H (for ∃E)
3. | | | Fa   H (for ~I)
4. | | | ~Fa   2, 3 ↔MP
5. | | | Fa & ~Fa   3, 4 &I
6. | | ~Fa   3–5 ~I
7. | | Fa   2, 6 ↔MP
8. | | P & ~P   6, 7 EFQ
9. | P & ~P   1, 2–8 ∃E
10. ~∃x(Fx ↔ ~Fx)   1–9 ~I

Since the conclusion '~∃x(Fx ↔ ~Fx)' is negative, we proceed by indirect proof. We hypothesize '∃x(Fx ↔ ~Fx)' for ~I at line 1, its representative instance 'Fa ↔ ~Fa' for ∃E at line 2, and 'Fa' for a second ~I at line 3. The obvious move at line 8 would have been to infer 'Fa & ~Fa' by &I, as we did at line 5. But if we do that here, then since 'Fa & ~Fa' contains 'a', the name of the representative individual, the ∃E rule would be inapplicable at line 9. Hence instead we use EFQ to obtain the arbitrary contradiction 'P & ~P'. Since this does not contain 'a', and since the other requirements on ∃E are met, the use of ∃E at line 9 is legitimate.

Exercise 8.2

Prove the following sequents:

1. ∃x(Fx & Gx) ⊢ ∃xFx & ∃xGx
2. ∃xFx ⊢ ∃x(Fx ∨ Gx)
3. ∃xFx → Ga ⊢ Fb → ∃xGx
4. ∃x~~Fx ⊢ ∃xFx

5. $\exists x F x \vdash \exists x \sim\sim F x$
6. $\sim\exists x F x \vdash \sim\exists x (F x \mathbin{\&} G x)$
7. $\vdash \sim\exists x (F x \mathbin{\&} \sim F x)$
8. $\vdash \exists x F x \leftrightarrow \exists y F y$
9. $\exists x (F x \vee G x) \vdash \exists x F x \vee \exists x G x$
10. $\exists x F x \vee \exists x G x \vdash \exists x (F x \vee G x)$

8.3 UNIVERSAL ELIMINATION

Universal elimination ($\forall$E) is the rule usually used for reasoning from universal premises. It is as simple as EI and is in a sense its opposite. The idea is this: Given that everything has certain characteristics, it follows that a particular individual has them. For example, if everything is located in space and time, then it follows that Alice is located in space and time. Using 'S' for "is located in space" and 'T' for "is located in time," we may symbolize that inference as '$\forall x (S x \mathbin{\&} T x) \vdash S a \mathbin{\&} T a$'. This sequent is provable by a single step of $\forall$E:

1. $\forall x (S x \mathbin{\&} T x)$ A
2. $S a \mathbin{\&} T a$ 1 $\forall$E

Stated formally, the rule is as follows:

Universal Elimination ($\forall$E)   Let $\forall\beta\Phi$ be any universally quantified formula and $\Phi^{\alpha}/_{\beta}$ be the result of replacing all occurrences of the variable β in Φ by some name α. Then from $\forall\beta\Phi$ infer $\Phi^{\alpha}/_{\beta}$.

In the inference above, $\forall\beta\Phi$ is '$\forall x (S x \mathbin{\&} T x)$', $\Phi^{\alpha}/_{\beta}$ is '$S a \mathbin{\&} T a$', β is 'x', and α is 'a'.

The application of $\forall$E is in most instances simple and obvious. Here it is used in a proof of the sequent '$\forall x (F x \to G x), F a \vdash G a$':

1. $\forall x (F x \to G x)$ A
2. $F a$ A
3. $F a \to G a$ 1 $\forall$E
4. $G a$ 2, 3 $\to$E

As with the other quantifier rules, more than one use of $\forall$E is required to eliminate more than one quantifier. This proof of the sequent '$\forall x \forall y \forall z ((L x y \mathbin{\&} L y z) \to L x z), L a b, L b c \vdash L a c$' provides a good illustration (the sequent makes intuitive sense if you read 'L' as "is longer than"):

1. $\forall x \forall y \forall z ((L x y \mathbin{\&} L y z) \to L x z)$ A
2. $L a b$ A
3. $L b c$ A

4. $\forall y \forall z((Lay \,\&\, Lyz) \rightarrow Laz)$ 1 $\forall$E
5. $\forall z((Lab \,\&\, Lbz) \rightarrow Laz)$ 4 $\forall$E
6. $(Lab \,\&\, Lbc) \rightarrow Lac$ 5 $\forall$E
7. $Lab \,\&\, Lbc$ 2, 3 &I
8. Lac 6, 7 $\rightarrow$E

It is crucial here to instantiate each variable with the right name. For example, at step 4 we could have used $\forall$E to obtain

4.' $\forall y \forall z((Lby \,\&\, Lyz) \rightarrow Lbz)$ 1 $\forall$E

but that would not have been useful with the assumptions given. Use of $\forall$E with multiple quantifiers and multiple names thus requires circumspection and careful planning.

Our final example, a proof of '$\exists x{\sim}Fx \vdash {\sim}\forall xFx$', contains several twists, requiring in addition to $\forall$E the use of EFQ with an $\exists$E strategy that in turn is nested in an indirect proof:

1. $\exists x{\sim}Fx$ A
2. | $\forall xFx$ H (for ~I)
3. | | ${\sim}Fa$ H (for $\exists$E)
4. | | Fa 2 $\forall$E
5. | | $P \,\&\, {\sim}P$ 3, 4 EFQ
6. | $P \,\&\, {\sim}P$ 1, 3–5 $\exists$E
7. ${\sim}\forall xFx$ 2–6 ~I

Since the conclusion is negative, we proceed by indirect proof, hypothesizing '$\forall xFx$' for ~I at line 2. The hypothesis at line 3 is a representative instance of assumption 1 for $\exists$E. As in the example at the end of Section 8.2, we use EFQ to obtain an arbitrary contradiction free of the name 'a' so that $\exists$E may be applied at line 6.

Exercise 8.3.1

Prove the following sequents:

1. $\vdash \forall xFx \rightarrow Fa$
2. ${\sim}Fa \vdash {\sim}\forall xFx$
3. $\forall x(Fx \rightarrow Gx), {\sim}Ga \vdash {\sim}Fa$
4. $\forall x(Fx \rightarrow Gx), Ga \rightarrow Ha \vdash Fa \rightarrow Ha$
5. $\forall x \forall y(Rxy \rightarrow Ryx), Rab \vdash Rba$
6. $\forall x(Fx \rightarrow Gx), \exists xFx \vdash \exists x(Fx \,\&\, Gx)$
7. $\forall x(Fx \rightarrow Gx), \exists x{\sim}Gx \vdash \exists x{\sim}Fx$
8. $\forall x(Fx \rightarrow Gx), {\sim}\exists xGx \vdash {\sim}\exists xFx$
9. $\forall x(Fx \rightarrow Gx), \forall x{\sim}Gx \vdash {\sim}\exists xFx$
10. $\forall xFx \lor \forall xGx, {\sim}Ga \vdash \forall xFx$

Exercise 8.3.2

Formalize this argument, using the symbol scheme given below:

> Triticale, an artificial cross between wheat and rye, is superior to both. Since wheat and rye are natural, this proves that it is not the case that everything natural is superior to everything artificial.

Names	One-Place Predicates	Two-Place Predicate	Three-Place Predicate
t — triticale	A — is artificial	S — is superior to	C — is a cross between
h — wheat	N — is natural		
r — rye			

Now attempt to prove the resulting sequent. If you symbolized just what was said, you will find that the sequent cannot be proved; it is in fact invalid. In attempting the proof, however, you should notice that adding a certain obvious assumption would make the sequent valid. Identify this assumption, formalize it, and then prove the resulting sequent.

8.4 UNIVERSAL INTRODUCTION

The last of the four quantifier rules is universal introduction ($\forall$I). Like $\exists$E, it makes use of a representative instance. Nevertheless, it is simpler, since it does not require a hypothetical derivation. To illustrate it, we shall consider this valid but unsound argument:

> All frogs are green.
> Everything is a frog.
> ∴ Everything is green.

To obtain the conclusion from these premises, we may reason as follows:

> Since all frogs are green, if Alice is a frog then Alice is green. And since everything is a frog, Alice is a frog. It follows that Alice is green. But since we have made no assumptions about Alice, she is a representative individual for any object whatsoever. What we have proved of her must be true of everything. Therefore everything is green.

The last step of this reasoning is a step of $\forall$I. Its validity depends upon the fact that nothing is assumed about Alice; that is, her name does not appear in any hypothesis whose derivation has not yet ended or in any assumption. This makes her a representative individual for everything in the domain of discourse. Thus what we prove of her could equally well have been proved of anything—which is why we can legitimately infer that everything is green.

If we symbolize the argument in the obvious way, we obtain the sequent '$\forall x(Fx \rightarrow Gx)$, $\forall xFx \vdash \forall xGx$'. Our reasoning may now be formalized as follows:

1.	$\forall x(Fx \rightarrow Gx)$	A
2.	$\forall xFx$	A
3.	$Fa \rightarrow Ga$	1 $\forall$E
4.	Fa	2 $\forall$E
5.	Ga	3, 4 $\rightarrow$E
6.	$\forall xGx$	5 $\forall$I

Step 6 is legitimate only because 'a' does not appear in any assumption or hypothesis so that we could validly have substituted any other name for 'a' in steps 3–5. This shows that we could have proved $G\alpha$ for any name α, which is why we may validly infer '$\forall xGx$' at step 6.

Here is the formal statement of the $\forall$I rule:

Universal Introduction ($\forall$I)   Let Φ be a formula containing a name α, and let $\Phi^{\beta}/_{\alpha}$ be the result of replacing all occurrences of α in Φ by some variable β not already in Φ. Then from Φ infer $\forall\beta\Phi^{\beta}/_{\alpha}$, provided that α does not occur in any hypothesis whose hypothetical derivation has not yet ended or in any assumption.

In terms of our example, Φ is 'Ga', α is 'a', β is 'x', $\Phi^{\beta}/_{\alpha}$ is 'Gx', and, consequently, $\forall\beta\Phi^{\beta}/_{\alpha}$ is '$\forall xGx$'. The qualification 'not already in Φ' is needed to ensure that we do not introduce quantifiers of the same variable with overlapping scopes and so infer something that is not even a formula.

To prove a universally quantified statement, then, we prove a representative instance of it, making sure that the representative individual is not named in any hypothesis whose hypothetical derivation has not yet ended or in any assumption. Then we apply $\forall$I. In annotating uses of $\forall$I, we cite only the line number of the representative instance.

With the addition of $\forall$I our quantifier rules are complete, and we can now prove any valid sequent of predicate logic that does not involve identity. Let's consider another simple example, a proof of the sequent '$\forall x(Fx \rightarrow Gx)$, $\forall x(Gx \rightarrow Hx) \vdash \forall x(Fx \rightarrow Hx)$':

1.	$\forall x(Fx \rightarrow Gx)$	A
2.	$\forall x(Gx \rightarrow Hx)$	A
3.	Fa	H (for $\rightarrow$I)
4.	$Fa \rightarrow Ga$	1 $\forall$E
5.	Ga	3, 4 $\rightarrow$E
6.	$Ga \rightarrow Ha$	2 $\forall$E
7.	Ha	5, 6 $\rightarrow$E

8.	Fa → Ha	3–7 →I
9.	$\forall x(Fx \rightarrow Hx)$	8 $\forall$I

The strategy of the proof is governed by the structure of the conclusion. Here the conclusion is the universal formula '$\forall x(Fx \rightarrow Hx)$', so we must prove a representative instance of it—that is, a conditional of the form Fα → Hα. To do that we proceed by conditional proof. We hypothesize 'Fa', taking 'a' as the name of the representative individual, at line 3. The conditional 'Fa → Ha' is proved at line 8. Since now at line 9 'a' does not appear in any hypothesis whose hypothetical derivation has not yet ended or in any assumption, we may apply $\forall$I, knowing that we could have proved Fα → Hα for any name α.

The next example combines $\forall$I with a reductio strategy. The sequent to be proved is '$\sim\exists xFx \vdash \forall x\sim Fx$':

1.	$\sim\exists xFx$	A
2.	Fa	H (for ~I)
3.	$\exists xFx$	2 $\exists$I
4.	$\exists xFx$ & $\sim\exists xFx$	1, 3 &I
5.	~Fa	2–4 ~I
6.	$\forall x\sim Fx$	5 $\forall$I

Since the desired conclusion is the universal formula '$\forall x\sim Fx$', to prove it by $\forall$I we need a representative instance of the form ~Fα. But this is negative, so to prove it we must hypothesize Fα and seek a contradiction. The name 'a' will do for α since it does not appear in any assumption and there are as yet (at step 1) no hypotheses. So at step 2 we hypothesize 'Fa' for indirect proof. Having obtained a contradiction at line 4, we deduce '~Fa' and then, as planned, apply $\forall$I to reach the conclusion at line 6. Though 'a' appears in the hypothesis 'Fa' at line 2, the derivation from that hypothesis has ended by line 6 (indeed, it ends at line 5) so that $\forall$I may legitimately be applied.

The following proof of '$\sim\forall xFx \vdash \exists x\sim Fx$' uses a double reductio strategy:

1.	$\sim\forall xFx$	A
2.	$\sim\exists x\sim Fx$	H (for ~I)
3.	~Fa	H (for ~I)
4.	$\exists x\sim Fx$	3 $\exists$I
5.	$\exists x\sim Fx$ & $\sim\exists x\sim Fx$	2, 4 &I
6.	~~Fa	3–5 ~I
7.	Fa	6 ~E
8.	$\forall xFx$	7 $\forall$I
9.	$\forall xFx$ & $\sim\forall xFx$	1, 8 &I
10.	$\sim\sim\exists x\sim Fx$	2–9 ~I
11.	$\exists x\sim Fx$	10 ~E

There is no obvious way to proceed once the assumption has been set out, so we hypothesize the negation of the desired conclusion for indirect proof at line 2. Now we notice that we could contradict assumption 1 if we could prove 'Fa' and then get '$\forall xFx$' by $\forall$I. To prove 'Fa' we work once again by indirect proof, hypothesizing '~Fa' at line 3. From there the rest of the proof plays itself out as planned.

The next example illustrates once again the utility of EFQ within quantifier proofs. It is a proof of the sequent '~∃xFx ⊢ ∀x(Fx → Gx)':

1.	~∃xFx	A
2.	⎮ Fa	H (for →I)
3.	⎮ ∃xFx	2 ∃I
4.	⎮ Ga	1, 3 EFQ
5.	Fa → Ga	2–4 →I
6.	∀x(Fx → Gx)	5 ∀I

We could have avoided the use of EFQ by hypothesizing '~Ga' for ~I at line 3, but this would have made the proof several steps longer. This sequent is of intrinsic interest, since it says that from the premise that nothing is F we may infer that all F are G. Here we see once again (recall the discussion in Section 7.3) the odd behavior of universally quantified material conditionals whose antecedent terms are empty.

As in propositional logic, the general strategy for proving a sequent in predicate logic is determined by the form of the conclusion or subconclusion for which we are aiming. The proof strategies in Table 8.1 supplement those given in Table 4.1 in Section 4.3 and should be used in combination with them. Thus, for example, if the conclusion to be proved is of the form '∀xFx → ∀xGx', which is a conditional, first apply the strategy for conditionals from Table 4.1. Thus we hypothesize '∀xFx' and aim to derive the subconclusion '∀xGx'. This subconclusion is of the form ∀βΦ so that we next apply the strategy for that form from Table 8.1. Using the two strategy tables together in this way, most problems can be solved fairly easily. However, some proofs in predicate logic demand ingenuity that cannot be encoded in a simple set of instructions.

Quantifier Exchange Rules

Eight derived rules are of particular importance in predicate logic. These are called the **quantifier exchange rules (QE)**:

From ∀βΦ, infer ~∃β~Φ.	From ∃βΦ, infer ~∀β~Φ.
From ~∀βΦ, infer ∃β~Φ.	From ~∃βΦ, infer ∀β~Φ.
From ∀β~Φ, infer ~∃βΦ.	From ∃β~Φ, infer ~∀βΦ.
From ~∀β~Φ, infer ∃βΦ.	From ~∃β~Φ, infer ∀βΦ.

The expression Φ in each of these rules is not a formula itself, but the result of replacing all occurrences of some name in a formula by the variable β. For example, we may take β as '*x*' and Φ as 'F*x*', or β as '*x*' and Φ as '(F*x* & G*x*)', or, again, β as '*y*' and Φ as '∃xL*xy*'. In each case the expression Φ is called an **open sentence**, and the variable β in such an open sentence is called a **free variable**.

We may verify that each instance of the quantifier exchange rules can be proved using only the fourteen basic rules (ten propositional rules and four quantifier rules) of predicate logic by proving the corresponding sequent in which β is

TABLE 8.1
Proof Strategies

If the conclusion or sub-conclusion you are trying to prove is of the form:	Then try this strategy:
$\exists\beta\Phi$	Work toward a subconclusion of the form $\Phi^\alpha/_\beta$, where α is a name that does not occur in Φ, in order to obtain $\exists\beta\Phi$ by $\exists$I. If there is an existential premise, it is likely that the subconclusion $\Phi^\alpha/_\beta$ will have to be derived hypothetically after a representative instance of this premise has been hypothesized for $\exists$E. In that case, to avoid misusing $\exists$E, obtain $\exists\beta\Phi$ by $\exists$I before ending the hypothetical derivation with $\exists$E. If all else fails, hypothesize $\sim\exists\beta\Phi$ and work toward a subconclusion of the form $\Theta \ \& \sim\Theta$ in order to obtain $\exists\beta\Phi$ by $\sim$I and $\sim$E.
$\forall\beta\Phi$	Work toward a subconclusion of the form $\Phi^\alpha/_\beta$, where α is a name that does not occur in Φ or in any assumption or hypothesis whose hypothetical derivation has not yet ended, in order to obtain $\forall\beta\Phi$ by $\forall$I. If there are universal premises, it is likely that some or all of them will have to be instantiated with α by $\forall$E before this can be done.

'x' and Φ is the open sentence 'Fx'. For given such a proof, it is easily seen that any instance of the corresponding rule may be proved by precisely the same sequence of steps—that is, by a proof of precisely the same form. Take the rule 'From $\sim\forall\beta\Phi$, infer $\exists\beta\sim\Phi$', for example. We proved the corresponding sequent '$\sim\forall xFx \vdash \exists x\sim Fx$' above. But by precisely the same steps we could have proved '$\sim\forall x(Fx \ \& \ Gx) \vdash \exists x\sim(Fx \ \& \ Gx)$' or '$\sim\forall yGy \vdash \exists y\sim Gy$' or '$\sim\forall y\exists xLxy \vdash \exists y\sim\exists xLxy$'—or any other sequent having the form indicated by the rule. To show this, we shall rewrite the proof of '$\sim\forall xFx \vdash \exists x\sim Fx$' in full generality, using the Greek metavariables β and Φ in place of the variable 'x' and the open sentence 'Fx', respectively. It is evident by inspection of this proof form that no matter which variable we use for β or which open sentence with free variable β we use for Φ, the resulting sequent can still be proved using only the basic rules:

1.	$\sim\forall\beta\Phi$			A
2.		$\sim\exists\beta\sim\Phi$		H (for $\sim$I)
3.			$\sim\Phi^\alpha/_\beta$	H (for $\sim$I)
4.			$\exists\beta\sim\Phi$	3 $\exists$I
5.			$\exists\beta\sim\Phi \ \& \sim\exists\beta\sim\Phi$	2, 4 &I
6.		$\sim\sim\Phi^\alpha/_\beta$		3–5 $\sim$I
7.	$\Phi^\alpha/_\beta$			6 $\sim$E

8.	$\quad\mid\qquad\qquad \forall\beta\Phi$	7 $\forall$I
9.	$\quad\mid\qquad\qquad \forall\beta\Phi$ & $\sim\forall\beta\Phi$	1, 8 &I
10.	$\sim\sim\exists\beta\sim\Phi$	2–9 $\sim$I
11.	$\exists\beta\sim\Phi$	10 $\sim$E

Here $\Phi^\alpha/_\beta$ is a formula that results from replacing each occurrence of β in the open sentence Φ by some name α not already in Φ. From this proof form it is clear that 'From $\sim\forall\beta\Phi$, infer $\exists\beta\sim\Phi$' is a derived rule.

In the same way, we can see for each of the other quantifier exchange rules that by proving its corresponding sequent, we have in effect shown that every instance of that rule can be proved using only the fourteen basic rules of predicate logic. That is, we can see that the quantifier exchange rules are in fact derived rules.

Exercise 8.4.1

In the text we verified that three of the eight quantifier exchange rules are derived rules by proving the sequents '$\exists x\sim Fx \vdash \sim\forall xFx$', '$\sim\exists xFx \vdash \forall x\sim Fx$', and '$\sim\forall xFx \vdash \exists x\sim Fx$'. Verify this for the other five quantifier exchange rules by proving the following sequents using only the fourteen basic rules:

1. $\forall xFx \vdash \sim\exists x\sim Fx$
2. $\exists xFx \vdash \sim\forall x\sim Fx$
3. $\forall x\sim Fx \vdash \sim\exists xFx$
4. $\sim\forall x\sim Fx \vdash \exists xFx$
5. $\sim\exists x\sim Fx \vdash \forall xFx$

Exercise 8.4.2

Prove the following sequents, using basic or derived rules:

1. $\forall x(Fx \rightarrow Gx) \vdash \forall x(\sim Gx \rightarrow \sim Fx)$
2. $\forall x(Fx \rightarrow Gx) \vdash \forall xFx \rightarrow \forall xGx$
3. $\forall x(Fx \rightarrow Gx) \vdash \forall x\sim(Fx \& \sim Gx)$
4. $\forall x(Fx \rightarrow \sim Gx) \vdash \forall x(Gx \rightarrow \sim Fx)$
5. $\forall x(Fx \rightarrow Gx), \sim\forall xGx \vdash \sim\forall xFx$
6. $\forall x(Fx \rightarrow Gx), \forall x\sim Gx \vdash \forall x\sim Fx$
7. $\forall x(Fx \rightarrow Gx), \sim\exists xGx \vdash \forall x\sim Fx$
8. $\forall x(Fx \rightarrow Gx), \sim\forall xGx \vdash \exists x\sim Fx$
9. $\forall xRxx \vdash \forall x\exists yRxy$
10. $\exists x\forall yRxy \vdash \forall y\exists xRxy$
11. $\vdash \exists x(Fx \& \sim Gx) \leftrightarrow \sim\forall x(Fx \rightarrow Gx)$
12. $\vdash \exists xFx \leftrightarrow \sim\forall x\sim Fx$
13. $\vdash \forall xFx \leftrightarrow \sim\exists x\sim Fx$
14. $\vdash \forall x(Fx \rightarrow Fx)$
15. $\forall x(\exists yFy \rightarrow Gx), Fa \vdash \forall xGx$

Exercise 8.4.3

Prove the sequents corresponding to the arguments formalized in Exercise 6.1, using basic or derived rules.

8.5 IDENTITY

To prove sequents involving identity, we need two more rules, =I and =E. The identity introduction rule is utterly simple:

Identity Introduction (=I)   Where α is any name, assert $\alpha = \alpha$.

In a sense, this is not even a rule of *inference,* since it employs no premise. It simply licenses us to assert a logical truth of the form $\alpha = \alpha$ at any line of a proof. Clearly this is a valid procedure since a logical truth must be true given any premises—or none at all. For annotation, we simply write '=I' to the right. Since no premise is used, no line number is listed. This proof of the sequent '$\forall x \forall y(x = y \rightarrow Rxy) \vdash Raa$' illustrates a simple use of =I:

1. $\forall x \forall y(x = y \rightarrow Rxy)$ A
2. $\forall y(a = y \rightarrow Ray)$ 1 $\forall$E
3. $a = a \rightarrow Raa$ 2 $\forall$E
4. $a = a$ =I
5. Raa 3, 4 $\rightarrow$E

The following proof of the theorem '$\vdash \sim\exists x \sim x = x$' exemplifies another typical use of =I:

1. | $\exists x \sim x = x$ H (for ~I)
2. | | $\sim a = a$ H (for $\exists$E)
3. | | $a = a$ =I
4. | | $P \mathbin{\&} \sim P$ 2, 3 EFQ
5. | $P \mathbin{\&} \sim P$ 1, 2–4 $\exists$E
6. $\sim\exists x \sim x = x$ 1–5 ~I

Since the desired conclusion '$\sim\exists x \sim x = x$' is negative, we hypothesize '$\exists x \sim x = x$' for indirect proof at line 1. But this is an existential formula, and so we hypothesize '$\sim a = a$', a representative instance of it, for $\exists$E at line 2. We can now contradict line 2 by applying =I at line 3, but to obtain a contradiction that does not contain the name 'a' of the representative individual, we must use EFQ. Steps of $\exists$E and ~I then complete the proof.

The elimination rule for identity is familiar from algebra as the rule that allows us to substitute equals for equals—but in logic, since we are not dealing only with quantities, it is more accurate to say "identicals for identicals." It is sometimes called the rule of **identity substitution.**

Identity Elimination (=E)   From a premise of the form $\alpha = \beta$ and a formula Φ containing either α or β, infer any formula which results from replacing one or more occurrences of either of these names by the other in Φ.

Uses of =E are annotated by citing two line numbers: the number of the line on which $\alpha = \beta$ occurs and the number of the line on which Φ occurs.

The validity of =E is fairly obvious, but to prove rigorously that it is valid takes considerable work, and we will postpone that task until Section 9.1. In the meantime, we shall simply use it. Here it is used in a simple proof of the theorem '$\vdash (Fa \,\&\, a = b) \rightarrow Fb$':

1.	Fa & a = b	H (for →I)
2.	Fa	1 &E
3.	a = b	1 &E
4.	Fb	2, 3 =E
5.	(Fa & a = b) → Fb	1–4 →I

The theorem is a conditional, so the overall strategy is conditional proof. With respect to the formal statement of the =E rule, $\alpha = \beta$ is 'a = b' and Φ is 'Fa'.

If α or β occurs more than once in Φ, then =E may be applied in several ways. For example, from the premises 'Laa' and 'a = b', =E enables us to infer 'Lab', 'Lba', or 'Lbb'. Actually, we can infer even more conclusions, since we can apply 'a = b' to itself—that is, take 'a = b' instead of 'Laa' as Φ. Thus from $\alpha = \beta$ (i.e., 'a = b') and Φ ('a = b' again) we may infer 'a = a' and 'b = b', each by a single step of =E. To get the conclusion 'b = a', however, takes two steps of =E, as in this proof of the sequent 'a = b $\vdash$ b = a':

1.	a = b	A
2.	b = b	1, 1 =E
3.	b = a	1, 2 =E

In the first step at line 2 we have as premises 'a = b' and 'a = b'. We use the first of these as $\alpha = \beta$ in the rule to replace the occurrence of 'a' in the second (which plays the role of Φ in the rule) with 'b' and hence to deduce 'b = b'. (Alternatively, 'b = b' could be obtained by a step of =I.) Then at step 3 we use 'a = b' again to replace the second occurrence of 'b' in 'b = b' (which is now playing the role of Φ) with 'a'. This cannot all be done in a single step, since the =E rule allows us to replace only one name at a time (though, as noted previously, we may replace several occurrences of it). To get from 'a = b' to 'b = a', we must replace 'a' with 'b' and 'b' with 'a'. Since we are replacing two distinct names, we need at least two steps.

Exercise 8.5.1

Prove the following sequents:

1. Fa, ~Fb ⊢ ~a = b
2. ⊢ $\forall x \forall y(x = y \rightarrow (Rxy \rightarrow Ryx))$
3. ⊢ $\exists x \; x = a$
4. ⊢ $\forall x \exists y \; x = y$
5. ⊢ $\forall x \; x = x$
6. ⊢ $\forall x(x = y \rightarrow y = x)$
7. ⊢ $\forall x \forall y \forall z((x = y \; \& \; y = z) \rightarrow x = z)$
8. ⊢ $\forall x \forall y(x = y \rightarrow (Fx \leftrightarrow Fy))$
9. $\forall x(x = a \lor x = b), \; \sim Fa \vdash \exists x Fx \rightarrow Fb$
10. $\forall x \forall y(Rxy \rightarrow x = y), \; Fa, \; \sim Fb \vdash \sim Rab$

Exercise 8.5.2

Prove the sequents corresponding to the arguments that were formalized in Exercise 6.3.

8.6 FUNCTIONS

The addition of function symbols to the language of predicate logic requires no new rules. However, because function symbols create new names (see Section 6.4), the quantifier and identity rules must be reinterpreted to allow for the new complex names they provide. *The names mentioned in the rules ∃I, ∀E, =I, and =E may be either simple or complex. However, the names of representative individuals used in the rules ∃E and ∀I must always be simple—that is, just lowercase letters 'a' through 't'.* To use a complex name for a representative individual would import into the proof information that would make that individual nonrepresentative.

To illustrate the use of function symbols in proofs, we shall prove two theorems governing one-place functions. The first of these, '⊢ $\forall x \forall y(x = y \rightarrow f(x) = f(y))$', says that for identical arguments, a function takes identical values:

1.	$a = b$	H (for →I)
2.	$f(a) = f(a)$	=I
3.	$f(a) = f(b)$	1, 2 =E
4.	$a = b \rightarrow f(a) = f(b)$	1–3 →I
5.	$\forall y(a = y \rightarrow f(a) = f(y))$	4 ∀I
6.	$\forall x \forall y(x = y \rightarrow f(x) = f(y))$	5 ∀I

Note the use of =I with the complex name 'f(a)' at line 2 and the quantification of simple names contained in complex names at steps 5 and 6.

The second of our two theorems, '⊢ ∀x∃y∀z(z = f(x) ↔ z = y)', says that for each argument (represented here by the variable 'x') a function has a unique value (represented by 'y'):

1. | b = f(a)   H (for →I)
2. b = f(a) → b = f(a)   1–1 →I
3. b = f(a) ↔ b = f(a)   2, 2 ↔I
4. ∀z(z = f(a) ↔ z = f(a))   3 ∀I
5. ∃y∀z(z = f(a) ↔ z = y)   4 ∃I
6. ∀x∃y∀z(z = f(x) ↔ z = y)   5 ∀I

Of special interest in this example is the use of ∃I with the complex name 'f(a)' at line 5.

Exercise 8.6

Prove the sequents corresponding to the arguments formalized in Exercise 6.4.

CHAPTER 9

CLASSICAL PREDICATE LOGIC: SOUNDNESS, COMPLETENESS, AND INEXPRESSIBILITY

Because it sometimes produces infinite trees, the tree test is not a decision procedure for predicate logic. In the first two sections of this chapter we shall prove that the tree test is nevertheless sound and complete. We also prove soundness and completeness for the derivation rules in Section 9.3. And finally in Section 9.4 we consider a wholly different reason predicate logic may be unable to decide the validity of an argument: It may not be able adequately to represent the argument's form.

9.1 SOUNDNESS OF THE TREE TEST

Recall that a test for validity is **sound** if whenever the test classifies a sequent as valid it is valid. A test is **complete** if (conversely) whenever a sequent is valid, the test classifies it as valid. Thus to say that a test is sound and complete is to say

(1) The test classifies a sequent as valid if and only if it is valid.

But if this is the case, it would seem that the test is, after all, a decision procedure—for wouldn't it have to give a correct answer in every case in order to be sound and complete?

Actually not. For statement (1) does not tell us exactly what will happen if the sequent is invalid. What it does tell us (by contraposition) is this:

(2) A sequent is invalid if and only if it is not the case that the test classifies it as valid.

Now there are two ways that the tree test might fail to classify a sequent as valid:

(i) the test might classify the sequent as *in*valid; that is, the tree might terminate with an open path, or

(ii) the test might not classify the sequent at all; it might go on forever and never return an answer.

This second possibility is not excluded by soundness and completeness. What soundness and completeness do guarantee is that the test always terminates with a correct answer when applied to a *valid* sequent. They also guarantee that if the test gives an answer for an invalid sequent, that answer will be correct. But for invalid sequents, soundness and completeness do not guarantee that the test always gives an answer. And we have seen that the tree test for predicate logic does indeed fail to classify some invalid sequents.

Is this a fault of the tree test (which could be remedied by some modification of the test, or, lacking that, by an entirely new test for validity)—or must any test inevitably fail in this way? We shall prove in Section 10.6 that any test must fail.

In this section and the next, we examine the proofs of soundness and completeness for the tree test for predicate logic with identity but without function symbols. We put function symbols aside (though consistency and completeness can still be proved if they are present), because retaining them would complicate the proofs considerably without much gain in insight.

Once again, a test for validity is *sound* if whenever that test classifies a sequent as valid, it is valid. In this section, we show that the tree test for predicate logic (with identity but without function symbols) is sound. As in the soundness proof for propositional logic in Section 5.8, we do this in two stages. First we prove that any tree constructed by finitely many applications of the rules from a consistent initial list contains an open path. Then we derive the soundness result as a corollary.

In Section 5.8, to prove that any tree constructed from a consistent initial list contains an open path, we reasoned as follows. Since the initial list is consistent, it is true on some valuation, which we called $\mathcal{V}$. Then we showed that any tree constructible from this list contains a path P all of whose formulas are true on $\mathcal{V}$. Since all formulas on P are true on $\mathcal{V}$, the path cannot contain both a formula and its negation (which could not both be true on any valuation). Hence P must be open. Our reasoning here is similar, except that the valuation on which all members of the path are true need not be the same as the valuation $\mathcal{V}$ which makes the initial list true. It may instead be derived from $\mathcal{V}$ by a series of expansions—one for each new name introduced to the path by $\exists$ or (in cases where the path contains a universal formula but no names) $\forall$. Hence we argue, not that the tree contains a path all formulas of which are true on $\mathcal{V}$, but that it contains a path all formulas of which are true *on some valuation*—the valuation in question being an expansion (or an expansion of an expansion, etc.) of $\mathcal{V}$.

Moreover, because the quantifier rules and the =E rule work by replacing names with variables or other names, we must ensure that such exchanges result in formulas with appropriate truth values. Formulas whose names (if any) may be replaced without change in truth value by other names denoting the same objects are called **extensional** formulas. The soundness proof depends on the assumption that all formulas are extensional. We shall prove this assumption in two different forms—a general version involving two expansions of a given valuation and a more particular version involving only a single valuation—before proving the soundness of the tree test.

The proof of the first general version proceeds by mathematical induction, using the concept of complexity. The **complexity** of a formula is the number of occurrences of logical operators it contains, not counting the identity operator. Thus the complexity of atomic formulas (including identity formulas) is 0. The complexity of '$\forall x(\sim Fx \rightarrow \sim Gx)$', for example, is 4, since there are four occurrences of operators, one each of '$\forall$' and '$\rightarrow$' and two of '$\sim$'.

Now consider the infinite series S of sets of formulas, whose first member is the set of all formulas of complexity 0, whose second member is the set of all formulas of complexity 0 or 1, whose third member is the set of all formulas of complexity 0, 1, or 2, and so on. (In general, for $n \geq 0$, the $(n + 1)$st member of S is the set of all formulas of complexity n or less.) We shall show that each set in this series has the property of containing only extensional members. (This is the property F in the induction schema of Section 5.5.) Since every formula must belong to some member of S, we may then conclude that all formulas are extensional. Formally, we define *extensionality* as follows:

DEFINITION A formula Φ is **extensional** iff for any valuation $\mathcal{V}$ of Φ and any object d of which both α and β are potential names with respect to $\mathcal{V}$, if α occurs in Φ and $\Phi^\beta/_\alpha$ is a result of replacing one or more occurrences of α in Φ by β, then $\mathcal{V}_{(\alpha,d)}(\Phi) = \mathcal{V}_{(\beta,d)}(\Phi^\beta/_\alpha)$.

The following lemma, then, demonstrates the extensionality of all formulas. (Incidentally, this lemma illustrates in great detail the strategy of arguing by cases—a strategy analogous to $\vee$E in the object language.)

METATHEOREM (General Extensionality Lemma): All formulas are extensional.

PROOF: We shall show by induction on the series S that all the members of each set in S are extensional. Since each formula, being obtained by finitely many applications of the formation rules, is of finite complexity, each must belong to some set in the series S (indeed, to infinitely many!). Thus it follows that all formulas are extensional.

Basis Case: We must show that the first item of S, the set of all formulas of complexity 0, has the property of containing only extensional members. Inspection of the formation rules reveals that a formula Φ of complexity 0 may have one of four forms. It may be a sentence letter, or a one-place predicate followed by a name, or an n-place predicate ($n > 1$) followed by n names, or an identity statement. We consider each form in turn. Take first the case in which Φ is a sentence letter. Then no names occur in Φ. Hence it is trivially the case that if α occurs in Φ and $\Phi^\beta/_\alpha$ is a result of replacing one or more occurrences of α in Φ by β, then $\mathcal{V}_{(\alpha,d)}(\Phi) = \mathcal{V}_{(\beta,d)}(\Phi^\beta/_\alpha).$[1] Consider, next, the case in which Φ is of the form $\Psi\gamma$, where Ψ is a one-place predicate and γ is a name. Let $\mathcal{V}$ be any valuation of Φ such that α and β are both potential names of d with respect to $\mathcal{V}$. We shall show by conditional proof that Φ is extensional.

Suppose for conditional proof that α occurs in Φ and $\Phi^\beta/_\alpha$ is a result of replacing one or more occurrences of α in Φ by β. Then since only one name, γ, occurs in Φ, γ is α. In other words, Φ is $\Psi\alpha$, and, likewise, $\Phi^\beta/_\alpha$ is $\Psi\beta$. Now by valuation rule 1,

$$\mathcal{V}_{(\alpha,d)}(\Psi\alpha) = T \text{ iff } \mathcal{V}_{(\alpha,d)}(\alpha) \; \varepsilon \; \mathcal{V}_{(\alpha,d)}(\Psi)$$

But, given that α and β are both potential names of d with respect to $\mathcal{V}$, the definition of an expansion implies that $\mathcal{V}_{(\alpha,d)}(\alpha) = d = \mathcal{V}_{(\beta,d)}(\beta)$. Moreover (since expansions do not change the extensions of predicates), $\mathcal{V}_{(\alpha,d)}(\Psi) = \mathcal{V}(\Psi) = \mathcal{V}_{(\beta,d)}(\Psi)$. Hence

$$\mathcal{V}_{(\alpha,d)}(\Psi\alpha) = T \text{ iff } \mathcal{V}_{(\beta,d)}(\beta) \; \varepsilon \; \mathcal{V}_{(\beta,d)}(\Psi)$$

However, again by valuation rule 1, $\mathcal{V}_{(\beta,d)}(\beta) \; \varepsilon \; \mathcal{V}_{(\beta,d)}(\Psi)$ iff $\mathcal{V}_{(\beta,d)}(\Psi\beta) = T$. Therefore

$$\mathcal{V}_{(\alpha,d)}(\Psi\alpha) = T \text{ iff } \mathcal{V}_{(\beta,d)}(\Psi\beta) = T$$

Hence by bivalence

$$\mathcal{V}_{(\alpha,d)}(\Psi\alpha) = \mathcal{V}_{(\beta,d)}(\Psi\beta)$$

Thus, since $\Psi\alpha = \Phi$ and $\Psi\beta = \Phi^\beta/_\alpha$,

$$\mathcal{V}_{(\alpha,d)}(\Phi) = \mathcal{V}_{(\beta,d)}(\Phi^\beta/_\alpha)$$

We have thus shown for any formula Φ of the form $\Psi\gamma$, where Ψ is a one-place predicate and γ is a name, that for any valuation $\mathcal{V}$ of Φ and any object d of which both α and β are potential names with respect to $\mathcal{V}$, if α occurs in Φ and $\Phi^\beta/_\alpha$ is a result of replacing one or more occurrences of α in Φ by β, then $\mathcal{V}_{(\alpha,d)}(\Phi) = \mathcal{V}_{(\beta,d)}(\Phi^\beta/_\alpha)$. That is, we have shown that all formulas consisting of a one-place predicate followed by a name are extensional. Next we show this for all formulas consisting of an n-place predicate followed by n names ($n > 1$). So we must consider the case in which Φ is of the form $\Psi\gamma_1, \ldots, \gamma_n$, where Ψ is an n-place predicate and $\gamma_1, \ldots, \gamma_n$ are names. Let $\mathcal{V}$ be any valuation of Φ such that α and β are both potential names of d with respect to $\mathcal{V}$.

Now suppose for conditional proof that α occurs in Φ and $\Phi^\beta/_\alpha$ is a result of replacing one or more occurrences of α in Φ by β.

---

[1] Since any conditional with a false antecedent is true!

Since α occurs in Φ, at least one of the names $\gamma_1, \ldots, \gamma_n$ must be α. Moreover, $\Phi^{\beta}/_{\alpha}$ is of the form $\Psi\delta_1, \ldots, \delta_n$, where for each of the names γ_i ($1 \le i \le n$) in the list $\gamma_1, \ldots, \gamma_n$, either $\gamma_i = \alpha$ and $\delta_i = \beta$, or $\gamma_i = \delta_i$. We shall show that in either case $\mathcal{V}_{(\alpha,d)}(\gamma_i) = \mathcal{V}_{(\beta,d)}(\delta_i)$.

Suppose, first, that $\gamma_i = \alpha$ and $\delta_i = \beta$. Then, given that α and β are both potential names of d with respect to $\mathcal{V}$, the definition of an expansion implies that $\mathcal{V}_{(\alpha,d)}(\gamma_i) = \mathcal{V}_{(\alpha,d)}(\alpha) = d = \mathcal{V}_{(\beta,d)}(\beta) = \mathcal{V}_{(\beta,d)}(\delta_i)$.

Therefore, if $\gamma_i = \alpha$ and $\delta_i = \beta$, then $\mathcal{V}_{(\alpha,d)}(\gamma_i) = \mathcal{V}_{(\beta,d)}(\delta_i)$.

Suppose, to consider the other possibility, that $\gamma_i = \delta_i$. Now there are three subcases. Either $\gamma_i = \alpha$ (not all occurrences of α need be replaced by β!) or $\gamma_i = \beta$ or neither (i.e., $\gamma_i \ne \alpha$ and $\gamma_i \ne \beta$).

Suppose, to take the first case, that $\gamma_i = \alpha$. Then, since $\mathcal{V}$ is a valuation of Φ and thus assigns some extension to γ_i, and since α is a potential name of d with respect to $\mathcal{V}$, the extension $\mathcal{V}$ assigns to γ_i must be d. That is, $\mathcal{V}(\gamma_i) = \mathcal{V}(\alpha) = d$. Therefore $\mathcal{V}_{(\alpha,d)}$ is a trivial expansion of $\mathcal{V}$ so that $\mathcal{V}_{(\alpha,d)}(\gamma_i) = \mathcal{V}(\gamma_i) = d$. Therefore, whether or not $\alpha = \beta$, by the definition of an expansion, $d = \mathcal{V}_{(\beta,d)}(\gamma_i)$. Hence, since $\gamma_i = \delta_i$, $d = \mathcal{V}_{(\beta,d)}(\delta_i)$. But then $\mathcal{V}_{(\alpha,d)}(\gamma_i) = \mathcal{V}_{(\beta,d)}(\delta_i)$.

Hence, if $\gamma_i = \alpha$, then $\mathcal{V}_{(\alpha,d)}(\gamma_i) = \mathcal{V}_{(\beta,d)}(\delta_i)$.

Suppose now, to take the second of these three subcases, that $\gamma_i = \beta$. Then again, since $\mathcal{V}$ is a valuation of Φ and so assigns some extension to γ_i, and since β is a potential name of d with respect to $\mathcal{V}$, $\mathcal{V}(\gamma_i) = \mathcal{V}(\beta) = d$. That is, $\mathcal{V}_{(\beta,d)}$ is a trivial expansion of $\mathcal{V}$ so that $\mathcal{V}_{(\beta,d)}(\gamma_i) = \mathcal{V}(\gamma_i) = d$. Hence, since $\gamma_i = \delta_i$, $\mathcal{V}_{(\beta,d)}(\delta_i) = d$. So, by the definition of an expansion, $d = \mathcal{V}_{(\alpha,d)}(\gamma_i)$. Therefore $\mathcal{V}_{(\alpha,d)}(\gamma_i) = \mathcal{V}_{(\beta,d)}(\delta_i)$.

Hence, if $\gamma_i = \beta$, then $\mathcal{V}_{(\alpha,d)}(\gamma_i) = \mathcal{V}_{(\beta,d)}(\delta_i)$.

Finally, to take the third subcase, suppose that γ_i is neither α nor β. Then, by the definition of an expansion, both $\mathcal{V}_{(\alpha,d)}$ and $\mathcal{V}_{(\beta,d)}$ must assign the same extension to γ_i that $\mathcal{V}$ does. Hence, since $\gamma_i = \delta_i$, $\mathcal{V}_{(\alpha,d)}(\gamma_i) = \mathcal{V}_{(\beta,d)}(\delta_i)$.

So, if γ_i is neither α nor β, then $\mathcal{V}_{(\alpha,d)}(\gamma_i) = \mathcal{V}_{(\beta,d)}(\delta_i)$. Therefore, in any of the three subcases in which $\gamma_i = \delta_i$, $\mathcal{V}_{(\alpha,d)}(\gamma_i) = \mathcal{V}_{(\beta,d)}(\delta_i)$. So, regardless of whether $\gamma_i = \alpha$ and $\delta_i = \beta$ or $\gamma_i = \delta_i$, $\mathcal{V}_{(\alpha,d)}(\gamma_i) = \mathcal{V}_{(\beta,d)}(\delta_i)$. Thus we know that for each i ($1 \le i \le n$), $\mathcal{V}_{(\alpha,d)}(\gamma_i) = \mathcal{V}_{(\beta,d)}(\delta_i)$. Now by valuation rule 2

$$\mathcal{V}_{(\alpha,d)}(\Psi\gamma_1, \ldots, \gamma_n) = \text{T iff } \langle \mathcal{V}_{(\alpha,d)}(\gamma_1), \ldots, \mathcal{V}_{(\alpha,d)}(\gamma_n)\rangle \, \varepsilon$$
$$\mathcal{V}_{(\alpha,d)}(\Psi)$$

Hence

$$\mathcal{V}_{(\alpha,d)}(\Psi\gamma_1, \ldots, \gamma_n) = \text{T iff } <\mathcal{V}_{(\beta,d)}(\delta_1), \ldots, \mathcal{V}_{(\beta,d)}(\delta_n)> \epsilon$$
$$\mathcal{V}_{(\alpha,d)}(\Psi)$$

But by the definition of an expansion (since expansions don't affect the denotations of predicates), $\mathcal{V}_{(\alpha,d)}(\Psi) = \mathcal{V}(\Psi) = \mathcal{V}_{(\beta,d)}(\Psi)$. Hence

$$\mathcal{V}_{(\alpha,d)}(\Psi\gamma_1, \ldots, \gamma_n) = \text{T iff } <\mathcal{V}_{(\beta,d)}(\delta_1), \ldots, \mathcal{V}_{(\beta,d)}(\delta_n)> \epsilon$$
$$\mathcal{V}_{(\beta,d)}(\Psi)$$

But, again by valuation rule 2, this implies that

$$\mathcal{V}_{(\alpha,d)}(\Psi\gamma_1, \ldots, \gamma_n) = \text{T iff } \mathcal{V}_{(\beta,d)}(\Psi\delta_1, \ldots, \delta_n) = \text{T}$$

But since $\Psi\gamma_1, \ldots, \gamma_n = \Phi$ and $\Psi\delta_1, \ldots, \delta_n = \Phi^\beta/_\alpha$, this means that

$$\mathcal{V}_{(\alpha,d)}(\Phi) = \text{T iff } \mathcal{V}_{(\beta,d)}(\Phi^\beta/_\alpha) = \text{T}$$

Hence by bivalence

$$\mathcal{V}_{(\alpha,d)}(\Phi) = \mathcal{V}_{(\beta,d)}(\Phi^\beta/_\alpha)$$

Thus we have shown for any formula Φ of the form $\Psi\gamma_1, \ldots, \gamma_n$ that for any valuation $\mathcal{V}$ and any object d of which both α and β are potential names with respect to $\mathcal{V}$, if α occurs in Φ and $\Phi^\beta/_\alpha$ is a result of replacing one or more occurrences of α in Φ by β, then $\mathcal{V}_{(\alpha,d)}(\Phi) = \mathcal{V}_{(\beta,d)}(\Phi^\beta/_\alpha)$. That is, we have shown that all formulas consisting of an n-place predicate followed by n names are extensional. It remains to be seen that all identity formulas are extensional, but the proof is left as an exercise. (The proof is much like that for n-place predicates ($n > 1$), except that it uses valuation rule 3 rather than valuation rule 2.) This establishes that all formulas of complexity 0 are extensional.

Inductive Step: Suppose, for our inductive hypothesis, that the nth member of series S contains only extensional formulas—that is, for all formulas Δ of complexity n or less, if Δ contains α and $\Delta^\beta/_\alpha$ is the result of replacing one or more occurrences of α in Δ by β, then $\mathcal{V}_{(\alpha,d)}(\Delta) = \mathcal{V}_{(\beta,d)}(\Delta^\beta/_\alpha)$. We must show that the $(n+1)$st set in S also contains only extensional formulas. That is, we must show that all formulas of complexity $n + 1$ are extensional. Now by the formation rules any formula of complexity $n + 1$ must have one of the following forms:

negation	biconditional
conjunction	existentially quantified formula
disjunction	universally quantified formula
conditional	

(All other formulas are atomic and hence of complexity 0, which is less than $n + 1$.) We must now show, given the inductive hypothesis, that no matter which of these forms a formula of complexity $n + 1$ has, that formula is extensional. I shall do this only for the case of conjunction, leaving the others (which are quite similar) as exercises. Consider any conjunction Φ of complexity $n + 1$, and let $\mathcal{V}$ be any valuation of Φ such that α and β are both potential names of d with respect to $\mathcal{V}$.

Suppose for conditional proof that α occurs in Φ and $\Phi^\beta/_\alpha$ is a result of replacing one or more occurrences of α in Φ by β. Now Φ, being a conjunction, is of the form $(\Delta$ & $\Theta)$ for some formulas Δ and Θ, and α must occur in Δ, or in Θ, or in both. Let $\Delta^\beta/_\alpha$ and $\Theta^\beta/_\alpha$ be the results, respectively, of the substitutions of β for α (if any) made in Δ and Θ to obtain $\Phi^\beta/_\alpha$ from Φ. Now by the valuation rule for conjunction (rule 5),

$$\mathcal{V}_{(\alpha, d)}(\Phi) = T \text{ iff } \mathcal{V}_{(\alpha, d)}(\Delta) = T \text{ and } \mathcal{V}_{(\alpha, d)}(\Theta) = T$$

But since Φ has complexity $n + 1$, each of Δ and Θ, having fewer operators than Φ itself, must be of complexity n or less. Hence by the inductive hypothesis,

$$\mathcal{V}_{(\alpha, d)}(\Delta) = T \text{ iff } \mathcal{V}_{(\beta, d)}(\Delta^\beta/_\alpha) = T \text{ and } \mathcal{V}_{(\alpha, d)}(\Theta) = T \text{ iff } \mathcal{V}_{(\beta, d)}(\Theta^\beta/_\alpha) = T$$

But, again by valuation rule 5,

$$\mathcal{V}_{(\beta, d)}(\Phi^\beta/_\alpha) = T \text{ iff both } \mathcal{V}_{(\beta, d)}(\Delta^\beta/_\alpha) = T \text{ and } \mathcal{V}_{(\beta, d)}(\Theta^\beta/_\alpha) = T$$

Thus

$$\mathcal{V}_{(\alpha, d)}(\Phi) = T \text{ iff } \mathcal{V}_{(\beta, d)}(\Phi^\beta/_\alpha) = T$$

So by bivalence,

$$\mathcal{V}_{(\alpha, d)}(\Phi) = \mathcal{V}_{(\beta, d)}(\Phi^\beta/_\alpha)$$

Therefore we have shown that for any conjunction Φ of complexity $n + 1$ and any valuation $\mathcal{V}$ of Φ such that α and β are both potential names of d with respect to $\mathcal{V}$, if $\Phi^\beta/_\alpha$ is the result of replacing one or more occurrences of α in Φ by β, then $\mathcal{V}_{(\alpha, d)}(\Phi) = \mathcal{V}_{(\beta, d)}(\Phi^\beta/_\alpha)$. We have shown, in other words, that all conjunctions of complexity $n + 1$ are extensional. By similar arguments, it can be shown that all formulas of complexity $n + 1$ having any of the other forms mentioned above are also extensional. Hence, given the inductive hypothesis, all members of the $(n + 1)$st set in series S are extensional.

Thus, if all members of the nth set in S are extensional, so are all members of the $(n + 1)$st. Hence, by mathematical induction, all the formulas in all the sets of S are extensional. Therefore all formulas are extensional.   QED

We now prove a second extensionality lemma, which is a simple corollary of the first lemma:

COROLLARY (Special Extensionality Lemma): Let α and β be any names and Φ any formula containing α, and let $\Phi^\beta/_\alpha$ be the result of replacing one or more occurrences of α in Φ by β. Then, if $\mathcal{V}(\alpha) = \mathcal{V}(\beta)$, $\mathcal{V}(\Phi) = \mathcal{V}(\Phi^\beta/_\alpha)$.

PROOF: Suppose $\mathcal{V}(\alpha) = \mathcal{V}(\beta)$. Then on $\mathcal{V}$ both α and β denote the same object, which we shall call d. Hence both are potential names of d with respect to $\mathcal{V}$. So by the general extensionality lemma, $\mathcal{V}_{(\alpha,d)}(\Phi) = \mathcal{V}_{(\beta,d)}(\Phi^\beta/_\alpha)$. But both $\mathcal{V}_{(\alpha,d)}$ and $\mathcal{V}_{(\beta,d)}$ are trivial expansions of $\mathcal{V}$ and hence are identical to $\mathcal{V}$. Thus $\mathcal{V}(\Phi) = \mathcal{V}(\Phi^\beta/_\alpha)$.

Therefore, if $\mathcal{V}(\alpha) = \mathcal{V}(\beta)$, then $\mathcal{V}(\Phi) = \mathcal{V}(\Phi^\beta/_\alpha)$.   QED

Incidentally, the validity of the inference rule =E, which we did not have the means to confirm in Section 8.5, follows directly from the special extensionality lemma. The proof is left as an exercise.

Having established these lemmas, we are now ready to prove the soundness of the tree test. As in Section 5.8, we prove first that if the initial list is consistent, there is an open path through any tree obtainable from it, and from this the soundness result follows as a corollary.

METATHEOREM: If an initial list of formulas of predicate logic with identity (but no function symbols) is consistent, then there is an open path through any (finished or unfinished) tree obtained from that list by finitely many applications of the tree rules.

PROOF: Suppose (for conditional proof) that some initial list of formulas of predicate logic with identity, call it L, is consistent. This means that there is some valuation on which all the members of L are true. Now let T be any tree constructed from L by finitely many applications of the tree rules for predicate logic. To create T, a series $T_1, \ldots, T_z$ of trees was successively constructed, whose first member T_1 was L, whose final member T_z is T, and whose $(n+1)$st member T_{n+1}, for each n ($1 < n \leq z$), was obtained from the nth, T_n, by the application of a single tree rule. We shall prove that each member of this series contains an open path, whence it follows that T itself contains an open path. To prove this, it suffices to show that every tree in the sequence contains a path all formulas of which are true

---

on some valuation. For if all formulas of a path are true on some valuation, then that path cannot contain both a formula and its negation (which cannot both be true on any valuation) or a formula of the form $\sim\alpha = \alpha$ (which cannot be true on any valuation), and hence must be open. We assumed above that there is some valuation on which all formulas of the initial list L are true. Then there must be some valuation $\mathcal{V}$ which makes all the members of L true but assigns no extensions to any names not in L, since any extensions assigned to names not in L could not affect the truth values of formulas in L. To prove that each tree in the series contains a path all of whose formulas are true on some valuation, it will be convenient to first prove a slightly stronger result, namely, that each tree in the series contains a path all formulas of which are true on some valuation *which assigns no extensions to names not on that path*. For this we use mathematical induction:

Basis Case: The first member of the series is T_1, which is L itself, and by hypothesis each member of L is true on $\mathcal{V}$ and hence true on some valuation (namely $\mathcal{V}$!). Moreover, $\mathcal{V}$, as noted above, assigns no extensions to names not appearing in L.

Inductive Step: Suppose (inductive hypothesis) that the nth item T_n of the series (where $1 \leq n < z$) contains a path P all of whose formulas are true on some valuation $\mathcal{V}'$ which assigns no extensions to names not on P. Now the $(n + 1)$st item, T_{n+1}, is formed by a single application of a rule to T_n. There are two possibilities concerning the point of application of this rule: Either the formula or formulas to which the rule is applied are on P or they are not. If the rule is applied to formulas on P, then by the inductive hypothesis these formulas are true on $\mathcal{V}'$. Hence the rule used can't have been $\sim$ or $\sim=$, which close paths, since neither a formula and its negation nor a negated self-identity can be true on any valuation. So it must have been one of the other rules. Now these rules, when applied to a path all of whose formulas are true on a valuation, yield at least one one-step extension all of whose formulas are true either on that valuation or (in the case of $\exists$—and $\forall$ when used to introduce a new name) on an expansion of that valuation with respect to the new name.[2] (Check this claim for each rule. The

---

[2] This is the case for $\exists$ and $\forall$, provided that the original valuation $\mathcal{V}'$ did not assign any extension to the new name; that is, it is a potential name for each object in the domain with respect to $\mathcal{V}'$. But these rules require that the new name not appear on the path P, and our inductive hypothesis ensures that $\mathcal{V}'$ assigns no extensions to names not on P.

reasoning for rules $\forall$ and $\exists$ requires the general extensionality lemma;[3] the special extensionality lemma is needed for =.) So at least one of the one-step extensions of P is a path of T_{n+1} all formulas of which are true on some valuation. (And if there is an expansion which gives a new name an extension, that name has been introduced to the path, so this expansion still assigns no extensions to names not on the path.) If, on the other hand, the formula or formulas to which the rule is applied are not on P, then nothing will be added to P in moving from T_n to T_{n+1}. Hence in this case P itself is a path of T_{n+1} all of whose formulas are true on $\mathcal{V}'$ and hence true on some valuation. So either way T_{n+1} contains a path all of whose formulas are true on some valuation which assigns no extensions to names not on that path.

Thus (by conditional proof) we have shown that for any n, if T_n contains a path all of whose formulas are true on some valuation which assigns no extensions to names not on that path, so does T_{n+1}. So (by mathematical induction) each tree in the sequence $T_1, \ldots, T_z$ contains a path all of whose formulas are true on some valuation which assigns no extensions to names not on that path. Hence T must itself contain a path all of whose formulas are true on some valuation. So (as explained above) T contains an open path.

Hence we have shown (by conditional proof) that if L is consistent, then there is an open path through any finished tree T obtainable from L by finitely many applications of the tree rules.   QED

Soundness now follows by essentially the same reasoning used in Section 5.8:

COROLLARY (Soundness): If the tree test classifies a sequent of predicate logic with identity (but no function symbols) as valid, it is in fact valid.

PROOF: Suppose (for conditional proof) that the tree test classifies a sequent $\Phi_1, \ldots, \Phi_n \vdash \Psi$ of predicate logic with identity (but no function symbols) as valid. This means that the tree's initial

---

[3] Suppose, for example, that $\exists$ is applied to some formula $\exists \beta \Phi$ to yield a new formula $\Phi^\gamma/_\beta$, which is the result of replacing each occurrence of β in Φ by some new name γ. Now, if there is some valuation $\mathcal{V}$ with domain $\mathcal{D}$ such that $\mathcal{V}(\exists \beta \Phi) = T$, then by valuation rule 10 there is some potential name α of some object d in $\mathcal{D}$ such that $\mathcal{V}_{(\alpha,d)}(\Phi^\alpha/_\beta) = T$. Now since γ is a new name, it is not assigned any value by $\mathcal{V}$, and so it is also a potential name for d. And since $\mathcal{V}_{(\gamma,d)}(\gamma) = \mathcal{V}_{(\alpha,d)}(\alpha) = d$, it follows by the general extensionality lemma that $\mathcal{V}_{(\gamma,d)}(\Phi^\gamma/_\beta) = \mathcal{V}_{(\alpha,d)}(\Phi^\alpha/_\beta) = T$. Therefore there is some expansion of $\mathcal{V}$—namely, $\mathcal{V}_{(\gamma,d)}$—that makes $\Phi^\gamma/_\beta$ true.

list is $\Phi_1, \ldots, \Phi_n, \sim\!\Psi$, and that all paths of the tree close after finitely many applications of the rules; hence after a finite number of applications of the rules this tree contains no open paths. But by the previous metatheorem, if the initial list is consistent, then there is an open path through any tree constructed from it by finitely many applications of rules. So (by modus tollens) the initial list is inconsistent. But then by the metatheorem proved at the end of Section 5.2 (a sequent is valid if and only if the set consisting of its premises and the negation of its conclusion is inconsistent), the sequent is valid. Therefore, if the tree test classifies such a sequent as valid, it is in fact valid.   QED

Exercise 9.1

1. In the basis case of the proof of the general extensionality lemma, we left unproved the assertion that all identity statements (statements of the form $\alpha = \beta$) are extensional. Prove this.
2. In the inductive step of the proof of the general extensionality lemma, we showed, given the hypothesis that all formulas of complexity n or less are extensional, that all conjunctions of complexity $n + 1$ are extensional. Complete the proof of this lemma by showing, given this hypothesis, that all negations, disjunctions, conditionals, biconditionals, existentially quantified formulas, and universally quantified formulas of complexity $n + 1$ are also extensional.
3. In the proof of the main metatheorem of this section, it is necessary to verify for each tree rule other than $\sim$ or $\sim\!=$ that when applied to a path all of whose formulas are true on some valuation $\mathcal{V}$, it yields at least one one-step extension of that path whose formulas are all true on $\mathcal{V}$ or on some expansion of $\mathcal{V}$. The propositional rules were covered in Section 5.8, and I did the checking for $\exists$ in footnote 3 of Chapter 9. Complete the necessary verifications for $\sim\!\forall$, $\sim\!\exists$, $\forall$, and $=$.
4. Prove, using the special extensionality lemma, that all instances of the inference rule $=$E are valid.

9.2 COMPLETENESS OF THE TREE TEST

A test for validity is **complete** if whenever an argument is valid, the test classifies it as valid. In this section we prove the completeness of the tree test for predicate logic with identity but no function symbols. As usual, we first prove a metatheorem and then derive the completeness result as a corollary. The metatheorem asserts that if a tree never closes, its initial list is consistent. To prove this, we use a strategy like that of Section 5.9. We begin by supposing for conditional proof that we have a tree that never closes. In propositional logic, where all trees are finished after a finite number of steps, this would simply mean that the finished tree contains an open path; but in predicate logic it is also possible that the tree fails to close because it is nonterminating, that is, infinite. Yet if it is nonterminating, we know by König's lemma (lemma 3, Section 5.7) that it contains an infinitely prolongable path. Hence (whether or not the tree is infinite) if it never closes, it contains a specific path that never closes. We saw in a practical way in Section 7.4 that such a path, whether infinite or not, defines a valuation $\mathcal{V}$ which makes each of its members, including the entire initial list, true.[4] But the existence of such a valuation establishes (by the definition of consistency) that the initial list is consistent, thus completing the conditional proof.

In outline, then, the proof is straightforward. The real work comes in defining $\mathcal{V}$ and proving that it really does make each member of the open path true. Here are the details:

METATHEOREM: If a tree consisting of formulas of predicate logic with identity (but no function symbols) never closes, then its initial list is consistent.

PROOF: Suppose for conditional proof that L is a list of formulas of predicate logic with identity (but no function symbols) which produces a tree that never closes. Then either L is nonterminating or it is not. If L is nonterminating, by König's lemma, it produces an infinitely prolongable path. If L is not nonterminating, then L yields a finished tree after finitely many applications of the rules; and this tree, since it never closes, contains at least one open path. Hence in either case L yields a path P which never closes. We now show how to define a valuation $\mathcal{V}$ that makes every formula on P (and hence every formula of L) true. The definition is as follows. Let the domain of $\mathcal{V}$ and the extensions it assigns to names be as described in Section 7.4— that is, the domain $\mathfrak{D}$ consists of a set of numbers, where the name 'a' denotes the number 1, 'b' denotes the number 2, and so on, except that where names flank identity signs each name has as its extension the lowest number designated by a name with which it is identified by an identity statement on P. This ensures that whenever two names flank an identity sign they designate the same number. For predicates, $\mathcal{V}$ is defined as follows:

---

[4] In particular, if we are testing for validity, $\mathcal{V}$ is the counterexample specified by that open path. If the path is infinitely prolongable, $\mathcal{V}$ may have an infinite domain.

if Φ is a zero-place predicate, then $\mathcal{V}(\Phi) = T$ iff Φ appears as a line on P;

if Φ is a one-place predicate, then for each number d in $\mathcal{D}$, $d \in \mathcal{V}('\Phi')$ iff there is a name α such that $\mathcal{V}(\alpha) = d$ and $\Phi\alpha$ appears as a line of P; and

if Φ is an n-place predicate ($n > 1$), then for any numbers $d_1, \ldots, d_n$ in $\mathcal{D}$, $<d_1, \ldots, d_n> \in \mathcal{V}('\Phi')$ iff there are names $\alpha_1, \ldots, \alpha_n$ such that for each i, $1 \leq i \leq n$, $\mathcal{V}(\alpha_i) = d_i$, and $\Phi\alpha_1, \ldots, \alpha_n$ appears as a line of P.

It is easy to verify that this definition makes all the atomic formulas, including identities, of P true on $\mathcal{V}$. Moreover, it makes all negations of atomic formulas true. For if the negation of an atomic formula Φ appears as a line on P, then Φ itself cannot appear on P; otherwise, applying the rules in the prescribed order, P would eventually close. And since Φ does not appear on P, it follows by the definition of $\mathcal{V}$ and the valuation rule for negation that $\mathcal{V}(\sim\Phi) = T$ (check this for each sort of atomic formula).

Suppose now for reductio that some formula of P is not true on $\mathcal{V}$. Then there must be some formula Ψ of P which is not true on $\mathcal{V}$, such that all formulas of P shorter than Ψ are true on $\mathcal{V}$. Now Ψ is neither an atomic formula nor the negation of an atomic formula, for otherwise Ψ would be true on $\mathcal{V}$, as noted above. Thus Ψ must be of one of the following forms:

conjunction	negated conjunction
disjunction	negated disjunction
conditional	negated conditional
biconditional	negated biconditional
universal	negated universal
existential	negated existential
double negation	

And since P never closes, the prescribed order of rule application guarantees that any rule which can be applied to Ψ eventually will be applied, as many times as possible. So the rule for one of the forms listed above must eventually be applied to Ψ as often as it can be.[5] Applying any of these rules except for $\sim\forall$ or $\sim\exists$ to any formula yields only shorter formulas. But even $\sim\forall$ and

---

[5] The identity rule might also be applied to formulas of any of these forms, but whether or not it is, still one of the rules listed must eventually be applied.

~∃ yield shorter formulas after two steps. Hence P will eventually contain at least one formula shorter than Ψ that is obtained from Ψ by at most two applications of these rules. But since Ψ is the shortest formula on P that is not true on $\mathcal{V}$, all formulas shorter than Ψ on P are true on $\mathcal{V}$. Hence all formulas on P obtained from Ψ by these rules are true on $\mathcal{V}$. But it is a property of each of the rules except for ∀ that if they yield only formulas true on $\mathcal{V}$ on some path, then the formula to which they were applied is true on $\mathcal{V}$. (As in Section 5.9, it is easy to check this claim, at least for each rule other than ∀.) In the exceptional case where Ψ is a universal formula, Ψ must be true on $\mathcal{V}$ if *every* formula derived from it by ∀ is true on $\mathcal{V}$, since $\mathcal{V}$ is constructed so that its domain contains only objects denoted by names on P, and since, given the prescribed order of application, ∀ will eventually be applied to Ψ for each name on P. But every formula derived from Ψ, being shorter than Ψ, must be true on $\mathcal{V}$. Hence Ψ itself, if it is a universal formula, must be true on $\mathcal{V}$. Thus we have shown that no matter what Ψ's form is, Ψ must be true on $\mathcal{V}$. But by hypothesis Ψ is not true on $\mathcal{V}$, and so we have a contradiction.

Thus, contrary to our reductio hypothesis, all formulas of P are true on $\mathcal{V}$. So in particular, each formula of the initial list L is true on $\mathcal{V}$, and hence L is consistent.

Hence, if such a tree never closes, then its initial list is consistent.   QED

COROLLARY (Completeness): If a sequent of predicate logic with identity (but no function symbols) is valid, the tree test classifies that sequent as valid.

PROOF: Suppose that $\Phi_1, \ldots, \Phi_n \vdash \Psi$ is a valid sequent of predicate logic with identity (but no function symbols). It follows by the metatheorem at the end of Section 5.2 (a sequent is valid if and only if the set consisting of its premises and the negation of its conclusion is inconsistent) that the set $\{\Phi_1, \ldots, \Phi_n, \sim\Psi\}$ is inconsistent. But by the previous metatheorem, if a tree whose initial list is this set never closes, then that initial list is consistent. Consequently (by modus tollens), it is not the case that the tree whose initial list is this set never closes; that is, this tree eventually does close. But this is to say that the tree test classifies the sequent $\Phi_1, \ldots, \Phi_n \vdash \Psi$ as valid.

> Therefore, if such a sequent is valid, then the tree test classifies that sequent as valid.   QED

We have now shown that the tree test is both sound and complete for predicate logic with identity but no function symbols; that is, it classifies a sequent of this logic as valid if and only if that sequent *is* valid. Conversely, this means that the tree test fails to classify a sequent as valid if and only if it is not valid. But failing to classify a sequent as valid is not the same thing as classifying it as invalid. Nonterminating trees fail to give an answer either way, and we know that such trees exist. So, though we are guaranteed a right answer if we apply the test to a valid sequent, and though we are guaranteed that if we apply the test to an invalid sequent and get an answer that answer will also be right, there is no guarantee that we will get any answer at all when we apply the test to an invalid sequent. This means, further, that if we apply the test to a sequent which we neither know to be valid nor know to be invalid, we can't be sure in advance that we will learn anything. The tree test for predicate logic, then, is not a decision procedure.

This raises the question of whether we might modify the tree test somehow to make it a decision procedure—or invent some wholly different procedure to decide the question of validity in predicate logic. The answer to this question is no. To prove that, we will need to say more precisely what a decision procedure is. We have defined a decision procedure as a terminating algorithm which determines for each sequent of a given logic whether or not that sequent is valid. The term in this definition which needs clarification is 'algorithm'. We shall clarify it in Chapter 10.

9.3 SOUNDNESS AND COMPLETENESS OF THE RULES OF INFERENCE

As in Section 5.10, we shall demonstrate the completeness of the inference rules by providing an algorithm for converting any tree for a valid sequent into a proof of that sequent. If Section 5.10 is not fresh in your mind, review it before reading this section, since what is said here requires an understanding of that earlier section. To expand the completeness result of Section 5.10 to predicate logic, we simply add to the algorithm described there the directions in Table 9.1, which tell how to construct portions of the proof that correspond to applications of the quantifier or identity rules in the tree.

If we now review the reasoning of the completeness proof in Section 5.10, we shall see that it still applies to the algorithm that includes the new directions in Table 9.1. (The relevant completeness proof for the tree rules of predicate logic is, of course, the one given in Section 9.2, not the proof for propositional logic given in Section 5.9. Note that the negated identity rule given in Table 9.1 ensures that each 'x' still stands for 'P & $\sim P$'.) Thus we can see that the inference rules for predicate logic are complete.

TABLE 9.1
Tree Rules and Corresponding Proof Steps

Tree Rule	Corresponding Step(s) in Proof
Universal Quantification ($\forall$) If a formula of the form $\forall\beta\Phi$ appears on an open path and α is a name that occurs in a formula on that path, write $\Phi^\alpha/_\beta$ (the result of replacing all occurrences of β in Φ by α) at the bottom of the path. If no formula containing a name appears on the path, then choose some name α and write $\Phi^\alpha/_\beta$ at the bottom of the path. In either case, *do not* check $\forall\beta\Phi$.	In either case, infer $\Phi^\alpha/_\beta$ from $\forall\beta\Phi$ by $\forall$E.
Negated Universal Quantification ($\sim\forall$) If an unchecked formula of the form $\sim\forall\beta\Phi$ appears on an open path, check it and write $\exists\beta\sim\Phi$ at the bottom of every open path that contains the newly checked formula.	Infer $\exists\beta\sim\Phi$ from $\sim\forall\beta\Phi$ by QE.
Existential Quantification ($\exists$) If an unchecked formula of the form $\exists\beta\Phi$ appears on an open path, check it. Then choose a name α that does not yet appear anywhere on that path and write $\Phi^\alpha/_\beta$, the result of replacing every occurrence of β in Φ by α, at the bottom of every open path that contains the newly checked formula.	Given $\exists\beta\Phi$, hypothesize $\Phi^\alpha/_\beta$. When a contradiction of the form 'P & $\sim P$' is deduced from $\Phi^\alpha/_\beta$ (all subsequent hypothetical derivations having ended), end the hypothetical derivation from $\Phi^\alpha/_\beta$ and deduce 'P & $\sim P$' by $\exists$E.
Negated Existential Quantification ($\sim\exists$) If an unchecked formula of the form $\sim\exists\beta\Phi$ appears on an open path, check it and write $\forall\beta\sim\Phi$ at the bottom of every open path that contains the newly checked formula.	Infer $\forall\beta\sim\Phi$ from $\sim\exists\beta\Phi$ by QE.
Identity (=) If a formula of the form $\alpha = \beta$ appears on an open path, then if another formula Φ containing either α or β appears unchecked on that path, write at the bottom of the path any formula Ψ not already occurring (checked or unchecked) on the path which results from replacing one or more occurrences of either of these names by the other in Φ. Do not check either $\alpha = \beta$ or Φ.	Infer Ψ from Φ and $\alpha = \beta$ by =E.
Negated Identity ($\sim$=) Close any open path on which a formula of the form $\sim\alpha = \alpha$ occurs.	Introduce $\alpha = \alpha$ by =I, then from $\alpha = \alpha$ and $\sim\alpha = \alpha$, deduce 'P & $\sim P$' by EFQ.

The soundness proof for the inference rules of predicate logic is also the same as the soundness proof in Section 5.10, except that the basis case now must take account of =I, and each of the six new inference rules must be checked in the induction to ensure that they yield valid corresponding sequents. The proofs are relatively straightforward and are left as an exercise. We thus are able to show that the inference rules for predicate logic are sound.

To summarize: The inference rules for predicate logic are both sound and complete. That is, a sequent is valid iff it can be proved. But we have been unable to formulate, as we did for propositional logic, a terminating algorithm for telling which sequents are valid and which are not. As a result, when given a sequent of predicate logic, we cannot always tell whether or not it is provable. In Chapter 10, we shall see that no terminating algorithm of any kind can decide that question in every case. In the meantime, however, we consider another reason we cannot always tell whether an argument is valid.

Exercise 9.3

1. Write out in full the completeness proof for the inference rules of predicate logic, using the completeness proof of Section 5.10 as a model.
2. Show that the soundness proof of Section 5.10 may still be applied to predicate logic by proving for each of the rules ∃I, ∃E, ∀I, ∀E, =I, and =E that when applied to lines whose corresponding sequents are valid, they yield a conclusion whose corresponding sequent is valid. (Hint: Some rules require the extensionality results of Section 9.1.)

9.4 INEXPRESSIBILITY

Predicate logic does not automatically decide the validity of every argument. Even if we manage to formalize an argument satisfactorily, there is no guarantee that we will be able to decide the validity of the corresponding sequent. But sometimes we cannot even get that far. In these cases the problem may lie in the **inexpressibility** in predicate logic of crucial elements of the argument's form.

The fact that some forms of reasoning are not expressible in predicate logic is hardly surprising. Predicate logic deals with a mere eight operators: '~', '&', '∨', '→', '↔', '∀', '∃', and '='—together with the operators expressible by combining these eight.[6] But why suppose that these are the only expressions whose semantics can affect validity? The validity of an argument form could conceivably depend, for example, on the semantics of certain predicates, such as 'is a part of' or 'is greater than'; adverbs, such as 'quickly' or 'necessarily'; or sentence operators, such as '. . . knows that . . .' or 'it should be the case that . . .'. In such cases,

---

[6] 'Neither . . . nor', for example, or 'the' (using Russell's theory of descriptions).

predicate logic might misjudge validity, for it takes no account of the semantics of such expressions.

A natural response to the problem of inexpressibility is to expand predicate logic to include more and more of these "nonstandard" operators. Part IV of this book explores that response. Not all logicians endorse it. 'Nonstandard' is an epithet used derisively by some, who argue that some or all of the operators we examine in Part IV are not really logical, or not really intelligible, or both, and that logic proper ends with predicate logic. This, however, is not my view.

In this section we consider some arguments whose validity is not decided, or seems to be incorrectly decided, by predicate logic. In each case we shall see that the problem originates with one or more expressions whose semantics is not fully representable in predicate logic. Then we consider ways of expanding predicate logic to accommodate the semantics of some of these terms. Our first example is

> This finger is part of this hand.
> This hand is part of my body.
> ∴ This finger is part of my body.

Using 'f' for 'this finger', 'h' for 'this hand', 'b' for 'my body', and 'P' for 'is a part of', this argument may be formalized as

> Pfh, Phb ⊢ Pfb

But while the argument is intuitively valid, the sequent is invalid. What has gone wrong?

The stock response is that this argument has a missing premise, namely, that if one thing is a part of a second and the second a part of a third, then the first is a part of the third. In symbols this is

> $\forall x \forall y \forall z ((Pxy \ \& \ Pyz) \rightarrow Pxz)$

Or we might add merely the relevant instance of this generalization:

> $(Pfh \ \& \ Phb) \rightarrow Pfb$

Adding either premise does indeed make the sequent valid in predicate logic, but it evades the question. We wanted to know whether the original argument had a valid form—not whether the argument that results from adding either premise does.

The point can be illuminated by a somewhat different example. Suppose someone were to claim that the argument

> All men are mortal.
> Socrates is a man.
> ∴ Socrates is mortal.

assumes the premise

> If all men are mortal and Socrates is a man, then Socrates is mortal.

so that the argument really is

> If all men are mortal and Socrates is a man, then Socrates is mortal.
> All men are mortal.
> Socrates is a man.
> ∴ Socrates is mortal.

This is clearly an arbitrary addition. Why stop here? We could as well argue that this augmented argument is still incomplete, since it in turn "really assumes" the further premise

> If it is the case that if all men are mortal and Socrates is a man, then Socrates is mortal, and in addition all men are mortal and Socrates is a man; then Socrates is mortal.

We have started on an infinite regress, so we had better call a halt. The only nonarbitrary stopping place is the original argument. It was valid as it stood.[7]

Analogously, the argument

> This finger is part of this hand.
> This hand is part of my body.
> ∴ This finger is part of my body.

is arguably valid as it stands. Why do some people want to add a premise to this argument, even though they would not be tempted to do so with the Socrates argument? The answer, I think, is that if they didn't postulate the hidden assumption, they would have to admit that predicate logic, which pronounces the argument's form *in*valid, gives the wrong result. The addition is made ad hoc, to salvage agreement between formalism and intuition. As a result, it is not the formalism that decides the argument's validity. The question of validity is decided by intuition before the decision to add or not to add a premise is made; then, since the form is seen to be valid, a premise is added to square predicate logic with intuition.

In this way, any argument that seems intuitively valid can be made formally valid by the addition of premises. But so can any argument that doesn't seem intuitively valid, even those that are egregiously *in*valid. There are many ways to make such arguments valid. One that always works is **conditionalization**. Given any sequent $\Phi_1, \ldots, \Phi_n \vdash \Psi$, simply conjoin the premises and make their conjunction the antecedent of a conditional whose consequent is the conclusion. Adding this conditional as a premise yields the valid sequent:

$$((\Phi_1 \& \ldots \& \Phi_n) \to \Psi), \Phi_1, \ldots, \Phi_n \vdash \Psi\text{[8]}$$

---

[7] Lewis Carroll, who was a logician as well as a writer of children's literature, discusses this regress of premises enlighteningly and entertainingly in a well-known article titled "What the Tortoise Said to Achilles," *Mind* 4 (1895): 278–80.

[8] I have suppressed brackets in the conditional's antecedent. They must be added to make the conditional a formula, but all ways of adding them are equivalent so that their exact placement does not matter.

So, for example, even such classical fallacies as the following *ad hominem* become valid in virtue of their "hidden" premises:

>   Bill believes that God exists.
>   Bill is an idiot.
> ∴   God does not exist.

Using conditionalization, the "hidden" premise is

>   If Bill believes that God exists and Bill is an idiot, then God does not exist.

With so flexible a procedure, it's no wonder that predicate logic can be made to yield correct results.

But because it can transform *any* argument into a valid argument, this procedure will err unless the decision to add or not to add premises is based on an accurate intuitive assessment of the validity of the argument before the addition of premises. It is informal intuition, not the formalism, that decides initially whether or not the argument is valid and thus guides our decision to add or not to add premises.

This is not to deny the general usefulness of adding premises. On the contrary, making unstated premises explicit is often essential to accurate argument analysis.[9] The point is only that it is possible to evaluate arguments intuitively before adding premises, as well as afterward, and that in many cases when we evaluate arguments before adding premises we seem to find them valid, though predicate logic pronounces their forms invalid. We can always compensate for

---

[9] But it is essential only where the suppressed premise is not logically true. The addition of a logically true premise does not alter the validity of an argument and so is merely redundant. That is why it is pointless to add a premise like 'If all men are mortal and Socrates is a man, then Socrates is mortal'. Likewise, the principle 'If one thing is a part of a second and the second a part of a third, then the first is a part of the third' is arguably a logical truth (by the semantics of the predicate 'is a part of'), though predicate logic takes no account of this. It would follow that adding this premise, too, is pointless, except to make predicate logic square with what we already know by intuition.

The addition of a premise that is not a logical truth is, by contrast, not redundant. In the argument

>   Jill is human.
> ∴   Jill is fallible.

for example, the nonlogical premise

>   All humans are fallible.

is suppressed and should for accuracy's sake be added, regardless of whether we are working informally or in the formalism of predicate logic. The question at issue here, of course, is "What counts as a logical truth?" One common answer is "any statement whose form is a valid formula of predicate logic." The burden of this section is to suggest that this answer might be too narrow.

A more thorough treatment of the problem of implicit premises may be found in John Nolt, *Informal Logic: Possible Worlds and Imagination* (New York: McGraw-Hill, 1984), chap. 4.

this, because we can always transform an invalid argument into a valid one by adding a premise. But still it seems that predicate logic incorrectly classifies the original.

Why? With our example, specifically, the argument's validity seems to hinge on the meaning (i.e., the semantics) of 'is a part of'. Except for the identity predicate, predicate logic makes no provision for representing the semantics of specific predicates. In fact, it systematically ignores their meanings. The sequent

Pfh, Phb ⊢ Pfb

which represents our argument could as well be used to symbolize the argument

      Fred praised Hannah.
      Hannah praised Bill.
∴   Fred praised Bill.

or any of an infinite number of other arguments, both valid and invalid, with wildly unrelated meanings. The meanings of individual predicates (other than the identity predicate) are lost in the process of formalization. Thus it can be argued that the appropriate form and the relevant semantics for this argument are *inexpressible* in predicate logic, just as the appropriate forms and the relevant semantics for quantificational arguments are inexpressible in propositional logic. Where validity depends on the semantics of terms other than the eight operators mentioned earlier, predicate logic is insensitive to it.[10]

In fact, predicate logic seems incapable of symbolizing whole categories of terms. Consider adverbs. Predicates are at least *syntactically* representable in predicate logic, though formalization strips away their meaning; but we don't even have the *syntax* to symbolize adverbs. In the argument

      Bill is working quietly.
∴   Bill is working.

for example, 'is working quietly' is a different predicate from 'is working' so that in predicate logic they must be represented by different predicate letters. But this conceals their obvious relatedness. Using 'b' for 'Bill', 'Q' for 'is working quietly', and 'W' for 'is working', we obtain

Qb ⊢ Wb

which is invalid. Yet the argument seems valid.

There is, however, a way of conceptualizing the argument's form within predicate logic that just might work. Donald Davidson has devised an ingenious analysis in which adverbs, prepositional phrases, predicates, and several other

---

[10] Some contemporary philosophers, notably W. V. O. Quine and Donald Davidson, deny that terms other than the logical operators have individualizable meanings. These philosophers hold that meaning is a holistic property of language that cannot be parceled out neatly to individual terms. Yet they seem to grant clear and distinct meanings to the classical logical operators. Why just these words and no others?

grammatical forms are treated as predicates of events.[11] It requires adding to each predicate a place for a variable interpreted over a domain of events. Instead of writing 'Bill is working' as 'Wb', Davidson would write it as '∃eWeb', which means "there is an event e such that e is a working by Bill."[12] Adverbs are symbolized as predicates of events. Thus 'Bill is working quietly' becomes '∃e(Web & Qe)', which means "there is an event e such that e is a working by Bill and e occurs quietly." Davidson would formalize our argument as

$$\exists e(Web \ \& \ Qe) \vdash \exists eWeb$$

which is valid in predicate logic. The logical relationship between 'is working' and 'is working quietly', which we had assumed to be inexpressible, is resolved into the familiar syntax of existential quantification and conjunction.

The same analysis applies to prepositional phrases. The argument

> Bill is working in the barn.
> ∴ Bill is working.

is also intuitively valid. For Davidson, the preposition 'in' is, like an adverb, simply an event-predicate, though it is binary rather than monadic. Using 'a' for 'the barn' and 'I' for 'is in', we can formalize this argument as

$$\exists e(Web \ \& \ Iea) \vdash \exists eWeb$$

which again is formally valid in predicate logic.

Davidson's analysis also handles gerunds and infinitives. The sentence 'Driving through Boston was harrowing', whose subject is the gerund 'driving through Boston', can be treated as

$$\exists e((De \ \& \ Teb) \ \& \ He)$$

where 'D' stands for 'driving', 'T' for 'through', 'b' for 'Boston', and 'H' for 'was harrowing'. The same formalization could be used for 'It was harrowing to drive through Boston', which uses the infinitive 'to drive through Boston' instead of the gerund.

Thus Davidson's analysis is widely applicable. But it succeeds only at the price of awkwardly complicating the syntax of predicates and of treating events as objects. As a result, it has its critics.

Yet this analysis stands for us as a caution. Because predicate logic contains no explicit symbols for adverbs and prepositions, it would be easy to conclude that it cannot deal with them. This, as Davidson reminds us, does not follow. The expressive capacity of predicate logic, intelligently deployed, may surprise us.

So far we have considered arguments whose intuitive validity seems obvious; the problem is that intuition doesn't agree with predicate logic. Whether our next

---

[11] "The Logical Form of Action Sentences," in Nicholas Rescher, ed., *The Logic of Decision and Action* (Pittsburgh: University of Pittsburgh Press, 1967).

[12] The letter 'e' is, of course, a name, not a variable, in our version of predicate logic. Davidson's notation differs from ours in this respect.

and final example is valid is *not* intuitively clear. Suppose Bad Bart, who is at this very moment oozing in through the window, is bent on murdering me and can be stopped only by being killed. Then (if I have time) I may reason as follows:

> I should live.
> It is necessarily the case that if I live Bad Bart dies.
> ∴   Bad Bart should die.

Is this valid, or not? If we try to translate the argument into predicate logic to find out, we are stymied. The argument's validity, or lack thereof, hinges on two expressions, 'ought to' and 'necessarily', for which we have devised no adequate representation in predicate logic. The form relevant to determining its validity is therefore apparently inexpressible. Fortunately, there are extensions of predicate logic, namely, modal deontic logics, in which this form can be expressed. Since these make their appearance in Section 13.1, we postpone further discussion of this argument until then.

Exercise 9.4

Each of the following arguments is, or might reasonably be thought to be, intuitively valid. Try to express the form of each in predicate logic. If you fail to produce a valid sequent, discuss the reasons for your failure. Don't add any premises!

1. Cindy is taller than Bob; so Bob isn't taller than Cindy.
2. I know that I am alive. Therefore I am alive.
3. He pried the safe open with a crowbar. Hence he pried something open.
4. Since this figure is square, it is equiangular.
5. There are more people than hairs on anyone's head. No one is completely bald. Consequently, at least two people have the same number of hairs on their heads.
6. Salt is sodium chloride. Consequently, if salt is soluble so is sodium chloride.
7. For each number there is a greater number. Thus there is no greatest number.
8. She was once a beauty queen. So it will always be the case that she was once a beauty queen.
9. If something is poisonous, it's dangerous. Therefore mercury is dangerous, because it is poisonous.
10. The pool is open whenever the lifeguard is on duty. The lifeguard is on duty now. So the pool is open now.
11. Since you have a right not to be killed, I have an obligation not to kill you.
12. God has all perfections. To exist is a perfection. Ergo, God exists.

10

CLASSICAL PREDICATE LOGIC: UNDECIDABILITY

At the end of Section 9.2, we asked whether, despite the failure of the tree test as a decision procedure for predicate logic, there might not be some other test which would provide a terminating algorithm that determines for each sequent of predicate logic whether or not that sequent is valid. To determine whether there is such a test, we need a precise definition of an algorithm. The first four sections of this chapter provide that definition by equating algorithms with the programs of an abacus, a primitive sort of computer. Then in Sections 10.5 and 10.6 we use this concept to explain and prove the undecidability of predicate logic with function symbols. Finally, in Section 10.7 we discuss the extent of this undecidability, showing, among other things, that it doesn't go away if we eliminate the function symbols.[1]

10.1 ABACI

In this section we discuss the design and operation of a rudimentary sort of computer called an **abacus** (plural **abaci**), or **register machine.** Our goal is to analyze the notion of an algorithm, which, as we shall see, turns out to be definable as an abacus program. Having understood this concept, we will be in a position to prove that predicate logic is undecidable—that is, it is in principle impossible to devise an algorithm that tells for any sequent of predicate logic whether or not it is valid.

Abaci should not be confused with the ancient counting devices of the same name, though they have some similar features. An abacus can be thought of as a series of bins, called **registers,** together with a **control mechanism** for moving **counters** (which you might think of as stones or marbles) one at a time into and out of these bins. (See Figure 10.1.) Programming an abacus means telling this mechanism when and where to add or remove a counter. *In theory,* the abacus has an unlimited number of registers and an unlimited supply of counters, and each

---

[1] For the material in this chapter, I am indebted to Richard Jeffrey's elegant treatment in *Formal Logic: Its Scope and Limits,* 3rd ed. (New York: McGraw-Hill, 1991), Chaps. 7 and 8.

FIGURE 10.1
Imaginative Representation of an Abacus (Register Machine)

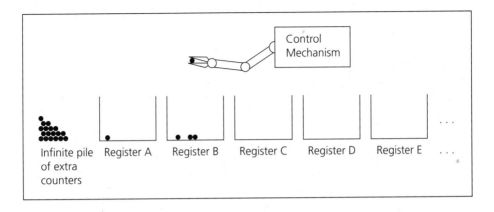

register can hold an unlimited number of counters. But in any real machine these quantities must be finite.

Abaci are simpler in design than ordinary computers, but they work in much the same way. Ordinary computers have a large number of registers, each of which is capable of storing a small number of zeros and ones, coded electronically. The list of zeros and ones in a register can be thought of as a number in binary code, and this number in turn may be regarded as representing the number of "counters" in the register. Programming a computer amounts to instructing its "control mechanism" (central processing unit) to move and manipulate these "counters," as in an abacus; but the instructions may be more sophisticated than just "add one" or "subtract one," which are the only commands an abacus "understands."

Yet this seemingly important difference between computers and abaci is actually rather superficial; for by giving the abacus sufficiently complex concatenations of "add one" and "subtract one" commands, we could make it mimic any of the operations of an ordinary computer. It would, however, be very slow, since it would have to perform many separate additions and subtractions to mimic a single operation of an ordinary computer.

Not only can an abacus do anything any actual computer can do; there is good reason to believe that it could do anything that any possible computer could do (this claim is called **Church's thesis,** which is the topic of Section 10.4). What is interesting, then, is to find out what an abacus can't do, since that sets limits on the capability of any possible computer.

But let's first see what an abacus *can* do. Suppose we want to program an abacus to add two numbers. For this we need two registers, register A and register B, to store the numbers. To add numbers x and y, we put x counters in register A and y counters in register B and instruct the machine to begin taking counters out of register B and to put a counter in register A for each one it removes from register B. The process is completed when register B becomes empty. Register A then contains $x + y$ counters, the sum of x and y.

FIGURE 10.2
The Two Operations That an Abacus Can Perform

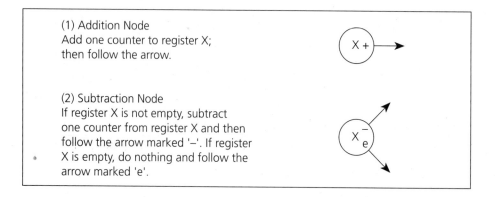

(1) Addition Node
Add one counter to register X;
then follow the arrow.

(2) Subtraction Node
If register X is not empty, subtract
one counter from register X and then
follow the arrow marked '–'. If register
X is empty, do nothing and follow the
arrow marked 'e'.

Putting the counters in the registers initially is not part of programming the machine. The program is merely a general list of instructions for creating a sum. What registers A and B contain to begin with is called the **input**. Once a program is written, we provide different inputs each time we run it. To program an abacus to do a particular task, we must analyze that task into an ordered series of simple operations. Fundamentally, an abacus can perform only two operations:

1. add a single counter to a specified register
2. remove one counter from a specified register, provided that it is not empty; if it is already empty, do nothing.

But these two operations can be combined and repeated in any order, and what is done after applying the second operation to a register depends on whether or not that register was empty when the operation began. The two operations are depicted in the diagrams in Figure 10.2. These diagrams are called **instruction nodes** (or just **nodes** for short). Don't confuse nodes with registers. The registers are not pictured in the diagrams, though the capital letters inside the circles (represented here by 'X') refer to them. Every abacus program can be written as a combination of addition and subtraction nodes, plus an entry arrow, which indicates where to start. The order in which the instructions are to be carried out is indicated by the way arrows from one node lead to another. Exactly one arrow emerges from each addition node. Its function is to point to the instruction to be followed after a counter has been added to the indicated register (register X in Figure 10.2). Exactly two arrows emerge from each subtraction node, one of which is marked with a minus sign and the other marked with an 'e'. The minus sign marks the arrow indicating the instruction to be followed next if a counter has been removed from the indicated register. The 'e' marks the arrow that is to be followed if the indicated register is empty when the node is first entered. Any number of arrows may lead into a node, and arrows may be stretched and bent to lead to any node, including the one from which they emerged.

To program the machine to add the number in register B to the number in register A, we analyze the process of adding in some suitable arrangement of the two fundamental abacus operations. Roughly, what we want the machine to do is this:

Remove a counter from register B.

Then add a counter to register A.

Remove another counter from register B.

And again add a counter to register A. . . .

Keep going like this until register B is empty; then stop.

It is easy to see that this set of instructions will result in the adding of the number in register B to the number in register A, no matter how many counters the two registers contain initially.

We can represent these instructions more perspicuously in a flow chart made up of addition and subtraction nodes:

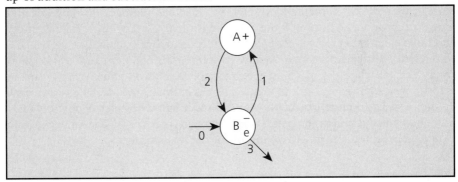

In this flow chart, the node for register A is an addition node and the node for register B is a subtraction node. The arrows are numbered for easy reference. (This is not, however, merely a convenience; it will be crucial later, when we describe the program in logical notation.) One and only one arrow leads into a flow chart; it is called the **entry arrow**. *The entry arrow must always be labeled as arrow 0,* as it is here, since the mechanism that operates the program always looks for the 0 arrow to begin the program. The numbering of the remaining arrows is arbitrary, but usually there is a more or less natural way to do it. Any arrow which, like arrow 3, leads out of the flow chart (i.e., which does not lead to further instructions) is called an **exit arrow**. Exit arrows are the program's stopping points. Not all abacus programs have them.

The operation of an abacus program can be thought of as taking place in a discrete series of numbered times. At each time, the machine is following an arrow in the program. Operations are performed between one time and the next. The program always begins with the machine on the entry arrow at time 0. To see how to read the flow chart, suppose we start the machine with three counters in register B and one in register A. Now at time 0 the machine is on arrow 0. Arrow 0 directs it to the node for register B (the bottom node), which gives it the following instruction:

> If register B is empty, move on to arrow 3.

> If register B is not empty, remove a counter from it and move on to arrow 1.

Since register B is not empty, the machine removes a counter, leaving two counters in register B, and moves on to arrow 1. It is on arrow 1 at time 1. Arrow 1 leads the machine to the node for register A (top node), where it obeys the instruction to add a counter to register A and move on to arrow 2. Thus at time 2 the machine is on arrow 2 with two counters in register B and two in register A. Arrow 2 leads the machine back to the bottom node. Since register B is still not empty, the machine again follows the instruction to remove a counter from register B and move on to arrow 1. So at time 3 it is on arrow 1 with one counter in register B and two in register A. It moves to the top node, adds a counter to register A, and passes on to arrow 2 again. Thus at time 4 the machine is on arrow 2 with one counter in register B and three in register A. It thus returns once again to the bottom node. Since register B still contains a counter, the machine removes this counter and moves to arrow 1. So at time 5 the machine is on arrow 1 with register B empty and three counters in register A. By time 6 it is on arrow 2 again, having added a counter to register A. Register A now contains four counters and register B is empty so that when the machine gets back to the bottom node, it passes on to arrow 3 instead of going back to arrow 1. Thus at time 7 the machine is on arrow 3, and, having no more instructions to follow, it halts. Register A now contains four counters, the sum of the initial values of registers A and B. The same program would likewise add any other two inputs for the two registers.

10.2 LOGICAL PROGRAMMING NOTATION

In this section we see how abacus programs can be written in logical notation.[2] The logical notation uses an $(n + 2)$-place predicate 'R', where n is the number of registers in the machine. We shall illustrate by referring to the adding program whose flow chart we constructed above. Since this program uses two registers, R will be a four-place predicate. The meaning of this predicate is as follows:

> 'R t w x y' means "At time t the machine is following arrow w with x counters in register A and y counters in register B."

This predicate thus allows us to describe the state of the machine at a given time. Each of the four places stands for a positive whole number. The first place following the predicate is always the time, the second always stands for the number of

---

[2] Because this notation allows free (unquantified) variables, program statements aren't formulas of predicate logic. But they become formulas if we quantify the variables—a fact of some importance, as we shall see in Section 10.6.

the arrow that the machine is following at that time, and the remaining places stand for the numbers of counters in the registers, the registers being listed in alphabetical order. That is, the third place stands for the number of counters in register A, the fourth place for the number of counters in register B, and so on. So, for example, the statement

> R 3 1 2 7

says:

> At time 3 the machine is on arrow 1 with 2 counters in register A and 7 in register B.

Arabic numerals such as '0', '1', or '147' are, grammatically speaking, just names. We could introduce them as new names into the predicate calculus, or we could think of them as abbreviations for symbols constructed from the numeral 0 and the successor sign. If we chose the latter course, we would write the number n as the zero symbol followed by n successor symbols (symbolized as apostrophes). Thus the numeral '5', for example, would be an abbreviation for

> 0'''''

We'll use the successor symbol primarily with variables. We'll generally write numerals in the more compact and familiar Arabic notation.

The program itself is written as a series of conditional statements, which say in effect, "If the machine is in such-and-such state at moment t, then at the next moment t' (i.e., $t + 1$) it should be in such-and-such a new state." (For the purposes of this chapter only, 't' counts as a variable.) For example, the statement

> R t 2 x 0 → R t' 3 x 0

tells the machine that if at time t it is on arrow 2 with x counters in register A and zero counters in register B, then at time t', it should be on arrow 3 with the same values in the two registers. This is part of the adding program discussed in the previous section. It tells the machine what to do if it enters the bottom node from arrow 2 and finds register B empty: Just go on to arrow 3; don't add or subtract anything.

To get the machine to add or subtract a counter, we use variables together with the successor sign. For example,

> R t 1 x y → R t' 2 x' y

says that if at time t the machine is on arrow 1 with x in register A and y in register B, then at t' it should be on arrow 2 with x' in register A and y in register B. This is the instruction corresponding to the top node of the flow chart. It tells the machine that when it is on arrow 1, it should add a counter to register A and then wind up on arrow 2. The following instruction illustrates subtraction:

> R t 0 x y' → R t' 1 x y

It tells the machine that if it is on the entry arrow (arrow 0) with x in register A and y' in register B, then at the next moment it should be on arrow 1 with register

A unchanged but one less counter (y counters) in register B. This is part of the instruction set for the bottom node of our flow chart. It is important to notice that this instruction is not applicable if register B is empty, for then register B could not contain y', that is, some nonnegative whole number y, plus one, counters. So we need a separate instruction for the case where the machine is on arrow 0 and finds register B empty:

$$R\ t\ 0\ x\ 0 \rightarrow R\ t'\ 3\ x\ 0$$

This says that if at time t the machine is on arrow 0 with x in register A and register B empty, the machine should move to arrow 3 without changing either register. This takes care of the case in which register B is empty when we start the adding program. In that case, adding register B, that is, zero, to register A will leave everything unchanged.

Only one more statement is needed to complete the program. We told the machine what to do if it is on arrow 2 and finds register B empty, but we haven't yet told it what to do if it is on arrow 2 and finds something in register B. From the flow chart, we see that the machine is supposed to take a counter out of register B and then go on to arrow 1; so we write

$$R\ t\ 2\ x\ y' \rightarrow R\ t'\ 1\ x\ y$$

The entire program, then, is

$$R\ t\ 0\ x\ y' \rightarrow R\ t'\ 1\ x\ y$$
$$R\ t\ 0\ x\ 0 \rightarrow R\ t'\ 3\ x\ 0$$
$$R\ t\ 1\ x\ y \rightarrow R\ t'\ 2\ x'y$$
$$R\ t\ 2\ x\ y' \rightarrow R\ t'\ 1\ x\ y$$
$$R\ t\ 2\ x\ 0 \rightarrow R\ t'\ 3\ x\ 0$$

The first two and last two statements of this program together constitute the instruction set for the bottom node of the flow chart. The third statement is the sole instruction for the top node.

The reason why the bottom node requires four statements while the top node requires only one is that the top node has only one arrow (arrow 1) entering it and only one (arrow 2) leaving, so all we have to do is tell the machine what to do in going from arrow 1 to arrow 2. But there are two ways to enter the bottom node (arrows 0 and 2) and two ways to leave it (arrows 1 and 3). Which arrow the machine takes out of this node depends on whether or not register B is empty. Thus we need to tell the machine when and how to go from arrow 0 to arrow 1 or arrow 3 (the first two statements) and when and how to go from arrow 2 to arrow 1 or arrow 3 (the last two statements). So it takes four statements to describe the bottom node, making a total of five statements for the program as a whole.

More generally, *the number of program statements needed to describe a node is the number of arrows coming into the node multiplied by the number of arrows going out.* When designing a program, you should always check it for completeness by figuring the number of statements required for each node and then adding these numbers to get the total number of statements for the program. If your program contains fewer statements, it's incomplete. If it contains more, you've written too much.

10.3 THE ABACUS PROGRAM

ABACUS is a computer program that enables you to construct, program, and run abaci that are simulated electronically within an ordinary computer. Though in theory an abacus has infinitely many registers, each with infinite capacity, these simulacra have at most seven registers (you get to choose the number), each of which holds a maximum of 32,767 counters. Because of the small number and capacity of their registers, they are not powerful enough to do any serious computing, much less to approach the performance of infinite abaci. But they do enable you to get a feel for how an abacus operates.

Getting ABACUS Started

ABACUS runs on any IBM-compatible personal computer. The program is stored in three files: ABACUS.EXE, ABACUS.MSG, and ABACUS.HLP. You start ABACUS from any directory containing these three files, by logging on to that directory and typing 'ABACUS'—without the quotation marks, of course!

ABACUS Program Editor

When you run the ABACUS program, the first thing you will see is a title, like the title page of a book. Press any key to remove the title. The editing screen will then appear. At the top of this screen are some abbreviated directions, and along the bottom is a menu of commands. The appearance of this menu means that you are ready to begin writing (creating), modifying, or running a program.

Creating Program Statements

To begin writing a program, press 'c' for 'CREATE' or use the arrow keys to move the highlighter to 'CREATE', and then press ENTER. If this is the first statement in your program, ABACUS will ask you to specify the number of registers you want to program. To know how many registers you need, you must have a pretty good idea of what your program will look like. I recommend sketching it out ahead of time, using a flow chart as described in Section 10.1. Once you start writing the program on the computer, you can't change the number of registers without rewriting everything you've done, so make sure you choose the right number before you begin.

If this is the first time you're using ABACUS, you might specify two registers and then experiment by writing the addition program described in Sections 10.1 and 10.2. When ABACUS says

Number of registers (1 - 7):

Just type

2

and then ENTER.

You are now ready to enter a program statement. The order in which you create statements is unimportant (ABACUS will arrange them in the order of their arrow numbers), but suppose we begin with the first statement of the adding program, that is,

$$R\ t\ 0\ x\ y' \rightarrow R\ t'\ 1\ x\ y$$

Now the first place after the R is always the same in all program statements. In the statement's antecedent it always designates some time t and in the consequent it designates the next time t'. ABACUS supplies the R predicates, arrows, and time variables for each statement automatically. Thus what appears on the screen after you specify the number of registers is

R t _
Enter initial arrow number

The program is asking for the second place following the R in the antecedent of the program statement, which in this case is 0. So type '0' and then press either ENTER or the space bar. The screen now looks like this:

R t 0 _
Enter initial value for register A

Register values are designated either by the numeral '0' or by variables (lowercase letters) with or without a single successor symbol. In the program statement we are writing, the initial value for register A is designated by the variable 'x'. So type 'x' and then press either the space bar or ENTER. The screen now looks like this:

R t 0 x _
Enter initial value for register B

The initial value for register B is 'y''. After you enter this, ABACUS supplies the arrow, the second R predicate, and the second time variable in your program statement, so you see this on the screen:

R t 0 x y' $\rightarrow$ R t' _
Enter final arrow number

The "final" settings are those mentioned in the consequent of the program statement. ABACUS has automatically set the final time (the first place following R in the consequent) to t' and is asking you for the arrow number, which should be 1. Enter this and then the final register values 'x' and 'y' to complete entry of the statement. The finished statement is now part of your program and is displayed at the top of the screen.

Correcting Errors

If you make a mistake while entering a statement, you can backspace over it and retype it, so long as you have not pressed ENTER or the space bar, which enters data into the program. If you have already entered the mistake, press ESC to abort the statement and start again.

If you've already entered an entire statment and then found that it contains a mistake, you can modify it. Use the vertical arrow or the Page Up, Page Down, Home, or End keys to move the highlighter to the statement you want to modify. Then press 'm' for MODIFY or use the horizontal arrow keys to move the highlighter at the bottom of the screen to MODIFY. Press ENTER. You will see a window like that used to create the statement originally, except that the statement to be modified is written at the top. Proceed as if you were creating the statement anew. When you finish typing it, the new version will replace the old in the program. If you decide you don't want to modify the statement before you finish typing, press ESC to abort the modification.

You can also delete a statement without replacing it. Choose the statement with the highlighter and then choose DELETE at the bottom of the screen and press ENTER.

If you want to delete all the statements from your program, choose ERASE from the bottom menu and press ENTER. This erases the program from active memory but doesn't affect any work that you've saved to a disk.

Saving Programs

To preserve a program once it has been written, you must save it to a disk file; otherwise, when you start a new program or turn the computer off, the program will be irretrievably lost. Programs saved to disk files are stored permanently in a magnetic medium, much as a tape recording is stored on a tape. Once saved, a program can be called up again into the program editor by using the GET command. To save a program, choose SAVE from the menu at the bottom of the screen and press ENTER. You will then see a message that looks like this:

Directory: A:\
Press ENTER to proceed, ESC to abandon, or type a new directory

Unless you are familiar with IBM operating systems and want to use this feature to save to a floppy disk, you should not have to change the directory, so don't worry about this. Just press ENTER. If the program has not already been named, you will be asked to name it. The name must consist of eight or fewer characters (no punctuation or spaces are allowed). After you type in the name and press ENTER, ABACUS writes the program on your disk, using the name you typed, together with the suffix ".ABA" to tag it as an ABACUS program file. You can use this name to retrieve the program later. *Caution: If you use the name of a file that is already on the disk, your current program will be written in place of the one that had that name originally, and the latter will be lost.*

Starting a New Program

If you are done working on one program and want to start another, save it if you want to preserve it, then choose NEW_PROGRAM from the menu at the bottom of the screen and press ENTER. The editing screen will be cleared and the old program will be erased from active memory. *Caution: If you don't save the old program before starting the new one, it will be lost.*

Quitting

To exit from ABACUS, simply press ESC. To prevent quitting by accident, ABA-CUS will ask if you really want to quit. Respond by typing 'y' for yes or 'n' for no. If you have a program in memory, ABACUS also asks whether you want to save it on the disk, to make sure that you don't accidentally quit without recording your work. If you're saving to a floppy disk, you can get your disk back by pressing the button next to the slot into which you put it.

Running Your Program

Once you have created a program with the program editor, it is ready to run. ABACUS provides a display which allows you to watch the registers changing from moment to moment. The counters are represented in the display by numbers.

To run your program, press 'r' from the editing menu. You will then see a new display called the input menu. Before starting your program, you must give ABACUS some input by specifying the initial number of counters in each register. To do this, press 'i' from the input menu. You will then be asked for the number of counters in each register. If you've written the addition program described in Sections 10.1 and 10.2, you might, for example, tell ABACUS to start with one counter in register A and three in register B. That would enable you to compare what you see on the screen with my earlier explanation of how the program runs.

Once you have entered the input, the ABACUS registers will appear at the right side of the screen along with their contents. Below them is a clock which ticks off the moments of time the program takes. You control the clock by pressing the ENTER key. Each time you press ENTER, the clock advances one moment. If you hold the ENTER key down, the clock ticks very rapidly. The speed of the clock controls the speed of the program, so you can make the program run as fast or as slowly as you like.

When ABACUS comes to a point in your program where it finds no more instructions (this will be an exit arrow if you've written the program correctly), the clock will stop and the message 'END PROGRAM' will appear on the screen. If you unexpectedly get this message to start with, then your program probably contains an error, and you need to get back to the program editor by typing 'r' to revise the program.

You can stop the program before it finishes by pressing ESCAPE (ESC).

Once you have stopped the program or it has finished by itself, ABACUS returns you to the input menu. From there, you can rerun the program with a new input, return to the program editor, or quit altogether.

Getting Programs from the Disk

Any program stored on the disk can be called up into the program editor by selecting GET from the editing menu and pressing ENTER. After seeing the message

Directory: A:\
Press ENTER to proceed, ESC to abandon, or type a new directory

and pressing ENTER again, you will see a display of the names of the programs on file. There is a highlighter in this display which can be shifted from name to name by using the arrow keys on the right side of your keyboard. Move the highlighter to the name of the program you want to call up and then press ENTER. The program will then appear on the screen, and you can run it or revise it as you like. If you revise it, be sure to save the revised version onto the disk before you quit.

You can also delete programs from the disk by selecting KILL and pressing ENTER. Notice that KILL is different from ERASE. ERASE removes a program from the screen but does not affect the disk. KILL deletes a program from the disk but does not affect what is on the screen.

Experiment and enjoy!

Exercise 10.3.1 (Creating Programs from Flow Charts)

Translate the following flow charts into logical notation, type them into the ABA-CUS program editor, run them to test them, and save them under the names indicated.

1. This program adds one to the quantity in register A and then halts. Save it under the name 'PLUS1'.

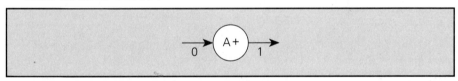

2. This one repeatedly adds one to the quantity in register A and never halts. Save it under the name 'COUNTS'.

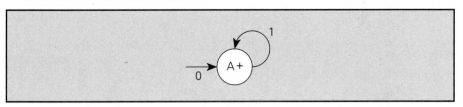

3. This one empties register A and then halts. Save it under the name 'EMPTY'.

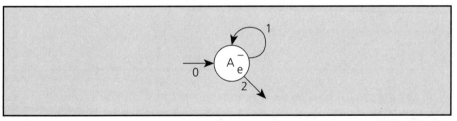

4. This one empties register A and then just keeps on running without effect. Save it under the name 'IDLER'.

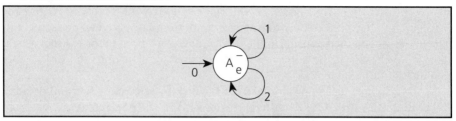

5. This one adds one to each of registers A and B, then halts; save it under the name 'EACH1'.

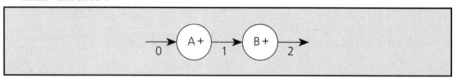

6. When started with register C empty, this program adds the contents of register B to register A while retaining the contents of register B. Save it under the name 'ADD'.

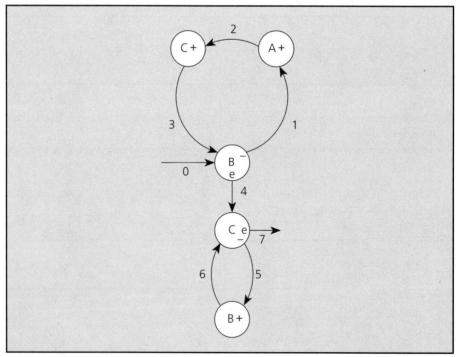

7. In the diagram below, ADD functions as part of a program to multiply the quantity in register A by the quantity in register B (registers C and D must

initially be empty). If n is the number in register A, this program moves the number n to register D (so that register A is empty), then adds the contents of register B to register A n times, keeping track of this addition by removing a counter from D each time. It winds up with the answer in register A and with the number that was originally in register B still there. Save this program under the name 'MULTIPLY'.

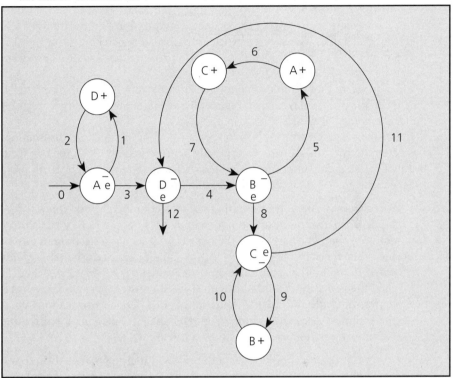

Exercise 10.3.2 (Creating Programs from Scratch)

To solve the following problems, you must invent the flow chart. Once you have drawn it and numbered the arrows (remembering to number the entry arrow as 0), write, test, and save the program as in PART I.

1. Write a program that adds two to the number in register A and then halts. Use only one register. Save this program under the name 'PLUS2'.
2. Often in computer programs, the numbers 1 and 0 are interpreted as the answers "yes" and "no," respectively.[3] Write a program which, started with any natural number in register A, answers the question "Is this number even?" If the number is even, it signals this by stopping with a 1 (yes) in register A. If

---

[3] The correspondence is, of course, arbitrary; we could let 1 be "no" and 0 be "yes," or adopt some other convention.

the number is odd, it signals this by stopping with a 0 (no) in register A. (Hint: This program can be done with a single register, but its flow chart will contain several nodes.) Save this program under the name 'EVEN'.

3. Write a program that determines for any natural number whether it is evenly divisible by three. That is, if it is divisible by three, the program should halt with a 1 in register A; if not, the program should halt with a 0 in register A. Use only one register. Save the program under the name 'DIV3'.

4. Write a one-register program that answers the question "Is this number less than four?" That is, when started with a number in register A, it outputs 1 if that number is less than four and 0 if it is four or greater. Save this program under the name 'LESS4'.

5. Write a program that doubles the number in register A. (Hint: Use two registers; when the program is started, register B must be empty.) Save this program under the name 'DOUBLER'.

6. Write programs to do truth tables for negation, conjunction, and disjunction. In a computer, truth values are typically represented by 0's and 1's. We'll follow the usual convention of using 0 for false and 1 for true. A truth table for conjunction, for example, will work like this:

> If registers A and B (representing the two conjuncts) both contain 1 as input, then the program should halt with 1 in register A (which we conventionally declare to be the answer register) and nothing in any of the other registers. (That is, if both conjuncts are true, the table yields true.) If some other combination of 0's and 1's is in registers A and B, then the program should halt with 0 in all registers. (Any other combination of truth and falsity yields falsehood.) Don't worry about what the program does with numbers greater than 1, since for a truth table we simply won't allow larger numbers as input.

The negation program should reverse the value in register A. The disjunction program should halt with a 1 in register A and 0 everywhere else if the input of either register A or register B was 1; otherwise, it will halt with 0 in all registers. Try to make these programs as simple as possible, using as few registers as possible. Save them under the titles 'NEG', 'CONJ', and 'DISJ'.

7. Write a program for the operator **neither . . . nor.** (Hint: This program might first compute disjunction as in problem 6 and then reverse the truth value of that computation.) Save this program under the label 'NOR'.

8. Write a two-register program that empties the contents of register A into register B, then empties the contents of register B into register A, then empties the contents of register A back into register B again, and so on infinitely. Make the program run infinitely even if both registers are initially empty. Save it under the name 'SISYPHUS'.

9. Write a program that answers the question "Are these two numbers equal?"; that is, it compares the contents of registers A and B and outputs a 1 in register A (with register B empty) if they are equal but 0 in both registers if they are unequal. Use only two registers. Save this program under the name 'EQUAL'.

10. Write a program to exchange the contents of registers A and B. When the program halts, all the other registers (if any) should be empty. Save this program under the name 'EXCHANGE'. (Hint: Use three registers.)

11. One important arithmetical function is min (short for minimum), a two-place function which, for any numbers x and y, gives as its value the smaller of the two. If both are equal to some quantity n, then min gives n as its value. More concisely:

$$\min(x, y) = x, \text{ if } x \leq y$$
$$\min(x, y) = y, \text{ if } x > y$$

Write a program that computes min. Given any two numbers x and y as input in registers A and B, your program should eventually halt with $\min(x, y)$ in register A and all other registers empty. (Hint: Use three registers.) Save this program under the name 'MIN'.

12. Write a program that computes the max (short for maximum) function, which is defined as follows:

$$\max(x, y) = x, \text{ if } x \leq y$$
$$\max(x, y) = y, \text{ if } y > x$$

That is, given any two numbers in registers A and B, this program halts with the larger of the two in register A and all other registers empty. Save this program under the name 'MAX'.

13. Write a program that does division. That is, given any dividend x in register A and any divisor y in register B, the program halts with the quotient (i.e., the number of times y goes into x) in register A and the remainder in register B. Thus, for example, if the input to register A is 14 and the input to register B is 3, the program gives the quotient 4 in register A with the remainder 2 in register B. Save this program under the name 'DIVIDE'. (Hint: The program will be lengthy and will require four registers.)

14. Write a program which when given any natural number n in register A (with all other registers empty) halts with n^2 in register A and all other registers empty. Save it under the name 'SQUARE'.

10.4 CHURCH'S THESIS

We have been examining the concept of an abacus in order to clarify the notion of an algorithm. Specifically, we shall claim that any algorithm can be represented as an abacus program, and any abacus program is an algorithm. In this sense, algorithms are just abacus programs, and vice versa. This claim is a version of **Church's thesis.**

But why should we accept Church's thesis? The answer is bound up with some remarkable developments in the history of logic. In the earlier section on algorithms, I mentioned the formalist program of reducing logic and mathematics to finite mechanical calculation. That research program was begun by the mathematician David Hilbert around the turn of the century. Central to the program, of course, was the development of a clear concept of mechanical computation, that is, of an algorithm. In the 1930s, Hilbert's work inspired a flurry of independent attempts to make this intuitive idea clear. Various authors defined the idea in various ways. Kurt Gödel, in developing his historic proof of the incompleteness of arithmetic, in effect characterized computation in terms of the notion of a recursive function. Alan Turing represented algorithms as programs for a simplified computer, now called a Turing machine. Alonzo Church developed yet a third characterization, using what he called the lambda calculus. The Russian mathematician A. A. Markov invented a fourth: Markov processes. And Emil Post created yet a fifth: Post productions. On the surface these ideas had little in common. But they all proved to be equivalent in the sense that any calculation performable by any of them was performable by all.

This was convincing evidence that algorithms were a precisely delineated "natural kind." Moreover, other ways of defining algorithmic process (such as the abacus or register machines used here) have also proven equivalent to these original formulations. Further, with the explosive development of computers and the theory of computation, millions of algorithms have been investigated. Yet no one has ever developed a process that appeared intuitively to be an algorithm, yet could not be performed by the procedures just mentioned. (There is no doubt about the converse; that is, it is clear that anything these procedures can do is an algorithm.) So today there is general agreement that algorithms are a precise and well-defined class of operations and that each of these procedures adequately characterizes that class.

This conviction, however, is not amenable to strict proof. It's a philosophical thesis, supported by extensive experience. It is called *Church's thesis,* because Church was one of the first thinkers to state it explicitly and to grasp its implications. (Alan Turing also hit upon it at about the same time so that it is sometimes called the **Church/Turing thesis.**) In its most general version, it asserts that each of the formulations mentioned earlier is an adequate characterization of the idea of an algorithm. We shall use a more specific version of it, namely, that *any algorithm can be represented as an abacus program.*

But how can abacus programs, which operate on counters, represent algorithms, which operate on sequences of symbols? The trick is to represent symbol sequences as numbers, or to devise a numerical encoding. An **encoding** is an effective way of assigning each of the things we want to talk about a distinct code number. This must be a nonnegative whole number so that it can be represented by counters in an abacus. The numbers we use for a given code need not be consecutive, but they may not be repeated; that is, distinct objects may not be assigned the same number (which would make the code ambiguous). Suppose, for example, that we want to encode the names of the three West Coast states: Washington, Oregon, and California. These will be represented in the abacus as numbers. One simple encoding looks like this:

Washington	Oregon	California
1	2	3

That is, the number 1 stands for the name 'Washington', 2 for 'Oregon', and 3 for 'California'. The order, of course, is arbitrary. Here is a different encoding, using the same numbers:

Washington	Oregon	California
3	2	1

Since the numbers need not be consecutive, the following is also a perfectly good encoding:

Washington	Oregon	California
363	0	1,297

But the numbering below is *not* an encoding, since here the number 2 is used ambiguously to stand for two different states:

Washington	Oregon	California
2	1	2

But, while the definition of the term "encoding" excludes ambiguities, it admits the possibility that two different numbers from the same code might stand for the same object, just as a person might have two different names. This is of little importance, however; the codes we consider will generally assign unique numbers to objects.

Encodings may be infinite as well as finite. Suppose, for example, that we wish to encode the following infinite series of formulas:

$$P, \quad \sim P, \quad \sim\sim P, \quad \sim\sim\sim P, \ldots$$

Perhaps the most natural ways to do so are

P,	~P,	~~P,	~~~P, ...
1	2	3	4 ...

and

P,	~P,	~~P,	~~~P, ...
0	1	2	3 ...

In each case, there is an algorithm that outputs a code number given a formula, and a second algorithm that outputs a formula given a code number. To go from formulas to code numbers (i.e., to **encode** the formulas), the algorithm for the first encoding is

Count the formula's negation signs and add 1.

And the algorithm for the second is

Count the formula's negation signs.

To go from a code number n to its corresponding formula (i.e., to **decode** the number), the algorithm for the first encoding is

Write 'P' and prefix it with $n - 1$ negation signs.

And the algorithm for the second encoding is

Write 'P' and prefix it with n negation signs.

If there exist algorithms both for encoding and for decoding, as there do in these cases, we shall say the numbering is **effective**.

We shall insist by definition that all encodings be effective in this sense. Numerical encodings of finite sets of symbol sequences (like the names for the western states) are automatically effective if given as lists, since a symbol sequence or its code number can always be found by a finite scan of the list. Infinite encodings are effective, though, only if specified by a rule that allows us to get both from code number to symbol sequence and from symbol sequence to code number by finitely many well-defined steps, that is, by a terminating algorithm.

In practice, most infinite numberings we are likely to invent are effective. But there are numberings that are noneffective in the sense that infinite calulations may be required to determine which code number stands for which object or which object stands for which code number. These numberings tend to be rather convoluted. For an example, consider the following numbering of the even positive integers:

If the series of base ten digits that express an even integer n appears in the decimal expansion of the number π, then let n encode itself; if not, let it be encoded by $n - 1$.

To illustrate, consider the number fourteen. The series of base ten digits that express this number is '14', that is, a '1' followed by a '4'. Now the decimal expansion of π is an infinite nonrepeating decimal, which begins as follows: 3.14159 . . . . Sequences of digits appear within it more or less randomly. The sequence '14' appears here (the second and third digits), and so in our numbering 14 numbers itself. In general, each even number will be numbered either by itself or by the odd number before it. But we may not be able to tell which, without completing an infinite operation. For example, consider the number 2,727,944. Does the base ten sequence which expresses it—namely, '2727944'—appear in the decimal expansion of π? Maybe. If we start cranking out the digits of π, we may eventually find it. But then again we may not. If in fact the base ten sequence never turns up, so that the code for 2,747,944 is 2,747,943, we'd have to search through the infinite decimal expansion of π to find out. Thus calculating a code from a number involves a potentially infinite operation. It is therefore noneffective. (Note that calculating the number from its code, however, is an effective procedure, assuming that we know that the code is a code. For if the code number is even, then it stands for itself, and if it is odd, it stands for itself plus one.)

It's not that our sample numbering is ill defined. The rule defining it is perfectly clear and exact. But it is not effective and therefore does not count as an encoding.

Exercise 10.4 (Doing Logic on a Computer)

One way to illustrate the use of numerical encodings is to write ABACUS programs that solve logic problems rather than numerical ones. Doing this for any substantial body of logic is a difficult programming task, but we can get some taste of how computers can perform logical as well as numerical operations by considering narrowly circumscribed ranges of problems. Consider, for example, the fragment of propositional logic whose character set is

$$\rightarrow \quad P \quad Q \quad R$$

and whose formulas are defined by the following formation rules:

    i. The sentence letters 'P', 'Q', and 'R' are formulas.
    ii. If Φ and Ψ are sentence letters, then $\Phi \rightarrow \Psi$ is a formula.

No formula of this fragment contains more than three characters. Now consider the following numerical encoding of the character set:

$$\begin{array}{cccc} \rightarrow & P & Q & R \\ 0 & 1 & 2 & 3 \end{array}$$

We extend this encoding to formulas as follows:

    i. If a formula is a sentence letter, its code number is just the code number for that letter.
    ii. If a formula is a conditional $\Phi \rightarrow \Psi$, its code number is four times the code number for Φ plus the code number for Ψ. (Thus, for example, the code number for 'P $\rightarrow$ Q' is $(4 \times 1) + 2 = 6$.)

This encoding of formulas does not specifically represent the conditional sign, but since that sign is the only logical operator available in this fragment of propositional logic, there is no need; we know in advance that every compound formula (i.e., formula represented by a number greater than three) is a conditional.

    To decode the number for a conditional, we divide by 4; the quotient is the number of the antecedent, and the remainder is the number of the consequent. Thus the number 11 represents the formula 'Q $\rightarrow$ R', since 11 divided by 4 is 2 (the code number for 'Q') with a remainder of 3 (the code number for 'R').

    Using this encoding, we can now program ABACUS to perform some simple logical tasks:

1. Write a program which, given the code for a conditional in register A and code numbers for sentence letters in registers B and C, answers the question "Is the sequent consisting of the premises represented in registers A and B and the conclusion represented in register C an instance of modus ponens?" That is, it halts with a 1 in register A and all other registers empty if this sequent is an instance of modus ponens and 0's in all registers if not.
2. Generalize the program from problem 1 to test the validity of *any* two-premise sequent expressible in this fragment of propositional logic. This involves testing not only for modus ponens, but also for hypothetical syllogism, for material implication, and for conclusions that are tautologous or merely repeat a premise.

This exercise shows how a computer can be programmed to "recognize" logical form and employ logical rules. Using the same ideas, we could devise encodings for all of propositional or predicate logic and develop software for performing deduction tasks, doing truth tables, or constructing trees. Programs to do these things would be much more complex than the programs of this exercise—but they would work in essentially the same way.

10.5 THE HALTING PROBLEM

Church's thesis tells us that any algorithm can be carried out by an abacus. But since an abacus operates only on counters, any data we enter into it must first be numerically encoded so that each potential item of input is represented by a specific number of counters. Thus, for example, if we wanted an abacus to do tree tests, we would have to devise a way to encode trees as numbers. This is complicated, but feasible. Individual formulas could be encoded along the lines illustrated in Exercise 10.4. But an encoding for whole trees would also have to include symbols representing check marks, X's, and some kind of punctuation to separate formulas and paths from one another. Given as input the code number of an initial list of formulas for a tree, the abacus would perform a series of arithmetic operations on these numbers and, if it halted, output a new number representing the completed tree.

Such an abacus program would not solve the decision problem for predicate logic, however; for when given an infinitely prolongable initial list it would run forever and thus fail to return an answer.

Yet even though for some lists of formulas such a program would be unable to detect consistency, *we* might be able to do so. The infinite trees we have seen so far are recognizable as infinite by the patterns of repetition they exhibit. We don't have to carry them out very far before we notice this. If all infinite trees exhibited such repetition, and if we could always recognize it, then the tree test coupled with our repetition-recognizing ability *would*, at least in principle, enable us to solve the decision problem. For once we recognized (via the repetition) that a tree was going infinite, we would know that it must contain at least one open path, and we could deduce that the initial list was consistent without finishing the tree.

But, alas, not all infinite trees are regularly repetitive. Some grow without any recognizable pattern. Their apparent randomness foils the attempt to make the tree test into a decision procedure by coupling it with a test for pattern repetition.

Thus we see that our inability to create a decision procedure using the tree test is not due simply to the fact that some trees are infinite. The deeper source of the failure is our inability to know for some trees whether they are infinite or not. More generally, the problem is our inability to recognize whether or not a given instance of a potentially infinite process is actually infinite.

So let's try another approach. Given an abacus program that constructs trees, we might, instead of looking for patterns of repetition in the trees themselves, simply ask: "Does this program eventually halt, when given as input the code number of a particular initial list of formulas?" If the answer were yes, then we could simply run the program to find out whether or not the initial list was consistent; and if the answer were no, then we would know that the tree was infinite and hence that the initial list was consistent. Either way, we'd have our answer.

This approach brings us to the **halting problem,** the problem of creating an algorithm that decides for each program and input whether or not that program halts given that input. A solution to the halting problem, then, would give us a solution to the decision problem.

However, like the construction of trees, the running of an abacus program is a potentially infinite process. Some abacus programs halt with a given input after a finite number of steps; others run forever. Among the nonhalters, some are readily recognizable as nonhalters by the patterns of repetition they exhibit; others exhibit complex, nonrepetitive behavior. With the latter, we may find ourselves in a state of ignorance like that produced by infinite nonrepetitive trees: We seem to have no way of knowing whether the process would end if only we were to carry it a few (or a few trillion) steps further, or whether it never ends. It seems unlikely, then, that we could ever produce an algorithm to decide whether or not programs halt. But can we be sure?

Astonishingly, we can. In this section we show that the very idea of a solution to the halting problem is self-contradictory. For if we had an algorithm (i.e., abacus program) that solved the halting problem, we could convert it into what we shall call a **reverse halting program.** But, as we shall see, a reverse halting program is a logically impossible object. Thus we conclude that the halting problem is unsolvable, and with that conclusion this section will end. By then we may strongly suspect that the decision problem is likewise unsolvable—but we will not yet have proof.

The proof comes in Section 10.6. Here we reverse direction. Having seen that a solution to the halting problem would also be a solution to the decision problem, we consider the converse: Would a solution to the decision problem also be a solution to the halting problem? The answer is yes; thus, in essence, the decision problem and the halting problem are one and the same. We prove this by showing how each abacus program and input can be translated into a sequent of predicate logic. A test to decide the validity of each such sequent would determine for the corresponding program and input whether or not that program halts with that input—and so would solve the halting problem. Having already seen that the halting problem is unsolvable, however, we must then infer that there can be no algorithmic test to decide the validity of each of these particular program-representing sequents. And this means that there can be no general solution to the decision problem.

In outline the central argument of this section and the next is as follows:

1. There is no reverse halting program for any encoding.
2. If there is an abacus program that solves the halting problem, then there is a reverse halting program for some encoding.

∴ 3. There is no abacus program that solves the halting problem. [from 1 and 2, by modus tollens]
   4. If predicate logic with function symbols is decidable, then there is an abacus program that solves the halting problem.
∴ 5. Predicate logic with function symbols is undecidable. [from 3 and 4, by modus tollens]

We prove premises 1 and 2 in this section, from which 3 follows immediately as a corollary. Then in Section 10.6 we prove premise 4, from which, together with 3, 5 follows, also as a corollary. When reading these proofs, there is some danger of getting lost in details. To keep your bearings, refer back to this five-step outline from time to time.

As we just noted, the halting problem is the problem of determining whether a given program eventually halts with a given input. We are entertaining the idea of a program that solves this problem—that is, a program that checks programs to see if they halt. But how could a program take a program as input? The trick, of course, is to encode the program taken as input as a number. This encoding must be effective; that is, there must be both an algorithm for encoding and an algorithm for decoding. This can be done; in fact, there are endlessly many ways to do it. We shall consider one example. Our encoding begins with programs as expressed in logical notation. Such programs are merely sequences of symbols. In fact, the logical notation can be thought of as consisting merely of ten primitive symbols:[4]

$$0 \quad t \quad x \quad y \quad z \quad \rightarrow \quad R \quad ' \quad * \quad .$$

You are familiar with the character for zero ('0'); the variables 't', 'x', 'y', and 'z'; the arrow representing the conditional; the predicate letter 'R'; and the successor symbol "'". The asterisk ('*') is added to make new variables in case we need more than the four listed here. Appending the asterisk to any variable produces a new variable. (Thus, for example, '$x***$' is a variable different from the variables 'x', '$x*$', and '$x**$'.) The final mark, the period, is a punctuation mark used to indicate the end of a program statement. Numbers (to designate register contents or arrows in the program) are written in this notation as the zero character followed by the appropriate number of successor marks.

Now to develop a numerical code for programs written in this notation, we first assign each character in the notation a digit from 0 to 9. Suppose we do it this way:

0	t	x	y	z	$\rightarrow$	R	'	*	.
0	1	2	3	4	5	6	7	8	9

---

[4] The number ten is serendipitous, since it allows us to use the familiar base ten notation in a very straightforward way. With character sets containing other numbers of primitive characters, the same thing can be done in other bases. This is confusing to people who are used to dealing in tens, but it is no problem for computers.

To translate a program written in logical notation into a code number, we rewrite the entire program on a single line, converting numerals to successor notation and placing periods after program statements (for variables other than 't', 'x', 'y', and 'z', it may be necessary to use the asterisk); then simply replace each character by its corresponding digit. The result, a single enormous number, is the program's numerical code. Consider, for example, the two-line program that we would write in the usual abacus notation as follows:

$$Rt0x' \rightarrow Rt'1x$$
$$Rt00 \rightarrow Rt'20$$

Rewriting this program as a single line in the new notation, we get

$$Rt0x' \rightarrow Rt'0'x \cdot Rt00 \rightarrow Rt'0''0 \cdot$$

And this codes up into the astronomical number

6102756170729610056170779

Any program can be encoded in this way. Moreover, the processes of encoding and decoding are both clearly algorithmic. Of course, not all numbers represent programs. The number 123, for example, represents the nonsense sequence 'txy'. But that's fine; code numbers need not be consecutive. In discussing the two kinds of halting problems, we will focus on what happens when we input code numbers for programs into programs. Keep in mind that the encoding of programs illustrated here is just one of infinitely many ways of encoding that are possible; it merely provides a concrete understanding of what an encoding of abacus programs looks like.

We are now ready to give a precise definition of what it means to solve the halting problem. *(NOTE: In this definition, and in the ensuing discussion and proofs, when we say of an input or output that it is placed in some register or registers, we assume unless otherwise specified that all other registers are empty.)*

DEFINITION   An abacus program GH is said to **solve the halting problem** iff there is an encoding of abacus programs such that when given any program number e from the encoding (placed in register A) and any nonnegative whole number i (placed in register B),

(i) GH stops with 1 in register A, if the program numbered e eventually halts when started with input i in register A,[5] and

(ii) GH stops with 0 in register A, if the program numbered e never halts when started with input i in register A.

---

[5] It will for our purposes be sufficient to restrict consideration of the behavior of programs examined by GH to cases in which their input is in register A (assuming all other registers to be empty); without this restriction we would need a coding scheme to represent the inputs to many registers as a single number; this is possible, but cumbersome, and so we'll avoid it.

The number *i* represents the input provided to the program numbered *e* in register A. We have specified the registers in which the inputs *i* and *e* and output of GH are to be placed merely for definiteness. A machine that in effect solved this problem but took input or produced output elsewhere could easily be converted into a machine that fits our definitions, by adding operations to transfer the input or output to the appropriate registers. Likewise, the specification of the output as being 0 or 1 is inessential. Any output scheme would do, so long as there was an effective way to tell which outputs stood for halting and which for not halting. But if there were an effective way to do this, then there would also be a way to program the machine to convert this nonstandard output into 0's or 1's as described earlier. (We might, for example, have as output any positive integer, the even ones standing for halting and the odd ones standing for nonhalting; then we would simply append a test for evenness to get the output to be either 0 or 1.) So, if there is any program that in effect solves this problem but doesn't fit our definitions, it can easily be converted into a program that solves the problem and does fit the definitions.

We are now poised to prove that a solution to the halting problem is impossible. To do this, we will show that if some abacus program did solve the halting problem, it would enable us to create a reverse halting program, the very idea of which is self-contradictory. The concept of a reverse halting program is convoluted; so rather than explaining it straight off, we'll first examine a simpler analog: Bertrand Russell's barber.[6]

Consider an adult male barber living in a certain village, who for any man of the village, shaves that man if and only if the man does not shave himself. This seems, on the face of it, perfectly possible. Each of the village men either shaves himself or is shaved by the barber, but not both. But trouble comes when we ask about the barber himself. Since for any man *M* of the village, the barber shaves *M* if and only if *M* does not shave himself, and since the barber himself is a man of the village, it follows that he shaves himself if and only if he doesn't shave himself. This is a contradiction, which shows that the very idea of such a barber is incoherent; no such barber can exist.[7]

---

[6] I call this Russell's barber, because it was Russell who invented the example, though for a different purpose than it serves here.

[7] The contradiction is the statement

(*) The barber shaves himself if and only if he doesn't shave himself.

which has the form 'S ↔ ~S'. This form is inconsistent, as you can check with a truth table or tree. Some people might be bothered by the fact that this contradiction is not in the usual 'P & ~P' form. If you are one of these people, consider the following argument, which deduces a standard form contradiction from statement (*):

Suppose for reductio that the barber shaves himself. Then by (*) and modus ponens he does not shave himself. Hence he both does and does not shave himself.

Hence we must reject the reductio hypothesis, and so we have shown that the barber does not shave himself. But then again by (*) and modus ponens he does shave himself. So it follows from (*) alone that the barber both does and does not shave himself.

Now a reverse halting program is like Russell's barber. But whereas the barber's task is to shave, the task of a reverse halting program is to respond to program code numbers given to it as input. Its response is to be the opposite of what the program indicated by the code number does when given its own number as input. That is, if the encoded program halts when given its own code number as input, the reverse halting program runs forever with that same code number as input. If the encoded program runs forever when given its own code number as input, the reverse halting program halts when given that number.

Consider, for example, the program P mentioned earlier:

$Rt0x' \to Rt'1x$
$Rt00 \to Rt'20$

P subtracts one from the input and halts—or, if the input is zero, halts without changing anything. Thus it halts no matter what input it is given. So, in particular, P halts if given its own program number, 61027561707296100561707709, as input.

When a reverse halting program is given a program number, however, it does just the opposite of what the program it stands for does with it. So, since P halts when given its own number, 61027561707296100561707709, as input, a reverse halting program would run forever given this number as input.

Thus, like Russell's barber, who does for each man the opposite with respect to shaving of what that man does in relation to himself, a reverse halting program does for each program the opposite with respect to halting of what that program does in relation to its own program number. More precisely:

DEFINITION A **reverse halting program** RH for an encoding of abacus programs is an abacus program which, when given a program number n from the encoding as input in register A, halts if and only if the program numbered n does not halt with input n in register A.

Now RH, being by definition an abacus program, must itself have a code number. And, just as we see that Russell's barber is an impossible object by asking whether or not he shaves himself, so we can see that RH is an impossible object by asking what it does when given its own code number as input:

METATHEOREM: There is no reverse halting program for any encoding.

PROOF: Suppose for reductio that there is some reverse halting program RH for some encoding. Then when given a program code number n as input in register A, RH halts if and only if the program numbered n does not halt with input n in register A. Now RH, being itself an abacus program, must have a code number r in the encoding. Hence in particular when given r as input in register A, RH

> halts if and only if the program numbered r (i.e., RH itself) does not
> halt with input r in register A. But this is a contradiction.
>   Hence there is no reverse halting program for any encoding.   QED

This establishes premise 1 of the argument outlined earlier. Our next task is to prove premise 2—that is, to show that if there were a solution to the general halting problem, that would enable us to build a reverse halting program.

METATHEOREM: If there is an abacus program that solves the halting problem, then there is a reverse halting program for some encoding.

PROOF: Suppose for conditional proof that some abacus program GH solves the halting problem. Then there is an encoding E of abacus programs such that given any program number e from E and input number i,

(i) GH stops with 1 in register A if the program numbered e eventually halts when started with input i in register A, and

(ii) GH stops with 0 in register A if the program numbered e never halts when started with input i in register A.

Since (we have assumed) GH exists, we can create a new program, GH+, by prefixing to GH a small program that puts a duplicate of the quantity in register A into register B, as shown:

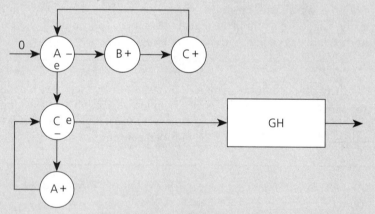

The Program GH+

We represent GH, which is a part of GH+, simply as a rectangle, since we don't know its internal structure. Given any program code number n from encoding E in register A, GH+ duplicates n in register B and then runs GH with the number n in both register A and register B. So when started with any program number n as input in register A,

> (i) GH+ stops with 1 in register A if the program numbered n eventually halts with input n, and
>
> (ii) GH+ stops with 0 in register A if the program numbered n never halts with input n.

In effect, GH+ answers the question "Does this program halt, given its own program number as input?" for any program. Now since we can build GH+, we can also build a slightly more complicated program RH by adding a two-node addendum to GH+, as illustrated below. The addendum consists of a program that halts if the output of GH+ is 0 and loops forever if the output of GH+ is 1.

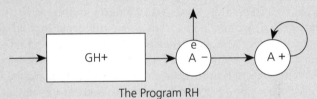

The Program RH

Since GH+ always halts when given program numbers as inputs (because it gives 0 and 1 as answers), it must have at least one exit arrow; we represent GH+ here as having exactly one, but the number doesn't matter. To construct RH we direct all the arrows to the first node of the addendum. Inspection of this flow chart reveals that when given a program number n as input in register A, RH halts if and only if the program numbered n does not halt with input n in register A. RH is thus a reverse halting program for the encoding E. Therefore, if there is an abacus program that solves the halting problem, then there is a reverse halting program for some encoding.   QED

We now use the two metatheorems just proved to draw the following corollary, which is the major result of this section (this is statement 3 in the outline given earlier):

> **COROLLARY:** There is no abacus program that solves the halting problem.
>
> PROOF: Immediate (by modus tollens) from the previous two metatheorems.

In particular, this means that we can't solve the decision problem for predicate logic simply by applying a halting test to a trees program—for the very good reason that a halting test is an impossible object. But maybe there is some specific halting test for trees programs, or maybe there is some other sort of algorithm altogether that could decide the validity of sequents of predicate logic . . .

No such luck.

10.6 THE UNDECIDABILITY OF PREDICATE LOGIC

We are now ready to prove the central result of this chapter—the undecidability of predicate logic.[8] The first proof of this result was published in 1936 by Alonzo Church; thus it has come to be known as **Church's theorem** (not to be confused with Church's *thesis* discussed in Section 10.4). Our version of Church's argument will proceed in two steps: statements 4 and 5 in the outline in Section 10.5. First, to prove statement 4, we shall show that given any program and any number as input, we can construct a sequent that is valid if and only if that program halts with that input. Thus, if we had an algorithmic test for validity, we could use it to create an abacus program that solves the halting problem by testing these sequents for validity. But since, as we saw in the previous section, no abacus program can solve the halting problem, it follows that there can be no solution to the decision problem. This is statement 5, the conclusion of the outline. Our next task is to prove statement 4. Notice that the proof of this statement, unlike our other proofs, uses Church's thesis as an assumption.

METATHEOREM: If predicate logic with function symbols is decidable, then there is an abacus program that solves the halting problem.

PROOF: Assume for conditional proof that predicate logic with function symbols is decidable. That is, there exists a terminating algorithm that determines for each of its sequents whether or not it is valid. Now by Church's thesis any algorithm can be represented by some abacus program. Hence there exists an abacus program, call it D, that determines for each sequent whether or not it is valid and does so in a finite number of steps. Since abacus programs take only numerically coded inputs, this means that there is some encoding E of the sequents of predicate logic such that when given a code number from E as input, D returns an output that effectively signals whether or not the sequent that has this code number is valid. We lose no generality if we assume that this output is 1 if the sequent is

---

[8] Specifically, our proof in this section applies to predicate logic with function symbols. Whether or not the identity predicate is included makes no difference, since we make no use of the identity predicate in our proof. In Section 10.7 we modify the proof to cover predicate logic without function symbols but with the identity predicate.

valid and 0 if it is not, since if the output is encoded in some other way, it is a trivial matter to convert it into a 0 or a 1. Similarly, we can always arrange it so that this output appears in register A. Thus we may suppose that given as input any number from the encoding E that represents some sequent F:

(i) D stops with 1 in register A if F is valid, and
(ii) D stops with 0 in register A if F is invalid.

Now for each abacus program P and nonnegative integer i we can effectively define an associated sequent in predicate logic such that P halts with input i if and only if the sequent associated with P and i is valid. (This is proved below—lemma 1.)

Using this construction, we can write a separate program, call it T (for translator), that takes as input a number representing a program P (in, we may suppose, our standard encoding of programs—or some other) and an integer i and then does two things:

(1) constructs a representation of the associated sequent for P and i, and
(2) converts this representation of the associated sequent into the code number for that sequent in E, and outputs this code number.

We know by Church's thesis that we can write an abacus program to do (1), for we can effectively define the construction of an associated sequent (this is done below). And again by Church's thesis we know that we can write a program to do (2), since E, being an encoding, is effective. Now we prefix D with T, so that T's output is fed directly into D. The result is a new program, H:

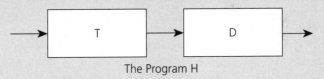

The Program H

Now if we start H with a code number for a program P and an integer i as input,

(i) H stops with 1 in register A if the program numbered e eventually halts when started with input i in register A, and
(ii) H stops with 0 in register A if the program numbered e never halts when started with input i in register A.

But this is to say that H solves the halting problem.
Hence we have shown that if predicate logic with function symbols is decidable, then there is an abacus program that solves the halting problem.   QED

The undecidability of predicate logic with function symbols (statement 5 of the outline) now follows as a simple corollary:

COROLLARY: Predicate logic with function symbols is undecidable.

PROOF: Immediate (by modus tollens) from the previous metatheorem and the fact (proved at the end of Section 10.5) that no abacus program can solve the halting problem.

To cinch the proof of the metatheorem on which this corollary depends, we need to confirm that in fact we can effectively define the sort of associated sequent described earlier. Here is the definition:

The associated sequent for a program with r registers and input n has two sorts of premises:

1. A statement of the form $R00i0 \ldots 0$. This statement asserts that at time 0 the machine is on arrow 0 with i counters in register A and all other registers empty.[9]
2. The program statements with their variables universally quantified.

And the conclusion of the associated sequent is defined as follows:

1. If there are one or more exit arrows, construct for each exit arrow a statement of the form $\exists t\, \exists x_1 \ldots \exists x_r\, R\, t\, e\, x_1 \ldots x_r$, where e is the arrow number, t is a variable representing time, and $x_1 \ldots x_r$ are variables indicating the contents of the registers. This statement says that the machine reaches arrow number e at some time with some input. Then make the conclusion the disjunction of all such statements. (The conclusion thus says that the program reaches one of the exit arrows.)
2. If there are no exit arrows, let the conclusion be the negation of the first premise so that the sequent is invalid.

The associated sequent for a given program and input is constructed so as to be valid if and only if the program eventually halts with that input.

Example: The associated sequent for the following program with input 5 is shown below:

---

[9] We assume they are empty because the halting problem (as defined in Section 10.5) concerns inputs to register A only, and we are here designing associated forms so that a test for their validity would solve the halting problem.

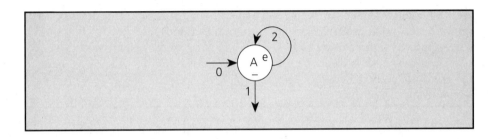

R005	(Machine state when program begins)
$\forall t(Rt00 \rightarrow Rt'20)$	
$\forall t\forall x(Rt0x' \rightarrow Rt'1x)$	
$\forall t(Rt20 \rightarrow Rt'20)$	
$\forall t\forall x(Rt2x' \rightarrow Rt'1x)$	(Superfluous)
$\therefore \quad \exists t\exists x Rt1x$	(Halt)

This program, of course, halts with input 5 (it just subtracts one and stops); accordingly, the associated sequent is valid. (The conclusion follows from the first and third premises.) If, however, instead of 'R005', we made the first premise 'R000', then the sequent would be invalid. This, too, is as it should be, for with an input of 0, the program does not halt; it runs forever, doing nothing.

Notice that for each moment the program is running, the premises of this sequent imply a true description of the state of the abacus at that moment. Trivially, for example, these premises imply

R005

which describes the machine state at time 0, simply because this is the first premise. This conclusion, together with the third premise, implies

R114

which describes the state of the machine at time 1, which is the point at which the program halts. If the first premise were 'R000' instead of 'R005', then the premises would imply the following infinite set of true descriptions:

1. R000   (given as the first premise)
2. R120   (from 1 and the second premise)
3. R220   (from 2 and the fourth premise)
4. R320   (from 3 and the fourth premise)
5. R420   (from 4 and the fourth premise)

    .
    .
    .

In general, where s is a number representing a time, e is a number representing an arrow, and $c_1, \ldots, c_r$ are numbers representing the contents of the registers, we shall call a statement consisting of the predicate R s e c_1 . . . c_r a **true description** of time s relative to a given input i and program P if and only if when P is started with input i, at time s it is on arrow e with $c_1, \ldots, c_r$ in the respective registers.

Our next task is to confirm the following assumption, which was made in the proof of the metatheorem:

LEMMA 1: A program halts given a certain input i if and only if its associated sequent for input i is valid.

PROOF: The conclusion is a biconditional. We must therefore prove two conditionals: If the program halts given input i, its associated sequent for input i is valid; and if its associated sequent for input i is valid, it halts given input i. This requires two conditional proofs. It is easy to see that if the associated sequent is valid, the program halts:

> For suppose the associated sequent for program P with input i is valid. Now its premises are true if P is given input i; thus since the sequent is valid, its conclusion must also be true if P is given input i. But its conclusion asserts that P eventually halts. Hence P eventually halts if given input i.

It remains to prove that if the program halts with input i, then its associated sequent for input i is valid.

> Suppose for conditional proof that the program eventually halts with input i. Then it halts at some time s on some exit arrow e with some numbers $c_1 \ldots c_r$ in the registers. Hence it did not halt before time s. Now we make the following assumption (proved as lemma 2 below): For any time t, if a program has not halted before t, the premises of its associated sequent validly imply a true description of time t. Thus by the lemma the premises of the associated sequent validly imply

> $$R\, s\, e\, c_1 \ldots c_r$$

> whence it follows validly that

> $$\exists t\, \exists y_1 \ldots \exists y_r\, R\, t\, e\, y_1 \ldots y_r$$

> which is the conclusion or a disjunct of the conclusion of the associated sequent. Hence the conclusion of the associated sequent validly follows from its premises; that is, the associated sequent is valid.

Thus P halts given input i if and only if its associated sequent for input i is valid.   QED

The only remaining work is to prove lemma 2.

LEMMA 2: For any time t, if a program has not halted before t, the premises of its associated sequent validly imply a true description of time t.

PROOF: The conclusion is a universal quantification over times, which are a linearly ordered series. Thus we can proceed by mathematical induction.

Basis Case: We must show that if a program has not halted before time 0, the premises of its associated sequent validly imply a true description of time 0. But since the first premise is a true description of time 0, this is obviously true.

Inductive Step: We must prove a conditional with a conditional antecedent and conditional consequent. That is, we must prove that if it is true that (if a program has not halted before t, the premises of its associated sequent validly imply the true description of time t), then it's true that (if a program has not halted before $t + 1$, the premises of its associated sequent validly imply the true description of time $t + 1$).

Suppose for conditional proof that if a program has not halted before t, the premises of its associated sequent validly imply the true description of time t. (This is the inductive hypothesis.) Now since what we are trying to prove is a conditional, we make another conditional proof hypothesis:

Suppose for conditional proof that a program has not halted before time $t + 1$. Then clearly it has not halted before time t. So by the inductive hypothesis (and modus ponens) the premises of its associated sequent validly imply the true description of time t. Now since it hadn't halted at time t, the machine must have been on some arrow that was not an exit arrow at time t. Call this arrow x. Since x was not an exit arrow, there must be some clause in the program description which tells the machine what to do when it is on arrow x. Given that the machine was on arrow x at time t, this clause will imply a true description of the machine at time $t + 1$. However, the universal generalization of this clause is a premise of the program's associated sequent. Hence, since the premises of that sequent validly imply a true description of time t, they also imply a true description of time $t + 1$, which was to be proved.

Thus we have shown, given the inductive hypothesis, that if a program has not halted before $t + 1$, the premises of its associated sequent validly imply the true description of time $t + 1$. QED

This completes the proof of the undecidability of predicate logic with function symbols. We have shown that there can be no algorithmic procedure for determining whether or not any sequent of predicate logic is valid. Some procedures (like the tree test) work for some sequents, but no procedure can work for all. No matter what algorithms we create, no matter how sophisticated or fast we make our computers, there will always be logic problems that we cannot solve.

And we have just proved that—logically!

10.7 HOW FAR DOES THE UNDECIDABILITY EXTEND?

Our proof of undecidability of predicate logic made explicit use of a function symbol (the successor symbol) in the construction of associated sequents. Thus, strictly speaking, what we have proved is that predicate logic with function symbols is undecidable. What if we dropped the function symbols? Would we still have an undecidable logic?

We can fairly easily show that the answer is yes, provided that we still have the identity predicate. The trick is to redefine the concept of an associated sequent, using a two-place predicate 'S' meaning "is the successor of" rather than the successor function symbol. To guarantee that S generates the appropriate implications, we will need to add two new premises to each associated inference. These are

$$\forall x \exists y Syx$$

which means (given a domain of numbers) that every number has at least one successor and

$$\forall x \forall y \forall z ((Syx \ \& \ Szx) \rightarrow y = z)$$

which means that each number has at most one successor. Together, these two statements imply that each number has exactly one successor. We didn't need to say this explicitly when we used the successor function symbol, since it is built into the logic of functions that each function has exactly one value per argument. More specifically, the corresponding formulas using the successor notation, that is, the formulas

$$\forall x \exists y \ y=x'$$

and

$$\forall x \forall y \forall z ((y = x' \ \& \ z = x') \rightarrow y = z)$$

are valid.

Notice that the second of our new assumptions about 'S' uses the identity predicate, which played no role in our old associated sequents. Thus, using this new kind of associated sequent, though we will be able to show the undecidability of predicate logic without function symbols, it will be predicate logic *with the identity predicate*.

In addition to adding these new premises to associated sequents, we need to rewrite the formulas comprising the sequents, using 'S' instead of "'". This calls for some rearrangement because of the grammatical differences between function symbols and predicates. Roughly, all the 'S' predicates get packed into antecedents of conditionals. The statement

$$\forall t \forall x (Rt0x \rightarrow Rt'0x')$$

for example, becomes

$$\forall z \forall y \forall t \forall x (Szx \rightarrow (Syt \rightarrow (Rt0x \rightarrow Ry0z)))$$

This procedure eliminates all occurrences of "'" but adds a new universal quantifier and a new occurrence of 'S' in the antecedent of a conditional for each so that formulas get cumbersome. That's why we didn't define associated sequents this way in the first place. Use of the successor function symbol makes both the abacus programming notation and the definition of an associated inference much simpler.

Even though these new-style associated sequents are more cumbersome, they work exactly the way the old ones did, and the undecidability proof of Section 10.6 can be redone, by substituting the new sort of associated sequent for the old sort in the proof. This changes it from a proof of the undecidability of predicate logic with function symbols to a proof of the undecidability of predicate logic without function symbols but with the identity predicate.

In fact, predicate logic remains undecidable if we eliminate the identity predicate as well, but we will not show that here.[10] In sum, the identity predicate and function symbols make no difference; predicate logic itself, with or without either, is undecidable. But why?

The answer, as the infinite trees of Section 7.4 suggest, is that the only counterexamples for some invalid sequents are counterexamples with infinite domains— domains constructible only by an infinite process. The ability to describe such infinities is one of predicate logic's virtues; without this ability, predicate logic would be of little use, for example, in higher mathematics, where it has in fact found many applications. But with this virtue comes the corresponding vice of undecidability.

For some uses, however, we do not need the full power of predicate logic: A mere part or fragment of predicate logic will do. We have already seen that one such fragment, propositional logic, is decidable. Are there other decidable fragments—fragments that include more than just propositional logic?

Indeed there are. One is the fragment obtained by dropping the existential quantifier from predicate logic without function symbols and requiring all universal quantifiers to take wide scope (i.e., not to occur within the scopes of operators that are not universal quantifiers). The resulting fragment of predicate logic,

---

[10] One way to do it is to use the sort of associated sequents just illustrated but eliminate the identity predicate by defining it in terms of the other predicates used in those sequents—namely, 'R' and 'S'. The technique for eliminating the identity predicate is explained in W. V. Quine, *Philosophy of Logic* (Englewood Cliffs, N.J.: Prentice-Hall, 1970), pp. 63–64.

though quantified, is, like propositional logic, decidable. It never generates infinite trees, because once each formula's initial string of quantifiers is instantiated for all names already on the path, no new names can appear and the tree can be finished simply by repeated application of the propositional rules. This is true even when we negate a universal conclusion to test for validity, which will yield an existential formula by ~∀. Once all the initial quantifiers of this formula are instantiated— by repeated steps of ~∀ and ∃[11]—this formula can generate no new names. Restricting predicate logic in this way would, of course, limit the things we could say, but it might be adequate for some uses.

Other fragments of predicate logic are decidable as well so that if we restrict our attention to certain classes of problems, we may sometimes be sure of getting an answer even if we are using quantifiers. Much technical work has been devoted to sorting out decidable fragments of predicate logic from the undecidable ones, but we shall pursue this theme no further.

Before we leave the topic of undecidability, one small but significant doubt needs airing. The proof of premise 4 in our outline of the undecidability proof assumed Church's thesis. But Church's thesis is not a logical truth. It is a well-confirmed empirical hypothesis—so well confirmed that by now it in effect defines the notion of an algorithm. It is conceivable, however, that we might some day discover something that is recognizably a computational process but which nevertheless is not representable as an abacus program. What we would say then would depend on whether we think of Church's thesis as an empirical hypothesis or a definition. If we think of it as an empirical hypothesis, we would say that it proved to be false. If we think of it as a definition, then we would simply announce the discovery of nonalgorithmic computational processes.

However we described it, such a discovery would undermine our proof of the undecidability of predicate logic, but it would by no means show that predicate logic is decidable. The new computational procedures might be no more capable of solving the decision problem than abacus programs are. This whole scenario, however, is highly speculative.

Exercise 10.7

Is the fragment of predicate logic that results from allowing only existential quantification and requiring these quantifiers to take wide scope decidable? Why or why not?

---

[11] Actually, having banned existential quantification, we would not really have the ∃ rule for trees; we would need instead a modified ~∀ rule which combined the functions of our current ~∀ and ∃ rules.

PART IV

EXTENSIONS OF CLASSICAL LOGIC

CHAPTER 11

LEIBNIZIAN MODAL LOGIC

11.1 MODAL OPERATORS

Prominent among philosophically important operators that are apparently inexpressible in predicate logic are **alethic** modifiers, such as 'must', 'might', 'could', 'can', 'have to', 'possibly', 'contingently', 'necessarily'. The term 'alethic' comes from the Greek word for truth, *alethea*. These words are said to express alethic modalities—that is, various modes of truth. **Modal logic,** in the narrowest sense, is the study of the syntax and semantics of these alethic modalities.

But the term is also used in a broader sense, to designate the study of other sorts of propositional modalities. These include **deontic** (ethical) **modalities** (expressed by such constructions as 'it ought to be the case that', 'it is forbidden that', 'it is permissible that', etc.); **propositional attitudes** (relations between sentient beings and propositions, expressed by such terms as 'believes that', 'knows that', 'hopes that', 'wonders whether', and so on); and **tenses** (e.g., the past, present, and future tenses as expressed by the various modifications of the verb 'to be': 'was', 'is', and 'will be').

The extension of the term 'modal' to these other forms of modality is no fluke; they share important logical properties with alethic modalities. For one thing, all of them can be regarded as operators on propositions. Consider, for example, these sentences, all of which involve the application of modal operators (in the broad sense) to the single proposition 'People communicate':

Alethic Operators

It is possible that people communicate.
It must be the case that people communicate.
It is contingently the case that people communicate.
It could be the case that people communicate.
It is necessarily the case that people communicate.

Deontic Operators

It is obligatory that people communicate.
It is permissible that people communicate.
It is not allowed that people communicate.
It should be the case that people communicate.

Operators Expressing Propositional Attitudes

Ann *knows that* people communicate.
Bill *believes that* people communicate.
Cynthia *fears that* people communicate.
Don *supposes that* people communicate.
Everyone *understands that* people communicate.
Fred *doubts that* people communicate.

Operators Expressing Tenses

It was (at some time) the case that people communicated.
It was always the case that people communicated.
It will (at some time) be the case that people communicate.
It will always be the case that people communicate.

There are, of course, many more operators in each category. And some of those listed, such as 'it is possible that' and 'it could be the case that' are, at least in some contexts, semantically identical or synonymous. With the exception of the operators expressing propositional attitudes, all of those listed here are monadic; they function syntactically just like the negation operator 'it is not the case that', prefixing a sentence to produce a new sentence. Thus, for example, the operators 'it is necessary that', usually symbolized by the box '□' and 'it is possible that', usually symbolized by the diamond sign '◇',[1] are introduced by adding this clause to the formation rules:

If Φ is a formula, then so are □Φ and ◇Φ.

The operators expressing propositional attitudes, however, are binary. But unlike such binary operators as conjunction or disjunction, which unite a pair of sentences into a compound sentence, propositional attitude operators take a name and a sentence to make a sentence. The place for this name may be quantified, as in 'Everyone understands that people communicate'.

Many modal operators have **duals**—operators which, when flanked by negation signs, form their equivalents. The operators '□' and '◇', for example, are duals, as the following sentences assert:

□Φ ↔ ~◇~Φ
◇Φ ↔ ~□~Φ

That is, it is necessary that Φ if and only if it is not possible that not-Φ, and it is possible that Φ if and only if it is not necessary that not-Φ.

There are other duals among these operators as well. Consider the deontic operator 'it is obligatory that', which we shall symbolize as 'O', and the operator 'it is permissible that', which we shall write as 'P'. These are similarly related:

OΦ ↔ ~P~Φ
PΦ ↔ ~O~Φ

That 'O' and 'P' should thus mimic '□' and '◇' is understandable, since obligation is a kind of moral necessity and permission a kind of moral possibility.

There are also **epistemic** (knowledge-related) duals. The operator 'knows that' is dual with the operator 'it is epistemically possible, for . . . that'—the former representing epistemic necessity (knowledge) and the latter epistemic possibility. (Something is **epistemically possible** for a person if *so far as that person knows* it might be the case.) Symbolizing 'knows that' by 'K' and 'it is epistemically possible for . . . that' by 'E', we have:

pKΦ ↔ ~pE~Φ
pEΦ ↔ ~pK~Φ

In English: p knows that Φ if and only if it is not epistemically possible for p that not-Φ; and it is epistemically possible for p that Φ if and only if p does not know that not-Φ ('p', of course, stands for a person).

There are temporal duals as well. Let 'P' mean 'it was (at some time) the case that' and 'H' mean 'it has always been the case that'. Then:

HΦ ↔ ~P~Φ
PΦ ↔ ~H~Φ

---

[1] Sometimes 'L' is used instead of '□' and 'M' instead of '◇'. These abbreviate the German terms for logical (*logische*)—that is, necessary—truth and possible (*mögliche*) truth.

Here 'H' represents a kind of past tense temporal necessity and 'P' a kind of past tense temporal possibility. A similar relationship holds between 'it always will be the case that' and 'it sometimes will be the case that' and between other pairs of temporal operators.

These systematic logical relationships bear a striking resemblance to two familiar laws of predicate logic:

$$\forall x \Phi \leftrightarrow \sim\exists x \sim\Phi$$
$$\exists x \Phi \leftrightarrow \sim\forall x \sim\Phi$$

Are these pairs of dual operators somehow analogous to quantifiers?

11.2 LEIBNIZIAN SEMANTICS

Leibniz, who was among the first to investigate the logic of alethic operators, in effect suggested that they are. His semantics for modal logic was founded upon a simple but metaphysically audacious idea: Our universe is only one of a myriad possible universes, or possible worlds. Each of these possible worlds comprises a complete history, from the beginning (if there is a beginning) to the end (if there is an end) of time.

Such immodest entities may rouse skepticism, yet we are all familiar with something of the kind. I wake up on a Saturday; several salient possibilities lie before me. I could work on this book, or weed my garden, or take the kids to the park. Whether or not I do any of these things, my ability to recognize and entertain such possibilities is a prominent feature of my life. For ordinary purposes, my awareness of possibilities is confined to my doings and their immediate effects on the people and things around me. Yet my choices affect the world. If I spend the day gardening, the world that results is a different world than if I had chosen otherwise. Leibnizian metaphysics, then, can be seen as a widening of our vision of possibility from the part to the whole, from mere possible situations to entire possible worlds.

Possible worlds figure most notoriously in Leibniz's theodicy. God, in contemplating the Creation, surveyed all possible worlds, says Leibniz, and chose to actualize only the best—ours. Since ours is the best of all possible worlds, the degree of evil or suffering it contains is unavoidable—as we would see if only we had God's wisdom.[2]

What interests the logician, however, is not how Leibniz used possible worlds to rationalize actual miseries, but how he used them to adumbrate an alethic modal semantics. On Leibniz's view:

□Φ is true if and only if Φ is true in all possible worlds.

---

[2] This has given rise to the quip that the optimist is one who, like Leibniz, thinks that ours is the best of all possible worlds, whereas the pessimist is one who is sure of it.

and

> $\Diamond \Phi$ is true if and only if Φ is true in at least one possible world.

The operators '$\Box$' and '$\Diamond$' are thus akin, respectively, to universal and existential quantifiers over a domain of possible worlds. So, for example, to say that it is necessary that $2 + 2 = 4$ is to say that in all possible worlds $2 + 2 = 4$; and to say that it is possible for the earth to be destroyed by an asteroid is to say that there is at least one possible world (universe) in which an asteroid destroys the earth.

Generalizing where Leibniz did not, we can extend his analysis to other modalities. Deontic operators are like quantifiers over morally possible (i.e., permissible) worlds—worlds that are ideal in the sense that within them all the dictates of morality are obeyed (exactly *which* morality is a question we shall defer!). Epistemic operators are like quantifiers over epistemically possible worlds—that is, over those worlds compatible with our knowledge (or, more specifically, with the knowledge of a given person at a given time). And tense operators act like quantifiers too—only they range, not over worlds, but over moments of time.

Time and possibility: an odd juxtaposition, yet illuminating, for there are rich analogies here. For one thing, just as there is a specific temporal moment, the present, which is in a sense uniquely real (for the past exists no longer, the future not yet), so there is a specific possible world, the actual world, which (for us at least) is uniquely real.

A second point of analogy is that in nonpresent moments objects have different properties from those they do now. I, for example, am now seated in front of a computer, whereas an hour or two ago I was riding my bike. Not all of what was true of me then is true of me now. In the same way, objects have properties different from those they actually have in nonactual worlds. I am a philosophy professor, but I could have been a farmer; that is, in some possible world I have the property of being a farmer, a property I do not actually have.

And just as an object (or a person) is typically not a momentary phenomenon, but has temporal duration—is "spread out," so to speak, through time—so too is an object "spread out" through possibilities. I am not just what I am at the moment; rather, I am an entire life, a yet-uncompleted history, from birth to death. Likewise, or so the analogy suggests, I am not merely what I actually am, but also my possibilities—what I could have been and could still be.[3]

Thus time and possibility share certain structural features, and their respective logics ought to reflect this fact. In Section 13.2 we shall see that to some extent they do. But in the meantime, we have run way ahead of Leibniz's conception of alethic modality. To Leibniz we now return, but with an anachronistic twist. We shall reformulate his insight about alethic operators in contemporary metatheoretic terms.

To begin, observe that a valuation for predicate logic in effect models a single world. It consists of a domain and assignments of appropriate extensions to pred-

---

[3] Cf. Martin Heidegger's contention that *Dasein* (human existence) *is* its possibilities and thus is more than it factually is; *Being and Time*, trans. John Macquarrie and Edward Robinson (New York: Harper & Row), pp. 68, 183–84, 185.

icates and names within that domain. In modal logic, we posit many possible worlds. A model for modal logic, then, should contain many "worlds," each with its own domain. And because the facts differ from world to world, that model should assign to each predicate not just a single extension, but an extension in each world. To keep things manageably (but preposterously) simple, consider a model representing just three possible worlds, w_1, w_2, and w_3. And (still oversimplifying) let's suppose that w_1 contains exactly four objects, α, β, γ, and δ; w_2 contains exactly two objects, β and γ; and w_3 contains exactly three objects α, δ, and ϵ:

World	Domain
w_1	$\{\alpha, \beta, \gamma, \delta\}$
w_2	$\{\beta, \gamma\}$
w_3	$\{\alpha, \delta, \epsilon\}$

Now suppose we want to interpret the one-place predicate 'B', which for the sake of definiteness we may suppose means "is blue." Since a thing may be blue in one world but not in another, we cannot assign this predicate a single set (the set of blue things), as we would have in predicate logic. Rather, we need to assign it a separate set in—or "at" (either preposition may be used)—each world. For each world w, the set assigned to 'B' at w then represents the things that are blue in w. Suppose we assign to 'B' the set $\{\alpha, \beta\}$ in w_1, $\{\ \}$ in w_2, and $\{\alpha, \delta, \epsilon\}$ in w_3. Then, according to our model there are two blue things in w_1 and none in w_2, and in w_3 everything is blue.

Because extensions differ from world to world (i.e., are world-relative) in modal logic, a valuation $\mathcal{V}$ now must take into account not only predicates, but also worlds, in assigning extensions. Thus we write

$$\mathcal{V}(\text{'B'}, w_1) = \{\alpha, \beta\}$$
$$\mathcal{V}(\text{'B'}, w_2) = \{\ \}$$
$$\mathcal{V}(\text{'B'}, w_3) = \{\alpha, \delta, \epsilon\}$$

to indicate that at world w_1 the set of things that satisfies the predicate 'B' (i.e., the set of blue things) is $\{\alpha, \beta\}$, and so on.

Truth, too, is now world-relative. Blue things exist in w_1 but not in w_2; thus the formula '$\exists x Bx$' ought to be true at w_1 but not at w_2. That is, $\mathcal{V}(\text{'}\exists x Bx\text{'}, w_1) =$ T, but $\mathcal{V}(\text{'}\exists x Bx\text{'}, w_2) =$ F. Accordingly, when we assign truth values to sentence letters, we shall have to assign each letter a truth value for each world. Let 'M', for example, mean "there is motion." We might let 'M' be true in w_1 but not in w_2 or w_3. Thus $\mathcal{V}(\text{'M'}, w_1) =$ T, but $\mathcal{V}(\text{'M'}, w_2) = \mathcal{V}(\text{'M'}, w_3) =$ F.

We shall assume, however, that names do not change denotation from world to world. Thus we shall assign to each name a single object, which may inhabit the domains of several possible worlds, and this assignment will not be world-relative. This models the metaphysical idea that people and things are "spread out" through possibilities, just as they are "spread out" through time. With respect to time, for example, the name 'John Nolt' refers to me now, but also to me when I was a child and to the old man whom (I hope) I will become. I occupy many moments, and my name refers to me at each of these moments. Analogously, I have many possibilities, and my name refers to me in each. When I consider that I could be a farmer, part of what makes this possibility interesting to me is that it is *my* possibility.[4] It is I, John Nolt, who could be a farmer; my name, then, refers not only to me as I actually am, but to me as I could be. I am a denizen of possibilities (that is, possible worlds), as well as times, and my name tracks me through these possibilities, just as it does through the moments of my life.

Names, then, as we shall understand them, are **rigid designators;** they refer to the same object in each world in which they refer to anything at all. The idea that names designate rigidly, due to Ruth Marcus and Saul Kripke,[5] is now widely, though not universally, accepted. Other semantic interpretations of names have been offered, but we shall not consider them here.

In our semantics we shall model rigid designation by representing the value assigned to a name α simply as $\mathcal{V}(\alpha)$, rather than as $\mathcal{V}(\alpha, w)$, which would represent the value assigned to α *at a world w*. The omission of the world variable indicates that the denotations of names are not world-relative.

The concept of rigid designation harbors a metaphysical presupposition: the doctrine of **transworld identity.** This is the idea that the same object may exist in more than one possible world. It is modeled in our semantics by the fact that we allow the same object to occur in the domains of different worlds. Most logicians who do possible worlds semantics take transworld identity for granted, though there are exceptions.[6]

Though a rigidly designating name refers to the same object in different worlds, that object need not be "the same" in the sense of having the same properties. I would have quite different properties in a world in which I was a farmer, but I would still be the same person—namely, me.

These ideas are reflected in the model introduced above. Object β, for example, exists in w_1 and w_2. It therefore exhibits transworld identity. Moreover, it is in the extension of the predicate 'B' in w_1, but not in w_2. Thus, though it is the same object in w_1 as it is in w_2, it is blue in w_1 but not in w_2. If we think of w_1 as the actual world, this models the idea that an object that is actually blue nevertheless *could be* nonblue (it is capable, for example, of being dyed or painted a different color, yet retaining its identity).

Suppose now that we use the name 'n' to denote object β, that is, let $\mathcal{V}('n') = \beta$. (Note the absence of a world-variable here; the denotation of a rigidly designat-

---

4 Of course not all possibilities are *my* possibilities. In a world in which my parents had never met, I would never have existed, and the name 'John Nolt' would not refer to anything in that world (unless, of course, there were a different person with that name—but then the name would simply be ambiguous; that person would not be me). My existence, in other words, is contingent. In our models, this contingency is represented by the fact that an object need not occur in the domain of each world.

5 See Kripke's *Naming and Necessity* (Cambridge: Harvard University Press, 1972).

6 Most notably David Lewis, in "Counterpart Theory and Quantified Modal Logic," *Journal of Philosophy* 65 (1968): 113–26.

ing name, unlike truth or the denotation of a predicate, is not world-relative.) Then we would say that the statement 'Bn' ("n is blue") is true in w_1, but not in w_2, that is, $\mathcal{V}(\text{'Bn'}, w_1) = \text{T}$, but $\mathcal{V}(\text{'Bn'}, w_2) = \text{F}$.

But what are we to say about the truth value of 'Bn' in w_3, wherein β does not exist? Consider some possible (but nonactual) stone. Is it blue or not blue in the actual world? Both answers are arbitrary. Similarly, it seems arbitrary to make 'Bn' either true or false in a world in which 'n' has no referent.

This problem cannot be satisfactorily resolved without either abandoning bivalence (so that 'Bn', for example, may be neither true nor false) or modifying the logic of the quantifiers. The first approach is perhaps best implemented by means of supervaluations, which are discussed in Section 15.3; the second by free logics, which are covered in Section 15.1. Discussion of either method now would perhaps complicate things beyond what we could bear at the moment. We shall therefore leave the question unsettled.

Valuation rules 1 and 2 below give truth conditions for atomic formulas at a world only on the condition that the extensions of the names contained in those formulas are in the domain of that world. The truth conditions at w for atomic formulas (other than identities) that contain names which denote no existing thing at w are left unspecified. (Identity statements are an exception, since their truth conditions are not world-relative.) Our semantics, then, will be deficient in this respect, though still usable in other respects. The deficiency will be remedied in Chapter 15.

A valuation, or model, then, consists of a set of things called **worlds,** each with its own domain of objects. In addition, it assigns to each name an object from at least one of those domains, and it assigns to each predicate and world an appropriate extension for that predicate in that world. An object may belong to the domain of more than one world, but it need not belong to domains of all worlds. Two different worlds may have the same domain. The full definition is as follows:

DEFINITION A **Leibnizian valuation** or **Leibnizian model** $\mathcal{V}$ for a formula or set of formulas of modal predicate logic consists of the following:

1. A nonempty set $\mathcal{W}_{\mathcal{V}}$ of objects, called the **worlds** of $\mathcal{V}$.
2. For each world w in $\mathcal{W}_{\mathcal{V}}$ a nonempty set $\mathcal{D}_w$ of objects, called the **domain** of w.
3. For each name or nonidentity predicate σ of that formula or set of formulas, an extension $\mathcal{V}(\sigma)$ (if σ is a name) or $\mathcal{V}(\sigma, w)$ (if σ is a predicate and w a world in $\mathcal{W}_{\mathcal{V}}$) as follows:
   i. If σ is a name, then $\mathcal{V}(\sigma)$ is a member of the domain of at least one world.
   ii. If σ is a zero-place predicate (sentence letter), $\mathcal{V}(\sigma, w)$ is one (but not both) of the values T or F.

> iii. If σ is a one-place predicate, $\mathcal{V}(\sigma, w)$ is a set of members of $\mathcal{D}_w$.
>
> iv. If σ is an n-place predicate $(n > 1)$, $\mathcal{V}(\sigma, w)$ is a set of ordered n-tuples of members of $\mathcal{D}_w$.

Given any valuation, the following valuation rules describe how truth and falsity are assigned to complex formulas:

Valuation Rules for Leibnizian Modal Predicate Logic

Given any Leibnizian valuation $\mathcal{V}$, for any world w in $\mathcal{W}_\mathcal{V}$:

1. If Φ is a one-place predicate and α is a name whose extension $\mathcal{V}(\alpha)$ is in $\mathcal{D}_w$, then

    $\mathcal{V}(\Phi\alpha, w) = \text{T iff } \mathcal{V}(\alpha) \, \varepsilon \, \mathcal{V}(\Phi, w);$

    $\mathcal{V}(\Phi\alpha, w) = \text{F iff } \mathcal{V}(\alpha) \, \not\varepsilon \, \mathcal{V}(\Phi, w).$

2. If Φ is an n-place predicate $(n > 1)$ and $\alpha_1, \ldots, \alpha_n$ are names whose extensions are all in $\mathcal{D}_w$, then

    $\mathcal{V}(\Phi\alpha_1, \ldots, \alpha_n, w) = \text{T iff } <\mathcal{V}(\alpha_1), \ldots, \mathcal{V}(\alpha_n)> \varepsilon \, \mathcal{V}(\Phi, w);$

    $\mathcal{V}(\Phi\alpha_1, \ldots, \alpha_n, w) = \text{F iff } <\mathcal{V}(\alpha_1), \ldots, \mathcal{V}(\alpha_n)> \not\varepsilon \, \mathcal{V}(\Phi, w).$

3. If α and β are names, then

    $\mathcal{V}(\alpha = \beta, w) = \text{T iff } \mathcal{V}(\alpha) = \mathcal{V}(\beta);$

    $\mathcal{V}(\alpha = \beta, w) = \text{F iff } \mathcal{V}(\alpha) \neq \mathcal{V}(\beta).$

For the next five rules, Φ and Ψ are any formulas:

4. $\mathcal{V}(\sim\Phi, w) = \text{T iff } \mathcal{V}(\Phi, w) \neq \text{T};$

    $\mathcal{V}(\sim\Phi, w) = \text{F iff } \mathcal{V}(\Phi, w) = \text{T}.$

5. $\mathcal{V}(\Phi \, \& \, \Psi, w) = \text{T iff both } \mathcal{V}(\Phi, w) = \text{T and } \mathcal{V}(\Psi, w) = \text{T};$

    $\mathcal{V}(\Phi \, \& \, \Psi, w) = \text{F iff either } \mathcal{V}(\Phi, w) \neq \text{T or } \mathcal{V}(\Psi, w) \neq \text{T, or both}.$

6. $\mathcal{V}(\Phi \lor \Psi, w) = \text{T iff either } \mathcal{V}(\Phi, w) = \text{T or } \mathcal{V}(\Psi, w) = \text{T, or both};$

    $\mathcal{V}(\Phi \lor \Psi, w) = \text{F iff both } \mathcal{V}(\Phi, w) \neq \text{T and } \mathcal{V}(\Psi, w) \neq \text{T}.$

7. $\mathcal{V}(\Phi \to \Psi, w) = \text{T iff either } \mathcal{V}(\Phi, w) \neq \text{T or } \mathcal{V}(\Psi, w) = \text{T, or both};$

    $\mathcal{V}(\Phi \to \Psi, w) = \text{F iff both } \mathcal{V}(\Phi, w) = \text{T and } \mathcal{V}(\Psi, w) \neq \text{T}.$

8. $\mathcal{V}(\Phi \leftrightarrow \Psi, w) = \text{T iff either } \mathcal{V}(\Phi, w) = \text{T and } \mathcal{V}(\Psi, w) = \text{T, or } \mathcal{V}(\Phi, w) \neq \text{T and } \mathcal{V}(\Psi, w) \neq \text{T};$

    $\mathcal{V}(\Phi \leftrightarrow \Psi, w) = \text{F iff either } \mathcal{V}(\Phi, w) = \text{T and } \mathcal{V}(\Psi, w) \neq \text{T, or } \mathcal{V}(\Phi, w) \neq \text{T and } \mathcal{V}(\Psi, w) = \text{T}.$

For the next two rules, $\Phi^\alpha/_\beta$ stands for the result of replacing each occurrence of the variable β in Φ by α, and $\mathcal{D}_w$ is the domain that $\mathcal{V}$ assigns to world w.

9. $\mathcal{V}(\forall_\beta\Phi, w) = \text{T iff for all potential names } \alpha \text{ of all objects } d \text{ in } \mathcal{D}_w,$

    $\mathcal{V}_{(\alpha, d)}(\Phi^\alpha/_\beta, w) = \text{T};$

    $\mathcal{V}(\forall_\beta\Phi, w) = \text{F iff for some potential name } \alpha \text{ of some object } d \text{ in } \mathcal{D}_w,$

    $\mathcal{V}_{(\alpha, d)}(\Phi^\alpha/_\beta, w) \neq \text{T}.$

10. $\mathcal{V}(\exists_\beta\Phi, w) = \text{T iff for some potential name } \alpha \text{ of some object } d \text{ in } \mathcal{D}_w,$

    $\mathcal{V}_{(\alpha, d)}(\Phi^\alpha/_\beta, w) = \text{T};$

    $\mathcal{V}(\exists_\beta\Phi, w) = \text{F iff for all potential names } \alpha \text{ of all objects } d \text{ in } \mathcal{D}_w,$

    $\mathcal{V}_{(\alpha, d)}(\Phi^\alpha/_\beta, w) \neq \text{T}.$

11. $\mathcal{V}(\Box\Phi, w) = \mathrm{T}$ iff for all worlds u in $\mathcal{W}_V$, $\mathcal{V}(\Phi, u) = \mathrm{T}$;
    $\mathcal{V}(\Box\Phi, w) = \mathrm{F}$ iff for some world u in $\mathcal{W}_V$, $\mathcal{V}(\Phi, u) \neq \mathrm{T}$.
12. $\mathcal{V}(\Diamond\Phi, w) = \mathrm{T}$ iff for some world u in $\mathcal{W}_V$, $\mathcal{V}(\Phi, u) = \mathrm{T}$;
    $\mathcal{V}(\Diamond\Phi, w) = \mathrm{F}$ iff for all worlds u in $\mathcal{W}_V$, $\mathcal{V}(\Phi, u) \neq \mathrm{T}$.

Since the valuation rules are a lot to swallow in one bite, we'll take the propositional fragment of the semantics by itself first and come back to the full modal predicate logic later. This simplifies the definition of a valuation considerably:

DEFINITION A **Leibnizian valuation** or **Leibnizian model** $\mathcal{V}$ for a formula or set of formulas of modal propositional logic consists of

1. A nonempty set $\mathcal{W}_V$ of objects, called the **worlds** of $\mathcal{V}$.
2. For each sentence letter σ of that formula or set of formulas and each world w in $\mathcal{W}_V$, an extension $\mathcal{V}(\sigma, w)$ consisting of one (but not both) of the values T or F.

Here worlds are like the (horizontal) lines on a truth table, in that each is distinguished by a truth-value assignment to atomic formulas—though not all lines of a truth table need be represented in a single model.

Consider, for example, the following valuation of the formula '(V ∨ W)' which we may suppose means "Sam is virtuous or Sam is wicked":

$\mathcal{W}_V = \{1, 2, 3, 4\}$
$\mathcal{V}(\text{'V'}, 1) = \mathrm{T}$ $\mathcal{V}(\text{'W'}, 1) = \mathrm{F}$
$\mathcal{V}(\text{'V'}, 2) = \mathrm{F}$ $\mathcal{V}(\text{'W'}, 2) = \mathrm{F}$
$\mathcal{V}(\text{'V'}, 3) = \mathrm{F}$ $\mathcal{V}(\text{'W'}, 3) = \mathrm{T}$
$\mathcal{V}(\text{'V'}, 4) = \mathrm{F}$ $\mathcal{V}(\text{'W'}, 4) = \mathrm{T}$

The "worlds" here are the numbers 1, 2, 3, and 4. (In a model, it doesn't matter what sorts of objects do the modeling.) In world 1, 'V' is true and 'W' is false—that is, Sam is virtuous, not wicked. In world 2, Sam is neither virtuous nor wicked. And in worlds 3 and 4, Sam is wicked, not virtuous.[7] Our model represents the situation in which Sam is both virtuous and wicked as impossible, since this situation occurs in none of the four possible worlds. In other words, only three of the four lines of the truth table for 'V ∨ W' are regarded as possible. This is arguably appropriate, given the meanings we have attached to 'V' and 'W'.

---

[7] In a sense, world 4 is redundant, since from the point of view of our model it differs in no way from world 3. But this sort of redundancy is both permissible and realistic. It may, for example, represent the idea that world 4 differs from world 3 in ways not relevant to the problem at hand; for example, Sam may be a sailor in world 3 but not in world 4. Of course, if the model were truly realistic, it would contain many more worlds representing many such irrelevant differences, but we are simplifying.

To understand more about how this model works, we must consider the valuation rules for propositional modal logic (rules 4–8 and 11–12 above). According to rule 6, for example, the statement 'V ∨ W' has the value T in a world w if and only if either 'V' or 'W' has the value T in that world, and it is false otherwise. Thus this statement is true in worlds 1, 3, and 4, but false in world 2. The rules for the other truth-functional propositional operators ('~', '&', '→', and '↔') are all similarly relativized to worlds.

The real novelty, though, and the heart of Leibniz's insight, lies in rules 11 and 12. Consider, for example, the statement '□~(V & W)', which according to our interpretation means "it is necessarily the case that Sam is not both virtuous and wicked." According to rule 11, this formula is true at a given world w if and only if the statement '~(V & W)' is true in all worlds. Now in our model '~(V & W)' is in fact true in all worlds. For there is no world in which both 'V' and 'W' are true; hence by rule 5, 'V & W' is not true in any world, and so by rule 4, '~(V & W)' is true in each world. This means by rule 11 that '□~(V & W)' is true in every world.

Similarly, the statement '◇V' ("it is possible that Sam is virtuous") is true in all worlds. For consider any given world w. Whichever world w is, there is some world u (namely, world 1) in which 'V' is true. Hence by rule 12, '◇V' is true in w.

Notice also that since '◇V' is true in all worlds, it follows by another application of rule 11 that '□◇V' ("it is necessarily possible that Sam is virtuous") is true in all worlds. In fact, repeated application of rule 11 establishes that '□□◇V', '□□□◇V', and so on are all true at all worlds in this model. The following meta-theorem exemplifies the formal use of modal semantics; use it as a model for Exercise 11.2.1:

METATHEOREM: For any world w of the model just described, $\mathcal{V}('□◇V', w) = T$.

PROOF: Let u be any world of this model, that is, $u \; \varepsilon \; \mathcal{W}_{\mathcal{V}}$. Since $\mathcal{V}('V', 1) = T$, it follows by rule 12 that $\mathcal{V}('◇V', u) = T$. Thus, for all u in $\mathcal{W}_{\mathcal{V}}$, $\mathcal{V}('◇V', u) = T$. Now let w be any world in $\mathcal{W}_{\mathcal{V}}$. It follows by rule 11 that $\mathcal{V}('□◇V', w) = T$.   QED

Exercise 11.2.1

Consider the following model:

$\mathcal{W}_{\mathcal{V}} = \{1, 2, 3\}$

$\mathcal{V}('P', 1) = T$	$\mathcal{V}('Q', 1) = F$	$\mathcal{V}('R', 1) = T$
$\mathcal{V}('P', 2) = F$	$\mathcal{V}('Q', 2) = F$	$\mathcal{V}('R', 2) = T$
$\mathcal{V}('P', 3) = T$	$\mathcal{V}('Q', 3) = T$	$\mathcal{V}('R', 3) = T$

Using the valuation rules, prove the following with respect to this model:

1. $\mathscr{V}(\text{'P} \lor \text{Q'}, 1) = \text{T}$
2. $\mathscr{V}(\text{'}\square\text{R'}, 1) = \text{T}$
3. For any world w in $\mathscr{W}_\mathscr{V}$, $\mathscr{V}(\text{'}\square\text{R'}, w) = \text{T}$
4. There is no world w in $\mathscr{W}_\mathscr{V}$ such that $\mathscr{V}(\text{'}\square\text{P'}, w) = \text{T}$
5. For any world w in $\mathscr{W}_\mathscr{V}$, $\mathscr{V}(\text{'}\Diamond \text{P'}, w) = \text{T}$
6. For any world w in $\mathscr{W}_\mathscr{V}$, $\mathscr{V}(\text{'}\sim\square\text{R'}, w) = \text{F}$
7. For any world w in $\mathscr{W}_\mathscr{V}$, $\mathscr{V}(\text{'}\Diamond \sim\text{R'}, w) = \text{F}$
8. For any world w in $\mathscr{W}_\mathscr{V}$, $\mathscr{V}(\text{'P} \lor \sim\text{P'}, w) = \text{T}$
9. For any world w in $\mathscr{W}_\mathscr{V}$, $\mathscr{V}(\text{'}\square(\text{P} \lor \sim\text{P})\text{'}, w) = \text{T}$
10. For any world w in $\mathscr{W}_\mathscr{V}$, $\mathscr{V}(\text{'}\sim\Diamond (\text{P \& } \sim\text{P})\text{'}, w) = \text{T}$

Our semantics is democratic: It treats all possible worlds as equals; none is singled out as uniquely actual. This models another prominent idea in modal metaphysics: the thesis of the **indexicality of actuality**. According to this doctrine, no world is actual in an absolute sense; each is actual from a perspective within that world but not from any perspective external to it. For those whose perspective (consciousness?) is rooted in other possible worlds, our world is merely possible, just as their worlds are merely possible for us. Actuality, then, is indexed to worlds (world-relative) in just the way truth is.

The thesis of the indexicality of actuality is much disputed. Logicians who think that actuality is not indexical may incorporate this idea into their semantics by designating exactly one world of each model as actual. But this bifurcates their concept of truth. They have, on the one hand, a notion of nonrelative or actual truth—that is, truth in the actual world—and, on the other, the same relative notion of truth (truth-in-a-world) that we use in defining possibility and necessity. I use the indexical conception of actuality here because it requires only one sort of truth (world-relative) and hence yields a simpler semantics.

Those who find the indexicality of actuality dizzying may appreciate the following analogy. Imagine you are a transcendent God, perusing the actual universe from creation to apocalypse. As you contemplate this grand spectacle, ask yourself: Which moment is the present?

In your omniscience you should see at once that this question is nonsensical. There is a present moment only for creatures situated within time, not for a God who stands beyond it. The present moment for me at noon on my third birthday is different from the present moment for me as I write these words, which is different from the present moment for you as you read this. None of these is *the* present moment, for there is no absolute present.[8] Presentness is indexed to moments of time—that is, relative to temporal position. If I have lived or will live at a given moment, then that moment is present to the temporal part of me that intersects it but not present to other temporal parts of me.

---

[8] This is not idle speculation; the thesis that there is no absolute present is central to Einsteinian relativity theory, which is the source of the best understanding of time available at the moment.

Analogously, according to the understanding that grounds our semantics, there is an actual world only for creatures situated within worlds, not for a God—or a modal semanticist—standing beyond them. A world in which I become a farmer is just as actual for that farmer (i.e., for that possible "part" of me) as the world I am currently experiencing is for the professorial portion of me that inhabits it. Neither of these, nor any other, is *the* actual world in some absolute sense, because actuality is always relative to a perspective within some possible world.[9]

That, at any rate, is one way of understanding the "democratic" semantics presented here: Models do not single out an actual world, because our model theory operates from a perspective beyond worlds from which no world is uniquely actual.

Having relativized truth to worlds, we must make compensatory adjustments in those metatheoretic concepts that are defined in terms of truth. Consistency, for example, is no longer merely truth on some valuation (model), for formulas are no longer simply true or false on a valuation; they are true or false *at a world* on a valuation. Thus we must revise our definitions of metatheoretic concepts as follows:

DEFINITION A formula is **valid** iff it is true in all worlds on all of its valuations.

DEFINITION A formula is **consistent** iff it is true in at least one world on at least one valuation.

DEFINITION A formula is **inconsistent** iff it is not true in any world on any of its valuations.

DEFINITION A formula is **contingent** iff there is a valuation on which it is true in some world and a valuation on which it is not true in some world.

DEFINITION A *set of formulas* is **consistent** iff there is at least one valuation containing a world in which all the formulas in the set are true.

DEFINITION A *set of formulas* is **inconsistent** iff there is no valuation containing a world in which all the formulas in the set are true.

DEFINITION Two formulas are **equivalent** iff they have the same truth value at every world on every valuation of both.

DEFINITION A **counterexample** to a sequent is a valuation containing a world at which its premises are true and its conclusion is false.

---

[9] Here we contradict Leibniz, who thought that actuality *was* something absolute—namely, whatever it was that God added to our possible world in order to create it (ours was, according to Leibniz, the only world God created). For a fuller discussion of the indexicality of actuality, see David Lewis, *On the Plurality of Worlds* (Oxford: Basil Blackwell, 1986), sec. 1.9, pp. 92–96.

DEFINITION A sequent is **valid** iff there is no world in any valuation on which its premises are true and its conclusion is not true.

DEFINITION A sequent is **invalid** iff there is at least one valuation containing a world at which its premises are true and its conclusion is not true.

Using these concepts, we now embark upon a metatheoretic exploration of Leibnizian modal semantics. Our first metatheorem confirms the truism that what is necessary is the case.

METATHEOREM: Any sequent of the form $\Box \Phi \vdash \Phi$ is valid.

PROOF: Suppose for reductio that some sequent of this form is not valid—that is, that there is some formula Φ, some valuation $\mathcal{V}$, and some world w of $\mathcal{V}$ such that $\mathcal{V}(\Box \Phi, w) = T$ but $\mathcal{V}(\Phi, w) \neq T$. Since $\mathcal{V}(\Box \Phi, w) = T$, it follows by valuation rule 11 that $\mathcal{V}(\Phi, u) = T$ for all worlds u in $\mathcal{W}_{\mathcal{V}}$. Hence in particular $\mathcal{V}(\Phi, w) = T$, which contradicts our supposition that $\mathcal{V}(\Phi, w) \neq T$.

Thus we have shown that any sequent of the form $\Box \Phi \vdash \Phi$ is valid. QED

The converse, of course, does not hold. What is need not be necessary. The Earth is populated; but this is not necessarily the case. (It might cease to be the case through any of a variety of catastrophic events, and indeed it might never have happened at all.) To vivify the next metatheorem, think of 'P' as meaning "the Earth is populated," and think of world 1 as the actual world and world 2 as a world in which the Earth is barren.

METATHEOREM: The sequent 'P $\vdash \Box$P' is invalid.

PROOF: Consider the valuation $\mathcal{V}$ whose set $\mathcal{W}_{\mathcal{V}}$ of worlds is $\{1, 2\}$ such that

$$\mathcal{V}(\text{'P'}, 1) = T$$
$$\mathcal{V}(\text{'P'}, 2) = F$$

Now since $\mathcal{V}(\text{'P'}, 2) \neq T$, there is some world u in $\mathcal{W}_{\mathcal{V}}$ (namely, world 2) such that $\mathcal{V}(\text{'P'}, u) \neq T$. Hence by rule 11, $\mathcal{V}(\text{'}\Box\text{P'}, 1) \neq T$. Therefore we have both $\mathcal{V}(\text{'P'}, 1) = T$ and $\mathcal{V}(\text{'}\Box\text{P'}, 1) \neq T$, which constitutes a counterexample. Thus the sequent is invalid. QED

On Leibnizian semantics what is necessary at one world is necessary at all; therefore, what is necessary is necessarily necessary. This is because necessity itself is truth in all worlds, and if something is true in all worlds, then it is true in all worlds that it is true in all worlds. The following metatheorem gives the details:

METATHEOREM: Any sequent of the form $\Box\Phi \vdash \Box\Box\Phi$ is valid.

PROOF: Suppose for reductio that some sequent of this form is not valid—that is, that there is some formula Φ, some valuation $\mathcal{V}$, and some world w of $\mathcal{V}$ such that $\mathcal{V}(\Box\Phi, w) = T$ but $\mathcal{V}(\Box\Box\Phi, w) \neq T$. Since $\mathcal{V}(\Box\Box\Phi, w) \neq T$, it follows by valuation rule 11 that $\mathcal{V}(\Box\Phi, u) \neq T$ for some world u in $\mathcal{W}_{\mathcal{V}}$. But then again by rule 11, for some world x in $\mathcal{W}_{\mathcal{V}}$, $\mathcal{V}(\Phi, x) \neq T$. However, since $\mathcal{V}(\Box\Phi, w) = T$, by rule 11, $\mathcal{V}(\Phi, y) = T$ for all worlds y in $\mathcal{W}_{\mathcal{V}}$ (in particular for world x); and so we have a contradiction.

Consequently, contrary to our supposition, any sequent of the form $\Box\Phi \vdash \Box\Box\Phi$ is valid.   QED

World variables ('w', 'u', 'x', and 'y', for example, in the previous metatheorem) are a pervasive feature of modal metalogic. Each such variable should be introduced with a metalinguistic quantifier to indicate whether it stands for all worlds or just some. Variables standing for a particular world may be repeated later in the proof if there is need to refer to that world again. Early in the previous metatheorem, for example, 'w' is introduced (via existential quantification: "there is a valuation $\mathcal{V}$ containing a world w") to stand for a particular world; later it is employed several times to refer to that same world. To avoid ambiguity, it is best to choose a typographically new variable for each quantification. Thus, for example, in the same proof, 'y' is used to make a universally quantified statement, and 'u' and 'x' to make separate existentially quantified statements.

Our next metatheorem proves one of the two biconditionals expressing the idea that '$\Box$' and '$\Diamond$' are duals. (The other is left as an exercise below.) In some systems one of these two operators is taken as primitive and the other is defined in terms of it using one of these biconditionals.

METATHEOREM: Any formula of the form $\Diamond\Phi \leftrightarrow {\sim}\Box{\sim}\Phi$ is valid.

PROOF: Suppose for reductio that some formula of this form is not valid. That is, for some formula Φ there exists a valuation $\mathcal{V}$ and world w of $\mathcal{V}$ such that $\mathcal{V}(\Diamond\Phi \leftrightarrow {\sim}\Box{\sim}\Phi, w) \neq T$. It follows by valuation rule 8 that either $\mathcal{V}(\Diamond\Phi, w) = T$ and $\mathcal{V}({\sim}\Box{\sim}\Phi, w) \neq T$ or $\mathcal{V}(\Diamond\Phi, w) \neq T$ and $\mathcal{V}({\sim}\Box{\sim}\Phi, w) = T$. We show that either case leads to contradiction.

　　Suppose, first, that $\mathcal{V}(\Diamond\Phi, w) = T$ and $\mathcal{V}({\sim}\Box{\sim}\Phi, w) \neq T$. Since $\mathcal{V}(\Diamond\Phi, w) = T$, by rule 12, $\mathcal{V}(\Phi, u) = T$ for some world u in $\mathcal{W}_{\mathcal{V}}$. Hence by rule 4 there is some world u in

$\mathcal{W}_\mathcal{V}$ at which $\mathcal{V}(\sim\Phi, u) \neq$ T. So by rule 11, $\mathcal{V}(\square\sim\Phi, w) \neq$ T. But we had assumed that $\mathcal{V}(\sim\square\sim\Phi, w) \neq$ T, whence it follows by rule 4 that $\mathcal{V}(\square\sim\Phi, w) =$ T; and so we have a contradiction.

Hence it is not the case that both $\mathcal{V}(\lozenge\Phi, w) =$ T and $\mathcal{V}(\sim\square\sim\Phi, w) \neq$ T.

Suppose now that $\mathcal{V}(\lozenge\Phi, w) \neq$ T and $\mathcal{V}(\sim\square\sim\Phi, w) =$ T. Since $\mathcal{V}(\lozenge\Phi, w) \neq$ T, by rule 12, $\mathcal{V}(\Phi, u) \neq$ T for all worlds u in $\mathcal{W}_\mathcal{V}$. Hence by rule 4 for all worlds u in $\mathcal{W}_\mathcal{V}$, $\mathcal{V}(\sim\Phi, u) =$ T. So by rule 11, $\mathcal{V}(\square\sim\Phi, w) =$ T. But we had assumed that $\mathcal{V}(\sim\square\sim\Phi, w) =$ T, whence it follows by rule 4 that $\mathcal{V}(\square\sim\Phi, w) \neq$ T; and so we have a contradiction.

Therefore it is not the case that both $\mathcal{V}(\lozenge\Phi, w) \neq$ T and $\mathcal{V}(\sim\square\sim\Phi, w) =$ T. Thus, since, as we saw above, it is also not the case that both $\mathcal{V}(\lozenge\Phi, w) =$ T and $\mathcal{V}(\sim\square\sim\Phi, w) \neq$ T, then contrary to what we had concluded above,

$\mathcal{V}(\lozenge\Phi \leftrightarrow \sim\square\sim\Phi, w) =$ T.

Thus we have shown that every formula of the form $\square\Phi \leftrightarrow \sim\lozenge\sim\Phi$ is valid.   QED

One of the most important consequences of the doctrine that names are rigid designators is the thesis expressed in the next metatheorem: the neccessity of identity. Kripke, who popularized this thesis in its contemporary form,[10] illustrates it with the following example. 'Phosphorus' is a Latin name for the morning star; 'Hesperus' is the corresponding name for the evening star. But the morning star and the evening star are in fact the same object, the planet we now call Venus. Hence the statement

Hesperus = Phosphorus

is true. Now if names are rigid designators, then since this statement is true, the object designated by the name 'Hesperus' in the actual world is the very same object designated by 'Hesperus' in any other world, and the object designated by the name 'Phosphorus' in the actual world is the same as the object designated by that name in any other world. Thus in every world both names designate the same object they designate in the actual world: the planet Venus. So 'Hesperus = Phosphorus' is not only true in the actual world but necessarily true.

Yet this conclusion is disturbing. So far as the ancients knew, Hesperus and Phosphorus could have been separate bodies; it would seem, then, that it is not necessary that Hesperus = Phosphorus.

But this reasoning is fallacious. The sense in which it was possible that Hesperus was not Phosphorus is the *epistemic* sense; it was possible *so far as the*

---

[10] *Naming and Necessity* (Cambridge: Harvard University Press, 1972).

ancients knew—that is, compatible with their knowledge—that Hesperus was not Phosphorus. It was not genuinely (i.e., alethically) possible. The planet Venus is necessarily itself; that is, it is itself in any possible world in which it occurs. And if names are rigid designators, then the names 'Hesperus' and 'Phosphorus' both denote Venus in every world in which Venus exists. Hence, given the dual doctrines of transworld identity and rigid designation (both of which are incorporated in our semantics), it is alethically necessary that Hesperus is Phosphorus, despite the fact that it is not epistemically necessary. Keep this example in mind while considering the metatheorem below.

METATHEOREM: Every sequent of the form $\alpha = \beta \vdash \Box\alpha = \beta$ is valid.

PROOF: Suppose for reductio that some sequent of this form is not valid. Then for some names α and β there is a valuation $\mathcal{V}$ and world w of $\mathcal{V}$ such that $\mathcal{V}(\alpha = \beta, w) = T$ and $\mathcal{V}(\Box\alpha = \beta, w) \neq T$. Since $\mathcal{V}(\Box\alpha = \beta, w) \neq T$, by rule 11 there is some world u in $\mathcal{W}_\mathcal{V}$ such that $\mathcal{V}(\alpha = \beta, u) \neq T$. Hence by rule 3, $\mathcal{V}(\alpha) \neq \mathcal{V}(\beta)$. But then again by rule 3, $\mathcal{V}(\alpha = \beta, w) \neq T$, which contradicts what we had said above.

Thus, contrary to our supposition, every sequent of the form $\alpha = \beta \vdash \Box\alpha = \beta$ is valid.   QED

Modal operators interact with the quantifiers of predicate logic in logically interesting ways. The last two metatheorems of this section illustrate this interaction.

METATHEOREM: The sequent '$\exists x Fx \vdash \exists x \Diamond Fx$' is valid.

PROOF: Suppose for reductio that '$\exists x Fx \vdash \exists x \Diamond Fx$' is not valid. Then there is some valuation $\mathcal{V}$ and world w of $\mathcal{V}$ such that $\mathcal{V}('\exists x Fx', w) = T$ and $\mathcal{V}('\exists x \Diamond Fx', w) \neq T$. Since $\mathcal{V}('\exists x Fx', w) = T$, it follows by rule 10 that for some potential name α of some object d in $\mathcal{D}_w$, $\mathcal{V}_{(\alpha,d)}(F\alpha, w) = T$. So for some world u (namely w) in $\mathcal{W}_\mathcal{V}$, $\mathcal{V}_{(\alpha,d)}(F\alpha, u) = T$. But then by rule 12, $\mathcal{V}_{(\alpha,d)}(\Diamond F\alpha, w) = T$. Hence, since d is in $\mathcal{D}_w$, by rule 10, $\mathcal{V}('\exists x \Diamond Fx', w) = T$, contrary to what we had supposed above.

Thus we have established that '$\exists x Fx \vdash \exists x \Diamond Fx$' is valid.   QED

The sequent says that given that something is F, it follows that something (that very same thing, if nothing else) is *possibly* F. This is a consequence of the fact that the actual world, which we may think of as w— and also u—in the proof, is also a possible world, so that whatever actually has a property also possibly has it. In the proof, the object which actually has the property F is object d. Since d has F in w, d has F in some possible world, i.e., possibly has F. It follows, then, that something possibly has F. This enables us to contradict the reductio hypothesis.

Our final metatheorem shows that from the fact that it is possible something is F, it does not follow that the world contains anything which itself is possibly F. Suppose, for example, that we admit that it is (alethically) possible that there are such things as fairies. (That is, there is a possible world containing fairies.) From that it does not follow that there is in the actual world anything which itself is possibly a fairy. The counterexample presented in the following metatheorem is a formal counterpart of this idea. Think of world 1 as the actual world, which (we assume) contains no fairies and world 2 as a world in which fairies exist. (The fairies are objects δ and ε.) Read the predicate 'F' as "is a fairy."

METATHEOREM: The sequent '$\Diamond \exists x Fx \vdash \exists x \Diamond Fx$' is invalid.

PROOF: Consider the following valuation $\mathcal{V}$ whose set $\mathcal{W}_{\mathcal{V}}$ of worlds is $\{1, 2\}$:

World	Domain
1	$\{\alpha, \beta, \chi\}$
2	$\{\alpha, \beta, \chi, \delta, \varepsilon\}$

where

$$\mathcal{V}(\text{'F'}, 1) = \{\ \} \qquad \mathcal{V}(\text{'F'}, 2) = \{\delta, \varepsilon\}$$

Now $\mathcal{V}(\text{'}\Diamond \exists x Fx\text{'}, 1) = T$. For $\mathcal{V}_{('a', \delta)}(\text{'}a\text{'})$—that is, δ—is in the domain of world 2 and $\mathcal{V}_{('a', \delta)} \varepsilon \mathcal{V}_{('a', \delta)}(\text{'F'}, 2)$ so that by rule 1, $\mathcal{V}_{('a', \delta)}(\text{'}Fa\text{'}, 2) = T$. Thus by rule 10, $\mathcal{V}(\text{'}\exists x Fx\text{'}, 2) = T$. And from this it follows by rule 12 that $\mathcal{V}(\text{'}\Diamond \exists x Fx\text{'}, 1) = T$.

However, $\mathcal{V}(\text{'}\exists x \Diamond Fx\text{'}, 1) \neq T$, for there is no member ω of the domain of world 1 which is in the extension of the predicate 'F' in any world. Hence by rule 1 there is no world u in $\mathcal{W}_{\mathcal{V}}$, name v and object ω in the domain of world 1 such that $\mathcal{V}_{(v, \omega)}(Fv, u) = T$. That is, by rule 12 there is no name v and object ω in the domain of world 1 such that $\mathcal{V}_{(v, \omega)}(\Diamond Fv, 1) = T$. So by rule 10, $\mathcal{V}(\text{'}\exists x \Diamond Fx\text{'}, 1) \neq T$.

Thus, since $\mathcal{V}(\text{'}\Diamond \exists x Fx\text{'}, 1) = T$ but $\mathcal{V}(\text{'}\exists x \Diamond Fx\text{'}, 1) \neq T$, we have a counterexample and the sequent is invalid.   QED

Notice that in the proof of this theorem we avoided the question of predication for nonexisting objects (which we have left unsettled). In this case it is the question whether the objects δ and ε, which are fairies in world 2, are also fairies in world 1, where they do not exist. Our valuation rules do not answer this question, but the sequent '$\Diamond \exists x Fx \vdash \exists x \Diamond Fx$' is invalid regardless of how it is answered.

Exercise 11.2.2

Prove the following metatheorems using Leibnizian semantics for modal predicate logic:

1. The sequent '$P \vdash \Diamond P$' is valid.
2. The sequent '$\Diamond P \vdash P$' is invalid.
3. The sequent '$\Diamond (P \& Q) \vdash \Diamond P \& \Diamond Q$' is valid.
4. The sequent '$\Diamond P \& \Diamond Q \vdash \Diamond (P \& Q)$' is invalid.
5. Every sequent of the form $\Phi \vdash \Box \Diamond \Phi$ is valid.
6. Every sequent of the form $\Diamond \Box \Phi \vdash \Box \Phi$ is valid.
7. For any formula Φ, if Φ is a valid formula, then so is $\Box \Phi$.
8. Every formula of the form $\Box \Phi \leftrightarrow \sim \Diamond \sim \Phi$ is valid.
9. Every sequent of the form $\Box \Phi \vdash \Diamond \Phi$ is valid.
10. Every sequent of the form $\Box (\Phi \rightarrow \Psi) \vdash (\Box \Phi \rightarrow \Box \Psi)$ is valid.
11. Every sequent of the form $\Box (\Phi \rightarrow \Psi) \vdash \sim \Diamond (\Phi \& \sim \Psi)$ is valid.
12. Every sequent of the form $\sim \Diamond (\Phi \& \sim \Psi) \vdash \Box (\Phi \rightarrow \Psi)$ is valid.
13. The sequent '$\Box P, P \rightarrow Q \vdash \Box Q$' is invalid.
14. Every formula of the form $\Box \alpha = \alpha$ is valid.
15. Every sequent of the form $\sim \alpha = \beta \vdash \Box \sim \alpha = \beta$ is valid.
16. Every sequent of the form $\Diamond \alpha = \beta \vdash \alpha = \beta$ is valid.
17. The sequent '$\forall x \Box Fx \vdash \Box \forall x Fx$' is invalid.
18. Every sequent of the form $\forall \beta \Box \Phi \vdash \forall \beta \Phi$ is valid.

11.3 A NATURAL MODEL?

Our model theory (semantics) deepens our understanding of the alethic modal operators, though to get interesting results we have had to make a metaphysical assumption or two along the way. Still we have not learned much about possibility per se. The models we have so far considered are all wildly unrealistic—because they contain too few worlds; because these "worlds" are not really worlds at all, but numbers; because their domains are too small; and because we never really said what the objects in the domains were. In this section we seek a more realistic understanding of possibility by correcting these oversimplifications.

In Section 7.2 we noted that, although most of the models we encounter even in predicate logic are likewise unrealistic (being composed of numbers with artificially constructed properties and relations) we can, by giving appropriate meanings to predicates and names, produce a *natural model*. A natural model is a model whose domain consists of the very objects we mean to talk about and whose predicates and names denote exactly the objects of which they are true on their intended meanings. A natural model for geometry, for example, might have a domain of points, lines, and planes. A natural model for subatomic physics might have a domain of particles and fields.[11]

A natural model for modal discourse will consist of a set of possible worlds—genuine worlds, not numbers—each with its own domain of possible objects. And that set of worlds will be infinite, since there is no end to possibilities.

But what *is* a possible world?

Leibniz thought of possible worlds as universes, more or less like our own. But how much like our own? Can a universe contain just one object? There is no obvious reason why not. Can it contain infinitely many? It seems so; in fact, for the century or two preceding Einstein, many astronomers thought that the actual universe really did. We have already said that there is a possible world in which I am a farmer. Is there one in which I am a tree?

This is a question concerning my **essence,** that set of properties which a thing must have in order to be me. What belongs to my essence? Being a professor is pretty clearly *not* essential to me. What about being (biologically) human? There are fairy tales in which people are turned into trees and survive. Do these tales express genuine possibilities? Such questions have no easy answers. Perhaps they have no answers at all.

Philosophers who think that the nature of things determines the answers are **realists** about essence. Realists believe that essences independent of human thought and language exist "out there" awaiting discovery. (Whether or not we *can* discover them is another matter.) Opposed to the realists are **nominalists,** who think that essences—if talk about such things is even intelligible—are not discovered, but created by linguistic practices. Where linguistic practices draw no sharp lines, there are no sharp lines; so if we say increasingly outrageous things about me (I am a farmer, I am a woman, I am a horse, I am a tree, I am a prime number . . .), there may be no definite point at which our talk no longer expresses possibilities. For nominalists, then, it is not to be expected that all questions about possibility have definite answers. (Extreme nominalists deny that talk about possibility is even intelligible.) The realist-nominalist debate has been going on since the Middle Ages; and, though lately the nominalists have seemed to have the edge, the issue is not likely to be settled soon.

To avoid an impasse at this point, we shall invoke a distinction that enables us to sidestep the problem of essence. Whether or not it is **metaphysically possible** (i.e., possible with respect to considerations of essence) for me to be a tree, it *does* seem **logically possible** (i.e., possible in the sense that the idea itself—in this case the idea of my being a tree—embodies no contradiction). Contradiction is perhaps a clearer notion than essence; so let us at least begin by thinking of our natural model as modeling logical, not metaphysical, possibility.

In confining ourselves to logical possibility, we attempt to think of objects as essenceless. What sorts of worlds are possible now? It would seem that a possible

---

[11] These would be models for theories expressed in predicate logic, not necessarily in modal logic.

world could consist of any set of objects possessing any combination of properties and relations whatsoever.

But new issues arise. Some properties or relations are mutually contradictory. It is a kind of contradiction, for example, to think of a thing as both red and colorless. Similarly, it seems to be a contradiction to think of one thing as being larger than a second while the second is also larger than the first. But these contradictions are dependent upon the meanings of certain predicates: 'is red' and 'is colorless' in the first example; 'is larger than' in the second. They do not count as contradictions in predicate logic, which ignores these meanings (see Section 9.4).

If we count them as genuine contradictions, then we must deny, for example, that there are logically possible worlds containing objects that are both red and colorless. If we refuse to count them as genuine contradictions, then we must condone such worlds. In the former case, our notion of logical possibility will be the **informal** concept introduced in Chapter 1. In the latter, we shall say that we are concerned with purely **formal** logical possibility.

Only if we accept the purely formal notion of logical possibility will we count as a logically possible world any set of objects with any assignment whatsoever of extensions to predicates. If we accept the informal notion, we shall be more judicious—rejecting valuations which assign informally contradictory properties or relations to things. We shall still face tough questions, however, about what counts as contradictory. Can a thing be both a tree and identical to me? That is, are the predicates 'is a tree' and 'is identical to John Nolt' contradictory? The problem of essence, in a new guise, looms once again. Only by insisting upon the purely formal notion of logical possibility can we evade it altogether.

In the next chapter the lovely simplicity of Leibnizian semantics will be shattered, so we might as well allow ourselves a brief moment of logical purity now. Let's adopt, then, at least for the remainder of this section, the formal notion of logical possibility.

Now, take any set of sentences you like and formalize them in modal predicate logic. The natural model for these sentences is an infinite array of worlds. Any set whatsoever of actual and/or merely possible objects is a domain for some world in this array. The predicates of the formalization are assigned extensions in each such set in all possible combinations (so that each domain is the domain of many worlds). Among these domains is one consisting of all the objects that actually exist and nothing more. And among the various assignments of extensions to predicates in this domain is one which assigns to them the extensions they actually do have. This assignment on this domain corresponds to the actual world. (Other assignments over the same domain correspond to worlds consisting of the same objects as the actual world does, but differing in the properties those objects have or the ways they are interrelated.) If our discourse contains any names, on the intended interpretation these names name whatever objects they name in the actual world; but they track their objects (i.e., continue to name them) through all the possibilities in which they occur.

11.4 INFERENCE IN LEIBNIZIAN LOGIC

Leibnizian propositional logic retains all the inference rules of classical propositional logic but adds new rules to handle the modal operators. Though we shall examine inferences involving identity, we shall not deal with quantifiers in this section, since the quantifier rules depend on how we resolve the question of predication for nonexisting objects. One reasonable way of resolving this question is to adopt a **free logic**—that is, a logic free of the presupposition that every name always names some existing thing. We shall consider free logics in Section 15.1, and we defer the treatment of modal inferences involving quantification to that section.

The nonquantificational Leibnizian logic that we will explore in this section adds to the rules of classical propositional logic and the classical rules for identity seven new inference rules (the names of most are traditional and of various origins):

Duality (DUAL)   From either of $\Diamond\Phi$ and $\sim\Box\sim\Phi$, infer the other; from either of $\Box\Phi$ and $\sim\Diamond\sim\Phi$, infer the other.

K rule (K)   From $\Box(\Phi \rightarrow \Psi)$, infer $(\Box\Phi \rightarrow \Box\Psi)$.

T rule (T)   From $\Box\Phi$, infer Φ.

S4 rule (S4)   From $\Box\Phi$, infer $\Box\Box\Phi$.

Brouwer rule (B)   From Φ, infer $\Box\Diamond\Phi$.

Necessitation (N)   If Φ has previously been proved as a theorem, then any formula of the form $\Box\Phi$ may be introduced at any line of a proof.

Necessity of identity ($\Box$=)   From $\alpha = \beta$, infer $\Box\alpha = \beta$.

It is not difficult to show that every instance of each of these rules is valid on a Leibnizian semantics—and indeed we did this for some of them in Section 11.2 (the rest were left as exercises).

The necessitation rule differs from the others in that it uses no premises but refers, rather, to theorems established by previous proofs. A theorem is a valid formula, a formula true in all worlds on all valuations. Therefore, if Φ is a theorem, $\Box\Phi$ and any formula of the form $\Box\Phi$ may be asserted anywhere in a proof without further assumptions. When we use the rule of necessitation, we annotate it by writing its abbreviation 'N' to the right of the introduced formula, followed by the previously proved theorem or axiom schema employed.

These seven inference rules, together with the rules of classical propositional logic and the identity rules =I and =E, constitute a system of inference that is sound and complete with respect to a Leibnizian semantics for the modal propositional logic with identity—but to show this is beyond our scope. The purely propositional rules (i.e., the ones other than =I, ≠E, and □=) comprise a logic known as S5.[12] This section is largely an exploration of the valid inferential patterns of S5.

We begin by proving the sequent 'P ⊢ ◊ P':

1. P		A
2.	□~P	H (for ~I)
3.	~P	2 T
4.	P & ~P	1, 3 &I
5. ~□~P		2–4 ~I
6. ◊ P		5 DUAL

The strategy is an indirect proof. Recognizing initially that ' ◊ P' is interchangeable with '~□~P', we hypothesize '□~P' for reductio. Using the T rule, the contradiction is obtained almost immediately. This yields '~□~P', which is converted into ' ◊ P' by DUAL at line 6.

The rules N and K are often used together to obtain modalized versions of various theorems and rules. The sequent '□(P & Q) ⊢ □P', for example, which is a modalized version of &E, is proved by using N and then K:

1. □(P & Q)	A
2. □((P & Q) → P)	N ((P & Q) → P)[13]
3. □(P & Q) → □P	2 K
4. □P	1, 3 →E

A similar but more sophisticated strategy utilizing N and K yields sequents involving possibility. Our next example is a proof of ' ◊ P ⊢ ◊ (P ∨ Q)', a modalized version of ∨I. Here we apply N to the theorem '~(P ∨ Q) → ~P', the contrapositive of 'P → (P ∨ Q)', which in effect expresses ∨I. (This strategy of applying N to contraposed nonmodal versions of the modal sequent we want to prove is typical when the modality involved is possibility.)

1. ◊ P	A
2. □(~(P ∨ Q) → ~P)	N (~(P ∨ Q) → ~P)[14]
3. □~(P ∨ Q) → □~P	2 K
4. ~□~P	1 DUAL
5. ~□~(P ∨ Q)	3, 4 MT
6. ◊ (P ∨ Q)	5 DUAL

Note the use of the derived rule modus tollens at line 5. Derived rules for classical propositional logic (see Section 4.4) are all available in Leibnizian modal logic.

N and K are used together once again in this derivation of the theorem '⊢ ◊ ~P → ~□P':

---

12 The name originates with the logician C. I. Lewis, whose pioneering work on modal logic dates from the first few decades of the twentieth century. Lewis explored a number of modal systems, which he christened with such unmemorable labels. Inexplicably, the labels stuck.

13 This theorem is problem 2 of Exercise 4.4.2.

14 See problem 6 of Exercise 4.4.2.

1.	◇~P	H (for →I)
2.	~□~~P	1 DUAL
3.	□(P → ~~P)	N (P → ~~P)[15]
4.	□P → □~~P	3 K
5.	~□P	2, 4 MT
6.	◇~P → ~□P	1–5 →I

However, a very different strategy may be used to prove the related theorem '⊢ □~P → ~◇P':

1.	□~P		H (for →I)
2.		◇P	H (for ~I)
3.		~□~P	2 DUAL
4.		□~P & ~□~P	1, 3 &I
5.	~◇P		2–4 ~I
6.	□~P → ~◇P		1–5 →I

Here, after hypothesizing the theorem's antecedent for conditional proof, we employ an indirect proof, hypothesizing '◇P' for reductio at line 2. The use of DUAL at line 3 immediately provides a contradiction, which is recorded at line 4, and the conclusion follows by easy steps of ~I and →I at lines 5 and 6.

The following proof of the sequent '□(P → Q) ⊢ □~Q → □~P', which is a kind of modalized version of modus tollens, displays further uses of N and K:

1.	□(P → Q)	A
2.	□((P → Q) → (~Q → ~P))	N ((P → Q) → (~Q → ~P))
3.	□(P → Q) → □(~Q → ~P)	2 K
4.	□(~Q → ~P)	1, 3 →E
5.	□~Q → □~P	4 K

The necessitation rule N is used at line 2 with the theorem '⊢ (P → Q) → (~Q → ~P)', which was proved in Section 4.4. In the use of K at line 3, Φ is 'P → Q' and Ψ is '~Q → ~P', but at line 5 Φ is '~Q' and Ψ is '~P'.

The B rule is used in the following proof of '◇□P ⊢ P':

1.	◇□P		A
2.		~P	H (for ~I)
3.		□◇~P	2 B
4.		□(◇~P → ~□P)	N (◇~P → ~□P)
5.		□◇~P → □~□P	4 K
6.		~□~□P	1 DUAL
7.		~□◇~P	5, 6 MT
8.		□◇~P & ~□◇~P	3, 7 &I
9.	~~P		2–8 ~I
10.	P		9 ~E

---

[15] See problem 3 of Exercise 4.4.2.

Note the use of N with the previously proved modal theorem '◇~P → ~□P' at line 4.

We next prove the theorem '⊢ ◇◇P → ◇P', using the S4 rule:

1.	◇◇P	H (for →I)
2.	□~P	H (for ~I)
3.	□□~P	2 S4
4.	□(□~P → ~◇P)	N (□~P → ~◇P)
5.	□□~P → □~◇P	4 K
6.	□~◇P	3, 5 →E
7.	~□~◇P	1 DUAL
8.	□~◇P & ~□~◇P	6, 7 &I
9.	~□~P	2–8 ~I
10.	◇P	9 DUAL
11.	◇◇P → ◇P	1–10 →I

This theorem can easily be strengthened to the biconditional '◇P ↔ ◇◇P', using the previously proved sequent 'P ⊢ ◇P' as a derived rule. This biconditional shows that repetition of possibility operators is in effect redundant in Leibnizian logic. The same can be shown for necessity operators—that is, '⊢ □P ↔ □□P', but the proof is left as an exercise.

As in propositional and predicate logic, we may use derived rules. We will not, however, bother to name them, since few have widely used names. Instead, we simply list the previously proved sequent to the right, together with the line numbers of the premises (if any) that are instances of the previously proved sequent's premises. (Rules derived from theorems have no premises, and we cite no lines for them.) This proof of '□(P → Q) ⊢ ◇P → ◇Q' uses the previously proved sequent '□(P → Q) ⊢ □~Q → □~P' as a derived rule at line 4:

1.	□(P → Q)	A
2.	◇P	H (for →I)
3.	□~Q	H (for ~I)
4.	□~Q → □~P	1 □(P → Q) ⊢ □~Q → □~P
5.	□~P	3, 4 →E
6.	~□~P	2 DUAL
7.	□~P & ~□~P	5, 6 &I
8.	~□~Q	3–7 ~I
9.	◇Q	8 DUAL
10.	◇P → ◇Q	2–9 →I

Notice the use of indirect proof with the duality rule to obtain '◇Q'.

As I pointed out in Section 4.4, proof of a sequent establishes the validity of any formula that shares that sequent's form. Thus, when we use a sequent as a derived rule, we may use any instance of it. The following proof of the sequent '~a = b ⊢ □~a = b' utilizes the previously proved sequent '□(P → Q) ⊢ ◇P → ◇Q' as a derived rule at line 5. This sequent is used, however, in the form '□(a = b → □a = b) ⊢ ◇a = b → ◇□a = b', where 'a = b' replaces 'P' and '□a = b' replaces 'Q'.

Similarly, the previously proved sequent '◇□P ⊢ P' is used in the form '◇□a = b ⊢ a = b' at line 7.

1.	~a = b	A
2.	~□~a = b	H (for ~I)
3.	◇a = b	2 DUAL
4.	□(a = b → □a = b)	N (a = b → □a = b)
5.	◇a = b → ◇□a = b	4 □(P → Q) ⊢ ◇P → ◇Q
6.	◇□a = b	3, 5 →E
7.	a = b	6 ◇□P ⊢ P
8.	a = b & ~a = b	1, 7 &I
9.	~~□~a = b	2–8 ~I
10.	□~a = b	9 ~E

At line 4 we use the necessitation rule with the theorem '⊢ a = b → □a = b'. We didn't actually prove this theorem, but its proof is trivial, given the □ = rule, and is left for an exercise below.

This proof shows that not only is identity necessary as the □ = axiom schema asserts, but also nonidentity is necessary—a result fully appropriate in light of the semantics of rigid designation.

Our next result establishes that whatever is possible is necessarily possible—that is, (on Leibnizian semantics) possible with respect to any world. The sequent expressing this idea is '◇P ⊢ □◇P':

1.	◇P	A
2.	□◇◇P	1 B
3.	□(◇◇P → ◇P)	N (◇◇P → ◇P)
4.	□◇◇P → □◇P	3 K
5.	□◇P	2, 4 →E

And finally we show that whatever is even possibly necessary is necessary. That is, the sequent '◇□P ⊢ □P' is provable:

1.	◇□P	A
2.	□(◇□P → P)	N (◇□P → P)
3.	□◇□P → □P	2 K
4.	□◇□P	1 ◇P ⊢ □◇P
5.	□P	3, 4 →E

Exercise 11.4

Prove the following sequents:

1. ⊢ a = b → □a = b
2. □P ⊢ □(P ∨ Q)
3. ⊢ □~~P → □P
4. ◇(P & Q) ⊢ ◇P
5. □Q ⊢ □(P → Q)

6. $\sim \Diamond P \vdash \Box(P \rightarrow Q)$
7. $\vdash \Box P \leftrightarrow \Box \Box P$
8. $\vdash \sim \Diamond (P \mathbin{\&} \sim P)$
9. $\Box P, \Box Q \vdash \Box(P \mathbin{\&} Q)$
10. $\Box P \vdash \Box\Box\Box P$

CHAPTER **12**

KRIPKEAN MODAL LOGIC

12.1 KRIPKEAN SEMANTICS

There is among modal logicians a modest consensus that Leibnizian semantics accurately characterizes logical possibility, in both its formal and informal variants. As we saw in Section 11.3, however, this does not tell us all we would like to know about informal logical possibility, because Leibnizian semantics does not specify which worlds to rule out as embodying informal contradictions. (Is the concept of a dimensionless blue point, for example, contradictory? What about the concept of a God-fearing atheist? The concept of a largest number?) Still, the semantic rules of Leibnizian logic as laid out in Section 11.2 and the inference rules of Section 11.4 do arguably express correct principles of both formal and informal logical possibility.

But logical possibility, whether formal or informal, is wildly permissive. Things that are logically possible need not be metaphysically possible (i.e., possible when we take essence into account). And things that are metaphysically possible need not be physically possible (i.e., possible when we take the laws of physics into account). It seems both logically and metaphysically possible, for example, to accelerate an object to speeds greater than the speed of light. But this is not physically possible. Moreover, what is physically possible need not be practically possible (i.e., possible when we take actual constraints into account). It is physically

334

possible to destroy all weapons of war, but it may not (unfortunately) be practically possible. Logical, metaphysical, physical, and practical possibility are all forms or degrees of alethic possibility. And there are, no doubt, other forms of alethic possibility as well. Furthermore there are, as we saw earlier, various non-alethic forms of "possibility": epistemic possibility, moral permissibility, temporal possibility, and so on. Does Leibnizian semantics accurately characterize them all—or do some modalities require a different semantics?

Consider the metatheorem, proved in Section 11.2, that any sequent of the form $\Box\Phi \vdash \Phi$ is valid. This seems right for all forms of alethic possibility. What is logically or metaphysically or physically or practically necessary is in fact the case. There are corresponding principles in epistemic, temporal, and deontic logic:

Modality	Principle	Meaning
Epistemic	$sK\Phi \vdash \Phi$	s knows that Φ; so Φ
Temporal	$H\Phi \vdash \Phi$	It has always been the case that Φ; so Φ
Deontic	$O\Phi \vdash \Phi$	It is obligatory that Φ; so Φ

The first is likewise valid. But the temporal and deontic principles are invalid. What was may be no longer, and what ought to be often isn't. Both temporal logic and deontic logic, then, have non-Leibnizian semantics.

Or, to take a more subtle example, consider sequents of the form $\Box\Phi \vdash \Box\Box\Phi$, which are also valid on a Leibnizian semantics. Some variants of this principle in different modalities are given below:

Modality	Principle	Meaning
Alethic	$\Box\Phi \vdash \Box\Box\Phi$	It is necessary that Φ; so it is necessarily necessary that Φ[1]
Epistemic	$sK\Phi \vdash sKsK\Phi$	s knows that Φ; so s knows that s knows that Φ
Temporal	$H\Phi \vdash HH\Phi$	It has always been the case that Φ; so it has always been the case that it has always been the case that Φ
Deontic	$O\Phi \vdash OO\Phi$	It is obligatory that Φ; so it is obligatory that it is obligatory that Φ

---

[1] Necessity can be understood here in any of the various alethic senses—logical, metaphysical, physical, practical, and so on.

The temporal and alethic versions are plausible, perhaps; but the epistemic and deontic versions are dubious. The epistemic version expresses a long-disputed principle in epistemology; it seems, for example, to rule out unconscious knowledge. And the deontic version expresses a kind of moral absolutism: The fact that something ought to be the case is not simply a (morally) contingent product of individual choice or cultural norms, but is itself morally necessary. These are controversial theses. We should suspect a semantics that validates them.

In fact, Leibnizian semantics seems inadequate even for some forms of alethic modality. Consider the sequent 'P ⊢ □ ◇ P' with respect to physical possibility. (This sequent is valid given a Leibnizian semantics; see problem 5 of Exercise 11.2.2.)

What does it mean for something to be physically possible or physically necessary? Presumably, a thing is physically possible if it obeys the laws of physics and physically necessary if it is required by those laws. But are the laws of physics the same in all worlds? Many philosophers of science believe that they are just the regularities that happen to hold in a given world. Thus in a more regular world there would be more laws of physics, in a less regular world fewer. If so, then the laws of physics—and physical possibility—are world-relative.[2] Leibnizian semantics treats possibility as absolute; all worlds are possible from the point of view of each. But our present reflections suggest that physical possibility, at least, is world-relative.

To illustrate, imagine a world, world 2, in which there are more physical laws than in the actual world, which we shall call world 1. In world 2, not only do all of *our* physical laws hold, but in addition it is a law that all planets travel in circular orbits. (Perhaps some novel force accounts for this.) Now in our universe, planets move in either elliptical or circular orbits. Thus in world 1 it is physically possible for planets to move in elliptical orbits (since some do), but in world 2 planets can move only in circular orbits. Since world 2 obeys all the physical laws of world 1, what happens in world 2, and indeed world 2 itself, is physically possible relative to world 1. But the converse is not true. Because what happens in world 1 violates a physical law of world 2 (namely, that planets move only in circles), world 1 is not possible relative to world 2. Thus the very possibility of worlds themselves seems to be a world-relative matter!

Kripkean semantics takes the world-relativity of possibility seriously. Within Kripkean semantics, various patterns of world-relativity correspond to different logics, and this variability enables the semantics to model a surprising variety of modal conceptions.

The fundamental notion of Kripkean semantics is the concept of **relative possibility** (which is also called **alternativeness** or **accessibility**). Relative possibility is the relation which holds between worlds x and y just in case y is possible relative to x. The letter '$\mathcal{R}$' is customarily used to express this relation in the metatheory. Thus we write

---

[2] I should confess that virtually everything I am saying here is controversial. But I have suppressed objections, not because I am confident that what I am saying here is true, but because I am trying to trace a line of thought that makes the transition from Leibnizian to Kripkean semantics intelligible. The metaphysics I spin out in the process should be regarded as illustration, not as gospel.

$x \mathcal{R} y$

to mean "*y* is possible relative to *x*" or "*y* is an alternative to *x*" or "*y* is accessible from *x*." (These are all different ways of saying the same thing.) So in the example just discussed it is true that $1\mathcal{R}2$ ("world 2 is possible relative to world 1"), but it is not true that $2\mathcal{R}1$. Each world is also possible relative to itself, since each obeys the laws which hold within it. Hence we have $1\mathcal{R}1$ and $2\mathcal{R}2$. The structure of this two-world model is represented in the following diagram, where each circle stands for a world and an arrow indicates that the world it points to is possible relative to the world it leaves:

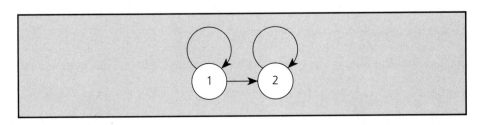

A Kripkean model is in most respects like a Leibnizian model, but it contains in addition a specification of the relation $\mathcal{R}$—that is, of which worlds are possible relative to which. This is given by defining the set of pairs of the form $<x, y>$ where *y* is possible relative to *x*. In the example above, for instance, $\mathcal{R}$ is the set

$$\{<1, 2>, <1, 1>, <2, 2>\}$$

The definition of a Kripkean model mimics that of a Leibnizian model, with the addition of the requirement that $\mathcal{R}$ be defined (item 2 below):

DEFINITION A **Kripkean valuation** or **Kripkean model** $\mathcal{V}$ for a formula or set of formulas of modal predicate logic consists of the following:

  1. A nonempty set $\mathcal{W}_{\mathcal{V}}$ of objects, called the **worlds** of $\mathcal{V}$.
  2. A relation $\mathcal{R}$, consisting of a set of pairs of worlds from $\mathcal{W}_{\mathcal{V}}$.
  3. For each world *w* in $\mathcal{W}_{\mathcal{V}}$ a nonempty set $\mathcal{D}_w$ of objects, called the **domain** of *w*.
  4. For each name or nonidentity predicate σ of that formula or set of formulas, an extension $\mathcal{V}(\sigma)$ (if σ is a name) or $\mathcal{V}(\sigma, w)$ (if σ is a predicate and *w* a world in $\mathcal{W}_{\mathcal{V}}$) as follows:
      i.   If σ is a name, then $\mathcal{V}(\sigma)$ is a member of the domain of at least one world.
      ii. If σ is a zero-place predicate (sentence letter), $\mathcal{V}(\sigma, w)$ is one (but not both) of the values T or F.
      iii. If σ is a one-place predicate, $\mathcal{V}(\sigma, w)$ is a set of members of $\mathcal{D}_w$.
      iv. If σ is an *n*-place predicate ($n > 1$), $\mathcal{V}(\sigma, w)$ is a set of ordered *n*-tuples of members of $\mathcal{D}_w$.

The addition of $\mathscr{R}$ brings with it a slight but significant change in the valuation rules for '□' and '◇'. Necessity at a world w is no longer simply truth in all worlds, but truth in all worlds that are possible *relative to w*. Likewise, possibility in w is truth in at least one world that is possible *relative to w*. Thus, instead of the valuation rules 11 and 12 for Leibnizian semantics (Section 11.2), Kripkean semantics has the modified rules:

11' $\mathscr{V}(\Box\Phi, w) = T$ iff for all worlds u such that $w\mathscr{R}u$, $\mathscr{V}(\Phi, u) = T$;
  $\mathscr{V}(\Box\Phi, w) = F$ iff for some world u, $w\mathscr{R}u$ and $\mathscr{V}(\Phi, u) \neq T$.
12' $\mathscr{V}(\Diamond\Phi, w) = T$ iff for some world u, $w\mathscr{R}u$ and $\mathscr{V}(\Phi, u) = T$;
  $\mathscr{V}(\Diamond\Phi, w) = F$ iff for all worlds u such that $w\mathscr{R}u$, $\mathscr{V}(\Phi, u) \neq T$.

No other valuation rules are changed.

Consider now a Kripkean model for propositional logic (which allows us to ignore the domains of the worlds), using the sentence letter 'P', which we interpret to mean "Planets move in elliptical orbits." Let $\mathscr{W}_{\mathscr{V}}$ be the set $\{1, 2\}$ and $\mathscr{R}$ be the set

$$\{<1, 2>, <1, 1>, <2, 2>\}$$

as mentioned and diagramed in the example recently discussed. Suppose further that

$$\mathscr{V}(\text{'P'}, 1) = T$$
$$\mathscr{V}(\text{'P'}, 2) = F$$

as in that example. (That is, planets move in elliptical orbits in world 1 but not in world 2.) Now the sequent 'P ⊢ □◇P', which was valid on Leibnizian semantics, is invalid on this Kripkean model. For $\mathscr{V}(\text{'P'}, 1) = T$, but $\mathscr{V}(\text{'}\Box\Diamond P\text{'}, 1) \neq T$. That is, world 1 provides a counterexample.

We can see that $\mathscr{V}(\text{'}\Box\Diamond P\text{'}, 1) \neq T$ as follows. Note first that the only world in $\mathscr{W}_{\mathscr{V}}$ accessible from world 2 is 2 itself; in other words, the only world u in $\mathscr{W}_{\mathscr{V}}$ such that $2\mathscr{R}u$ is world 2. Moreover, $\mathscr{V}(\text{'P'}, 2) \neq T$. Hence for all worlds u in $\mathscr{W}_{\mathscr{V}}$ such that $2\mathscr{R}u$, $\mathscr{V}(\text{'P'}, u) \neq T$. So by rule 12', $\mathscr{V}(\text{'}\Diamond P\text{'}, 2) \neq T$. Therefore, since $1\mathscr{R}2$, there is some world x in $\mathscr{W}_{\mathscr{V}}$ (namely, world 2) such that $1\mathscr{R}x$ and $\mathscr{V}(\text{'}\Diamond P\text{'}, x) \neq T$. It follows by rule 11' that $\mathscr{V}(\text{'}\Box\Diamond P\text{'}, 1) \neq T$. We restate this finding as a formal metatheorem:

> **METATHEOREM:** The sequent 'P ⊢ □◇P' is not valid on Kripkean semantics.
>
> **PROOF:** As given above.

Moreover, neither of the other sequents mentioned in this section—'□P ⊢ P' and '□P ⊢ □□P'—is valid, either. Let's take '□P ⊢ P' first.

METATHEOREM: The sequent '□P ⊢ P' is not valid on Kripkean semantics.

PROOF: Consider the following Kripkean model for propositional logic. Let the set $\mathcal{W}$ of worlds be {1, 2} and the accessibility relation $\mathcal{R}$ be the set {<1, 2>, <2, 2>}, and let

$$\mathcal{V}(\text{'P'}, 1) = F$$
$$\mathcal{V}(\text{'P'}, 2) = T$$

Now $\mathcal{V}(\text{'P'}, 2) = T$ and 2 is the only world possible relative to 1; that is, 2 is the only world u such that $1\mathcal{R}u$. Hence for all worlds u such that $1\mathcal{R}u$, $\mathcal{V}(\text{'P'}, u) = T$. Therefore by rule 11', $\mathcal{V}(\text{'□P'}, 1) = T$. But $\mathcal{V}(\text{'P'}, 1)$ ≠ T. Therefore '□P ⊢ P' is not valid on Kripkean semantics.   QED

This result poses a problem. Intuitively, '□P ⊢ P' is (or ought to be) valid on the alethic and epistemic interpretations. But it should not come out valid on the deontic interpretation (which, to distinguish it from the other interpretations, we usually write as 'OP ⊢ P') or on the temporal interpretation discussed above.

The reasoning for the deontic interpretation is straightforward. Think of world 1 as the actual world, world 2 as a morally perfect world, and 'P' as expressing the proposition "Everything is morally perfect." Then, of course, 'P' is true in world 2 but not in world 1. Moreover, think of $\mathcal{R}$ as expressing the relation of permissibility or moral possibility. Now world 2 is morally permissible, both relative to itself and relative to world 1 (because what is morally perfect is surely morally permissible!). But world 1 is not morally permissible, either relative to itself or relative to world 2, because all kinds of bad (i.e., morally impermissible) things go on in it. Our model, then, looks like this:

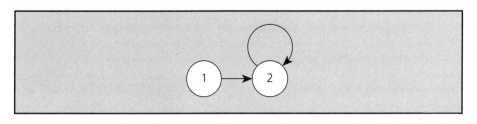

Now since in this model every world that is morally permissible relative to the actual world is morally perfect (since there is, in the model, just one such world, world 2), it follows (by the semantics for '□', i.e., formally, rule 11') that it ought to be the case in world 1 that everything is morally perfect, even though that is not the case in world 1. Thus, when we interpret '□' as "it ought to be the case that,"[3] we can see how '□P ⊢ P' can be invalid. Kripkean semantics, then, seems

---

[3] We could, of course, have used the symbol 'O' instead of '□' to express the deontic reading, but we are considering several different readings simultaneously here.

right for the deontic interpretation, but wrong for the epistemic, temporal, and alethic interpretations.

But in fact Kripkean semantics is applicable to the other interpretations, as well, provided that we are willing to relativize our concept of validity. The key to this new conception can be found by reexamining the proof from an alethic viewpoint. From this viewpoint the proof is just wrong. Surely, if it is alethically necessary that *P*, then *P*. But where is the mistake?

It lies, from the alethic point of view, in the specification of $\mathcal{R}$. The alethic sense of possibility requires that *every* world be possible relative to itself, for what is true in a world is certainly alethically possible in that same world. But the relation $\mathcal{R}$ used in the proof does not hold between world 1 and itself. The model is therefore defective from an alethic point of view.

To represent the alethic intepretation, we must insist that $\mathcal{R}$ be **reflexive**— that each world in the set $\mathcal{W}_\mathcal{V}$ of worlds be possible relative to itself. Thus the model given above as a counterexample is not legitimate for the alethic interpretation. *The only admissible models—the only models that count—for the alethic interpretation are models whose accessibility relation is reflexive.* This is also true for the epistemic modalities, but not for the deontic or temporal ones.

This suggests the following strategy: Each of the various modalities is to be associated with a particular set of admissible models, that set being defined by certain restrictions on the relation $\mathcal{R}$. Validity, then, for a sequent expressing a given modality is the lack of a counterexample among *admissible* models for the particular sorts of modal operators it contains. Other semantic notions (consistency, equivalence, and the like) will likewise be defined relative to this set of admissible models, not the full range of Kripkean models. In this way we can custom-craft a different semantics for each of the various modalities.

Let us, then, require admissible models for alethic or epistemic modalities, but not for the deontic or temporal ones, to be reflexive. Then we must redefine the notion of a valid sequent as follows:

> A sequent is **valid relative to a given set of models (valuations)** iff there is no model in that set containing a world in which the sequent's premises are true and its conclusion is not true.

To say that a sequent is valid relative to Kripkean semantics in general is to say that it has no counterexample in any Kripkean model, regardless of how $\mathcal{R}$ is structured.

With this new relativized notion of validity, we can now prove that all sequents of the form $\Box\Phi \vdash \Phi$ *are* valid—relative to the class of reflexive models:

METATHEOREM: All sequents of the form $\Box\Phi \vdash \Phi$ are valid relative to the set of models whose accessibility relation is reflexive.

PROOF: Suppose for reductio that this is not the case—that is, for some formula Φ there exists a valuation $\mathcal{V}$ whose accessibility relation $\mathcal{R}$ is reflexive and some world w of $\mathcal{V}$ such that $\mathcal{V}(\Box\Phi, w)$ = T and $\mathcal{V}(\Phi, w) \neq$ T. Now since $\mathcal{V}(\Box\Phi, w)$ = T, by rule 11' $\mathcal{V}(\Phi, u)$ = T, for every world u such that $w\mathcal{R}u$. But since $\mathcal{R}$ is reflexive, $w\mathcal{R}w$. Therefore $\mathcal{V}(\Phi, w)$ = T, which contradicts what we had concluded above.

Thus we have shown that all sequents of the form $\Box\Phi \vdash \Phi$ are valid relative to the set of models whose accessibility relation is reflexive. QED

We may say, then, that all sequents of the form $\Box\Phi \vdash \Phi$ are valid when '$\Box$' is interpreted as an alethic or epistemic operator, but not if we interpret it as a deontic or temporal operator of the sort indicated earlier. But the validity of all sequents of this form is the same thing as the validity of the T rule introduced in Section 11.4. Thus we may conclude that the T rule is valid for some modalities but not for others.

It is the reflexivity of the accessibility relation that guarantees that sequents of the form $\Box\Phi \vdash \Phi$ are valid. Such sequents were valid as a matter of course on Leibnizian semantics, where it is assumed that each world is possible relative to each, and hence that each world is possible relative to itself. Accessibility in Leibnizian semantics is therefore automatically reflexive. But Kripkean semantics licenses accessibility relations that do not link each world to each, thus grounding the construction of logics weaker in various respects than Leibnizian logic.

Just as the reflexivity of $\mathcal{R}$ guarantees the validity of $\Box\Phi \vdash \Phi$, so other requirements on $\mathcal{R}$ correspond to other modal principles. Principles which hold for all Kripkean models apply to all the logics encompassed by Kripkean semantics. Those which hold only in restricted classes of Kripkean models (such as models in which $\mathcal{R}$ is reflexive) are applicable to some intepretations of the modal operators but not to others.

We noted above that the principle $\Box\Phi \vdash \Box\Box\Phi$ seems plausible for temporal and alethic modalities, but questionable for deontic and epistemic ones. This principle is in fact just the S4 rule discussed in Section 11.4. It is valid on Leibnizian semantics, as we saw in the previous chapter, but it is invalid on Kripkean semantics, since, for example, the instance '$\Box P \vdash \Box\Box P$' is invalid:

METATHEOREM: The sequent '$\Box P \vdash \Box\Box P$' is not valid on Kripkean semantics.

PROOF: Consider the following Kripkean model for propositional logic. Let the set $\mathcal{W}$ of worlds be {1, 2, 3} and the accessibility relation $\mathcal{R}$ be the set {<1, 2>, <2, 3>}, and let

$\mathcal{V}$('P', 1) = T
$\mathcal{V}$('P', 2) = T
$\mathcal{V}$('P', 3) = F

> Now $\mathcal{V}$('P', 2) = T and 2 is the only world possible relative to 1; that is,
> 2 is the only world u such that $1\mathcal{R}u$. Hence for all worlds u such that
> $1\mathcal{R}u$, $\mathcal{V}$('P', u) = T. Therefore by rule 11', $\mathcal{V}$('□P', 1) = T. However, since
> $2\mathcal{R}3$ and $\mathcal{V}$('P', 3) ≠ T, by rule 11', $\mathcal{V}$('□P', 2) ≠ T. And since $1\mathcal{R}2$ and
> $\mathcal{V}$('□P', 2) ≠ T, again by rule 11', $\mathcal{V}$('□□P', 1) ≠ T. Therefore, since
> $\mathcal{V}$('□P', 1) = T and $\mathcal{V}$('□□P', 1) ≠ T, we have a counterexample, and so
> '□P ⊢ □□P' is not valid on Kripkean semantics.   QED

Yet the S4 rule *is* valid relative to models whose accessibility relation is transitive.
The relation $\mathcal{R}$ is **transitive** if and only if for any worlds x, y, and z, if $x\mathcal{R}y$ and
$y\mathcal{R}z$, then $x\mathcal{R}z$. Think of this in relation to physical possibility. We said that a
world y is physically possible relative to a world x if and only if y obeys the same
physical laws (and perhaps some additional physical laws as well). That is,

$x\mathcal{R}y$ if and only if y obeys all the physical laws that hold in x.

Now clearly if y obeys all the laws that hold in x and z obeys all the laws that hold
in y, then z obeys all the laws that hold in x. That is, if $x\mathcal{R}y$ and $y\mathcal{R}z$, then $x\mathcal{R}z$.
So the accessibility relation for physical possibility is transitive. The next meta-
theorem shows how we get from this fact about the accessibility relation to the
conclusion that all sequents of the form $□\Phi ⊢ □□\Phi$ are valid, where '□' is interpreted
as physical necessity.

> **METATHEOREM:** All sequents of the form $□\Phi ⊢ □□\Phi$ are valid rela-
> tive to the set of models whose accessibility relation is transitive.
>
> **PROOF:** Suppose for reductio that this is not the case—that is, for some
> formula Φ there exists a valuation $\mathcal{V}$ whose accessibility rela-
> tion $\mathcal{R}$ is transitive and some world x of $\mathcal{V}$ such that $\mathcal{V}(□\Phi, x)$
> = T and $\mathcal{V}(□□\Phi, x)$ ≠ T. Now since $\mathcal{V}(□\Phi, x)$ = T, by rule 11',
> $\mathcal{V}(\Phi, u)$ = T for every world u such that $x\mathcal{R}u$. But since $\mathcal{V}(□□\Phi,$
> $x)$ ≠ T, by rule 11' there is a world y such that $x\mathcal{R}y$ and $\mathcal{V}(□\Phi,$
> $y)$ ≠ T. And since $\mathcal{V}(□\Phi, y)$ ≠ T, again by rule 11' there is a
> world z such that $y\mathcal{R}z$ and $\mathcal{V}(\Phi, z)$ ≠ T. Now since $x\mathcal{R}y$ and
> $y\mathcal{R}z$, and $\mathcal{R}$ is transitive, it follows that $x\mathcal{R}z$. But we saw above
> that $\mathcal{V}(\Phi, u)$ = T for every world u such that $x\mathcal{R}u$. So in partic-
> ular $\mathcal{V}(\Phi, z)$ = T, contrary to what we just concluded.
> Thus all sequents of the form $□\Phi ⊢ □□\Phi$ are valid relative to the set of
> models whose accessibility relation is transitive.   QED

For our last example, we return to the principle $\Phi ⊢ □◇\Phi$, which was valid
on Leibnizian semantics (indeed, it is just the B rule introduced in Section 11.4)
but seemed invalid for physical possibility. (The fact that planets move in elliptical
orbits does not mean that it is *necessarily possible* that planets move in elliptical

orbits, for there are physically possible worlds in which planetary orbits are necessarily circular and hence in which elliptical orbits are impossible.) The property of $\mathcal{R}$ that would make this sequent valid is symmetry. $\mathcal{R}$ is **symmetric** if and only if for any worlds x and y, if $x\mathcal{R}y$, then $y\mathcal{R}x$. The accessibility relation for physical possibility is not symmetric, since a world with our physical laws plus some "extra" laws would be physically possible relative to our world, but ours would not be physically possible relative to it (since our world violates its "extra" laws). Logical possibility, however, presumably does have a symmetric accessibility relation—assuming (as is traditional) that the laws of logic are the same for all worlds. The final metatheorem in this section shows why symmetry guarantees the validity of $\Phi \vdash \square \lozenge \Phi$.

METATHEOREM: All sequents of the form $\Phi \vdash \square \lozenge \Phi$ are valid relative to the set of models whose accessibility relation is symmetric.

PROOF: Suppose for reductio that this is not the case—that is, for some formula Φ there exists a valuation $\mathcal{V}$ whose accessibility relation $\mathcal{R}$ is symmetric and some world x of $\mathcal{V}$ such that $\mathcal{V}(\Phi, x) =$ T and $\mathcal{V}(\square \lozenge \Phi, x) \neq$ T. Now since $\mathcal{V}(\square \lozenge \Phi, x) \neq$ T, by rule 11' there is a world y such that $x\mathcal{R}y$ and $\mathcal{V}(\lozenge \Phi, y) \neq$ T. And since $\mathcal{V}(\lozenge \Phi, y) \neq$ T, by rule 12' for all worlds u such that $y\mathcal{R}u$, $\mathcal{V}(\Phi, u) \neq$ T. But $\mathcal{R}$ is symmetric; and so since $x\mathcal{R}y$ it follows that $y\mathcal{R}x$. Thus since for all worlds u such that $y\mathcal{R}u$, $\mathcal{V}(\Phi, u) \neq$ T, it follows in particular that $\mathcal{V}(\Phi, x) \neq$ T. But we concluded above that $\mathcal{V}(\Phi, x) =$ T, which is a contradiction.

So, contrary to our hypothesis, $\Phi \vdash \square \lozenge \Phi$ is valid relative to the set of models whose accessibility relation is symmetric.   QED

We have said so far that the accessibility relation for all forms of alethic possibility is reflexive. For physical possibility, I have argued that it is transitive as well. And for logical possibility it seems also to be symmetric. Thus the accessibility relation for logical possibility is apparently reflexive, transitive, *and* symmetric. It can be proved, though we shall not do so here, that these three characteristics together define the logic S5, which is characterized by Leibnizian semantics. That is, making the accessibility relation reflexive, transitive, and symmetric has the same effect on the logic as making each world possible relative to each.

Leibnizian semantics can in fact be viewed as a special case of Kripkean semantics—the case in which we restrict admissible models to those whose accessibility relation is **universal**, that is, those in which each world is accessible from each. Universal relations are, of course, automatically reflexive, transitive, and symmetric. Thus, for example, any sequent which is valid in all reflexive models is also valid in all universal models. Sequents valid on Leibnizian semantics can from the Kripkean perspective be regarded as sequents valid relative to the special class of models with universal accessibility relations. Since Leibnizian semantics seems appropriate for logical possibility, from a Kripkean point of view logical possibility is characterized by the class of Kripkean models with universal accessibility relations.

If we drop the requirement of symmetry, we lose the law $\Phi \vdash \Box \Diamond \Phi$ (the inference rule B of Section 11.4), and principles derivable from it, and obtain a weaker logic, S4, which is a good candidate for being the logic of physical possibility.

Logics for the other modalities involve other principles and other properties of $\mathcal{R}$, many of which are disputed. The chief merit of Kripkean semantics is that it opens up new ways of conceiving and interrelating issues of time, possibility, knowledge, obligation, and so on. For each we can imagine a relevant set of worlds (or moments) and a variety of ways an accessibility relation could structure this set and define an appropriate logic. This raises intriguing questions that, were it not for Kripke's work, we never would have dreamed of asking.

Exercise 12.1

Prove the following metatheorems. [Note that saying that a form is valid relative to the set of all Kripkean models is just another way of saying that it is (unqualifiedly) valid on Kripkean semantics.]

1. $\Phi \vdash \Diamond \Phi$ is valid relative to the set of models whose accessibility relation is reflexive.
2. $\Diamond \Diamond \Phi \vdash \Diamond \Phi$ is valid relative to the set of models whose accessibility relation is transitive.
3. $\Diamond \Box \Phi \vdash \Phi$ is valid relative to the set of models whose accessibility relation is symmetric.
4. '$P \vdash \Diamond P$' is not valid relative to the set of all Kripkean models.
5. '$\Diamond \Diamond P \vdash \Diamond P$' is not valid relative to the set of all Kripkean models.
6. '$\Diamond \Box P \vdash P$' is not valid relative to the set of all Kripkean models.
7. $\Box(\Phi \rightarrow \Psi) \vdash \Box \Phi \rightarrow \Box \Psi$ is valid relative to the set of all Kripkean models.
8. $\Box \Phi \vdash \Diamond \Phi$ is valid relative to the set of models whose accessibility relation is reflexive.
9. $\Diamond \Phi \lor \Diamond \sim\Phi$ is valid relative to the set of models whose accessibility relation is reflexive.
10. $\sim\Diamond(\Phi \,\&\, \sim\Phi)$ is valid relative to the set of all Kripkean models.

12.2 INFERENCE IN KRIPKEAN LOGICS

In Section 11.4 we introduced the full Leibnizian logic S5. Since then we have seen that some of the rules of S5 are inappropriate for certain forms of modality. The T rule (from $\Box \Phi$ infer Φ), for example, is plainly invalid when '$\Box$' is taken to express obligation, as it is in deontic logics. We have now seen that this rule was validated by the reflexivity of the accessibility relation. Likewise, the B rule (from Φ infer

□◇Φ), which is validated by the symmetry of the accessibility relation, seems invalid for physical possibility. And again the S4 rule (from □Φ infer □□Φ), which is validated by the transitivity of the accessibility relation, is of questionable validity for several modalities.

Just as Kripkean *semantics* permits nonreflexive, nonsymmetric, or nontransitive accessibility relations, which are fragments, as it were, of the full universal accessibility relation of Leibnizian semantics, so Kripkean *logics* may be fragments of the full Leibnizian logic S5. Less metaphorically, Kripkean logics may lack some of the rules of inference (either basic or derived) that are available in S5.

There are, however, certain rules that are valid relative to the set of all Kripkean models. These rules, in other words, have no counterexamples no matter how severely we diminish the accessibility relation. Three rules in particular are fundamental in this way:

Duality (DUAL)   From either of ◇Φ and ~□~Φ, infer the other; from either of □Φ and ~◇~Φ, infer the other.

K rule (K)   From □(Φ → Ψ), infer (□Φ → □Ψ).

Necessitation (N)   If Φ has previously been proved as a theorem, then any formula of the form □Φ may be introduced at any line of a proof.

These rules are common to all Kripkean modal logics. Together with the ten basic rules of classical propositional logic they constitute a logic that is sound and complete relative to the set of all Kripkean models. This logic is known as the system K (for Kripke!). In other words, a sequent of propositional modal logic (modal logic without the identity predicate or quantifiers) is provable in the system K iff it has no counterexample in any Kripkean model.[4]

K itself is not very interesting. But by adding various rules to K we may obtain differing logics that are useful for different purposes. Each rule corresponds to a particular structural requirement on the accessibility relation. Imposing new structural requirements diminishes the range of admissible models—models that may serve as counterexamples. Thus imposing new structural requirements on $\mathcal{R}$ increases the number of valid rules. Among systems we have considered, the one with the most structural requirements is S5, for whose admissible models $\mathcal{R}$ must be reflexive, transitive, and symmetric. In a sense S5 is the maximal Kripkean logic, since it is sound and complete for the most restrictive class of models, the class of models whose accessibility relation is universal. (Though reflexivity, transitivity, and symmetry don't entail universality, the class of all universal models determines the same logic, S5, as the class of reflexive, transitive, and symmetric models does.)

---

[4] Proofs of the soundness and completeness of a great variety of Kripkean systems may be found in Brian F. Chellas, *Modal Logic: An Introduction* (Cambridge: Cambridge University Press, 1980), chap. 3.

Table 12.1 summarizes some characteristics of five important Kripkean logics. But there are, in fact, infinitely many Kripkean logics, dozens if not hundreds of which have received detailed treatment. Table 12.1, then, presents only a small sample.

Exercise 12.2

Note that in the problems below it is not safe to use the sequents proved in Section 11.4 as derived rules, since these were proved using the full logic of S5 and the systems in which we are working are fragments of S5 in which certain rules are unavailable. Nevertheless, some of the strategies illustrated in that section may be useful here.

I.   Construct proofs for the following sequents in the system K:
  1. $\sim\Diamond P \vdash \Box\sim P$
  2. $\sim\Box P \vdash \Diamond\sim P$
  3. $\vdash\Box(P \rightarrow P)$
II. Construct proofs for the following sequents in the system D:
  1. $\vdash \Diamond(P \rightarrow P)$
  2. $\vdash \sim\Box(P \mathbin{\&} \sim P)$
  3. $\sim\Diamond P \vdash \sim\Box P$
  4. $\Box\Box P \vdash \Box\Diamond P$
III. Construct proofs for the following sequents in the system T:
  1. $\Box P \vdash \Diamond P$
  2. $\sim\Diamond P \vdash \sim P$
  3. $\sim P \vdash \sim\Box P$
IV. Construct proofs for the following sequents in the system S4:
  1. $\vdash \Diamond P \leftrightarrow \Diamond\Diamond P$
  2. $\Diamond\sim\Box P \vdash \Diamond\sim P$
  3. $\sim\Diamond P \vdash \Box\sim\Diamond P$

12.3 STRICT CONDITIONALS

We have until now been using the material conditional, symbolized by $\rightarrow$', to render the English operator 'if . . . then' into formal logic. This practice, as we noted in Section 3.1, is, strictly speaking, illegitimate. The material conditional is at best only a loose approximation to 'if . . . then'. Many inferences which are valid for the material conditional are invalid for English conditionals. Consider, for example:

$P \vdash a \rightarrow P$

Socrates grew to manhood.
∴   If Socrates died as a child, then Socrates grew to manhood.

$\sim P \vdash P \rightarrow Q$

Socrates did not die as a child.
∴   If Socrates died as a child, then Socrates grew to manhood.

TABLE 12.1
Some Important Kripkean Propositional Modal Logics

Logic	Basic Rules*	Accessibility Relation	Application
K	**DUAL** From either of ◇Φ and ~□~Φ, infer the other; from either of □Φ and ~◇~Φ, infer the other. **K** From □(Φ → Ψ), infer (□Φ → □Ψ). **N** If Φ has previously been proved as a theorem, then any formula of the form □Φ may be introduced at any line of a proof.	No restrictions	Minimal Kripkean logic
D	**DUAL, K,** and **N,** together with: **D** From □Φ infer ◇Φ.	Serial (see Section 13.1)	Good candidate for minimal deontic logic
T	**DUAL, K,** and **N,** together with: **T** From □Φ infer Φ.	Reflexive	Minimal alethic logic
S4	**DUAL, K, N,** and **T,** together with: **S4** From □Φ infer □□Φ.	Reflexive, transitive	Good candidate for logic of physical possibility; closely related to intuitionistic logic (see Section 16.2)
S5	**DUAL, K, N, T,** and **S4,** together with: **B** From Φ infer □◇Φ.	Reflexive, transitive, symmetric	Logic of logical possibility, perhaps other kinds of possibility as well (see Section 13.2)

*In addition to the ten rules of classical propositional logic.

It is not the case that if Socrates was a rock then Socrates was a man.
∴ Socrates was a rock, but not a man.

If we eliminate auto accidents, then we save thousands of lives.
If we nuke the entire planet, then we eliminate auto accidents.
∴ If we nuke the entire planet, then we save thousands of lives.

If the Atlantic is an ocean, then it's a polluted ocean.
∴ If the Atlantic is not a polluted ocean, then it's not an ocean.

In each case, the premises are true and the conclusion is false in the actual world, using our ordinary understanding of the conditional. Yet in each case, the argument is valid if we interpret 'if . . . then' as the material conditional. The last two arguments have forms that at first glance appear to be paradigms of good reasoning: hypothetical syllogism,

$$A \rightarrow B, B \rightarrow C \vdash A \rightarrow C$$

and contraposition,

$$A \rightarrow B \vdash {\sim}B \rightarrow {\sim}A$$

(sometimes called "transposition"). Yet these forms are apparently invalid for 'if . . . then'.

C. I. Lewis, the inventor of S4, S5, and other modern modal systems, was one of the first formal logicians to investigate the disparity between English and material conditionals. Lewis noticed that ordinary English conditionals seemed to express, not just a truth function, but a necessary connection between antecedent and consequent. Defying skepticism about the intelligibility of the concept of necessary connection, Lewis introduced in 1918 a new conditional, represented by the symbol '$\exists$', which incorporated this idea. $\Phi \dashv \Psi$ is true if and only if it is impossible for both Φ to be true and Ψ false. $\Phi \dashv \Psi$ is true, in other words, if and only if it is necessarily the case that if Φ then Ψ, where 'if . . . then' signifies the material conditional. Thus '$\exists$' is often introduced as a defined operator into modal systems using the definition

$$\Phi \dashv \Psi \text{ iff } \Box(\Phi \rightarrow \Psi)$$

An equivalent definition in terms of the possibility operator is

$$\Phi \dashv \Psi \text{ iff } {\sim}\Diamond(\Phi \, \& \, {\sim}\Psi)$$

Translated into Kripkean semantics, the truth conditions for the strict conditional are as follows:

$\mathcal{V}(\Phi \dashv \Psi, w) = T$ iff for all worlds u such that $w\mathcal{R}u$ and $\mathcal{V}(\Phi, u) = T$, $\mathcal{V}(\Psi, u) = T$
$\mathcal{V}(\Phi \dashv \Psi, w) = F$ iff for some world u such that $w\mathcal{R}u$, $\mathcal{V}(\Phi, u) = T$ and $\mathcal{V}(\Psi, u) \neq T$

The strict conditional is in some respects a better approximation to English conditionals than is the material conditional. But the closeness of the approximation depends in part upon which brand of alethic necessity we intend the strict conditional to express. Usually, the necessity built into the connection expressed by English conditionals seems to be something more like practical than physical, metaphysical, or logical necessity. So, though $\mathcal{R}$, like all alethic accessibility relations, should be reflexive, it is doubtful that it need also be transitive and symmetric (as the accessibility relation for logical possibility probably is). Accordingly, we adopt as **admissible for strict conditionals** all and only those Kripke models in which $\mathcal{R}$ is reflexive.

We began this section with five arguments, the forms of the first three of which were as follows:

$$B \vdash A \rightarrow B$$
$$\sim A \vdash A \rightarrow B$$
$$\sim(A \rightarrow B) \vdash A \ \& \sim B$$

All three arguments are valid, reading '→' as the material conditional, but all are outrageous reading '→' as an English conditional. (Indeed, the first two have often been called the "paradoxes of material implication.") Yet, if we replace '→' by '⌐3', we get the reasonable result that none of the three arguments is valid.

Let's consider the sequent 'B ⊢ A ⌐3 B' first. To facilitate comparison with the first argument above, think of 'B' as meaning "Socrates grew to manhood" and 'A' as meaning "Socrates died as a child." Socrates did, of course, grow to manhood; yet it is (or was) possible for him to have died as a child and not grown to be a man. So the premise is true and the conclusion false. To represent this counterexample formally we need two worlds: world 1, representing the actual world, a world in which Socrates did grow to be a man, and a merely possible world, world 2, in which he died as a child:

METATHEOREM: The sequent 'B ⊢ A ⌐3 B' is invalid relative to the admissible models for strict conditionals.

PROOF: Consider the Kripkean model $\mathcal{V}$ in which

$\mathcal{W}_{\mathcal{V}} = \{1, 2\}$	$\mathcal{V}(\text{'A'}, 1) = F$
$\mathcal{R} = \{<1, 1>, <1, 2>, <2, 2>\}$	$\mathcal{V}(\text{'B'}, 1) = T$
	$\mathcal{V}(\text{'A'}, 2) = T$
	$\mathcal{V}(\text{'B'}, 2) = F$

This model is admissible for strict conditionals, because $\mathcal{R}$ is reflexive. Since $1\mathcal{R}2$, $\mathcal{V}(\text{'A'}, 2) = T$, and $\mathcal{V}(\text{'B'}, 2) \neq T$, it follows that $\mathcal{V}(\text{'A} \ⵣ3\ B\text{'}, 1) \neq T$. Thus, since $\mathcal{V}(\text{'B'}, 1) = T$, the sequent is invalid.   QED

The same counterexample establishes the invalidity of the sequent '~A ⊢ A ⌐3 B'. In the actual world, Socrates did not die as a child, which makes '~A' true; but, since it was possible (relative to the actual world) that he did and never grew to manhood, 'A ⌐3 B' is false. Proof of the invalidity of this sequent is left to the reader (see the exercise at the end of this section).

The sequent '~(A ⌐3 B) ⊢ A & ~B' is also invalid. The fact that A does not necessitate B tells us nothing about the truth values of either A or B. The formal treatment of this problem is left entirely to the reader.

Though reasoning in these counterintuitive patterns is not valid for the strict conditional, many natural and familiar patterns—modus ponens and modus tollens, for example—are valid. So far, then, the strict conditional seems to answer accurately to our understanding of 'if . . . then' in English.

But the situation is not as tidy as it seems. The last two of our five arguments have the forms hypothetical syllogism and contraposition, respectively. These forms, as we saw, seem invalid for English conditionals, but they are valid for the strict conditional. We shall prove this for contraposition only, leaving the proof for hypothetical syllogism as an exercise:

METATHEOREM: The sequent 'A ⊰ B ⊢ ~B ⊰ ~A' is valid relative to the admissible models for strict conditionals.

PROOF: Suppose for reductio that this sequent is invalid relative to the admissible models. Then there exists some admissible model containing a world w such that $\mathcal{V}($ 'A ⊰ B', $w) = $ T and $\mathcal{V}($ '~B ⊰ ~A', $w) \neq$ T. Since $\mathcal{V}($ '~B ⊰ ~A', $w) \neq$ T, there exists a world u such that $w_{\mathcal{R}}u$, $\mathcal{V}($ '~B', $u) = $ T and $\mathcal{V}($ '~A', $u) \neq$ T. Hence by the valuation rule for negation $\mathcal{V}($ 'A', $u) = $ T and $\mathcal{V}($ 'B', $u) \neq$ T. But since $w_{\mathcal{R}}u$, this implies that $\mathcal{V}($ 'A ⊰ B', $w) \neq$ T, and so we have a contradiction.

Therefore the sequent 'A ⊰ B ⊢ ~B ⊰ ~A' is valid relative to the admissible models for strict conditionals.   QED

The fact that it makes hypothetical syllogism and contraposition valid might be seen as an advantage, rather than a disadvantage of the strict conditional. These are, after all, common and persuasive forms of reasoning. But since they are apparently invalid for at least some English conditionals, their validity for the strict conditional is in fact a disadvantage, insofar as the strict conditional is supposed to accurately analyze the English.

The disparity beween strict and English conditionals also crops up in "paradoxes" reminiscent of the paradoxes of material implication. These concern the sequents '□B ⊢ A ⊰ B' and '~◇A ⊢ A ⊰ B', both of which are "paradoxically" valid. Reading '⊰' as an English conditional, we can produce preposterously invalid instances. For example:

It is necessarily the case that humans are mortal.
∴ If humans are immortal, then humans are mortal.

and

It is impossible for Socrates to be a rock.
∴ If Socrates is a rock, then Socrates is a chihuahua.

In both cases (thinking of the necessity or possibility invoked in the premise as practical rather than, say, logical), the premise is true and the conclusion (understood as an English conditional) is false. Thus it is rash to identify even strict conditionals with their English counterparts.

Exercise 12.3

Prove the following metatheorems for the logic of strict conditionals—whose admissible models are all Kripkean models in which $\mathscr{R}$ is reflexive.

1. The sequent '~A ⊢ A ⥽ B' is invalid.
2. The sequent '~(A ⥽ B) ⊢ A & ~B' is invalid.
3. The sequent '□B ⊢ A ⥽ B' is valid.
4. The sequent '~◇A ⊢ A ⥽ B' is valid.
5. The formula 'A ⥽ A' is valid.
6. The sequent 'A ⥽ B, A ⊢ B' is valid.
7. The sequent 'A ⥽ B, ~B ⊢ ~A' is valid.
8. The sequent 'A ⥽ B, B ⥽ C ⊢ A ⥽ C' is valid.
9. The sequent 'A, B ⊢ A ⥽ B' is invalid.
10. The sequent 'A, ~B ⊢ ~(A ⥽ B)' is valid.

12.4 LEWIS CONDITIONALS

What, then, does the English 'if . . . then' mean? Logicians are divided on this question, and it is presumptuous even to assume that English conditionals all mean the same thing. But for a good many English conditionals, the best answer I know of is this picturesque morsel from David Lewis:

> 'If kangaroos had no tails, they would topple over' seems to me to mean something like this: In any possible state of affairs in which kangaroos have no tails, and which resembles our actual state of affairs as much as kangaroos having no tails permits it to, the kangaroos topple over.[5]

More generally, we may say:

> *If* Φ *then* Ψ is true in a world w iff in all the worlds most like w in which Φ is true, Ψ is also true.

Contrast this with similarly stated truth conditions for the strict conditional:

> Φ ⥽ Ψ is true in a world w iff in all the worlds possible relative to w in which Φ is true, Ψ is also true.

Here, of course, we have to specify the relevant sense of possibility; that is, we have to know which form of alethic modality we are dealing with.

Lewis's truth conditions, however, do not require us to specify the sort of possibility we intend. The antecedent of the conditional does that automatically. We are to consider, not all practically, or physically, or logically possible worlds, but rather all the worlds most like ours in which the antecedent is true.

---

[5] *Counterfactuals* (Cambridge: Harvard University Press, 1973), p. 1. The following analysis uses the truth conditions given on p. 25, which prevent vacuous truth.

As a result, Lewis's truth conditions do not flounder, as those for the strict conditional do, when the antecedent is impossible. With the strict conditional, if there are no possible worlds in which the antecedent is true, then, trivially, the consequent is true in all such worlds—no matter what that consequent may say. Thus, as we saw, given that it is impossible for Socrates to be a rock and reading 'if . . . then' as a strict conditional using the practical sense of possibility, we must concede that the absurd sentence 'If Socrates is a rock, then Socrates is a chihuahua' is true.

Lewis's semantics avoids this consequence. Having not found any practically possible worlds in which the antecedent is true, we do not simply punt and declare the conditional true; rather, rising to the challenge, we consider more and more remote possibilities. In our example, since it seems impossible, even in the metaphysical sense, for Socrates to be a rock, we must extend our consideration all the way out to mere logical possibilities before finding worlds in which he is. When we come to the first of these (i.e., those most like the actual world—so that, despite the fact that in them Socrates is a rock, as much as possible of the rest of the world is as it actually is), we stop. Then we ask: Is Socrates a chihuahua in all of these worlds? The answer, pretty clearly, is no. And so the sentence 'If Socrates is a rock, then Socrates is a chihuahua' is false.

Though this example is artificial, the general procedure is not. When considering whether or not a statement of the form *if* Φ *then* Ψ is true, we do in fact imagine things rearranged so that Φ is true and then try to determine whether under these new conditions Ψ would also be true. But we do this conservatively, excluding ways of making Φ true that are wilder than necessary. That is, we try to keep as much as possible of our world unchanged. Most of us would assent to the conditional 'if kangaroos had no tails, they would topple over', even though we can envision worlds in which kangaroos have no tails but do not topple over because, for example, there is no gravity. But the conditional asks us only to entertain the possibility of depriving kangaroos of tails. Depriving them of gravity too is impertinent; it changes the world in ways not called for by the conditional's antecedent. Hence, depriving kangaroos of gravity is not relevant to determining the truth value of the conditional.

Yet there may be more than one equally conservative way of changing the world to make the antecedent true. Consider the conditional 'if forests were not green, then they would not be so beautiful.' Now there are many worlds equally minimally different from ours in which the antecedent is true: worlds in which forests are brown or blue or yellow, and so on. Only if we regarded the consequent as true in all of these worlds would we assent to the conditional. If we regarded brown forests, but not blue, as more beautiful than green, we would judge the conditional false. That's why Lewis stipulates that *if* Φ *then* Ψ is true iff among *all* the worlds (plural) most like *w* in which Φ is true, Ψ is also true.

The one element required by Lewis's semantics that has not appeared in any model we have considered so far is a measure of "closeness" or similarity among worlds. While Lewis uses these terms, I prefer to think in terms of degree of possibility; where Lewis would speak of worlds as being more or less similar to a given world, I regard them as being more or less possible relative to that world.

There are two reasons for this. First, it allows us to make the transition to Lewis's semantics without introducing the entirely new concept of similarity; the only change we need make is to think of $\mathscr{R}$ as having degrees, rather than being an all-or-nothing affair. Second, similarity is symmetric; A is precisely as similar to B as B is to A. But, as we have seen, $\mathscr{R}$ should not, in general, be assumed to be symmetric.

How might a model treat $\mathscr{R}$ as a matter of degree? The simplest way would be to set up some arbitrary scale (say, from 0 to 1), where 0 represents complete lack of relative possibility and 1 the highest degree of relative possibility. Presumably, then, each world is maximally possible relative to itself, that is, has degree 1 of $\mathscr{R}$ to itself, and all other worlds are less possible relative to it.

Such a numerical scale is, however, not quite satisfactory. There is no a priori reason to suppose that degrees of relative possibility can be ordered like the real numbers from 0 to 1. A more abstract mathematical treatment of order could address this problem but would introduce complexities beyond the scope of this book. We shall, then, at the risk of slight (and not very significant) oversimplification, suppose degrees of $\mathscr{R}$ can be ranked along a 0 to 1 scale.

Accordingly, instead of treating $\mathscr{R}$ as a set of pairs, as we did before, we may treat it as a set of triples, in which the third member is a number from 0 to 1, indicating the degree to which the second member is possible relative to the third. Thus for a model consisting of worlds 1 and 2, we might have, for example:

$$\mathscr{R} = \{<1, 1, 1>, <1, 2, 0.7>, <2, 1, 0>, <2, 2, 1>\}$$

This means that worlds 1 and 2 are each fully possible relative to themselves, world 2 is possible relative to world 1 with a degree of 0.7, and world 1 is not at all possible relative to world 2. Rather than writing this all out in English, let's use the notation $\mathscr{R}(1, 2) = 0.7$ to mean that the degree to which world 2 is possible relative to world 1 is 0.7. We shall stipulate that

(1) each pair of worlds in the model must be assigned a number from 0 to 1

and that

(2) no pair of worlds may be assigned more than one number

so that for any worlds x and y in the model, $\mathscr{R}(x, y)$ will exist and will be unique. (Where in a Kripkean model we would say that it is not the case that $x\mathscr{R}y$, now we shall say $\mathscr{R}(x, y) = 0$.) We further stipulate that

(3) for any worlds x and y, $\mathscr{R}(x, y) = 1$ iff $x = y$.

This implies that no world is as possible relative to a world x as x itself is. A **Lewis model,** then, will be exactly like a Kripkean model except for these differences in $\mathscr{R}$.

Lewis represents his conditional formally as the binary operator '$\square\!\!\rightarrow$', and we shall do likewise. But we shall differ from Lewis in reading this operator simply as "if . . . then." Lewis reads $\Phi \;\square\!\!\rightarrow\; \Psi$ as "if Φ were the case, Ψ would be the case," confining his analysis to so-called subjunctive or counterfactual conditionals. But

I am persuaded that this analysis is more broadly applicable.[6] Its formal truth clause is as follows:

$\mathcal{V}(\Phi\ \Box\!\!\rightarrow \Psi, w) = \mathrm{T}$ iff there is some world u such that $\mathcal{V}(\Phi, u) = \mathrm{T}$, and there is no world z such that $\mathcal{R}(w, z) \geq \mathcal{R}(w, u)$, $\mathcal{V}(\Phi, z) = \mathrm{T}$, and $\mathcal{V}(\Psi, z) \neq \mathrm{T}$.

This is just a transcription in our new terminology of the informal truth conditions given above. The world u is some arbitrary one of the worlds most possible relative to the actual world in which the antecedent Φ is true. We are saying, in other words, that $\Phi\ \Box\!\!\rightarrow \Psi$ is true at w iff

1. Φ is true in some world u, which is such that
2. there is no world at least as possible relative to w as u is in which Φ is true and Ψ is not.

Clause 2 implies that Ψ is true in u, as well as in any worlds more possible relative to w in which Φ is true. Putting both clauses together, this is to say that in all the worlds most possible relative to w in which Φ is true, Ψ is also true. The corresponding falsity clause is

$\mathcal{V}(\Phi\ \Box\!\!\rightarrow \Psi, w) = \mathrm{F}$ iff for all worlds u such that $\mathcal{V}(\Phi, u) = \mathrm{T}$ there is some world z such that $\mathcal{R}(w, z) \geq \mathcal{R}(w, u)$, $\mathcal{V}(\Phi, z) = \mathrm{T}$, and $\mathcal{V}(\Psi, z) \neq \mathrm{T}$.

If we wish to retain the operators '$\Diamond$' and '$\Box$', we can do so in the Kripkean fashion, by stipulating that for any worlds x and y, $x\mathcal{R}y$ iff $\mathcal{R}(x, y) \neq 0$. That is, y counts as accessible from x if and only if y is accessible to even the slightest degree from x. This allows the standard Kripkean clauses to be used for these operators.

We shall illustrate the use of Lewis semantics first by proving that modus ponens is valid for a Lewis conditional:

METATHEOREM: The sequent 'A $\Box\!\!\rightarrow$ B, A $\vdash$ B' is valid for Lewis models.

PROOF: Assume for reductio that this sequent is invalid; that is, there is a Lewis model containing a world w such that $\mathcal{V}$('A $\Box\!\!\rightarrow$ B', $w) = \mathrm{T}$, $\mathcal{V}$('A', $w) = \mathrm{T}$, and $\mathcal{V}$('B', $w) \neq \mathrm{T}$. Now by the definition of a Lewis model, for any world u, $\mathcal{R}(w, w) \geq \mathcal{R}(w, u)$. Hence for all worlds u, there is some world z, namely w, such that $\mathcal{R}(w, z) \geq \mathcal{R}(w, u)$, $\mathcal{V}$('A', $z) = \mathrm{T}$, and $\mathcal{V}$('B', $z) \neq \mathrm{T}$. Hence, in particular, for all worlds u such that $\mathcal{V}$('A', $u) = \mathrm{T}$, there is some world z such that $\mathcal{R}(w, z) \geq \mathcal{R}(w, u)$, $\mathcal{V}$('A', $z) = \mathrm{T}$, and $\mathcal{V}$('B', $z) \neq \mathrm{T}$. But this is to say that $\mathcal{V}$('A $\Box\!\!\rightarrow$ B', $w) \neq \mathrm{T}$, and so we have a contradiction.

Hence the sequent 'A $\Box\!\!\rightarrow$ B, A $\vdash$ B' is valid for Lewis models.   QED

---

[6] See Michael Kremer, "'If' Is Unambiguous," *Nous* 21 (1987): 199–217, for a fuller discussion of this point.

It turns out, however, that contraposition and hypothetical syllogism, which we saw were invalid for English conditionals, are both also invalid for Lewis's conditionals. We shall prove this for contraposition, leaving hypothetical syllogism as an exercise. To set the stage, consider the invalid instance of contraposition mentioned above:

> If the Atlantic is an ocean, then it's a polluted ocean.
> ∴ If the Atlantic is not a polluted ocean, then it's not an ocean.

According to Lewis, we evaluate a conditional by considering the worlds most similar to (or, in my terms, most *possible* relative to) the actual world in which the antecedent is true. In the case of this argument's premise, there is only one such world—the actual world itself—for the Atlantic is in fact an ocean. We now check to see if the consequent is true among all members of this (one-membered) class of worlds. And indeed it is, for the Atlantic *is* a polluted ocean. Therefore the premise is true in the actual world.

We then subject the conclusion to the same procedure. The conclusion's antecedent is not true in the actual world, so we must move in imagination out to those worlds most like the actual world (or most *possible* relative to the actual world) in which the Atlantic is pristine. Presumably, there are many approximately equally possible ways in which this could have happened. The Industrial Revolution might never have occurred; or we might have developed an ecological conscience before it did; or we might have developed technology for cleaning up oceans. The details matter little; for, whatever we imagine here, it will not include the Atlantic's being transmuted into something other than an ocean. That possibility is much wilder than these others. It seems not even to be a metaphysical possibility, but merely a logical one. The others are all physical, if not practical, possibilities. In none of these more "homey" possibilities is the Atlantic not an ocean. Therefore the conditional's consequent is false in all the worlds most like the actual world in which its antecedent is true. And so the conditional is false.

We can model this counterexample with a domain of two worlds: world 1, representing the actual world, and world 2, representing one of the "homey" worlds in which the Atlantic is pristine but remains an ocean. Read 'A' as "the Atlantic is an ocean" and 'B' as "the Atlantic is a polluted ocean":

METATHEOREM: The sequent 'A $\Box\!\!\rightarrow$ B $\vdash$ ~B $\Box\!\!\rightarrow$ ~A' is invalid for Lewis models.

PROOF: Consider the model $\mathcal{V}$ defined as follows:

$$\mathcal{W}_{\mathcal{V}} = \{1, 2\} \qquad\qquad \mathcal{V}(\text{‘A’}, 1) = T$$
$$\mathcal{R} = \{<1, 1, 1>, <1, 2, 0.7>, <2, 1, 0.5>, \qquad \mathcal{V}(\text{‘B’}, 1) = T$$
$$<2, 2, 1>\} \qquad\qquad\qquad\qquad \mathcal{V}(\text{‘A’}, 2) = T$$
$$\mathcal{V}(\text{‘B’}, 2) = F$$

This meets conditions 1–3 and so is a Lewis model. Clearly there is no world z such that $\mathcal{R}(1, z) \geq \mathcal{R}(1, 1)$, $\mathcal{V}(\text{‘A’}, z) = T$, and $\mathcal{V}(\text{‘B’}, z) \neq T$. But

$\mathcal{V}$('A', 1) = T. Hence there is a world u, namely world 1, such that $\mathcal{V}$('A', u) = T and there is no world z such that $\mathcal{R}(1, z) \geq \mathcal{R}(1, u)$, $\mathcal{V}$('A', z) = T, and $\mathcal{V}$('B', z) $\neq$ T. Therefore $\mathcal{V}$('A $\square\!\!\rightarrow$ B', 1) = T. Now there is only one world u such that $\mathcal{V}$('~B', u) = T: This is world 2. Yet $\mathcal{R}(1, 2) \geq \mathcal{R}(1, 2)$, $\mathcal{V}$('~B', 2) = T, and $\mathcal{V}$('~A', 2) $\neq$ T. Thus for all worlds u such that $\mathcal{V}$('~B', u) = T, there is some world z, namely world 2, such that $\mathcal{R}(1, z) \geq \mathcal{R}(1, u)$, $\mathcal{V}$('~B', z) = T, and $\mathcal{V}$('~A', z) $\neq$ T. But this is to say that $\mathcal{V}$('~B $\square\!\!\rightarrow$ ~A', 1) = F. Thus since, as we saw above, $\mathcal{V}$('A $\square\!\!\rightarrow$ B', 1) = T, it follows that the sequent 'A $\square\!\!\rightarrow$ B ⊢ ~B $\square\!\!\rightarrow$ ~A' is invalid.   QED

Further investigation of Lewis's semantics reveals many more respects in which his conditionals fit our intuitions about English conditionals (see the exercise below). Of the conditionals we have examined, Lewis's is surely the best approximation to the English. But whether it is uniquely *correct* as a formal semantics for the English conditional remains a disputed question.

Exercise 12.4

Prove the following metatheorems for '$\square\!\!\rightarrow$' using Lewis models.

1. The sequent 'A $\square\!\!\rightarrow$ B, ~B ⊢ ~A' is valid.
2. The sequent 'A $\square\!\!\rightarrow$ B, B $\square\!\!\rightarrow$ C ⊢ A $\square\!\!\rightarrow$ C' is invalid.
3. The sequent '~A ⊢ A $\square\!\!\rightarrow$ B' is invalid.
4. The sequent 'B ⊢ A $\square\!\!\rightarrow$ B' is invalid.
5. The sequent '~(A $\square\!\!\rightarrow$ B) ⊢ A & ~B' is invalid.
6. The sequent 'A, B ⊢ A $\square\!\!\rightarrow$ B' is valid.
7. The sequent 'A, ~B ⊢ ~(A $\square\!\!\rightarrow$ B)' is valid.
8. The sequent 'A $\square\!\!\rightarrow$ C ⊢ (A & B)$\square\!\!\rightarrow$ C' is invalid.
9. The sequent '$\square$B ⊢ A $\square\!\!\rightarrow$ B' is invalid.
10. The sequent '~$\Diamond$A ⊢ A $\square\!\!\rightarrow$ B' is invalid.

CHAPTER 13

DEONTIC AND TENSE LOGICS

13.1 A MODAL DEONTIC LOGIC

Deontic logic has often been studied as it was presented (briefly) in Chapter 12—independently of alethic logic, using Kripke-style models whose accessibility relations represent permissibility rather than alethic possibility. Though this approach has been fruitful, more can be learned by considering deontic and alethic operators together in the same model. Some important deontic principles, such as Immanuel Kant's dictum that ought implies can, involve both deontic and alethic elements (the 'can' signifies some form of alethic possibility). These principles remain unexamined when deontic logic is studied in isolation.

To do modal and deontic logic together, we need two pairs of monadic modal operators: '□' and '◇' to express necessity and possibility, and 'O' and 'P' to represent obligation and permission. Thus we also need two accessibility relations: an alethic relation, which we represent, as before, by the letter '$\mathcal{R}$', and a deontic relation, which we represent by the letter '$\mathcal{S}$'. For any two worlds x and y, $x\mathcal{R}y$ if and only if y is possible relative to x, and $x\mathcal{S}y$ if and only if y is morally permissible relative to x.

What it means for y to be morally permissible relative to x is a question that lies outside logic. Presumably, for a utilitarian like Jeremy Bentham or John Stuart Mill it means that, relative to the conditions that hold in x (the kinds of sentient

357

beings, desires, and so on that exist there), world y is a world in which happiness is maximized. For a deontologist like Kant it might mean that in y all actions accord with the moral law that holds in x—and perhaps for Kantians the same moral law holds in all worlds so that any world that is permissible relative to one world is permissible relative to them all. The logic to be presented here is compatible with these interpretations, as well as others, and does not decide between them.

The valuation rules are just like those for Kripkean modal logic except that we need two new clauses for the deontic operators. These mirror the clauses for '$\Box$' and '$\Diamond$', except that they have $\mathcal{S}$ in place of $\mathcal{R}$:

13. $\mathcal{V}(\mathbf{O}\Phi, w) = \text{T}$ iff for all worlds u such that $w\mathcal{S}u$, $\mathcal{V}(\Phi, u) = \text{T}$;
    $\mathcal{V}(\mathbf{O}\Phi, w) = \text{F}$ iff for some world u, $w\mathcal{S}u$ and $\mathcal{V}(\Phi, u) \neq \text{T}$.
14. $\mathcal{V}(\mathbf{P}\Phi, w) = \text{T}$ iff for some world u, $w\mathcal{S}u$ and $\mathcal{V}(\Phi, u) = \text{T}$;
    $\mathcal{V}(\mathbf{P}\Phi, w) = \text{F}$ iff for all worlds u such that $w\mathcal{S}u$, $\mathcal{V}(\Phi, u) \neq \text{T}$.

Because we want $\mathcal{R}$ and $\mathcal{S}$ to represent specific kinds of accessibility relations, we shall make certain restrictions on admissible models. We saw in Section 12.1 that all alethic accessibility relations are reflexive. So we shall require this of $\mathcal{R}$.

Deontic accessibility relations, as we saw, are generally not reflexive. However, we might want them to meet another, somewhat weaker condition —namely, that each world has at least one permissible alternative. More precisely, the relation $\mathcal{S}$ must be such that for every world w, there is a world u such that $w\mathcal{S}u$. Such a relation is called **serial**, because if $\mathcal{S}$ meets this condition, then starting with any world w_1, there must be a world w_2 such that $w_1\mathcal{S}w_2$ and then a world w_3 such that $w_2\mathcal{S}w_3$, and then a world w_4 such that $w_3\mathcal{S}w_4$, . . . and so on in an endless series. Nothing prevents some or all of these worlds from being identical with one another. Thus, for example, if we have just one world w such that $w\mathcal{S}w$, $\mathcal{S}$ is still serial. In other words, the series may run in a circle as well as a line—and in other more complex ways. In general, all reflexive relations are serial. However, not all serial relations are reflexive.

The reason for wanting $\mathcal{S}$ to be serial is that otherwise every statement, including every contradiction, is obligatory at some world. Seriality is therefore a kind of consistency condition on morality; if the accessibility relation is not serial, the demands of our morality are (at least under some conditions) inconsistent. The following metatheorem proves this:

METATHEOREM: If $\mathcal{S}$ is not serial, then there is a world w such that $\mathcal{V}(\mathbf{O}\Phi, w) = \text{T}$ for any formula Φ.

PROOF: Suppose that $\mathcal{S}$ is not serial. This means that there is a world w such that it is not the case that $w\mathcal{S}u$ for any world u. Now consider any formula Φ. Since there are no worlds u such that $w\mathcal{S}u$, trivially $\mathcal{V}(\Phi, u) = \text{T}$ for all worlds u such that $w\mathcal{S}u$. Hence by valuation rule 13, $\mathcal{V}(\mathbf{O}\Phi, w) = \text{T}$.

Thus we have shown that if $\mathcal{S}$ is not serial, then there is a world w such that $\mathcal{V}(O\Phi, w) = T$ for any formula Φ.   QED

Here Φ may be any formula, including any contradiction.[1]

Ideally, at least, we want a consistent morality. Hence we define an **admissible model for modal deontic logic** as a Kripkean model that includes a reflexive relation $\mathcal{R}$ and a serial relation $\mathcal{S}$ on the set $\mathcal{W}_{\mathcal{V}}$ of worlds. Validity and related semantic concepts will now be defined relative to such admissible models, as described in Section 12.1.

Having defined our semantics, we can now see what it does. To begin, we can prove the standard dual relationships between **O** and **P**:

METATHEOREM: Any formula of the form $O\Phi \leftrightarrow {\sim}P{\sim}\Phi$ is valid relative to the class of admissible models.

PROOF: Suppose for reductio that for some formula Φ, $O\Phi \leftrightarrow {\sim}P{\sim}\Phi$ is not valid, that is, there exists an admissible model $\mathcal{V}$ containing a world w such that $\mathcal{V}(O\Phi \leftrightarrow {\sim}P{\sim}\Phi, w) \neq T$. By valuation rule 8, either $\mathcal{V}(O\Phi, w) = T$ and $\mathcal{V}({\sim}P{\sim}\Phi, w) \neq T$ or $\mathcal{V}(O\Phi, w) \neq T$ and $\mathcal{V}({\sim}P{\sim}\Phi, w) = T$. We show that this leads to contradiction.

Suppose, first, that $\mathcal{V}(O\Phi, w) = T$ and $\mathcal{V}({\sim}P{\sim}\Phi, w) \neq T$. Since $\mathcal{V}(O\Phi, w) = T$, it follows by rule 13 that for all worlds u such that $w\mathcal{S}u$, $\mathcal{V}(\Phi, u) = T$. Hence by rule 4 there is no world u such that $w\mathcal{S}u$ and $\mathcal{V}({\sim}\Phi, u) = T$. Hence by rule 14, $\mathcal{V}(P{\sim}\Phi, w) \neq T$, whence it follows by rule 4 that $\mathcal{V}({\sim}P{\sim}\Phi, w) = T$. But we had supposed that $\mathcal{V}({\sim}P{\sim}\Phi, w) \neq T$, and so we have a contradiction.

Hence it is not the case that $\mathcal{V}(O\Phi, w) = T$ and $\mathcal{V}({\sim}P{\sim}\Phi, w) \neq T$. By similar reasoning we can also show that it is not the case that $\mathcal{V}(O\Phi, w) \neq T$ and $\mathcal{V}({\sim}P{\sim}\Phi, w) = T$. Thus, contrary to what we had concluded above, $\mathcal{V}(O\Phi, w) = \mathcal{V}({\sim}P{\sim}\Phi, w)$, and so again we have a contradiction.

Thus we have shown that any formula of the form $O\Phi \leftrightarrow {\sim}P{\sim}\Phi$ is valid.   QED

We also, of course, have the dual result:

---

[1] An analogous problem would arise in alethic logic if we allowed nonserial relations there. But we have banned them, having required alethic accessibility relations to be reflexive, and hence serial.

> **METATHEOREM:** Any formula of the form $P\Phi \leftrightarrow {\sim}O{\sim}\Phi$ is valid relative to the class of admissible models.

The proof is left as an exercise.

Of more philosophical interest is Immanuel Kant's famous thesis that ought implies can. In the notation of modal deontic logic, this is the principle that $O\Phi \rightarrow \Diamond\Phi$. Logic does not require this thesis; we can envision an arrangement of possibility and permissibility for which it does not hold. Suppose, for example, that we ought to preserve the Earth's biosphere but are nevertheless fated to destroy it. Then using 'A' to mean "we preserve the biosphere," 'OA' would be true and '$\Diamond$ A' false in our world. Kant in effect denies that there can be such a genuine moral tragedy; but modal deontic logic does not support him. In the following metatheorem, think of world 1 as the actual world and world 2 as what ought to be. World 1 is the only world in the model that is possible relative to world 1; this models the idea that what actually happens is "fated," or the only thing that could happen. World 2 is the only world that is permissible relative to world 1, but world 2 is not possible relative to world 1; this models the idea that what ought to be is impossible.

> **METATHEOREM:** The formula 'OA $\rightarrow \Diamond$ A' is not valid relative to the class of admissible models.
>
> **PROOF:** Consider the model $\mathcal{V}$ in which
>
> $$\mathcal{W}_\mathcal{V} = \{1, 2\} \qquad \mathcal{V}(\text{'A'}, 1) = F$$
> $$\mathcal{R} = \{<1, 1>, <2, 2>\} \qquad \mathcal{V}(\text{'A'}, 2) = T$$
> $$\mathcal{S} = \{<1, 2>, <2, 2>\}$$
>
> This model is admissible, since $\mathcal{R}$ is reflexive and $\mathcal{S}$ is serial. Since 2 is the only world u in this model such that $1\mathcal{S}u$ and since $\mathcal{V}(\text{'A'}, 2) = T$, it follows that $\mathcal{V}(\text{'A'}, u) = T$ for all worlds u such that $1\mathcal{S}u$. Thus by rule 13, $\mathcal{V}(\text{'OA'}, 1) = T$. But since 1 is the only world u such that $1\mathcal{R}u$, and since $\mathcal{V}(\text{'A'}, 1) \neq T$, there is no world u such that $1\mathcal{R}u$ and $\mathcal{V}(\text{'A'}, 1) = T$. Hence by rule 12, $\mathcal{V}(\text{'}\Diamond\text{A'}, 1) \neq T$. But then since both $\mathcal{V}(\text{'OA'}, 1) = T$ and $\mathcal{V}(\text{'}\Diamond\text{A'}, 1) \neq T$, by rule 7, $\mathcal{V}(\text{'OA} \rightarrow \Diamond\text{A'}, 1) \neq T$; and so 'OA $\rightarrow \Diamond$ A' is not valid.   QED

The notion that ought implies can would seem to be grounded more in the warm cosmic optimism of the Age of Enlightenment than in cold logic. But the whole story is not yet told; it takes a new twist at the end of this section.

Meanwhile, let's consider a more practical application. Unsophisticated reasoners often argue in the following pattern:

OB, A → B ⊢ OA

For instance:

> We ought to eliminate AIDS. If we adopt a policy of strict quarantine of AIDS victims, we eliminate AIDS. Therefore, we ought to adopt a policy of strict quarantine of AIDS victims.

With respect to this sequent, 'we eliminate AIDS' is 'B' and 'we adopt a policy of strict quarantine of AIDS victims' is 'A'. The fallacy is obvious: There may be better policies that would achieve the same goal—like finding a cure. That is, we can envision a world, call it *w*, in which AIDS ought to be eliminated (i.e., is eliminated in all of *w*'s morally permissible alternatives) and in which a quarantine would eliminate AIDS, but in which it is not the case that we ought to quarantine (i.e., there is a morally permissible alternative world in which we do not quarantine). We can model this counterexample with just two worlds—world 1, which we may think of as the actual world, and world 2, a possible and permissible alternative to world 1 in which AIDS is eliminated by some means other than quarantine. Here is what the model looks like in formal terms:

METATHEOREM: The sequent 'OB, A → B ⊢ OA' is invalid relative to the class of admissible models.

PROOF: Consider the model $\mathscr{V}$ in which

$$\mathscr{W}_{\mathscr{V}} = \{1, 2\} \qquad\qquad \mathscr{V}(\text{‘A’}, 1) = F$$
$$\mathscr{R} = \{<1, 1>, <1, 2>, <2, 1>, <2, 2>\} \qquad \mathscr{V}(\text{‘B’}, 1) = F$$
$$\mathscr{S} = \{<1, 2>, <2, 2>\} \qquad\qquad \mathscr{V}(\text{‘A’}, 2) = F$$
$$\mathscr{V}(\text{‘B’}, 2) = T$$

This model is admissible, since $\mathscr{R}$ is reflexive and $\mathscr{S}$ is serial. Since 2 is the only world *u* in the model such that $1\mathscr{S}u$, and since $\mathscr{V}(\text{‘B’}, 2) = T$, it follows that $\mathscr{V}(\text{‘B’}, u) = T$ for all *u* such that $1\mathscr{S}u$. Hence by rule 13, $\mathscr{V}(\text{‘OB’}, 1) = T$. But since $1\mathscr{S}2$ and $V'(\text{‘A’}, 2) \neq T$, by rule 13, $\mathscr{V}(\text{‘OA’}, 1) \neq T$. Moreover, since $\mathscr{V}(\text{‘A’}, 1) \neq T$, $\mathscr{V}(\text{‘A} \to \text{B’}, 1) = T$ by rule 7. Thus, since $\mathscr{V}(\text{‘OB’}, 1) = T$, $\mathscr{V}(\text{‘A} \to \text{B’}, 1) = T$, and $\mathscr{V}(\text{‘OA’}, 1) \neq T$, the sequent is invalid.   QED

The next metatheorem illustrates a valid pattern of deontic reasoning:

METATHEOREM: The sequent 'OA, O(A → B) ⊢ OB' is valid relative to the class of admissible models.

PROOF: Suppose for reductio that this sequent is invalid; that is, there is an admissible model in which there is a world *w* such that $\mathscr{V}(\text{‘OA’}, w) = T$, $\mathscr{V}(\text{‘O(A} \to \text{B)’}, w) = T$, and $\mathscr{V}(\text{‘OB’}, w) \neq T$.

Since $\mathcal{V}(\text{'OB'}, w) \neq T$, by rule 13 there is a world u such that $w \mathcal{S} u$ and $\mathcal{V}(\text{'B'}, u) \neq T$. But since $\mathcal{V}(\text{'OA'}, w) = T$ and $w \mathcal{S} u$, it follows, again by rule 13, that $\mathcal{V}(\text{'A'}, u) = T$. And since $\mathcal{V}(\text{'A'}, u) = T$ and $\mathcal{V}(\text{'B'}, u) \neq T$, it follows by rule 7 that $\mathcal{V}(\text{'(A} \rightarrow \text{B)'}, u) \neq T$. Finally, since $w \mathcal{S} u$, it follows again by rule 13 that $\mathcal{V}(\text{'O(A} \rightarrow \text{B)'}, w) \neq T$. But we said above that $\mathcal{V}(\text{'O(A} \rightarrow \text{B)'}, w) = T$, and so we have a contradiction.

Thus, contrary to our hypothesis, the sequent 'OA, O(A $\rightarrow$ B) $\vdash$ OB' is valid.   QED

It's now time to take up some business left unfinished at the end of Section 9.4. This concerns the argument

I should live.
It is necessarily the case that if I live Bad Bart dies.
∴   Bad Bart should die.

We saw in our earlier discussion that the form of this argument is not straightforwardly representable in predicate logic. But it is easily representable in modal deontic logic. Using 'A' for 'I live' and 'B' for 'Bad Bart dies', the form is:

OA, □(A → B) $\vdash$ OB

This is invalid. For, as in the case of ought implies can, maybe what we have here is a genuine moral tragedy. Perhaps what ought to be the case is that no life is lost, even though, given the circumstances, this *can't* be the case. We can thus use a counterexample similar to the one used to refute the thesis that ought implies can. Once again, world 1 is the actual world—in which, we shall suppose, Bart gets me. (I hesitated too long in my moral deliberations.) World 2 represents what ought to be—a world in which we both live, but which, unfortunately, is impossible relative to world 1.

METATHEOREM: The sequent 'OA, □(A → B) $\vdash$ OB' is invalid relative to the class of admissible models.

PROOF: Consider the model in which

$\mathcal{W}_{\mathcal{V}} = \{1, 2\}$	$\mathcal{V}(\text{'A'}, 1) = F$
$\mathcal{R} = \{<1, 1>, <2, 2>\}$	$\mathcal{V}(\text{'B'}, 1) = F$
$\mathcal{S} = \{<1, 2>, <2, 2>\}$	$\mathcal{V}(\text{'A'}, 2) = T$
	$\mathcal{V}(\text{'B'}, 2) = F$

This model is admissible, since $\mathcal{R}$ is reflexive and $\mathcal{S}$ serial. Now $\mathcal{V}(\text{'A'}, 1) \neq T$; hence by rule 7, $\mathcal{V}(\text{'A} \rightarrow \text{B'}, 1) = T$. Since 1 is the only world u such that $1 \mathcal{R} u$, by rule 11, $\mathcal{V}(\text{'}\square(A \rightarrow B)\text{'}, 1) = T$. Moreover, 2 is the only world u such that $1 \mathcal{S} u$. Therefore, since $\mathcal{V}(\text{'A'}, 2) = T$, it follows that $\mathcal{V}(\text{'OA'}, 1) = T$; and since $\mathcal{V}(\text{'B'}, 2) \neq T$, it follows that $\mathcal{V}(\text{'OB'}, 1) \neq$

T. Thus, since $\mathcal{V}('OA', 1) = T$, $\mathcal{V}('\square(A \rightarrow B)', 1) = T$, and $\mathcal{V}('OB', 1) \neq T$, the sequent is invalid.   QED

We have been examining a conception of modal deontic logic according to which not every permissible world is possible. This is reasonable if we are talking about practical or physical possibility. It is permissible, for example, for you to leap up from the earth's surface thirty feet into the air (so long as you don't harm anything in the process). The fact that this is not practically or physically possible (given your physical constitution) seems irrelevant. But if we are talking about *logical* possibility things get cloudier. Are there permissible situations or worlds that are *logically* impossible? On the one hand, it seems pointless to prohibit logical impossibilities, since they can't happen anyway. On the other, since logical impossibilities are not coherently conceivable, one might argue that talk of them is uninterpretable. On this view, there are no permissible logical impossibilities, because there are no logical impossibilities of any kind. Every permissible world, then, is logically possible.

Let's adopt this second view. We noted earlier that Leibnizian semantics, which makes each world possible from each, seems adequately to model logical possibility. In the Kripkean framework, Leibnizian semantics corresponds to the special class of models whose accessibility relation $\mathcal{R}$ is **universal.** ($\mathcal{R}$ is universal iff for all worlds x and y, $x\mathcal{R}y$.) Now, if we superimpose a deontic accessibility relation upon a universal alethic relation (representing logical possibility), we obtain a model appropriate for characterizing the interaction of deontic modality with logical possibility. In such a model, since each world is possible relative to each, every world permissible relative to a given world is also possible relative to that world. The universality of the alethic accessibility relation, then, implies that what is permissible is also possible. Possibility and permissibility, which before had gone their separate ways, become interestingly interrelated.

Let's define a **universal modal deontic model** as an admissible modal deontic model in which $\mathcal{R}$ is not merely reflexive, but universal. We may now reconceive the semantic concepts of validity, consistency, and so on as relative to the class of universal modal deontic models. The operators '$\diamond$' and '$\square$' thus model specifically logical possibility and necessity.

If we now reopen the question of whether ought implies can—thinking of "can" this time in the logical sense—we discover that things have changed. The Kantian thesis *is* valid relative to this new class of models:

METATHEOREM: The formula '$OA \rightarrow \diamond A$' is valid relative to the set of universal models.

PROOF: Suppose for reductio that this formula is not valid relative to this class; that is, there is a universal model containing a world w such that $\mathcal{V}('OA \rightarrow \diamond A', w) \neq T$. Then by rule 7, $\mathcal{V}('OA', w) = T$ and $\mathcal{V}('\diamond A', w) \neq T$. Since the model is universal, $\mathcal{S}$ is serial;

so there is some world u such that $w \mathscr{S} u$. Since $w \mathscr{S} u$ and $\mathscr{V}(\text{'OA'}, w) = T$, by rule 13, $\mathscr{V}(\text{'A'}, u) = T$. But, again since the model is universal, $\mathscr{R}$ is universal; hence $w \mathscr{R} u$. Thus since $w \mathscr{R} u$ and $\mathscr{V}(\text{'A'}, u) = T$, by rule 12, $\mathscr{V}(\text{'} \Diamond A \text{'}, w) = T$, contrary to what we said above.

Thus 'OA → ◊ A' is valid relative to the set of universal models.   QED

This result, however, wouldn't have helped Kant, for he clearly intended the 'can' in his principle 'ought implies can' to express practical possibility.

As the following exercise illustrates, the validity 'ought implies can' is only one of many changes that our logic undergoes if we move from our former notion of admissible models to universal models—that is, from physical or practical to logical possibility.

Inferentially, our modal deontic logic requires separate rules for the modal and deontic operators. The rules DUAL, K, and N (see Section 11.4), being valid for all Kripkean logics, are valid for both sets of operators. Since we have required $\mathscr{S}$ to be serial, we have the rule D (from OΦ infer PΦ) for the deontic operators (the proof of its validity is left as an exercise below). If we merely require $\mathscr{R}$ to be reflexive, we need for the modal operators only the additional rule T, but if we require $\mathscr{R}$ to be universal, we must employ the full Leibnizian logic, including T, B, and S4. These rules, then, constitute logics that are sound and complete relative to the semantics presented here.

Exercise 13.1.1

For each of the following sequents, prove metatheoretically either that it is valid or that it is invalid, relative to the class of admissible models in which $\mathscr{R}$ is reflexive and $\mathscr{S}$ is serial. Where the sequent is invalid, describe a counterexample informally, as well as giving the formal proof. Does the validity of any inference change if we require $\mathscr{R}$ to be universal in admissible models?

1. A ⊢ OA
2. OA ⊢ A
3. OA ⊢ PA
4. □A ⊢ PA
5. □A ⊢ OA
6. P(A & B) ⊢ PA
7. OA, OB ⊢ O(A & B)
8. PA, PB ⊢ P(A & B)
9. OA, A → B ⊢ OB
10. A, O(A → B) ⊢ OB
11. A, (A → OB) ⊢ OB
12. PA, O(A → B) ⊢ PB
13. PA, P(A → B) ⊢ PB
14. PA, □(A → B) ⊢ PB

Exercise 13.1.2

Prove that the following formulas are valid relative to the class of models in which $\mathscr{R}$ is reflexive and $\mathscr{S}$ serial:

1. ~P(A & ~A)
2. O(A ∨ ~A)
3. ~(OA & O~A)
4. ~(□A & □~A)
5. PA ∨ P~A

13.2 A MODAL TENSE LOGIC

"What then is time?" asks St. Augustine. "I know what it is if no one asks me what it is; but if I want to explain it so someone who has asked me, I find that I do not know."[2]

Ordinarily we understand time as a linearly ordered sequence of moments. We have a position in time, the present moment. All other moments lie in either the past or the future. The present constantly advances toward the future, and this advance gives time a direction. The past is a continuum of moments stretching behind us, perhaps to infinity. It is unalterable. Whatever has been is now necessarily so. The future, however, is not frozen into unalterability but alive with possibilities. Starting with the present, events could take various alternative courses. There is, in other words, more than one possible future. Though only one of these courses of events will in fact be realized (we may not, of course, know which one), still the others are genuinely possible, in a way that alternative pasts are not genuinely possible.

These intuitions suggest a model on which time is like a tree with a single trunk (the past) that at a certain point (the present) begins to split and split again into ramifying branches (various possible futures). As time moves forward, the lower branches (formerly live possibilities, lost through passage of time) disappear. Only one path through the tree represents the actual course of time, that is, the actual world. More and more of the path is revealed as time moves on and lower branches vanish. If time were finite, eventually all the branches representing merely possible futures would disappear and only this single path from trunk to branch tip would remain: the entire history of the actual world from the beginning to the end of time. But we might also think of time as infinite—at least toward the future and perhaps also backward into the past. If time is infinite toward the past, then the tree's trunk extends endlessly downward, never touching ground; and if time is infinite toward the future, then its branches stretch endlessly upward, never touching the sky. In either case, we might picture at least a part of the tree like the diagram in Figure 13.1.

[2] *Confessions*, book X, chap. 14.

FIGURE 13.1
A Picture of Time

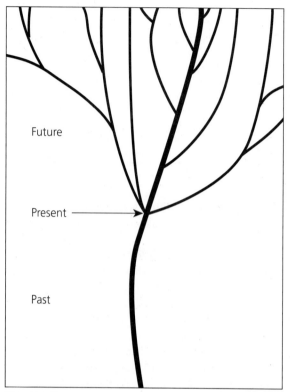

The thick line represents the actual world. The thinner lines represent temporal portions of merely possible worlds that share the actual world's past. Specific times are represented by points on any of the lines.

It would be rash to claim that this picture of time is true. Time, according to relativity physics, is inseparable from space and relative to motion, and though it is experienced as past, present, and future, these may not be "objective" features of time itself. Even if they are, our picture may well be inaccurate for the very distant past (in the vicinity of the big bang) and for the very distant future, because we do not fully understand the behavior of time at these extremes. Moreover, if the world is deterministic, then possible alternative futures (the thin branches) are merely illusions. But this is not the place for a detailed physical or philosophical discussion of the nature of time. The logic presented in this section should be regarded not as the one true tense logic, but as an example of a tense logic that accords reasonably well with our everyday understanding of time. The literature on tense logic is replete with logics for relativistic time, discrete time, circular time, ending time, and so on, all of which differ substantially from the logic presented here.[3]

A **tense logic** is a logic that includes operators expressing tense modifications. The logic we shall consider here is a modal[4] tense logic because it contains alethic modal operators in addition to tense operators. It has four tense operators:

H—it has always been the case that
P—it was (at some time) the case that
G—it will always be the case that
F—it will (at some time) be the case that

These are all monadic operators on sentences. The first two and last two are duals. That is, on any reasonable semantics, the following are valid formulas:

$$H\Phi \leftrightarrow \sim P \sim \Phi$$
$$P\Phi \leftrightarrow \sim H \sim \Phi$$
$$G\Phi \leftrightarrow \sim F \sim \Phi$$
$$F\Phi \leftrightarrow \sim G \sim \Phi$$

Using these four operators, we can express a great variety of tense modifications. Here are some examples:

Group I

GHΦ It will always be that it has always been that Φ. [Intuitively, this means that Φ is the case at all times—past, present, and future.]

FHΦ It will be the case that it has always been that Φ. [Φ has always been the case and will continue to be for some time.]

HΦ It has always been the case that Φ.

PHΦ It was the case that it had always been that Φ. [There was a time before which it was always the case that Φ.]

HPΦ It has always been that it had (at some time) been the case that Φ. [That is, there have always been times past at which Φ was the case, but these may have occurred intermittently.]

PΦ It was the case that Φ.

GPΦ It will always have been that Φ.

FPΦ It will be the case that it has (at some time) been that Φ.

---

[3] The classic source for many of these variants is Arthur Prior, *Past, Present and Future* (Oxford: Oxford University Press, 1967). Prior's use of Polish notation may be a barrier for readers accustomed to the more unusual notation employed in this book, but with a little practice one can easily adapt to it. Many variants of tense logic are also discussed in Nicholas Rescher and Alasdair Urquhart, *Temporal Logic* (New York: Springer-Verlag, 1971).

[4] 'Modal' here is used in its narrow sense, as a synonym for 'alethic'.

Group II

HGΦ   It has always been the case that it would always be that Φ. [Φ is the case at all times—past, present, and future.]

PGΦ   It was (at some time) the case that it always would be that Φ.

GΦ   It always will be the case that Φ.

FGΦ   It will (at some time) be the case that it will always be that Φ. [That is, there will come a time after which Φ is always the case.]

GFΦ   It will always be the case that it will sometimes be the case that Φ. [Moments at which Φ is the case will always lie in the future, though perhaps intermittently.]

FΦ   It will be the case that Φ.

HFΦ   It has always been that it will be the case that Φ.

PFΦ   It was (at some time) the case that it would (later) be the case that Φ.

An adequate tense logic will, for example, determine which of these statement forms imply which others, but of course it will do a good deal more than that. (In fact, on the assumption that there is no first or last moment of time—an assumption discussed below—each formula of either group implies all formulas listed below it in the same group; and the first members of the two groups are equivalent, as are the last.)

There is in most tense logics no special operator for the present tense. To assert that Φ is presently the case, we simply assert Φ. We anticipate, then, that sequents such as the following are valid:

FHA ⊢ A
A ⊢ HFA
PGA ⊢ A
A ⊢ GPA

Our intuitive picture of time includes multiple possible futures. Indeed, each path through the tree from the base of the trunk (if it has a base) to the tip of a branch (if branches have tips) represents a complete possible world. These possible worlds share a portion of their histories with the actual world but split off at some specific time. This is a picture we often use in decision making. Suppose I am considering whether to go to the mountains for a hike or just stay at home and relax this weekend. These are (we assume) real possibilities, though undoubtedly not the only ones. Corresponding to each is at least one possible world—that is, at least one course of events that the world might take from the beginning of time through and beyond the moment of my decision. Suppose I decide to hike and I carry out that intention. Then the world (or one of the worlds) in which I hike is the actual world, and the worlds in which I stay at home that weekend are possible but nonactual. In these nonactual worlds, everything up to the moment of my decision occurs exactly as it does in the actual world, though events depart from their actual course more or less dramatically thereafter.

When the weekend is over, I may say, "Though I could have stayed home, I can't now go back and change the past; it is now necessarily the case that I went hiking," mixing tenses and alethic modalities in ways that our picture nicely illustrates. To say that I could have stayed home is to say that up to the beginning of the weekend a world in which I stayed home (represented by a path up the trunk through one of the thin branching lines) was possible. This branch, however, has disappeared as time has moved on. To say that my having gone hiking is now necessary is to say that I did go hiking in all currently possible worlds, a circumstance represented in our picture by the fact that all currently possible worlds have exactly the same past as the actual world (the tree has but one trunk).

What we have been thinking of as the disappearance of the tree's lower branches can also be understood in Kripkean terms as the termination of accessibility. In a sense these "vanished" branches are still there; they still represent worlds that are possible in some absolute sense. But these worlds are no longer possible relative to (i.e., no longer accessible from) the actual world. In tense logic, in other words, accessibility is time-relative. Thus to represent alethic modalities in familiar Kripkean fashion in the context of tense logic, we must add a temporal index to the accessibility relation $\mathcal{R}$. Instead of saying flatly that world w_2 is accessible from world w_1, we must specify a time relative to which accessibility is asserted. Thus we shall write, for example, '$w_1\mathcal{R}w_2t$' to indicate that w_2 is accessible from w_1 at time t.[5] Worlds in which I stayed home on the weekend in question are accessible from the actual world prior to my leaving, but not thereafter.

Truth, already relativized to worlds in alethic modal logic, must in tense logic be further relativized to times. It is true now that I am sitting at my computer, but this will not be true a few hours hence. Thus the statement 'I am sitting at my computer' is true at one time and not at another within the actual world. Moreover, though it is true now in the actual world, it is not true in a world (possible until very recently) in which I got up and went for a snack a moment ago. Thus a statement may have different truth values at different times within the same world and different truth values at the same time within different worlds. Valuations for predicates (including zero-place predicates) must, accordingly, be indexed to both worlds and times. We shall write, for example, '$\mathcal{V}(\Phi, t, w) = T$' to indicate that formula Φ is true at time t in world w. But we shall treat names, as before, as rigid designators, relativizing their denotations neither to worlds nor to times.

Now times (or, as many authors prefer, "moments") do not just occur randomly within worlds, but successively in a strict linear order. In fact, a world may simply be defined as a linear progression of times. To do this formally, we must specify the relation by which the times are ordered. We shall call this the **earlier**

---

[5] It is customary in tense logic to dispense with a separate Kripkean semantics for the alethic operators and to analyze possibility and necessity in terms of the tenses. See, for example, Robert P. McArthur, *Tense Logic* (Dordrecht: D. Reidel, 1976), chap. 3, or Rescher and Urquhart, *Temporal Logic,* chap. XII. But elegant versions of this procedure badly distort the meaning either of the tense operators or of the alethic operators, and more accurate ones are cumbersome and inelegant. Thus I depart from the custom.

than relation and represent it as 'ε'. Thus '$t_1\varepsilon t_2$' means that time t_1 is earlier than time t_2. To say that the times comprising a world are **linearly ordered** is to say that for any times t_1 and t_2 belonging to the same world, either $t_1\varepsilon t_2$ or $t_2\varepsilon t_1$ or $t_1 = t_2$. This implies that the moments comprising a given world can all be arrayed, as in our intuitive picture, as points along a single (possibly curved but more or less vertical) line, with each earlier moment beneath all later moments.

ε, moreover, must in general be **transitive**—that is, for any times t_1, t_2, and t_3, if $t_1\varepsilon t_2$ and $t_2\varepsilon t_3$, then $t_1\varepsilon t_3$—for it violates our conception "earlier" to think of t_1 as earlier than t_2 and t_2 as earlier than t_3 but not t_1 as earlier than t_3.[6]

Finally, we must recognize that even domains, which in alethic logic were relativized to worlds, must now be relativized to times as well. Objects come into and go out of existence as time passes. Thus within a single world what exists at one time differs from what exists at another. But also at a given time what exists in one world may differ from what exists in another. I am now poised over a soap bubble, ready to pop it with my finger. If I choose to do so, then a moment afterward the actual world contains one less soap bubble than exists at the very same moment in the world that would have been actual had I not poked.

Having made these observations, we are now ready to say what a formal model for modal tense logic looks like:

DEFINITION   A **model** or **valuation** $\mathcal{V}$ for a formula or set of formulas of modal tense logic consists of the following:

1. A nonempty set $\mathfrak{I}$ of objects called the **times** of $\mathcal{V}$.
2. A transitive relation ε, consisting of a set of pairs of times from $\mathfrak{I}$.
3. A nonempty set $\mathcal{W}_{\mathcal{V}}$ of objects, called the **worlds** of $\mathcal{V}$.
4. Corresponding to each world w, a set $\mathfrak{I}_w$ of times called the **times in w**[7] such that for any pair of times t_1 and t_2 in this set, either $t_1\varepsilon t_2$ or $t_2\varepsilon t_1$ or $t_1 = t_2$.
5. For each world w and time t in w, a nonempty set $\mathcal{D}_{(t,w)}$ of objects, called the **domain** of w at t.
6. For each name or nonidentity predicate σ of that formula or set of formulas, an extension $\mathcal{V}(\sigma)$ (if σ is a name) or $\mathcal{V}(\sigma, w)$ (if σ is a predicate and w a world in $\mathcal{W}_{\mathcal{V}}$) as follows:
   i. If σ is a name, then $\mathcal{V}(\sigma)$ is a member of $\mathcal{D}_{(t,w)}$ for at least one time t and world w.

---

[6] We might also be tempted to insist that ε is **irreflexive** (i.e., for all times t, it is not the case that $t\varepsilon t$) and **asymmetric** (i.e., for all times t_1 and t_2, if $t_1\varepsilon t_2$ then not $t_2\varepsilon t_1$). But we will resist these temptations. Making ε irreflexive and asymmetric would prevent us from modeling the kind of circular time envisioned in Nietzsche's idea of the eternal recurrence and from envisioning other interesting kinks in time, and there seems to be no a priori reason to rule such models out.

[7] This definition permits us to write the more intuitive expression 't is in w' rather than the formal '$t\,\varepsilon\,\mathfrak{I}_w$'. There is no point in trying to remember the meanings of too many symbols.

ii. If σ is a zero-place predicate (sentence letter), and t is in w, then $\mathcal{V}(\sigma, t, w)$ is one (but not both) of the values T or F.

iii. If σ is a one-place predicate and t is in w, $\mathcal{V}(\sigma, t, w)$ is a set of members of $\mathcal{D}_{(t,w)}$.

iv. If σ is an n-place predicate ($n > 1$), and t is in w, $\mathcal{V}(\sigma, t, w)$ is a set of ordered n-tuples of members of $\mathcal{D}_{(t,w)}$.

Notice that this definition allows worlds to share times, though it permits what is true at a time in a given world to be false at that same time in a different world (as happens after worlds diverge). A world need not contain all times. One world may begin or end sooner than another, and some might be temporally infinite—having no beginning and no end. And worlds need not share any times at all. There may be worlds with times wholly distinct from ours. However, the earlier-than relation transcends worlds in the sense that if $t_1 \mathcal{E} t_2$, t_1 is earlier than t_2 in any world that includes both of these times. Our definition even allows us to model worlds that skip times—jumping as it were from an earlier time to one much later. I doubt that we have much use for such models, but it is harmless to suppose that logic does not rule them out.

Notice, finally, that our definition of a model does not include a specification of the alethic accessibility relation $\mathcal{R}$. This is because $\mathcal{R}$ is definable in terms already available to us. Specifically, we may say that world w_2 is accessible from w_1 at time t iff w_2 has exactly the same history as w_1 up to time t.[8] If w_2 differs in any respect from w_1 before t, then w_2 is no longer possible relative to w_1, for otherwise the past would not be necessary. (Note, however, that in order to be accessible from w_1 at time t, w_2 need not diverge from w_1 precisely at time t; the divergence of the two worlds may yet lie some distance into the future.) Two worlds w_1 and w_2 **have the same history** iff they consist of the same moments up to time t and every atomic formula that is true at a given moment before t in one is true at the same moment in the other, that is, if they meet conditions 1–3 of the following definition:

DEFINITION Given a model $\mathcal{V}$ for a formula or set of formulas, then for any worlds w_1 and w_2 and time t of $\mathcal{V}$, $w_1 \mathcal{R} w_2 t$ iff

1. t is a time in both w_1 and w_2,

---

[8] We assume here that if two worlds that are exactly alike up to a certain time t are both possible (i.e., members of the set of *possible* worlds), then nothing that occurs in either world before that time dictates which of their two courses events must follow from t onward. Hence at t either world is possible relative to the other. This assumption seems reasonable, but as we shall see below it implies a very strong alethic logic, S5. Alternatively, we might have insisted that having the same initial history up to t is a necessary, though not sufficient, condition for accessibility at t. This would permit a variety of weaker alethic logics.

> 2. w_1 and w_2 contain the same times up to t; that is, for all times t', if $t' \varepsilon t$, then t' is in w_1 iff t' is in w_2, and
>
> 3. w_1 and w_2 have the same atomic truths at every moment up to t; that is, for all times t' such that $t' \varepsilon t$, $\mathfrak{D}(t', w_1) = \mathfrak{D}(t', w_2)$, and for all predicates Φ, $\mathcal{V}(\Phi, t', w_1) = \mathcal{V}(\Phi, t', w_2)$.

Since names are not relativized to either worlds or times, stipulating that all times up to t have the same domains and give predicates the same extensions in both worlds insures that the truth values of atomic formulas are the same in both worlds up to t. It also guarantees that most nonatomic formulas have the same truth values in w_1 and w_2—but not that all nonatomic formulas do. We should expect, for example that a formula of the form $\mathbf{F}\Phi$ might have different truth values in w_1 and w_2 even at times before t, since though the two worlds' histories up to t are the same, their futures need not be.

Notice that we require for accessibility only that a world share its history with a given world *up to* the time t in question. Thus, for example, a world may be accessible from the actual world, even if it differs at the present moment, provided only that its past history is exactly the same. If instead we required sameness *up to and including* t we would make not only the past but also the present necessary. For then only worlds exactly like the actual world at t would be accessible from the actual world at t so that anything that happens at t happens necessarily at t. This conflicts with the intuition that our present choices are not determined. It must be admitted, however, that either definition of $\mathcal{R}$ is metaphysically presumptuous. It is a matter of whether we choose to locate the earliest point of potential freedom or contingency in the present moment or the immediate future. Our semantics places it in the present.

It is not difficult to see from our definition of the accessibility relation that $\mathcal{R}$ is reflexive, symmetric, and transitive—in the sense that, for any worlds w_1, w_2, and w_3 and any time t in them:

$w_1 \mathcal{R} w_1 t$
if $w_1 \mathcal{R} w_2 t$, then $w_2 \mathcal{R} w_1 t$
if $w_1 \mathcal{R} w_2 t$ and $w_2 \mathcal{R} w_3 t$, then $w_1 \mathcal{R} w_3 t$.

Together with the valuation rules to be stated below, this implies that the alethic logic associated with our version of modal tense logic is S5. However, it is not this alethic logic that interests us here, but the logic of the tense operators. The semantics for this logic is given by our previous definitions together with the following valuation rules. Rules 1–12 are just the Kripkean rules for alethic modal logic, relativized to times as well as worlds. The novelty lies in rules 13–16. We omit falsity rules here, since the list is getting long. But no matter; apart from cases of nondenoting names, which we shall ignore, a formula is still false iff it is not true.

Valuation Rules for Modal Tense Logic

Given any valuation $\mathcal{V}$ of modal tense logic whose set of worlds is $\mathcal{W}_V$, for any world w in $\mathcal{W}_V$ and time t in w:

1. If Φ is a one-place predicate and α is a name whose extension $\mathcal{V}(\alpha)$ is in $\mathcal{D}_{(t,w)}$, then $\mathcal{V}(\Phi\alpha, t, w) = T$ iff $\mathcal{V}(\alpha) \, \varepsilon \, \mathcal{V}(\Phi, t, w)$.
2. If Φ is an n-place predicate ($n > 1$) and $\alpha_1, \ldots, \alpha_n$ are names whose extensions are all in $\mathcal{D}_{(t,w)}$, then
$$\mathcal{V}(\Phi\alpha_1, \ldots, \alpha_n, t, w) = T \text{ iff } <\mathcal{V}(\alpha_1), \ldots, \mathcal{V}(\alpha_n)> \varepsilon \, \mathcal{V}(\Phi, t, w)$$
3. If α and β are names, then $\mathcal{V}(\alpha = \beta, t, w) = T$ iff $\mathcal{V}(\alpha) = \mathcal{V}(\beta)$.

For the next five rules, Φ and Ψ are any formulas:

4. $\mathcal{V}(\sim\Phi, t, w) = T$ iff $\mathcal{V}(\Phi, t, w) \neq T$
5. $\mathcal{V}(\Phi \,\&\, \Psi, t, w) = T$ iff both $\mathcal{V}(\Phi, t, w) = T$ and $\mathcal{V}(\Psi, t, w) = T$
6. $\mathcal{V}(\Phi \vee \Psi, t, w) = T$ iff either $\mathcal{V}(\Phi, t, w) = T$ or $\mathcal{V}(\Psi, t, w) = T$, or both
7. $\mathcal{V}(\Phi \rightarrow \Psi, t, w) = T$ iff either $\mathcal{V}(\Phi, t, w) \neq T$ or $\mathcal{V}(\Psi, t, w) = T$, or both
8. $\mathcal{V}(\Phi \leftrightarrow \Psi, t, w) = T$ iff $\mathcal{V}(\Phi, t, w) = \mathcal{V}(\Psi, t, w)$

For the next two rules, $\Phi^\alpha/_\beta$ stands for the result of replacing each occurrence of the variable β in Φ by α, and $\mathcal{D}_{(t,w)}$ is the domain that $\mathcal{V}$ assigns to world w at time t.

9. $\mathcal{V}(\forall\beta\Phi, t, w) = T$ iff for all potential names α of all objects d in $\mathcal{D}_{(t,w)}$, $\mathcal{V}_{(\alpha,d)}(\Phi^\alpha/_\beta, t, w) = T$
10. $\mathcal{V}(\exists\beta\Phi, t, w) = T$ iff for some potential name α of some object d in $\mathcal{D}_{(t,w)}$, $\mathcal{V}_{(\alpha,d)}(\Phi^\alpha/_\beta, t, w) = T$
11. $\mathcal{V}(\Box\Phi, t, w) = T$ iff for all worlds u such that $w\mathcal{R}ut$, $\mathcal{V}(\Phi, t, u) = T$
12. $\mathcal{V}(\Diamond\Phi, t, w) = T$ iff for some world u such that $w\mathcal{R}ut$, $\mathcal{V}(\Phi, t, u) = T$
13. $\mathcal{V}(H\Phi, t, w) = T$ iff for all times t' in w such that $t'\varepsilon t$, $\mathcal{V}(\Phi, t', w) = T$
14. $\mathcal{V}(P\Phi, t, w) = T$ iff for some time t' in w, $t'\varepsilon t$ and $\mathcal{V}(\Phi, t', w) = T$
15. $\mathcal{V}(G\Phi, t, w) = T$ iff for all times t' in w such that $t\varepsilon t'$, $\mathcal{V}(\Phi, t', w) = T$
16. $\mathcal{V}(F\Phi, t, w) = T$ iff for some time t' in w, $t\varepsilon t'$ and $\mathcal{V}(\Phi, t', w) = T$

Since truth is now relativized not only to worlds, but to times, we must once again revise the definitions of our chief semantic concepts:

DEFINITION A formula is **valid** iff it is true at all times in all worlds on all of its valuations.

DEFINITION A formula is **consistent** iff it is true at at least one time in at least one world on at least one valuation.

DEFINITION A formula is **inconsistent** iff it is not true at any time in any world on any of its valuations.

DEFINITION A formula is **contingent** iff there is a valuation on which it is true at some time in some world and a valuation on which it is not true at some time in some world.

DEFINITION A *set of formulas* is **consistent** iff there is at least one valuation containing a world in which there is a time at which all the formulas in the set are true.

DEFINITION A *set of formulas* is **inconsistent** iff there is no valuation containing a world in which there is a time at which all the formulas in the set are true.

DEFINITION Two formulas are **equivalent** iff they have the same truth value at every time in every world on every valuation of both.

DEFINITION A **counterexample** to a sequent is a valuation containing a world in which there is a time at which its premises are true and its conclusion is not true.

DEFINITION A sequent is **valid** iff there is no world in any valuation containing a time at which its premises are true and its conclusion is not true.

DEFINITION A sequent is **invalid** iff there is at least one valuation containing a world in which there is a time at which its premises are true and its conclusion is not true.

The primary application of modal tense logic is in clarifying our understanding of the relation between time and possibility. One of the perennial philosophical issues concerning that relation is the question of determinism. Determinism is the thesis that at any given time the only possible world is the actual world—that, in terms of our picture, the tree of time has no thin branches.

There are many arguments purporting to prove this thesis. It has been argued, for example, that since God knows everything that will happen, the course of events cannot deviate from what God foresees and is therefore determined. Other possibilities are illusory. This argument depends, however, on a dubious theological premise.

More cogent, at least initially, are arguments that aim to deduce determinism not from assumptions about God's foreknowledge, but from assumptions about the structure of time itself. As an example, consider the following argument, which purports to show that anything that happens has always been predetermined (i.e., has always necessarily been going to happen):

Suppose that as a matter of fact, a certain event happens—for example, that you read this logic book. Then it has always been the case that you would read this logic book. Therefore it was always necessary that you would read this book. Since the same reasoning can be applied to any actual event, anything that happens was always destined to happen.

The core of this argument consists of two inferences, which, using 'R' for 'You read this book', we may formalize as follows:

R ⊢ HFR
HFR ⊢ H□FR

Analysis of these inferences provides a good illustration of the uses of our semantics. The first is valid. Intuitively, we can see this as follows. Suppose for reductio that this inference is invalid—that you are now at this moment, t, reading this book, but that it is not the case that you have always been going to read this book. Since you have not always been going to read this book, there was a time earlier than t, call it t', at which it is not the case that you were going to read this book.

But then it was true at t' that at all later moments you would not read this book. Since in particular the current moment t is later than t', it follows that you are not reading this book now at t—which contradicts what we said above. Hence the first inference is valid. Here is the same reasoning in strict metatheoretic terms:

METATHEOREM: 'R ⊢ HFR' is valid.

PROOF: Suppose for reductio that this sequent is invalid; that is, there is a valuation $\mathscr{V}$ containing some world w in which there is a time t such that $\mathscr{V}('R', t, w) = T$ and $\mathscr{V}('HFR', t, w) \neq T$. Since $\mathscr{V}('HFR', t, w) \neq T$, by valuation rule 13 there is some time t' in w such that $t'\varepsilon t$ and $\mathscr{V}('FR', t', w) \neq T$. But then by rule 16 for all times t'' in w such that $t'\varepsilon t''$, $\mathscr{V}('R', t'', w) \neq T$. Now since t is in w and $t'\varepsilon t$, this means in particular that $\mathscr{V}('R', t, w) \neq T$, which contradicts our conclusion above that $\mathscr{V}('R', t, w) = T$.

Therefore 'R ⊢ HFR' is valid.   QED

However, the second inference, 'HFR ⊢ H□FR', is invalid. To show this, we must construct a model on which the premise is true and the conclusion false. Intuitively, the model will consist, at minimum, of two diverging worlds, the actual world w_1 and a merely possible world w_2. In the actual world w_1, you have (we shall assume) at the present moment just begun to read this book. In w_1, then, the premise that you have always been going to read this book is true. Now w_2 is exactly like w_1 right up to the present moment. In w_2, however, you never at any time read this book. Thus the conclusion 'H□FR' is false in w_1, because it has not always been the case that you would neccessarily read this book. Up to the present moment it was still possible for you not to be going to read this book, since you had the option represented by w_2.

To make this informal reasoning rigorous, we must formalize this counter-example. We aim to make it simple—though that also makes it unrealistic. Our model need contain only two times, a past time t_1 and the present t_2, and two worlds, w_1 and w_2, each containing both times.[9] (The future plays no role in this example, nor do changes in the past that would require more than one past time in either world.) The sentence letter 'R' will be false at t_1 and true at t_2 in the actual world w_1 and false at both t_1 and t_2 in the merely possible world w_2. It is, of course, arbitrary which objects we use to represent the times and worlds. We might, for example, use the negative numbers -1 and -2 to represent worlds w_1 and w_2 and the positive numbers 1 and 2 to represent times t_1 and t_2, respectively. But doing so would make the proof harder to follow. We shall therefore dispense with this step and simply call the worlds (whatever they are) w_1 and w_2 and the times t_1 and

---

[9] Technically, we could get by even without the past moments, but the resulting model is so counterintuitive that it does not make a good illustration.

t_2. These stipulations define the model. Having done that, the only work that remains is to apply the truth clauses for the operators to verify that this model does indeed make the premise 'HFR' true and the conclusion 'H□FR' false:

METATHEOREM: 'HFR ⊢ H□FR' is invalid.

PROOF: Consider the valuation $\mathcal{V}$ whose set ℐ of times is $\{t_1, t_2\}$, whose earlier-than relation ε is $\{<t_1, t_2>\}$ and whose set of worlds is $\{w_1, w_2\}$. The set of times for both worlds is $\{t_1, t_2\}$; that is, both the times of this valuation are in both worlds, and further:

$$\mathcal{V}(\text{'R'}, t_1, w_1) = F \qquad \mathcal{V}(\text{'R'}, t_1, w_2) = F$$
$$\mathcal{V}(\text{'R'}, t_2, w_1) = T \qquad \mathcal{V}(\text{'R'}, t_2, w_2) = F$$

(Since we are dealing here with propositional logic, it is unnecessary to stipulate domains for the various worlds at various times.)

Now time t_2 is in world w_1, $t_1 \varepsilon t_2$ and $\mathcal{V}(\text{'R'}, t_2, w_1) = T$. Hence by rule 16, $\mathcal{V}(\text{'FR'}, t_1, w_1) = T$. But t_1 is the only time t' in w_1 such that $t' \varepsilon t_2$. Hence for all times t' in w_1 such that $t' \varepsilon t_2$, $\mathcal{V}(\text{'FR'}, t', w_1) = T$. Thus by rule 13, $\mathcal{V}(\text{'HFR'}, t_2, w_1) = T$.

Further, t_2 is the only time t' in world w_2 such that $t_1 \varepsilon t'$. And $\mathcal{V}(\text{'R'}, t_2, w_2) \neq T$. Hence by rule 16, $\mathcal{V}(\text{'FR'}, t_1, w_2) \neq T$. Now by the definition of $\mathcal{R}$, $w_1 \mathcal{R} w_2 t_1$ (since t_1 is a time in both w_1 and w_2 and—trivially!—w_1 and w_2 contain the same times up to t and have the same atomic truths at every moment up to t). Since, then, $w_1 \mathcal{R} w_2 t_1$ and $\mathcal{V}(\text{'FR'}, t_1, w_2) \neq T$, by rule 11, $\mathcal{V}(\text{'□FR'}, t_1, w_1) \neq T$. And since t_1 is a time in w_1 and $t_1 \varepsilon t_2$, it follows by rule 13 that $\mathcal{V}(\text{'H□FR'}, t_2, w_1) \neq T$.

We have now shown that $\mathcal{V}(\text{'HFR'}, t_2, w_1) = T$ and $\mathcal{V}(\text{'H□FR'}, t_2, w_1) \neq T$; hence 'HFR ⊢ H□FR' is invalid.   QED

Have we, then, refuted determinism? Of course not. We have refuted only one argument for it. And this refutation employs a semantics based on controversial assumptions about time and possibility. Indeed, it is a semantics designed from the outset to represent nondeterministic time—time with many possible futures. That it yields counterexamples to deterministic arguments is therefore no wonder. The determinist could well retort that we have used the wrong semantics and hence the wrong logic, that the true semantics represents time not as a branching tree but as a single nonbranching line, and that our semantics simply begs the question.

Logic alone cannot settle this issue. For any purported solution, one can always ask whether the correct semantics, and hence the correct logic, has been used. But here opinions will differ. One can be extremely conservative, allowing into one's semantics only the most strictly logical presuppositions or one can be more venturesome, adopting presuppositions with a metaphysical tinge. (I have been somewhat venturesome, for example, in assuming that ε is transitive and, within worlds, linear, and also in assuming that accessibility amounts to shared history; the determinist, who makes the strong assumption that only one world is possible at any given time, is more venturesome still.) Conservative logics, which operate with fewer presuppositions, are less controversial. But, because they validate fewer inferences, they are also less interesting. The most interesting tense logics venture some way into the hazy borderland between logic and metaphysics.

Though it leaves the problem of determinism unsolved, logical analysis of arguments for determinism is not merely an empty exercise. Surely we clarify our conceptions if we take the time to formalize them and relate them to various models. Moreover, the fact that we can *model* nondeterministic time shows that there is no contradiction in its conception—so far, at least, as we have conceived it. Even if real time is wholly unlike our models, the existence of these models shows that a nondeterministic universe cannot be ruled out on logical grounds alone. There is a logic of nondeterministic time, whether or not time itself is deterministic.

We now turn to some general features of our modal tense logic. Note, first, that tense logic reflects the most fundamental patterns of modal reasoning. In addition to the dualities already mentioned, we have, corresponding to the rule of necessitation in modal logic, this rule: If Φ is valid then so are $H\Phi$ and $G\Phi$. Similarly, corresponding to the Kripke rule K, every sequent of either of the following forms is valid:

$$H(\Phi \to \Psi) \vdash (H\Phi \to H\Psi)$$
$$G(\Phi \to \Psi) \vdash (G\Phi \to G\Psi).$$

However, since the relation ε need not be reflexive, we do not have the principles

$$H\Phi \vdash \Phi$$
$$G\Phi \vdash \Phi$$

which correspond to the T rule $\Box\Phi \vdash \Phi$. These principles are incorrect for tense logic since the first says that whatever has always been true in the past is still true and the second that whatever will always be true in the future is true already. To both of these theses there are easy counterexamples.

Two interesting principles that are not valid on our semantics are

$$P\Phi \to PP\Phi$$
$$F\Phi \to FF\Phi$$

The first asserts that if there was a time at which Φ was the case then there was a (presumably more recent) time at which it had already been that Φ; the second asserts that if there will be a time at which Φ is the case then there will be a (presumably still earlier) time at which Φ is going to be the case. These schemata express the thesis that time is **dense**—that between any two times there exists a third. Any model some of whose worlds contain only finitely many times falsifies this thesis. Since time as we experience it certainly seems to be dense, we might want to build density into our definition of a model. We could do this by requiring that ε be a dense as well as transitive relation—that is, by requiring that for any times t_1 and t_2 in a world w, if $t_1 \varepsilon t_2$, then there exists a time t_3 in w such that $t_1 \varepsilon t_3$

and $t_3 \varepsilon t_2$. That would imply, among other things, that all worlds contain infinitely many times, and it would make the two density principles valid.

All instances of the converses of the density principles

$$PP\Phi \rightarrow P\Phi$$
$$FF\Phi \rightarrow F\Phi$$

are, by contrast, valid on our semantics. This can be shown from our stipulation in the definition of a valuation that ε is transitive.

Tense logic displays some interesting oddities if time has a first or last moment. If there is a first moment—that is, a moment t at which time begins—in some world w, for example, then at that world and time $P\Phi$ is false for any formula Φ, even if Φ is valid. This is because there is no time t' in w such that $t'\varepsilon t$ and $\mathcal{V}(\Phi, t', w) = T$ so that by valuation rule 14, $\mathcal{V}(P\Phi, t, w) \neq T$. But the real oddity is that $H\Phi$ is true at t for any formula Φ, even if Φ is a contradiction. This is because, since there are no times t' in w such that $t'\varepsilon t$ and $\mathcal{V}(\Phi, t', w) \neq T$ (since there are no times t' in w such that $t'\varepsilon t$), it follows trivially that for all times t' such that $t'\varepsilon t$, $\mathcal{V}(\Phi, t', w) = T$ so that by valuation rule 13, $\mathcal{V}(H\Phi, t, w) = T$.

As a matter of fact, the formula 'PH(A & ~A)', which says that there was a time at which the contradiction 'A & ~A' had always been the case, is a way of asserting that there was a first moment in time. Similarly, 'FG(A & ~A)' says in effect that there will be a last moment in time. It follows, then, that '~PH(A & ~A)' and '~FG(A & ~A)' assert, respectively, that time has no first moment and no last moment. However, this is not the same as asserting that time has gone on or will go on forever. Suppose that time will end exactly one second from now, but that there still will be a moment of time ½ second from now, ¾ second from now, ⅞ second from now, and so on. Then there will be no last moment, even though time does not go on forever. There is no way in our version of tense logic to say that time goes on forever, since our logic deals only with the topological properties of time (i.e., roughly, with time's "shape"), rather than with its duration. Logics dealing with duration are called **chronological logics** or **metric temporal logics,** but they are beyond the scope of this book.[10]

Some of the valid formulas of tense logic have no analogs in the other modal logics we have studied. Among these are the following "mixing axioms" (so called because they mix past and future operators):

$$\Phi \rightarrow GP\Phi$$
$$\Phi \rightarrow HF\Phi$$

The first of these asserts that if Φ then it will always be that Φ was the case; the second asserts that if Φ then it always had been that Φ would be the case.

Likewise peculiar to tense logic are these axioms of past and future linearity:

$$(P\Phi \ \& \ P\Psi) \rightarrow (P(\Phi \ \& \ \Psi) \lor ((P(\Phi \ \& \ P\Psi) \lor P(P\Phi \ \& \ \Psi)))$$
$$(F\Phi \ \& \ F\Psi) \rightarrow (F(\Phi \ \& \ \Psi) \lor ((F(\Phi \ \& \ F\Psi) \lor F(F\Phi \ \& \ \Psi)))$$

---

[10] For an account of metric temporal logics, see Rescher & Urquhart, *Temporal Logic,* chap. X.

The first asserts that if Φ and Ψ are both the case in times past, then they are both the case at the same past moment, or Ψ is the case before Φ, or Φ is the case before Ψ. The second is an analogous assertion about the future. The validity of these principles follows from our stipulation in the definition of a valuation that time within a world is linear.

We have designed our semantics (primarily through the definition of the relation $\mathscr{R}$) to model the notion that the past is necessary. Thus we might expect that all formulas of the form $\mathbf{P}\Phi \rightarrow \Box\mathbf{P}\Phi$ turn out to be valid. This is almost, but not quite, true. All formulas of this form in which Φ contains no occurrence of either of the future operators 'F' or 'G' are valid. But the use of 'F' or 'G' would allow us to make statements about what is going to be true in the future, and since the future need not be determined on our semantics, their inclusion may result in false instances.

To see why, let's consider a world w and a time t in w at which Alice, standing on the edge of a precipice with a hang glider, decides to leap—a thing she has never done before. Suppose also that this decision was voluntary; that is, though in w she decides to leap and actually takes the plunge, she need not have done so. In other words, there is some other possible world u which has the same history as w up to t, in which her decision at time t is not to leap. In u, we shall suppose, she stays put, deciding then and there that hang gliding is not for her and never attempting it again. In w, then, at some time after t Alice is hang gliding, but in u she never hang glides. Let's use the letter 'A' to stand for 'Alice is hang gliding.' Then 'PFA $\rightarrow \Box$PFA', which is an instance of the general form $\mathbf{P}\Phi \rightarrow \Box\mathbf{P}\Phi$, is false in w at t. For consider some time t' in w that is earlier than t. Then clearly 'FA' is true at t' in w. Hence 'PFA' is true at t in w. However, '$\Box$PFA' is false at t in w. This is because 'A' is false at all times in u. Hence in u there is no time before t at which 'FA' is true. So 'PFA' is false at t in u. Hence, since u is accessible from w at t (both worlds having the same history up to t), '$\Box$PFA' is false at t in w. It is, in other words, not necessary at t in w that it was the case that Alice would hang glide—for at t, the moment of her decision, a world in which she would never leap was still possible.

Though instances of $\mathbf{P}\Phi \rightarrow \Box\mathbf{P}\Phi$ may not be valid when Φ contains **F** or **G**, still, from those instances not containing **F** or **G**, all of which *are* valid, we can see that our semantics incorporates a strong form of the doctrine of **essentiality of origin**. Any object which now actually exists has, as a matter of necessity, the entire past it actually did have, from the moment of its origin up to the present. Worlds whose history deviates from ours at some time before now are now no longer possible relative to the actual world, though they may once have been possible.

You probably have noticed that principles of tense logic tend to come in pairs—one principle for the past and one for the future. This suggests a general principle, known as the **mirror image rule**:

> If Φ is a valid formula, then so is the formula Ψ obtained from Φ by replacing each occurrence of **G** by **H** and each occurrence of **F** by **P**, or vice versa.

The mirror image rule justifies, for example, an inference from 'A $\rightarrow$ GPA' to 'A $\rightarrow$ HFA' and vice versa.

This rule is, in fact, valid for semantic systems that make the past and future topologically symmetrical. Our semantics is not one of these, however, since we have designed it to make past but not future events necessary. Consequently, not all instances of the mirror image rule are valid on our semantics. For example, though the formula 'PA → □PA' is valid, as noted previously, the corresponding formula 'FA → □FA' is contingent.

Finally, let us take note of an interesting principle involving the interaction of quantification with modal and tense operators—Murphy's law: "Whatever can go wrong will." Using 'W' for 'goes wrong', we might at first blush just literally transcribe this principle as '$\forall x(\Diamond Wx \to FWx)$', but that misinterprets the tenses. It says, "Whatever can *now* go wrong will at some future time go wrong." But it is truer to the intent to say that whatever can *at some future time* go wrong will at some future time go wrong, that is:

$$\forall x(\Diamond FWx \to FWx)$$

Our nondeterministic semantics provides countermodels to this thesis, but a deterministic semantics does not.

Exercise 13.2.1

Prove that the following sequents are valid on our semantics for modal tense logic:

1. FHA ⊢ A
2. FHA ⊢ HA
3. PA ⊢ GPA
4. PPA ⊢ PA
5. HA & PB ⊢ P(A & B)
6. GA → FA ⊢ ~G(A & ~A)
7. GHA, FA ⊢ HGA

Hint: It is important to the proofs of the last three problems that the sentence letter 'A' does not contain the operators 'F' or 'G':

8. PA ⊢ □PA
9. $\Diamond$FHA ⊢ A
10. A ⊢ $\Diamond$HFA

Exercise 13.2.2

Prove that the following sequents are invalid:

1. PA ⊢ A
2. PA ⊢ $\Diamond$A
3. □A ⊢ FA
4. □PA ⊢ P□A
5. PA ⊢ PPA

Exercise 13.2.3

Prove that the following formulas are not valid:

1. A ∨ (PA ∨ FA)
2. FA → □FA
3. FA ∨ F~A
4. P(A ∨ ~A)
5. ∀x(◇FW*x* → FW*x*)

CHAPTER $\boldsymbol{14}$

HIGHER-ORDER LOGICS

14.1 HIGHER-ORDER LOGICS: SYNTAX

Consider the following obviously valid inference:

> Al is a frog.
> Beth is a frog.
> ∴ Al and Beth have something in common.

We might symbolize this in predicate logic by 'Fa, Fb ⊢ ∃xHabx', where 'H' is a three-place predicate meaning "___ and ___ have ___ in common." But this sequent is invalid and so does not capture the relevant features of the argument. What Al and Beth have in common, of course, is the property expressed by the predicate 'F', the property of being a frog. This is the "something" referred to in the conclusion. 'Something' normally indicates the presence of existential quantification, but in this case the quantification seems to generalize not the places occupied by the names, but the place occupied by the predicate. The form, in other words, appears to be this:

Fa, Fb ⊢ ∃X(Xa & Xb)

where 'X' is not a specific predicate, but a variable replaceable by predicates—a variable that stands for properties. Thus the conclusion asserts that there is a property X which both Al and Beth have—or, more colloquially, that they have something in common.

If we allow such quantification, then many ideas not previously expressible in any direct way become formally expressible. We may formalize 'Everything has some property', for example, as '$\forall x \exists Y Y x$'. Notice that we now need two styles of variables, one for properties (uppercase variables) and one for individuals (lowercase variables). A logic which quantifies over both individuals and properties of individuals is called a **second-order logic,** as opposed to systems such as classical predicate logic, which quantify only over individuals and are therefore called **first-order logics.** It is also possible to quantify over properties of properties, as in this inference:

> Socrates is snub-nosed.
> Being snub-nosed is an undesirable property.
> ∴ Socrates has a property that has a property.

Here being undesirable is asserted to be a property of the property of being snub-nosed. Using the extra-large typeface symbol 'U' to stand for 'is undesirable', the equally large variable 'Y' to quantify over properties of properties,[1] 's' for 'Socrates', and 'N' for 'is snub-nosed', we may express this inference as

$$Ns, \, UN \vdash \exists X(Xs \,\&\, \exists Y Y X)$$

'N' occupies the predicate position in the first premise but the subject position in the second, where it is treated as a name for the property of being snub-nosed. Logics which quantify over properties of properties in this fashion are called **third-order logics.** And there are fourth-order logics, fifth-order logics, and so on. Any logic of the second order or higher is called a **higher-order logic.** Higher-order logics use a different type of variable for each domain of quantification (individuals, properties of individuals, properties of properties of individuals, and so on). An infinite hierarchy of higher-order logics is called a **theory of types.**

Higher-order logic was invented by Gottlob Frege late in the nineteenth century as a way of analyzing the concept of a natural number. To understand Frege's idea, let's consider the number two. What, exactly, is this number? It seems to be a property of some sort, since it is exemplified by various things: world wars in the twentieth century, wings of a hummingbird, truth values of classical logic, letters in the word 'ox', poles of the Earth—to mention a few. Consider, in particular, the last of these, the poles. In what sense do the poles exemplify twoness? Certainly not individually. The North Pole does not exemplify twoness. Neither does the South Pole. Each pole by itself is just a single thing. What exemplifies twoness is not the poles taken individually, but the set defined by the property of being a pole—i.e., the set that contains just the two poles. Twoness, then, is a property of this set or its defining property, not of the individual letters. Frege defined twoness as the property of being a property with two exemplars. On this analysis, the

---

[1] This difference is usually marked by special subscripts or superscripts, but for the simple illustrations given here, variation in size is more graphic.

property of being a pole has the higher-order property of twoness because it is exemplified by two individual objects.

Frege's idea is readily formalizable in second-order logic. Let the first-order predicate 'P' stand for 'is a pole'. Then, using ordinary first-order logic, we can say that there are exactly two poles, as follows:

$$\exists x \exists y (\sim x = y \;\&\; \forall z (Pz \leftrightarrow (z = x \lor z = y)))$$

(The general technique for symbolizing expressions of this sort is explained in Section 6.3.) More generally, using the predicate variable 'X', we can say that exactly two things have property X like this:

$$\exists x \exists y (\sim x = y \;\&\; \forall z (Xz \leftrightarrow (z = x \lor z = y)))$$

This expression is in effect a one-place predicate whose instances are properties rather than individuals. If we replace 'X' by a predicate expressing a property exemplified by exactly two individuals, the resulting formula is true. If we replace 'X' by any other predicate of individuals, it is false. Using our convention of extra-large typeface to indicate predicates of properties, we may thus abbreviate this expression as '$2X$', where '2' is a predicate meaning "has the property of being exemplified by two individuals." Formally, we can do this by adopting a definition of the following form:

$$\forall X (2X \leftrightarrow \exists x \exists y (\sim x = y \;\&\; \forall z (Xz \leftrightarrow (z = x \lor z = y))))$$

To say that there are exactly two poles, we may now simply write '$2P$'. This means that the property of being a pole has the property of being exemplified by two individuals. Similar analyses may be offered of the other natural numbers. So, for example,

$$\forall X (0X \leftrightarrow \sim\exists y Xy)$$
$$\forall X (1X \leftrightarrow \exists x \forall y (Xy \leftrightarrow y = x))$$
$$\forall X (3X \leftrightarrow \exists x \exists y \exists z (((\sim x = y \;\&\; \sim x = z) \;\&\; \sim y = z) \;\&\; \forall w (Xw \leftrightarrow ((w = x \lor w = y) \lor w = z))))$$

and so on.

Higher-order logic enables us to quantify over these numbers and introduce still higher-order predicates that apply to them (such as 'is prime' or 'is greater than'). Thus it provides the resources to construct arithmetic—and much of the rest of mathematics—in what appear to be purely logical terms.[2] For this reason Frege and also Alfred North Whitehead and Bertrand Russell,[3] writing near the beginning of the twentieth century, held that mathematics itself is nothing more than logic. More precisely, they argued that all mathematical ideas can be defined

---

[2] The details of this construction are beyond the scope of this book. The classic introduction to them is Bertrand Russell's *Introduction to Mathematical Philosophy* (London: Allen and Unwin, 1919).

[3] The arguments of Whitehead and Russell were developed in their historic three-volume work, *Principia Mathematica* (Cambridge: Cambridge University Press, 1910–1913).

in terms of purely logical ideas and that all mathematical truths are logical truths. This thesis, known as **logicism,** has, however, met with serious technical difficulties and is now in disrepute.[4]

In addition to providing an analysis of number, second-order logic provides an analysis of identity. Identity can be defined in terms of second-order quantification and the biconditional by a principle known as **Leibniz's law.** (However, we shall not adopt this definition but will retain the identity sign as a separate, primitive operator.) This is the principle that objects are identical to one another if and only if they have exactly the same properties. In formal terms:

$$a = b \leftrightarrow \forall X(Xa \leftrightarrow Xb)$$

Leibniz's law itself is sometimes further analyzed into two subsidiary principles, the **identity of indiscernibles:**

$$\forall X(Xa \leftrightarrow Xb) \rightarrow a = b$$

and the **indiscernibility of identicals:**

$$a = b \rightarrow \forall X(Xa \leftrightarrow Xb)$$

The first of these formulas says that objects that have exactly the same properties are identical, and the second says that identical objects have exactly the same properties. Leibniz's law is equivalent to their conjunction.

Higher-order quantifiers may range not only over properties but over relations as well. For example, the argument

> Al loves Beth.
> ∴   Al has some relation to Beth.

may be formalized as 'Lab ⊢ ∃ZZab'.[5]

Analogies, to take another example, are often expressed in the form

> a stands to b as c stands to d.

For instance:

> Washington D.C. is to the USA as Moscow is to Russia,

---

[4] For good accounts of the demise of logicism, see Rudolf Carnap's "The Logicist Foundations of Mathematics" and Kurt Gödel's "Russell's Mathematical Logic," both in D. F. Pears, ed., *Bertrand Russell: A Collection of Critical Essays* (New York: Doubleday, 1972). See also Paul Benacerraf and Hilary Putnam, eds., *Philosophy of Mathematics: Selected Readings,* 2nd ed. (New York: Cambridge University Press, 1983).

[5] It is common practice in higher-order logic to mark variables standing for n-place predicates with the superscript or subscript 'n'; but since we require that a quantified variable always occurs both with the quantifier and at least once later in the formula, this is unnecessary, for we can tell which sort of predicate the variable stands for by counting the names after one of the later occurrences of the variable in the formula. Thus we know that in '∃ZZab', 'Z' is a variable ranging over two-place relations, for in its second occurrence it is followed by two names.

the analogy here being the relationship between a country and its capital city. The general assertion that there is such an analogy among four particular items may be formalized as

$$\exists Z(Zab \mathbin{\&} Zcd)$$

This says that there is some respect in which a stands to b as c stands to d.

Many important generalizations in logic are naturally formulated as higher-order sentences. Take, for example, the assertion that every asymmetric relation is irreflexive. An **asymmetric** relation is one such that if it holds between x and y it does not hold between y and x. An **irreflexive** relation is one that does not hold between any object and itself. Accordingly, 'All asymmetric relations are irreflexive' may be formalized as

$$\forall Z(\forall x\forall y(Zxy \rightarrow {\sim}Zyx) \rightarrow \forall x{\sim}Zxx)$$

Type hierarchies involving relations can be extraordinarily complex. For the remainder of this chapter we shall confine our consideration just to second-order logic, since much of what is novel about type theory appears already at the second order.

Some second-order logics allow quantification not only of one-place and many-place predicates, but of zero-place predicates (sentence letters) as well. On such logics, for example, we may infer from the valid formula 'P ∨ ~P' the formula '$\forall X(X \vee {\sim}X)$', which may be interpreted as "every proposition is such that either it or its negation holds." But the interpretation of such formulas is problematic, unless we regard propositions as truth values—in which case it is trivial. So we will not discuss this sort of quantification here.

The syntax of second-order logic is like that of first-order predicate logic (including the identity predicate), with two exceptions: (1) We now reserve the capital letters 'U' through 'Z', which before were predicates, to be used with or without subscripts as **predicate variables,** and (2) we add the following clause to the formation rules:

If Φ is a formula containing a predicate Ψ, then any expression of the form $\forall\Delta\Phi\Delta/\Psi$ or $\exists\Delta\Phi\Delta/\Psi$ is a formula, where $\Phi\Delta/\Psi$ is the result of replacing one or more occurrences of Ψ in Φ by some predicate variable Δ not already in Φ.

This is just like the quantifier clause for predicate logic, except that it concerns predicates and predicate variables, rather than names and individual variables.

Exercise 14.1

Formalize the following arguments in second-order logic, using the interpretation suggested below. All of these arguments are valid.

Names	One-Place Predicates	Two-Place Predicate
a—Al	H—is human	L—loves
b—Bud	M—is mortal	
	P—is perfect	

1. All humans are mortal. Therefore all humans have something in common.
2. Al is human. No humans are perfect. Therefore there is at least one property which Al has and at least one which he doesn't have.
3. All objects are such that there is no property which they both have and lack. Therefore, for any object and any property, either it has that property or it does not.
4. Al is Bud. Therefore Al and Bud have exactly the same properties.
5. Everything is either human or nonhuman; therefore there is a single property which every object has.
6. Everything is identical to itself; therefore there is some relation which everything has to itself.
7. Al loves himself. Therefore not all relations are irreflexive.
8. Some relations are asymmetric. Therefore some relations are irreflexive.

14.2 SECOND-ORDER LOGIC: SEMANTICS

We have been treating one-place predicate variables informally as ranging over properties and n-place predicate variables ($n > 1$) as ranging over relations. But what *are* properties and relations? The usual answer is that properties are sets and n-place relations are sets of n-tuples. This is also the answer we shall give, though it leads to some counterintuitve consequences. Since, for example, there is only one empty set (see Section 7.1), it also follows that there is only one property that is had by no objects. We must concede, for instance, that the properties of being a purple kangaroo and of being a frictionless machine (neither of which is had by any object), though nominally distinct, are actually the same property. There are more sophisticated notions of what properties and relations are, but these would take us into the field of intensional logic, which is beyond the scope of this book.[6]

One advantage of treating properties and relations as sets or sets of n-tuples is that it makes generalization of the notion of a valuation to second-order logic elegant and easy. We may define a **valuation** for second-order logic in just the way we did for first-order predicate logic; it is just a domain together with an assignment of appropriate extensions to predicates and names. We must, however,

---

[6] There is no easy introduction to intensional logic. Some of the most interesting work remains that of Richard Montague. See his *Formal Philosophy* (New Haven, Conn.: Yale University Press, 1974).

generalize the idea of an expansion of a valuation and provide additional valuation rules for second-order quantification.

To illustrate, let's take the formula '∃XXa', which says that object a has some property—that is, on our current interpretation, is a member of some set. This is clearly true. What makes it true is that we can always drop the quantifier and substitute some one-place predicate Φ for 'X', which we can interpret so as to make Φa true. (The simplest way to do this is to let $\mathcal{V}(\Phi)$ be the set whose sole member is the object denoted by 'a'.) In other words, '∃XXa' is true iff we can expand our language with a possibly new predicate Φ interpreted so as to make Φa true. To state this formally we must define the concept of a second-order expansion. Instead of introducing a new name that denotes an object in the domain, as in a first-order expansion, a second-order expansion adds a new n-place predicate that denotes a set of objects (if $n = 1$) or n-tuples (if $n > 1$) from the domain.

To simplify this definition and the valuation rules that follow, we shall regard a set of objects as a set of one-tuples so that instead of the awkward phrasing 'set of objects (if $n = 1$) or n-tuples (if $n > 1$)', we may say simply 'set of n-tuples ($n > 0$)'. We now define the notion of a potential characterizer and a second-order expansion. These are perfectly analogous to the first-order conceptions of a potential name and expansion.

DEFINITION Let $\mathcal{V}$ be any valuation, Ψ any n-place predicate ($n > 0$), and $\mathcal{N}$ any set of n-tuples of objects in the domain of $\mathcal{V}$. Then Ψ **potentially characterizes** $\mathcal{N}$ with respect to $\mathcal{V}$ if and only if $\mathcal{V}$ does not assign some extension other than $\mathcal{N}$ to Ψ. (In other words, Ψ potentially characterizes $\mathcal{N}$ if and only if either $\mathcal{V}(\Psi) = \mathcal{N}$ or $\mathcal{V}$ assigns nothing to Ψ.)

DEFINITION Let $\mathcal{V}$ be any valuation, $\mathcal{N}$ any set of n-tuples ($n > 0$) from the domain of $\mathcal{V}$, and Ψ any n-place predicate which potentially characterizes $\mathcal{N}$ with respect to $\mathcal{V}$. Then the **second-order expansion** $\mathcal{V}_{(\Psi,\mathcal{N})}$ of $\mathcal{V}$ with respect to $\mathcal{N}$ and Ψ is the valuation which has the same domain as $\mathcal{V}$ and which assigns the same extensions to the same predicates and names, but which *in addition* assigns to Ψ the extension $\mathcal{N}$, if $\mathcal{V}$ does not already assign Ψ an extension. If $\mathcal{V}$ already assigns $\mathcal{N}$ to Ψ, then $\mathcal{V}_{(\Psi,\mathcal{N})}$ is just $\mathcal{V}$.

Now to the valuation rules of first-order predicate logic, we add the following new clauses. Let Δ be any n-place predicate variable ($n > 0$) and $\Phi(\Psi/\Delta)$ the result of replacing all occurrences of the Δ in Φ by Ψ. Then:

11. $\mathcal{V}(\forall\Delta\Phi) = T$ iff for all sets $\mathcal{N}$ of n-tuples from $\mathcal{D}$ and for all n-place predicates Ψ that potentially characterize $\mathcal{N}$, $\mathcal{V}_{(\Psi,\mathcal{N})}(\Phi(\Psi/\Delta)) = T$;
     $\mathcal{V}(\forall\Delta\Phi) = F$ iff for some set $\mathcal{N}$ of n-tuples from $\mathcal{D}$ and some n-place predicate Ψ that potentially characterizes $\mathcal{N}$, $\mathcal{V}_{(\Psi,\mathcal{N})}(\Phi(\Psi/\Delta)) \neq T$.
12. $\mathcal{V}(\exists\Delta\Phi) = T$ iff for some set $\mathcal{N}$ of n-tuples from $\mathcal{D}$ and some n-place predicate Ψ that potentially characterizes $\mathcal{N}$, $\mathcal{V}_{(\Psi,\mathcal{N})}(\Phi(\Psi/\Delta)) = T$;

$\mathcal{V}(\exists\Delta\Phi) = F$ iff for all sets $\mathcal{N}$ of n-tuples from $\mathcal{D}$ and for all n-place predicates Ψ that potentially characterize $\mathcal{N}$, $\mathcal{V}_{(\Psi,\mathcal{N})}(\Phi(\Psi/\Delta)) \neq T$.

Using this semantics, we can see, for example, that the formula '$\exists XXa$', which we considered earlier, is not merely true on some particular valuations but is a valid formula.

METATHEOREM: '$\exists XXa$' is valid.

PROOF: Suppose for reductio that there is some valuation $\mathcal{V}$ such that $\mathcal{V}('\exists XXa') \neq T$. Then by valuation rule 12, for all sets $\mathcal{N}$ of one-tuples (objects) from $\mathcal{D}$ and for all one-place predicates Φ that potentially characterize $\mathcal{N}$, $\mathcal{V}_{(\Phi,\mathcal{N})}(\Phi a) \neq T$. Now (by the definition of a valuation) $\mathcal{V}$ assigns to the name 'a' some object d in $\mathcal{D}$. It follows in particular that for the one-place predicate 'F' and the set $\{d\}$, $\mathcal{V}_{('F',\{d\})}('Fa') \neq T$. This means, by valuation rule 1, that it is not the case that $\mathcal{V}_{('F',\{d\})}('a') \; \varepsilon \; \mathcal{V}_{('F',\{d\})}('F')$, that is, it is not the case that $d \, \varepsilon \, \{d\}$—which is a contradiction.
Therefore '$\exists XXa$' is true on all valuations.   QED

Trees in second-order logic are just like those for first-order predicate logic, except that they employ four new rules—two each for each of the two new second-order quantifiers. Except for the universal quantifier rule, they are little different from the corresponding rules for first-order quantifiers. The existential rule is:

Second-Order Existential Quantifier (2∃)   If an unchecked formula of the form $\exists\Delta\Phi$, where Δ is an n-place predicate variable, appears on an open path, check it. Then choose an n-place predicate Ψ that does not yet appear anywhere on that path and write $\Phi(\Psi/\Delta)$, the result of replacing every occurrence of Δ in Φ by Ψ, at the bottom of every open path that contains the newly checked formula.

We may use this rule to show, for example, that the form '$\exists X(Xa \& Xb) \vdash a = b$' is invalid. (Just having at least one property in common does not guarantee identity!) Here is the tree:

1.	$\sqrt{}\,\exists X(Xa \& Xb)$	Premise
2.	$\sim a = b$	Negation of conclusion
3.	$\sqrt{}\,Fa \& Fb$	1 2∃
4.	Fa	3 &
5.	Fb	3 &

The tree exhibits a counterexample in a domain of two distinct individuals, both of which have the property F.

The tree rules for negated quantifiers are exactly like those for first-order predicate logic, except that they mention predicate variables instead of individual variables:

Negated Second-Order Existential Quantification (2~∃) If an unchecked formula of the form ~∃ΔΦ (where Δ is a predicate variable) appears on an open path, check it and write ∀Δ~Φ at the bottom of every open path that contains the newly checked formula.

Negated Second-Order Universal Quantification (2~∀) If an unchecked formula of the form ~∀ΔΦ (where Δ is a predicate variable) appears on an open path, check it and write ∃Δ~Φ at the bottom of every open path that contains the newly checked formula.

The following tree uses 2~∀ and 2∃ to show that '$a = b \vdash \forall X(Xa \rightarrow Xb)$' is valid:

1. $a = b$ Premise
2. $\checkmark \sim\forall X(Xa \rightarrow Xb)$ Negation of conclusion
3. $\checkmark \exists X\sim(Xa \rightarrow Xb)$ 2 2~∀
4. $\checkmark \sim(Fa \rightarrow Fb)$ 3 2∃
5. Fa   4 ~→
6. ~Fb   4 ~→
7. Fb   1, 5 =
8. ×   6, 7

The second-order universal quantification rule, however, is more complicated. To see the need for the complication, consider the following example. It is certainly true (indeed valid) that if Al has any property then Al does not not have that property. In symbols: $\forall X(Xa \rightarrow \sim\sim Xa)$. It ought to follow in particular that if Al is loved then Al is not not loved. But the property of being loved is, on at least one useful formalization denoted not by a simple predicate, but by the complex expression '$\exists xLxy$', where 'L' is a two-place predicate meaning "loves." The complex expression reads, "There is something that loves y," or, more simply, "y is loved." Correspondingly, 'Al is loved' is '$\exists xLxa$'. Thus what follows as an instance of '$\forall X(Xa \rightarrow \sim\sim Xa)$' is '$\exists xLxa \rightarrow \sim\sim\exists xLxa$'.

Notice that to obtain this instance we had to replace the predicate variable 'X' in '$\forall X(Xa \rightarrow \sim\sim Xa)$' not by a single one-place predicate, but by the entire expression '$\exists xLxy$'. In the process, the place of the unquantified variable 'y' was taken by the name 'a'.

Now let's consider a more sophisticated example. It is also true (and valid) that for any relation, if Al has that relation to Beth, then something has that relation to Beth—that is, $\forall Z(Zab \rightarrow \exists xZxb)$. And from this it ought to follow (since nonidentity is a relation) that if Al is not identical to Beth, then something is not identical to her—that is, $\sim a = b \rightarrow \exists x\sim x = b$. Now the relation of nonidentity is expressed by the complex formula '$\sim x = y$'. To obtain '$\sim a = b \rightarrow \exists x\sim x = b$' as an instance of '$\forall Z(Zab \rightarrow \exists xZxb)$', we remove the quantifier and replace each occurrence of the predicate variable 'Z' by '$\sim x = y$', substituting the first name or variable following that occurrence of 'Z' for 'x' and the second name or variable following that occurrence of 'Z' for 'y'. It is this sort of substitution that makes the universal quantification rule somewhat difficult to express.

Notice that expressions such as '$\exists x Lxy$' and '$\sim x = y$' are not officially formulas, since they contain unquantified variables. They are, rather, expressions that could be obtained by removing initial first-order quantifiers from quantified formulas. The unquantified variables in such expressions are known as **free variables**, and such an expression containing exactly n free variables is called an **n-place open sentence**. Thus '$\exists x Lxy$' is a one-place open sentence, because it has one free variable, 'y', and '$\sim x = y$' is a two-place open sentence. What we count in determining the number of places is the number of distinct variables, not the number of occurrences of variables. So, for example, '$Lxx \lor \sim Lxx$' is a one-place open sentence, even though its one variable occurs four times.

An instance of a second-order universally quantified formula, then, is a formula obtained by removing the quantifier with its attached n-place predicate variable and replacing remaining occurrences of that variable with an n-place open sentence so that names and variables wind up in the right places in the manner illustrated above. More precisely:

DEFINITION Let Δ be an n-place predicate variable and Ψ be an n-place open sentence whose free variables (in no particular order) are $\alpha_1, \ldots, \alpha_n$. Then an **instance** of a formula of the form $\forall \Delta \Phi$ with respect to Ψ is the formula that results from replacing each occurrence of $\Delta \beta_1, \ldots, \beta_n$ in Φ, where $\beta_1, \ldots, \beta_n$ are lowercase variables or names, with $\Psi(\beta_1/\alpha_1, \ldots, \beta_n/\alpha_n)$, the result of replacing each occurrence of the lowercase variables $\alpha_1, \ldots, \alpha_n$ in Ψ by $\beta_1, \ldots, \beta_n$, respectively.

Being an instance is an easier thing to show than to say! Having gotten this far, however, we should not find the universal quantifier rule too difficult:

Second-Order Universal Quantification (2∀)   If a formula of the form $\forall \Delta \Phi$, where Δ is an n-place predicate variable, appears on an open path and Ψ is any n-place open sentence whose predicates (excluding the identity predicate) and names all occur on that path, then write any instance of $\forall \Delta \Phi$ with respect to Ψ at the bottom of the path. *Do not* check $\forall \Delta \Phi$.

The following tree uses the second-order universal rule (2∀) to show that the form '$Fa \vdash \exists X Xa$' is valid:

1.	Fa	Premise
2.	$\checkmark \sim \exists X Xa$	Negation of conclusion
3.	$\forall X \sim Xa$	2 2$\sim \exists$
4.	$\sim Fa$	3 2$\forall$
5.	$\times$	1, 4

Here we may think of the one-place open sentence that replaces the predicate variable 'X' at step 4 simply as 'Fx'—or 'Fy', and so on: The choice of the lower-case variable is arbitrary. Notice that in accordance with the rule 'Fx' contains no names or predicates not already on the path.

Sometimes, however, the path may contain no names or predicates at all. In that case we can still form instances by using the identity predicate, for which explicit exception is made in the rule. Consider this tree, which shows that the assertion that something has some property, '$\exists X \exists y X y$', is valid:

1. $\checkmark \sim\exists X \exists y X y$ Negation of given
2. $\forall X \sim\exists y X y$ 1 2-∃
3. $\checkmark \sim\exists y\, y = y$ 2 2∀
4. $\checkmark \forall y \sim y = y$ 3 ~∃
5. $\sim a = a$ 4 ∀
6. ✕   5

Here we may think of the open formula replacing 'X' at step 3 as '$x = x$'.

Finally, let's use the tree rules to demonstrate a mildly surprising result—namely, that being identical to something amounts just to having every property that thing has (or, more properly, belonging to every set it belongs to). That is, we are going to show that the formula '$a = b \leftrightarrow \forall X(Xa \rightarrow Xb)$' is valid. This is an apparently stronger version of Leibniz's law, which asserts that two things are identical iff they have exactly the same properties, that is: $a = b \leftrightarrow \forall X(Xa \leftrightarrow Xb)$. It turns out, however, that if b has all of a's properties, then as a matter of logic a has all of b's—so that the two formulations are really equivalent. Intuitively, we can see this as follows. Suppose for reductio that b has all of a's properties but that a does not have all of b's. Then there is some property F that b has but a doesn't. Since a doesn't have F, then a has the property $\sim$F. And since b has all of a's properties, it follows that b has $\sim$F, and hence has both F and $\sim$F—a contradiction. That explains the equivalence of '$\forall X(Xa \rightarrow Xb)$' and '$\forall X(Xa \leftrightarrow Xb)$'. Here is the tree that shows that '$a = b$' and '$\forall X(Xa \rightarrow Xb)$' are equivalent (i.e., that '$a = b \leftrightarrow \forall X(Xa \rightarrow Xb)$' is valid):

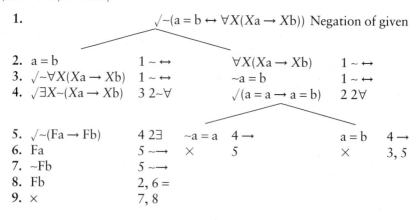

1. $\checkmark \sim(a = b \leftrightarrow \forall X(Xa \rightarrow Xb))$ Negation of given

2. $a = b$ 1 ~ ↔ $\forall X(Xa \rightarrow Xb)$ 1 ~ ↔
3. $\checkmark \sim\forall X(Xa \rightarrow Xb)$ 1 ~ ↔ $\sim a = b$ 1 ~ ↔
4. $\checkmark \exists X \sim(Xa \rightarrow Xb)$ 3 2-∀ $\checkmark (a = a \rightarrow a = b)$ 2 2∀

5. $\checkmark \sim(Fa \rightarrow Fb)$ 4 2∃ $\sim a = a$ 4 → $a = b$ 4 →
6. Fa   5 ~→   ✕   5   ✕   3, 5
7. $\sim$Fb   5 ~→
8. Fb   2, 6 =
9. ✕   7, 8

The trick here is in the right branch at step 4 where we instantiate the predicate variable 'X' in '$\forall X(Xa \rightarrow Xb)$' with the one-place open sentence '$a = y$' to obtain '$(a = a \rightarrow a = b)$'. '$\forall X(Xa \rightarrow Xb)$' asserts that b has every property that a has. We take that quite strictly, concluding that if a has the property being identical with a (expressed by the formula '$a = y$'), then b also has this property.

Second-order logic has a big surprise in store when we consider the questions of soundness, completeness, and decidability. Second-order logic is undecidable, of course, since it contains first-order predicate logic, and we proved in Section 10.6 that first-order predicate logic is undecidable. That means that some invalid forms in second-order logic have infinite trees. No surprise there. But though the tree rules for second-order logic are provably sound, it can be shown that no validity test for second-order logic is complete. That is, every test, including the tree test, fails to recognize some valid forms as valid. This surprising and frustrating fact is a consequence of Gödel's historic proof of the incompleteness of arithmetic, which is beyond the scope of this book.[7]

Exercise 14.2.1

Prove the following metatheorems:

1. '$\forall XXa \vdash Fa$' is valid.
2. '$Fa \vdash \forall XXa$' is invalid.
3. '$\exists X\forall yXy$' is valid.
4. '$\exists X\forall y{\sim}Xy$' is valid.

Exercise 14.2.2

Test the following formulas for validity, using trees:

1. $\exists XXa \rightarrow Fa$
2. $\forall X\forall yXy$
3. $\exists Z\forall xZxx$
4. $\exists ZZab$
5. $\forall Z(\forall x\forall y(Zxy \rightarrow {\sim}Zyx) \rightarrow \forall x{\sim}Zxx)$
6. $\forall Z(\forall x(Zax \rightarrow Zbx) \rightarrow a = b)$

---

[7] If you would like to pursue these matters, I heartily recommend George Boolos and Richard Jeffrey, *Computability and Logic*, 2nd ed. (Cambridge: Cambridge University Press, 1980).

PART V

NONCLASSICAL LOGICS

CHAPTER 15

MILDLY NONCLASSICAL LOGICS

All the logics we have examined until now have presupposed that (1) the logical meaning of a statement is its truth conditions, (2) all statements are either true or false but not both, and (3) every name refers to some existing thing. The logics we have developed under these assumptions are called **classical logics.** But while these assumptions are justifiable for some applications of logic, for others they are not. In this chapter and the next we raise specific challenges to these assumptions. The result, as we shall see, is not anarchy or chaos but an intriguing plurality of **nonclassical logics.** In this chapter we focus on some relatively tame departures from classicism (hence the chapter title). In the next we shall consider more radical deviations. This division is, however, somewhat arbitrary, and some logicians regard some of the developments even of this chapter as beyond the pale.

15.1 FREE LOGICS

Where α is any name, $\exists x\ x = \alpha$ is valid in classical predicate logic. Such formulas count as logical truths, not for any deep metaphysical reason, but merely because in our definition of a valuation for predicate logic we have stipulated that each name must refer to something. But that is not the case in ordinary language. 'Vulcan', 'Pegasus', 'Phlogiston', 'the ether', 'Bilbo Baggins', 'Hamlet', 'the Easter Bunny', 'the Loch Ness Monster', and so on are names that do not refer to any existing thing. Thus classical predicate logic cannot allow such names, on pain of asserting the existence of something that does not exist.

This problem is not confined to fictional names. Even a perfectly respectable name, like 'Arkansas', becomes problematic in modal logic, which may entertain the possibility of worlds in which Arkansas does not exist. In such a world, '$\exists x\ x =$ a' is plainly false, reading 'a' as 'Arkansas'; but according to classical predicate logic, '$\exists x\ x = a$' is a logical truth. Nor is the difficulty confined to alethic modalities. It arises too in tense logic, where we may, for example, consider the actual world at times before Arkansas existed. At such times, once again, '$\exists x\ x = a$' surely ought to be false.

Indeed, related difficulties arise where no names are used at all. The formula '$\exists x\ x = x$', which may be read as "something self-identical exists" or even just "something exists," is also classically valid. Its validity results from the stipulation in the classical definition of a valuation that domains are nonempty. This stipulation is made to ensure that names have something to denote. But, while true, '$\exists x \; x = x$' seems not to be a genuine *logical* truth. "Why is there something, and not rather nothing?" asks the philosopher Martin Heidegger; and the answer, if there is one, surely does not lie in the semantic conventions of classical predicate logic. No merely logical response can placate such questioning. A more modest logic would allow empty domains and would therefore have no such theorems as '$\exists x \; x = x$'.

There is good reason, then, to seek a logic capable of handling nondenoting names, names denoting objects that do not exist at a given world, and, perhaps, empty domains. Such a logic is called a **free logic,** because it is free from the presupposition that a name must denote some existing thing. The development of free logics has followed two different strategies.

The first strategy is simply to allow some names to have no denotation at all. This seems most appropriate in the case of fictional names or theoretical names (like 'the ether') that turn out to have been based on misconceptions. This strategy requires a modification of the valuation rules for atomic sentences containing names, since it is ordinarily presupposed that the names denote something. In classical predicate logic, for example, we expressed the valuation rule for atomic formulas with one-place predicates as follows:

1. If Φ is a one-place predicate and α is a name, then $\mathcal{V}(\Phi\alpha) = \text{T}$ iff $\mathcal{V}(\alpha) \; \varepsilon \; \mathcal{V}(\Phi)$.

But where α has no denotation, $\mathcal{V}(\alpha)$ does not exist, so this rule must be supplemented by some additional convention.

There are various ways of handling nondenoting names. We might, for example, make $\mathcal{V}(\Phi\alpha)$ false whenever α does not denote. Or we might allow either truth value to be assigned to such formulas—modeling, for example, our intuition that although Hamlet does not exist, it is true that he is a character in one of Shakespeare's plays, but false that he is buried in Rome. We might also make $\Phi\alpha$ truth-valueless when α does not denote. This third choice is best implemented in a supervaluational semantics of the sort discussed in Section 15.3. There it will be seen on at least one natural rendering to lead not to free logic, but to a classical logic with a nonstandard semantics. The first two options for handling nondenoting names are problematic in various ways and will not be considered here.[1]

The second strategy for developing free logics is to retain the idea that all names denote but to represent some of the things names may denote as not existing. This is accomplished by defining two domains: one representing actually existing objects, the other representing both existing and nonexisting objects. Names may denote any object in the second and wider domain, but the familiar existential and universal quantifiers range only over the narrower domain of existing things.

---

[1] An excellent survey of the options is found in the essay "Free Logics" by Ermanno Bencivenga in D. Gabbay and F. Guenthner, eds., *Handbook of Philosophical Logic, Volume III: Alternatives to Classical Logic* (Dordrecht: D. Reidel, 1985).

This is called a **Meinongian semantics,** after the philosopher Alexius Meinong, who held that names or definite descriptions that do not denote existing things nevertheless denote objects which, though they do not exist, have "being."

Meinongian semantics is especially suited to various forms of modal logic (including tense logics). In an alethic modal logic, it is usually implemented by defining two domains. The first of these, called the **inner domain,** is world-relative and represents, as usual, the domain of objects existing in that world. The second, called the **outer domain,** is, according to the version of Meinongian semantics I shall describe, not world-relative. The outer domain represents the set of all things that can be named, including all things in the inner domains of one's own world as well as merely possible things and perhaps also fictional things—even if these exist in no possible world. It thus contains all the objects that exist in any world of the model and maybe some other objects as well. (In a tense logic, the inner domain of a time is, analogously, the set of things existing at that time; the outer domain contains all things existing at any time in the same time sequence—and perhaps also some things, like fictional objects, that exist outside this sequence.)

On a Meinongian semantics, the formula '$\exists x \; x = a$' is true at a given world w if and only if the object denoted by 'a' is in that world's inner domain. If this object is not in w's inner domain, but only in the outer domain—that is, if it does not exist at w—then '$\exists x \; x = a$' is false at w.

Moreover, on Meinongian semantics, since names need not denote existing objects, there is no reason not to allow the inner domains of some worlds to be empty, thus falsifying '$\exists x \; x = x$' at those worlds.

Further, Meinongian semantics provides a way of completing the truth conditions for atomic formulas of modal predicate logic, which we left incomplete in Section 11.2. For example, where $\mathcal{D}_w$ is the (classical) domain of world w, we there defined the truth conditions for an atomic formula of the form $\Phi\alpha$ as follows:

> If Φ is a one-place predicate and α is a name whose extension $\mathcal{V}(\alpha)$ is in $\mathcal{D}_w$, then
> $\mathcal{V}(\Phi\alpha, w) = \text{T iff } \mathcal{V}(\alpha) \; \varepsilon \; \mathcal{V}(\Phi, w);$
> $\mathcal{V}(\Phi\alpha, w) = \text{F iff } \mathcal{V}(\alpha) \; \not\varepsilon \; \mathcal{V}(\Phi, w).$

The problem is that while the extension of a name need not be a member of $\mathcal{D}_w$, the extensions of predicates are in classical modal logic confined to $\mathcal{D}_w$. Given this restriction, we intentionally formulated the truth conditions to say nothing about the truth value of $\Phi\alpha$ if $\mathcal{V}(\alpha) \not\varepsilon \mathcal{D}_w$ (i.e., if α denotes an object that does not exist in w), for it would have been arbitrary to stipulate truth conditions where we had assigned no extensions to justify them. Thus, for example, if 'a' names Arkansas, 'S' is a predicate meaning "is a state," and w is a world in which Arkansas does not exist, these truth conditions say nothing about the truth value of 'Sa' at w. There simply is no structure within classical modal semantics on which to base such a truth value.

Meinongian semantics provides the needed structure. In a Meinongian semantics, $\mathcal{D}_w$ becomes the inner domain of world w and there is in addition an outer domain, which we shall call $\mathcal{I}$. The extensions of predicates, instead of being confined to $\mathcal{D}_w$, are now defined for the outer domain $\mathcal{I}$. So, for example, for a one-place predicate Φ, $\mathcal{V}(\Phi, w)$ is now a subset of $\mho$ rather than of $\mathcal{D}_w$. Similarly, each name denotes an object in $\mho$, though the extension of a name—in contrast to that of a predicate—is always rigid, that is, not world-relative. On Meinongian semantics it becomes part of the task of constructing a model to stipulate for each predicate and each world not only which existing objects that predicate is true of in that world, but also which nonexisting objects it is true of in that world. We define extensions of predicates at worlds not simply for all the actual objects in those worlds, but for all nameable objects.

Such a semantics does not automatically decide whether it is true or false that Arkansas is a state in a world in which Arkansas doesn't exist. We must make that decision in defining the extension of the predicate 'is a state' for the various worlds. The choice itself seems largely a matter of convention or stipulation. But the semantics does allow us to model this choice once we have made it. There is nothing in the classical semantics of Section 11.2 that allows us even to model it.

While the extensions of predicates and names are chosen from the outer domain $\mho$, we retain the standard quantifier rules, according to which quantifiers range only over the inner domain $\mathcal{D}_w$. Thus, if we decide to make 'Sa' ("Arkansas is a state") true in some world w where neither Arkansas nor any other state exists (i.e., no member of $\mathcal{V}('S', w)$ is in $\mathcal{D}_w$), then even though 'Sa' is true in w, '$\exists xSx$' is false there. So one way in which Meinongian semantics differs from classical semantics is that it makes the rule $\exists$I invalid.

Since nothing essential to the understanding of free logic hinges on whether we take a Kripkean or Leibnizian approach to modality, we shall here adopt the simpler Leibnizian approach, ignoring the accessibility relation $\mathcal{R}$. We thus characterize a valuation $\mathcal{V}$ as follows:

DEFINITION A **Meinongian valuation** or **Meinongian model** $\mathcal{V}$ for a formula or set of formulas of modal predicate logic consists of

1. A nonempty set $\mathcal{W}_V$ of objects, called the **worlds** of $\mathcal{V}$,
2. A nonempty set $\mho$ of objects, which is called the **outer domain** of $\mathcal{V}$,
3. For each world w in $\mathcal{W}_V$ a possibly empty subset $\mathcal{D}_w$ of $\mho$, called the **inner domain** of w,
4. For each name or nonidentity predicate σ of that formula or set of formulas, an extension $\mathcal{V}(\sigma)$ (if σ is a name) or $\mathcal{V}(\sigma, w)$ (if σ is a predicate and w a world in $\mathcal{W}_V$) as follows:
   i. If σ is a name, then $\mathcal{V}(\sigma)$ is a member of $\mho$,
   ii. If σ is a zero-place predicate (sentence letter), then $\mathcal{V}(\sigma, w)$ is one (but not both) of the values T or F.
   iii. If σ is a one-place predicate, then $\mathcal{V}(\sigma, w)$ is a set of members of $\mho$.
   iv. If σ is an n-place predicate ($n > 1$), then $\mathcal{V}(\sigma, w)$ is a set of ordered n-tuples of members of $\mho$.

We may now complete the valuation rules for atomic formulas containing n-place predicates, $n > 0$. These rules need no longer be restricted to the case in which the extensions of the relevant names are in $\mathcal{D}_w$. Instead, they now read simply:

1. If Φ is a one-place predicate and α is a name, then

$$\mathcal{V}(\Phi\alpha, w) = T \text{ iff } \mathcal{V}(\alpha) \, \varepsilon \, \mathcal{V}(\Phi, w);$$
$$\mathcal{V}(\Phi\alpha, w) = F \text{ iff } \mathcal{V}(\alpha) \, \not\varepsilon \, \mathcal{V}(\Phi, w).$$

2. If Φ is an n-place predicate ($n > 1$) and $\alpha_1, \ldots, \alpha_n$ are names, then

$$\mathcal{V}(\Phi\alpha_1, \ldots, \alpha_n, w) = T \text{ iff } <\mathcal{V}(\alpha_1), \ldots, \mathcal{V}(\alpha_n)> \varepsilon \, \mathcal{V}(\Phi, w);$$
$$\mathcal{V}(\Phi\alpha_1, \ldots, \alpha_n, w) = F \text{ iff } <\mathcal{V}(\alpha_1), \ldots, \mathcal{V}(\alpha_n)> \not\varepsilon \, \mathcal{V}(\Phi, w).$$

These rules give us the truth conditions for atomic formulas under all conditions, not just under the condition that the objects denoted by the names are in $\mathcal{D}_w$.

The other valuation rules may be stated precisely as in Section 11.2. Specifically, we have for the existential quantifier:

$$\mathcal{V}(\exists\beta\Phi, w) = T \text{ iff for some potential name } \alpha \text{ of some object } d \text{ in } \mathcal{D}_w,$$
$$\mathcal{V}_{(\alpha,d)}(\Phi^\alpha/_\beta, w) = T;$$
$$\mathcal{V}(\exists\beta\Phi, w) = F \text{ iff for all potential names } \alpha \text{ of all objects } d \text{ in } \mathcal{D}_w,$$
$$\mathcal{V}_{(\alpha,d)}(\Phi^\alpha/_\beta, w) \neq T.$$

But because of the revised definition of a valuation, the logic of the quantifiers has been substantially altered. We noted informally a few paragraphs back that the rule of existential introduction ($\exists$I) is invalid on this semantics, for there might be a world (or time) in which it is true that Arkansas is a nonexisting state. In fact, to turn this into a formal counterexample, we may for simplicity's sake suppose that there is only one possible world, w, in which neither Arkansas nor anything else exists. This is the strategy of the following metatheorem (in which the number 1 is a surrogate for Arkansas):

METATHEOREM: The sequent 'Sa $\vdash \exists x Sx$' is invalid on Meinongian semantics.

PROOF: Consider the Meinongian valuation $\mathcal{V}$ such that

$$\mathcal{W}_{\mathcal{V}} = \{w\} \qquad \mathcal{V}(\text{'a'}) = 1$$
$$\mathcal{I} = \{1\} \qquad \mathcal{V}(\text{'S'}, w) = \{1\}$$
$$\mathcal{D}_w = \{\ \}$$

Since $1 \, \varepsilon \, \{1\}$, it follows that $\mathcal{V}(\text{'a'}) \, \varepsilon \, \mathcal{V}(\text{'S'}, w)$ and hence (by valuation rule 1) that $\mathcal{V}(\text{'Sa'}, w) = T$. However, since $\mathcal{D}_w = \{\ \}$, there is no potential name α of some object d in $\mathcal{D}_w$ such that $\mathcal{V}_{(\alpha,d)}(S\alpha, w) = T$. Therefore $\mathcal{V}(\text{'}\exists x Sx\text{'}, w) \neq T$, and so the sequent is invalid. **QED**

Because inner domains may be empty, as the previous metatheorem illustrates, the logic itself does not presuppose the existence of anything. In particular, the assertion that something exists, '$\exists x\ x = x$' is no longer valid as it is in classical logic:

METATHEOREM: The formula '$\exists x \; x = x$' is not valid on Meinongian semantics.

PROOF: Consider the Meinongian valuation $\mathcal{V}$ such that

$$\mathcal{W}_\gamma = \{w\}$$
$$\mathcal{I} = \{1\}$$
$$\mathcal{D}_w = \{\;\}$$

Since $\mathcal{D}_w = \{\;\}$, there is no name α of some object d in $\mathcal{D}_w$ such that $\mathcal{V}_{(\alpha,d)}(\alpha = \alpha, w) = T$. Therefore $\mathcal{V}('\exists x \; x = x', w) \neq T$, and so '$\exists x \; x = x$' is not valid.   QED

Formulas of the form $\exists x \; x = \alpha$ are true at a world w iff $\mathcal{V}(\alpha) \; \varepsilon \; \mathcal{D}_w$—that is, iff the object denoted by α is a member of the set of things that actually exist at w. Thus $\exists x \; x = \alpha$ means "α exists." It is customary to abbreviate such formulas using the symbolism '$E!\alpha$', which, again, may simply be read as "α exists." We saw with our first metatheorem that existential introduction (or existential generalization) is invalid on a Meinongian semantics, but a restricted version of it still holds, as the following metatheorem shows:

METATHEOREM: Any sequent of the form $\Phi^\alpha/_\beta, E!\alpha \vdash \exists \beta \Phi$, where $\Phi^\alpha/_\beta$ is the result of replacing each occurrence of the variable β in Φ by the name α, is valid on Meinongian semantics.

PROOF: Suppose for reductio that $\Phi^\alpha/_\beta, E!\alpha \vdash \exists \beta \Phi$ is invalid—that is, there is some Meinongian valuation $\mathcal{V}$ and world w of $\mathcal{V}$ such that $\mathcal{V}(\Phi^\alpha/_\beta, w) = T$ and $\mathcal{V}(E!\alpha, w) = T$ but $\mathcal{V}(\exists x \Phi, w) \neq T$. Since $\mathcal{V}(E!\alpha, w) = T$—that is, $\mathcal{V}(\exists x \; x = \alpha, w) = T$—it follows by the valuation rule for the existential quantifier that there is some potential name γ of some object d in $\mathcal{D}$ such that $\mathcal{V}_{(\gamma,d)}(\gamma = \alpha, w) = T$. Hence by the valuation rule for identity, $\mathcal{V}_{(\gamma,d)}(\gamma) = \mathcal{V}_{(\gamma,d)}(\alpha)$. But by the definition of an expansion (see Section 7.2), $\mathcal{V}_{(\gamma,d)}(\gamma) = d$, and so $\mathcal{V}_{(\gamma,d)}(\alpha) = d$. Moreover, since $\mathcal{V}$ is a valuation of $\Phi^\alpha/_\beta$ and so assigns some extension to α, it follows (again by the definition of an expansion) that $\mathcal{V}_{(\gamma,d)}(\alpha) = \mathcal{V}(\alpha)$. So $\mathcal{V}(\alpha) = d$. Hence α is a potential name of d with respect to $\mathcal{V}$. Thus, since $\Phi^\alpha/_\beta$ contains α and $\mathcal{V}(\Phi^\alpha/_\beta, w) = T$, $\mathcal{V}(\exists x \Phi, w) = T$, contrary to our supposition.

Therefore all sequents of the form $\Phi^\alpha/_\beta, E!\alpha \vdash \exists \beta \Phi$ are valid.   QED

So, for example, we might reason concerning a particular rabbit named Allison:

Allison is a rabbit.
Allison exists.
∴   Some rabbit exists.

In symbols:

> Ra, E!a ⊢ ∃xRx

This is a simple sequent of the form $\Phi^{\alpha}/_{\beta}$, E!α ⊢ ∃βΦ, which is the subject of the preceding metatheorem.

Having provided a Meinongian semantics for quantified Leibnizian modal logic, we can now take care of the unfinished business of supplying inference rules for the quantifiers of Leibnizian modal logic. The rules given here apply to free logic in general, not just to modalized forms of free logic. As with classical predicate logic, we need an introduction and elimination rule for each of the quantifiers. But all four of these rules require slight modification. Since, for instance, the name 'a' need not denote anything in the actual or present situation, to infer '∃xFx' from the premise 'Fa', we need the additional premise '∃x x = a'. Similarly, to infer 'Fa' from the premise '∀xFx', we need that same additional premise. Indeed, each of the classical quantifier rules must be modified by the addition of this kind of existence statement at one place or another:

Free Existential Introduction (F∃I)   Let Φ be any formula containing some name α and $\Phi^{\beta}/_{\alpha}$ be the result of replacing at least one occurrence of α in Φ by some variable β not already in Φ. Then from Φ and ∃x x = α infer ∃β$\Phi^{\beta}/_{\alpha}$.

Free Existential Elimination (F∃E)   Let ∃βΦ be any existential formula, Ψ any formula, and α any name that occurs neither in Φ nor in Ψ. And let $\Phi^{\alpha}/_{\beta}$ be the result of replacing all occurrences of the variable β in Φ by α. Then, given a derivation of Ψ from the hypothesis $\Phi^{\alpha}/_{\beta}$ & ∃x x = α, end the hypothetical derivation and from ∃βΦ infer Ψ, provided that α does not occur in any other hypothesis whose hypothetical derivation has not ended or in any assumption.

Free Universal Introduction (F∀I)   Let Φ be a formula containing a name α, and let $\Phi^{\beta}/_{\alpha}$ be the result of replacing all occurrences of α in Φ by some variable β not already in Φ. Then given a derivation of Φ from the hypothesis ∃x x = α, end the hypothetical derivation and infer ∀β$\Phi^{\beta}/_{\alpha}$, provided that α does not occur in any other hypothesis whose hypothetical derivation has not yet ended or in any assumption.

Free Universal Elimination (F∀E)   Let ∀βΦ be any universally quantified formula and $\Phi^{\alpha}/_{\beta}$ be the result of replacing all occurrences of the variable β in Φ by some name α. Then from ∀βΦ and ∃x x = α infer $\Phi^{\alpha}/_{\beta}$.

By adding F∃I, F∃E, F∀I, and F∀E to the seven rules listed in Section 11.4, we obtain a logic that is sound and complete with respect to the Meinongian semantics outlined here. That is, a sequent of modal predicate logic is provable in that logic iff it has no counterexample in our Meinongian semantics. Like classical predicate logic, however, and for essentially the same reasons, this logic is undecidable.

We now illustrate this inferential system with a few simple proofs. We begin with the sequent '$\forall x(Fx \rightarrow Gx)$, Fa, $\exists x\, x = a \vdash \exists xGx$':

1. $\forall x(Fx \rightarrow Gx)$ A
2. Fa   A
3. $\exists x\, x = a$ A
4. Fa $\rightarrow$ Ga   1, 3 F$\forall$E
5. Ga   2, 4 $\rightarrow$E
6. $\exists xGx$ 3, 5 F$\exists$I

Without the premise '$\exists x\, x = a$', this proof would fail, for 'a' might refer to a nonexisting object that has the property F but not the property G, even though all actual things having F also have G. Notice that, unlike their classical counterparts which utilize only one premise each, F$\forall$E and F$\exists$I always require two premises. Uses of these rules must therefore be annotated with two line numbers.

This proof of the theorem '$\vdash \forall x(Fx \rightarrow \exists yFy)$' illustrates the use of the rule F$\forall$I:

1. | $\exists x\, x = a$ H (for F$\forall$I)
2. | | Fa   H (for $\rightarrow$)
3. | | $\exists yFy$ 1, 2 F$\exists$I
4. | Fa $\rightarrow \exists yFy$ 2–3 $\rightarrow$I
5. $\forall x(Fx \rightarrow \exists yFy)$ 1–4 F$\forall$I

Unlike classical universal introduction, F$\forall$I requires a hypothetical derivation. The hypothesis (which is introduced in this proof at line 1) is always of the form $\exists x\, x = \alpha$, where α denotes a representative individual—that is, an individual about which we have made no particular assumptions, except that it exists. The hypothesis at line 2 is for conditional proof. Notice that while '$\forall x(Fx \rightarrow \exists yFy)$' is a theorem, instances of it, such as 'Fa $\rightarrow \exists yFy$' are not theorems, since the name 'a' need not denote an existing thing.

The next proof illustrates F$\exists$E and the integration of free logic with modal principles. It is a proof of the sequent '$\exists xFx \vdash \exists x \Diamond Fx$':

1. $\exists xFx$ A
2. | Fa & $\exists x\, x = a$ H (for F$\exists$E)
3. | Fa   2 &E
4. | $\Diamond$ Fa   3 P $\vdash \Diamond$P[2]
5. | $\exists x\, x = a$ 2 &E
6. | $\exists x \Diamond Fx$ 4, 5 F$\exists$I
7. $\exists x \Diamond Fx$ 1, 2–6 F$\exists$E

---

[2] This sequent, which was proved in Section 11.4, is used here as a derived rule in the manner described in that same section.

At line 2 we hypothesize a conjunction. The first conjunct is a representative instance of the existential formula at line 1, using the name 'a' as the representative individual. The second asserts that the object denoted by 'a' exists. From this conjunctive hypothesis ($\Phi^\alpha/_\beta$ & $\exists x\ x = \alpha$ in the statement of the F∃E rule), we derive the formula '$\exists x \Diamond Fx$' (Ψ in the statement of the F∃E rule). This hypothetical derivation enables us to infer '$\exists x \Diamond Fx$' from '$\exists x Fx$' by F∃E at line 7.

We now prove the theorem '$\vdash \forall x Fx \rightarrow (\sim Fa \rightarrow \sim \exists x\ x = a)$':

1.	$\forall x Fx$	H (for →I)
2.	$\sim Fa$	H (for →I)
3.	$\exists x\ x = a$	H (for ~I)
4.	Fa	1, 3 F∀E
5.	Fa & $\sim Fa$	2, 4 &I
6.	$\sim \exists x\ x = a$	3–5 ~I
7.	$\sim Fa \rightarrow \sim \exists x\ x = a$	2–6 →I
8.	$\forall x Fx \rightarrow (\sim Fa \rightarrow \sim \exists x\ x = a)$	1–7 →I

The strategy is a simple reductio nested within two conditional proofs.

Finally, we prove the sequent '$\Box \forall x Fx, \Diamond \exists x\ x = a \vdash \Diamond Fa$'. This proof illustrates the use of several modal rules together with free logic. Note especially the use of the previous theorem with the N rule at line 3:

1.	$\Box \forall x Fx$	A
2.	$\Diamond \exists x\ x = a$	A
3.	$\Box(\forall x Fx \rightarrow (\sim Fa \rightarrow \sim \exists x\ x = a))$	N ($\forall x Fx \rightarrow (\sim Fa \rightarrow \sim \exists x\ x = a)$)
4.	$\Box \forall x Fx \rightarrow \Box(\sim Fa \rightarrow \sim \exists x\ x = a)$	3 K
5.	$\Box(\sim Fa \rightarrow \sim \exists x\ x = a)$	1, 4 →E
6.	$\Box \sim Fa \rightarrow \Box \sim \exists x\ x = a$	5 K
7.	$\sim \Box \sim \exists x\ x = a$	2 DUAL
8.	$\sim \Box \sim Fa$	6, 7 MT
9.	$\Diamond Fa$	8 DUAL

Exercise 15.1.1

Construct proofs for the following sequents in free Leibnizian predicate logic:

1. $\exists x\ x = a, \sim Fa \vdash \sim \forall x Fx$
2. $\forall x \Box Fx \vdash \forall x Fx$
3. $\forall x Fx \vdash \forall x \Diamond Fx$
4. $\vdash \forall x\ x = x$
5. $\vdash \sim \exists x \Diamond \sim x = x$
6. $\exists x\ x = a \vdash \exists x\ x = x$
7. $\exists x \sim Fx \vdash \sim \forall x Fx$
8. $\exists x\ x = a \vdash \exists x \Box x = a$
9. $\vdash (Fa \ \& \ \exists y\ a = y) \rightarrow \exists y Fy$
10. $\exists y \Box (Fy \ \& \ \exists x\ x = y) \vdash \Box \exists y Fy$

Exercise 15.1.2

Prove the following metatheorems:

1. Every instance of F∀E is a valid sequent on Meinongian semantics.
2. The sequent '∀xFx ⊢ Fa' is invalid on Meinongian semantics.
3. The sequent '□∀xFx ⊢ ∀x□Fx' is invalid on Meinongian semantics.
4. The sequent '∀x□Fx ⊢ □∀xFx' is invalid on Meinongian semantics.

15.2 MULTIVALUED LOGICS

In Section 3.1, I summarily announced that we would consider only two truth values, T and F, and that we would assume that each statement had exactly one of these truth values in every possible situation. We have followed that policy ever since. But there are reasons not to be satisfied with it. There are, for example, sentences which, though grammatically well formed, seem to have no intelligible meaning. Suppose someone says, for example, "Development digests incredulity." This might be a striking metaphor of some kind, but what it means, if anything, is hardly clear. One might argue that it is simply false. Then 'Development does not digest incredulity' is true. But this statement is hardly more intelligible than the first. We might, then, decide to rule them both out of court; they both, we might conclude, are neither true nor false. Against this conclusion, some have objected that since neither sentence is really intelligible, neither makes a statement, and where no statement is made there is nothing that can be either true or false. The question of truth or falsity simply does not arise. On this view, unintelligible sentences do not challenge the principle of bivalence because that principle applies only to statements.

A different, and perhaps stronger, challenge to the principle of bivalence stems from reference failure. Consider, for example, the statement 'The Easter Bunny is a vegetarian'.[3] In one sense, this is not true, since there is no Easter Bunny. But if we conclude that it is false, then we must assent to 'The Easter Bunny is not a vegetarian'. Is he, then, a carnivore? The problem, of course, is that since the term 'The Easter Bunny' does not pick out an object of which we may predicate either vegetarianism or nonvegetarianism, it seems misleading to think of these sentences as either true or false. We might reasonably conclude, then, that because of the reference failure they are neither. Notice that here it is less plausible to argue that no statement has been made. We understand perfectly well what it means to say that the Easter Bunny is a vegetarian. But what is asserted seems not to be either true or false.

---

[3] We are here regarding 'The Easter Bunny' as a proper name, rather than a definite description. Thus it is by no means obvious that we could successfully deal with this reference failure by appealing to Russell's theory of descriptions.

Semantic paradox supplies even stronger arguments against the principle of bivalence. Consider the following sentence, which we shall call S:

Sentence S is false.

Here we can actually offer a metalinguistic proof that it is neither true nor false. For suppose for reductio that it is true. Then what it says (that it is false) is correct, and so it is false. It is, then, on this supposition both true and false, which contradicts the principle of bivalence. Suppose, on the other hand, that it is false. Then, since it says of itself that it is false, it is true. Hence once again it is both true and false, in contradiction to the principle of bivalence. Hence, from the principle of bivalence itself, we derive by reductio both the conclusion that this sentence is not true and the conclusion that it is not false. It is, then, certainly not bivalent.

One might also reject bivalence on metaphysical grounds. Jan Łukasiewicz, who constructed the first multivalued semantics early in the twentieth century, held that contingent statements about the future do not become true until made true by events. Suppose, for example, that a year from now you decide to write a novel. Still it is not true *now* that a year from now you will decide to write a novel; the most that is true now is that it is possible that you will and possible that you won't. Only when you actually do decide a year hence does it become true that a year earlier you were going to decide to write a novel a year hence. Obviously, Łukasiewicz's conception of time is different from that presented in Section 13.2, where we modeled a nondeterministic time in which contingent statements about the future may be true at present. Łukasiewicz assumed that the present truth of contingent statements about the future implies determininsm. In any case, the idea that the truth of a contingent statement does not "happen" until a specific moment in time, whether right or not, is of logical interest. It implies that many statements about the future are neither true nor false now so that there is some third semantic status, which Łukasiewicz called 'possible' or 'indeterminate', in addition to truth and falsity.

There may also be more mundane, practical grounds for rejecting bivalence. The designers of a computer database of propositions, for example, might want to list some propositions as true, some as false, and others as *unknown*. There is, of course, no *metaphysical* basis for the third value in this case. The propositions listed as unknown may all in fact be true or false. But in practice the inferential routines used with the database may work best if they embody a non-bivalent logic.

Finally, phenomena of vagueness might motivate us to reject bivalence. The seemingly simple and clear sentence 'This is a car' asserted of a midsize sedan is certainly true. Asserted of an eighteen-wheeler it is certainly false. But what if it is asserted of a van? Many people feel that such assertions are "sort of true, but not exactly true." Since, like 'car', virtually all words are somewhat vague, for virtually all statements there are borderline situations in which we are hesitant to say that the statement is either true or false. But the notion that truth comes in degrees leads beyond consideration of a mere third alternative to truth and falsity into the realm of infinite valued and fuzzy logics (see Section 16.1).

All of these considerations seem to point to the existence or usefulness of at least one new truth value in addition to truth and falsity. Let us, for the moment, posit just one, which we shall call I or "indeterminate." Adoption of this third truth value requires substantial revision of the valuation rules and of truth tables for propositional logic. For one thing, a valuation may assign not just T or F to a sentence letter, but also I. For another, we will have to decide how the logical operators should treat the new value—and there is not just one way to do this. We shall assume that formulas governed by the operators have their usual truth values when their components are all true or false. But what values should complex formulas take in cases in which one or more of the components have the value I? Two general policies suggest themselves:

1. Indeterminacy of the part should infect the whole so that, if a complex formula has an indeterminate component, then the formula as a whole should be indeterminate.
2. If the truth value of the whole is determined on a classical truth table by the truth or falsity of some components, even if other components are indeterminate, then the whole formula should have the value so determined.

The difference between these two policies is easily seen in the case of disjunction. Suppose that the sentence letter 'P' has the value T and that the letter 'Q' has the value I. Then what is the truth value of 'P ∨ Q'? According to the first policy, the indeterminacy of 'Q' infects the whole formula so that the truth value of 'P ∨ Q' should be I. But on the second policy, we must recognize that the truth of either disjunct is classically sufficient for the truth of the disjunction, and so the truth value of 'P ∨ Q' should be T.

It is not obvious which of these policies is preferable. Indeed, one may be preferable for some applications, the other for others. Thus we shall discuss them both and, toward the end of this section, add a third to the mix.

In the late 1930s the Russian logician D. A. Bochvar proposed a three-valued semantics for propositional logic based on the first policy—namely that the indeterminacy of a part infects the whole. This semantics is encapsulated in the following truth tables:

Φ	~Φ	Φ	Ψ	Φ & Ψ	Φ ∨ Ψ	Φ → Ψ	Φ ↔ Ψ
T	F	T	T	T	T	T	T
F	T	T	F	F	T	F	F
I	I	T	I	I	I	I	I
		F	T	F	T	T	F
		F	F	F	F	T	T
		F	I	I	I	I	I
		I	T	I	I	I	I
		I	F	I	I	I	I
		I	I	I	I	I	I

Notice that, whereas in classical logic for formulas or formula sets containing n sentence letters there are 2^n valuations (horizontal lines on the truth table), in three-valued logic there are 3^n. The truth table for a binary operator, for example, has nine lines.

The valuation rules for Bochvar's logic reflect this new complexity. We shall not state them all, but the rules for '~' and '&' may serve as examples:

$\mathcal{V}(\sim\Phi) = T$ iff $\mathcal{V}(\Phi) = F$.
$\mathcal{V}(\sim\Phi) = F$ iff $\mathcal{V}(\Phi) = T$.
$\mathcal{V}(\sim\Phi) = I$ iff $\mathcal{V}(\Phi) = I$.

$\mathcal{V}(\Phi\ \&\ \Psi) = T$ iff both $\mathcal{V}(\Phi) = T$ and $\mathcal{V}(\Psi) = T$.
$\mathcal{V}(\Phi\ \&\ \Psi) = F$ iff either $\mathcal{V}(\Phi) = F$ and $\mathcal{V}(\Psi) = T$, or $\mathcal{V}(\Phi) = T$ and $\mathcal{V}(\Psi) = F$, or $\mathcal{V}(\Phi) = F$ and $\mathcal{V}(\Psi) = F$.
$\mathcal{V}(\Phi\ \&\ \Psi) = I$ iff either $\mathcal{V}(\Phi) = I$ or $\mathcal{V}(\Psi) = I$, or both.

The resulting logic has some striking features. For one thing, all of those formulas which were classically tautologous (i.e., valid by their truth tables) are on Bochvar's semantics tautologies no longer. The classical tautology 'P → P', for example, has the value I in the case in which 'P' has the value I. It is not, therefore, true on all valuations and hence not a tautology. In fact, every formula of ordinary propositional logic is indeterminate on any Bochvar valuation in which any one of its sentence letters is indeterminate. Those formulas which were tautologies in classical logic still, however, have a special character: There is no valuation on which they are false. But they are not tautologies, as we have defined that term.

We might, of course, broaden our definition of tautology. We could say that a tautology is any formula which is not false on any line of its truth table—that is, which is either true or indeterminate on all lines. Then the classical tautologies would count as tautologies, even on Bochvar's semantics. Thus it comes down to a question of which truth values we shall accept as **designated**—that is, which values count toward tautologousness. If a statement must be true on all lines of its truth table to count as a tautology, then T is the only designated value. If a statement need merely be either true or indeterminate on all valuations, then both T and I are designated values. For Bochvar, only T was designated.

The definition of validity itself presents us with similar choices. In a bivalent logic, it makes no difference whether we say that a sequent is valid iff

> there is no valuation on which its premises are all true and its conclusion is untrue

or

> there is no valuation on which its premises are all true and its conclusion is false.

Given bivalence, untruth and falsity are the same thing. In a multivalued logic, however, the difference between the two definitions is substantial, for there may be valuations on which the premises are true and the conclusion is indeterminate. Should these count as counterexamples? If we think so, we will adopt the first definition of validity. If we think not, we will adopt the second. Bochvar adopted the first, and it is the one we shall use here. *Indeed, we stipulate now that we shall for the purposes of this section (and particularly the exercise at the end) retain the wording of all the definitions of semantic concepts presented in Chapter 3.*

Another interesting feature of Bochvar's semantics is that it invalidates a number of sequents that at least some logicians have regarded as suspect. The so-called "paradoxes of material implication," for example:

$$Q \vdash P \to Q$$
$$\sim P \vdash P \to Q$$

though valid in classical logic, are on Bochvar's semantics invalid. In the first case, the counterexample is the valuation on which 'Q' is true and 'P' indeterminate, which makes the premise true and the conclusion indeterminate (hence untrue). In the second, the counterexample is the valuation on which 'P' is false and 'Q' indeterminate. Indeed, the invalidity of these sequents is an instance of the following general principle:

METATHEOREM: Let $\Phi_1, \ldots, \Phi_n \vdash \Psi$ be a sequent of ordinary propositional logic (as defined by the formation rules of Chapter 2). Then on Bochvar's semantics, if $\{\Phi_1, \ldots, \Phi_n\}$ is consistent and Ψ contains a sentence letter not found in $\Phi_1, \ldots, \Phi_n$, then that sequent is invalid.

PROOF: Suppose that $\{\Phi_1, \ldots, \Phi_n\}$ is consistent and Ψ contains a sentence letter not found in $\Phi_1, \ldots, \Phi_n$. Since $\{\Phi_1, \ldots, \Phi_n\}$ is consistent, there is some Bochvar valuation $\mathcal{V}$ of $\Phi_1, \ldots, \Phi_n$ that makes each of these formulas true. But now consider the valuation $\mathcal{V}'$, which is just like $\mathcal{V}$ except that in addition it assigns the value I to each of the sentence letters that appear in Ψ but not in $\Phi_1, \ldots, \Phi_n$. $\mathcal{V}'$ makes $\Phi_1, \ldots, \Phi_n$ true but Ψ indeterminate, and so $\mathcal{V}'$ is a counterexample, which proves the sequent invalid.

Therefore, if $\{\Phi_1, \ldots, \Phi_n\}$ is consistent and Ψ contains a sentence letter not found in $\Phi_1, \ldots, \Phi_n$, then that sequent is invalid.   QED

In stating this metatheorem I said explicitly that the formulas in question were to be formulas "of ordinary propositional logic (as defined by the formation rules of Chapter 2)." The reason for this qualification is that Bochvar added a novel operator to his logic, and the metatheorem does not apply to formulas containing this novel operator.

Following Susan Haack, I shall symbolize this operator as 'T', since it means in effect "it is true that."[4] Like negation, it is a monadic operator, so to add it to our language we adopt this new formation rule:

If Φ is a formula, so is $T\Phi$.

The truth table for 'T' is

Φ	$T\Phi$
T	T
F	F
I	F

That is, if a formula Φ is true, then it is true that Φ. But if Φ is false or indeterminate, then it is not true that Φ.

This "truth operator" gives Bochvar's logic a new twist, for any formula of which it is the main operator is bivalent. And though, as we saw above, Bochvar's logic contains no tautologies among the formulas of ordinary propositional logic, it does have tautologies. These, however, are all formulas containing the truth operator. Here are some examples:

$TP \rightarrow TP$
$TP \lor \sim TP$
$T(P \lor \sim P) \lor (\sim TP \;\&\; \sim T\sim P)$

Notice, by contrast, that '$TP \lor T\sim P$' is not tautologous, for it is false when 'P' is indeterminate.

Bochvar hoped that his new semantics would solve the problem of semantic paradox. Consider, for example, the semantically paradoxical sentence that we have called S:

Sentence S is false.

We argued above that S is neither true nor false. But if we adopt Bochvar's semantics, there is a third option: It might have the value I. Suppose, then, that it does. In that case, using the sentence letter 'S' to represent sentence S, though the formula 'S' has the value I, the formula 'TS' has the value F, for it is in fact not true that sentence S is false.

This three-valued approach seems neatly to dissolve the paradox. Unfortunately, however, a new paradox emerges to take its place. Let U be the sentence:

Sentence U is untrue.

As before, suppose for reductio that this sentence is true. Then what it says is correct, and so it is untrue. Hence it is both true and untrue—a contradiction. Therefore it is not true. It follows, on Bochvar's semantics, that it has one of the

---

[4] *Philosophy of Logics* (Cambridge: Cambridge University Press, 1978), p. 207.

values F or I. But in either case it is untrue, and so what it says is correct; hence it is true. Once again we have a contradiction—despite the third value.

Bochvar's semantics does not, therefore, provide a general solution to semantic paradoxes—nor does any other three-valued or multivalued semantics. If semantic paradox is the problem, multivalued semantics is not the solution.

Bochvar, as we have seen, settled upon the first of the valuational policies mentioned above—the policy of making indeterminacy of a part infect the whole. The second policy is to assign truth values to the whole even if some components are indeterminate, so long as the truth or falsity of the remaining components is sufficient to determine the truth value of the whole by the classical valuation rules. This second policy results in a different set of truth tables:

Φ	~Φ	Φ	Ψ	Φ & Ψ	Φ ∨ Ψ	Φ → Ψ	Φ ↔ Ψ
T	F	T	T	T	T	T	T
F	T	T	F	F	T	F	F
I	I	T	I	I	T	I	I
		F	T	F	T	T	F
		F	F	F	F	T	T
		F	I	F	I	T	I
		I	T	I	T	T	I
		I	F	F	I	I	I
		I	I	I	I	I	I

The three-valued propositional semantics expressed by these tables was first proposed by S. C. Kleene. (Kleene also investigated Bochvar's system independently.) As with Bochvar's logic, we may also introduce the operator 'T', which has the same truth table as before.

On Kleene's semantics, as on Bochvar's, classically tautologous formulas are nontautologous. For, as on Bochvar's semantics, any statement of ordinary propositional logic all of whose atomic components have the truth value I has itself the truth value I; hence, for any formula, there is always a valuation (namely, the valuation that assigns I to all of its sentence letters) on which that formula is not true.

Yet Kleene's logic differs from Bochvar's in that it makes most of the classical inference patterns, including the paradoxes of material implication, valid. There are, however, some exceptions: In particular, inferences to what are classically tautologies from irrelevant premises still fail. The sequent 'P ⊢ Q → Q', for example, though classically valid, is invalid on Kleene's semantics, for the valuation on which 'P' is true and 'Q' indeterminate is a counterexample.

Kleene's semantics assigns the classical values T and F to more complex formulas than Bochvar's semantics does. Łukasiewicz, who was the first to explore three-valued logic, proposed a semantics that goes even further in this direction. Łukasiewicz's semantics is like Kleene's, except that where Kleene makes the conditional and biconditional indeterminate when both their components are indeterminate, Łukasiewicz makes them true. Łukasiewicz's semantics is thus expressed by the following truth tables:

Φ	$\sim\Phi$	Φ	Ψ	$\Phi \,\&\, \Psi$	$\Phi \vee \Psi$	$\Phi \rightarrow \Psi$	$\Phi \leftrightarrow \Psi$
T	F	T	T	T	T	T	T
F	T	T	F	F	T	F	F
I	I	T	I	I	T	I	I
		F	T	F	T	T	F
		F	F	F	F	T	T
		F	I	F	I	T	I
		I	T	I	T	T	I
		I	F	F	I	I	I
		I	I	I	I	T	T

Again we may augment Łukasiewicz's semantics with Bochvar's operator 'T', which has the same truth table as before.

Łukasiewicz's semantics, unlike Kleene's or Bochvar's, makes some of the classical tautologies valid; 'P → P', 'P → (P ∨ Q)', '(P & Q) → P', and 'P ↔~~P', for example, are each true on all Łukasiewicz valuations. But the classical tautologies 'P ∨ ~P' (the law of excluded middle) and '~(P & ~P)' (the law of noncontradiction) are nontautologous, because each takes the value I when 'P' itself is indeterminate. Some classical tautologies may even be false on Łukasiewicz's semantics. '~(P ↔ ~P)', for example, is false when 'P' is indeterminate.

On Łukasiewicz's semantics, as on Kleene's, most of the familiar classically valid sequents remain valid. An exception is the inference of certain classical tautologies from unrelated premises. For example, 'P ⊢ Q ∨ ~Q' is invalid since its premise is true while its conclusion is indeterminate in the case in which 'P' has the value T and 'Q' the value I. Anomalously, however, 'P ⊢ Q → Q' remains valid.

Moreover, Łukasiewicz's semantics dispenses with the classical logical equivalences between ~(Φ & ~Ψ) or ~Φ ∨ Ψ and Φ → Ψ, precisely because of this case. For although Φ → Ψ is true when both Φ and Ψ are indeterminate, both ~(Φ & ~Ψ) and ~Φ ∨ Ψ are indeterminate in that case. Some logicians find these features inelegant.

The move to three-valued systems suggests still further generalizations to semantics allowing four or more values—perhaps even infinitely many values. Some of the early semantics for modal logic, for example, used four values: contingently true, contingently false, necessarily true, and necessarily false, with the first two as designated values. And there are many other variants—too many to catalogue here.[5]

One can also, of course, create multivalued predicate logics. This generally requires some adjustment of the definition of a valuation and of the valuation rules for atomic formulas. We might, for example, as in free logics, allow names to lack referents. Then either all or some of the formulas containing these names could be stipulated to have the truth value I. Or we could attempt to dichotomize atomic

---

[5] A good source for further study is Alasdair Urquhart, "Many-Valued Logic," in D. Gabbay and F. Guenthner, eds., *Handbook of Philosophical Logic, Volume III: Alternative to Classical Logic* (Dordrecht: D. Reidel, 1985).

formulas into those that are meaningful and those that are meaningless, assigning the latter the value I. Or, if we are doing tense logic, we might design our models so that atomic statements about the future always receive the value I. But again, we shall not bother with the details of these variations.

Exercise 15.2.1

Construct truth tables to test each of the following formulas for tautologousness (validity) on the semantics of Łukasiewicz, Kleene, and Bochvar, respectively (that is, do three tables for each formula), and record your results by writing 'tautologous' or 'nontautologous' next to each table:

1. $P \lor \sim P$
2. $P \to P$
3. $(P \to Q) \leftrightarrow (\sim P \lor Q)$
4. $TP \to P$
5. $P \to TP$
6. $(P \lor \sim P) \lor (\sim TP \;\&\; \sim T\sim P)$

Exercise 15.2.2

Use truth tables to test each of the following sequents for validity on each of these three semantics. (Recall that, according to the definition given in Chapter 3 and still in effect here, a counterexample is a valuation on which all the premises are true and the conclusion is untrue.) Record your results by writing 'valid' or 'invalid' next to each table:

1. $P \to Q, P \vdash Q$
2. $P \vdash \sim (Q \;\&\; \sim Q)$
3. $P \vdash P \lor Q$

15.3 SUPERVALUATIONS

The motive for moving to multivalued logics is that certain kinds of propositions seem to be neither true nor false. This leads some logicians to posit a third value: neutral, possible, indeterminate—or something of the sort. But once we have added a third truth value, why not a fourth, a fifth, and so on? One way to stem this regress is to stipulate that propositions that are neither true nor false do not have some *other* truth value; they have no truth value at all. Such propositions are said to exhibit **truth-value gaps.** But how, then, could we calculate the truth value of a complex formula if, for example, some of its component propositions have no truth value?

The simplest response would be to declare all such formulas truth-valueless. The result would be just like Bochvar's three-valued semantics, except that in the truth tables where Bochvar's logic has an 'I', this semantics would have a blank.

Or one could create truth tables like those for other forms of three-valued logic. But this approach is hardly novel, differing in no essential respect from three-valued logics themselves.

A more interesting method—and one that, unlike most multivalued logics, preserves the validity of all classical inference patterns—is the technique of supervaluations invented by Bas van Fraassen.[6] In propositional logic, a supervaluational semantics assigns to sentence letters the value T, or the value F, or no value at all. We shall call such an assignment a **partial valuation.** (Note that at one extreme some partial valuations assign truth values to all the sentence letters of a formula or set of formulas and, at the other, some assign no truth values at all.) The truth values of complex formulas, however, are not calculated by truth tables directly from the truth values of their components. Rather, the calculation takes into account all of what are called the *classical completions* of a given partial valuation.

Let s be any partial valuation. Then a **classical completion** of s is a *classical valuation* (one that assigns each sentence letter in the relevant formula or set of formulas one and only one of the values T or F) that fills in all the truth-value gaps left by s. In other words, a classical completion of s does not change any truth-value assignment to a sentence letter that has already been made by s, but merely supplements assignments made by s, giving each sentence letter of the given formula or set of formulas a truth value. Since each truth-value gap can be filled in by the assignment either of T or of F, each partial valuation, unless it is classical to begin with,[7] has more than one classical completion. Consider, for example, the formula '$(P \vee Q)$ & $(R \vee S)$', and let s be the partial valuation of this formula that assigns the value T to both 'P' and 'R' but no value to 'Q' or 'S'. Then s has with respect to this formula four classical completions, corresponding to the four ways of assigning truth value to the sentence letters 'Q' and 'R'. Each classical completion of s is represented by a horizontal line in the truth table below:

P	Q	R	S	(P	$\vee$	Q)	&	(R	$\vee$	S)
T	T	T	T	T	T	T	T	T	T	T
T	T	T	F	T	T	T	T	T	T	F
T	F	T	T	T	T	F	T	T	T	T
T	F	T	F	T	T	F	T	T	T	F

The columns under 'P' and 'R' list only T's, because these are the values assigned by the partial valuation s, and they are retained in each classical completion.

To determine the truth value of the compound formula '$(P \vee Q)$ & $(R \vee S)$', we expand s into a new nonclassical valuation $\mathcal{V}_s$ called the **supervaluation** of s.

[6] See his "Singular Terms, Truth Value Gaps, and Free Logic," *Journal of Philosophy* 63 (1966): 481–95.

[7] The definition of a partial valuation given above treats classical valuations as special cases of partial valuations. Thus, if s is a partial valuation which is also classical, the classical completion of s is s itself.

This is done by calculating the truth value of '(P ∨ Q) & (R ∨ S)' on each of the classical completions of $\mathcal{S}$, using the valuation rules of classical logic, as in the table above. If '(P ∨ Q) & (R ∨ S)' is true on each of these classical completions (as the table shows that it is), then '(P ∨ Q) & (R ∨ S)' is true on the supervaluation $\mathcal{V}_{\mathcal{S}}$. If it had been true on none of them, then it would have been false on $\mathcal{V}_{\mathcal{S}}$. And if it had been true on some but not others, then it would have been assigned no truth value on $\mathcal{V}_{\mathcal{S}}$.

A supervaluation, then, is constructed in two stages. First, we define a partial valuation $\mathcal{S}$, which assigns to each sentence letter the value T, or the value F, or no value. Next, at the second stage, we construct all the classical completions of $\mathcal{S}$ and use the classical valuation rules to calculate the truth values of complex formulas on each of these classical completions. A formula Φ (whether atomic or complex) is then assigned a truth value by the supervaluation $\mathcal{V}_{\mathcal{S}}$ if and only if all the classical completions of $\mathcal{S}$ agree on that truth value; if not, $\mathcal{V}_{\mathcal{S}}$ assigns no value to Φ. More formally:

DEFINITION A **supervaluational model** of a formula or set of formulas consists of

1. a **partial valuation** $\mathcal{S}$, which assigns to each sentence letter of that formula or set of formulas the value T, or the value F, or no value. We use the notation '$\mathcal{S}(\Phi)$' to denote the value (if any) assigned to Φ by $\mathcal{S}$.

2. A **supervaluation** $\mathcal{V}_{\mathcal{S}}$ of $\mathcal{S}$ that assigns truth values $\mathcal{V}_{\mathcal{S}}(\Phi)$ to formulas Φ according to these rules:

> $\mathcal{V}_{\mathcal{S}}(\Phi) = $ T iff for all classical completions $\mathcal{S}'$ of $\mathcal{S}$, $\mathcal{S}'(\Phi) = $ T;
> $\mathcal{V}_{\mathcal{S}}(\Phi) = $ F iff for all classical completions $\mathcal{S}'$ of $\mathcal{S}$, $\mathcal{S}'(\Phi) = $ F;
> $\mathcal{V}_{\mathcal{S}}$ assigns no truth value to Φ otherwise.

Supervaluations may leave truth-value gaps, not only in atomic formulas but in complex formulas as well. Consider, for example, the partial valuation $\mathcal{S}$ of 'P ∨ Q' that assigns F to 'P' and no value to 'Q'. Then the corresponding supervaluation $\mathcal{V}_{\mathcal{S}}$ assigns no value to 'P ∨ Q'. For on the classical completion that makes 'Q' true this formula is true, but on the classical completion that makes 'Q' false, this formula is false. Thus, since the classical completions of $\mathcal{S}$ do not agree on 'P ∨ Q', the formula receives no truth value on the supervaluation $\mathcal{V}_{\mathcal{S}}$.

One might suppose that supervaluations just mimic Kleene's three-valued semantics (which assigns as many classical truth values as possible)—with a blank in place of the truth value I. But this is not so. Supervaluational semantics is not truth-functional. That is, it does not provide a table for calculating the truth value of a formula from the truth values of its parts. Consider disjunctions, for example, in the case in which both disjuncts lack truth value. Some of these are truth-valueless on supervaluations, but some are true. Take, for instance, the partial valuation $\mathcal{S}$ of the formula 'P ∨ Q' that makes both 'P' and 'Q' truth-valueless.

Then both disjuncts 'P' and 'Q' and the disjunction 'P $\lor$ Q' are truth-valueless on the corresponding supervaluation $\mathcal{V}_{\mathcal{S}}$, because all three formulas are true on some classical completions of $\mathcal{S}$ and false on others. But contrast this valuation with the partial valuation $\mathcal{T}$ of the formula 'P $\lor$ ~P' on which 'P' has no truth value. Here there are two classical completions of $\mathcal{T}$—one that makes 'P' true and one that makes 'P' false. And again both disjuncts are truth-valueless on the corresponding supervaluation $\mathcal{V}_{\mathcal{T}}$ because each disjunct is true on one of the classical completions of $\mathcal{T}$ and false on the other. Yet the disjunction 'P $\lor$ ~P' itself, since it is classically valid, is true on every classical completion of $\mathcal{T}$. So, although 'P $\lor$ Q' is truth-valueless on the supervaluation on which both of its disjuncts are truth-valueless, 'P $\lor$ ~P' is true on the supervaluation on which both of its disjuncts lack truth value. It follows that disjunction cannot be represented by a truth table in a supervaluational semantics. The other binary operators are likewise non-truth-functional.

In a supervaluational semantics we may retain the classical definitions of such semantic terms as validity and consistency, but we must now understand the valuations mentioned in their definitions as supervaluations. Thus, for example, a *formula* is **valid** iff it is true on all supervaluations; and a *sequent* is **valid** iff there is no supervaluation on which its premises are true and its conclusion is untrue. (And, of course, there are two ways of being untrue: being false and being truth-valueless.)

Surprisingly, the logic that results from these stipulations is just classical propositional logic—even though, as we have seen, its semantics differs significantly from that of classical logic. Thus, for example, an inference is valid on supervaluational semantics if and only if it is valid on classical bivalent semantics, despite the fact that the former, but not the latter, permits truth-value gaps. Let's prove this:

> **METATHEOREM:** Let $\Phi_1, \ldots, \Phi_n, \Psi$ be any formulas of propositional logic. Then the sequent $\Phi_1, \ldots, \Phi_n \vdash \Psi$ is classically valid iff it is valid on supervaluational semantics.
>
> **PROOF:** Suppose for conditional proof that $\Phi_1, \ldots, \Phi_n \vdash \Psi$ is classically valid. That is, there is no classical valuation on which $\Phi_1, \ldots, \Phi_n$ are all true and Ψ is untrue.
>
> Now suppose for reductio that this sequent is invalid on supervaluational semantics. Then there is a supervaluation $\mathcal{V}_{\mathcal{S}}$ such that $\Phi_1, \ldots, \Phi_n$ are all true on $\mathcal{V}_{\mathcal{S}}$ but $\mathcal{V}_{\mathcal{S}}(\Psi)$ $\neq$ T. Thus there is a partial valuation $\mathcal{S}$ of $\{\Phi_1, \ldots, \Phi_n, \Psi\}$, each of whose classical completions makes $\Phi_1, \ldots, \Phi_n$ true but at least one of whose classical completions makes Ψ untrue. But a classical completion is by definition a classical valuation, and we saw above that there is no classical valuation on which $\Phi_1, \ldots, \Phi_n$ are all true and Ψ is untrue. Thus we have a contradiction.

> Therefore, contrary to our hypothesis, $\Phi_1, \ldots, \Phi_n \vdash \Psi$ is valid on supervaluational semantics.
>
> So, by conditional proof, if $\Phi_1, \ldots, \Phi_n \vdash \Psi$ is classically valid, then it is valid on supervaluational semantics.
>
> Now suppose for conditional proof that $\Phi_1, \ldots, \Phi_n \vdash \Psi$ is valid on supervaluational semantics. Then there is no supervaluation on which $\Phi_1, \ldots, \Phi_n$ are all true and Ψ is untrue. Thus there is no partial valuation of $\{\Phi_1, \ldots, \Phi_n, \Psi\}$, each of whose classical completions makes $\Phi_1, \ldots, \Phi_n$ true and at least one of whose classical completions makes Ψ untrue. In particular, none of the partial valuations of $\{\Phi_1, \ldots, \Phi_n, \Psi\}$ which assigns truth values to all the sentence letters in these formulas is such that each of its classical completions makes $\Phi_1, \ldots, \Phi_n$ true and at least one of its classical completions makes Ψ untrue. Hence, since every classical valuation is just the unique classical completion of some partial valuation which assigns truth values to all sentence letters, it follows that there is no classical valuation on which $\Phi_1, \ldots, \Phi_n$ are all true and Ψ is untrue. Thus $\Phi_1, \ldots, \Phi_n \vdash \Psi$ is classically valid.
>
> Therefore, once again by conditional proof, if $\Phi_1, \ldots, \Phi_n \vdash \Psi$ is valid on supervaluational semantics, then it is classically valid. Thus we have shown that $\Phi_1, \ldots, \Phi_n \vdash \Psi$ is classically valid iff it is valid on supervaluational semantics.   QED

Let's now extend supervaluational semantics to predicate logic. It may appear that supervaluations are especially suited to those forms of free logic which permit truth-value gaps (see Section 15.1). For just as supervaluations model our ability to make assertions that are neither true nor false by permitting truth-valueless formulas, so such free logics model our ability to give names to things that do not exist by permitting denotationless names. But at least one natural supervaluational semantics for predicate logic leads, not to free logic, but (as in the propositional case) to a logic whose inferences are classical but whose semantics is nonbivalent.

We extend supervaluational semantics to predicate logic by beginning as in propositional logic with partial valuations. A **partial valuation** for predicate logic is an assignment of the usual sorts of extensions in a nonempty domain to names and predicates and of truth values to sentence letters. It need not, however, assign extensions to all (or any) of the names and sentence letters. That is, it may leave names denotationless or sentence letters truth-valueless. Partial valuations must, however, assign extensions to all n-place predicates ($n > 0$)—though, as in classical predicate logic, n-place predicates may still be made "denotationless" by being assigned the empty set. A **classical completion** of a partial valuation for predicate logic, then, is simply a classical valuation for predicate logic that assigns the same values that $\mathscr{s}$ does but fills in the gaps where $\mathscr{s}$ assigns no values. Then we stipulate that for each partial valuation $\mathscr{s}$, formulas are true on the supervaluation $\mathscr{V}_\mathscr{s}$ of $\mathscr{s}$

iff they are true on all classical completions of $\mathscr{S}$—that is, true no matter what object in the domain we assign to the denotationless names or what truth value we assign to truth-valueless sentence letters. Similarly, formulas are false on $\mathcal{V}_s$ iff they are false on all classical completions of $\mathscr{S}$.

This makes most, but not all, atomic formulas containing nondenoting names truth-valueless. If, for example, a partial valuation assigns to the one-place predicate 'P' the entire domain as its extension, then for any name α, even if α is denotationless, Pα is true on the corresponding supervaluation, since no matter which object in the domain we could assign to α, Pα will be true. Similarly, if the extension of 'P' is { }, then Pα is false, regardless of whether or not α has denotation. However, if the extension of 'P' contains some but not all of the objects in the domain, then Pα is truth-valueless when α lacks denotation, since some assignments of denotation to α would make Pα true while others would make it false. Various generalizations of these results also hold for relational predicates.

All formulas of the form $\alpha = \alpha$ are true on all supervaluations—a pleasing result. However, where α and β are different names one or both of which are denotationless, $\alpha = \beta$ is truth-valueless, unless the domain contains but one object.

This semantics validates the inferences:

$$\text{Fa} \vdash \exists x \text{Fx}$$

and

$$\forall x \text{Fx} \vdash \text{Fa}$$

which are invalid on free logics. Indeed, the resulting logic is—despite the truth-value and denotation gaps—plain old classical predicate logic. The semantics presented here is, however, only one of several ways to implement supervaluational predicate logics. Other, generally more complicated, semantic variations yield logics more akin to the free logics of Section 15.1.[8]

In both propositional and predicate logic, supervaluational semantics allows us to retain all the inferential structure of classical logic while abandoning the semantic principle of bivalence. It is thus an interesting compromise between classical and nonclassical logics.

Exercise 15.3

1. Prove that a formula of propositional logic is classically valid iff it is valid on supervaluational semantics.
2. Prove that the inferences 'Fa $\vdash \exists x$Fx' and '$\forall x$Fx $\vdash$ Fa' are valid on the supervaluational semantics for predicate logic sketched in this section.

---

[8] For a discussion of these semantic alternatives, see Ermanno Bencivenga, "Free Logics," in D. Gabbay and F. Guenthner, eds., *Handbook of Philosophical Logic, Volume III: Alternatives to Classical Logic* (Dordrecht: D. Reidel, 1985), especially pp. 402–12.

16

RADICALLY NONCLASSICAL LOGICS

16.1 INFINITE VALUED AND FUZZY LOGICS

Consider the following argument:

> A global population of 1,000,000,000 is sustainable.
> If a global population of 1,000,000,000 is sustainable, so is a global population of 1,000,000,001.
> ∴ A global population of 1,000,000,001 is sustainable.

Is this sound? The reasoning (which is just modus ponens) seems valid, and the premises are true—or at least *almost* true. But if we iterate the same reasoning 999 billion times, like this:

> A global population of 1,000,000,000 is sustainable.
> If a global population of 1,000,000,000 is sustainable, so is a global population of 1,000,000,001.
> ∴ A global population of 1,000,000,001 is sustainable.
>
> If a global population of 1,000,000,001 is sustainable, so is a global population of 1,000,000,002.
> ∴ A global population of 1,000,000,002 is sustainable.
>   .
>   .
>   .

∴   A global population of 999,999,999,999 is sustainable.
If a global population of 999,999,999,999 is sustainable, so is a global population of 1,000,000,000,000.
∴   A global population of 1,000,000,000,000 is sustainable.

we obtain an egregiously false conclusion.

The trouble seems to lie in the iteration of "almost true" premises of the form

If a global population of n is sustainable, so is a global population of $n + 1$.

Early in the sequence of inferences these premises lead to conclusions that are either wholly true or approximately true. But as they are used to draw conclusion after conclusion, the conclusions become less and less true so that by the end of the sequence we arrive at a conclusion that is wholly false.

It is obvious that no particular statement in this sequence is the source of the error. All the conditional premises are true, or nearly so. Rather, there is a gradual progression from truth into error. The reason we cannot locate the error in any single premise is that the predicate 'is sustainable' is vague. There are paradigm cases: populations that are clearly sustainable and populations that are clearly unsustainable. But there are also intermediate cases in which it is "sort of true" but "sort of false" that the population is sustainable. Our vague notion of sustainability defines no sharp boundary at which a population of n is sustainable, but a population of $n + 1$ is not. Rather, as the numbers increase it becomes less and less true that the population is sustainable.

The novelty of this explanation is that it makes truth a matter of degree. There are, it appears, not just two truth values, but a potential continuum of values, from wholly false to wholly true. If we take this gradation of truth value seriously, the result is an infinite valued semantics.

The obvious way to represent these truth values is on a scale from 0 to 1 with 0 being wholly false and 1 being wholly true. Then, in propositional logic, instead of assigning propositions just the values T or F, a valuation may assign them any real number from 0 to 1. This, of course, forces us to revise the valuation rules for the operators. It is by no means obvious how to do this. Several options are available, as we saw in Section 15.2, when we move from two values to three; many more present themselves when we contemplate an infinity of values. We shall sample only one infinite-valued semantics—one of the simplest.

Consider, first, the negation operator. If Φ is wholly true, then $\sim\Phi$ is wholly untrue and vice versa. Likewise, it seems reasonable to suppose that if Φ is three-quarters true, $\sim\Phi$ is only one-quarter true. Thus, as a general rule $\sim\Phi$ has all the truth that Φ lacks and vice versa. More formally,

1. $\mathcal{V}(\sim\Phi) = 1 - \mathcal{V}(\Phi)$

This gives negation many of the properties we expect it to have. It follows from this definition, for example, that the double negation of a formula has the same truth value as the formula itself. That is,

$$\begin{aligned}
\mathcal{V}(\sim\sim\Psi) &= 1 - \mathcal{V}(\sim\Psi) && \text{By valuation rule 1}\\
&= 1 - (1 - \mathcal{V}(\Psi)) && \text{By valuation rule 1}\\
&= 1 - 1 + \mathcal{V}(\Psi) && \text{By algebra}\\
&= \mathcal{V}(\Psi) && \text{By algebra}
\end{aligned}$$

A conjunction would seem to be as true as the least true of its conjuncts. The truth conditions for conjunctions are best expressed using the notation 'min(x, y)' to indicate the minimum or least of the two values x and y—or the value both 'x' and 'y' express if $x = y$. Thus, for example, $\min(0.25, 0.3) = 0.25$ and $\min(1, 1) = 1$. The valuation rule for conjunctions, then, is

2. $\mathcal{V}(\Phi \,\&\, \Psi) = \min(\mathcal{V}(\Phi), \mathcal{V}(\Psi))$

Again, we can prove some familiar properties. A conjunction of the form $\Psi \,\&\, \Psi$, for example, has the same truth value as Ψ:

$$\begin{aligned}
\mathcal{V}(\Psi \,\&\, \Psi) &= \min(\mathcal{V}(\Psi), \mathcal{V}(\Psi)) && \text{By valuation rule 2}\\
&= \mathcal{V}(\Psi) && \text{By definition of min}
\end{aligned}$$

Disjunctions are as true as the most true of their disjuncts. This idea may be expressed by the notation 'max(x, y)', which indicates the maximum or greatest of the two values x and y, or the value both variables express if $x = y$:

3. $\mathcal{V}(\Phi \lor \Psi) = \max(\mathcal{V}(\Phi), \mathcal{V}(\Psi))$

We can now show, for example, that generalizations of De Morgan's laws hold on this semantics. For example, $\mathcal{V}(\sim\Phi \,\&\, \sim\Psi) = \mathcal{V}(\sim(\Phi \lor \Psi))$:

$$\begin{aligned}
\mathcal{V}(\sim\Phi \,\&\, \sim\Psi) &= \min(\mathcal{V}(\sim\Phi), \mathcal{V}(\sim\Psi)) && \text{By valuation rule 2}\\
&= \min((1 - \mathcal{V}(\Phi)), (1 - \mathcal{V}(\Psi))) && \text{By valuation rule 1}\\
&= 1 - \max(\mathcal{V}(\Phi), \mathcal{V}(\Psi)) && \text{By algebra}^1\\
&= 1 - \mathcal{V}(\Phi \lor \Psi) && \text{By valuation rule 3}\\
&= \mathcal{V}(\sim(\Phi \lor \Psi)) && \text{By valuation rule 1}
\end{aligned}$$

There are many ways of dealing with conditionals; again we shall choose one of the simplest. We shall assume that a conditional is wholly true if its consequent is at least as true as its antecedent, but that if the consequent is less true than the antecedent by some amount x, then the conditional is less than wholly true by that amount. If, for example, $\mathcal{V}(\Phi) = 0.3$ and $\mathcal{V}(\Psi) = 0.4$, then $\mathcal{V}(\Phi \to \Psi) = 1$, since the degree of truth of the consequent exceeds that of the antecedent. If, however, the values are reversed, so that $\mathcal{V}(\Phi) = 0.4$ and $\mathcal{V}(\Psi) = 0.3$, then, since the antecedent's degree of truth exceeds the consequent's by 0.1, the conditional is that much less than wholly true; in other words, $\mathcal{V}(\Phi \to \Psi) = 1 - 0.1 = 0.9$. These truth conditions can be expressed by the equation

4. $\mathcal{V}(\Phi \to \Psi) = 1 + \min(\mathcal{V}(\Phi), \mathcal{V}(\Psi)) - \mathcal{V}(\Phi)$

If Ψ is at least as true as Φ—that is, $\mathcal{V}(\Phi) \le \mathcal{V}(\Psi)$—then $\min(\mathcal{V}(\Phi), \mathcal{V}(\Psi)) - \mathcal{V}(\Phi) = 0$ and so $\mathcal{V}(\Phi \to \Psi) = 1$. If $\mathcal{V}(\Phi) > \mathcal{V}(\Psi)$, then $\min(\mathcal{V}(\Phi), \mathcal{V}(\Psi)) - \mathcal{V}(\Phi) = \mathcal{V}(\Psi)$

---

[1] The algebraic principle used here is that $\min(1 - x, 1 - y) = 1 - \max(x, y)$.

$- \mathcal{V}(\Phi)$ so that $\mathcal{V}(\Phi \to \Psi) = 1 + \mathcal{V}(\Psi) - \mathcal{V}(\Phi) = 1 - (\mathcal{V}(\Phi) - \mathcal{V}(\Psi))$; that is, the conditional is less than wholly true by the amount $\mathcal{V}(\Phi) - \mathcal{V}(\Psi)$.

Notice that $\Phi \to \Psi$ is wholly false only if $\mathcal{V}(\Phi) = 1$ and $\mathcal{V}(\Psi) = 0$. Otherwise, it has some degree of truth—that is, $\mathcal{V}(\Phi \to \Psi) > 0$.

For the biconditional, we shall assume that its truth value is 1 iff the truth values of its components are equal and that otherwise it is less than wholly true by the amount of their difference. Thus, if $\mathcal{V}(\Phi) = \mathcal{V}(\Psi)$, then $\mathcal{V}(\Phi \leftrightarrow \Psi) = 1$. But if, say, $\mathcal{V}(\Phi) = 0.3$ and $\mathcal{V}(\Psi) = 0.7$ so that the difference between $\mathcal{V}(\Phi)$ and $\mathcal{V}(\Psi)$ is 0.4, then $\mathcal{V}(\Phi \leftrightarrow \Psi) = 1 - 0.4 = 0.6$. These truth conditions are expressible by the equation

5. $\mathcal{V}(\Phi \leftrightarrow \Psi) = 1 + \min(\mathcal{V}(\Phi), \mathcal{V}(\Psi)) - \max(\mathcal{V}(\Phi), \mathcal{V}(\Psi))$

This makes the truth value of $\Phi \leftrightarrow \Psi$ equal to that of $(\Phi \to \Psi) \mathbin{\&} (\Psi \to \Phi)$, as the following equations show:

$\mathcal{V}((\Phi \to \Psi) \mathbin{\&} (\Psi \to \Phi))$

$=$	$\min(\mathcal{V}(\Phi \to \Psi), \mathcal{V}(\Psi \to \Phi))$	By valuation rule 2
$=$	$\min((1 + \min(\mathcal{V}(\Phi), \mathcal{V}(\Psi)) - \mathcal{V}(\Phi)), (1 + \min(\mathcal{V}(\Psi), \mathcal{V}(\Phi)) - \mathcal{V}(\Psi)))$	By valuation rule 4
$=$	$\min((1 + \min(\mathcal{V}(\Phi), \mathcal{V}(\Psi)) - \mathcal{V}(\Phi)), (1 + \min(\mathcal{V}(\Phi), \mathcal{V}(\Psi)) - \mathcal{V}(\Psi)))$	By algebra[2]
$=$	$1 + \min(\mathcal{V}(\Phi), \mathcal{V}(\Psi)) + \min(-\mathcal{V}(\Phi), -\mathcal{V}(\Psi))$	By algebra[3]
$=$	$1 + \min(\mathcal{V}(\Phi), \mathcal{V}(\Psi)) - \max(\mathcal{V}(\Phi), \mathcal{V}(\Psi))$	By algebra[4]
$=$	$\mathcal{V}(\Phi \leftrightarrow \Psi)$	By valuation rule 5

These valuation rules yield familiar systems if we restrict the number of truth values. If we consider just the values 1 and 0, taking 1 as T and 0 as F, then these rules define the classical semantics for propositional logic. If we allow a third value, ½, and take it to be I, these rules yield Łukasiewicz's three-valued semantics. In fact Łukasiewicz was the first to state these rules, though he had in mind applications not to problems of vagueness, but to the problem of future contingents.

Knowledge of these correlations can be used to generate counterexamples to certain specific theses in the infinite-valued semantics. For example, we may wonder whether 'P ∨ ~P' is valid (true on all valuations), which in the context of fuzzy logic means having the value 1 on all valuations. We saw, however, in Section 15.2 that this formula is invalid on Łukasiewicz's semantics, the counterexample being the case in which $\mathcal{V}(\text{'P'}) = I$. Since I translates into the value ½ on the infinite-valued semantics, the truth-value assignment $\mathcal{V}(\text{'P'}) = \frac{1}{2}$ should also produce a counterexample here. Indeed it does:

---

[2] For clearly $\min(x, y) = \min(y, x)$.

[3] Here we appeal to the fairly obvious fact that $\min((x - y), (x - z)) = x + \min(-y, -z)$.

[4] This inference relies on the fact that $\min(-x, -y) = -\max(x, y)$.

METATHEOREM: The formula 'P ∨ ~P' is not valid on this infinite-valued semantics.

PROOF: Consider the valuation $\mathcal{V}$ such that $\mathcal{V}$('P') = ½. Now by valuation rule 3, $\mathcal{V}$('P ∨ ~P') = max($\mathcal{V}$('P'), $\mathcal{V}$('~P')), which is by valuation rule 1 max($\mathcal{V}$('P'), $(1 - \mathcal{V}$('P'))). But since $\mathcal{V}$('P') = ½, this is just max(½, $(1 - ½)$) = max(½, ½) = ½. Thus, since $\mathcal{V}$('P ∨ ~P') = ½, 'P ∨ ~P' is not valid.   QED

It is interesting to note, however, that the truth value of formulas of the form Φ ∨ ~Φ can never drop below ½. These formulas, though not in all instances valid, are always at least half true!

This does not hold for all classically valid formulas, however. We saw that the classical tautology '~(P ↔ ~P)' is false on Łukasiewicz's three-valued semantics when P is indeterminate. Similarly, on the infinite-valued semantics $\mathcal{V}$('~(P ↔ ~P)') = 0 when $\mathcal{V}$('P') = ½.

And, as on Łukasiewicz's three-valued semantics, some formulas—those of the form Φ → Φ, for example—are valid despite the infinity of values:

METATHEOREM: For any formula Φ, Φ → Φ is valid on the infinite-valued semantics.

PROOF: Let Φ be any formula. By valuation rule 4, $\mathcal{V}$(Φ → Φ) = 1 + min($\mathcal{V}$(Φ), $\mathcal{V}$(Φ)) − $\mathcal{V}$(Φ) = 1 + $\mathcal{V}$(Φ) − $\mathcal{V}$(Φ) = 1 + 0 = 1. Hence Φ → Φ is valid.   QED

In general, formulas which are classically valid may take any truth value on the infinite-valued semantics, though those of particular forms may be confined to a particular range of values or even to one value.

With infinitely many truth values available, we also have various choices for what counts as valid reasoning. We might, for example, define the concept of validity in either of these ways:

1. A sequent is valid iff there is no valuation on which its premises are wholly true and its conclusion is not wholly true (i.e., one which the truth value of the premises is 1 but the truth value of the conclusion is less than 1).
2. A sequent is valid iff there is no valuation on which the lowest of the truth values of its premises exceeds the truth value of its conclusion.

Or, generalizing definition 2, we might even make validity itself a matter of degree:

3. A sequent is valid to degree 1 iff it is valid by definition 2; it is valid to degree $1 - x$ iff there is no valuation on which the lowest of the truth values of its premises exceeds the truth value of its conclusion by more than x, where $x > 0$.

On definition 3, for example, the sequent 'Q ⊢ P ∨ ~P' is valid to degree ½. For the highest value 'Q' can have is 1, whereas the lowest value 'P ∨ ~P' can have is ½. Thus there is no valuation on which the truth value of the premise exceeds the truth value of the conclusion by more than ½. Hence this sequent is valid to degree $1 - ½ = ½$.

A sequent is valid to degree 1 according to definition 3 iff it is valid by definition 2. And any sequent valid by definition 2 is also valid by definition 1, though the converse does not hold. There are other possible definitions of validity as well. None is uniquely correct. Rather, on an infinite-valued semantics the concept of validity splinters into an array of concepts.

In particular cases, various concepts of validity may coincide. For example, the sequent 'P & Q ⊢ P' is valid on definitions 1 and 2 and hence valid to degree 1 on definition 3. But in other cases, different concepts of validity yield different results. Consider, for example, modus ponens in the form of the sequent 'P, P → Q ⊢ Q'. While valid on definition 1, this sequent is invalid on definition 2 and valid only to degree ½ on definition 3. For on the valuation $\mathcal{V}$ such that $\mathcal{V}(\text{'P'}) = ½$ and $\mathcal{V}(\text{'Q'}) = 0$:

$$
\begin{aligned}
\mathcal{V}(\text{'P} \to \text{Q'}) &= 1 + \min(\mathcal{V}(\text{'P'}), \mathcal{V}(\text{'Q'})) - \mathcal{V}(\text{'P'}) \quad \text{By valuation rule 4} \\
&= 1 + \min(½, 0) - ½ \\
&= 1 + 0 - ½ \\
&= ½
\end{aligned}
$$

On $\mathcal{V}$, therefore, both premises have the value ½ but the conclusion has the value 0. Thus there is a valuation (namely, $\mathcal{V}$) on which the lowest of the truth values of the premises exceeds the truth value of the conclusion, and so the sequent is invalid by definition 2. This example also shows that the sequent is valid at most to degree ½ on definition 3. To show that it is valid exactly to degree ½ takes more work, but we have already seen what we need to see.

Let's now return to the problem with which we began this section. We note first that conditionals of the form

If a global population of n is sustainable, so is a global population of $n + 1$

are not wholly true on our semantics. For at high values of n, each statement of the form

A global population of $n + 1$ is sustainable

is slightly less true than each statement of the form

A global population of n is sustainable.

To obtain the truth value of the conditional, we subtract the difference between the values of these two statements from 1. Thus each such conditional has a truth value slightly less than 1.

Moreover, we have just seen that with less than perfectly true premises modus ponens may yield conclusions that are less true than either of the premises. Hence it is now intelligible how even with premises that are almost wholly true, the truth values of successive conclusions by modus ponens may diminish. A long sequence of such inferences, then, may lead us from near truth to absolute falsehood.

As this example illustrates, infinite-valued semantics holds considerable promise for the semantic treatment of at least some kinds of vague inferences. But it is not wholly satisfactory. Though we might agree, for example, that the truth value of 'A global population of 6,000,000,001 is sustainable' is slightly less than the truth value of 'A global population of 6,000,000,000 is sustainable', there is no fact of the matter as to what these numerical truth values are. Is the truth value of the first statement, for example, 0.3? 0.5? 0.9? And what, exactly, is the numerical difference between the truth values of the two statements?

Part of our inability to answer lies in our ignorance. We don't understand the earth as an ecosystem well enough to know, except within a very broad range, what populations are sustainable. But part of the problem lies also in the vagueness of the term 'sustainable'. Even if we knew everything there is to know about the earth, we would at best be able to offer only artificially precise numbers for truth values, because the concept of sustainability is essentially vague and qualitative, lacking any rigorously quantifiable structure.

In the mid-1960s, Lofti Zadeh set out to improve upon infinite-valued semantics by making the truth values themselves imprecise. That is, instead of assigning to a statement like 'A global population of 6,000,000,000 is sustainable' an arbitrarily precise numerical truth value, Zadeh proposed that we assign it an imprecise range of values. By this he meant not merely an interval of values (say, the interval between .4 and .5, which itself is a precisely defined entity), but a *fuzzy* interval of values. A fuzzy interval is a kind of fuzzy set. And a **fuzzy set** is a set for which membership is a matter of degree.

Most concepts, Zadeh argued, define not classical sets, but fuzzy sets. Take the concept of redness. Some things are wholly and genuinely red. But others are almost red, somewhat red, only a little bit red, and so on. So, whereas fresh blood or a red traffic light might be fully a member of the set of all red things, the setting sun might be, say, halfway a member and a peach only slightly a member. Now in fuzzy-set theory, membership is assigned strict numerical values from 0 to 1, like the truth values in infinite-valued semantics. But in defining truth values, Zadeh compounds the fuzziness. He might, for example, define a truth value AT (almost true), which is a fuzzy set of numerical values in which, say, numbers no greater than 0.5 have membership 0, 0.6 has membership 0.3, 0.7 has membership 0.5, 0.9 has membership 0.8, and 0.99 has membership 0.95. Such a fuzzy set of numerical values is for Zadeh a truth value. A logic whose semantics is based on such fuzzy truth values is called a **fuzzy logic.**

If infinite-valued semantics presents a bewildering array of choices of truth conditions and semantic concepts, fuzzy logic compounds the complication. Already in infinite-valued predicate logic, the extensions assigned to predicates must be fuzzy sets; for if they were classical sets, atomic formulas containing n-place predicates ($n > 0$) would always be either true or false. So, for example, the predicate 'is red' has as its extension the fuzzy set of red things described above. Consequently, infinite-valued semantics has the following truth clause for one-place predicates Φ and names α:

$\mathcal{V}(\Phi\alpha) = x$ iff $\mathcal{V}(\alpha)$ is a member of the fuzzy set $\mathcal{V}(\Phi)$ to degree x.

But on Zadeh's fuzzy semantics the extensions of predicates are structures still more complex than fuzzy sets, structures which, when applied to the extensions of names, yield fuzzy truth values. The valuation rules for the operators, and the semantic concepts of validity, consistency, and so on, must all be redefined once again to accommodate these fuzzy values. In the process these concepts "splinter" even more wildly than concept of validity does in infinite-valued logic.

Yet despite the complication upon complication, arbitrariness remains. Zadeh suggests that a fuzzy logic should not employ all possible fuzzy truth values (a very large set of values indeed!), but only a small finite range of them, and that it should correlate them with such natural language expressions as 'very true', 'more or less true', and so on. But *which* fuzzy set of numbers corresponds to the English expression 'more or less true'? And why should we suppose that precisely that set is what we mean when we say that a particular sentence is more or less true? The choice of any particular fuzzy value is just as arbitrary as the assignment of a precise numerical truth value to a vague statement. The arbitrariness does not go away; it is merely concealed in the complexity.

Arbitrariness notwithstanding, fuzzy logic has found useful application in artificial intelligence devices. But it has also acquired a certain unwarranted mystique. Many people are attracted to the idea of a (warm and?) fuzzy logic because it sounds as if it might offer relief from overtaxing precision. As a result of this popularity, the term 'fuzzy logic' is often used loosely. In popular science publications it may mean no more than an infinite-valued logic—or even statistical or just plain muddle-headed reasoning.

Exercise 16.1

Prove the following metatheorems using infinite-valued semantics:

1. The sequent 'P & Q ⊢ P' is valid on definitions 1 and 2 of validity and valid to degree 1 on definition 3.
2. The sequent 'P, P → Q ⊢ Q' is valid on definition 1.
3. The formula '~(P & ~P)' is not valid (i.e., does not always have the value 1).

16.2 INTUITIONISTIC LOGICS

All the logics thus far considered have as their fundamental semantic concept the notion of truth. Truth is usually understood as a kind of correspondence between propositions or thoughts and reality. But many philosophers, believing that we have no access to reality as it is in itself, doubt that we can ever attain truth in this sense. I may think that the soup is boiling and then go to the stove and see that it is. In this sense I may confirm my thought that the soup is boiling. But my seeing or hearing (or even touching) the soup does not, so this line of reasoning goes, reveal the soup as it is in reality, but only the soup as I see or hear or feel it. I may, in other words, compare my thought with the soup *as perceived by me,* but never with the soup as it is *in itself.* But if I can never know the relation between my thought and reality itself, then I can never know truth. And if truth is something unknowable, then perhaps our semantics should be based on something more empirical.

One suggestion is to base our semantics on relations not between thought and reality, but between thought and evidence—relations such as proof, warrant, or confirmation. My perception of the soup is a form of evidence that proves, warrants, or confirms my thought or assertion that the soup is boiling. Thus thought or assertion, which I experience, is compared with evidence, which I also experience, rather than with reality or the world, which I allegedly never experience as it is in itself. Another word for such direct experience is 'intuition'. Accordingly, the resolve to restrict semantics to entities that can be made evident to direct experience is called **intuitionism.**

Intuitionists reject the traditional notion of truth because it posits a world-as-it-is-in-itself—something we never experience as such—as that to which thought or assertion corresponds. For the intuitionist this world-in-itself is irrelevant to semantics. Having gone this far, one might even be tempted to conclude that there is no such thing as the world as it is in itself. Some prominent philosophers have drawn this conclusion.

Others have accepted this conclusion only in regard to certain kinds of reality. The originator of intuitionism, L. E. J. Brouwer, was concerned primarily with mathematics, not with the world in general. He held that mathematical objects (numbers, functions, sets, etc.) exist only insofar as we construct them or define the means for their construction. The propositions of mathematics, then, are not true in the sense of corresponding to some independently existing reality, but rather merely confirmable, refutable, or neither, by the evidence of our calculations and proofs.

Lately others—most notably Michael Dummett—have held that even the semantics of ordinary discourse is best understood as intuitionistic. Dummett's view is less "subjectivistic" than that of earlier intuitionists. He holds that what constitutes the meanings of terms must be publicly observable; otherwise, our ability to learn language would be inexplicable. Thus we learn the meanings of terms by observing them in use and so associating them with publicly evident assertibility conditions. Meaning, then, is constituted, not by truth conditions (for truth, as we know, is not always publicly evident!), but by assertibility conditions. To know the meaning of a term is to know the publicly evident conditions under which it is appropriate to assert various sentences containing it.

Regardless of whether intuitionism is confined to a specific domain, or applied universally, the strategy is always the same: Replace the traditional concept of truth with some notion of warrant or evidence. This warrant or evidence may be regarded more or less subjectively, as was the case with the original intuitionists, or as publicly accessible, as in Dummett. We shall use the general term **confirmation** to stand for all of these notions of warrant or evidence. Replacement of truth by confirmation subtly shifts the meaning of each formula or statement. To assert a formula Φ is to say not that it corresponds to reality, but that it is evident, warranted, or (in our jargon) *confirmed.* In the domain of mathematics, Brouwer interpreted this to mean that we have a proof of Φ; in more ordinary contexts, it means that the assertion of Φ is warranted. Correlatively, to assert ~Φ is to say that Φ is refutable. In mathematics, this means that we have a disproof of Φ—typically the derivation of a contradiction from Φ; in ordinary contexts, it means that the denial of Φ is warranted.

But not every proposition is either confirmed or refuted; indeed, not every proposition *can* be either confirmed or refuted, even in principle. Consider, to use one of Brouwer's examples, this proposition, which we shall symbolize as 'P':

> There are seven consecutive sevens in the decimal expansion of the number π, that is, 3.141 . . . .

If there are seven consecutive sevens, say, in the first million (or billion or trillion) digits of this decimal expansion, then we can know conclusively that there are simply by calculating that many digits. In fact, though I don't, someone may know this already, since π has in fact been calculated by computers to many millions of digits. But suppose that no matter now far we calculate, we never find seven consecutive sevens. Then, since neither we nor our computers (both being finite creatures) can calculate all the infinitely many digits of this decimal expansion, then (provided there is no noncalculational way to decide the question—and there does not seem to be) proposition P is in that case neither confirmable nor refutable, even in principle. There can, in other words, never, not even in principle, be suffi-cient evidence to confirm the disjunction 'P ∨ ~P', whose intuitionistic meaning is that 'P' is either confirmed or refuted. Hence intuitionists reject, even as an ideal, the law of excluded middle, Φ ∨ ~Φ, which they read as asserting that Φ is either confirmed or refuted.

The reasons for this rejection appear, perhaps even more clearly, in nonmath-ematical examples. It is unlikely, for example, that we will ever either confirm or refute certain statements about the past. Maybe the statement that Napoleon ate breakfast on September 9, 1807, is one of these. It is, from a classical point of view, either true or false that Napoleon did so. But the intuitionist is not interested in, and may not even believe in, truth in this sense. Interested, rather, in what we can (at least in principle) have warrant to believe, she has replaced the notion of truth with the idea of confirmation.

So far, this sounds like little more than a three-valued logic, the values being "confirmed," "refuted," and "neither." But it is more subtle than that.

We can begin to appreciate the subtlety by considering the inference rule of double negation, or ~E (from ~~Φ, infer Φ), which is valid in both classical and multivalued systems; it is invalid in intuitionistic logic. For to an intuitionist, since negation signifies refutation, ~~Φ means "it is refuted that Φ is refuted." But sup-pose we somehow refute the view that the proposition that Napoleon ate breakfast on September 9, 1807, is refuted. That is not tantamount to confirming this prop-osition; it may only demonstrate our ignorance. Hence from ~~Φ an intuitionist may not in general infer Φ. This is a drastic departure both from classical logic and from multivalued logics based on the notion of truth!

Moreover, if intuitionistic logic were three-valued in the way suggested above, then the intuitionistic operator '~' would have a truth (or, rather, confir-mation!) table that would tell how to calculate the value of ~Φ from the value of

FIGURE 16.1
Possible Semantic Classification of a Statement Φ According to Intuitionism

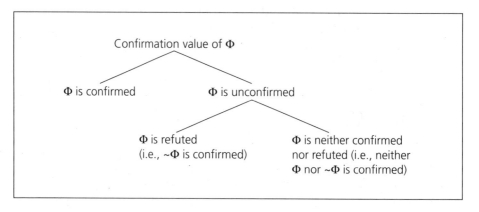

Φ. But there can be no such table. For suppose the value of Φ were "neither," that is, neither confirmed nor refuted. Then ~Φ could not have the value "confirmed," since that would mean that it is confirmed that Φ is refuted and hence that Φ itself is refuted, rather than having the value "neither." But the meaning assigned by the intuitionist to '~' does not determine which of the other two values ("neither" or "refuted") ~Φ ought to have. We saw in the preceding paragraph that ~Φ might be refuted though Φ is "neither." But it might also be "neither" if Φ is "neither"; that is, both the proposition Φ that Napoleon ate breakfast on September 9, 1807, and its negation may be neither confirmed nor refuted. Thus when Φ is "neither," ~Φ may be either refuted or "neither." It follows that intuitionist propositional logic is non-truth-functional (or, more accurately, non-confirmation-functional). That is, the semantic values assigned to a complex formula in a given situation cannot in general be calculated merely from the values of its subformulas in that situation. Thus no confirmation-functional three-valued logic will suffice.

The most natural formal semantics for intuitionistic logic is in fact *bivalent* (two-valued). We shall think of the values as "confirmed" and "unconfirmed" and abbreviate them 'C' and 'U', though in the literature they are usually written as 'T' and 'F' or '1' and '0'.

Refutation, on this semantics, is merely a subspecies of nonconfirmation. More specifically, Φ is refuted if and only if ~Φ is confirmed—in which case Φ has the value U and ~Φ the value C. Φ may, however, have the value U even if ~Φ also has the value U. Figure 16.1 illustrates the relations of these concepts.

The particular version of this bivalent semantics which I shall present here was developed by Saul Kripke.[5] It has illuminating connections to Kripkean se-

---

[5] See Kripke's "Semantical Analysis of Intuitionistic Logic I," in J. Crossley and M. Dummett, eds., *Formal Systems and Recursive Functions* (Amsterdam: North Holland, 1963), pp. 92–129. My presentation in this section is based on this article.

mantics for modal logic—in particular, for the modal system S4. If the material on Kripkean semantics in Section 12.1 is not fresh in your mind, it might be helpful to review it before reading on.

A Kripke model $\mathcal{V}$ for intuitionistic logic, like Kripkean models for modal logics, specifies a set $\mathcal{W}_{\mathcal{V}}$ of "possible worlds" and an accessibility relation $\mathcal{R}$ on those worlds. However, the modality represented by the model is not alethic possibility, but a specific kind of **epistemic possibility**—that is, possibility relative to what has been confirmed. If we think of possible worlds as *worlds,* then their possibility consists in the fact that everything that is the case within them is consistent with the available evidence.

But this is not the most illuminating way to think of possible worlds. Indeed, the central idea of intuitionism is to avoid positing such worlds-in-themselves and to formulate a semantics only in terms of the available evidence. It is better, then, to regard these "worlds" as representations of states of evidence—that is, of the total evidence available to a person or culture at a given time. In each such state, propositions are categorized not as true or false, but as confirmed or unconfirmed. Now a proposition which is confirmed in an evidential state w must also be confirmed in every evidential state that is epistemically possible with respect to w. For example, if I have confirmed (by calculation, say) that $472 + 389 = 861$, then in every evidential state that is consistent with my current evidence, $472 + 389 = 861$. It is, in other words, epistemically necessary for me that $472 + 389 = 861$. *Confirmation is thus a kind of epistemic necessity.*

Accordingly, the confirmation of a proposition Φ in a given evidential state w must be represented semantically not merely by the assignment of the value C to Φ at w, but by the assignment of the value C to Φ at w and at all "worlds" (evidential states) accessible from w.

This is a fundamental difference from the way truth is modeled in Kripkean semantics for classical modal logic. In classical Kripkean models, if we make a sentence letter Φ true in a given world of some model, that does not prevent us from making Φ false in any other world of that model. We may distribute the truth values for a given sentence letter among worlds in any pattern we like, regardless of how the accessibility relation is structured. (The same principle applies to the extensions of predicates in modal predicate logic.) Not so on the Kripkean semantics for intuitionistic logic. Because confirmation, unlike truth, is a kind of necessity, not every distribution of confirmation values is admissible. If we assign to Φ the value C at one "world" w of our model, then we must also assign C to Φ at every "world" u such that $w \mathcal{R} u$.

Consequently, as we follow accessibility relations out from a given world, the set of confirmed propositions can only get larger or, at minimum, remain constant; it never decreases.

Some accounts of intuitionistic logic suggest that $\mathcal{R}$ be understood temporally so that accessible evidential states are those we might arrive at through time as we learn more. But this interpretation is misleading, particularly for nonmathematical applications. What we confirm in the future may contradict what we confirm in the present, if only because (from a classical standpoint) the world has changed in the meantime. In reality it may also happen that evidence we obtain in the future contradicts our present evidence, even if the relevant facts haven't changed, because our present evidence is mistaken. (What I think is the boiling of the soup, for example, may turn out on closer inspection to be only the play of shadow from a nearby fan.) Kripkean semantics, however, never allows anything confirmed in an evidential state accessible from w to conflict with anything confirmed in w. Therefore $\mathcal{R}$ is best understood as taking us not to possible *future* states of evidence, but to states that, consistent with the evidence we have currently, we might *now* enjoy if we could now have more evidence.[6]

Because $\mathcal{R}$ expresses this specific kind of epistemic possibility (namely, consistency with current evidence), $\mathcal{R}$ must have a specific structure. It must, first of all, be reflexive—at least if we suppose (as Kripke does) that evidential states are noncontradictory, that is, self-consistent.

Moreover, $\mathcal{R}$ must be transitive. That is, if an evidential state w_2 is consistent with (accessible from) another state w_1, and a third state w_3 is consistent with w_2, then w_3 is consistent with w_1. This follows from the assumption noted above that every proposition confirmed in a particular evidential state w is also confirmed in all evidential states accessible from w. For then if $w_1\mathcal{R}w_2$ and $w_2\mathcal{R}w_3$, all the propositions confirmed in w_1 are also confirmed in w_2 and all of those confirmed in w_2 are confirmed in w_3. Hence all of those confirmed in w_1 are confirmed in w_3. But this means that w_3 is consistent with the evidential state w_1 so that (since $\mathcal{R}$ represents consistency with current evidence) $w_1\mathcal{R}w_3$.

Finally, with respect to predicate logic, we must assign a domain to each evidential state. Intuitively, this domain represents the objects whose existence we have confirmed. Since it is epistemically possible for there to be objects whose existence we have not confirmed, we allow that as we move out from a given evidential state along a trail of accessibility, the domain may grow. But it may not diminish, for if the existence of an object is confirmed, then it is not epistemically possible for that object not to exist. That is, if $w_1\mathcal{R}w_2$, then the domain of w_2 must include all the objects in the domain of w_1 and maybe some additional objects as well. With these principles in mind we make the following definition:

DEFINITION A **Kripkean valuation** or **Kripkean model** $\mathcal{V}$ for a formula or set of formulas of intuitionistic predicate logic consists of the following:

1. A nonempty set $\mathcal{W}_{\mathcal{V}}$ of objects, called the **worlds** or **evidential states** of $\mathcal{V}$.
2. A reflexive, transitive relation $\mathcal{R}$, consisting of a set of pairs of worlds from $\mathcal{W}_{\mathcal{V}}$.
3. For each world w in $\mathcal{W}_{\mathcal{V}}$ a nonempty set $\mathcal{D}_w$ of objects, called the **domain of w**, such that for any worlds x and y, if $x\mathcal{R}y$, then $\mathcal{D}_x$ is a subset of $\mathcal{D}_y$.

---

[6] It is, of course, possible to provide explicitly for such future (and also past) states of evidence by adding tense operators to Kripkean intuitionistic logic.

4. An assignment to each name α in that formula or set of formulas of an extension $\mathcal{V}(\alpha)$ that is a member of the domain of at least one world.

5. An assignment to each predicate Φ and world w in that formula or set of formulas, an extension $\mathcal{V}(\Phi, w)$ such that

    i. If Φ is a zero-place predicate, $\mathcal{V}(\Phi, w)$ is one (but not both) of the values C or U such that if $\mathcal{V}(\Phi, w) = C$, then for all u such that $w\mathcal{R}u$, $\mathcal{V}(\Phi, u) = C$.

    ii. If Φ is a one-place predicate, $\mathcal{V}(\Phi, w)$ is a set of members of $\mathcal{D}_w$ such that if $d \in \mathcal{V}(\Phi, w)$, then for all u such that $w\mathcal{R}u$, $d \in \mathcal{V}(\Phi, u)$.

    iii. If Φ is an n-place predicate ($n > 1$), $\mathcal{V}(\Phi, w)$ is a set of ordered n-tuples of members of $\mathcal{D}_w$ such that if $<d_1, \ldots, d_n> \in \mathcal{V}(\Phi, w)$, then for all u such that $w\mathcal{R}u$, $<d_1, \ldots, d_n> \in \mathcal{V}(\Phi, u)$.

Now, rather than the *truth conditions* for complex formulas, we give what we might call their **confirmation conditions**. Let Φ and Ψ be any formulas and $\mathcal{V}$ any valuation of Φ and Ψ whose accessibility relation is $\mathcal{R}$. Then

1. If Φ is a one-place predicate and α is a name, then $\mathcal{V}(\Phi\alpha, w) = C$ iff $\mathcal{V}(\alpha) \in \mathcal{V}(\Phi, w)$;
   $\mathcal{V}(\Phi\alpha, w) = U$ iff $\mathcal{V}(\alpha) \notin \mathcal{V}(\Phi, w)$.

2. If Φ is an n-place predicate ($n > 1$) and $\alpha_1, \ldots, \alpha_n$ are names, then
   $\mathcal{V}(\Phi\alpha_1, \ldots, \alpha_n, w) = C$ iff $<\mathcal{V}(\alpha_1), \ldots, \mathcal{V}(\alpha_n)> \in \mathcal{V}(\Phi, w)$;
   $\mathcal{V}(\Phi\alpha_1, \ldots, \alpha_n, w) = U$ iff $<\mathcal{V}(\alpha_1), \ldots, \mathcal{V}(\alpha_n)> \notin \mathcal{V}(\Phi, w)$.

3. If α and β are names, then $\mathcal{V}(\alpha = \beta, w) = C$ iff $\mathcal{V}(\alpha) = \mathcal{V}(\beta)$;
   $\mathcal{V}(\alpha = \beta, w) = U$ iff $\mathcal{V}(\alpha) \neq \mathcal{V}(\beta)$.

For the next five rules, Φ and Ψ are any formulas:

4. $\mathcal{V}(\sim\Phi, w) = C$ iff for all u such that $w\mathcal{R}u$, $\mathcal{V}(\Phi, u) \neq C$.
   $\mathcal{V}(\sim\Phi, w) = U$ iff for some u such that $w\mathcal{R}u$, $\mathcal{V}(\Phi, u) = C$.

5. $\mathcal{V}(\Phi \,\&\, \Psi, w) = C$ iff both $\mathcal{V}(\Phi, w) = C$ and $\mathcal{V}(\Psi, w) = C$.
   $\mathcal{V}(\Phi \,\&\, \Psi, w) = U$ iff either $\mathcal{V}(\Phi, w) \neq C$ or $\mathcal{V}(\Psi, w) \neq C$, or both.

6. $\mathcal{V}(\Phi \vee \Psi, w) = C$ iff either $\mathcal{V}(\Phi, w) = C$ or $\mathcal{V}(\Psi, w) = C$, or both.
   $\mathcal{V}(\Phi \vee \Psi, w) = U$ iff both $\mathcal{V}(\Phi, w) \neq C$ and $\mathcal{V}(\Psi, w) \neq C$.

7. $\mathcal{V}(\Phi \rightarrow \Psi, w) = C$ iff for all u such that $w\mathcal{R}u$, $\mathcal{V}(\Phi, u) \neq C$ or $\mathcal{V}(\Psi, u) = C$, or both.
   $\mathcal{V}(\Phi \rightarrow \Psi, w) = U$ iff for some u such that $w\mathcal{R}u$, $\mathcal{V}(\Phi, u) = C$ and $\mathcal{V}(\Psi, u) \neq C$.

8. $\mathcal{V}(\Phi \leftrightarrow \Psi, w) = C$ iff for all u such that $w\mathcal{R}u$, $\mathcal{V}(\Phi, u) = \mathcal{V}(\Psi, u)$.
   $\mathcal{V}(\Phi \leftrightarrow \Psi, w) = U$ iff for some u such that $w\mathcal{R}u$, $\mathcal{V}(\Phi, u) \neq \mathcal{V}(\Psi, u)$.

For the next two rules, $\Phi^\alpha/_\beta$ stands for the result of replacing each occurrence of the variable β in Φ by α, and $\mathcal{D}_w$ is the domain that $\mathcal{V}$ assigns to world w.

9. $\mathcal{V}(\forall\beta\Phi, w) = C$ iff for all worlds u such that $w\mathcal{R}u$ and for all potential names α of all objects d in $\mathcal{D}_u$, $\mathcal{V}_{(\alpha,d)}(\Phi^\alpha/_\beta, u) = C$;

$\mathcal{V}(\forall\beta\Phi, w) = \mathrm{U}$ iff for some world u such that $w\mathcal{R}u$, and some potential name α of some object d in $\mathcal{D}_u$, $\mathcal{V}_{(\alpha,d)}(\Phi^\alpha/_\beta, u) \neq \mathrm{C}$.

10. $\mathcal{V}(\exists\beta\Phi, w) = \mathrm{C}$ iff for some potential name α of some object d in $\mathcal{D}_w$, $\mathcal{V}_{(\alpha,d)}(\Phi^\alpha/_\beta, w) = \mathrm{C}$;

$\mathcal{V}(\exists\beta\Phi, w) = \mathrm{U}$ iff for all potential names α of all objects d in $\mathcal{D}_w$, $\mathcal{V}_{(\alpha,d)}(\Phi^\alpha/_\beta, w) \neq \mathrm{C}$.

The clauses for atomic formulas, identity, conjunction, disjunction, and the existential quantifier are the same as in Kripkean or Leibnizian modal logic, except that we have replaced 'T' with 'C' and 'F' with 'U'. But the clauses for negation, the conditional and the biconditional, and the universal quantifier are novel.

The negation operator expresses not merely nonconfirmation, but refutation. Refutation is a kind of epistemic impossibility. Intuitively, $\sim\Phi$ is confirmed (i.e., Φ is refuted) iff current evidence precludes any possibility of the confirmation of Φ. Formally, $\sim\Phi$ is confirmed in a given evidential state w iff no state in which Φ is confirmed is compatible with (accessible from) w. Thus negation is an epistemic impossibility operator; '$\sim$' has the same semantics in intuitionistic logic as '$\square\sim$'— or, equivalently, '$\sim\diamond$'—in Kripkean modal logic.

To assert $\Phi \rightarrow \Psi$ is to say that any epistemically possible state that confirms Φ also confirms Ψ. Formally, $\Phi \rightarrow \Psi$ is confirmed in an evidential state w iff in each evidential state compatible with (accessible from) w, either Φ is not confirmed or Ψ is confirmed. Except for the replacement of truth by confirmation and falsehood by nonconfirmation, the semantics for the intuitionistic conditional is the same as that for the classical strict conditional (see Section 12.3).

The biconditional is in effect a conjunction of strict conditionals. To assert $\Phi \leftrightarrow \Psi$ is to say that no epistemically possible state differentiates the two.

The universal quantifier '$\forall$' means "for all epistemically possible objects," rather than just "for all objects whose existence has been confirmed." It has the same semantics as '$\square\forall$' in Kripkean modal logic. To assert $\forall\beta\Phi$ in intuitionistic logic, then, is not just to say that Φ is confirmed to apply to all objects whose existence has been confirmed, but to assert that Φ has been confirmed to apply to all objects whose existence is compatible with our current evidential state.

The intuitionistic meanings of conjunctions, disjunctions, and existential statements are, by contrast, more direct analogues of their classical meanings. To assert $\Phi \mathbin{\&} \Psi$ is to assert that both Φ and Ψ are confirmed. To assert $\Phi \vee \Psi$ is to assert that at least one of these disjuncts is confirmed. And to assert $\exists\beta\Phi$ is to claim confirmation of the existence of an object to which Φ applies.

This new semantics requires new definitions for the fundamental semantic concepts. We shall call a *sequent* **intuitionistically valid** iff there is no intuitionistic Kripke model containing some evidential state in which the sequent's premises are confirmed and its conclusion is not confirmed. Intuitively, this means that any evidence that confirmed the premises would also confirm the conclusion. A *formula* is **intuitionistically valid** if it is confirmed in all evidential states in all intuitionistic Kripke models. A formula is **intuitionistically inconsistent** iff there is no evidential state in any intuitionistic Kripke model in which it is confirmed. And so on. We now demonstrate formally some of the ideas discussed informally above:

METATHEOREM: The formula 'P ∨ ~P' is not intuitionistically valid.

PROOF: Consider the valuation $\mathcal{V}$ whose set $\mathcal{W}_{\mathcal{V}}$ of worlds is {1, 2} and whose relation $\mathcal{R}$ is {<1, 1>, <2, 2>, <1, 2>} such that

$$\mathcal{V}('P', 1) = U \qquad \mathcal{V}('P', 2) = C$$

(Clearly $\mathcal{R}$ is reflexive and transitive and $\mathcal{V}$ meets the conditions on confirmation value assignments imposed by the definition of a valuation.) Since $\mathcal{V}('P', 2) = C$ and $1\mathcal{R}2$, there is some world u (namely, 2) such that $1\mathcal{R}u$ and $\mathcal{V}('P', u) = C$. Thus by valuation rule 4, $\mathcal{V}('\sim P', 1) \neq C$. So, since $\mathcal{V}('P', 1) \neq C$, by rule 6 $\mathcal{V}('P \vee \sim P', 1) \neq C$. Hence 'P ∨ ~P' is not intuitionistically valid.   QED

The model here represents an evidential state (world 1) in which 'P' is neither confirmed nor refuted, but relative to which it is epistemically possible that 'P' be confirmed (world 2).

This same evidential state provides a counterexample to the inference from '~~P' to 'P'. In this case, because world 2 holds out the possibility that 'P' may yet be confirmed, it is refuted that 'P' is refuted—that is, '~~P' is confirmed—even though 'P' is unconfirmed. Here is the proof:

METATHEOREM: The sequent '~~P ⊢ P' is intuitionistically invalid.

PROOF: Consider the valuation $\mathcal{V}$ whose set $\mathcal{W}_{\mathcal{V}}$ of worlds is {1, 2} and whose relation $\mathcal{R}$ is {<1, 1>, <2, 2>, <1, 2>} such that

$$\mathcal{V}('P', 1) = U \qquad \mathcal{V}('P', 2) = C$$

(As above, $\mathcal{R}$ is reflexive and transitive and $\mathcal{V}$ meets the conditions on confirmation value assignments imposed by the definition of a valuation.)

Now, as before, since $\mathcal{V}('P', 2) = C$ and $1\mathcal{R}2$, there is some world u (namely, 2) such that $1\mathcal{R}u$ and $\mathcal{V}('P', u) = C$. Thus by valuation rule 4, $\mathcal{V}('\sim P', 1) \neq C$.

Moreover, since $\mathcal{V}('P', 2) = C$ and $2\mathcal{R}2$, there is some world u (namely, 2) such that $2\mathcal{R}u$ and $\mathcal{V}('P', u) = C$. Thus by valuation rule 4, $\mathcal{V}('\sim P', 2) \neq C$.

We have now seen that $\mathcal{V}('\sim P', 1) \neq C$ and $\mathcal{V}('\sim P', 2) \neq C$. But 1 and 2 are the only worlds u such that $1\mathcal{R}u$. Hence for all worlds u such that $1\mathcal{R}u$, $\mathcal{V}('\sim P', u) \neq C$. Thus again by rule 4, $\mathcal{V}('\sim\sim P', 1) = C$. But $\mathcal{V}('P', 1) \neq C$. Therefore '~~P ⊢ P' is intuitionistically invalid.   QED

The inference from 'P' to '~~P', however, remains valid, as in classical logic. The proof is as follows:

> **METATHEOREM:** The sequent 'P ⊢ ~~P' is intuitionistically valid.
>
> **PROOF:** Suppose for reductio that this is not the case; that is, there is some intuitionistic Kripkean model $\mathcal{V}$ with accessibility relation $\mathcal{R}$ and some world w of $\mathcal{V}$ such that $\mathcal{V}('P', w) = C$ but $\mathcal{V}('~~P', w) \neq C$. Since $\mathcal{V}('~~P', w) \neq C$, there is by valuation rule 4 some world u such that $w\mathcal{R}u$ and $\mathcal{V}('~P', u) = C$. And since $\mathcal{V}('~P', u) = C$, again by rule 4, for all worlds x such that $u\mathcal{R}x$, $\mathcal{V}('P', x) \neq C$. Now since $\mathcal{V}$ is an intuitionistic Kripkean model, $\mathcal{R}$ is reflexive, and so $u\mathcal{R}u$. Thus in particular $\mathcal{V}('P', u) \neq C$. However, again since $\mathcal{V}$ is an intuitionistic Kripkean model and $\mathcal{V}('P', w) = C$, it follows that $\mathcal{V}('P', y) = C$ for all worlds y such that $w\mathcal{R}y$. Hence in particular, since $w\mathcal{R}u$, $\mathcal{V}('P', u) = C$, which contradicts our previous conclusion.
> Therefore the sequent 'P ⊢ ~~P' is intuitionistically valid.   QED

Many classically valid formulas remain valid in intuitionistic logic. 'P → P' is an example:

> **METATHEOREM:** The formula 'P → P' is intuitionistically valid.
>
> **PROOF:** Suppose for reductio that this is not the case; that is, there is some intuitionistic Kripkean model $\mathcal{V}$ with accessibility relation $\mathcal{R}$ and some world w of $\mathcal{V}$ such that $\mathcal{V}('P → P', w) \neq C$. Then by valuation rule 7, for some world u such that $w\mathcal{R}u$, both $\mathcal{V}('P', u) = C$ and $\mathcal{V}('P', u) \neq C$. But this is absurd.
> Therefore 'P → P' is intuitionistically valid.   QED

Though intuitionism dispenses with the law of excluded middle, it retains the classical principle that anything follows from a contradiction:

> **METATHEOREM:** The sequent 'P, ~P ⊢ Q' is intuitionistically valid.
>
> **PROOF:** Suppose for reductio that this is not the case; that is, there is some intuitionistic Kripkean model $\mathcal{V}$ with accessibility relation $\mathcal{R}$ and some world w of $\mathcal{V}$ such that $\mathcal{V}('P', w) = C$ and $\mathcal{V}('~P', w) = C$, but $\mathcal{V}('Q', w) \neq C$. Since $\mathcal{V}('~P', w) = C$, by valuation rule 4, for all worlds u such that $w\mathcal{R}u$, $\mathcal{V}('P', u) \neq C$. But since $\mathcal{V}$ is an intuitionistic Kripkean model, $\mathcal{R}$ is reflexive

so that $w\mathcal{R}w$. Hence in particular, $\mathcal{V}('P', w) \neq C$, which contradicts our supposition.

Accordingly, 'P, ~P ⊢ Q' is intuitionistically valid.   QED

In intuitionistic natural deduction, the rule EFQ that allows us to infer anything from a formula together with its negation replaces the now-invalid classical negation elimination rule: from ~~Φ, infer Φ. The other natural deduction rules are unchanged.

Also in intuitionism, we lose the interdefinability of most operators. The operators '~', '&', '∨', and '→' must all be taken as primitive, though $\Phi \leftrightarrow \Psi$ is definable as $(\Phi \rightarrow \Psi) \& (\Psi \rightarrow \Phi)$. This means, for example, that it is not the case that $\Phi \rightarrow \Psi$ is confirmed iff ~$\Phi \vee \Psi$ is. For $\Phi \rightarrow \Psi$ asserts that any evidential state in which Φ is confirmed is also one in which Ψ is confirmed (confirmation of Φ is automatically confirmation of Ψ). But ~$\Phi \vee \Psi$ asserts that we have either confirmation of ~Φ or confirmation of Ψ. We may confirm $\Phi \rightarrow \Psi$ without confirming ~$\Phi \vee \Psi$.

I said earlier in this section that Kripke's semantics for intuitionistic propositional logic is illuminatingly connected to his semantics for the modal logic S4—the classical modal logic determined by the stipulation that the accessibility relation $\mathcal{R}$ be reflexive and symmetric. The connection can be seen by observing that in intuitionistic semantics confirmation is a kind of necessity and refutation a kind of impossibility. That is, to assert that Φ is confirmed is to assert that Φ is confirmed in all accessible worlds (under the presumption that accessibility is reflexive and transitive), and to assert that Φ is refuted is to assert that Φ is not confirmed in any accessible world.

Indeed, any formula Φ of intuitionistic logic can be translated into a formula Ψ of modal logic such that Φ is valid in intuitionistic logic iff Ψ is valid in S4 and Φ follows intuitionistically from a set of premises iff Ψ follows in S4 from the translations of those premises. Using $\tau(\Phi)$ to stand for the translation of intuitionistic formula Φ into the language of S4, the following rules stipulate recursively how the translation may be carried out. For any formulas Φ and Ψ:

1. If Φ is atomic, then $\tau(\Phi) = \Box\Phi$
2. $\tau(\sim\Phi) = \Box\sim\tau(\Phi)$
3. $\tau(\Phi \& \Psi) = \tau(\Phi) \& \tau(\Psi)$
4. $\tau(\Phi \vee \Psi) = \tau(\Phi) \vee \tau(\Psi)$
5. $\tau(\Phi \rightarrow \Psi) = \Box(\tau(\Phi) \rightarrow \tau(\Psi))$
6. $\tau(\Phi \leftrightarrow \Psi) = \Box(\tau(\Phi) \leftrightarrow \tau(\Psi))$
7. $\tau(\forall\beta\Phi) = \Box\forall\beta\tau(\Phi)$
8. $\tau(\exists\beta\Phi) = \exists\beta\tau(\Phi)$

Comparing the valuation rules and the definition of an intuitionistic valuation to the corresponding rules and definitions of Kripkean semantics for classical modal logic makes the rationale for these rules clear. The operators '&', '∨', and '∃' work essentially the same way in intuitionistic logic as in S4, so the translations of conjunctions and disjunctions are straightforward. But atomic formulas, negations, conditionals, biconditionals, and universally quantified formulas are all, if confirmed, confirmed necessarily, so their translations always introduce an occurrence of the necessity operator. Take, for example, the inference 'P ⊢ ~~P', which is intuitionistically valid. To translate this, we apply the following steps:

$$
\begin{array}{lll}
\daleth(P) \vdash \daleth(\sim\sim P) & = & \Box P \vdash \daleth(\sim\sim P) & \text{By rule 1} \\
& = & \Box P \vdash \Box\sim\daleth(\sim P) & \text{By rule 2} \\
& = & \Box P \vdash \Box\sim\Box\sim\daleth(P) & \text{By rule 2} \\
& = & \Box P \vdash \Box\sim\Box\sim\Box P & \text{By rule 1}
\end{array}
$$

The translated sequent at the end of this list is valid in S4.

Or consider, for example, the formula 'P ∨ ~P', which is not intuitionistically valid. Its translation runs as follows:

$$
\begin{array}{lll}
\daleth(P \vee \sim P) & = & \daleth(P) \vee \daleth(\sim P) & \text{By rule 4} \\
& = & \Box P \vee \daleth(\sim P) & \text{By rule 1} \\
& = & \Box P \vee \Box\sim\daleth(P) & \text{By rule 2} \\
& = & \Box P \vee \Box\sim\Box P & \text{By rule 1}
\end{array}
$$

This last formula is not valid in S4. We can via such translations reduce any problem in intuitionistic logic to an equivalent problem in S4.

In summary, the decision to take confirmation rather than truth as the fundamental semantic concept yields a logic with some, but not all, of the features of classical logic.

Exercise 16.2

Prove that each of the following sequents is valid on Kripkean intuitionistic semantics:

1. P & Q ⊢ P
2. P, Q ⊢ P & Q
3. P, P → Q ⊢ Q
4. P ⊢ P ∨ Q
5. ~P, P ∨ Q ⊢ Q
6. P → Q, Q → R ⊢ P → R

Prove that the following are not intuitionistically valid:

7. P → Q ⊢ ~P ∨ Q
8. ~P → ~Q ⊢ Q → P

Prove that the following are intuitionistically inconsistent:

9. P & ~P
10. ~(P → P)

16.3 RELEVANCE LOGICS

Relevance logic (also called **relevant logic**) is a form of logic that does not count an inference valid unless its premises are relevant to its conclusion. All the logics we have considered until now validate irrelevant inferences. In particular, the sequent 'P, ~P ⊢ Q' is valid in every system we have surveyed. And though most of the nonclassical logics we have considered lack some of the valid formulas of classical logic, still the formulas which are valid in those systems validly follow from any set of premises, whether relevant or not.

In relevance logic, by contrast, an argument is valid only if there is some relevant connection between its premises and its conclusion. But the nature of this connection is disputed. Relevantists generally agree, however, on three things:

1. Inconsistent premises do not imply every proposition, but only propositions relevantly related to them.
2. A valid formula does not validly follow from every set of premises, but only from premises relevant to it.
3. There is a kind of conditional that is true only if its antecedent and consequent are relevantly connected.

How might one justify these theses?

Advocates of classical logic often argue that there is no problem in allowing inconsistent premises to imply any conclusion; since inconsisent premises cannot all be true, arguments which employ them are always unsound and hence always negligible. But is it safe for all applications of logic to assume that inconsistencies are never the case? Consider, for example, the domain of statutory law.[7] Statutes are enacted by legislatures. Once in effect, they create certain legal "realities," which shape our social and political institutions. But legislatures can make mistakes and even, on occasion, contradict themselves. A legislature may, for example, pass one law which implies that under certain conditions a corporation is liable and a second law which implies that under those same conditions that corporation is not liable, the contradiction remaining for some time unnoticed. Since corporate liability is constituted wholly by the law (there is no independent fact of the matter), the result may be a situation in which a corporation both is and is not liable. In practice, of course, there are procedures for resolving such contradictions. But they can arise and they persist until resolved. Similar contradictions may arise in other humanly constructed realms, such as games and fiction—and perhaps even in semantics itself, in the case of such paradoxical sentences as 'This sentence is not true' (see Section 15.2).

To grant, on the basis of such examples, that inconsistencies are sometimes the case while retaining classical logic is disastrous. If the law contains a true contradiction, for example, then using classical logic we may *soundly* infer that

---

[7] A relevance logic for statutory law is outlined in John Nolt, Grayfred B. Gray, Donald R. Ploch, and Bruce J. MacLennan, "A Logic for Statutory Law," *Jurimetrics Journal* 35 (Winter 1995): 121–51.

everyone is guilty of embezzlement, that bologna is blue, and infinitely many other absurdities. It would be useful, then, to have for the domain of law and for other domains that may admit contradictions a logic which allows only relevant conclusions to be validly derived from these contradictions. Unlike most other forms of logic, this new logic would isolate the consequences of contradictions, preventing them from "infecting" irrelevant areas of knowledge. Logics according to which contradictions do not imply all propositions are said to be **paraconsistent**. Relevance logics are paraconsistent logics.

But we need not hold that there actually are true contradictions to have reservations about such reasoning. Contradictions are frequently encountered in hypothetical reasoning, and even there it seems odd, if not worse, to reach a contradiction and then infer something wholly irrelevant.

It seems similarly perverse to "prove" a valid formula from an irrelevant premise. Suppose, for example, that someone challenges us to prove that nothing is both alive and not alive and that we argue as follows:

> Abe Lincoln was truthful.
> ∴   Nothing is both alive and not alive.

(In symbols this might be 'Ta ⊢ ~∃x(Ax & ~Ax)'.) Now the premise is true and the reasoning is classically valid, so the argument is sound. But to respond this way to a person who was genuinely puzzled about whether something might be both alive and not alive would be flippant, to say the least. It is perfectly evident that the premise of this argument does not prove, support, or provide any evidence for its conclusion. In that sense, the argument is not valid. We seem, then, to have an intuitive, nonclassical notion of validity. Relevantists hope to formalize that notion.

Finally, relevantists hold that there is a "natural" conditional that is true only if its antecedent and consequent are relevantly connected. Using '⇒' to express this conditional, the proposition 'Snow is white ⇒ Rome is in Italy', for example, is false because its antecedent and consequent, though both true, are irrelevant to one another. None of the conditionals we have considered so far, not even Lewis conditionals, require relevance for their truth so that the relevantist's understanding of 'if' is distinctive. In particular, where 'A' and 'B' express unrelated propositions, relevantists object to inferences such as:

> A, B ⊢ A □→ B

which is valid for the Lewis conditional,

> B ⊢ A → B
> ~A ⊢ A → B

which are valid for the material and intuitionistic conditionals, and

> □B ⊢ A → B
> ~◇A ⊢ A → B

which are valid for all the conditionals we have so far studied, except for the Lewis conditional and the conditional of Bochvar's multivalued logic. For the conditionals of relevance logic, none of these sequents are valid.

A great variety of semantics have been offered for relevance logics. Some of these incorporate a non-truth-functional form of relevant conjunction, called **fusion,** which seems to have no straightforward natural language equivalent. Indeed, in some of the most interesting forms of relevance logic, fusion is employed in the metalanguage to define validity.[8] Treatment of the semantics of fusion is, however, beyond the scope of this book.

Here I will present a simple truth-functional relevance semantics for propositional logic without conditionals. This semantics can be extended to conditionals, but not very happily.[9] No one has yet produced a completely satisfying semantics for relevance logic as a whole.

The essence of this semantics is a radical rejection of bivalence. Classically a sequent is valid iff it lacks a counterexample. This leads us to accept such sequents as 'P, ~P ⊢ Q' and 'P ⊢ Q → Q' as valid. Relevance logicians find this definition too permissive. There are two ways to tighten it up. The first is to incorporate some additional criterion of relevance into the definition of validity. The second is to retain that definition but liberalize our notion of a counterexample to allow novel counterexamples capable of invalidating sequents like those just mentioned. The semantics we shall examine here uses the second method.

A counterexample is a valuation which makes the premises, but not the conclusion, of a sequent true. But what sort of valuation could make the premises of 'P, ~P ⊢ Q' both true or the conclusion of 'P ⊢ Q → Q' untrue?

Actually, we have already seen valuations on which 'Q → Q' is not true. It is not true, for example, on the three-valued semantics of either Kleene or Bochvar when 'Q' has the value I. Thus, in general, a three-valued logic can provide counterexamples to sequents whose conclusions are classical tautologies. But a counterexample to 'P, ~P ⊢ Q' would have to make both 'P' and '~P' true. What sort of valuation could do *that?*

Both premises could, perhaps, be true if 'P' were both true and false. For in that case '~P' would also, presumably, be both true and false. Hence both premises would be true, and both would also be false. Semantics which permit the assignment of both values to a proposition are called **dialethic** (literally, "two-truth"). To see how such a semantics might have some practical application in the field of law, consider this instance of 'P, ~P ⊢ Q':

> Corporation X is liable.
> Corporation X is not liable.
> ∴   Bologna is blue.

To this argument we can imagine the following counterexample. Suppose that the legislature has enacted contradictory laws which make it both true and false that Corporation X is liable. Then since it is true that Corporation X is liable, the first

---

[8] See Stephen Read, *Relevant Logic* (Oxford: Basil Blackwell, 1988).

[9] The best effort I know of is that of Graham Priest and Richard Sylvan, in "Simplified Semantics for Basic Relevant Logics," *Journal of Philosophical Logic* 21 (1992): 217–32. The extension of the semantics presented here to conditionals is presented on pp. 228–30 of that article.

premise is true. And since it is false that Corporation X is liable, the second premise is true. But the conclusion, let us agree, is not true. Of course the premises are both false as well. But if we define a counterexample as a situation in which the premises are true and the conclusion is not true, this situation fits that definition.

Originally, however, in Chapter 1, we characterized an informal counterexample as a *coherently conceivable* situation in which the premises are true and the conclusion untrue. It is not so clear that the situation I have described is coherently conceivable. In one sense it is. Contradictory legislation can be enacted. But in another sense it is not *coherently* conceivable for a proposition to be both true and false. Dialetheicists in effect propose a liberalization of our notion of coherence so that we can coherently conceive such contradictions in certain situations. Let's humor them.

We might fear that their proposal would generate counterexamples everywhere, leading us to a wholesale denial of validity. In fact, however, the new counterexamples it produces (classical counterexamples still stand) apply only to sequents that we would generally recognize as irrelevant. Dialetheicism does not invalidate, for example, the sequent 'P & Q ⊢ P' (simplification). Any truth-value assignment (whether dialethic or not) that makes the premise true must also make the conclusion true; there is no counterexample. Of course if 'P' is both true and false and 'Q' is true, then the premise is both true and false and so is the conclusion. Hence the premise is true and the conclusion false. But this is still not a counterexample, for we have defined a (formal) counterexample as a valuation on which the premises are all true and the conclusion is *not* true. The conclusion of this inference might be false when the premise is true—and false as well—but in any case this conclusion cannot fail to be true when the premise is true. Thus simplification remains valid on a dialethic semantics.

For the same reason 'P & ~P ⊢ P' is valid, though 'P & ~P ⊢ Q' is not. Contradictions thus have consequences—but only relevant consequences.

Before going on, we ought to be more explicit about the semantics we are using. Recall that we are considering only the nonconditional fragment of propositional logic. Since this logic is purely propositional, a valuation can be merely an assignment of truth values to sentence letters. But since propositions may receive either value, neither, or both, it is convenient to think of what is assigned to a sentence letter as a *set* of truth values. Any of these four sets may be assigned:

   {T}   {F}   {T, F}   { }

More precisely:

DEFINITION A **dialethic valuation** or **dialethic model** for a formula or set of formulas of propositional logic is an assignment of one, but not more than one, of the sets {T}, {F}, {T, F} or { } to each sentence letter in that formula or set of formulas.

As usual, truth values are assigned to complex formulas by valuation rules. These rules mimic the classical rules as closely as possible. Where some components of a complex formula Φ lack truth value but values of the other parts suffice to determine the value (or values) of Φ by classical truth tables, then that truth value is what is assigned to Φ. (This is in effect the procedure of Kleene's multivalued semantics, but with truth value-gaps instead of a third truth value.) Where one or more components of a formula have both values, then the value(s) of that formula are calculated classically for both.

For example, suppose that $\mathcal{V}('P') = \{T, F\}$ and $\mathcal{V}('Q') = F$. What is $\mathcal{V}('P \& Q')$? Since 'Q' is false (and not true), the classical truth table makes 'P & Q' false both in the case in which 'P' is true and in the case in which 'P' is false. Hence, regardless of whether we combine the falsity of 'Q' with the truth of 'P' or with the falsity of 'P', we get the same result: 'P & Q' is false. Therefore $\mathcal{V}('P \& Q') = \{F\}$.

If, however $\mathcal{V}('P') = \{T, F\}$ and $\mathcal{V}('Q') = T$, then $\mathcal{V}('P \& Q') = \{T, F\}$. For in combining the truth of 'Q' with the truth of 'P' we see that 'P & Q' is true, and in combining the truth of 'Q' with the falsity of 'P' we see that 'P & Q' is false.

The following valuation rules express these principles in full generality:

1. $T \varepsilon \mathcal{V}(\sim\Phi)$ iff $F \varepsilon \mathcal{V}(\Phi)$.
   $F \varepsilon \mathcal{V}(\sim\Phi)$ iff $T \varepsilon \mathcal{V}(\Phi)$.
2. $T \varepsilon \mathcal{V}(\Phi \& \Psi)$ iff $T \varepsilon \mathcal{V}(\Phi)$ and $T \varepsilon \mathcal{V}(\Psi)$.
   $F \varepsilon \mathcal{V}(\Phi \& \Psi)$ iff $F \varepsilon \mathcal{V}(\Phi)$ or $F \varepsilon \mathcal{V}(\Psi)$, or both.
3. $T \varepsilon \mathcal{V}(\Phi \vee \Psi)$ iff $T \varepsilon \mathcal{V}(\Phi)$ or $T \varepsilon \mathcal{V}(\Psi)$, or both.
   $F \varepsilon \mathcal{V}(\Phi \vee \Psi)$ iff $F \varepsilon \mathcal{V}(\Phi)$ and $F \varepsilon \mathcal{V}(\Psi)$.

These rules may also be represented, though less compactly, as four-valued truth tables:

Truth Table for Negation

Φ	~Φ
{T}	{F}
{F}	{T}
{T, F}	{T, F}
{ }	{ }

Truth Table for Conjunction

Φ	Ψ	Φ & Ψ
{T}	{T}	{T}
{T}	{F}	{F}
{T}	{T, F}	{T, F}
{T}	{ }	{ }
{F}	{T}	{F}
{F}	{F}	{F}
{F}	{T, F}	{F}
{F}	{ }	{F}
{T, F}	{T}	{T, F}
{T, F}	{F}	{F}
{T, F}	{T, F}	{T, F} *(continued)*

{T, F}	{ }	{F}
{ }	{T}	{ }
{ }	{F}	{F}
{ }	{T, F}	{F}
{ }	{ }	{ }

Truth Table for Disjunction

Φ	Ψ	Φ ∨ Ψ
{T}	{T}	{T}
{T}	{F}	{T}
{T}	{T, F}	{T}
{T}	{ }	{T}
{F}	{T}	{T}
{F}	{F}	{F}
{F}	{T, F}	{T, F}
{F}	{ }	{ }
{T, F}	{T}	{T}
{T, F}	{F}	{T, F}
{T, F}	{T, F}	{T, F}
{T, F}	{ }	{T}
{ }	{T}	{T}
{ }	{F}	{ }
{ }	{T, F}	{T}
{ }	{ }	{ }

Notice that where Φ and Ψ have exactly one truth value each, these are just the classical truth tables, and that in other cases these tables retain as much as possible of the classical valuation rules.

Just as bivalent truth tables can be used to establish the validity or invalidity of sequents in classical propositional logic, so these tables can be used to demonstrate the validity or invalidity of sequents in the nonconditional fragment of propositional relevance logic. We simply construct the table according to the valuation rules or truth tables for the operators and then scan it, looking for a line on which the premises are all true (whether or not they are also false) and the conclusion is not true (whether or not it is false). The following table, for example, demonstrates the validity of one version of De Morgan's laws (in fact, all versions of De Morgan's laws are valid on this semantics):

P	Q	P	∨	Q	⊢	~	(~P	&	~Q)
{T}	{T}		{T}			{T}	{F}	{F}	{F}
{T}	{F}		{T}			{T}	{F}	{F}	{T}
{T}	{T, F}		{T}			{T}	{F}	{F}	{T, F}
{T}	{ }		{T}			{T}	{F}	{F}	{ }
{F}	{T}		{T}			{T}	{T}	{F}	{F}
{F}	{F}		{F}			{F}	{T}	{T}	{T}
{F}	{T, F}		{T, F}			{T, F}	{T}	{T, F}	{T, F}
{F}	{ }		{ }			{ }	{T}	{ }	{ }

{T, F}	{T}	{T}	{T}	{T, F}	{F}	{F}
{T, F}	{F}	{T, F}	{T, F}	{T, F}	{T, F}	{T}
{T, F}	{T, F}	{T, F}	{T, F}	{T, F}	{T, F}	{T, F}
{T, F}	{ }	{T}	{T}	{T, F}	{F}	{ }
{ }	{T}	{T}	{T}	{ }	{F}	{F}
{ }	{F}	{ }	{ }	{ }	{ }	{T}
{ }	{T, F}	{T}	{T}	{ }	{F}	{T, F}
{ }	{ }	{ }	{ }	{ }	{ }	{ }

There is no horizontal line on which the premise is true and the conclusion untrue, and hence no counterexample, though there are lines on which both the premise and the conclusion have the value {T, F}. In fact, the table shows that 'P ∨ Q' and '~(~P & ~Q)' are logically equivalent.

Somewhat surprisingly, however, disjunctive syllogism fails. The following table shows that the sequent 'P ∨ Q, ~P ⊢ Q' is invalid for dialethic relevance logic:

P	Q	P	∨	Q,	~P	⊢	Q
{T}	{T}		{T}		{F}		{T}
{T}	{F}		{T}		{F}		{F}
{T}	{T, F}		{T}		{F}		{T, F}
{T}	{ }		{T}		{F}		{ }
{F}	{T}		{T}		{T}		{T}
{F}	{F}		{F}		{T}		{F}
{F}	{T, F}		{T, F}		{T}		{T, F}
{F}	{ }		{ }		{T}		{ }
{T, F}	{T}		{T}		{T, F}		{T}
{T, F}	{F}		{T, F}		{T, F}		{F}
{T, F}	{T, F}		{T, F}		{T, F}		{T, F}
{T, F}	{ }		{T}		{T, F}		{ }
{ }	{T}		{T}		{ }		{T}
{ }	{F}		{ }		{ }		{F}
{ }	{T, F}		{T}		{ }		{T, F}
{ }	{ }		{ }		{ }		{ }

On the tenth line of the table, the one on which 'P' has the value {T, F} and 'Q' the value F, we see that the premises are both true (and false) but the conclusion is untrue. This valuation is a counterexample. (So also is the valuation displayed on the twelfth line).

Informally, it may help to conceive the counterexample once again in legal terms. Suppose that 'P' stands for 'Corporation X is liable', which has turned out to be both true and false in the way described above, and suppose that 'Q' stands for 'The Constitution is invalid'. Then since Corporation X is liable, the disjunction 'Either Corporation X is liable or the Constitution is invalid' is also true. But since 'Corporation X is liable' is also false, the second premise, 'Corporation X is not liable', is true. Still this does not mean that the Constitution is invalid!

The invalidity of disjunctive syllogism (DS) may seem a high price for relevance, but in fact if we allow DS and also allow ∨I, the sequent 'P, ~P ⊢ Q' becomes provable at once:

1. P   A
2. ~P   A
3. P ∨ Q   1 ∨I
4. Q   2, 3 DS

Since any relevance logic must reject this sequent, relevance logicians have generally regarded DS as invalid.

Some, however, have rejected ∨I (or both DS and ∨I) instead. The rejection of ∨I is more in keeping with the criterion of relevance suggested in Section 1.3—that an inference is relevant only if any idea that occurs in the conclusion also occurs in at least one of the premises—for ∨I apparently violates this criterion by introducing a disjunct that may have nothing to do with any of the previously asserted premises.

To obtain a dialethic relevance logic that satisfies this criterion, we could adopt the Bochvar idea that the indeterminacy of the part infects the whole (see Section 15.2)—using the value { }, of course, instead of the value I. Thus, for example, while on the dialethic semantics given above a disjunction whose disjuncts have the values { } and T is true, on this Bochvar-inspired semantics, such a disjunction has the value { }. This makes ∨I invalid and, more generally, guarantees the invalidity of any sequent whose conclusion contains an "idea" (sentence letter) not occurring in its premises, thereby satisfying the criterion of Section 1.3. However, the resulting logic, which lacks both ∨I and DS, is extremely weak.

This is the problem with relevance logics generally: Those that satisfy some of our intuitions about relevance tend to be objectionable in other ways. Thus, though many relevance logics have been invented, none has emerged as clearly right or best.

Before leaving the topic of relevance logic, we ought to say a word about relevant conditionals. Relevance logic was initially developed to formalize the idea of **entailment,** or relevant implication. An entailment conditional, like a strict conditional in classical modal logic, expresses a kind of necessary connection between antecedent and consequent; but for the entailment conditional that connection must also be relevant. Thus, whereas a strict conditional is automatically true whenever its antecedent is impossible or its consequent necessary, an entailment conditional might be false under these conditions if the relevant connection was lacking.

Because entailment is a kind of necessary connection, many attempts to formulate a semantics for entailment have employed a modified Kripkean possible worlds approach. The most prominent of these replace the Kripkean accessibility relation $\mathcal{R}$ with one or two three-place relations on worlds, which are used to define the truth conditions for the entailment conditional. There are several ways of doing this, however, and all have their problems.[10]

---

[10] Read, *Relevant Logic,* and Priest and Sylvan, "Simplified Semantics for Basic Relevant Logics," discuss various forms of Kripkean semantics for relevance logics with entailment. See notes 8 and 9, respectively.

Exercise 16.3.1

Use truth tables to determine whether or not the following sequents are valid on the dialethic semantics for relevance logic given above:

1. $P \vdash P$
2. $P \vdash P \vee \sim P$
3. $P \vdash Q \vee \sim Q$
4. $P \vdash P \vee Q$
5. $P, Q \vdash P$

Exercise 16.3.2

Create dialethic truth tables for the operators '$\sim$', '$\&$', and '$\vee$' to implement Bochvar's idea (mentioned above) that the indeterminacy of the part infects the whole (i.e., that if a component of a formula has the value { }, so does the entire formula). Then test the five sequents of Exercise 16.3.1 with these new truth tables.

16.4 A NONMONOTONIC LOGIC: PROLOG

We often reason from assumptions that we accept provisionally but do not really know to be true. As we gain information, we may find that these assumptions were wrong. Then conclusions that we had taken to be true may turn out to be false. Of course, if we always reasoned deductively from true premises, this could never happen. But if our assumptions are unreliable it can happen despite our reasoning deductively.

Classical deductive reasoning does not make explicit allowance for mistaken assumptions. If we begin with a body of information (premises) and then add further information (new premises) that contradict what we originally assumed, we are still able to infer all the conclusions that followed from the original body of information. For example, if we begin with these assumptions:

1. Offer is valid if not prohibited.
2. The offer is not prohibited.

we may validly infer:

C. The offer is valid.

But suppose assumption 2 was just a presumption which we later find out to be false. Then we have a new piece of information, which contradicts it:

3. The offer is prohibited.

But if we simply add 3 to 1 and 2, the conclusion C, though no longer justified, is still provable. Obviously, then, we need not only to add premise 3 to our stock of information *but also to delete premise 2 and conclusion C*. But within classical logic there exists no formal mechanism for doing this.

There is, of course, the mechanism of reductio ad absurdum. But reductio rejects suppositions that were made in order to be refuted by the derivation of a contradiction. The situation here is different. We were not making the supposition that the offer is not prohibited in order to refute it. Rather, we believed it and reasoned with it nonhypothetically—until we found out that it, specifically, was false. Since this assumption is not singled out as hypothetical by our formalism, when we deduce a contradiction the formalism does not tell us which assumption to reject. Should we reject 2 or 3—or even 1? Classical logic is indifferent to all of these choices. It allows us to do any of these things—or to continue drawing random conclusions from the contradictory amalgam of premises 1, 2, and 3.

What ought to be rejected, however, is 2; and the reason it ought to be rejected is that it was merely a kind of "default" assumption, which the new information specifically refuted. If we want a formalism that makes the right choice here, then we need to build into it a distinction between **categorical assumptions** (assumptions proper, those explicitly asserted to be true) and **presumptions** (those not explicitly asserted but taken to be true merely by default and subject to refutation by new information). Presumptions remain in effect unless and until they are specifically refuted, at which time they are rejected, along with whatever conclusions depend on them.

Reasoning that incorporates a mechanism enabling new premises to refute old presumptions or their consequences is called **nonmonotonic.** Classical reasoning is **monotonic** (one-directional) in the sense that by adding new premises to a premise set we can only add to the conclusions validly derivable from them. In nonmonotonic reasoning, by contrast, new premises may, by refuting presumptions, subtract from as well as add to the set of validly derivable conclusions.

Nonmonotonic logics may have many applications. Visual information processing, for example, seems to involve something analogous to nonmonotonic inference. Given incomplete information (when looking, say, at a crowd from a distance), the visual system seems to utilize certain "default" hypotheses. We tend, for example, to see in terms of familiar patterns; thus, "assuming" in the absence of contrary information that what is before me is familiar, I may see the face of a friend—only to have that face resolve itself on closer inspection into the unfamiliar visage of a stranger. The seeing of the friend is a kind of conclusion drawn on the basis of a presumption of familiarity. The new information provided by the closer look is akin to a set of new premises that refute that presumption and replace the initial conclusion with a new one: The face is that of a stranger. In view of these analogies, simulations of this visual processing on a computer might naturally treat it as a form of nonmonotonic inference.

There are many systems of nonmonotonic logic, but we shall consider just one: PROLOG (PROgramming in LOGic), a computer programming language designed for artificial intelligence applications.[11] PROLOG is designed to facilitate the programming of logical inferences on a computer. Given a set of premises

---

[11] Unlike **machine languages,** such as the language of the ABACUS programs described in Sections 10.1–10.3, **programming languages** like PROLOG do not give specific directions as to what changes to make in which registers or storage units

(consisting of the PROLOG program) together with a statement in the form of a question called the **query,** the PROLOG system returns an answer to the query. It does this by using a built-in algorithm to determine whether the query statement follows from these premises. The logic by which it does so, however, is nonmonotonic and radically nonclassical.

To understand this logic, it is important to note that PROLOG was designed not primarily to model presumptive reasoning, but to maximize computational efficiency. In PROLOG, falsehood may be represented by the absence of a positive assertion. Thus the computer's memory is not occupied with negative statements and the program need not invoke special computational routines to handle them. This streamlines the program's operation. But because this streamlining was the main design goal, PROLOG is cumbersome and primitive as a device for representing presumptive reasoning. Still it is useful as an example, since among nonmonotonic systems that have real applications it is one of the simplest.

There are many variants of PROLOG, and each incorporates, in addition to its inferential capabilities, the ability to direct a number of other tasks (such as erasing the screen, or creating and writing to files) that are essential to the operation of computers but logically unimportant. We shall therefore consider only the logical core of PROLOG, as opposed to these nonlogical parts of the language.

Moreover, we shall consider only propositional PROLOG, not the full PROLOG language (which, like classical predicate logic, has variables that may be universally quantified).[12] This will enable us to focus on nonmonotonic reasoning while avoiding extraneous complications associated with this implicit universal quantification.

The atomic formulas, or **atoms,** of propositional PROLOG are not sentence letters, as in propositional logic, but concatenations of lowercase letters and (occasionally) numerals that usually represent natural language sentences. Spaces are indicated by underline marks. Thus the English sentence 'The offer is valid' could be represented in PROLOG as 'the_offer_is_valid'.

PROLOG has three logical operators: a generalized conditional operator ':-', which is usually read as "if"; a conjunction operator, written as a comma; and a negation operator, which is written simply as 'not', but which, unlike '~', comes with a pair of brackets. Conditionals are written consequent first, and their antecedents are often written on a new line and indented. Moreover, if the antecedent is conjunctive, it is customary to write each conjunct on a new line. Thus, for example, the statement 'Offer is valid if not prohibited and not taxed' might be written as follows:

---

in a particular kind of machine. Because they ignore such specifics, they may be used on computers of many different designs. However, a programming language must first be translated into the machine language for the particular kind of machine on which it is to be used. This is accomplished by a machine-specific translating program called a **compiler.** The compiler in effect tells the computer how to carry out the details of the tasks the programmer specifies in the programming language.

12 In PROLOG, however, the universal quantifiers are implicit—that is, there are no symbols for them—and there are no existential quantifiers.

offer_is_valid :-
     not(offer_is_prohibited),
     not(offer_is_taxed).

Conjunctions need no brackets, since all ways of bracketing them are equivalent so that there is no possibility of ambiguity.

I said that ':-' is a generalized conditional operator, because although it functions as a conditional when provided with an antecedent and a consequent, the antecedent, or the consequent, or both may be omitted. To see what ':-' means in these cases and to understand how all the meanings are related, it is helpful to think of a conditional of the form Φ :- $\Psi_1, \ldots, \Psi_n$ as the classically equivalent disjunction $\Phi \lor \sim\Psi_1 \lor \ldots \lor \sim\Psi_n$.[13] The formula :- $\Psi_1, \ldots, \Psi_n$, then, is just this disjunction without the first disjunct—that is, $\sim\Psi_1 \lor \ldots \lor \sim\Psi_n$. Consequently, :- $\Psi_1, \ldots, \Psi_n$ asserts that at least one of $\Psi_1, \ldots, \Psi_n$ is false—that is, that not all of $\Psi_1, \ldots, \Psi_n$ are true. Similarly, Φ :- is just $\Phi \lor \sim\Psi_1 \lor \ldots \lor \sim\Psi_n$ with all disjuncts but the first missing. It is therefore simply a redundant way of asserting Φ. The clause ':-' is a "disjunction" with no disjuncts; it is called the **empty clause**. Since there are no disjuncts, there is no way for this "disjunction" to be true, and so the empty clause is a contradiction; it invariably receives the value F.

We define a **literal** as an atom or an expression of the form not(Φ), where Φ is an atom. A formula of PROLOG is known as a **clause**:

DEFINITION If $\Psi_1, \ldots, \Psi_n$ ($n \geq 0$) and Φ are literals, the following are **clauses**:

    :- $\Psi_1, \ldots, \Psi_n$
    Φ :- $\Psi_1, \ldots, \Psi_n$

Nothing else counts as a clause.

This definition is PROLOG's sole formation rule. The notation '$\Psi_1, \ldots, \Psi_n$' stands for a sequence of literals separated by commas, that is, an n-membered conjunction—or a single literal in the case $n = 1$. In the case $n = 0$, this definition makes the symbol ':-' and all formulas of the form Φ :- clauses. ':-', as we noted earlier, is the empty clause. Clauses of the form Φ :- may simply be written as Φ, since in that case ':-', as we also noted earlier, is redundant.

Where Φ :- $\Psi_1, \ldots, \Psi_n$ is a clause, Φ is called the **head** and $\Psi_1, \ldots, \Psi_n$ the **tail** of the clause. Some clauses have no head, some have no tail, some have neither a head nor a tail, and some have both.

Notice that conditionals may not occur as subformulas of conditionals or conjunctions and that only atoms may be negated. Even with the language thus

---

[13] Notice that I am using the notation of propositional logic here, not the notation of PROLOG, though I am omitting unnecessary brackets; PROLOG does not contain the operators '$\lor$' and '$\sim$'.

restricted, it is possible to translate any statement of propositional logic into a list of PROLOG clauses.

Two classes of clauses, in particular, must be singled out, because each serves a different function:

DEFINITION A **program clause** is a clause with a head.

DEFINITION A **goal clause** is a clause with a tail but without a head.

A list of program clauses is called a **program.**[14] The program functions as a set of assumptions that are categorically asserted to be true. A goal clause, by contrast, represents a conclusion to be proved or refuted.

PROLOG's logical semantics is bivalent. The valuation rules for PROLOG's operators are as follows (here $n > 0$):

1. $\mathcal{V}(\Phi :\text{-} \Psi_1, \ldots, \Psi_n) = \text{T}$ iff $\mathcal{V}(\Phi) = \text{T}$ or $\mathcal{V}(\Psi_1) \neq \text{T}$ or $\ldots$ or $\mathcal{V}(\Psi_n) \neq \text{T}$;
   $\mathcal{V}(\Phi :\text{-} \Psi_1, \ldots, \Psi_n) = \text{F}$ iff $\mathcal{V}(\Phi) \neq \text{T}$ and $\mathcal{V}(\Psi_1) = \text{T}$ and $\ldots$ and $\mathcal{V}(\Psi_n) = \text{T}$.
2. $\mathcal{V}(:\text{-} \Psi_1, \ldots, \Psi_n) = \text{T}$ iff $\mathcal{V}(\Psi_1) \neq \text{T}$ or $\ldots$ or $\mathcal{V}(\Psi_n) \neq \text{T}$;
   $\mathcal{V}(:\text{-} \Psi_1, \ldots, \Psi_n) = \text{F}$ iff $\mathcal{V}(\Psi_1) = \text{T}$ and $\ldots$ and $\mathcal{V}(\Psi_n) = \text{T}$.
3. $\mathcal{V}(\Phi:\text{-}) = \text{T}$ iff $\mathcal{V}(\Phi) = \text{T}$;
   $\mathcal{V}(\Phi:\text{-}) = \text{F}$ iff $\mathcal{V}(\Phi) \neq \text{T}$.
4. $\mathcal{V}(\text{'}:\text{-'}) = \text{F}$.
5. $\mathcal{V}(\text{not}(\Psi)) = \text{T}$ iff $\mathcal{V}(\Psi) \neq \text{T}$;
   $\mathcal{V}(\text{not}(\Psi)) = \text{F}$ iff $\mathcal{V}(\Psi) = \text{T}$.

To understand these rules, it is useful to think of conditionals as disjunctions in the way suggested earlier. Though they concern an unfamiliar operator, these rules are perfectly classical. PROLOG's departure from classicism lies, as we shall see, not in its valuation rules, but in its handling of presumptions.

Notice that in the case $n = 1$, ':- $\Psi_1, \ldots, \Psi_n$' and 'not(Ψ_1)' are semantically identical. They are not, however, syntactically identical. ':-' may prefix conjunctions, whereas 'not' prefixes only atoms; moreover, ':-Ψ' is always a goal clause and may not appear in programs. Though the operator 'not' is available in all practical implementations of PROLOG, PROLOG was first conceived as a theoretical language that did not include this operator. 'Not' was added to give PRO-

---

[14] In most actual implementations what we are calling the program is divided into the **program proper** and the **database.** The program proper consists mainly of conditionals (clauses with both heads and tails) that represent more or less enduring principles, whereas the database consists mainly of atoms (clauses with heads but no tails) that represent the facts or the state of a computation at the moment. Usually databases are more fluid, being updated frequently. The distinction between the program proper and the database is, however, pragmatic, not logical (from a logical point of view, both consist of program clauses functioning as categorical assumptions), and we will take no further notice of it here.

LOG more expressive power for practical applications, and this accounts for the partial redundancy.

PROLOG systems incorporate a proof procedure called a **resolution algorithm** to check arguments for validity. These arguments are all of a particular type. Their premises are a program, and their conclusion is a query to be tested against that program. (To keep things simple, we shall consider only atomic queries.) The resolution algorithm aims to construct a proof of the query from the program. The strategy is always reductio. Hence, where Φ is the query, the proof takes the program clauses as assumptions and hypothesizes the goal clause :- Φ, which is in effect the negation of Φ (see valuation rule 2 in the case $n = 1$). To these clauses, the algorithm now applies certain inference rules. If the application of these rules produces the empty clause (a contradiction), the procedure classifies the conclusion as true by reductio. If, however, there comes a point at which all possible moves with the rules have been made and the empty clause has not been deduced, then the procedure classifies the conclusion as false. It may also happen that the rules can be applied infinitely.[15] Propositional PROLOG has only three inference rules. The first of these is just a notational variant of the classical ~I. We shall call it **reductio ad absurdum:**

Reductio Ad Absurdum (RAA) Given a derivation of the empty clause ':-' from a hypothesis :- Φ, end the derivation and infer Φ :-.

As we just noted, :- Φ is in effect the negation of Φ, and Φ :- is just Φ written as a program clause (appending ':-' does not change Φ's meaning).

The second rule of inference, the **resolution rule,** is more novel:

Resolution Rule (R) Given clauses of the forms :- $\Phi, \Psi_1, \ldots, \Psi_n$ and Φ :- $\Theta_1, \ldots, \Theta_m$ ($n \geq 0$ and $m \geq 0$), infer :- $\Theta_1, \ldots, \Theta_m, \Psi_1, \ldots, \Psi_n$.

To see how the resolution rule works, we shall consider a small PROLOG program, which might be a fragment of a tree identification program. This program consists of four clauses:[16]

> tree_is_a_jack_pine :-

---

[15] The program consisting of the single clause 'p :- p', for example, fails to halt when given the query 'p'. PROLOG's resolution algorithm is therefore not a decision procedure, though certain closely related algorithms are. The availability of potentially infinite procedures makes PROLOG a more flexible programming tool than it would have been otherwise.

[16] In a real implementation, the first two of these clauses would belong to the program proper (see footnote 11), whereas the second two would probably belong to the database, representing, for example, our current observations.

>   tree_has_needles_4_cm_long,
>   needles_are_divergent

needles_are_divergent :-
>   needles_spread_away_from_one_another

needles_spread_away_from_one_another :-

tree_has_needles_4_cm_long :-

These constitute our assumptions.

Now suppose that we present this system with the query whether the tree in question is a jack pine. A query is a request to try to prove a conclusion; in this case the conclusion is 'tree_is_a_jack_pine'. Thus the problem is to prove the sequent whose premises are the four clauses listed above and whose conclusion is 'tree is_a_jack_pine'. In a running PROLOG program, if the proof is successful, the computer responds that the query is true. And because PROLOG presumes that what is not stated in or implied by its program is false, if the attempt to prove this sequent failed, the computer would report that 'tree_is_a_jack_pine' is false.

We shall first construct the proof purely syntactically, just to show how the resolution rule works. Then we shall consider what the proof means.
PROLOG's overall proof strategy, as noted above, is reductio; it attempts to derive a contradiction from what is in effect the negation of the conclusion. We begin as usual in a reductio strategy by listing the assumptions, which are simply the program clauses and hypothesizing the "negation" of the conclusion:

1. tree_is_a_jack_pine :-
>   tree_has_needles_4_cm_long,
>   needles_are_divergent   A
2. needles_are_divergent :-
>   needles_spread_away_from_one_another   A
3. needles_spread_away_from_one_another :-   A
4. tree_has_needles_4_cm_long :-   A
5. | :- tree_is_a_jack_pine   H

Now in a PROLOG proof, goal clauses direct strategy. So we look to line 5, the only goal clause, to find out how to proceed. The resolution rule says that given a goal clause of the form :- $\Phi, \Psi_1, \ldots, \Psi_n$ and a program clause of the form $\Phi :- \Theta_1, \ldots, \Theta_m$ ($n \geq 0$ and $m \geq 0$), we may infer the goal clause :- $\Theta_1, \ldots, \Theta_m, \Psi_1, \ldots, \Psi_n$. Now the clause at line 5 is of the form :- $\Phi, \Psi_1, \ldots, \Psi_n$, where Φ = 'tree_is_a_jack_pine' and $n = 0$. And the clause at line 1 is of the form $\Phi :- \Theta_1, \ldots, \Theta_m$, where Θ_1 = 'tree_has_needles_4_cm_long', Θ_2 = 'needles_are_divergent', and $m = 2$. Thus we may infer :- $\Theta_1, \ldots, \Theta_m, \Psi_1, \ldots, \Psi_n$, which in this case (since $m = 2$ and $n = 0$) is just :- Θ_1, Θ_2—that is,

6. | :- tree_has_needles_4_cm_long,
>   needles_are_divergent   1, 5 R

The remainder of the proof proceeds by similar applications of R. The complete proof is:

1. tree_is_a_jack_pine :-
        tree_has_needles_4_cm_long,
        needles_are_divergent   A
2. needles_are_divergent :-
        needles_spread_away_from_one_another   A
3. needles_spread_away_from_one_another :-   A
4. tree_has_needles_4_cm_long :-   A
5. | :- tree_is_a_jack_pine   H
6. | :- tree_has_needles_4_cm_long,
            needles_are_divergent   1, 5 R
7. | :- needles_are_divergent   4, 6 R
8. | :- needles_spread_away_from_one_another   2, 7 R
9. | :-   3, 8 R
10. tree_is_a_jack_pine :-   5–9 RAA

The empty clause (a contradiction) emerges at line 9, allowing us to reject the hypothesis at line 10. To grasp the syntactic features of this final step, notice that the goal clause at line 8 is of the form :- $\Phi, \Psi_1, \ldots, \Psi_n$, where Φ = 'needles_spread_away_from_one_another' and $n = 0$. Similarly, the program clause at line 3 is of the form Φ :- $\Theta_1, \ldots, \Theta_m$, where $m = 0$. Thus we may infer :- $\Theta_1, \ldots, \Theta_m, \Psi_1, \ldots, \Psi_n$, which in this case (since $m = 0$ and $n = 0$) is just ':-'.

So far, all of this is just meaningless symbol manipulation. But its meaning will come alive when we give it a semantics. Actually, PROLOG proofs may usefully be interpreted from either of two distinct semantical perspectives: the **logical semantics** defined in part by the valuation rules above, and a **procedural semantics,** according to which the clauses in the proof are not declarative statements, but rather instructions to the computer. We shall employ both perspectives, though our account of the procedural semantics will be very informal.

We begin with the logical semantics. Here it will be useful to translate the proof into the more familiar notation of propositional logic, using the following interpretation scheme:

J   tree_is_a_jack_pine
L   tree_has_needles_4_cm_long
D   needles_are_divergent
S   needles_spread_away_from_one_another

Rather than treating PROLOG conditionals directly as conditionals, we shall translate them into equivalent disjunctions (see valuation rule 1). The following proof in propositional logic corresponds step-for-step to the PROLOG proof above:

1. J ∨ (~L ∨ ~D)   A
2. D ∨ ~S   A
3. S   A
4. L   A
5. | ~J   H (for ~I)
6. | ~L ∨ ~D   1, 5

7.	~D	4, 6
8.	~S	2, 7
9.	S & ~S	3, 8 &I
10. J		5–9 ~I and ~E

This, understood classically, is what the PROLOG proof *means* from a logical point of view. Lines 6–8 are all obtained by variants of disjunctive syllogism (DS) that are obviously valid. (In fact, in this format the resolution rule can be seen as a kind of generalization of DS, though some of its instances are a good bit more complex than DS itself. R also serves the function of &I at line 9!) Thus from the logical perspective, this PROLOG proof is just an ordinary derivation in classical propositional logic, despite the unfamiliarity of the resolution rule.

Of course we can't quite be satisfied with this. The fact that the resolution rule produces a valid derivation in this case doesn't show that it is always valid. ('Valid' here has its usual classical meaning.) To have confidence in a rule, especially a rule of this complexity, we need to prove that it is valid. So we shall:

METATHEOREM: All instances of the resolution rule are valid.

PROOF: Suppose for reductio that some instance of the resolution rule is not valid; that is, for some literals $\Theta_1, \ldots, \Theta_m, \Psi_1, \ldots, \Psi_n$ ($n \geq 0$ and $m \geq 0$) and atom Φ there exists a valuation $\mathcal{V}$ such that $\mathcal{V}(:\text{-}\,\Phi, \Psi_1, \ldots, \Psi_n) = T$, $\mathcal{V}(\Phi :\text{-}\,\Theta_1, \ldots, \Theta_m) = T$, and $\mathcal{V}(:\text{-}\,\Theta_1, \ldots, \Theta_m, \Psi_1, \ldots, \Psi_n) \neq T$. Since $\mathcal{V}(:\text{-}\,\Theta_1, \ldots, \Theta_m, \Psi_1, \ldots, \Psi_n) \neq T$, by valuation rule 2, $\mathcal{V}(\Theta_1) = T$ and . . . and $\mathcal{V}(\Theta_m) = T$ and $\mathcal{V}(\Psi_1) = T$ and . . . and $\mathcal{V}(\Psi_n) = T$.

Now suppose, again for reductio, that $\mathcal{V}(\Phi) = T$. Then $\mathcal{V}(\Phi) = T$ and $\mathcal{V}(\Psi_1) = T$ and . . . and $\mathcal{V}(\Psi_n) = T$ so that by rule 2, $\mathcal{V}(:\text{-}\,\Phi, \Psi_1, \ldots, \Psi_n) \neq T$, which contradicts what we said above.

Hence $\mathcal{V}(\Phi) \neq T$. But then since $\mathcal{V}(\Theta_1) = T$ and . . . and $\mathcal{V}(\Theta_m) = T$, it follows by rule 1 that $\mathcal{V}(\Phi :\text{-}\,\Theta_1, \ldots, \Theta_m) \neq T$, again contradicting a conclusion above.

Therefore all instances of the resolution rule are valid.   QED

The resolution rule is therefore just as legitimate as modus ponens. Its complexity makes it a bit of a nuisance for humans to use, but it is an efficient rule for machine computation.

So much for the logical perspective. Now let's reconsider the same proof (the PROLOG original, not the translation) procedurally, as the running of a computer program. From this perspective it takes on a wholly different meaning. A goal clause, for example, instead of being read as a negative declarative statement, is an instruction to the computer to pursue the goal of proving the first literal to the right of the ':-' symbol. (The literals to the right of this first literal, if any, represent a succession of such proof goals, to be attempted later if this first goal succeeds.) That is why goal clauses are called *goal clauses*. Indeed, on the procedural semantics, we may read the symbol ':-' prefixing a goal clause as the English phrase 'try to prove'. Thus, for example, the clause on line 5 instructs the computer to try to prove that the tree is a jack pine. The computer responds by scanning down the existing proof for clauses whose head is 'tree_is_a_jack_pine'. Line 1 contains such a clause.

Now a program clause of the form $\Phi :\text{-} \Psi_1, \ldots, \Psi_n$, such as is found on line 1, is on the procedural interpretation the following conditional instruction: To prove Φ, prove $\Psi_1, \ldots, \Psi_n$. Line 1 therefore tells the computer that it could prove that the tree is a jack pine if it could show that the tree has needles 4 cm long and that these needles are divergent. Thus proving these two things becomes the computer's intermediate goal at line 6. Once again the computer scans down the existing proof and determines that at line 4 it is given that the tree has needles 4 cm long. The first of the two goals has thus been attained. Hence at line 7 the computer deletes this first goal, leaving only the second: to prove that the needles are divergent. It scans down the list yet again and finds at line 2 the conditional instruction: To prove that the needles are divergent, prove that they spread away from one another. So proving that they spread away from one another becomes the goal at line 8. Again the computer scans down the proof and notes that at line 3 it is given that the needles spread away from one another. Thus the last goal is attained, and there is no more work to be done. The empty clause at line 9 may be read as an instruction to stop and output the result that the query has been proved, that is, that the tree is a jack pine.

In all of this it may be seen that on the procedural interpretation the resolution rule is not merely an inference rule, but a device for prioritizing goals and deleting them once they are achieved.

These two semantic viewpoints, the logical and the procedural, provide equally correct and mutually illuminating understandings of PROLOG proofs. Neither uniquely represents what is *really* going on; they are just two different ways of understanding what is from a computational point of view a purely syntactic exercise in symbol manipulation. When dealing with PROLOG programs, it is useful to keep them both in mind.

PROLOG has a third inference rule, the **negation as failure rule,** which (since it is the source of PROLOG's nonmonotonicity) is more interesting than the other two. To see how it works, we shall return to the problem with which we began this section. We shall take as our sole premise the clause

offer_is_valid :-
    not(offer_is_prohibited).

Our query is 'offer_is_valid'. We are thus seeking a proof of the sequent 'offer_is_valid :- not(offer_is_prohibited) ⊢ offer_is_valid'. We will examine the reasoning first from a procedural point of view.

This sequent represents a query, the conclusion 'offer_is_valid', addressed to a very simple program consisting of one program clause, the premise. The query sets the goal of trying to prove 'offer_is_valid', that is, of determining whether the program makes 'offer_is_valid' true. To do this, the computer scans the program for instructions. In this case the query matches the head of the one and only program clause, which gives the instruction: to prove 'offer_is_valid' prove 'not(offer_is_prohibited)'. But how can we prove this? PROLOG's method is to set as its next goal a proof of 'offer_is_prohibited'. We shall represent the attempt to prove this as a hypothetical derivation subsidiary to the main proof. The first step is to hypothesize ':- offer_is_prohibited', which from a logical point of view amounts to hypothesizing the negation of 'offer_is_prohibited'. As with the main proof itself, the strategy of this hypothetical derivation, then, is reductio; we aim to deduce the contradiction ':-'. From a procedural point of view, however, to hypothesize ':- offer_is_prohibited' is simply to establish the subsidiary goal: prove 'offer_is_prohibited'. If the hypothetical derivation yields a contradiction, this goal succeeds, which means that the prior goal of proving 'not(offer_is_prohibited)' fails. But if all possible moves are exhausted and we still have not attained a contradiction, then the subsidiary goal of proving 'offer_is_prohibited' fails. It is at this point that PROLOG makes its great nonclassical leap, for it counts the failure to prove a clause Φ as a proof of not(Φ). The mechanism by which it does so is the *negation as failure* rule. Use of this rule, in other words, enables us to deduce 'not(offer_is_prohibited)'. But, as we saw earlier, this suffices to establish 'offer_is_valid' and thus complete the proof. That is the reasoning in a nutshell. Now let's consider it more formally. We begin with a more explicit statement of the negation as failure rule:

Negation as Failure Rule (NF)   Given a derivation from the hypothesis :- Φ in which ':-' is not deduced after R and NF have been used as many times as possible, end the hypothetical derivation and infer not(Φ) :-.

Now let's construct a formal proof of the sequent 'offer_is_valid :- not(offer_is_prohibited) ⊢ offer_is_valid'. We begin as before by assuming the premise and hypothesizing the result of transforming the conclusion or query into a goal clause:

1. offer_is_valid :- not(offer_is_prohibited)   A
2. | :- offer_is_valid   H

From a logical point of view, ':- offer_is_valid' is the negation of 'offer_is_valid'. From a procedural point of view, it is the instruction "prove 'offer_is_valid'."

':- offer_is_valid' is a goal clause (headless clause). As noted above, the structure of the goal clauses in a proof determines the strategy. A goal clause must have one of two forms:

:- $\Phi, \Psi_1, \ldots, \Psi_n$
:- not(Φ), $\Psi_1, \ldots, \Psi_n$

where Φ is an atom, $\Psi_1, \ldots, \Psi_n$ are literals, and $n \geq 0$. With clauses of the first form there is no choice but to use the resolution rule; if the rule is not applicable, the clause cannot be used. But with clauses of the second form, though we can still use the resolution rule, a second strategy is available: Hypothesize Φ and, depending on whether or not the ensuing hypothetical derivation eventually yields a contradiction, end this hypothetical derivation either by RAA or by NF.

':- offer_is_valid' is of the first form (where Φ is 'offer_is_valid' and $n = 0$), so it requires the resolution rule. But the resolution rule is applicable to a goal clause only if the first conjunct of its tail is the head of some other rule. In this case the first and only conjunct is 'offer_is_valid', which is the head of the clause at line 1 so that the resolution rule is applicable. In terms of the statement of the resolution rule above, Φ = 'offer_is_valid', $n = 0$, Θ_1 = 'not(offer_is_pro-hibited)', and $m = 1$. The rule tells us to infer :- $\Theta_1, \ldots, \Theta_m, \Psi_1, \ldots, \Psi_n$, that is, ':- not(offer_is_prohibited)':

1.	offer_is_valid :- not(offer_is_prohibited)	A
2.	:- offer_is_valid	H
3.	:- not(offer_is_prohibited)	1, 2 R

Since ':- not(offer_is_prohibited)' is of the form :- not(Φ),$\Psi_1, \ldots, \Psi_n$, where $n = 0$, and since 'not(offer_is_prohibited)' does not match the head of any other clause, the next step, as explained above, is to hypothesize ':- offer_is_prohibited' for either RAA or NF:

1.	offer_is_valid :- not(offer_is_prohibited)	A
2.	:- offer_is_valid	H
3.	:- not(offer_is_prohibited)	1, 2 R
4.	:- offer_is_prohibited	H

We must now see whether this new hypothesis will yield a contradiction. This hypothesis is of the form :- Φ,$\Psi_1, \ldots, \Psi_n$, where Φ is 'offer_is_prohibited' and $n = 0$. Hence the only rule that might be applicable to it is the resolution rule. But there is no clause of the form offer_is_prohibited :- $\Theta_1, \ldots, \Theta_m$, which would be needed to apply the resolution rule. We have also exhausted our options with the other goal clauses at lines 2 and 3. Therefore the attempt to prove 'offer_is_prohibited' has failed.

Now the negation as failure rule says that if we have hypothesized :- Φ and failed to deduce ':-' after R and NF have been used as many times as possible, we should end the hypothetical derivation and infer not(Φ) :-. In this case Φ = 'offer_is_prohibited'. Thus the next step in the proof is this:

1.	offer_is_valid :- not(offer_is_prohibited)	A
2.	:- offer_is_valid	H
3.	:- not(offer_is_prohibited)	1, 2 R
4.	:- offer_is_prohibited	H
5.	not (offer_is_prohibited) :-	4–4 NF

Now we go back and check the remaining goal statements to see if anything further can be done. Clause 3 is of the form :- Φ,$\Psi_1, \ldots, \Psi_n$, where Φ is 'not(offer_is_prohibited)' and $n = 0$. And clause 5 is of the form Φ :- $\Theta_1, \ldots, \Theta_m$, where $m = 0$. Hence the resolution rule allows us to infer $\Theta_1, \ldots, \Theta_m, \Psi_1, \ldots, \Psi_n$, that is, ':-'. This is a contradiction, which permits us to apply RAA and complete the proof:

1.	offer_is_valid :- not(offer_is_prohibited)	A
2.	:- offer_is_valid	H
3.	:- not(offer_is_prohibited)	1, 2 R
4.	| :- offer_is_prohibited	H
5.	not (offer_is_prohibited) :-	4–4 NF
6.	:-	3, 5 R
7.	offer_is_valid :-	2–5 RAA

Steps 6 and 7 can be understood either procedurally or logically. From a procedural perspective, we have at line 5 met the goal of proving 'not(offer_is_prohibited)', the goal listed on line 3. This goal may then be eliminated, leaving ':-', the empty goal to be accomplished. There is, in other words, nothing more to be done. We have proved 'offer_is_valid'; we need only to record this at line 7.

From a logical point of view, by contrast, the clause on line 3 is a double negation of 'offer_is_prohibited' (see valuation rules 2 and 5), whereas the clause on line 5 is just its negation. Hence these two lines yield a contradiction, which may be expressed in PROLOG by the empty clause ':-'. This enables us to reject the hypothesis at line 2 and so infer 'offer_is_valid'.

In constructing this proof I followed a strategy which ought now to be expressed more explicitly. This strategy is the **resolution algorithm.** To apply it, first list the program statements as assumptions, followed by the hypothesis :- Φ, where Φ is the conclusion (query), and then begin with step 2:

1. If an unfinished hypothetical derivation ends with ':-', apply RAA, then go to step 2; if not, just go on to step 2.
2. If there is a clause of the form :- $\Phi, \Psi_1, \ldots, \Psi_n$ ($n \geq 0$) and another clause of the form Φ :- $\Theta_1, \ldots, \Theta_m$ ($m \geq 0$) and R has not yet been applied to these two, apply R to them and go back to step 1; otherwise, go on to step 3.
3. If there is a clause of the form :- not(Φ), $\Psi_1, \ldots, \Psi_n$ ($n \geq 0$), but :- Φ has not been hypothesized, hypothesize :- Φ and go back to step 1; otherwise, go on to step 4.
4. If there is a hypothetical derivation that has not yet ended, then the attempt to deduce ':-' within this derivation has failed; apply NF; then go back to step 2. If there is no hypothetical derivation that has not yet ended, stop; the proof is complete and the formula on the last line is the answer to the query.

I have stated this algorithm a bit loosely. In actual implementations there are strict directions for scanning down the proof to locate the first unused formula of a given type. These details matter to programmers, but we need not bother with them.

If you were attentive to the earlier exposition, you might have been bothered by the fact that I did not annotate hypotheses with a rule name. The algorithm explains why. When we introduce a hypothesis—either when we hypothesize negation of the conclusion or when we follow step 3 of the algorithm—we may not know which of the two rules RAA or NF will be used to end the hypothetical derivation. To hypothesize the negation of a formula is in effect to treat that formula as a query. If that hypothesis leads to contradiction, we will apply RAA and conclude that the original formula is true. If not, we will apply NF. Which rule we will eventually use depends on how the proof goes after the hypothesis has been made. So we don't know how to annotate the hypothesis until the hypothetical derivation has ended. But by then there is no point in annotating it at all, since the annotation functions merely to remind us of our strategy as we construct the proof.

If the rule NF bothered you, it should have. It is, in fact, invalid, for it enabled us to prove the plainly invalid sequent

offer_is_valid :- not(offer_is_prohibited) ⊢ offer_is_valid.

Consider, for example, a possible situation in which the offer is prohibited and is invalid. More formally, let $\mathcal{V}$('offer_is_valid') ≠ T and $\mathcal{V}$('offer_is_prohibited') = T. By valuation rule 5 this makes $\mathcal{V}$('not(offer_is_prohibited)') ≠ T so that $\mathcal{V}$('offer_is_valid :- not(offer_is_prohibited)') =T by valuation rule 1. Thus we have a counterexample.

Many logicians are apt to conclude at this point that PROLOG is simply a botched attempt to make logic simple enough to meet the computational demands of computers. (PROLOG *can* reason efficiently from large databases, which is what it was designed to do; systems employing more classical forms of logic are less efficient). But there is another perspective from which PROLOG's logic is not utterly irrational. It all depends on how we understand the sequent itself. The sequent we proved has only one *assumption*. But PROLOG operates not only with assumptions, but also with *presumptions* that are not explicitly stated. Specifically, for any atom Φ, if Φ is not deducible from the program, then not(Φ) is a presumption. There are, then, indefinitely many presumptions, one of which is 'not(offer_is_prohibited)'. If we count these, too, as premises, then the resulting sequent *is* valid; the conclusion follows by modus ponens. In that case, the alleged counterexample turns out to be a simple mistake. By setting $\mathcal{V}$('offer_is_prohibited') = T, we make the premise 'not(offer_is_prohibited)' false; but a counterexample must make all the premises true.

Thus, if we count presumptions as actual premises, PROLOG's reasoning is purely classical. On this conception, the negation as failure rule is not a genuine rule of inference at all, but a device for identifying relevant presumptions and inserting them as premises into proofs. When we prove a sequent, then, we should actually list all the clauses obtained by NF in the proof as premises. But since these presumptions are identified in the process of constructing the proof, on this view we don't really know which sequent we are proving until we have proved it! This is very odd.

If, on the other hand, we do not count presumptions as premises, then we avoid this oddity. On this view, NF is a genuine inference rule so that PROLOG's presumptions, instead of being treated as premises, are built right into its logic, making that logic radically nonclassical. In that case, the conclusion 'offer_is_valid' really does follow from the premise 'offer_is_valid :- not(offer_is_prohibited)'. But then adding new premises may defeat the presumption that the offer is not prohibited (a presumption made automatically by the logic, unless there is explicit information to the contrary). Thus, for example, the following sequent is not provable by PROLOG's logic:

> offer_is_valid :- not(offer_is_prohibited), offer_is_prohibited ⊢ offer_is_valid.

Thus PROLOG, as we said at the outset, is nonmonotonic. The additional information 'offer_is_prohibited' defeats the presumption 'not(offer_is_prohibited)' and cancels the implication to the conclusion 'offer_is_valid'.

In fact, if a PROLOG program consisting of these premises is presented with the query 'offer_is_valid', it answers 'false'. The reasoning is as follows:

1.	offer_is_valid :- not(offer_is_prohibited)	A
2.	offer_is_prohibited :-	A
3.	:- offer_is_valid	H
4.	:- not(offer_is_prohibited)	1, 3 R
5.	:- offer_is_prohibited	H
6.	:-	2, 5 R
7.	offer_is_prohibited :-	5–6 RAA
8.	not(offer_is_valid) :-	3–7 NF

The offer is now presumed not to be valid, since the attempt to prove that it is valid (lines 3–7) has failed.

PROLOG may at first seem too arcane for practical application; but once one gets used to how it handles presumptions, it begins to seem natural. Moreover, if one can manage to formulate a program so that it implies as true just those propositions in the relevant field of knowledge that are in fact true, then PROLOG's logic gives the same results as classical logic. But even if not, the results obtained from a PROLOG program are readily intelligible. And PROLOG has been used in the construction of much useful software—including the ABACUS program supplied with this book.

Exercise 16.4

Prove the following sequents, using PROLOG's resolution algorithm (premises are separated with semicolons to avoid confusion with the conjunctive commas):

1. p:-q,t; s:-t; q:-r,s; t:-; r:- ⊢ p
2. p:-q,not(r); q:-; r:-s ⊢ p
3. p:-q,not(r); q:-; r:-s; s:- ⊢ not(p)

16.5 CONCLUSION: LOGICAL PLURALISM

Is there a uniquely true logic? This book's answer, obviously, is no. Classical logic has dominated the field, particularly in mathematics, and it has the advantage of simplicity, but it is not the best logic for all applications. The advent of artificial intelligence systems has spurred the creation of hundreds of alternative logics for specific applications. Some, like PROLOG, sacrifice strict logical validity to computational efficiency. Others make use of three or more semantic values, because for some applications classical two-valued semantics is too restrictive. (We don't always know which propositions in our database are true or false, so we can't always make an accurate two-valued assignment—or we may want to grant these propositions degrees of truth and falsity.) The pressure toward nonclassical concessions is especially acute when we attempt to design intelligent systems that use something akin to natural language. Here we encounter in bewildering complexity problems of relevance, nonsense, semantic paradox, reference failure, and so on, all of which raise challenges to the classical principle of bivalence. And even on the most fundamental issues, such as whether a semantics should be based on confirmation or on truth, there are deep disagreements; intuitionists take the former view, classicists the latter.

Moreover, there are motives for rejecting classicism that we have not even mentioned in this book. The weird behavior of the most fundamental particles of matter, for example, has convinced some physicists that the subatomic world is best characterized by a form of nonclassical logic called **quantum logic**.[17] And, to take a very different example, some researchers in cognitive science believe that thought should be understood as operating not primarily on propositions, but on image-like structures. The main difference between a proposition and an image is that a proposition is composed of definite and discrete units (represented by names, predicates, logical operators, etc.), whereas an image is continuous in the sense that its parts may shade and blur off into one another. Inference, in this view, is not the discrete deduction of one proposition of others, but the continuous transformation of images into new images. Such transformations, some researchers now speculate, may form the subject matter of wholly new logics called **continuous logics**. This work, however, is still in its infancy.

Despite these manifold developments, some logicians still believe that beneath all the novelties, complexities, practicalities, and concessions to our various inabilities lies a philosophically pure logic, a unique language of ideal reason. Maybe. But if so, we are far from discerning it. On the contrary, the tendency of philosophical logic in the past century has been almost entirely toward greater diversity, rather than greater unity.

As a result, many logicians, your author among them, have grown mightily skeptical of the idea of a single true or best logic. Each logic, or at least each semantically interpreted logic, carries with it its own notion of truth. What could it mean to talk of the truth of a logic itself? Is there some overarching notion of truth against which we might compare individual logics and find them more or less true? If so, no one has articulated it. And what could it mean to say that one logic is *best*? Best for what?

Logics are tools. And just as there is no single tool that is simply and unqualifiedly best, so too there is no single logic that is simply and unqualifiedly best. *Best* is always relative to an application. For pounding nails, a hammer is best; for cutting wood, a saw. Likewise with logics.

---

[17] For a good account of quantum logic, see Maria Luisa Dalla Chiara, "Quantum Logic," in D. Gabbay and F. Guenthner, eds., *Handbook of Philosophical Logic, Volume III: Alternatives to Classical Logic* (Dordrecht: D. Reidel, 1985), pp. 427–69.

INDEX

abacus, 268–288
ABACUS program, 275–283, 287–288
accessibility, 336–344
  degrees of, 352–356
  in deontic logic, 357–358
  in intuitionistic logic, 431–433
  in tense logic, 369–372
'accordingly', 17
actual world, 318–319
adjective, 166
adverb, 265–266
affirming the antecedent, 27, 28
affirming the consequent, 27, 28, 54
alethic modality, 307–308, 334–336, 340
algorithm, 129–133, 283–286
  terminating, 132
'all', 15, 161–164. *See also* universal quantifier
alternativeness. *See* accessibility
analogy, 385–386
'and', 15, 29, 33. *See also* conjunction
antecedent, 27
argument, 3–6
  of a function, 181, 200
argument by cases. *See* constructive dilemma
argument form, 25–38. *See also* sequent
argument indicator, 17
assertibility conditions, 40. *See also* confirmation
ASSOC. *See* association
associated sequent, 297–301
association, 106
assumption, 80–81
  categorical, 448
asymmetric relation, 370*n*, 386
'at least', 176
'at most', 176–177
atomic formula, 32, 171–172, 175
  in PROLOG, 449
Augustine, St., 365
'aut', 44
axiom, 133
axiom schema, 108–112

B (Brouwer) rule, 328, 344
basis case, 124
'because', 17
Bentham, Jeremy, 357
biconditional, 29. *See also* 'if and only if'
  elimination rule, 86

introduction rule, 86
material, 49
metatheorem, 119–120
rule for trees, 71
truth conditions for, 49–50
biconditional modus ponens, 106
biconditional modus tollens, 106
bivalence, 40, 406–407
Bochvar, D. A., 408–412, 414, 440
brackets, 31–32, 38, 171, 172, 175
Brouwer, L. E. J., 428
'but', 33

chain of inference, 79–82
character count, 134
character set
  for an algorithm, 130–131
  for predicate logic, 171
  for propositional logic, 36–37
chronological logic, 378
Church, Alonzo, 284, 296
Church's theorem, 296
Church's thesis, 269, 283–286
classical completion, 415, 418
classical logic, 6, 40, 397
clause, 450
coherence, 7
COM. *See* commutation
commutation, 106
compiler, 449*n*
completeness
  of inference rules for predicate logic,
    259–260
  of inference rules for propositional logic, 83,
    145–153
  of tree test for predicate logic, 245–246,
    255–259
  of tree test for propositional logic, 133–134,
    142–144
complex formula, 32
computational procedure, 129–130
conclusion, 3
conclusion indicator, 17
conditional, 19, 27, 34. *See also* 'if'; 'if . . . then';
  'only if'; conditional proof
  elimination rule, 84
  introduction rule, 90–91
  Lewis, 351–356